BURT FRANKLIN RESEARCH AND SOURCE WORKS SERIES No. 43

THE CAMERALISTS

THE CAMERALISTS

THE PIONEERS OF GERMAN SOCIAL POLITY

BY
ALBION W. SMALL

BURT FRANKLIN RESEARCH AND SOURCE WORKS SERIES No. 43

BURT FRANKLIN
New York 25, N. Y.

Published by
BURT FRANKLIN
514 West 113th Street
New York 25, N. Y.

First Published
Chicago **1909**

PRINTED IN U.S.A.

TABLE OF CONTENTS

PREFACE

Like its predecessor in this series, *Adam Smith and Modern Sociology*, the present book is a mere fragment. It deals with a single factor of the social process in the German States. It finds this factor already effective in 1555. It does not attempt to trace each link in the chain of continuity from that date. It reviews the most important seventeenth-century writers in the line of sequence, but the emphasis of the book falls in the eighteenth century. I have carefully excluded the problem of relations between this literary factor and other social elements, and I have purposely refrained from estimating its ratio of importance among the formative forces of the period. Conclusions of that order must come from a larger synthesis, for which the present study supplies merely a detail.

To justify my belief that the labor which this book cost was well spent, it would be necessary to prove first, that Americans have much to gain from better understanding of the Germans; and second, that just appreciation of the present social system of the Germans is impossible for Americans unless they are willing to trace it historically. These propositions must be left, however, without the support of argument, merely as the author's profession of faith.

To readers of English only, cameralism is virtually a lost chapter in the history of the social sciences. Although everything now belonging to German polity has a part of its heredity in that type of social theory, not every reputable student of the social sciences in America could correctly define the term, and few could name more than one or two writers to whom it is properly applied.

In a word, the cameralists were a series of German writers, from the middle of the sixteenth to the end of the eighteenth century, who approached civic problems from a common viewpoint, who proposed the same central question, and who developed a coherent civic theory, corresponding with the German system of administration at the same time in course of evolution. To the cameralists the central problem of science was the problem of the state. To them the object of all social theory was to show how the welfare of the state might be secured. They saw in the welfare of the state the source of all other welfare. Their key to the welfare of the state was revenue to supply the needs of the state. Their whole social theory radiated from the central task of furnishing the state with ready means.

For reasons to be mentioned later, allusions to the cameralists in English books, whether original or translated, are more frequent among the economists than elsewhere. If, however, we consult the two handbooks of the history of economic theory in most frequent use by students in this country, we find that they barely allude to cameralism, and their historical perspective would be clearer if they did not mention the subject at all. In the second edition of Cossa,[1] Klock, Becher, Hornigk (*sic*), and Schröder are disposed of in a paragraph of about seventy words, and another paragraph two lines longer, in the chapter on the physiocrats (!), mentions the "Chamber Sciences," as represented by Justi and Sonnenfels only. The third edition of the same book, or the volume which took the place of a third edition, translated under the title *An Introduction to the Study of Political Economy*, mentions the same three Austrians, and adds a couple of lines on Seckendorff in the section on "Industrial Freedom;" it mentions Gasser, Dithmar, and Darjes in the section on "Professional Chairs, Newspapers, and Academies;" it gives a paragraph each to Justi and Son-

[1] Translated under the supervision of Jevons, with the title, *Guide to the Study of Political Economy;* original first edition, 1876, second, 1878, translation, 1880.

nenfels, in the section entitled "Bureaucratic and Professorial Eclecticism;" and then, after a few statements thirty-four pages later, about the "German Physiocrats," it for the first time finds its bearings among German thinkers with Rau, who began to write a generation after cameralism in the strict sense had passed its prime. Ingram evidently abstracted from Roscher, by some principle of selection which does not appear, a dozen names of German "mercantilists" of the cameralistic period. The summary way in which he disposes of them shows that he had no first-hand knowledge of these writers, and that he utterly misapprehended their place in the history of German thought. If one were so fortunate as to learn the names of the cameralists, and turned to Palgrave for more information, little would be found beyond repetition of scraps gathered from Roscher; and these so disconnected that they would hardly pique curiosity to pry farther. All the other English aids to knowledge of cameralism are so scattered that an adequate introduction to the subject by means of them would be out of the question.

During the last generation, American readers of German appear to have relied, as a rule, for information about early phases of German economic thought, chiefly upon two writers, Kautz[1] and Roscher.[2]

Of Kautz it is enough to say that he was of the rear guard of the rhetoricians. His book is wonderfully plausible if not lucid reading. Its early pages appear to express methodological conclusions which the maturest scholarship has not superseded. Unfortunately, the author's own procedure, as it appears in the body of the book, shows that for him these

[1] Julius Kautz, *Die geschichtliche Entwickelung der National-Oekonomik und ihrer Literatur*, Wien, 1860.

[2] Wilhelm Roscher, *Geschichte der National-Oekonomik in Deutschland*, München, 1874. In the following pages, if nothing appears to the contrary, this work is referred to whenever the author's name is used.

imposing propositions had merely the force of impotent generalities. His actual method is first, derivation, by some occult means, of certain general principles under which to subsume the economists of the period; then, second, use of the writers of the period as so many illustrations of the principles. When projected upon this vicious circle, the course of thought in successive stages falls into alluring symmetry. A little inquiry into the facts, however, shows that these pleasing constructions are mainly fictitious.

For example, Kautz locates the second of his three great divisions of economic ideas "between the end of the Middle Ages and Adam Smith." This second period he interprets as that of independent investigation, "in which the national-economic ideas and principles were no longer mixed and combined with the political, legal, and religious systems of theory, but were presented as a totality of peculiar special cognitions."[1] The truth of this generalization depends upon the standard used for measurement of relative bondage to conventionality and independence of it. Compared with the age of the schoolmen the period from Martin Luther to Adam Smith was of course intellectually free. On the other hand, if contemporaries of Kautz had gone back to the economic and political theorists of the intermediate period, with no preparation but nineteenth-century ideas, they would have been amazed at the degree in which social thinking of all sorts was paralyzed by dogmatic prepossessions. Even if Kautz's generalization had been qualified in a way to make it valid, use of it as a premise from which to deduce interpretation of the economic theories of the period was like finding a sufficient explanation of the course of American experience since 1776 in terms of the mere negative condition of independence from England. Anyone who can have patience with discursive essays upon long-distance impressions of the development of economic

[1] *Loc. cit.*, p. 25.

theory would find Kautz impressive. As a guide to critical study of the actual process he is impossible.

Whatever our estimate, on the other hand, of the "historical school," and of Roscher's contributions to economic theory, there can be no doubt about the value of his services to economic history. The volume cited above, on the history of economic theory in Germany, has served as an almost unchallenged authority on the subject for a generation. Those who have had most occasion to work in the field which this book surveys will be most sincere in their gratitude to the author. The present volume could surely not have been written if Roscher had not blazed the way.

Nevertheless, the farther I went in the studies which this book reports, the more my wonder grew that German scholarship had not yet produced a work which would be as evident an advance upon Roscher as he was upon Kautz. For obvious reasons such a book must be written in Germany. At the same time, comparison of the perspective of foreign scholars may be worth something as an aid in establishing the viewpoint from which the evolution of German social theories should be reconsidered.

It is approximately true that knowledge of the cameralists as a group has remained as it was left by Roscher. The most general thesis of the present work is that the cameralists have not yet come to their own in the assignment of historical values. In other words, while acknowledging my debt to Roscher, I find it necessary to impeach his authority.

In the first place, Roscher was essentially a collector, not an interpreter. Yet, although his chief merit was as an assembler of details, I have still been surprised at the number of times in which I have found him apparently in error about matters of fact. It was not my affair to find out whether these slips were more his fault or his misfortune. At his time the evidence which would have corrected the errors of detail may not have been accessible. At all events, the writers in *Die allgemeine deutsche Biographie* almost invariably justify more or less important modifications in Roscher's accounts of the individual careers of the cameralists. My own study of these writers has been confined to their books. For such biographical introduction as was necessary I have relied throughout, unless exception is noted, upon the work just named, whenever it differed from Roscher.

But the chief issue with Roscher is much more radical. For a generation the world's interpretation of the cameralists has virtually been stereotyped in the form which he cast. The more specific thesis of the present work is that his version of the cameralists utterly misses their real meaning. It is a blur produced by a combination of methodological fallacy and historical nearsightedness. German scholars alone are within reach of the means fully to reconstruct the history if the thesis is sustained. I hope I am right, however, that the very distance from the bulk of the sources, which compels attention to the main movement of thought, confers a distinct advantage in making out the larger meanings of the body of literature in question.

In order to justify this challenge of venerable tradition, account must be taken of the immediate antecedents of Roscher's book. In 1858 Leopold Ranke submitted to the Bavarian Royal Academy of Sciences a plan for a series of twenty-four volumes on the history of the sciences in Germany. The subjects of those volumes in the series which are most intimately related to the present issue are: (1) *Geschichte;* (2) *Kriegswissenschaft;* (3) *Jurisprudenz;* (4) *Allgemeines Staatsrecht und Politik;* (5) *Nationalökonomie und kameralistische Fächer;* (6) *Landwirthschaftslehre.* For the convenience of the writers available, and for facility of popular exposition, these subdivisions were doubtless more suitable than any others that might have been proposed. As a programme for critical research, however, the standards of today being the criterion, that division of labor surrendered the work in advance to preconception and misconstruction. A precisely analogous fallacy would be involved in a scheme today to parcel out among different scholars, in accordance with present national boundaries, an analysis of the political conditions of Europe at the time of Charlemagne. The political map of Europe in the ninth century was not as it is today, and analysis based on the contrary assumption would deserve rejection without a hearing. But the inchoate social sciences, from the middle of the sixteenth century to the end of the eighteenth, were no more homogeneous and coterminous with scientific categories at the middle of the nineteenth century than national frontiers of the ninth century retain their places in the twentieth. In other words, the Bavarian Academy did not undertake to find the centers in the past from which the evolution of the social sciences could be traced step by step and process by process. On the contrary, it sponsored a plan which called for a conventionalizing of previous centuries in terms of nineteenth-century classification. This scheme ruthlessly inverted the rule which had been the first great historiographical commandment with promise since Savigny and Niebuhr.

The result was a conspicuous vindication of the violated principle. The sort of analysis which the present volume reports very early unearths the fact that the conventional division of labor in the series threw the data out of their relations and retarded discovery of their meaning. In particular it assigned the cameralists to Roscher,[1] while it estopped analysis of them at their proper center within the scope of Bluntschli.[2] Using the terms in the sense in which they are understood in the United States today, the cameralists were not primarily economists. They were primarily political scientists. This

[1] Under title (5) above.

[2] Title (4) above.

single perception demonstrates the unreliability of both Roscher and Bluntschli upon the cardinal question of the meaning of the cameralists for the evolution of the sciences in Germany. The first critical question to be answered in an interpretation of the cameralists is: *What was their specific purpose, the center from which they proceeded, the interest which gave the respective ratings to all their other interests?* Rarely is this question answered as promptly and as decisively as in the case of the cameralists. The answer exhibits in cameralism the germination, not of an academic abstraction, but of a whole civic polity.

Turning to the defect of historical nearsightedness, a typical symptom may be taken from Bluntschli.[1] He says:

> The Germans applied their attention tardily to general civic science (*Staatswissenschaft*). In the sixteenth century Italians and Frenchmen, in the seventeenth Dutchmen and Englishmen, and in the eighteenth Englishmen and Frenchmen were far in advance. Only by degrees did the Germans overtake these leaders, and presently it was their fortune, through diligence and thoroughness of investigation, through moral earnestness of endeavor, and through the loftiness of their standpoint and the energy of their thinking, to equal the foremost and to win general recognition.

In a certain sense the first two of these propositions are as true as the last. At the same time, this conventional judgment is in large part a mere survival of that obsession which filled Germany, and to a certain extent the rest of Europe, during the eighteenth century, with awe and fear of everything political made in France. In effect Bluntschli follows Weitzel[2] in canceling the cameralists from the account, while he discusses other Germans of much less real importance for civic science. Von Mohl had meanwhile written,[3] and had really given the

[1] *Loc. cit.*, p. xiv.

[2] *Geschichte der Staatswissenschaft*, 2 vols., 1832–33.

[3] *Geschichte und Literatur der Staatswissenschaften*, 3 vols., 1855–58.

cameralists more credit than Bluntschli allows, though he does not in principle vary from tradition. It is not necessary, if it were possible, to cloud the title of other countries to respect for their achievements in the political sciences. My contention is that the Germans were not as sterile in this field as it has been their own fashion to suppose. In fact there was no more virile political thinking in Europe in the seventeenth and eighteenth centuries than that of the German cameralists. I do not say that it was as profound, as abstract, as highly generalized, as political works of the first rank produced by other nations. It was suited to the occasions which set its task. It was constructive. It was effective. As in the case of all theory, in comparison with its practical counterpart, it is impossible to demonstrate how much the cameralism of the books was cause and how much effect of the cameralism of the bureaus. I do not raise that question. The same dilemma is at least as pertinent to Grotius or Locke or Montesquieu as to the cameralists; and on the ground of probable influence upon affairs the case of the latter does not on the whole suffer by comparison with any political theorists whatsoever. Moreover, the plea that neither the letter nor the spirit of these technologies in any great degree molded the actual political practices of the time would, by parity of reasoning, exclude every great human document from rank among the formative forces of the period that produced it. This arbitrary measure of meaning factors in history would leave among admitted social forces not a single standardizing formulation of human conduct, from the New Testament to Magna Charta and the last three amendments to the American Constitution.

At all events the cameralists of the books did their share toward systematizing the polity which was most intensively developed by the Germans. Their works contain in embryo everything which has made the German system today the most effective economizer of national energy in the world. If a tree should be known by its fruits, scholars in general, and the Germans in particular, have grossly blundered in slighting the sturdy stock from which the mighty growth of German civic theory and practice has developed.

There is a contrast between Roscher's method of approaching the material and my own in another respect. Roscher attempts in general to exhibit the cameralists in national groups, in connection with the administrative policies of their respective princes. That he is unable strictly to carry out this plan is evident from the titles of his chapters, from the twelfth to the twentieth inclusive, viz.: "The Dutch School and the Mercantile System;" "The Conservative National Economics of the Middle of the Seventeenth Century;" "The National Economics of the Last Great German Polyhistorian;" "The Austrian National Economics under Leopold I;" "The Prussian National Economics under the Great Elector;" "Leibniz and the Beginnings of the Halle School;" "The National Economics of Friedrich Wilhelm I;" "The National Economics of Frederick the Great;" "The Older Eclectics of the Eighteenth Century."

My plan, on the contrary, ignored the merely national relations of the respective authors, and treated them as nearly as possible chronologically, and as phenomena of a coherent tendency of thought. It can hardly be claimed that the last word has been said by or for either of these methods. I would simply point out that each has its advantages, and that the employment of both, at their highest efficiency, and in co-operation with each other, will doubtless be involved in the programme of future historians of this period.

There is nowhere between the lines of this book a wish to glorify German bureaucracy at the expense of American republicanism. The advantage to Americans of understanding German institutions will not come from adopting or even imitating them, but from adapting whatever may be learned from their workings to the improvement of our own institutions. The aim of this book is accordingly to find a point of departure for interpretation of German social theories and practices through their own process of evolution. The Hegelians would say it is a typical manifestation of the nature of things that the German and American polities should tend to complete each other. The one starts with the assumption of the state as the social unit. The other starts with the assumption of the individual as the social unit. Experience has shown that neither assumption is the whole truth, that each assumption is part of the truth, and that the social problem rests hard upon the need of a reconstruction which shall organize these two phases of the truth into a convincing basis for present social action. I venture again to express my belief that a service may be rendered to the American side of this assimilation by promoting acquaintance with the spirit of German polity. Taking it for granted that the best way to understand the German type of society and of social theory is through their evolution, I have undertaken to show that the trunk line of this evolution from the Reformation to the French Revolution is marked by the cameralists.

This book is not a contribution to the social sciences in the sense that it draws upon previously unknown sources. The cameralists have been catalogued over and over again.[1] Additional sources will doubtless be assembled when German scholars interest themselves in recovering this portion of their history. My effort has been rather to determine a new standpoint for explaining the sources. Nor is an attempt to put the cameralists in their proper historical perspective new in itself. Not to speak of interpretations attempted while the

[1] Exhaustive study of the literature of cameralism should take, as its base of operations, Baumstark, *Cameralistische Encyklopädie*, 1835. The state of tradition about the meaning of the cameralists is ocular proof, however, that it is a far cry from bibliography to interpretation.

cameralistic series in the strict sense was still incomplete, we may date the beginnings of historical treatment of cameralism from Rossig.[1] Almost without exception these reviews of cameralism have been so indiscriminate that the meaning of the movement has been obscured, if not positively misrepresented. Thus, to take the most important instance, Roscher, in consequence of begging the methodological question at the outset, makes a hodgepodge of identities by jumbling together survivals of mediaeval legalism like Besold, political scientists of the obsolescent not the evolving type like Bornitz, political philosophers of massive mold like Pufendorf, historical philosophers like Möser, metaphysical philosophers like Leibniz, Wolff, and Kant, and incidentally the cameralists. Not by a valid process of analysis, but by sheer force, Roscher reduces these unlike quantities to the common denominator "economist." In the same way, and perhaps even more fallaciously, Bluntschli had joined together heterogeneous elements as a continuous series in political science. I do not deny that every type of theory reacts upon every other type; but it is juvenile to assume that in any age the influence of a metaphysician and of a historian, for example, upon each other's peculiar type of thinking, is as direct and intense as that of two metaphysicians or two historians. Sometimes such cross-fertilization is more fruitful than in-and-in breeding. Again it is not. Neither is it to be assumed in a given case without proof. Nor can it be taken for granted that propositions occurring casually in one theory, but belonging primarily to another, may be carried over at face value into the theory to which they secondarily belong. For instance, a theologian might cull from every economic author of the last fifty years passages which carry some sort of theological implications. Those implications might or might not have been apparent to the authors them-

[1] *Versuch einer Geschichte der Oekonomie und Cameralwissenschaft*, 2 vols., 1781.

selves and intended by them. In any event it would be absurd to make a history of theology for the last fifty years by patching together such passages with others which were immediately theological in their premises and purpose. Before a truthful expression of one type of theory can be made in terms of another the mental latitude and longitude of each group of theorists, and even of each individual theorist, must be accurately determined, and corrections must be made accordingly in the presumptive force of their formulas. Neither Bluntschli nor Roscher properly recognized this principle. It is a marvel therefore that German scholarship has permitted the books of these authors so long to hold their place as standard accounts of the process of evolution in the German social sciences. The following pages are devoted to determining the group equation of the cameralists only.

Meanwhile the little book of Marchet[1] deserves much more attention than it seems to have received, either in Europe or in this country. Indeed, I could not have expressed myself as above about the persistent authority of Roscher if I could trace in recent German literature any considerable tendency to countenance Marchet's secession. The chief reason for the neglect will doubtless be found in the tacit assumption that, since Bluntschli and Roscher, German social theory previous to the nineteenth century is to be considered as a closed incident. I must acknowledge that Marchet has very largely anticipated my conclusions, particularly upon the fabulous character of tradition with respect to German mercantilism as a theory, and as to the doctrine of population. Any competent scholar was bound to reach similar results if he analyzed the sources instead of repeating hearsay.

[1] *Studien über die Entwickelung der Verwaltungslehre in Deutschland von der zweiten Hälfte des 17. bis zum Ende des 18. Jahrhunderts.* Von Dr. Gustav Marchet, o. ö. Professor an der k.-k. Hochschule für Bodencultur in Wien. München, 1885 (pp. viii + 437).

Until I had reached my own conclusions from examination of the original writers, I deliberately ignored the commentators as far as possible. Marchet was accordingly merely a name to me until I had completed my manuscript. This was fortunate, because if I had been familiar with his work I could not have been sure of the independence of my own judgment. In matters of detail Marchet notes particulars which I had omitted, others which I had not discovered, about Seckendorff, Becher, Hornick, Schröder, and Justi. His estimate of Hornick is especially notable, as he had the advantage of access to his book and other evidence which I could not obtain. On the other hand, comparison of my own method, and its resulting interpretation, with Marchet's tends to confirm my belief that I am on the right track. In the first place, the extent to which Marchet relies on the generalization *eudaemonism* to explain the political philosophy of the time too closely resembles the method of Kautz. In the second place, Marchet is not sufficiently free from the prime fallacy of Roscher. He does not perceive that he has to deal with several distinct types of theorists. These must be analyzed in turn, with reference to their respective centers of attention, before a valid synthesis of their unlike doctrines is possible. That is, the same sort of analysis to which this volume subjects the cameralists must be performed upon several distinct groups of thinkers, e. g., the general philosophers, the political philosophers, the moral philosophers, etc. Since this particular analysis has not been applied rigorously by Marchet to the cameralists as such, or to either of the other groups included in his survey, his book, with all its merits, leaves these theorists still not properly differentiated, and not interpreted strictly by the functional meaning of each, in the whole process of developing a system of social doctrines.

Schmoller has rescued the method of Roscher from futility by projecting the large survey within which all details of civic development, particularly in Germany, must be located. In his more intensive historical work Schmoller has dealt immediately with industrial and administrative development more than with the growth of theories. Analysis of the cameralists therefore explains one of the systems of communication, so to speak, that penetrated the territory in which Schmoller's primacy among explorers is secure. His monograph, *Mercantilism*, is the best introduction that can be recommended for the present volume. The relation of his more extended and technical treatment of the subject to the present study is indicated in the first chapter of this book.

In the following pages I have tried to present a digest of everything in the writings of the leading cameralists which is necessary to an impartial conclusion about their meaning for the German social sciences. Accordingly I offer in this volume a source book containing the most pertinent evidence about the real significance of the cameralists. These sources put each reader in possession of the means of testing my conclusions, and of estimating the cameralists for himself. The only preconception which I carried to the study of these theorists was the historical commonplace that they must be allowed to speak for themselves, and from their own standpoint, whatever that might prove to be. This commonplace has had at best fitful respect among social theorists or historians of social theory.

My chief interest in the cameralists is least of all antiquarian. I want to know what can be learned from them that is of permanent use for sociological methodology. My suspicions were early aroused that the fate which had befallen them would turn out to enforce certain primary methodological laws in application to the social sciences; and first of all the law that every historical actor must be judged primarily with reference to his immediate purposes, not as though his purposes were those of the moment at which the judgment was passed. I suspected that some of the *non sequiturs* which are epidemic in the social sciences would be found undisguised in a comparison of the cameralists as they really were with the tradition of them in the histories. It seemed to me that, if this turned out to be the case, exposure of the bad logic, in an example so far in the past that it enlists no partisan prejudice, would do more to promote valid reasoning upon current questions in the social sciences than possible direct refutations of contemporary argument. I therefore undertook a laborious historical search, not chiefly from historical interest, but for specifically methodological purposes. If historical valuations of the cameralists had mistreated them, I wanted to ferret out the precise flaw in the process, as a concrete warning against parallel miscarriages of judgment at present.

All that I knew about the cameralists, when I began this study, I had learned from Roscher. On the general grounds indicated above, I decided that if Roscher's composite picture of so many different types did justice to each, and to the synthesis of them, it would be an amazing coincidence; and I determined to find out for myself whether such a phenomenon had occurred. I first studied Justi, and at once made out indications which had not appeared in Roscher's report. It was evident moreover that there were more intimate relations than a mere chronological before-and-after between Justi and other writers. Following this clue, I abstracted from Roscher's heterogeneous collection of men who had more or less directly affected economic ideas a group with like marks of species. German civic theory in general so evidently proceeds from or at least through this type of thinkers that the finding marks forthwith furnish the fixed points from which to interpret the whole evolution of German social science. Whether the record proves to contain exhibits of methodological principles, either in the breach or in the observance, is discussed in the concluding chapter.

I have intentionally disobeyed the rules of good writing by retaining in the text many German words, instead of trying to propose English equivalents. This was for two chief reasons: first, that translation unavoidably interprets, and in the present connection it almost certainly interprets anachronistically. Any terms by which we might translate leading concepts of the cameralists, unless they might be careful circumlocutions, would impute to them shades of meaning which would really be ours, not theirs. In another class of cases I have gone still farther in retaining German terms or even considerable quotations, when I judged that the matter in hand would have value only for readers somewhat familiar with German. This was both for the sake of precision and to retain local color.

With the same purpose in view I have deliberately chosen awkward renderings of many German expressions. By so doing I have most accurately indicated the ideas of the various authors. In many ways their thought was not as our thought, and it is a falsification of history to make them speak as men would now. American conceptions of the growth and meaning of German social theory have been confused by neglect of translators to count with this elemental fact. This has been amply emphasized in the body of the book, but I add a typical instance from a different source. While writing this preface I had occasion, in another connection, to consult the English version of Heeren's *Geschichte des europäischen Staatensystems.*[1] Of European states from the beginning of the sixteenth century, Heeren is made to say:

At first, therefore, the royal authority in these kingdoms was everywhere much limited. Without the aid of the nobility no important war could be carried on; without the consent of the cities no taxes could be levied. Without standing armies (a small

[1] Originally published 1808–9. I refer to the fifth edition (1830), Vol. IX of the *Historische Werke*, p. 16. The English translation appeared in 1864 under the title, *A Manual of the History of the Political System of Europe and Its Colonies.* The passage is on p. 11.

beginning excepted), without *political economy*[1] (for no art was known but that of getting money), there existed, in reality, at this time no power, in the present acceptation of the word.

In the first place, Heeren's own proposition about *Staatswirthschaft* was a generality which would not bear rigorous criticism. In the second place, whether the author had a correct idea in mind or not, the term *Staatswirthschaft* itself has to be credited with a different content for every period of which it is positively or negatively predicated. It did not even have the identical connotations when Heeren's last edition was published which it had carried when the book first appeared; and never and nowhere had it meant precisely what writers or readers in England in 1864 understood by the phrase "political economy." Still further, as the following clause stands in the quotation it furnishes a second illustration of the need of paraphrase fairly to represent the original. The author's real meaning would be conveyed by the substitute: "the financial administration of states did not go beyond programmes for raising revenues." Standing by themselves, these particular instances are not of firstrate importance. They are merely samples of thousands scattered through English literature of the social sciences. The aggregate effect of unhistorical renderings of German terms, added to the unsatisfactory condition of the German tradition itself, is a state of regrettable misinformation among English readers about the actual course of development in German social theory and practice. I have tried, therefore, to report the cameralists in language that reflects the partial analysis actually in their minds, and which does not represent them as using nineteenth- and twentieth-century concepts of Germans, still less of Englishmen or Americans.

[1] The italics are mine, and the author's word is *Staatswirthschaft*. The next clause in parenthesis reads: *man kannte nur die Kunst, Geld aufzubringen*.

It has been my intention also to retain all archaisms and other peculiarities, even to obvious typographical errors, in quotations, titles, etc., in order to represent the exact state of the texts used. My notes, however, were reorganized several times, and were recopied by several hands. Moreover, space limits compelled me to omit an appendix which would have occupied 150 pages. It was to contain the tables of contents of the principal books cited, and other illustrative material. The retrenchment compelled frequent alterations in the body of the book. At the time of revising the proof most of the volumes used had necessarily been returned to libraries in this country and Germany. I have not been unmindful of the duty of verification, but it was thus not strictly within my power. I fear therefore that, although I have fortified myself as well as circumstances would permit against material errors, in matters of form the citations contain inaccuracies which might have been removed if the sources had been longer at my disposal. The capitalization, spelling, punctuation, etc., must accordingly be taken as illustrating rather than precisely transcribing the passages cited.

My most grateful thanks are due to the *Königliche Bibliothek* at Berlin for the loan of a large number of the cameralistic works without which this book could not have been written. My obligations are equally real for similar assistance from the libraries of Harvard, Columbia, and Cornell and for important information from the British Museum.

ALBION W. SMALL

January 1, 1909

CHAPTER I

INTRODUCTION TO CAMERALISM

Every theory, system, science is in some way a reflection of the prevailing purposes of the time in which it developed.

No hypothesis about the precise nature of the cause and effect concerned is concealed in this commonplace. We need not raise that question. Enough that in some way or other, which it is not necessary to discuss at this point, our philosophies echo the dominant purposes of the time that produced them.

If we attempt to detach a system of thought from the whole scheme of activities impelled by the prevailing systems of purposes, and if we try to set forth the meaning of that thought as though it had no connection with those purposes, the result is inevitable misinterpretation.

The same effect follows unintentional not less than deliberate separation of a body of thought, in which we are especially interested, from the surrounding circumstances of its development. It is like abstracting a plant from the soil and atmosphere which are the media of its existence, and then expecting it both to grow and to reveal the abstract process of its previous growth.

Speaking particularly of the social sciences, their crudeness at present is in part the result of arbitrary dismemberment of the process of which science is an interpretation, and consequent substitution of fictitious processes, more or less remote from one another and meaningless for one another. We have then, so far as we depend upon these sciences for knowledge, a collection of ghosts stalking abroad in defiance of all known laws, and apparently tending less and less to explain reality.

A single instance in which this has occurred on a rather large scale furnishes the primary motive of this book. We are to deal with cameralists and cameralism. A history of neither is to be attempted. At most this book may be called a brief of the argument which a history would have to complete if it were to satisfy sociologists.

An authentic interpretation of cameralism necessarily gives the most prominent place, in the center of the picture, to Justi. In order however rightly to estimate Justi, the work of other cameralists before and after his time must be analyzed and compared with his system. For the purposes of this survey then we shall regard cameralism as beginning with Seckendorff,[1] and ending with Sonnenfels.[2] A history of cameralism would have to begin more than a century before these pioneers. It would trace beginnings earlier than the time of Elector August of Saxony (1553–86) and Landgrave Philipp of Hesse (1518–67). It would follow changes of form, content, relations, and name, and it would be obliged to show, finally, that present differences between German and English institutions must be stated partially in terms of the persistence in the one case of a cameralistic tradition which was never naturalized in the other.

Lexis, in Conrad's *Handwörterbuch*, under the title "Kameralwissenschaft," states that the emperor Maximilian I established several *Reichskammer*, e.g., the *Kammergericht*, 1495, and that in the course of the sixteenth century the type of administration began to be developed in the chief states of the Empire. If we refer to this infancy of the system and of its technology, we are obliged to set our boundaries back so as to include among the writers Melchior von Osse, whose *Testament* was written in 1555, and Georg Obrecht, whose *Fünf unterschiedliche Secreta Politica* appeared in Strassburg in 1617. These authors will presently be discussed at some length.

Readers who use English only know cameralism chiefly

[1] *Teutsche Fürstenstaat*, 1655.

[2] *Grundsätze der Policey, Handlung und Finanz*, 1765.

through the historians of economics. The interpretation of cameralism in English tradition arbitrarily wrests the thing and its science from the setting in which it is intelligible. Exaggerating almost to paradox, we may say that cameralism was not a theory and practice of economics but of politics. Cameralism was a technique and a theory of administering a peculiar type of state in a society constructed out of peculiar types of purposes. To be sure, economic conditions and purposes formed their share of the circumstances to which cameralism was an adaptation. The argument which will follow is not an attempt to turn the flank of the economic interpretation of history. No issue is raised with those who insist that the ultimate elements of all factors of social situations are economic. Be that as it may, the actors in a given social situation think of the elements with which they are dealing as different in kind, and they construct their systems of theory and practice accordingly. Cameralism raised, directly and deliberately, no fundamental questions of pure economics. It was primarily a theory and a technique of government. Solution of problems of the nature and laws of wealth is *logically* antecedent to governmental institutions, to be sure, but until the last quarter of the eighteenth century the principle had been generally ignored. Governmental theory dealt with economic problems of course. Instead of formulating these separately as economic problems, however, it recognized no economic problems of the degree of generality familiar since Adam Smith's time. It dealt with economic relations as merely incidental to the application of governmental principles, and the latter, as proclaimed at the time, were in many respects narrowly provincial.

The situation which actually existed in Germany in the seventeenth and eighteenth centuries was a resultant of purposes which were conditioned first by these chief objective factors, viz., the soil and climate of the country; the state of the arts required for using natural resources; the domestic industrial structure, and the foreign trade relations; the ecclesiastical organization; the Holy Roman Empire; the character of the states within the Empire, and outside of it in Europe including nearer Asia; the prizes for national competition in the wealth of the Americas, the Levant, and the remote East; and the personal equation of the citizens. Then, second, there were firstrate subjective factors, which may be scheduled as the contemporary science, the theology or philosophy, the legal tradition both from Roman and Teuton sources, the political philosophy, and the rule-of-thumb conclusions which passed as wisdom in the conduct of life, from individual habit to the policies of states.

In this situation, as a matter of fact, the idea of the state and of government dominated all the other factors. So far as interests of the state could be distinguished, they settled the relative importance of everything else. The purposes of the state were paramount. The cameralists were servants of the state. Cameralism was the system elaborated by the chief agents of the rulers, partly as mere classification of practices which rulers had already adopted; partly as ways and means of accomplishing more of the purposes which the state proposed.

But in order properly to prepare for intelligent interpretation of cameralism still simpler elements of the situation must be called to mind.

In the first place, we must remember that the German territorial sovereignties in the period of the Reformation were essentially more like a typical Virginia plantation, in the most flourishing days of the Old Dominion, than like any political unit with which modern Americans are familiar. Even if the prince controlled territories which it would not be extravagant to describe as big farms, it was long before the operations of management were transformed from the primitive type of the big landed estate to a definitive civic structure. The administration of German states developed by a process which it does not fall within the scope of this book to trace, from the status in which the consort of the prince presided in person over the revenues of the principality, almost as directly as the New England farmer's wife managed her dairy. The advisers and chief functionaries, who gradually acquired the meaning which we find them possessing in the cameralistic period, were genetically differentiations of this proprietary relation and policy. The lord of the estate was to their minds, whatever their particular philosophy, a fixed term in the equation of life. They were powerless to think of a social order as rational which did not revolve about him as a regulator.

The great majority of the people in the German states, the peasants and artisans particularly, were regarded by the wisest men of the time as incapable of successful initiative. As an estimate of actual conditions the judgment was undoubtedly correct. The people were accordingly held to be dedicated by dispensation of Providence and the laws of nature to the condition of wardship, and to be fit for action only under authority. The fallacy of this generalization need not concern us. It is a historical fact and force. The ruler and his government were quite consistently seen in the most plausible light when they were contemplated as fulfilling the duties of guardianship over these industrially and politically incompetent masses. Under the circumstances paternalism was not an arrest of development; still less in principle an abuse of power. Whether in operation or in theory, it was the ideal expression of the situation.

Again, from the beginning, the German states were involved in a struggle for existence. With the kind of necessity here concerned we have now nothing to do, beyond recognizing it as a factor taken for granted by the statesmen of the period. In fact the most importunate problem for every German state was, in its own calculation, that of self-maintenance, and especially by control of an adequate military force.

The cameralists of the books, as distinguished from the cameralists of the bureaus, although the former class was usually recruited from the latter, were the men who worked out for publication, and especially for pedagogical purposes, the system of procedure in accordance with which German governments were supposed to perform their tasks. As a rule these men were employed in administrative positions of some sort, and spoke to a certain extent from experience. They were not mere academic theorists. *We may characterize these cameralists of the books as the group of writers distinguished from their contemporaries and from earlier and later theorists by constructing a "science" or group of "sciences" around the central consideration of the fiscal needs of the prince.* We might coin the name "*fiscalists*," and it would be more appropriate to their actual character than either of the terms by which they have been known. Under the circumstances to which we have referred, the most constant and pressing need of the ruler was ready money. The men who elaborated the theory of government for these German states had virtually to answer this question: *What programme must a wise government adopt, in order first and foremost to be adequately supplied with ready money, and thus able to discharge the duties of the state in their various orders of importance?* The most typical of these men expressed this paramount consideration very positively and frankly. One of the reasons why later cameralists used superficially different formulations of the same essential régime, was that the fiscal systems had become relatively fixed, and could be taken for granted. The less conventionalized portions of the system, and especially the idealized versions of its aims, could then come in for a larger share of attention; and there was more room for speculative excursions into the wider political philosophy or the deeper metaphysics by which later writers hoped to buttress the system.

In the rough, the chronic condition of the European nations

during the cameralistic period was war, and the primary task of governments, especially in Germany, was creation of readiness for war. The fiscal policy which was the rule in Europe during the period is known as the mercantile system.[1] This policy, as a cardinal political fact, is a datum presupposed by the present study. As Schmoller says (p. 57):

If we pause for a while to consider this foreign and external policy of the European states of the seventeenth and eighteenth centuries—which it has hitherto been the custom to regard as the essential feature of the mercantile system—it is not, of course, our purpose to describe the details of its several forms. The general features of its regulation are well enough known. Difficulties were put in the way of the importation of manufactured goods; and their production and exportation were favored by the prohibition of the export of raw materials, by bounties on export, and by commercial treaties. Encouragement was given to domestic shipping, to the fisheries, and to the coasting trade by restricting or forbidding foreign competition. Commerce with the colonies, and the supplying of them with European wares, was reserved for the mother country. The importation of colonial produce had to take place directly from the colony itself, and not by way of other European ports; and everywhere an attempt was made to establish *direct* trading relations by great privileged trading companies, and by state aid in manifold ways. . . . . The general features are known; the details have even yet not been subjected to due scientific investigation. Our only purpose here is to grasp the fundamental ideas of the system; which, naturally, found varying expressions, here in high duties, there in low, here in the prevention, there in the encouragement of the corn trade. The thought pursued everywhere was this: as competition with other countries fluctuated up and down, to cast the weight of the power of the state into the scales of the balance *in the way demanded in each case by national interests*.

[1] *Vide* Schmoller, *The Mercantile System and Its Historical Significance* (Macmillan, 1902). Translated from the *Studien über die wirthschaftliche Politik Friedrichs des Grossen* (1883), published in the first issue of Schmoller's *Jahrbuch* (1884).

We have accepted Schmoller's general hypothesis in explanation of the mercantilist system. His view must be taken as representing, in its main features, the consensus of present historical scholarship. He epitomizes it in this form:[1]

Our purpose was to show by a particular example, that of Brandenburg, that during the course of the period from the fifteenth to the seventeenth century, the creation of the German territorial state was not merely a political but also an economic necessity. . . . We have to do with a great historical process by which local sentiment and tradition were strengthened, the social and economic forces of the whole territory consolidated, important legal and economic institutions created; by which, further, the forces and institutions thus united were led to a battle of competition with other territories, involving numerous shiftings of toll, confiscation of goods and ships, embargoes and staple-fights, prohibitions of importation and exportation and the like; while, within the country itself, old antagonisms softened and trade became more free.

To so powerful and self-contained a structure and so independent and individual a policy as the town had reached in an earlier age, the German territory scarcely anywhere attained . . . . yet this very time—the second half of the sixteenth century, and the seventeenth century—was an epoch which gave every inducement for an economic transformation. The way was already clear, out of the narrow circle of the small territory into the larger union of forces possible only in the great state. . . . These forces all converging impelled society to some large economic reorganization on a broader basis, and pointed to the creation of national states with a corresponding policy. . . . Everywhere, save in Germany, economic bodies were stretching out and becoming political; everywhere new state systems of economy and finance were arising, able to meet the new needs of the time. Only in our Fatherland did the old economic institutions become so petrified as to lose all life; only in Germany were the foreign trade, the manufacturing skill, the supply of capital, the good economic usages, connections and traditions, which the country had possessed up to 1620, more and more completely lost.

[1] *Loc. cit.*, pp. 43 ff.

And it was not simply the external loss in men and capital which brought about this retrogression of Germany, during a period of more than one century, in comparison with the Powers of the West; it was not even the transference of the world's trading routes from the Mediterranean to the ocean that was of most consequence; it was the lack of politico-economic organization, the lack of consolidation in its forces. What, to each in its time, gave riches and superiority first to Milan, Venice, Florence, and Genoa; then later to Spain and Portugal; and now to Holland, France, and England, and, to some extent to Denmark and Sweden, was a *state* policy in economic matters as superior to the territorial as that had been to the municipal. Those states began to weave the great economic improvements of the time into their political institutions and policies, and to bring about an intimate relation between the one and the other. States arose, forming united, and therefore strong and wealthy economic bodies, quite different from earlier conditions; in these, quite unlike earlier times, the state organization assisted the national economy and this the state policy; and, quite unlike earlier times too, public finance served as the bond of union between political and economic life. It was not only a question of state armies, fleets, and civil services, it was a question rather of unifying systems of finance and economy which should encompass the forces of millions and whole countries, and give unity to their social life. There had always been great states; but they had been bound together neither by traffic nor by the organization of labor nor by any other like forces. The question now was—with a great society divided into social classes widely different from one another and complicated by the division of labor—to bring about, as far as possible, on the basis of common national and religious feelings, a union for external defense and for internal justice and administration, for currency and credit, for trade interests and the whole economic life, which should be comparable with the achievements, in its time, of the municipal government in relation to the town and its environs. This was no mere fancy of the rulers; it was the innermost need of the higher civilization itself that such enlarged and strengthened forms of social and economic community should come into existence. . . . The whole internal history of the seventeenth and eighteenth centuries, not only in Germany, but everywhere else, is summed up in the opposition of the economic policy of the state to that of the town, the district, and the several Estates; the whole foreign history is summed up in the opposition to one another of the separate interests of the newly rising states, each of which sought to obtain and retain its place in the circle of European nations, and in that foreign trade which now included America and India. . . . .

Only he who thus conceives of mercantilism will understand it; in its innermost kernel it is nothing but state making—not state making in a narrow sense, but state making and national-economy making at the same time; state making in the modern sense, which creates out of the political community an economic community, and so gives it a heightened meaning. The essence of the system lies not in some doctrine of money, or of the balance of trade; not in tariff barriers, protective duties or navigation laws; but in something far greater, namely, in the total transformation of society and its organization, as well as of the state and its institutions, in the replacing of a local and territorial economic policy by that of the national state. With this accords the fact lately pointed out with regard to the literary history of the movement, that what is peculiar to all the mercantilist writers is not so much the regulations of trade which they propose for the increase of the precious metals as the stress they lay on the active circulation of money, especially within the state itself.[1]

The last sentence in this quotation from Schmoller suggests the peculiar relation of the cameralists to mercantilism upon which we shall try to show that their writings prove tradition to be misleading. Mercantilism, the instinctive national policy of states in the process of evolution, while at the same time in miscellaneous struggle with other states, was the most prominent objective reality in the civic life of the time. On the other hand, later writers about mercantilism have created

[1] For Schmoller's later views on this main theme, and especially for bibliography of the various phases of the subject, *vide Grundriss*, Index, title "Mercantilismus," etc.

a grotesque mythology of the political and economic theory supposed to have been held by the supporters of the policy. The present study does not extend to mercantilistic theorists outside of Germany. While we are prepared, in the proper place, to challenge the credibility of this mythology as it applies to other countries, our propositions in this book refer not merely to German theorists alone, but to the cameralistic group among those theorists. The cameralists are generally reputed to have been typical mercantilists, in the sense that they are alleged to have taught certain economic doctrines implied by the mercantilistic policy. One of the results of appeal to the cameralistic books themselves is proof that mercantilism in the supposed sense, that is, as a specific system of false economic generalizations, cannot be found in these sources.

Adam Smith did much to create belief in this mythological mercantilism. When we analyze his chapter on "The Principle of the Commercial or Mercantile System,"[1] we find that it produced its effect in this direction more by innuendo than by precise assertion. The chapter begins with the sentence:

> That wealth consists in money, or in gold and silver, is a popular notion which naturally arises from the double function of money, as the instrument of commerce, and as the measure of value.

The poison in the sentence gets its venom in part by association with the title of Book IV, "Of Systems of Political Economy," and with the subtitle of chap. i. The reader understands Smith to imply that there have been systems of "political economy" based on the idea that "wealth consists in money, or in gold and silver;" and that there was a "commercial or mercantile system" which posited this principle. It turns out in the first place that Smith did not distinguish, in this part of his work, between "political economy" as a theory, and economic policy. He asserts that interested parties have succeeded

[1] *Wealth of Nations*, Book IV, chap. i.

in persuading nations to act as though money were the only wealth, and thereupon he indulges in a homily upon the absurdity of that idea. Nevertheless, he concludes[1] that a system of "political economy" which rested on this absurdity widely prevailed. Thus he says:

> The two principles being established, however, that wealth consisted in gold and silver, and that those metals could be brought into a country which had no mines only by the balance of trade, or by exporting to a greater value than it imported; it necessarily became the great object of political economy (*sic*) to diminish as much as possible the importation of foreign goods for home consumption, and to increase as much as possible the exportation of the produce of domestic industry.

A history of the growth of this mercantilistic myth would be instructive, and it is to be hoped that it will some day be written. We may content ourselves with a single comparatively modern and somewhat more full-grown version of the same fiction, this time by a writer who may fairly be presumed to have included the Germans more directly in his generalization than was probably the case with Smith.[2] This historian of political science says:

> The Mercantile System, then, or Colbertism, was the first attempt to put the fundamental principles of the theory of management [*Wirthschaftslehre*] on a scientific and orderly basis. *The central point of the same was the attribution of exclusive value to the precious metals.*[3] Consequently the effort in every possible way to acquire gold and silver, and to retain the same: hence also the anxiety for a favorable balance of trade. The means relied upon were: exclusive (*sic*) promotion of the transforming industries, and of foreign trade, especially attainable through privileges, advances of capital, precise regulations for industries, monopolies, favorable commer-

[1] Bax ed., Vol. I, p. 450.

[2] Von Mohl, *Geschichte und Literatur der Staatswissenschaften*, III. Bd. (1858), p. 296.

[3] Italics mine.

cial treaties and exclusive relations with colonies; then prohibition of the export of the precious metals, and of raw materials fit for domestic manufacture.

Nothing is easier than to show conclusively the incorrectness of the fundamental idea, as well as the impropriety of the means employed. It would therefore be a waste of time to stop for discussion of the absolute truth of the system. At the same time, the question of its relative value for the times and circumstances is not to be disposed of in the same way. It has long since been observed by others that this first system of political economy (*sic*) was not a product of minds exploring truth with a distinctly conscious purpose. It was rather the generalization of the actual programme of certain eminent statesmen, particularly Colbert.[1] It is equally easy to prove, however, that the essential fundamental idea of these statesmen, and therewith of the system built upon it, emerged necessarily from the economic condition of Europe after the middle of the seventeenth century. The accumulation of great sums of money for defraying the costs of war and supplying the luxury of courts was the involuntary task of the officials intrusted with the management of states. This task could be discharged easiest, not to say solely, by constant increase of the export of goods. These were wanted in the newly accessible parts of the world, and would be paid for in gold and silver. *Of a basing of popular welfare, and therewith of the income of the crown, upon more prosperous agriculture, not a word could be said;* partly because of the lack of all rational knowledge of agricultural economy on the part of the landed gentry, together with the utterly suppressed condition of the peasantry, partly because the development of this source of wealth could not keep pace with the above-mentioned need.

Such mixtures of *Wahrheit und Dichtung* are the substitutes for objective interpretation of the cameralistic period which our generation has inherited, and we have accepted them almost

[1] Von Mohl fails to discover, and consequently helps to add vogue to, the fallacy of the whole generalization. He does not perceive that the generalizers put into the system what they thought it should be made responsible for, instead of finding out what its followers actually thought.

without question. How far from the truth was the last sentence in the quotation may be inferred from the bibliography of agriculture published by Zincke.[1]

Now the fact is that "mercantilism" as political economy, in the sense at present associated with that term, in contrast with political policy, did not exist among the cameralists. This was, first, because political economy was not born till after their time, and second, because such material for political economy as was contained in their theories was wonderfully sound, as far as it went, on the meaning of money and the precious metals. It is as absurd to charge the theorists of the mercantilistic period with the economic vagaries of which (by inference from the opportunistic policies of the governments which they served, and which they themselves to a certain extent approved) our modern logic might prove them constructively guilty, as it would be to charge the economists of England today with dogmas which might be deduced from generalization of British policy in the Boer war. Mercantilism, the policy, was war more than it was philosophy. It was the practical answer to the practical question, *What is the practical thing for our state to do under present circumstances?* A situation might easily be imagined in which, with a war to be fought at a distance with a strong nation, the people of the United States, irrespective of party affiliations or economic principles, might afford a certain type of reasoners all the evidence they would want for the assertion, "The people of the United States all believe that *coal* is the only wealth." The conclusion would have essentially the same sort of logical support, and would have the same degree of validity, which examination of the sources discovers in the case of the cameralists and their alleged

[1] *Vide* below, p. 242; cf. p. 256. The blurred view of the cameralists given by Cohn is still more notable, because Cohn's book has probably influenced the thinking of many times more students than von Mohl's. *Vide Grundriss der Nationalökonomie*, 1885, pp. 99, 100.

mercantilism. They certainly believed in a mercantilistic policy. They certainly did not believe in the mercantilistic political economy which has been charged to them by an age that does not understand the meaning of the policy.

Tradition has dealt quite as uncritically with cameralistic beliefs about population. They have been represented as directly contrary to the Malthusian principle. The cameralists have been supposed to believe unlimited increase of the number of citizens both possible and desirable. In reality the Malthusian problem never distinctly appeared above their horizon. Their beliefs about population were substantially the same beliefs which the traffic managers of our western railroads, and the farmers of the prairie states act upon every year of abundant crops. They assume that hands enough are not to be had for harvesting. The cameralists knew as well as modern economists do that there was a limit beyond which more mouths could not be fed. They did not qualify their statements about population quite as carefully as men must who have in mind the Malthusian chapter in economic theory. Substantially, however, they held tenable views of the subject as far as they went, and their efforts to promote population would propably be duplicated today, under parallel circumstances, by the most convinced Malthusians in the world.

Perhaps the most radical misunderstanding of the cameralists, especially on this side of the Atlantic, is in connection with their theories of absolutism. To Americans, absolutism is so unthinkable as a principle of political philosophy, that nothing tolerable can be credited to theories in which such a postulate is a factor. But Americans would have become much profounder political philosophers than they are, if they had been patient enough to learn a little more about the part which the fiction of absolutism has performed in the process of civic evolution. They might have become more docile if they had perceived that the European superstition of the absolutism of rulers differs more in degree than in kind from the American superstition of the absolutism of the constitution. The truth is, each of these illusions was a legal fiction which promoted social control by expressing in the most vivid way practicable the enormous value of obedience to the accepted authorities. Each of these fictions was the idiom in which an age said, in its most impressive way, "The law must be obeyed." Americans have been taught so exclusively the dark phases of absolutistic régimes that they resent suggestion of factors in the case which they have not considered. While absolutism as a principle is indefensible, it has been of incalculable service as a makeshift; and sometimes, notably in the case of most of the cameralists, the absolutistic element which occupied the place of honor in the formal philosophy of the state was subordinated in effect by the moral force of judgments which made steadily in the direction of more authentic civic principles.

But we must indicate the central motive of the cameralists in a positive way. Apart from all details, whether on the credit or debit side, *the salient fact about the cameralistic civic theory was its fundamental assumption of the paramount value of the collective interests, or in other words the subordination of the interests of the individual to the interests of the community.* The absolutistic state, of which cameralism was the theory, used means and methods which are out of the question for democracies. That same absolutistic state maintained certain scales of social value, and arrived at certain types of concrete result, to which democracies thus far have not attained. Whether we will or no, human experience is social. The type of association is more important to the continuous process of human achievement than the choices of individuals. Whether any society has found the just balance between social ascendency and individual liberty, the principle that social ascendency must practically outrank private preference is vital to civilization. Whether the Germans have overemphasized the collectivistic principle, future centuries must decide. Even if Americans are unprepared to concede that our democracy has given individualism too much license, it will be the part of wisdom for us to inspect the achievements of German collectivism without deciding in advance that they contain nothing from which Americans can derive instruction.

Whether the collectivistic principle is ever beneficially to modify democracy or not, there is hardly room for debate upon the proposition that in sheer economy of social efficiency Germany has no near rival among the great nations. Whether the method of this achievement costs more than it is worth, is an open question. That, in view of what it has accomplished, it is worth understanding, is beyond dispute. The explanation of the German type of success cannot be reached without calculating the significance of the cameralists.

It has passed into a world's proverb that the German schoolmaster won the campaign of Sedan. It would be a superficial version of that approximate truth, if the schoolmaster in the case were supposed to be the pedagogue who taught the men in the three columns that crossed the Rhine. The school in which the wonderful proficiency of modern Germany was trained was its whole civic system. No part of the machinery of modern history has been regarded more contemptuously by the rest of the world than the petty German principalities. They were ignoble and obstructive enough, to be sure, but this is not the complete account. Each, with its minute cameralistic organization, functioned like the drill sergeants with the raw levies. The incapable masses of the German people were divided into squads, and disciplined for civic duties, and after the dull drill of centuries were delivered over to the united nation as the most completely socialized citizens in modern European history.

Without attempting to determine the precise degree of

influence which each theorist, or the government behind him, exerted upon the development of cameralism, we may begin with a rapid sketch of the more prominent text-writers. In general it is needless to bring into this account biographical material in addition to that to be found in *Die allgemeine deutsche Biographie*. While it is necessary to base our work upon the presumption of familiarity with Roscher,[1] the argument of this book is a direct challenge of the correctness of Roscher's interpretation.[2] We shall go to the writings of the cameralists themselves for direct evidence of the presumptions, the content, and the sociological significance of their system.

The term *Kammer*, derivatives of which have been transliterated into English to denote a theory and practice for which Englishmen have no exact equivalent, is itself a variant of the Latin *camera*, in turn from the Greek Καμάρα.[3] Cameralism was the routine of the bureaus in which the administrative employees of governments, first of all in the fiscal departments, did their work; or in a larger sense it was systematized governmental procedure, the application of which was made in the administrative bureaus.

Roscher distinguishes in the second half of the seventeenth

[1] *Geschichte der National-Oekonomik in Deutschland.*

[2] While Roscher partially corrects an error, yet he rehabilitates it at the same time in another form: *Zur Geschichte der englischen Volkswirthschaftslehre*, p. 122.

[3] Liddell and Scott: "anything with a vaulted roof or arched covering;" Heyse, *Fremdwörterbuch:* "*camera* or *Kammer* in the more restricted sense is the apartment where the counselors charged with administration of the revenues of a principality assembled: then the persons themselves, *Kammerräthe* and *Kammer-Assessoren*." *Cameralia*, or *Cameral-Wissenschaften*, were the theories on which administration of the revenues proceeded; in a wider sense the term was applied to the sciences of the state in general. A cameralist was one who understood these sciences either theoretically or in practice.

century three principal tendencies among the German national economists:[1]

first a *practical-conservative* tendency, which had its chief seat in the small territories of middle Germany and was best represented by Seckendorff. Then a *purely scientific* tendency, belonging almost wholly in the north of Germany, where as typical contrasts Pufendorf and Conring loom up. A third group, viz., the *practical-progressive*, attaches itself most closely in part to Austria, in part to the great Electors.

It begs the question at the outset, to use the phrase with which Roscher begins detailed discussion of these tendencies. To speak of "the conservative national economics"[2] in the second half of the seventeenth century in Germany is to imply that there already was a systematic economics in the sense in which that phrase was understood two hundred years later, when Roscher wrote. It is certainly not true that an economic theory existed in Germany at that time in the sense carried by the phrase in England since Adam Smith. It would be

[1] *Geschichte der National-Oekonomik in Deutschland*, p. 237. I shall urge later (p. 49; cf. pp. 195, 196) that it is necessary to supply English-speaking students with a commentary on this term, if they are to be protected against misconceptions of historical facts. The term "*National-ökonomik*" corresponds with what existed in Germany in the seventeenth and eighteenth centuries, only if it has the force of the phrase "national management." This management included morals, education, religion, politics, diplomacy, war, and finance, much more directly and intensively than it concerned itself with economic questions as understood in England and America. It is an anachronism therefore to credit Germany, before Adam Smith's critique of economic relations was imported and domesticated, with an economic science in the British sense. The men in Germany who theorized about civic interests before the close of the eighteenth century were political scientists after their kind. They were political economists only in a secondary and incidental sense. This distinction is crucial for the interpretation of all the social sciences in Germany from this point.

[2] *Loc. cit.*, p. 238.

less difficult to support a claim that economics in Germany in the second half of the nineteenth century was merely a more highly developed form of the theory which constituted the social science of the cameralists. This would however at best be a misleading version of the facts. Economic science in Germany was merely a subordinate and subconscious factor in the cameralistic theory of governmental management. It had not gained independence as a science of wealth relations, irrespective of the forms of government under which they exist. The económic presumptions of the cameralists, whether essentially sound or not, were at first merely the folklore of homely thrift, not critical analyses of general economic relations. In the seventeenth and eighteenth centuries the center of social interest was civic, not economic. With this theorem as our point of departure we are bound to arrive at a revised version of the economic theories of the period.[1]

[1] Readers who want the author's conclusions, but who are unwilling to examine his evidence, may pass from this point to the last chapter.

CHAPTER II

THE CIVICS OF OSSE

If the purpose of this book were to trace minutely the evolution of cameralism, our problem would lead back into investigation of generations of men, princes and their servants, of whom Osse was in many ways typical. Such an inquiry would take us far beyond the scope of the present study. It would be rather an investigation of the history of German political institutions in general, especially after the Reformation, than interpretation of a single quasi-academic factor in that civic development. It would bring to the center of attention quite different types of evidence from that to which this argument is restricted. Osse functioned chiefly as an agent of princes at a time when the territorial sovereignty of the German rulers was still undecided, and when the administration of German states was in an early formative stage. His activity as an author was relatively accidental, yet his influence in this character was incomparably more lasting than in any other. He is cited here, however, rather as a means of marking the relativity of the writers to be noticed more at length, than as properly within the bounds of the present survey.

Osse was born in the hamlet of Ossa, near the obscure town of Geithain, in 1506. He studied law at Leipzig, was "scholarly, conscientious, laborious, gentle and deeply pious."[1] He served for a time in the army; for several years he occupied the chief lectureship in law at Leipzig; in 1537 he was mentioned by Zarncke as *consiliarius Misnensis;* he remained a counselor of Herzog Georg till the death of the latter; passed to the service of Herzog Moritz, 1541; the same year was released by Moritz to enter the service of the elector Johann

[1] Diestel in *Allgemeine deutsche Biographie,* title "Osse."

Friedrich, where he remained as chancellor for six years. There are confusions in dates at this period, but after employment of uncertain length at Meiningen, Osse was in 1547 made *Hofrichter* in Leipzig. In 1550 he represented the elector at the Diet of Augsburg. On account of ill health he withdrew from his judgeship in 1555, and composed the document which is his chief title to a place in history. He died in 1556.

A more searching inquiry into the personal record of Osse is unnecessary. In spite of the author's own usage, and that of his editor Thomasius, which we follow, Roscher uses the form "Ossa," corresponding to the acepted spelling of his birthplace.

It appears further that, in spite of his prestige at Leipzig, Osse was not in full favor with the Saxon theologians. The complete story of this phase of his career would take us far afield, in the general culture-history of the period, and we must pass it with a mere hint. Philipp Melanchthon soundly berated Osse and five other advisers of Herzog Moritz, and he embellished one of his denunciations with the couplet:

Hiengen die Sechs an einen Strick.
Das wär Sachsen und Meissen Glück.[1]

The editor, Thomasius, implies that the reputation thus referred to made Osse uncomfortable at the court of Johann Friedrich, and accounts for his resignation. Thomasius protests, however, that he can find no adequate ground for Osse's bad repute with the elector. While declining to enter into the merits of the case, he submits this consideration, viz.:

Philipp Melanthon (*sic*) was no angel himself, and there are proofs enough that not everything which came from Melancthon as a judgment of other men can be taken as a divine truth or an infallible gospel.

At bottom, the case against Osse appears to have been that his break with traditional religious ideas was not as com-

[1] *Testament*, ed. Thom., 1717, "Vorrede," p. 10.

plete as the Lutherans demanded. He was accused of being still at heart a papist. In commenting upon this charge, Thomasius furnishes the interesting item that Osse's copious quotations from the Vulgate, instead of the Lutheran version, were among the most damaging evidences of his guilt.

We turn directly to the *Testament*, the document which entitles its author to rank as a forerunner of the seventeenth- and eighteenth-century cameralists.[1] It is a monograph written in the last year of its author's life, and by command of his prince, and was intended, both by prince and his emeritus adviser, to serve the purpose for which Adam Smith later invoked the hypothesis of "the impartial spectator."

The form in which the document is now most accessible is the edition of Christian Thomasius, the man who is reputed to have been the first in Germany to introduce the innovation of academic lectures in the vulgar language. At the time of his discovery of the document, he was an important factor in the influence of the University of Halle, of which he is called one of the founders. We shall have occasion to refer to him again in his proper chronological place. At present we need to cite only a few details in which he has thrown light upon Osse.

[1] *D. Melchiors von Osse "Testament." Gegen Hertzog Augusto Churfürsten zu Sachsen. Sr. Churfürst. Gnaden Räthen und Landschafften. 1556. Anitzo zum ersten mahl völlig gedruckt. Auch hin und wieder durch nutzliche Anmerckungen Erläutert. Nebst einer Vorrede und Anhang von einen Versuch kleiner "Annalium" den damahligen Zustand so wohl bey Hofe als auf Universitäten desto deutlicher sich einzubilden. Zum Gebrauch des Thomasischen "Auditorii." Halle im Magdeburgisch. A. MDCCXVII.* A portion of the author's special title-page to the body of the document reads: "Welchergestalt eine Christliche Obrigkeit ingemein, in ihrem Regiment mit Gottes Hülffe eine gottselige, weissliche vernünfftige und rechtmässige Justicien erhalten kan. Darum auch Erwehnung geschieht von dem Regiment. Gerichtbarkeit und Policey der löblichen Chur- und Fürstenthum Sachsen, Thüringen, und Meissen, Hochermeldtem Churfürsten zuständig."

In the first place, Thomasius says, in the Preface to the document, that he was first shown the imperfect manuscript, (apparently in 1707) in the *Fürstliche Bibliothek* at Wolffenbüttel. He adds that up to that time it was unknown to him, and he had not even seen the portions that had been printed. Later he bought the full manuscript at an auction. Thomasius appears to have recognized in Osse a man after his own heart. Replying to the supposed challenge, Why publish the book of a man about whom so many suspicions existed? he says (*Vorrede*, p. 16):

The author is the first of those counselors known to us who gave their opinion as to the way in which the judicial system is to be improved. The first usually breaks the ice, and cannot accomplish all, but he leaves the rest to his successors.

The document as we have it occupies, with the editor's notes, 548 pages. In the same binding, and filling 264 pages, is Thomasius' collection of materials on the history of the University of Leipzig. The title of the collection is *Ein kleiner Versuch von Annalibus*. The editing of Osse's work was in Thomasius' mind a propagandist measure, and as he regarded improvement of the educational system as the key to the whole problem, it was appropriate to issue the seemingly unlike documents together. It appears that Thomasius wanted to publish a treatise on political reform, with reference both to the Roman and the Canon law. The difficulties proved too great, and he chose to make Osse's document the vehicle of some of his ideas. His notes on the text number 271. The *Testament* itself contains only 118 sections. Although the notes are in much smaller type than the text, a rough estimate shows that they fill, in the aggregate, about one-half the whole space. If we should fully analyze both text and notes, we should find in them two separate monuments, of two stadia of development in political philosophy, previous to that marked by the most complete form of cameralism. For that reason we shall not undertake here a detailed account either of Osse or of Thomasius. Their determining purpose was not identical with that of cameralism proper. On the whole, they had their center in other groups, with which this book does not attempt to deal. We may simply note in these two writers certain germs which must be examined in more developed form in later theorists.

One who knew nothing of the history of the German language, or of its geographical variations, who assumed that its growth was in a straight line, and who drew conclusions from literary form alone, would promptly place Osse's *Testament* much later than Obrecht's *Secreta Politica;*[1] perhaps even later than Becher.[2] Of course the use of Latin by the side of German in the Obrecht collection strengthens the impression of age. Osse's syntax, as well as his vocabulary, approaches closer than that of either of these writers to modern usage. According to Thomasius' statement (*Vorrede*, p. 33), this is not to be attributed to the editor. He says that he changed little or nothing in the style, with the single exception of substituting the word *oder* in frequent cases for Osse's word *aber*. Osse's own statement of his reason for writing in German is as follows:

> The motives which have moved me to set down my opinions in the German language, are not for the sake of His Electoral Grace, who, God be praised, was in his youth thoroughly instructed in the Latin tongue and good arts, but rather the consideration that this memorial might come to the knowledge of laymen, untaught in the Latin language, and the desire that they might not be hindered in reading it by the intermixture of many Latin words.[3]

Osse begins the *Testament* with a paragraph which we translate as closely as possible:

> It is among all wise people beyond dispute, that every magistracy (*Obrigkeit*) may prove and make evident its virtue and aptitude in

[1] *Vide* pp. 40 ff. below.

[2] *Vide* pp. 107 ff. below.

[3] *Zuschrifft*, pp. 8 ff.

two ways. First, in time of war, through manly deeds, good sagacious projects, and protection of their lands and subjects, second, in time of peace, through ordering and maintaining of good godly righteous government, judiciary, and *Policey*.[1] For with these two every magistracy should necessarily be adorned and supplied, in order that in every time of war and peace they (*sic*) may be able well to govern, protect, control and defend their own.

Osse then enlarges briefly upon the duties which belong to the ruler in time of war; but he dismisses this side of the case as beyond his competence. As to the other class of duties, he continues (p. 33):

As to what concerns the government in times of peace, I will write, as much as God vouchsafes me grace, for He is the ground on which all must be built which is good, and wherever such ground is lacking there follows no permanent building.

The author promises to set down truly all that he has observed in the service of five electors of Saxony, the fifth then living. He frequently repeats that he is doing this not of his own motion, but at the command of the elector. We may safely assume that the passage immediately following represents Osse's fundamental opinions as well as they could be pictured. He says (p. 33):

Such a command I am not at liberty to disregard, and for this reason I lay down first of all the following ground. All that I hereafter write will be built upon it. It must also be observed with special diligence.

Government over men is such a high, precious and wonderful thing, that no human being, no matter how excellent in understanding, reason and wit, is to be intrusted with exercising it according to his own will, caprice and opinion, for such government is a higher thing than that the exercise of it could belong to one over others who by nature are of one origin with him, which same may be known from all races of animals, since a flock of sheep does not allow itself

[1] The reasons for allowing this term to stand in its German form will appear later.

to be ruled by a sheep, nor a drove of horses or cattle by one of their own kind, but rather for such government something else is necessary, which is higher and better than the other beasts. Now man, who in many ways surpasses the other animals, for the like reason, since man must be governed, he must be governed by something higher and more excellent than man himself, if the government is to be stable. Since now nothing more excellent can be found in this world than man . . . . who is yet fallible, and has much in common with the beasts, ... and even in case a man were found who could be moved from the right by no irregular affections, he would be subject to mortality, and no one would know what would happen with his successors, therefore almighty God, out of special grace to human kind, has ordained the means of the common written law [*der ordentlichen beschriebenen Recht und Gesetze*] whereby to keep the temper of magistrates and judges in the right way, in order that the same may govern others and render justice without any hindrance of inordinate inclinations and affections, and when one considers the usefulness of such a divinely given means, one finds that this ordination of rights and laws is one of the highest benefits and gifts with which God has blessed men here in this life, for such laws and rights were in the beginning ordained by wise honorable people after necessary consideration, not from friendship, love or hate, but in general without all inordinate affections and inclinations. . . . . When now such common right and law is ordained, even if those who act contrary to it are punished in accordance with it, ... no one has occasion for complaint, but everyone is satisfied, since we know that justice has been done to one as well as to another, and that so impatience and uproar of the subjects is avoided.[1]

A little later (p. 37) the conclusion is drawn still more distinctly:

[1] The uneasiness of Thomasius over the traditional doctrines about "*beschriebene Gesetze*" (*vide* Roscher, *in re* Thomasius) begins to show itself in the note in this passage, viz., "the written laws are by no means to be preferred to the customs" (*Gewohnheiten*). The naïve reasoning which Osse represents was an effective means of control so long as people accepted it at face value. Revolution was certain wherever it was repudiated without substitution of a constructive theory.

Hence follows that it is a human duty to hold the common rights and laws in honor, to esteem them high, and to subject oneself to them with patience, as the means whereby common peace, repose and welfare are maintained. And that also the established magistracy is under obligation to protect such right and law, to enforce it and to govern according to it, not oppressing anyone by acting contrary to it. For there can be no doubt that as the powers that be are ordained of God (*Ad. Rom.* 13) likewise also human rights and laws by the powers that be, so that they flow from the providence and special destiny of almighty God. . . . Accordingly everyone should remember that if he disobeys the magistrate and escapes punishment, yet he is not assured of escaping the punishment of almighty God.[1]

At the opening of the second part, Osse says that, in order rightly to understand his reflections as a whole, it is necessary to read what he has said in the first part about all Christian governments. As to electoral Saxony in particular, he adds, it has been the object of special divine favor. He specifies as a fundamental blessing, that the government is not elective but hereditary, and exclusively in the male line.[2] The consequence is (p. 204) that the best people in the country are retained in the service of the court, and the good customs and laws continue undisturbed. The country has therefore grown in power, resources, public buildings, and otherwise. Then follows this passage:

And since every government in temporal affairs is of two parts [*auf zweyerley stehet*], namely government (*sic*) and *Policey*, and then the judiciary and justice, it is in order that the aforenamed

[1] Entirely aside from the familiar dogmatic basis of this argument, Osse's use of the terms "*beschriebene*" and "*geschriebene Rechte*"—apparently without variation of concept—plainly shows that the argument got some of its plausibility from a peculiar form of the ambiguous middle hidden in the logic, i. e., the ecclesiastico-theological associations of the terms "*heilige Schrift*," "*geschrieben*," etc., were carried over to all written laws.

[2] Thomasius at once challenges this dictum, on the ground that debates over "the best form of government" are mere pedantries.

land in this respect also should be blessed of God before many other lands. For, in the first place, as respects the government, "*hochermeldeter Churfürst*" ordered his court with many dignified people, with counts, nobles, doctors, etc., who hear the causes presented, reflect upon these matters, weigh and consult, and with timely advice render true and right decisions. "*Seine Churfürst. Gn.*" has also filled the civic offices with functionaries, with orders that each shall receive what is due, and that justice shall always be rendered to the subjects. For in this country, God be praised, domestic peace is maintained, and many wholesome publications appear against oppression and irregular administration. Moreover, in this land there is a good and proper coinage, whereby the people are impelled to trade with one another in all the things which they need, whereby the revenues of the prince from commerce increase [*Zöll und Geleit*], etc. . . . . For where there is good coinage there is much trade, and where is much trade and people . . . . the land in general has improvement and prosperity, etc.

This passage may be used as a way mark. In the German states at the middle of the sixteenth century, there were officials and administration enough, but measured by the cameralism of the middle of the eighteenth century the officials were unorganized, and the administration unspecialized and unsystematized. Men of Osse's time were in contact with rudiments of all the governmental activities which have developed since, but these were relatively inchoate and confused. We have distinctly disclaimed the purpose of venturing into study of the evolution of cameralism, either theoretical or applied. Our composite picture of the academic side of it merely draws in a few lines from this embryonic period.

Osse enumerates as another blessing of the country the founding of "drey Fürsten-Schulen, als Meissen, Pforten, Grimma,[1] und zwo treffentliche Universitäten und hohe Schulen."[2] The author refers to these schools as particularly

[1] The two first in 1543, the last 1550 (Thomasius).

[2] Leipzig, 1409. Wittenberg, 1502.

to prepare men for official positions and to give them training in legal knowledge. Thomasius comments to the effect that the papacy was influential enough largely to nullify the benefits of these foundations. Then mention is made of the two *Hoffgerichte* held by the elector, the one at Leipzig, the other at Wittenberg, and the *Schöppen* are also praised as beneficent institutions,[1] and besides the other higher and lower courts held by prelates and nobles on their estates, there are many hundred *Land-Gerichte*, "so that, by the grace of God a praiseworthy justice is present in these lands." Moreover the country possesses a specially fine *Policey*,[2] and all affairs are arranged in good order, and we meet fine, courteous, affable persons in all stations.[3] In addition many natural and acquired advantages are enumerated which contribute to the happiness of the country.

Yet in spite of all these blessings, the author finds that it is possible for abuses to creep in. He finds this danger first in the administration of justice. His earliest attention is given then to the means of avoiding these evils. The caution with which he approaches the subject is again outspoken in protestations of obedience to the command of the prince; and the author refers besides to the demands of the common welfare (*gemeinen Nutz*) of all classes in the country, and of many

[1] These courts were supposed to secure justice in minor cases by a fair combination of official and lay persons. Thomasius has an important note (p. 210) on the quarrels in the law faculties over *Schöppenstuhle*. *Vide* pp. 208 and 310.

[2] Thereupon Thomasius tartly comments, "I will not undertake to judge what sort of a thing a fine or a nasty *Policey* may be." We shall not go into Osse's discussion of *Policey* in detail, because it suits our purpose to deal with the maturer form of the system particularly as reflected in Justi. *Vide* below, p. 436 *et passim.*

[3] Americans receive no more elementary impression in Germany than that the concept *gute Ordnung* fills the place in German life-philosophy which the notion "freedom" occupies in ours.

surrounding countries, as justifying attempts at improvement, in spite of the opposition of those whose selfish interests are on the side of things as they are.

Osse finds the root of all the difficulties which he has in mind, in the lack of properly taught and trained men to take the places of responsibility in the state. This fundamental opinion accounts for the extent to which his argument turns upon improvement in the universities. He recurs to the three reasons which he had assigned in secs. XCIV–XCVI of Part I, for unsatisfactory conditions in public life, viz.: (*a*) defective training of children, (*b*) omission to admit young men to the councils of their elders, (*c*) frequent changes in office, and he adds a fourth, viz., favoritism to relatives and friends. This excludes men of more talent from public careers, or from the places which they would be more competent to fill. The first means suggested for correcting the evil is a system of secret representatives of the prince at the universities. Their duty should be to pick out young men of promise, and to recommend them for appointments. Thereupon follow all the propositions for the improvement of schools and universities. With respect to the latter, Osse restricts himself almost exclusively to the "*arme betrübte und fast gefallene Universität Leipzig,*" because he professes ignorance of the facts at Wittenberg (pp. 258 ff.). As a source of information about conditions within and around the University of Leipzig at the middle of the sixteenth century the succeeding chapters are highly important. In this connection Thomasius' Appendix of 264 pages must again be mentioned.[1] As will appear however when the systematic cameralists are before us, the principal questions around which

[1] *Ein kleiner Versuch von Annalibus von Anno 1409 bis 1629. Eine etwas genauere Einsicht in die Historie von Ursprung und Fortgang der Universitäten in Deutschland, sonderlich der Universität Leipzig und Wittenberg, und denen in denenselben entstandenen Zänchereyen unterschiedener Facultäten ingleichen des eingeführten langweiligen Processes, und was vermittelst dieser Zänckereyen vor Unruhe an den Chur- und*

cameralistic theory was built up had not yet risen upon Osse's horizon. His document is useful for our purpose merely as a picture of undifferentiated confusion, with which to compare the highly articulated system of two centuries later. The Table of Contents is worth consideration. The titles of chapters must be understood to stand for a series of indictments of everything which might be classed under those heads at Leipzig, and enough evidence appears to create a prima-facie case in favor of the author's substantial correctness. Here then was a single group of symptoms which impressed men of Osse's type as calling for correction. In later chapters the reasons will appear why we must be content with a bare reference to this earlier type of social theory.

This first chapter on the specific subject of justice (chap. xiv) is a fine and typical specimen not merely of Osse's style, but of the moral valuations which were current among the more academic thinkers. The contrast between the objective facts of institutions and conduct on the one hand, and frequent and almost proverbial formulations of abstract moral standards on the other, is perhaps nowhere more evident than in this period. We may simply record in passing that citations might easily be made from the literature of this period, which would compare favorably in moral import with generalizations of the same order in any subsequent generation. The essential demands upon justice, as presented in this chapter, are that it shall be (1) unpartisan, (2) impersonal, (3) incorruptible.[1]

To this particular chapter on justice Thomasius adds a long note (p. 435) to this effect:

Fürstlichen Sächsischen Höfen verursacht worden, zu erlangen, zu desto bessern Verstand des von D. Melchior von Osse auf Churfürst Augusti Allergnädigsten Befehl A. 1555 verfertigten und 1556 übergebenen Rechtlichen Bedenckens. Zum Gebrauch des Thomasischen Auditorii.

[1] The first half at least is a rather notable apostrophe to Justice, and the remainder shows that lofty ideals of practical application were not without witnesses.

The author has, to be sure, said much that is good and useful about justice. He has however forgotten the best and most necessary, namely, that for good and righteous justice it is necessary that the same shall be *administered as promptly as possible*, and that justice shall not be tediously suspended.

In fact, Osse expresses himself with sufficient clearness on this point in the seventh and eighth sections of the same chapter.

Then follows an account of the evils actually existing in the Saxon courts, and suggestions for their correction. The same general scheme is followed in the succeeding chapters in the division on justice. Distinguishing the chapter on *Policey* from the latter for purposes of emphasis, and because the subject occupies such a unique position in the cameralistic period, we must give our attention to the editor, although, as we have intimated, he ought not properly to be considered in the series of writers with whom we are chiefly concerned, and although the chronological order is disarranged by attention to him here. Osse begins the chapter on *Policey* with a remark to this effect: Aristotle and the greater part of the ancient wise men have held that a good *Policey* of a land or a city requires four "pieces," viz., "*Princeps*," "*Concilium*," "*Praetorium*," and "*Populus*." These the author translates, "a ruler or overlord; good wise counsel; unpartisan, good judicature, and a pious obedient people."[1] As in the case of an earlier reference to *Policey*, Thomasius at once takes the cue, and his note is an important symptom. Beginning with bibliographical references which form one of the lines of evidence by which we trace the influence of authors to be discussed later,[2] Thomasius continues (p. 500):

[1] "*Ein Regent und Ober-Herr; guter weiser Rath; unpartheyische gute Gerichtbarkeit, und ein fromm gehorsam Volck.*"

[2] He first calls to mind the note referred to above (p. 30), and then cites: "aus dem ersten Theil die *relation* und *judicium* von *Clapmarii*

This very year there appeared at *Franckfurth am Mayn* a book entitled *Entwurff einer wohleingerichteten Policey.* It contains seven sheets. The author, who does not give his name, assumes that the flourishing condition of the financial system of a state must rest upon four chief pillars, namely *Policey*, fiscus, commerce, and taxation. The *Policey* has to do with the internal and external condition (*Verfassung*) of the state.[1] The internal condition consists in part of a vigorous society, namely, (1) in a vigorous growth of the inhabitants, partly in a joyous life, both of the soul, namely, (2) in a religious worship, (3) in virtuous conduct, and (4) praiseworthy education; and of the body, in its sustenance, and satisfaction, through (5) abundance of necessary, useful, and superfluous means-of-life, (6) robust health, and (7) peaceful security. The external condition consists (8) in the good order of people, things, and places, and (9) in a convenient ornamentation of city and country. On the contrary, every state is disintegrated and disordered through (1) decline of population, (2) disregard of religion, (3) vicious life, (4) neglect of education, (5) lack of sustenance and increase of the pauper class, (6) epidemics and plagues, (7) turbulence, revolts, and private quarrels, (8) irregular confusion of social strata, affairs, and places, (9) uncultivated lands and badly ordered towns. For promotion of the different kinds of good works, and removal of the evil, the author proposes in general the establishment

arcanis rerumpublicarum, von Faust's *consiliis pro aerario*, von Obrechts *Politischen Bedencken*, von Klokii *de Aerario*, von der *Fürstlichen Machtkunst oder unerschöpflichen Goldgrube*, von des Freyherrn von Schrötern *Fürst. Schatz und Rent-Cammer* (*nota* 39, p. 81; *nota* 41, pp. 96 ff., *nota* 76, pp. 152 ff.) ingleichen von der *Einfältigkeit der Haushaltungs-Regeln* (*nota* 40, p. 95).

[1] One of the anachronisms in English interpretation of German thought has come in through premature translation of this word *Verfassung* by our modern term "constitution." Unless direct evidence to the contrary appears in rare cases, the word should never be understood to mean "constitution" in the modern sense, until the beginning of the struggle for constitutions. I believe I fairly represent what the word meant to the author cited and even to Thomasius by the vague word "condition." The remainder of the quotation supports this view.

of a *Policey* bureau, the members of which should be charged with (1) giving their earnest attention to the above points, (2) averting harmful occurrences, (3) controlling disorder, or (4) bringing complaints before the proper tribunals, (5) maintaining reliable watchmen and detectives, (6) conducting unexpected visitations and inquisitions, (7) keeping a watchful eye on peaceful persons, things, and places in the state, (8) to that end drawing useful ordinances relating to persons and things, (9) responsibility for observance of the same. Thereupon the author enlarges upon each of these nine points of good *Policey*, especially upon the population, religion, virtuous conduct, good kinds of education, riches, health, security, order and adornment of a state, especially upon the means of securing these things, and of avoiding the opposite. Now the author deserves praise, in the first place [continues Thomasius], for attempting to treat of political things in a brief and very well-connected and rather clear didactic fashion, in contrast with the condition of which I have so often complained, viz., that there has been scarcely an attempt in universities at such pedagogy in political things. Indeed everyone who reads this writing will find in it much whose truth he will comprehend, and the introduction or abolition of which he will agree with the author in finding highly desirable for the state. He will accordingly be pleased that in a few hours' reading he has learned from the author more well-connected truths than if he had spent two years with political works written according to the Aristotelian method. . . . .

Thomasius then refers to a second monograph of the same author, another tract also published by him this year, viz., *Politische Gedanken, welcher gestalt Monarchen und Könige, Republiquen und Fürsten, nebst ihren Reichen, Ländern und Unterthanen, durch eine leichte methode mächtig und reich seyn oder werden können;* and he continues:

In this connection much remains to be said in order to make such a tract complete. I will attempt, however, to mention only the principal things, as suggested by this brief introduction. (1) It is to be wished that the author had explained somewhat more clearly how the *Policey* system should be distinguished from the fiscal, commercial and taxing systems. He observes at the outset, to be sure, that the fiscal system should deal with the *Oeconomie*[1] of the country and the domains of sovereigns; the commercial systems with trade and business [*Handel und Wandel*], with the appertaining occupations and professions; the taxing system with the arrangements for contribution to the state, and he promises to expand his thoughts upon these three neighboring pillars. After he thereupon announces, however, that the *Policey* has charge of the internal and external condition [*Verfassung*] of a state, one is not without reason for the opinion that, because the fiscal, commercial and taxing systems also belong to the internal or external condition of the state, these three pieces must also be counted as parts of the *Policey* system. And if one should say that the *Policey* system is here understood in a restricted sense, namely, so far as the same takes account of the well-being [*Wohlseyn*] of the subjects, since on the other hand the fiscal and taxing systems aim at the well-being of the rulers, this difference might have been announced at once without circumlocution by the author, but on the other hand it would then not be clear how the commercial system is distinguished from the *Policey* system, especially as everyone understands that the same belongs to the fifth chapter, and the author also there recommends the commercial system as a necessary part of the same. (2) It is very serious that the author regards all these four pillars not as the ground of a peaceful and virtuously reasonable state, but as a ground of the increasingly prosperous fiscal system, and that at the beginning of the second tract he lays down this rule as a basis: "All considerable rulers must attend to their sole ultimate purpose [*eintzigen Endzweck*] and highest interest, viz., to become powerful and (supplying from the title the words carefully omitted in this passage) rich."[2] For although in the present tract he chatters about religion and virtue,

[1] The reasons for not translating this term will appear later. *Vide* Index, title "Economy and Related Terms."

[2] A part of the reason for introducing Osse at all in this book is the value of these editorial notes upon his monograph in throwing light on contemporary estimates of the cameral system. Thomasius here puts his finger upon the central trait of cameralism, and it is astonishing that later writers have so far lost account of this clue to the whole theory.

it is on the other hand very suspicious when, at the beginning of the second chapter (p. 18), he announces that he will not inquire whether religion is an invention of the clergy and statesmen, who introduced it for spiritual or secular purposes, but it will be enough that the same furnished the chief foundation of a state. In the same spirit (on p. 5), in reciting the satisfactions of the body he places riches first, and gives precedence to the same not only over health but also over peaceful security. Indeed, in chapter i, §6, p. 9, he recommends polygamy as a serviceable means of increasing the population. Again he refers to regulation and limitation only of houses of prostitution, where they are to be tolerated for reasons of state, etc., etc. Who the author is, I will not disclose, although I discovered his identity a short time after I had read his two tracts and had made these notes. Meanwhile he has sufficiently betrayed himself when, in the tract, *How Great Lords May Become Rich* (p. 11), he cites a *Discurs* published by his father in 1655. . . .

It is evident that after writing note 105 above referred to (p. 30) Thomasius saw a great light, partly through the eyes of this unnamed writer, on the place of *Policey* in the administrative system. So much of the note is quoted, however, not primarily for its connection with Thomasius, but because the *rêsumê* of the document will be useful for comparison later. At the same time a few sentences should be added from the paragraph in Osse to which Thomasius' note is appended.[1] They continue his reference to the different divisions of administration. Osse says:

Everything should be directed toward keeping these four parts in good condition, if one is to maintain a good *Policey*, for a lord and ruler is in three respects under obligations to the people divinely intrusted to him; namely, that he should maintain the same in good prosperous circumstances, which occurs when the people [*das Volck*] lives virtuously, and some among them are promoted to learning, and to good arts, and many wise and learned people are in their number, from whom the rest may receive good instruction, and they

[1] *Vide* above, p. 33.

are not left to wander in the darkness of ignorance, and everything through which such promotion of things useful to the community is hindered is either prevented or averted by the ruler.

The foregoing is of firstrate importance when we generalize the civic assumptions of the cameralists.

It is to be noted that Osse could say, "Praise God, this land is already provided with an honorable, good, and praiseworthy *Policey*" (p. 506).[1] He could offer only certain very cautious and vague suggestions about details. For instance, he calls attention to conflicts of interests between rural and urban populations, which tended to injustice toward the former, through the tendency to concentrate certain rural occupations, such as brewing, in the towns (p. 509). Thomasius comments on the justice of his position, in spite of the foolishness of the grounds on which it is based, viz., that in Roman law trade was prohibited to the nobility. Again, Osse denounces the inhumanity of many of the nobility toward the widows and orphans of their dependents, and calls upon the elector to appoint a supervisor to act as a guardian of such dependent persons, and to secure their rights against conscienceless nobles. In the third place, he urges upon the elector correction of practice in the criminal courts, and especially prevention of illegal resort to torture. Increase of the amount of light and air in prisons; certain sumptuary reforms, on the ultimate ground (p. 516) that luxury drains money from the country; attempts to prevent rise in the price of meat; appointment of trustees to keep heirs from squandering their estates, are substantially all the further changes which Osse was able to recommend.

The *Testament* proper closes with these considerations. An appendix of seventeen pages, including the editor's notes, is added, with the title, *Additio Gemeine des Heil. Reichs*

[1] As evidence that this part of the administration was well guarded, he cites the *Policey- und Landes-Ordnung*, published by Elector August in 1555, "in *Corpore Juris Saxonici*, tom. I, pp. 31 biss 59 zu lesen."

Wohlfarth belangende. It replies to the hypothetical question, Supposing the conduct advised in the *Testament* were strictly adopted in Saxony, would it not all be in vain, because of the disorder in the Holy Roman Empire at large? The unhappy condition of the Empire was attributed by Osse to three causes: (1) the religious quarrels, (2) the weakening of the judicial authority of the Empire, (3) disregard of *Landfrieden* within the Empire. In discussing the situation he puts the emphasis almost entirely on the first point. The whole matter is primarily political in another sense from that in which the cameralists are to be considered, and it is not therefore material to our inquiry.[1]

Although Thomasius' *Versuch von Annalibus* is not directly germane to our purpose, its presence in the same volume with the *Testament* is excuse for alluding to it again. It is professedly an attempt to stimulate the neglected study of history. It is a collection of data principally concerning education in Saxony. It covers the period 1409–1629. To the student of Saxon history, and especially of the University of Leipzig, it would be an extremely valuable secondary source.

[1] Thomasius insists (p. 532) that Osse's omission to mention in this connection the Religious Peace of Augsburg (September 25, 1555) strengthens the suspicion that he was not a good Lutheran, but at heart a papist. As the *Testament* was dated December, 1555, and as the *Additio* was written later, failure to mention it, the editor thinks, points to the author's lack of sympathy with any arrangement in the nature of a *modus vivendi* between the contending forces. Osse's own professions do not tend to confirm this hypothesis.

CHAPTER III

THE CIVICS OF OBRECHT

The only writer whom it is necessary to mention between Osse and Obrecht is Georg Engelhard von Löhneyss (sometimes written Löhneis, Löhneissen, etc.). Although his name frequently occurs in the cameralistic books, there is no reason to regard him as an important contributor to cameralistic science. Thomasius (*Vorrede zum Testament*, p. 25) intimates that Löhneyss borrowed much without credit from Osse. I have been unable to obtain any of his writings. Inama says of him:[1]

He was of an aristocratic Palatine family. He was first Master of the Horse at the court of Elector August of Saxony. In 1583 he entered the service of Heinrich Julius of Braunschweig-Wolfenbüttel, first as *Stallmeister*, then as *Berghauptmann*. At both courts he had rare opportunities for training in the practical administrative technique of the time. Each court was supposed to have a model administrative system. August was an eminent and tireless administrator, Heinrich Julius the best trained jurist among contemporary rulers. At the same time these courts were noted for their display. From his purchased estates Löhneyss bore the title "Erbherr in Remlingen und Neundorf." For a while he had his own printing establishment, particularly to secure proper publication of his own writings. His three chief works were printed here.[2] The latter part of his life is without traces in the confusion of the Thirty Years' War. His printing establishment and the stock of his books were

[1] *All. d. Bib., in loc.*

[2] Viz., (1) *Della Cavelleria. S. de arte equitando, exercitiis equestribus et torneamentis, gründlicher Bericht von allem was zu der löblichen Reiterei gehörig, und einem Cavalier zu wissen von Nöthen, auch Chur und Wartung der Pferde und wie man dieselben auf allerhand Manier abrichten und zäumen soll*, 1609, 2d ed., 1624; (2) *Bericht vom Bergwerk, wie man dieselben bauen und in guten Wohlstand bringen soll*, 1617; (3) *Aulico-*

destroyed in the course of that struggle. Seckendorff, in his *Vorrede*, praised the *Hof-Staat- und Regierungskunst;* yet like the rest of the author's writings it has no special scientific weight. Still his chief cameralistic work stands, in riches of content and enlightened judgment, as well as practical insight, far above the mass of theoretical political products, and forms an immediate preparation for the flourishing period of German cameralistics inaugurated by Seckendorff's *Teutscher Fürstenstaat.*

The biography of Georg Obrecht is best epitomized in Eisenhart's sketch:[1]

Obrecht was born in Strassburg in 1547, and died in the same city in 1612. As a young man he studied in Paris. After escaping the massacre of St. Bartholomew, which cost the loss of his library, he went to Basel and obtained there the degree of Doctor of Laws in 1574. In 1575 he was made Professor of Law in Strassburg, and he retained the position to the end of his life. As the fleeting glory of Wittenberg began to fade, Strassburg assumed the spiritual leadership of Protestant Germany. Along with Giffen and Gothofredus, it was chiefly Obrecht who founded the fame of the Strassburg academy. He held various offices and dignities besides his professorship. In 1604 he was made a noble of the empire, and in 1609 he received the title of Palgrave.

For the purposes of this book Obrecht is important as the author of a single volume.[2] The chief significance of the five

politica oder Hof-Staats- und Regierungskunst, 1622–24, republished 1679. Apparently the last was identical with the book often referred to under the title *Teutscher Regentenstaat* (*vide* Roscher, p. 116). There are good reasons for the suspicion that Löhneyss has been mentioned by many writers who neglected to state that their knowledge of him was at second hand.

[1] *All. d. Bib., in loc.*

[2] *Fünff underschiedliche Secreta Politica, von Anstellung, Erhaltung und Vermehrung guter Policey, und von billicher, rechtmässiger und nothwendiger, Erhöhung eines jeden Regenten Jährlichen Gefallen und Einkommen. Allen Hohen und Nidern Obrigkeiten, besonders dess Heiligen Römischen Reichs Ständen, in diesen letzten und hochbetrangten*

monographs which make up the volume is disclosed at once in the Preface by the author's son, Joannes Thomas Obrecht ("J. C. et Comes Palatinus Caesareus"). As editor he gives an account of the origin and purpose of the different monographs. Attention is piqued at once by the statement, "I printed the book at my own expense, and secretly."[1] According to the editor's explanation, the essays are the outgrowth and development of a central purpose, which is stated in connection with the account of the first document. In a word, the wars with the Turks had made the question of money to pay expenses importunate. In the year 1590 Obrecht Sr. had publicly discussed certain theses *de principijs belli.* In that discussion he had maintained, among other things, that in order to carry on successful war, and to defend their lands, governments (*Obrigkeiten*) must be provided with an abundance of money (*mit einem starcken Gelt Nervo*). He had also announced that he would be ready, on a more favorable occasion, to go into detail as to the ways in which this *Nervus belli* might be obtained "through Christian, righteous, and proper means."

A single remark of a relatively obscure writer would be of little weight in supporting a general hypothesis. If there were any doubt that this problem of ways and means for the maintenance of military operations was desperate in every German state, it would be necessary to set down this item for what it is worth, and to go into the political records of Germany for evidence of the fiscal conditions. This has been done so

Zeiten zum besten. Hiebevor gestellet durch Georgium Obrechtum, J. C. Sacri Palatij Comitem, Reipub. Argentinens. Advocatum, & Academiae Antecessorem. Hernacher im Jahr 1617 zum Truch befördert, und biss anhero ingeheim gehalten: Nunmehr aber zu männigliches Nutzen publicirt, und mit nothwendigen Registern verbessert. "Lectio lecta placet, decies repetita placebit" (351 pp. with indexes).

[1] "Auf meinen Costen, in geheim und *sub secreto,*" *Vorrede,* p. 1.

fully, however, by German historians that no question remains about the main facts. Our problem is to interpret the phenomena of cameralism as one of the outgrowths of the times in which these facts existed. Here then was a single theorist. He confronted a situation which vexed all types of men theoretically or practically concerned with questions of civic polity in Germany. The key to the situation, as he saw it, was the need of more money to strengthen the state for war, in particular, as well as for other purposes. With this as his clue, he reasoned to the best of his ability, and the result was a scheme, on paper, which may fairly be called a respectable first draft of a programme which was later worked out in detail, and quite in the same spirit, by the cameralists. Without prejudging the theories of later writers, and without generalizing at this point about the extent to which the object of subsequent thinkers was identical with that of Obrecht, we must define his purpose clearly, and make it the explanation of his proposals. In a word, he wanted to show how civic authorities might solve their most importunate problem of commanding the sinews of war, and of providing for the more ordinary expenses of government. His whole discussion centers about this theme.

The son does not tell why it was thought necessary to keep the monographs secret. Apparently the essential reason was that such subjects were thought to be matters for the rulers and the learned alone, and that either the monographs themselves were not sufficiently matured for publication, or that no public existed, outside of a select circle, intelligent or responsible enough to profit by reading them. So far as evidence appears in the volume itself, Obrecht's theories contained nothing calculated to arouse governmental hostility. At the worst they might be regarded as well intended but visionary.

On the contrary, as the editor further states, Rudolf II called for Obrecht's opinion on the fiscal problem, and he accordingly wrote the first monograph. This document contains 59 pages, with an index of 6 pages, and is chiefly in Latin.[1]

It is not clear whether the editor means to imply that his father's further opinion was demanded from high quarters, or whether the above occasion spurred him to further study. At all events the account continues to the effect that Obrecht diligently searched the *Politicorum scripta*, so far as they were available, and tested them by the Word of God, in order to learn which doctrines were to be rejected, and which, as precious pearl and gems, should be loyally retained, and by the grace of God so set forth and applied that no one could have a grievance against them. The outcome of this study was the second monograph.[2]

Of this *Bedencken* the editor affirms that it was calculated to inspire confidence, both in rulers and subjects, on the one hand that the proposed means would be sufficient, and on the other hand that the demands of the government would not be unreasonable.

Obrecht, however, did not fully trust his own judgment about such important matters. He did not venture to call the

[1] Its special title reads: *Georgii Obrechti, etc. Discursus Bellico-politicus. Invictissimo et Augustissimo Principi ac Domino, Dn. Rudolpho Laudatissimae Memoriae. II Romanorum Imperatori, Anno M. DC. IV. ab Authore humilima animi devotione oblatus, in quo quomodo advursus Turcicum Tyrannum bellum commodè geri possit, quam felicissime ostenditur.*

[2] Beginning with the initials of the ascription, "Auspice Deo Triuno Optimo Maximo," the title-page reads: "*Politisch Bedencken und Discurs: Von Verbesserung Land unnd Leut, Anrichtung guter Policey. Und fürnemblich von nutzlicher Erledigung grosser Aussgaben, und billicher Vermehrung eines jeden Regenten und Oberherren Jährlichen Gefällen und Einkommen.*" This monograph occupies 135 pages, without index. Its main propositions are in German, and they are fortified by copious quotations in Latin from the *Politicorum scripta*, the same ranging from legendary sayings of Servius Tullius, to dicta of contemporary authorities in canonical and civil law.

proposal complete until he had consulted, either in person or in correspondence, during several years, "under pledge of silence," eminent theologians, "and highly experienced statesmen." With this assistance the *Discurs* was finished in 1609.[1]

The third document in the series is in form an independent monograph, but the editor says it was drawn from the *Bedencken* and was intended to show more plainly how the ideas in the former treatise could be applied. It was finished in 1610. It contains 46 pages.[2]

[1] There is a discrepancy of no material importance for our purpose, between the younger Obrecht and Thomasius with reference to this monograph. The latter states (Osse, p. 87) that the *Politisches Bedencken* was printed at Strassburg in the year 1606; that is, three years earlier than it was completed, if the former is correct. Thomasius adds that a copy of this first edition was in his possession. This appears to make him a competent witness so far, especially as he quotes enough of the remainder of the title to make the identity of the monograph rather certain. From the context, however, it is plain that Thomasius had never seen the edition of 1617, in which the document in question was virtually the second chapter. Of that edition he says, upon the authority of Deckher, "*descriptis Adespotis*, p.m. 335. . . . . The other, presumably somewhat enlarged, appeared in the year 1617." He further states that copies of the latter edition, at some date which he does not mention, sold for one hundred *Gulden*. To account for this he quotes that writer as follows: "Testata est Republ. Argentinensis, adferendo omnis exemplaria suae Cancellariae nolle se consilia civis fui, quae illi in proxi pessime cessere, omnibus palam fieri." Thomasius concludes that this "confiscation" was the reason for the scarcity price. The inference is plausible enough, but the only reason that can be surmised for calling in the book is similar to parents' motives for keeping some books which they find profitable for themselves out of reach of their children.

A little later in the Preface, the editor says of the third document in the volume, the *Aerarium Sanctum*, "so biss *dato* niemanden *communiciret* worden." The date referred to must mean that on which the collection was published, 1617.

[2] The title and general outline indicate its scope, viz., *Constitutio von nothwendiger und nützlicher Anstellung eines Aerarij Sancti. Durch welches fürnemblich die Beforderung und Erhaltung gemeiner Wohlfahrt*

Having gone so far in his studies, Obrecht discovered that something more was necessary. He concluded that the entire life of sovereigns and subjects must be conducted in accordance with the dictates of thrift and morality, or *the means would still be lacking to provide the necessary revenues.* Accordingly he harked back to Roman exploitation of "*Censum et Censuram,*" and he elaborated a scheme of *Policey*, partly prompted by his conception of the Roman system, partly appropriating contemporary police arrangements, and partly a speculative proposal. The significant point is that the animus of the whole undertaking was *the proposal to devise means by which adequate revenues might be assured to the state.* At the same time, and this is a trait that runs through the whole cameralistic régime, the total morale of the people was to be improved, primarily to be sure for state purposes, but none the less improvement of the physical, mental, and moral life conditions of all the people was an avowed and prominent part

gesucht und erlangt wird; Beschrieben und angestellt von Georgio Obrechto, etc.

I. Ein sondere *Constitutio* und Ordnung, de Iudiciario Vectigali.

II. Von sechs Ordnungen, in welchen die *bona Fisci*, dem *Aerario Sancto* zugeeignet werden: 1. *Ordinatio*, von oeden und unerbawten Güteren; 2. *Ordinatio, de Bonis Vacantibus:* 3. *Ordinatio de Bonis perditis, & prodererelicto habitis*, item de bonis peregrinorum, & Thesauris; 4. *Ordinatio*, de Bonis Ereptitiis; 5. Ordinatio, *de Bonis Damnatorum et Proscriptorum;* 6. *Ordinatio, de Bonis incestas Nuptias contrahentium;*

III. Von vier Ordnungen, durch welche *ratione bonorum subditorum* das *Aerarium Sanctum* mit vielen starcken Jährlichen Gefällen, und Einkommen versehen wird: 7. *Ordinatio, de Bonis subditorum in ultima aliqua voluntate Aerario Sancto relictis;* 8. *Ordinatio, de Bonis Subditorum, qui in ultima aliqua voluntate, extraneis personis* aliquid reliquerunt: 9. *Ordinatio, de Bonis subditorum, qui sine herede lineae ascendentis & descendentis decedunt, & in Linea collaterali tantum ultra septimum gradum heredes post se relinquunt:* 10. *Ordinatio*, von einer nothwendigen, und hochnutzlichen Fewr-Ordnung.

IV. *De Fine huius Constitutionis*, und wahin oberklärte *reditus* können, und sollen verwendet werden.

of the programme. It was not stated by the cameralists (Justi possibly excepted) as an end-end. It was emphasized with cumulative insistence as a means-end, and this factor became one of the distinguishing elements in German polity.[1] The fifth and last document or "*secretum*" in the series is referred to as the *Aerarium Liberorum*. Ostensibly it was a plan of savings and endowment insurance for children. The author avows quite frankly, however, that in essence it is a detail in his fiscal scheme. In a word, parents were to lay by, in the hands of the government, certain regular amounts, to receive interest at 6 per cent., and to be paid to the children named

[1] The so-called "*Constitution*," in which this scheme of *Policey* is outlined, contains only 31 pages. Its title-page is as follows:

Ein sondere Policey-Ordnung, und Constitution, durch welche ein jeder Magistratus, vermittels besonderen angestellten Deputaten, jederzeit in seiner Regierung, eine gewisse Nachrichtung haben mag, I. *Wie es gleichsam mit seiner ganzen Policey, als eines Politischen Leibs, und allen desselberen Gliederen, den Underthanen beschaffen.* II. *Wie gemelter Policey, derselben Gliederen, und Administration, auff: und zunemmen zubefürderen, ab: und undergang zuverhüten. So dann zum* III. *Wie auch die gemeine Wolfarth, so auss vorgedachten dreyen Stücken herkompt, zuvermehren, und zu erhalten seyen, Allen Oberkeiten, in diesen letzten, verkehrten, und gefährlichen Zeiten, hochnotwendig, und in viel Weg nutzlich samt einer kurtzen Information, und Erklärung, auch einem Appendice.*

The "*Information*" and "*Erklärung*," together with the Appendix, occupy 32 pages. The inscription of the former reads: "Kurtze *Information* und Erklärung. In welchen die *Precia Inscriptionum bestimbt*, und die Nutzbarkeiten welche auss den *inscriptionibus, inscriptionum Documentis & Albis*, wie auch aus Anordnung der *Deputaten*, sowol *privatim*, als *publice* zuerlangen seind, kürtzlich deducirt werden, Zu besserem Verstand, unnd Nachrichtung, voriger Policey Ordnung, und *Constitution* angestellt." The special title of the *Appendix* is: "Von underschiedenen *Inscriptionum Documentis*."

The passage in which the editor accounts for the writing of the *Constitution* contains so many side-lights upon the impulses of the document, which would disappear in a translation, that it would have been quoted in full in an appendix if space had permitted.

as beneficiaries on arrival at a certain age. If, however, a child died before reaching the specified age, both principal and interest should belong to the government. Since, however, this forfeiture would occur only in consequence of "a special dispensation of God," the editor seriously argues that the scheme, for which he might have quoted Italian precedents, ought not to be considered inequitable, but rather on the whole as favorable to parents as to the government.[1]

Beyond this general analysis of the book, our purpose calls merely for a few notes about incidentals in its contents. Considering the volume then as an exhibit of a coherent scheme of fiscal administration, we may abstract certain items of evidence bearing upon tendencies in fundamental political theory which the scheme exhibits.

After a brief address to the emperor, the chapter "*Billico-Politicus*" opens the discussion with a highly pedantic introduction upon the topic: *Quae ad Constitutionem Belli Turcici necessaria sint.* This is like stopping when the house is afire, to settle the metaphysical question, What is necessary to constitute a house afire? The author nevertheless gravely enumerates as the elements in the situation: "*Jus; Summus Magistratus; Hostes; Justa Causa; et Legitima Belli Susceptio.*" In ten pages these implications are expanded, and through brief discussion of the "mature deliberation" which must precede war, the way is paved for the actual problem of the tract, viz., enumeration of all available sources of revenue. Without entering into any of the technical details scheduled,

[1] The monograph contains 56 pages, including an Appendix of 10 pages, and in addition an Index of 8 pages. The title-page reads: *Constitutio und Ordnung. Von einem Hochnützlichen Aerario Liberorum, in welches, von den Elteren, allerhand Summen Gelts, fürnemblich ihren Newgebornen Kinderen, und in eventum ihnen selbs, auch der Obrigkeit, und Gemeiner Wohlfahrt zum besten angelegt werden: Sampt allerhand Erklärungen, und zweyen Kinder Rechnungen. Beschrieben unnd angestellt von Georgio Obrechto etc.*

we may notice that the sources of revenue named are classed under two general heads: first, those which impose a burden upon the persons supplying the revenue; second, those that impose no burden.[1] This distinction often reappears in the cameralistic books. In general it does not correspond with the ideas which would be attached to the terms today. A "burdensome" tax was one which impaired the citizen's means of maintaining his standard of life. A "non-burdensome" tax was one which left the means of livelihood intact, but might theoretically absorb all increments of profit.[2]

A single observation will suffice in connection with the second class of resources. The author names first among the fiscal means which impose no burden upon the persons who supply the revenue, "*bona oikonomia.*" In the text he uses the Greek form **οἰκονομίαν**. He explains that he means by it good administration in general. That is, all functionaries are to exhibit fidelity and diligence, they are not to incur needless expenses, they are to exercise frugality and parsimony, and thus to have in hand the means with which to meet unforeseen demands. This observation is necessary, because a cardinal datum for interpretation of the cameralists is that they did not have the idea, and consequently did not have a word

[1] I. *De necessariarum rerum comparatione: &c. praecipuè de modis, quibus cum onere subditorum pecunia comparari possit.* II. *De modis quibus sine onere subditorum pecunia compariri possit; et praecipuè de bona Oeconomia et de venditione vel oppigneratione bonorum.*

[2] We may merely name the four classes of resources which the author mentions under the first head, viz., (1) imposition of taxes; (2) extraordinary taxes; (3) "*si annui reditus atque census, sique portoria et vectigalia augentur*" (and without entering into the question of the precise connotation of these terms at the date of the book, the author's illustrations permit us to render them in general, income, property, and poll taxes, customs and excise); (4) certain ordinances (*constitutiones*) which may yield something to the treasury. In a sense the second monograph, and in a much more literal sense the third, fourth, and fifth papers are elaborations of the author's meaning under this head.

for "economics" in the sense attached to that term in nineteenth-century English usage. In this early instance, "*bona oikonomia*" evidently contained the rudiments, but only the rudiments, of the concept later represented by such a term as *Staatshaushaltung*. In the second half of the eighteenth century, as we shall see, the Greek term was often reserved for agricultural management only. In the intermediate period its meaning was unprecise. Our concern at this point is merely to indicate the inchoate condition of the stage of administrative theory represented by Obrecht, and in particular to put on record this early use of a term which, in translations into English, has been the innocent occasion of cardinal misjudgments of essential factors in the development of German social theories.

The remaining titles in the monograph refer to details of the fiscal resources of the time which yield nothing for our purpose.[1]

The second document opens with a series of specifications which picture most vividly the desperate financial straits of contemporary German rulers, from the emperor down to the minor princes. Incidentally the author furnishes cumulative evidence that the "biological analogy" was as serviceable a working tool for him as for some of the nineteenth-century sociologists.[2] The exhibit and the estimate of money as the

[1] This will be evident from headings of the remaining subdivisions: viz., "De novorum Acceptorum et redituum constitutione: et praecipue de modis quibus mediantè justitiae administratione accepta augeri possunt."

"De modis quibus sine Iustitiae administratione accepta atque reditus absque onere subditorum augeri possunt."

"De Commeatu Pabuli et Frumenti, item de armis, et de ijs rebus, quae ad arma pertinent comparandis."

"De Praecedentibus ad constitutionem belli accommodandis."

[2] Thus, "Sintemal wie in einem Natürlichen Leib, die nervi ***prima animalis sensus et motus instrumenta***, auch *causa actionum* seind: also ***in corpore civili***, oder in einer ***Republica***, als in einem Fürstenthumb,

vital force of governments lead to succinct statement of the purpose of the pamphlet, viz., to call the attention of rulers and governors to the necessity of diligent reflection about these things, and of adopting the means to be proposed, or better ones, in the interest of themselves and their subjects. The terms in which the author further urges these claims first reflect very plainly the inchoate, undifferentiated, and unorganized stage of civic administration in German states, and secondly, they contain a touch which marks an early form of a moral consideration not at that time very effective, but later of co-ordinate rank with the requirements for offensive and defensive strength against external enemies. In a word Obrecht argues that without money properly to pay civil employees, rulers cannot protect the people against the injustices of their own servants. He observes in this connection that "although there are to be sure many *magistri*, as Bodinus calls them," who are always well equipped with means of raising money, yet usually these means tend not merely to burden the subjects but completely to strip them. No one appears to point out means which would be just and lucrative, and at the same time serviceable for all sorts of improvement. He proposes, therefore, to present a scheme which would satisfy these requirements.

The body of the essay is divided on the lines drawn in the previous paper, viz., first, means for raising revenues by bur-

Graffschafft, Herrschafft, und in fürnemmen Stätten, seind Gelt und Gut gleichsam die *nervi*, und *instrumenta*, ohn welche kein *Respublica*, angericht, gebessert, und so wol zu Friedens Zeit, als in Kriegs Emperungen, unnd anderen hochbetrangten Zuständen, erhalten werden kan, etc." A little later the figure continues: "Dann welcher gestalt Gelt und Gut nit weniger Reipublicae von nöhten seind, als im Menschlichen Leib seind die *nervi sentientes*, welche von dem Hirn entspringen sollen; ebner massen Gelt und Gut gebührlicher weiss zuerlangen, gehört einer jeden Oberkeit zu, die gleichsam in *Republica*, als *in corpore civili*, anstatt Hirns ist, und hat solch *corpus* vollkömmlich zu regieren, etc."

dening the subjects; second, means which would not burden the subjects. This whole range of governmental problems is put under the head, "Oeconomica administratio." In general the scheme is merely an amplification of ideas contained in the earlier essay. The specific propositions do not concern us, but the conditions which were to be met and the status of reasoning about them may be somewhat more approximately understood by reference to the titles of chapters.[1]

If this were a history of administrative technique, or of administrative technology, Obrecht's book would furnish many details which would mark a stage in the process. As we are in search of the fundamental conceptions and ultimate purposes of cameralism, these details are interesting only in so far as they bear testimony about those conceptions and purposes. Not because they immediately yield much information on these points, but for use later in connection with other evidence, we may note a few items of more than merely administrative significance.

In the first place, Obrecht seems to have understood in a general way the impolicy of debasing the coinage. Thus he says (p. 108):

> That today certain mammon brothers, in search of selfish gain, seek all sorts of private advantage with the different coins, that they diminish and weaken the same in weight and value [*Schrott und Korn*] is directly contrary to all laws, also to various edicts of the Holy Empire with respect to coinage, and brings with it beyond all doubt the curse of God and temporal punishment.

In the second place, Obrecht represents a stage and type of political thinking in which the traditional taboo of commerce and trade as pursuits for members of the nobility began to be called in question. Thus, after citing a number of opinions on the conventional side, he asserts (p. 111):

[1] These were to have appeared in an appendix.

I however regard commerce as in a way necessary for a republic; and so necessary, indeed, that it cannot be separated from the body of the republic. For merchants are in the body of the republic, as it were, attendants, carriers, feet, etc. . . . . consequently, I hold it as more honorable than despicable when noble and high persons carry on trade for the sake of lightening the burdens of their subjects, and of discharging public obligations with the least difficulty.

To this item should be added a later passage, viz. (p. 122):

A ruler and overlord should make it an object of diligent attention that in his towns and country regions, so far as opportunity allows, all sorts of traders should be located. For the traders not only bring into the country all sorts of necessary wares, at their own cost and risk, but they also draw out of the country those wares of which the country has a superabundance. . . . . But a ruler should look out for the following four points: I, that the merchants should carry on no forbidden traffic, nor should they bring forbidden wares into the country, nor carry them out to forbidden places; II, that no scarcity, nor hindrance of the subjects in disposing of their wares, should be brought about by the merchants; III, that they should make no harmful and usurious bargains but their transactions should all tend to the common advantage, and not to the injury of their neighbors; IV, that the merchants should be protected against all unjust violence, for this is to the advantage not only of the merchants themselves, but of the subjects in general.

In the third place, Obrecht schedules encouragement of navigation as a means of enlarging a state's revenues. He seems to have no suspicion of questions about "balance of trade," but pleads artlessly for "provision of vessels that may bring all sorts of goods and wares from foreign ports, that the same may be sold again."

Fourthly, he proposes advances from the princely chest, to merchants who bring in foreign goods. The chief reason for this proposal seems to be that the interest on the advances would be a considerable source of profit to the prince.

Fifth, Obrecht recommends purchase by government of

certain food stuffs, wine, etc., to be held as a resource against possible scarcity prices, and then to be sold at reasonable rates, to the advantage both of government and subjects.

Promotion of artisanship is also urged, and for similar reasons. At the same time dangers from improper combinations of hand-workers are suggested, and severe punishments for misusing such organization are recommended. In connection with the advice that, to promote trade and crafts, fairs and markets should be arranged, a bare hint of the later population doctrine appears, viz. (p. 127):

And it is beyond all doubt that when all the above is set in operation with zeal, it will be to the advantage of rulers and overlords in this respect further, that they will have more populous and better appointed towns and territories, and that in consequence the various revenues will be strongly increased and improved.

Disapproval of debts to foreigners, which later became a cameralistic dogma, appears here as a mild preference: thus (p. 129):

If a ruler is burdened with many and heavy foreign interest charges . . . . it is advisable that he raise the amount from his subjects who have loanable money, and pay the interest to them rather than to foreigners, for in this way expenses and losses may be avoided.

The first paragraph of the chapter, "Constitutio Aerarij Sancti," furnishes another direct testimony, the stronger because it was inadvertent, as to the central purpose which was molding administrative theory and policy. It is a passage which distinctly locates the moving springs of cameralism. Translated according to the spirit rather than the letter it is as follows:

Since it is known to all of good understanding, and an open secret, and attested by daily experience, that in these last troublous times there is scarcely a government whose ordinary resources are not daily and hourly exhausted, and therefore scarcely one can at all times be happily administered and maintained in constant security by means of the ordinary revenues; but on the contrary unless by the side of these customary revenues a government institutes, with the utmost care, through all sorts of just and righteous means, a special and extraordinary treasury, such a government and *Policey*, at a time of unforeseen war, revolts, and other dangers, will stand unprotected and open to pillage and enemies, and in the presence of such danger and violence it can neither be protected nor administered. And although by extraordinary efforts under such circumstances money may be raised, yet if the money is collected, and the imminent danger is averted, yet another danger immediately follows, namely, that the growing burden of interest charges will ruin the state, as was the case with the Greek republics, and especially Lacedaemonia, which were ruined by borrowing from the Persian and Egyptian kings. Hence it is necessary to show how these dangers may be overcome by an extraordinary treasury.

As we shall attempt to show, this problem of ways and means to cover the expanding fiscal needs of the state was the central purpose which gave peculiar character to cameralism. All the incidental tenets of this technology, whether they were the opinions of exceptional writers or substantially the consensus of all, must be interpreted by their connection with this main interest.

This particular *Constitutio* is partly in the form of an ordinance to be promulgated by rulers: partly in the ordinary essay form on the merits of certain fiscal propositions. It contains nothing further in principle necessary for our purpose.

In the fourth document, *Policey Ordnung*, Obrecht displays foresight which entitles him to higher rank in the rolls of German political writers than the historians of his own country have assigned. In general, subsequent events conformed to his views, and the *Policey* system afterward developed, to which we must give so much attention in later portions of this book, was entirely contained in principle in his proposals. Without attempting to prove this in detail, we may briefly note the standpoint from which his suggestions issued and the aims which he had in view.

In the Introduction the author points out that all publicists have had regard for two considerations, and have urged them upon magistrates, viz., first, the census and censorship, "the fulcra and pillars of politics, and the supports on which all *Policey* must rest;" second, "reliable information and sufficient science possessed by every magistrate concerning the structure and organization of the *Policey*."

As to the first of these points, Obrecht states that existing administration makes use of census and censorship, yet in no adequate fashion; indeed, he holds that if it were possible the forms in use should be altogether abolished, and more adequate systems substituted. He concedes that such abrupt change would be impracticable, and in the case of the census particularly recommends that the methods now in use be retained.

With reference to the censorship, however, he declares that its policy may be essentially either preventive or punitive. Just here Obrecht's foresight is exceptional. He declares that police programmes of his time know nothing of preventive policies. The chief emphasis of the document falls therefore on the outline of a police policy calculated to improve the morale of the people, and thus not merely to diminish vice and crime, but to raise the general efficiency of the population. Without asking the question here whether this is a proper function of governments, we have to observe at the outset that German political theory progressively assumed that such guardianship and promotion of public morals formed a necessary part of governmental responsibility. Obrecht was accordingly a pioneer among post-Reformation thinkers in striking out a path which became one of the trunk lines of later administrative theory.[1]

[1] The introduction is such a vivid reflection of the situation within which Obrecht wrote that it would have been reproduced in full if space had permitted.

The Preface to the proposed *Constitution*, which is drafted in the form of a royal rescript, reiterates the underlying purpose of the proposition in terms which a translation cannot properly represent, but the substance is approximately this:

The following Police Order and Constitution, with its seven Sanctions [*Sanctionibus*] is ordained by us especially that we may every year, and as far as practicable at all times, have reliable information how matters stand with all our subjects, young and old, rich and poor, in all parts of our jurisdiction and territory, and also how matters stand with our whole *Policey*, and all of its branches, and how, in this later wholly perverted time, they may be protected against ruin, and may be sustained in constant integrity; and how we may bring it about, after ascertaining all the facts, that our subjects may rightly, well and usefully bring up their children, and themselves lead a Christian, worthy life, and thus so conduct themselves that they may be to their children, to us their divinely appointed rulers, to their neighbor, and to the common weal, a blessing and an honor, to their own temporal and eternal advantage.

The first *Sanction* covered a system of registration of births, both legitimate and illegitimate; the second, registration and guardianship of orphans and widows; the third, registration and supervision of young men "nearer their twentieth than their twenty-third year;" the fourth, registration and continued observation of all other male persons, above the twenty-third year, "in order that we may have direct knowledge of the character of all these persons under our whole government:" the fifth, registration of marriage intentions;[1] the

[1] For the reason parenthetically assigned: Because "*Matrimonia*" are "von den *Politicis* recht und wol *principia Urbium, seminaria Rerumpublicarum, et fundamenta Rei familiaris* genandt werden." In this connection the plan contemplates the appointment of officials who should censor the wedding customs, particularly with reference to extravagant outlays. One of the ends in view was to prevent squandering of the savings with which housekeeping must be set up. The word here used for that idea is worth our notice. The phrase is: "auss welchem sie ihre *Oeconomi* anstellen sollen."

sixth, registration of intentions of immigrants to become citizens, and of other cases of change of residence by strangers or subjects; seventh, registration of deaths, including certain related details, particularly concerning surviving heirs.

The explanations subjoined to this third paragraph, or chapter, take up in turn the seven "sanctions," and propose details, beginning with the price to be paid for each type of registration, and including arguments intended to show the benefits that would accrue, first to individuals, then to the public, from adoption of the programme. For example, we find at once (p. 215) the suggestion that each child registered under the first "sanction," should receive *ein Geburtsbrieff;* obviously an early, if not the earliest proposal of a detail of police technique which later became a matter of course.

On the side of the public advantages of the proposed programme, Obrecht urges, still under the device of a supposed ordinance or rescript (pp. 229 ff.), that, at all times, both in war and peace, governments would be able to administer more intelligently; they could maintain the common welfare (*Gemeine Wolfart*) with more intelligence and energy; they could also come to the assistance of the subjects more directly and efficiently; they could, fourth, through the fidelity of the various sorts of ***Deputaten*** contemplated in the programme, in many ways promote the common advantage (*Gemeinen Nutz*) better than without such organization.

It cannot be said that this final schedule of reasons for adopting the programme is likely to affect the modern reader as very convincing. The underlying fiscal purpose, viz., the collection of fees from the different registrations, is too obvious, while the advantages urged are both vague and problematical. The same is more evidently true of the insurance of children proposed in the last document, on which further comment is unnecessary.[1] These things do not, however, diminish the

[1] *Vide* above, p. 47.

evidential value of such a writer as Obrecht. Whether he actually exerted much influence or little, either upon administrative organization or upon academic theory, his book reflects beginnings of theoretical and practical tendencies in ways which make their essential impulses much more evident than they appear in their later more complex variations.

CHAPTER IV

THE CAMERALISTICS OF SECKENDORFF

Veit Ludwig von Seckendorff was born in 1626 and died in 1692. His most persistent influence was exerted through two books, *Der Teutsche Fürsten Staat*, and *Der Christen Staat*.[1] For our purposes, these books, rather than details of Seckendorff's life, are all-important. Enough of his biography may be noted, however, to indicate the interests for which he spoke. In childhood, Seckendorff was taught at home, while his father was most of the time in the wars. He was later sent to school in Coburg and Mühlhausen. In 1636 he went with his mother to Erfurt, where the foundations of his more mature knowledge were laid. He is said to have composed Latin orations at the age of eleven. He was a companion of two Württemburg princes in 1639. He attracted the attention of Herzog Ernst of Gotha, who sent him to the Gotha *Gymnasium* in 1640. Soon after this his father was beheaded on the charge of intended defection to the emperor. The family was provided for, however, in recognition of the father's previous services. The son went the same year to the University of Strassburg, where for several years he studied philosophy, jurisprudence, and history. In 1645, on his way to continue study at Erfurt, he visited the court of Gotha. This was the turning-point of his life. The duke gave him 200 *Thaler* for a visit to the Low Countries, and on his return appointed him *Hofjunker* and superintendent of the ducal library. In these positions his chief duty was to summarize selected books and recite their contents to the duke in his leisure hours, on Sundays

[1] Instead of reducing the various forms of these titles to a single style, the usage of the passages from which they have been cited has been followed.

or during journeys. In 1652, in his twenty-seventh year, he became *Hof- und Justitienrath*. The first of his important books, the *Fürsten Staat*, was written in 1655. "It may be regarded as a sort of handbook of German civil law, and was valued as such; on the other hand, it had the special approval of contemporaries, because it contained a systematic arrangement of rules and prescriptions for a well-regulated governmental administration, based on the model of the existing government of Gotha." Seckendorff was soon promoted to the position of *Geheimer Hof- und Kammerrath im Verwaltungsdienst*, and in 1664 to the highest dignity in the duchy, that of chancellor. His services were especially valued in finance, but he was also a power in political, ecclesiastical, and educational reform. He collaborated (1666) with the scholars Artopoeus and Böckler on a *Compendium historiae ecclesiasticae*, intended primarily for the *Gymnasium* in Gotha, but afterward widely used. In 1664 he accepted the call of Duke Moritz of Sachsenzeitz, as *Kanzler und Consistorial-Präsident*. He retained the position till the death of Moritz in 1681, then resigned all his responsibilities except that of *Landschaftsdirector von Altenburg*, and retired to his estate, Menselwitz, near Altenburg. The *Christen Staat* (1685) did much to promote the tendency toward pietism, although the author was not himself strictly a pietist. In reply to the Jesuit de Maimbourg (*Histoire du Luthéranism*, Paris, 1680) Seckendorff wrote in an incredibly short time a work which must still be consulted by all historians of the Reformation.[1] He arrived at Halle, as chancellor of the new university, October 31, 1692, but died December 18 following.[2]

[1] *Commentarius historicus et apologeticus de Lutheranismo seu de reformatione*, 1688–92.

[2] Th. Kolde, in *All. d. Bib.*, title "Seckendorff," and Roscher, *in loc.* This account should be compared with Seckendorff's own recollections in the dedication of *Der Christenstat*.

Seckendorff's close relations with Duke Ernst of Gotha were prime factors in his career. Ernst was eminent among the petty princes of his century. His reputation for piety was popularized in the nickname "Praying Ernst," and he was later known as "Ernst the Pious." His ecclesiastical laws have been called a complete course in pastoral theology. He was the father of twenty-two children, and in the management of his household and of his state he was regarded as an edifying example. Seckendorff systematized Duke Ernst's scheme of life. He virtually composed Ernst's practices as a manager into a didactic treatise. According to the Preface of the second edition of *Der Fürsten Staat*, his original intention was to treat only of rules for a single German principality, evidently Gotha, but his plan was afterward extended to include all German states of the secularized Protestant class.

Roscher regards it as a second cardinal fact in Seckendorff's career that, shortly before his death, he gave up the life of retirement upon his estate, to accept the chancellorship of the new University of Halle. The reasons for Roscher's opinion that this change was significant are not apparent. It was a generation after his most important book appeared, and six years after publication of the volume next in importance. Such migrations were by no means exceptional, and in this instance nothing can be inferred from the incident which has the slightest bearing upon Seckendorff in the only relation in which he was significant for Roscher's professed purpose, viz., interpretation of the history of German economics. This emphasis upon a merely personal detail is characteristic. Roscher's service to science was principally in assembling details. He was much less successful in estimating their value.

Seckendorff is classified by Roscher as conservative, in the sense of adhering to the old ways, while he was liberal, in the sense of thinking freely, if the phrase may be accommodated to the rigors of his time. He was not attracted by the innovations in the *Zeitgeist* of his period, but clung to the traditions of the generations before the Thirty Years' War. In this respect he was in nearly the same antithesis with leading publicists and mercantilists of his time, that is, to the theories of Leopold I and of the Great Elector, in which Sully stood to Colbert, or in the eighteenth century, Justus Möser to the political scientists of the time of Frederick the Great and Joseph II.

Moreover, Seckendorff was attached to the Reformation type of piety, and in spite of the tendency of the time in the other direction, he gave his political doctrines a strong religious shading.

Roscher further characterizes Seckendorff as "in civic life no more an absolutist than in court life he was a sycophant." This is true in the sense that he dared to regard the will of God as paramount to the will of the prince; but it is not true in the sense that he believed any power on earth was justified in holding the prince to account for his acts. In other words, political theory had virtually outgrown the conception that the will of the prince was the highest moral law, but it still retained the conception that the will of the prince was the ultimate civic law. Seckendorff was consequently the mouthpiece of the type of German state in the middle of the seventeenth century in which the assumption was fundamental. We shall speak of this as *quasi-absolutism.* Absolutism in the strictest sense it was not. From the point of view of modern democracy it was virtual absolutism. That is, it was a theory that no one but God had a right to discipline the prince, because he was responsible only to that divine power by whose grace he had been made sovereign over a defined group of men.[1]

We have then to deal, not with the first, but with one of the early doctrinaires and officiating administrators of the type of state thus indicated. Their task was to systematize the

[1] For confirmation of this judgment *vide* below, pp. 73 ff.; cf. doctrine of Schröder, pp. 137 ff.

administrative routine of that type of state. The theory and the application were not so sharply distinguished as they have been in later times. The work of the cameralists was so to serve their quasi-absolute lords that the power and efficiency of their states would be developed, and that their purposes with reference to competing states would be promoted. All the doctrines of the cameralists were in fact centered about this main purpose, and all their theories and judgments must be understood accordingly.[1]

As a side-light upon the foregoing propositions, scarcely anything could be more illuminating than the dedication of *Der Fürsten Staat.* Because our language makes an exact rendering of the ceremonial titles and phrases impossible, we quote the form of address in the original, viz.: *Dem Durchläuchtigsten, Hochgebornen Fürsten und Herrn, Herrn Johann Georgen Erb-Printzen der Chur- und Hertzogen zu Sachsen, Jülich, Cleve und Bergk, Landgrafen in Thüringen, Mark-*

[1] For the conditions of the Peace of Westphalia which furnished the general setting within which the problems of the several states of Germany are to be explained, *vide* Tillinghast's Ploetz, p. 316, following K. F. Eichhorn, *Deutsche Staats- u. Rechtsgeschichte*, IV, 522 ff. The most useful outline of the condition of Germany in the period in which Seckendorff wrote is in Bryce, *Holy Roman Empire*, chap. xx. *Vide* Tillinghast, *loc. cit.*, p. 371. "The Emperor was Leopold I, 1658–1705. After 1663 permanent diet at Regensburg, consisting of the *representatives* of the eight electors, the sixty-nine ecclesiastical, the ninety-six secular princes, and the imperial cities. (A miracle of tedious legislation, often degenerating into a squabble for precedence. 'A bladeless knife without a handle'.) *Corpus Catholicorum* and *Corpus Evangelicorum* (the corporate organizations of the Catholic and the evangelical estates, the latter being the most important. This organization of the Protestant estates had existed, in fact, since the latter half of the sixteenth century, but it was legally recognized in the Peace of Westphalia, when it was decreed that in the diet matters relating to religion and the church should not be decided by a majority, but should be settled by conference and agreement between the Catholic and Protestant estates, as organized corporations.)."

grafen zu Meissen, auch Ober- und Nieder-Lausznitz, Grafen zu der Marck und Ravensberg, Herrn zu Ravenstein, &c. Meinem gnädigsten Herrn, &c. Durchläuchtigster, Hochgebohrner, Gnädigster Fürst und Herr, &c.

The quaintness of expression in the extremely adroit and non-committal dedication itself cannot be reproduced in English. The translation can convey only the substance of the thought, the most obvious peculiarity of which is the rhetorical device of suggestion, instead of direct statement. It is as follows:

The wisdom, through which kingdoms, principalities, and lands are happily governed, is in its origin divine, in itself it is lordly and incomparable, and comprehends in its scope and generality all that which is found piecemeal in other sciences. It is within the circumference of each land the indispensable sun, through which everything is illuminated, warmed, and nourished. It is to be compared with an inexhaustible sea, into which all other wisdoms and arts flow, and through high and occult art, for the common welfare, is again discharged and distributed through the whole land. It is an evergreen of Paradise of all the most beautiful and useful plants, of the virtues and good ordinances, each of which in its turn and place bears grateful fruits. This wisdom King Solomon prayed the Allwise to grant for his royal office, with which he received also the greatest treasures and riches of the world as an additional gift. Foolish therefore those who would penetrate into the secrets of governments without the attendance and favor of this goddess. All those fall into gross sin who, apart from the divinely appointed and by nature sanctioned way, instead of such excellent royal and lofty science, in the name of the state and of politics, offer perverse and crafty counsel which plunges themselves and whole lands into ruin. For what reasons and occasions, Most Gracious Lord, I was moved to the publication of the present little-worthy work, in which, according to the slight measure of my feeble powers, I sought to bring together a few beams of this bright illuminating sun, certain drops from this great sea, and certain fruits from such a general world-garden, and according to opportunity to make them useful for the lands and principalities of our German fatherland, is to a certain extent set forth in the Preface, wherein also, with humblest apologies to your most illustrious highness, it is explained through what motive I allowed myself to seek, under your eminent name, protection for this very imperfect book. May it please you most graciously to accept this public expression of my most submissive zeal, as I hereby in humility and highest veneration most obediently profess it, and with your gracious permission I remain

His Most Illustrious Highness'
Most Submissive
VEIT LUDWIG VON SECKENDORFF

According to the standards of the time, this wretched stuff was not fulsome, it was merely conventional. Something of the sort, often much more extravagant, occurs in the dedications of most of the cameralistic books. We shall allow this sample to stand for all. It is turgid of course, but in that respect it fairly reflects the stage of thought which it attempted to express. The style was appropriate to the confused thinking which prevailed about everything pertaining to social relations. But this is merely incidental. The main thing is that these forms, dictated by tradition in one respect, yet artfully artless in another, fairly represent the attitude of the cameralists toward the interests of men in civic society. It was fundamentally an attitude of worship toward a supposed superior personage endowed with a prerogative of control over a group of inferior and subject persons. The social science of the time was an effort so to mobilize the attitude that the states which counted upon it as their chief asset could prosper.

In order to provide ourselves with a background for the doctrines which we are to analyze, we should from step to step parallel with this analysis unroll the general picture of German and European politics. For this part of the process recourse must be had to the historians. We can merely in passing make note of the dependence of such a study as this upon their larger work. Of the situation just before our time of departure Bryce writes:

To all parties alike the result of the Thirty Years' War was thoroughly unsatisfactory—to the Protestants, who had lost Bohemia, and were still obliged to hold an inferior place in the electoral college and in the Diet; to the Catholics, who were forced to permit the exercise of heretical worship and leave the church lands in the grasp of sacrilegious spoilers: to the princes, who could not throw off the burden of imperial supremacy: to the Emperor, who could turn that supremacy to no practical account. No other conclusion was possible to a contest in which everyone had been vanquished and no one victorious: which had ceased because, while the reasons for war continued, the means of war had failed. Nevertheless, the substantial advantage remained with the German princes, for they gained the formal recognition of that territorial independence whose origin may be placed as far back as the days of Frederick the Second, and the maturity of which had been hastened by the events of the last preceding century. It was, indeed, not only recognized, but justified as rightful and necessary. For while the political situation, to use a current phrase, had changed within the last two hundred years, the eyes with which men regarded it had changed still more. Never by their fiercest enemies in earlier times, not once by Popes or Lombard republics in the heat of their strife with the Franconian and the Swabian Caesars, had the Emperors been reproached as mere German kings, or their claim to be the lawful heirs of Rome denied. The Protestant jurists of the seventeenth century were the first persons who ventured to scoff at the pretended lordship of the world, and declare their empire to be nothing more than a German monarchy, in dealing with which no superstitious reverence need prevent its subjects from making the best terms they could for themselves, and controlling a sovereign whose religious predilections bound him to their ecclesiastical enemies. . . . .

The Peace of Westphalia is an era in the history of the Holy Empire not less clearly marked than the coronation of Otto the Great, or the death of Frederick the Second (1250). As from the days of Maximilian I (1493–1519) it had borne a mixed or transitional character, well expressed by the name Romano-Germanic, so henceforth it is in everything but title purely and solely a German Empire. Properly, indeed, it was no longer an Empire at all, but a Federation, and that of the loosest sort. For it had no common treasury, no efficient common tribunals, no means of coercing a refractory member; its states were of different religions, were governed according to different forms, were administered judicially and financially without any regard to each other. The traveller by rail in central Germany used, up till 1866, to be amused to find, every hour or two, by the change in the soldiers' uniforms, and in the colour of the stripes on the railway fences, that he had passed out of one and into another of its miniature kingdoms. Much more surprised and embarrassed would he have been a century earlier, when, instead of the present twenty-two, there were three hundred petty principalities between the Alps and the Baltic, each with its own laws, its own court (in which the ceremonious pomp of Versailles was faintly reproduced), its little army, its separate coinage, its tolls and custom-houses on the frontier, its crowd of meddlesome and pedantic officials, presided over by a prime minister who was often the unworthy favorite of his prince and sometimes the pensioner of a foreign court. This vicious system, which paralyzed the trade, the literature and the political thought of Germany, had been forming itself for some time, but did not become fully established until the Peace of Westphalia, by finally emancipating the princes from imperial control, had left them masters in their own territories. The impoverishment of the inferior nobility, and the decline of the commercial cities caused by a war that had lasted a whole generation, removed every counterpoise to the power of the electors and princes, and made absolutism supreme just where absolutism is least defensible, its states too small to have any public opinion, states in which everything depends on the monarch, and the monarch depends on his favorites. After A. D. 1648 the provincial estates or parliaments became obsolete in most of these principalities, and powerless in the rest. Germany was forced to drink to its very dregs the cup of feudalism, feudalism from which all the sentiment that once ennobled it had departed.[1]

If then we disregard on the one hand the theologians, on

[1] *Loc. cit.*, p. 389; *vide* Lowell, *Governments and Parties in Continental Europe*, Vol. I, pp. 231–36.

the other hand the legists, each group in its way acting rather as ballast or as a brake in the several states than as a propulsive force, the positive social science of Germany from the Peace of Westphalia to the Napoleonic peril was the theory useful in the administrative bureaus of these quasi-absolute states. Our purposes will draw a sharp line between the technical details of this theory and the general social ideas which the theories implied, on the one hand as their basis and on the other hand as their aims. The technical details we shall ignore, except as they are necessary for making out the more important general ideas. Our principal question is, What conceptions of social relations were peculiar to the cameralists, and what bearing have cameralistic theories upon the problems of social science in general?

To assist in fixing landmarks, we may say that Seckendorff was the Adam Smith of cameralism. The evidence now in order is first and chiefest in the two volumes already named. We shall first examine *Der Fürsten Staat.*[1]

The Preface, in archaic and bungling fashion, indicates that the purpose of the book is not to discuss general political ideas, nor forms of government in the abstract, but to furnish an account of the operative machinery of a typical German state. Of this preface, we may note, first, that it indicates knowledge of only one previous writer in precisely this field, viz., "an experienced courtier, Herr Löhneisen."[2] Seckendorff states, however, that he did not have the book at hand when he wrote, and that only a dim recollection of its contents was in his mind. His book was rather the result of his own

[1] Herrn Veit Ludwigs von Seckendorff, etc., *Teutscher Fürsten Staat, nun zum fünfftenmal übersehen und auffgelegt, Auch mit einer ganz neuen Zugabe. Sonderbahrer und wichtiger Materien um ein grosses Theil vermehret. . . . . Anno MDCLXXIIX.* In my revision of this chapter I have been able to refer only to this fifth edition.

[2] *Vide* above, p. 40, and Roscher, p. 116.

observation. Second, the author thinks that his description of a medium-sized state may easily be adapted either to the largest or the smallest members of the German civic family. Third, the author deliberately excludes consideration of the abuses which occur in the management of states. He confesses that so many of them are within his knowledge that it is difficult not to write satirically about government, but on the whole he thinks it better to describe administration as it is intended to be, rather than as it really is. Fourth, the author protests that he has not consciously or intentionally said anything in the book which invades the sanctity of imperial or princely prerogative. The fact that such an explanation could be thought of at all is a cardinal symptom of the arbitrariness of the régime which it reflects. Fifth, the Preface ends with a devout invocation of the divine blessing upon the emperor and all the members of the imperial system. Nothing in this petition could be construed as a direct assertion that these governments are peculiarly sacred. The mixture of politics and piety, however, is quite in character with what is otherwise in evidence about the dominant civic conceptions.

The book is divided into four parts. The first and shortest (22 pages) is merely a demand for a description of the external characteristics of a state, from the geographical and typographical features, the condition of cultivation and improvement, to the governmental and social structure. The second part (278 pages) approximately includes the subjects which Justi afterward assigned both to *Staatskunst* and to *Policey*, i. e., it treats "of the government and organization [*Verfassung*[1]] of a land and principality in spiritual and secular affairs." The third part (266 pages), on the properties and revenues of a ruler, corresponds with the *Finanzwissenschaft*, or *Cameral-*

[1] The translation "constitution" is avoided because it carries associations which would be largely anachronistic if referred to the quasi-absolute type of state. *Vide* p. 34 above.

wissenschaft in the restricted sense, of the later cameralists. Instead of a fourth part, co-ordinate with the first three, 198 pages are devoted to a more specific scheme of organization, in accordance with the foregoing discussion. The editions after 1664 contain an appendix of 208 pages, consisting of notes upon various passages in the body of the book.

While the contents of Seckendorff's system should be rearranged in another form, to show most distinctly their relations to cameralism as a whole, we must be content to sketch them in brief, so far as they are important for our purpose, in the order in which they appear in *Der Fürsten Staat* and *Der Christen Staat*.

Seckendorff begins the former book by calling attention to the unreliability, for purposes of precision, of most previous attempts to exhibit in print the exact conditions of German states and the consequent need of accurate accounts (pp. 30–32). These accounts should contain precise descriptions not only of the form of government of the state in question, the particular subject with which Seckendorff proposes to deal, and for subsequent treatment of which he hopes his book will serve as a model; but they should also describe the external conditions of the country, to which all rulers and magistrates must accommodate their policies. Because the present book does not refer to a specific country alone, he says, it can offer on the latter division of the subject only a tentative (*unverfänglich*) model or scheme in accordance with which the necessary description of the external conditions of each country may be worked out (p. 33). The scheme proposed is in brief as follows:

First, an account of the name, origin, and circumstances of the principality; viz., (*a*) whence the designation is derived; (*b*) how the sovereignty over this territory arose; (*c*) the geographical and topographical peculiarities of the territory; (*d*) the need of maps which shall show these facts (pp. 33–35). Second, an account of the subdivisions of the country and dependencies; i. e., (*a*) according to natural boundaries; (*b*) according to various artificial arrangements; (*c*) the distribution of the territory among various officials; (*d*) the subdivisions of magisterial and judicial jurisdictions in the country; (*e*) more specific description of each subdivision of the country under this scheme; (*f*) streets, bridges, and passes (pp. 35–41). Third, an account of the qualities and fertility of the territory; i. e., (*a*) the fertility of countries in general; (*b*) varieties of productivity of countries; (*c*) special topics to be treated in the description of the fertility of particular countries (pp. 41, 42). Fourth, an account of the inhabitants of the country; viz., (*a*) the uncertainty of the natural disposition of people;[1] (*b*) class divisions of the inhabitants;[2] (*c*) somewhat more essential marks of difference;[3] (*d*) personal and peculiar qualities of the sovereign[4] (pp. 49, 50). Fifth, a roster of the servants of the ruler and of the government (p. 50).

If the present purpose were to write a history of cameralism, it would be necessary to analyze these beginnings of a tech-

[1] It appears that amateur social psychologists had already brought rash generalizations about the character of peoples into disrepute. Seckendorff demands that judgments of that nature shall be based on adequate examination of the facts, instead of accidental and fragmentary evidence. He also points out that many characteristics of people which are attributed to their "natural traits" are due rather to their bringing up and their food supply (*Aufferziehung und Nahrung*); a decidedly farsighted paragraph (p. 43).

[2] The criterion in mind here is essentially that of civic and ecclesiastical structure, on the administrative side.

[3] Here the reference is to social differences which reflect group interests not primarily official, but the analysis suggested is very crude. It names differences of religion, differences connected with differentiation of a learned class, differences between the imperial and the local nobility, differences between the status of burghers in free cities and those of other cities, etc.

[4] The specifications under this head concern chiefly the traditions which hedge about the succession. They are of an entirely different order, according to modern methodology, from those with which the chapter began: i. e., they are political, constitutional, legal, not physical.

nology, in order to trace, first, the development of consciousness of the problems, administrative and theoretical, to be solved, and second, the development of the technique for dealing with those problems. Our concern, however, is not with these details. Our object is to visualize the relation which cameralism bore to the problems of social science in general. The first book of *Der Fürsten Staat* has no bearing upon this purpose beyond its use in confirming the theorem that cameralism was essentially a phase of the quasi-absolutism which was the central factor in the machinery of the social process in Germany from the Reformation to the French Revolution. There was nothing in the programme of description marked out in this book except the fourth and fifth categories which would not be equally in place in a democratic country. As it stands in Seckendorff's scheme, however, it is a plan for taking account of the stock with which a quasi-absolutism has to do business.

The second part directly addresses the task of planning the administration of the state, and it still more directly confirms our theorem of quasi-absolutism. Chap. i deals with the government, sovereignty (*Hoheit*), and authority of ruling princes in general.[1] Under this head the analysis proceeds: First, The government of a country is by no means an autocracy (*eigenwillige Herrschaft*). The distinction, as Seckendorff saw it, between an autocracy and the typical German

[1] I do not think it is necessary to enter into any of the constantly recurring questions about theoretical relations of the princes to the Empire. In practice, from this time on, the titular head of the Empire was virtually only one of the most powerful among the scores of rival quasi-sovereign princes in Germany, the ruler of Prussia looming up more and more as his most formidable competitor. The political plot, down indeed to the Franco-Prussian war, turned in the first instance upon the fluctuating success of these principal actors in controlling the lesser princes. I take the liberty of using the term sovereignty in connection with these rulers and states, because in relation to their subjects it was so nearly an unqualified fact that the modifications of the fact through relations to the Empire were relatively trivial.

state of his time, which we describe as a quasi-absolutism, may best be indicated in a translation of his own words. He says (pp. 52 ff.):

In German lands, God be praised, we have no knowledge of a power exercised by a single man in the country, who regards himself as the highest, and who, with or without right, uses the greatest power upon all the others for his profit and advantage, according to his will and caprice alone, as a master is in the habit of domineering over his chattel men servants and maid servants. On the other hand the princely government in the German principalities and lands, as in almost every rightly and wisely ordered *Policey*, is nothing else than the supreme and highest dominion of the properly ruling territorial prince or lord, which is enforced and exercised by him over the estates and subjects of the principality, also over the land itself and its appurtenances, for the maintenance and promotion of the common profit and welfare, and for the administration of justice.

If ideals were realities, German states at this period could not be classed as absolutistic in spirit and in essence, whatever they were in form. The fallacy which it required the Revolution to expose was that this type of pious statement of the purposes of government was not protected by effective safeguards against the arbitrariness of rulers on whose talent and virtue the realization of the ideal depended. In other words, the rulers were to such an extent the final judges of what was involved in "profit and welfare," and they had so large liberty to decide that whatever was "profit and welfare" for themselves was identical with the good of the people and the state, that the régime which cameralism represented was qualified autocracy, from the modern point of view. We shall see what some of the qualifications were, and we shall see that the cameralists in general were opposed to any further qualifications which would tend to make the ruler more responsible to the people. The cameralists did much to raise the standards which a benevolent despot should adopt. They did virtually nothing directly to raise the standards of the citizens' rights to insist that their rulers should adopt them. Within limits, to be sure, but with a scope which developing civic consciousness presently found intolerable, the princes were the sole judges of what was good for their peoples and states. Cameralism was the technique and the philosophy of states in which this situation was taken for granted.

In the second place (p. 53) Seckendorff brings the sovereignty of the prince into stronger light by comparing it with the subject condition of everybody else in the state. "When we thus ascribe this supreme authority to the person of the territorial lord alone, or thereby set aside all other persons in a country, whom we have already described in the first part, although they also are empowered with certain lordship and authority either by the prince himself and his ancestors, as well as by other foreign governments. . . . . All these, however powerful and rich they are, in comparison with the prince, are to be regarded severally and collectively as mere subjects."

In the next paragraph (p. 54) the author bases this doctrine on (1) the ancient tradition, (2) the feudal concession of lordship by the emperor to the territorial prince, (3) the recognition of the supreme authority of the prince by the other estates and subjects of the country by taking the customary oath of allegiance to him.

Confirmation of the claim is found further (p. 56) in the fact that other high personages, even of the rank of count, no longer use the form with reference to themselves, "by the grace of God," nor does such a person speak or write of himself as "we." The prince uses that form, and therewith he expresses his tenure of the supreme governing station, by the will of God, and his preferment over his subjects.

On the other hand, as previously asserted, the government of a principality consists in achieving and maintaining the common advantage and well-being, in spiritual and wordly things (p. 56). Thereupon Seckendorff moralizes: "The final purpose of all human actions and deeds is the honor of God, for which the human race was especially created. Particularly however is it seemly for those high authorities who are God's deputies on earth to see that the honor of their sovereign heavenly overlord is sought in all things, etc." (p. 57).

In further commentary on the sacred functions of the prince, the argument continues: "In former times the clergy deprived princes of large parts of their sacred prerogatives, but since a large part of Germany, more than a hundred years ago, turned to evangelical religion by adopting the Augsburg Confession, the princes have resumed those sacred offices which belonged to them."

In the third place, the prerogative of the prince in worldly administration may be specified under four heads (p. 58): First, in establishing his own power and dignity, so that he will be able to suppress disorders, and will have prestige enough to make his government efficient in gaining its ends; second, he has to establish power, good laws and ordinances in the country, by which righteousness, peace, and repose, and the means[1] of the country and of the people will be brought into being, and maintained, the evil punished, and the good promoted; third, the supreme jurisdiction in the country belongs to the prince, that is, to pronounce the law between his subjects in case they quarrel, and to enforce the findings according to the desert of each; fourth, it is his duty to establish and use all the means whereby the foregoing institutions may be set in motion and administered in case of need against disobedient subjects or foreign enemies and aggressors.

Chap. ii treats of the qualification of the sovereignty of the prince by his relations to the Empire. In sec. 1, on the "*Reichs Hoheit*" over the German principalities, Seckendorff continues in substance: "In order that the opinion may not be inferred from the previous chapter that any German *Landes-Herrschaft* is absolutely free, we have to call attention to the fact that we are speaking of countries within the *Roman Empire of the German Nation*, of which the imperial majesty is the supreme head. It follows that each German country is under the emperor and the Empire. This involves the

[1] The word *Vermögen* is an extremely loose term in cameralistic usage. We shall have to call attention to it frequently. It may mean "wealth," oftener it means wealth plus everything else, from bodily strength to the arts and sciences and a strong army, which is a civic resource. The colorless term "means" is therefore chosen as a rendering.

consequence that a German prince or *Landes-Herr* is not responsible alone to his conscience toward God the Almighty for his government and actions, but that he is also under obligations, and in many ways bound by his sworn duties to pay the due respect and obedience to the regularly chosen ruling Roman emperor and to the Empire, and to all that the imperial majesty, with the electors, princes, and estates of the Empire have ordained and may ordain" (pp. 60, 61).

This section, with the remainder of the chapter, is ample commentary upon Roscher's judgment cited above (p. 62; *vide* Roscher, p. 243), that Seckendorff was a champion of the old order. To him the Empire was still a vital reality. There can of course be no valid interpretation of German history, not merely in the seventeenth and eighteenth centuries, but even to the present moment, which does not trace the actual workings of this survival among the other factors which complicated the collisions of interests after the Empire became more a theory than a fact. It is as unnecessary for our present purpose as it would be impossible to compress into a brief formula the incalculable variety of modifications which the increasingly spectral reminiscence called the Empire wrought upon the changing political situations of the period in which cameralism developed. The most essential consideration is this: On the score of absolutism there was no essential difference for the masses between the graded feudal type of sovereignty represented by the Empire, and the quasi-absolute type represented by the would-be independent German princes, with slowly increasing modifications, down to the Franco-Prussian War. Democracy made progress directly or indirectly toward its own by collisions of interests among which, sometimes for weal and sometimes for woe, the imperial interest was a factor. If our present task were to enter upon analysis of the forces which played upon one another in Germany from Seckendorff to Sonnenfels, the imperial factor would constantly be a meaning term in the equation, though with a steadily diminishing coefficient. For our present purpose the perception suffices that however power and authority were divided between princes and emperor, the net result for the people of Germany was quasi-absolutism as the foundation course of their social structure. The quarrels between the shadowy imperial sovereign and the matter-of-fact territorial sovereigns, whether of major or minor importance in their immediate effects upon the evolution of constitutionalism, as the next species of political order in Germany, were in principle negligible from our present point of view. They were merely details in the administration of control, which was quasi-absolutism, however it was distributed. To the ordinary German citizen the presence or absence of the imperial factor in the political situation simply meant one privileged player more or less in the game in which in any event he was only a pawn. We may therefore cancel Seckendorff's imperialism from our calculation, for it was of no significance for our main consideration, viz., the essential relation of government to citizens, which was the major premise of cameralism.

For parallel reasons we need not concern ourselves with the class of questions which Seckendorff raises in chap. iii, viz., the relation of the prince to the hereditary or customary rights of certain other persons, particularly agnates of the princely house. These rights may vary from claim to petty prerogative to presumptive share in the sovereignty. However these items are arranged, they are, as it were, family matters among the quasi-absolute few, and the political tutelage of the many remains unaffected.

In chap. iv on the other hand we come upon limitations of quasi-sovereignty which were in the last analysis of a more democratic character. One of the most constant difficulties of the modern student of conditions under the régime of "benevolent despotism" is to understand how there can have been an irreducible minimum of law for the individual and for non-privileged groups which the quasi-autocrats were bound to respect. Of course the explanation is that the equilibrium of controlling and of controlled groups at any moment is a resultant of forces which have previously passed through many other forms of adjustment. In the conflicts of interests out of which German civilization of the seventeenth century took shape, a great body of tradition defining the rights of citizens had been accepted as settled. In the cameralistic period this body of tradition represented a mass of social inertia, compared with which imperial claims were merely casual grit in the political running gear, while the prerogatives of territorial princes were to a considerable extent recent acquisitions. These customs, which insured a great body of relatively satisfactory private rights, were in a large degree inconsistent with the autocratic type of sovereignty which the princes represented. Yet the customary laws were often more firmly established than the sovereignties, and whatever the theories of divine right, respect for ancient private rights was the price which the quasi-absolutisms had to pay for tenure of their balance of power. The critical fact in the quasi-absolutisms of this period, from our present point of view, was that the people, in the modern sense, had no initiative in legislation, and a minimum of influence upon public policies which might at last decide whether their ancient private rights were worth having. At the same time there was a body of law which in general amounted to much more of a real limitation upon the conceivable autocracy of the princes, from the democratic side, than the shadowy remainder of the older régime exerted from the imperial side. In the passage next in order (pp. 72 ff.) the nature of these limitations of absolutism is briefly indicated.

In the first place "the subjects in a country are not slaves." The alternative description of what they are is formulated in syntax as cloudy as the idea which it attempts to express. Its substance is that "subjects are under the righteous government of authorities divinely appointed to guard the welfare of their bodies and souls according to Christian, Godly, natural and imperial law, and that they are always to be protected and cherished by this government according to the cardinal principles of a commendable form of government, according to the circumstances of the German principalities, as will be set forth in the remainder of the book."

Thus there are particular rights and powers [*Befügnisse*] of subjects which the ruler is bound to respect, not merely because they are matters of conscience and of ultimate accountability to God, but because of certain externally binding obligations. For instance, either the ruler or his predecessors may have promised or conceded something, or it is incumbent upon him because it is involved in general German laws and principles, or it is in accordance with ancient tradition.[1] Thus the prince must, in the first place, have a care for the maintenance of religion, according to both custom and usage of the country. In the second place the prince must listen to the complaints of subjects against one another, and must execute justice between them. In the third place the subjects may rightfully claim that the ruler may not act in a tyrannical manner toward their possessions. In the fourth place, if he has entered into agreements with the estates or subjects of his land, the ruler may not act contrary to his promises, without the consent of said estates or subjects. If it becomes necessary to change the traditional order, as will often be the case in matters of taxation, it is proper that the ruler should grant a hearing to the estates, and that he gain their consent, in order to avoid serious complications. Besides these chief points there are many others, with reference to which the ruler, "although not from obligation, yet from praiseworthy

[1] It should be observed that while Seckendorff probably thought he was thus defining freedom, from our angle of vision he was simply drawing the outlines of quasi-absolutism. The ruler was relatively free to decide for himself whether and in what particulars he would respect these limitations, and what specific actions respect for them demanded. The subjects were not free to hold him strictly responsible to the law, or to take part in making new laws. They were thus at the mercy of the caprice of the prince to such an extent that their ancient liberties might at any moment virtually be nullified.

and excellent custom, takes council with the estates, and hears their loyal opinions, although he is not immediately bound thereby" (p. 76).[1]

Chap. v enters upon analysis of the secular administration. The first theorem is that the prince should himself administer the weightiest affairs of his land and not leave them to his servants (p. 84). The fulfilment of this condition consists first in the effort of the prince to obtain a thorough acquaintance with the circumstances of his land (*die eigentliche Beschaffenheit seines Landes umbständlich zu wissen*).[2]

Chap. vi enters into particulars about organization of a chancellery, but it contains nothing that contributes in principle to our inquiry. It continues the impression however that its specifications

[1] A general description of a *Landtag* follows (pp. 77 ff.). The whole discussion is typical of a state of things already referred to, and to be emphasized later, viz., that during the cameralistic period there was growing definiteness of opinion about the things wanted of governments. Very little appears in the writings of the cameralists to show that their eyes were opening to the need of some reinforcement of these wants beyond the irresponsible will of the rulers. In other words, the cameralists formulated governmental standards which involved more and more consideration of the wants of the people. They do not come out into the open with any theories of effective sanctions for these popular demands.

[2] The context elaborates the proposition by making it equivalent to a demand that the prince shall know all that is in the programme of the cameralists—a naïve way of reiterating the supreme importance of cameralism! The astonishing thing, to the modern mind, in the elaboration of this theorem is that its tone is that which we might expect in a tutor toward a prince in his early teens. One wonders whether the author was really addressing rulers, or was actually attempting to make the reading public believe that his picture of what a prince ought to be was a correct likeness of rulers as they were. One wonders too whether the theorems about the selection of the servants of the prince (pp. 89–92) could have been intended as exhortations. They are so axiomatic that no one at all acquainted with government could be expected to express any other views for public consumption. The fact that they were usually disregarded at will by the quasi-absolute rulers was a large part of the social logic which ultimately abolished absolutism.

about the qualifications and duties of civil servants constitute a highly idealized picture of the desirable, rather than a literal analysis of actual, official traits.

Chap. vii recurs to the first cardinal division of governmental functions[1] "which consists in maintaining the sovereign power and dignity in themselves" (p. 102).

At this point we come upon the plainest exhibition of that peculiarity of cameralism which for the purposes of this interpretation is fundamental. Cameralism posited the dignity and power of the government as the foremost consideration. Whether this is a tenable position we are not now concerned to inquire. Our primary object is to make plain that, this being the fundamental principle of cameralism, all the subsequent contents of the system must be understood strictly in their relations to this center. If they are detached from this base, and treated as though they were taught as universals by the cameralists, or with the same emphasis in relation to some other center, the whole meaning of cameralism as a phase of social science is radically misinterpreted. Suppose we say that Abraham Lincoln's "government of the people, for the people, by the people" means that the foremost aim of the state is what the people want, because they want it. Whether this would be a tenable principle we are also not now concerned to inquire. It is obvious at a glance, however, that the latter formula taken as a major premise of soial theory would tend to arrange institutions and policies in a system very different from that which would follow from the cameralistic assumption. The cameralistic principle tended to exalt government to the rank of an end in itself. The alternative suggested would tend to subordinate government to the rank of a means, to be employed in one way or another according to circumstances, and to be respected much or little in proportion to what it proved to be worth. Meanwhile, all sorts of

[1] *Vide* above, p. 76.

variations of judgment would occur between people who reasoned from one and the other basis, about almost everything with which governments have to do. It might turn out that from the one standpoint it would appear, in given circumstances, that taxes should be high, armies large, governmental employees many, individual initiative distrusted, commercial policies exclusive, etc., while from the other standpoint the opposite conclusions would be equally plausible. If we are interpreting incidentals of a theory, it makes all the difference in the world, therefore, what the basic presumptions of the theory are.

Roscher taught his generation to interpret the cameralists as economists, or at least English-speaking readers and imitators have understood him so to teach. As we have said above,[1] that interpretation is a cardinal error. The cameralists were primarily political scientists, and with a theory which prejudged economic questions that had not yet arisen in abstract form, but which came later into the center of debate. The judgments which the cameralists passed on such matters as population, money, taxes, trade, were dictated by the particular type of political preconception which they adopted. That is, they were estimates of political expediency under certain assumed conditions, among them being the presumption of the paramount worth of the government and its incarnation, the ruler. These cameralistic judgments were not passed upon economic questions in the shape in which they arose when economic problems were abstracted and generalized, instead of being treated as details subordinate to political preconceptions. In so far as we find economic theory in the cameralistic systems at all, therefore, we have to understand it as virtually an answer to the question, What, in the given case, best promotes the purposes of the quasi-absolutism which is the main consideration? Whether the cameralists judged sanely on that question or not, the answer was not intended by them

[1] *Vide* Preface, p. xiii.

to fit the primarily economic questions which were later raised; and it is a historical fallacy to summon them as witnesses on questions which never came within the range of their reckoning.

The chapter (vii) in which maintenance of the sovereign power and dignity is discussed occupies, with its prefixed summary, eighty-two pages. This is a natural and proportional allotment of space to correspond with the prominence which the theory assigns to the subject. It is altogether inconsistent with the supposition that the book was attempting to frame a social theory in which economic problems, as understood since Adam Smith, should receive due attention. We need to notice the chapter only enough to illustrate what we have said about its character as a symptom of partiality for a type of political structure.

In the first place, the chapter deals very largely with details which a modern democrat would lightly waive aside as mere matters of ceremonial, and good form. On the other hand, the first important stipulation is of another kind, viz., that the prince must annually verify the boundary lines of his territories to make sure that his neighbors are not encroaching (p. 116); and the next follows naturally, viz., that as a last resort force must be used to end the aggression (p. 117). The specifications under the head of protection of the princely dignity with respect to the emperor (pp. 119 ff.) are largely ceremonial pedantries, but if they pertain to matters of importance they touch the location of authority, not the principle of authority itself; that is, they refer to balance between the imperial and the princely prerogative. The insistence (p. 123) upon stickling about the terms of treaties, hereditary dispositions, primogeniture, etc., betrays systematic cultivation of princely self-consciousness, more than care for more important interests which might be endangered by laxness about precedents and technicalities. Specification of the regalia, the revenues, etc., would belong under this head in any system which made room for government at all, and Seckendorff's treatment of them here is in no respect peculiar. The political type for which he spoke becomes conspicuous, however, when he turns to the means which must be used to maintain the person and dignity of the prince himself (pp. 129 ff.). The safety and comfort of the chief magistrate will always be of importance in a civilized state but Seckendorff raises details of the most trifling sort, like matters of petty etiquette, or the kinds of amusements proper to the prince, to a degree of prominence which would be possible only under arbitrary preconceptions about the relative values of political persons (e. g., pp. 175 ff.). Parts of the chapter are prolegomena to a plan of mental and moral education for young princes (e. g., pp. 136, 137, and 138–164). No doubt all this is pertinent to the author's purpose, but the pathos of it is that it is exhortation to which no power in the state was supposed to be justified in compelling the prince to listen. Other parts of the chapter (e. g., pp. 135, 136) are appeals to the piety of the prince, and rather broad hints that if his intelligence is not equal to his responsibilities, he may by prayer and consultation with wise advisers obtain from God the necessary guidance. This is also very sound advice under the circumstances, but it all emphasizes the crucial presumption that government by a prince relatively irresponsible to his subjects must be taken for granted. The principles and policies and working rules of such a government were the matter in hand. No question was admitted which would go behind this presupposition of the divine right of such a type of government and ruler. All the subdivisions of the cameralistic system turned around this primary reservation.

Nothing in this interpretation of Seckendorff is a reflection upon the loftiness of his views or upon their value as a formulation of the ideals which might make benevolent despotism tolerable. On the contrary his theory was on a plane so high that a modern reader is bound to suspect him of secreting between the lines of his treatise conclusions which he does not state. One can hardly doubt that these conventional formulations, whether intentionally or not, actually were elements of the social dynamics steadily making for more equitable distribution of political power. On the surface, however, no hint of the moral appears that if princes do not observe these counsels of righteousness and prudence their occupation will presently be gone. Whether or not such men as Seckendorff and Justi, not to say Sonnenfels, had any premonition of the test awaiting quasi-absolutism, their high ideals of government, and of the character which rulers should maintain, must have been factors in sharpening the perception of citizens that the reality was too often in glaring contrast with the standard. The cameralists must thus be scheduled as among the factors which contributed indirectly to the political reconstructions of the nineteenth century. Our present business, however, is to show just what cameralism was, in theory and in practice, in order to find the explanation of the changes in theory and in practice which impended. In a word, the best elements in the cameralistic theory were essentials of good government for which the system of quasi-absolutism furnished no sufficient guarantee. A reversal of the cameralistic presumptions was therefore inevitable. Instead of starting with the paramount value of the quasi-absolutistic type of government, and making political and social theory a technique of maintaining it, post-cameralistic philosophy posited certain popular purposes as paramount, and then proceeded to adopt the governmental means by which their ends might be attained.

Chap. viii approaches the classes of subjects which for the modern mind must be central and essential in political principles and programmes, viz., "the establishment of good order and laws for the welfare and common benefit of the Fatherland." (*Vide* above, p. 76.) That is, Seckendorff is now occupying the standpoint indicated by the preamble of the Constitution of the United States. In this chapter he begins to outline the things which in his judgment would make for ends corresponding with the later specifications, "form a more perfect union, establish justice, insure domestic tranquillity, provide for the common defense, promote the general welfare, and secure the blessings of liberty to ourselves and our posterity." The essential difference in the two situations was that cameralism gave hostages to quasi-absolutism before it entered upon this division of the inquiry. Its answer, therefore, was foreordained to be in terms of the interests of the type of government assumed as paramount; while the American constitution-makers imagined themselves free from all political preconceptions; they supposed they were judging questions of popular welfare upon their merits, and they believed that they were acting upon the principle of framing political institutions solely for their probable utililty as means to popular ends. However actual bias may have vitiated the American presumption of political impartiality, there was a distinct contrast in principle between the republican attitude and that of the cameralists. The latter, as we have said, formulated their problem as principally a question of the welfare of the preordained quasi-absolutism, thus at the outset making the government primary and the people secondary. The latter formulated their problem as a question of the welfare of presumably equal citizens, thus at the outset making the people primary and the government secondary. Only so far as the welfare of equal citizens and the welfare of quasi-absolute governments involve identical relations could correspondence be expected between systems starting from such contradictory principles.

Because our inquiry makes the history of administrative technique merely incidental, our plan does not require analysis of Seckendorff's cameralism on its administrative side. We are trying to discover the relation of the cameralists to general problems of social science. In so far as Justi proves to be representative of the cameralists, his system will presently be exhibited in considerable detail, as typical in spirit and purpose, while at the same time more highly elaborated in structure than the schemes of his predecessors.

Seckendorff begins his outline of the governmental processes by which the peace and prosperity of the land are to be promoted, by repeating that "the power and authority to establish such ordinances pertains to the territorial lord and ruler alone, and it is his duty to promote them according to his best understanding and knowledge" (p. 192). At the same time he declares (p. 193): "The object of such ordinances in general is that by means of them justice, peace and prosperity [*Auffnehmen*], or the welfare of the land and of the people, may be sought."

We shall have occasion frequently to point out that, during this quasi-absolutistic period, inchoate ideas of popular welfare were expressed side by side with formulas of the paramount importance of the government. The solution of the problems of adjustment thus presented is simply this: In effect, the ideas of the primacy of governmental and dynastic interests prevailed until the democratic period changed the balance. Previous to the democratic revolutions, popular welfare was always construed, in case of conflict, as a phase of governmental welfare. Meanwhile expression of popular interests in more and more distinct form must have weakened the force of the governmental presumption long before the consequences of the change were visible in more democratic institutions.

In general Seckendorff represents the perspective of political desirability as follows:

Peace, or the internal concord of the country, and security against enemies, are the consequence of justice, and this in turn will be promoted by peace and concord, so that it is true, according to the teaching of King David, that the two kiss each other, and the one without the other does not exist. Finally, prosperity and welfare are established chiefly upon these two precious gifts of God, but they are manifest especially in abundant sustenance and growth of the number of the people, and in their means, conduct and manners. The supreme purpose (*sic*) of all these is the salutary maintenance of the *Policey* or of the whole government, in its honor, power and sovereignty, and the last aim is the honor of God, as we have elsewhere shown (p. 193).

Accordingly Seckendorff regards it as the task of government, and so of cameralism, to provide an organization and a technique which will not only secure peace and order, but the good morals of the citizens (p. 195). An extended discussion follows of details in which the state, partly through the secular administration, partly through the ecclesiastical and educational system, must curb vice and plant the seeds of virtue in the people.

If it were a part of our purpose to weigh the merits and defects of quasi-absolutism or paternalism as compared with democracy, this might be the proper point for undertaking the process. Instead of that, the occasion may be taken for a single remark by way of caution and qualification, viz.: Our constant appeal to democracy in contrast with paternalism does not imply disregard for the historic mission of paternalism. Certain national groups have reached a stage of development after which persistence of paternalism would have involved arrest of progress. Other groups have at the same time progressed more securely and rapidly under the guidance of paternalism than would have been probable or perhaps possible with any other form of control. German populations in the seventeenth and eighteenth centuries were unquestionably illustrations of the latter situation. We are not impeaching German quasi-absolutism in its character as a stage of evolution. We are trying to expose its fallacy when proposed as an a-priori principle.

Resuming the problem of securing peace and concord, Seckendorff indicates as means thereto (pp. 201 ff.): good organization of justice and the use of wholesome laws; (2) strict prohibition of self-enforcement of suppressed rights; (3) good organization and readiness for action of the personnel of civic control.

On the means of guarding the health and increasing the numbers of the people, Seckendorff indicates a governmental programme extending from the maintenance of midwives and nurses, the support of orphans, the subsidizing of physicians and surgeons,[1] to inspection of foods, of water supplies, measures for cleaning and draining towns, etc.

Passing to problems of securing to the people means of support, Seckendorff's programme includes (pp. 204 ff.): (1) the intention on the part of government that no subject shall lack means of securing the necessities of life, "except as a special punishment and providence of God, or by his own fault;" (2) that the surplus or special products of the country shall be specially conserved as a means of securing in exchange from other countries their necessary and useful products. Details under this programme are scheduled to the number of twelve, viz., (1) the fundamental provision, i. e., the good education of youth; (2) adequate ordering of all means of making the land yield support;[2] (3) special attention to those goods which are most generally necessary, i. e., the products of the field, of grazing, of forestry, of the iron, spinning, weaving, and wool trades; (4) proportional attention to the more vulgar occupations, i. e., of day-laborers and common servants; (5) ordinances regulating prices; (6) abolition of usury; (7) regulation of weights and measures; (8) certain classes of sumptuary laws, i. e., feasting and celebration; (9) other types of sumptuary laws, i. e., clothing, etc.; (10) discouragement of use of foreign wares as clothing and food; (11) suppression of various classes of parasites, e. g., gamblers, fakirs, fraudulent bankrupts, etc.; (12) just management of income-producing properties belonging to communities.

Thereupon follows a similar outline, under five heads, of measures to be employed in getting the most advantage from a country's surplus products, viz. (pp. 214 ff.): (1) Special account is to be made of the peculiar products of the country, and special provision made for their encouragement; (2) the influences of government must be exerted to maintain the zeal of the people for continuing these specially advantageous occupations; (3) encouragement must

[1] The use of the word *Balbierer* tells its own story of the degree ot differentiation which the professions had then attained.

[2] The section suggests a curiously unassorted mixture of physical and moral devices, from compulsion of each industrial class to stick to its traditional occupations, to moral discipline of apprentices and artisans.

be given to traders from other countries to purchase these goods; (4) special attention must be given to regulation of subjects who want to carry on foreign trade in these goods; (5) the people must be protected by regulation of domestic trade against various kinds of fraud.

In these two series of categories we have in embryo the *Policeywissenschaft* worked out in so much greater detail, and with so much more orderly arrangement, by a succession of writers up to Justi. Seckendorff's schedules call for two comments only: first, they show farseeing discernment of factors which must always be rather elementary in the prosperity of communities; second, they are crude judgments about wise ways and means for securing these desirable details. In other words, Seckendorff's technology was a collection of very premature conclusions about social causes and effects. The situations to which such judgments were supposed to apply had not been generalized, and the validity of these rough and ready judgments had not been adequately tested. That is, Seckendorff's embryonic *Policeywissenschaft*, from the viewpoint of our present analysis, was merely a collection of provisional working rules, one effect of which was presently (in the time of Adam Smith) to produce an effective demand for radical reconsideration of the presuppositions on which governmental relations to all economic activities had been based. In comparison with Justi, Seckendorff formulated these rules in a very loose fashion. They reflected the fundamental policies of quasi-absolutism plainly enough, however, and progress in systematizing these policies merely intensified their absolutistic character.

Chap. ix (pp. 218–39) deals with the organization of the courts. There is no question of principle between quasi-absolutistic and democratic theories of government, as to the fundamental conception that the government must administer justice. In this respect there is nothing peculiar to cameralistics which calls for our attention. If we were making a study of comparative juridical institutions, the systems of courts in Germany during the cameralistic period would of course occupy an important subdivision of the treatment. The purposes of this book neither require nor permit an attempt to consider that branch of German administration.

For similar reasons we may neglect chap. x (pp. 240–59), which deals very summarily with the means of executing the decrees of courts and with the war powers of governments. Chaps. xi–xiv (pp. 260–328) deal with the general subject of the relation of the ruler to ecclesiastical administration, under which rubric educational administration is included. Here again details are not material for our purpose. We may observe that, so far as space is an index, Seckendorff makes these subjects six times more prominent in his general theory of the state than Justi does in the same connection.[1] This difference probably corresponds with the emphasis actually placed by the two men upon the ecclesiastical side of government. Seckendorff appears to have had no doubts whatever that the divine order of the universe necessarily worked through divinely ordained princes, in whom secular and religious prerogatives were indissoluble. Justi had no other views for publication. He accepted the ecclesiastical organization as he found it, and though he expressed a good deal of contempt for some of its workings he did not venture to offer a theory of its place in the governmental scheme essentially different from that assigned to it by Seckendorff.

Reference to the Table of Contents and comparison of Parts III and IV with the corresponding portions of Justi's system[2] will afford all the evidence it falls within our purpose to cite about the place of Seckendorff in the development of the technique of the subject. We may pass, then, from this

[1] *Vide* the corresponding passage in *Staatswissenschaft*, i.e., pp. 122–32.

outline of the more important of his two books to a brief analysis of *Der Christen Stat*.

Our account of Seckendorff would be incomplete without examination of the version of his views published thirty years later than the volume just described. This book would be more properly classified primarily as a religious exhortation than as a political treatise. Since the relations between religion and politics were more in evidence at the time of its composition than they are at present, more may be learned from a disquisition of this type, about the shadings of contemporary political doctrines, than could safely be inferred from a similar book today. So far as possible, we shall confine our notice to certain features of the book which throw light upon the author's cameralistic theories.[1]

An incidental touch in the dedication, all the more significant because it was casual, yet at the same time conventional, was the assumption that the descendants of the prince to whom the book was dedicated would continue to exercise his prerogatives "to the end of the world." If there was any speculation in the mind of cameralistic authors to the effect that the structures of states might be changed in the course of time, such vain imaginings were kept below the surface. The strong

[1] The title-page reads: *Herrn Veit Ludwig's von Seckendorff Christen-Stat. In Drey Bücher abgetheilet. Im Ersten wird von dem Christenthum an sich selbst, und dessen Behauptung, wider die Atheisten und dergleichen Leute; Im Anderen von der Verbesserung des Weltlichen, und Im Dritten des Geistlichen Standes, nach dem Zweck des Christenthums gehandelt. Darbey unterschiedliche merckliche Stellen, aus alten und neuen Autoribus, in besonderen Additionen zur Bekräftigung und Nachdencken angehängt zu befinden.* Leipzig, verlegts. Joh. Friedrich Gleditsch. M.DC.XCIII. This second edition (first dated April 18, 1685) is the only one that I have seen. It is apparently a reprint of the first, without change. Nothing appears in it to show whether it was given to the printer by the author, or by an editor after his death. The body of the book, after a dedication, preface, etc.. occupying 38 pages, consists of 719 pages. The *Additiones* and Index occupy 570 pages.

probability is, in Seckendorff's case at least, that no such fancy had ever disturbed conventional reflections.

The Preface recites that, twenty years earlier, when the author was in service at the court of Moritz of Saxony, that prince, his consort, and some of the younger members of the family were greatly disturbed by symptoms of "atheism" among persons who were regular or occasional visitors at court. The impulse of Pascal's writings led Seckendorff to attempt a refutation of atheism, and this constitutes the substance of the first part of the present book. As the author describes this portion of his work, it was purely theoretical. It found such a favorable reception at court, however, that he was encouraged to expand it, and especially to show "how the many and great evils in all classes were best to be remedied, if the ground of Godliness were rightly considered, and its chief aim were kept in sight as the guide of all human actions." In order to carry out this idea, "the three so-called chief strata [*Haupt-Stände*] and their doings" were taken into particular consideration, with especial reference to the requirements of Christianity upon them. While this reflection was still in progress (1681) the death of the elector so changed the situation that the author was able to retire and give more time to writing. He mentions Philipp Jacob Spener of Franckfurt as among those who read parts of his manuscript and made useful suggestions. The pains which he takes to excuse the failings of the book, on the ground that he had always been a man of affairs and not a scholar, savor more of vanity than of modesty. They affect one as the pettiness of an amateur who was not too zealous about the substance of his message to be fussy about the impression he would make with respect to immaterial details of form.

The first book of *Der Christen-Stat* contains nothing which need occupy our attention.[1] It is simply a layman's apolo-

[1] The reasons are obvious from the title, viz., *Das Erste Buch, Von dem Christenthum an sich selbst, wie es wider die Atheisten, Deisten und*

getic for religion as formulated in the Augsburg Confession. Seckendorff states in his Preface that belief in this body of doctrine was handed down to him from ancestors who gave their adherence to it during the lifetime of Luther. It has its chief interest not as an interpretation of Lutheranism. For that we should go to the theologians. It has merely a secondary value as a statesman's attempt to commend Lutheranism primarily to men of his own class. It is a document of more significance for the religious than for the cameralistic side of German experience.[1]

The second book sets forth the ways in which true religion, as expounded in the previous book, should be applied in the reform of civic conduct.[2] Seckendorff recurs to a division of citizens which he often employs, viz., the spiritual, the secular, and the domestic strata.[3] He admits that in a way the third of these strata includes the others. For this reason he discusses it first.

Heuchler, durch äusserliche Gründe zu behaupten, und worinnen es ingemein bestehe. Of course this whole theological background must have its full reckoning in a calculus of the various social factors of the period. It must be kept in mind as the ultimate sanction to which the principles of statecraft were referred by the cameralists in Lutheran states, as a parallel sanction was appealed to in states which adopted other confessions. We simply cannot consider it here in detail.

[1] Among the curiosities of this chapter is an argument for the existence of God based on an *ad hominem* appeal to the current belief in the existence of ghosts. "Whosoever admits the existence of spirits, must also admit God as the supreme and highest spirit." The plausibility of the argument was also derived in part from the double meaning of the word *Geist*.

[2] *Das Andere Buch, Von der Verbesserung der Stände nach dem Grund des Christenthums und dessen Haupt-Zwecks, nemlich der wahren und ewigen Glückseligkeit, insonderheit aber von Verbesserung des Haus-Standes, wie auch des weltlichen Regiments.*

[3] "*Den Geistlichen, Weltlichen und Haus-Stand.*" The problem which the word "*Stand*" in this sense always presents to the English translator is only partially solved by the rendering "stratum."

He distinctly formulates the purpose of this second book in this way: "To show that all strata would be most surely reformed according to the rule of Christianity and its chief purpose." His initial aim is to show that if this reform should first take place in domestic life it would make all other civic improvement easier.

The argument proceeds from this premise (p. 188):

> The happiness of the domestic stratum, or of each separate human being, regardless of accidental social status, is to be sought approximately in this, that one may have health, food, clothing, and other comforts and necessities of life; then further, according to circumstances of age and time, that he may marry well, beget children, live long, and come to no exceptional end. To this must be added the common civic well-being [*bürgerliche Wolfarth*], the freedom or right to associate with his own, to be thereby in appropriate respect or honor, also to enjoy peace and protection against wrong and violence.

One is reminded that certain familiar traits of human nature are not modern inventions, by a reflection which follows this schedule, viz.:

> Most people seek to fix the blame and to locate the cause of evils and misfortunes at the wrong point. Each is more ready to blame another than himself. Hence arise envy, hatred, hostility, resistance and embitterment against those who live in better fortune, especially against government.

All sorts of impotent complaints, the author adds, are accordingly lodged against rulers, and at last against God, while people ought rather to ask themselves whether they are themselves in any way the authors of their own troubles. Then follows homely exhortation, in the name of religion, to observe commonplace rules of prudence in connection with body and estate. These rules are urged as having a peculiarly Christian content and force, to be sure, but that fact does not affect the essential purport and tendency of the argument.

The fundamental prudence of good bodily habits, of temperance, of frugality, are presented in their proper relations to subsequent conditions of happiness.

Then follows an equally judicious chapter on the domestic virtues. With mere changes of detail in the illustrations, it would serve fairly well as the syllabus of a lecture, or indeed of a series of lectures, in a modern sociological course on the family.

The argument then passes to the second of the "strata," but it would be more in accordance with later usage to say that the rest of the book amounts to a treatise on practical Christian ethics in the social as distinguished from the individual phases of conduct, and of course with the theology of the Augsburg Confession as the constant presupposition. With very crude grouping and analysis of the kinds of activity treated, the discussion in a way covers the whole range of conduct in the state, as it presented itself to Seckendorff's understanding.

The first main proposition is to the effect that all the difficulties encountered in civic life come from spurious Christianity. Beginning with enumeration of types of petty neighborhood quarrels, and pointing out their departure from Christian precepts and ideals, the author treats in a similar way the grosser vices and crimes. Incidentally, and by departing rather obviously from his text, he introduces in the fifth chapter an excursus of more interest for our purpose than his proper argument. It is an observation bearing on the doctrine of population, and seems to have only a forced relation to the context. He says:

When one however undertakes to speak of the common means of support and the freedom of citizens, and of the measures necessary for improving their condition in these respects, a considerable difference must be taken into account between countries: for the situation is of one sort in the case of those which derive their ordinary support from agriculture, and of another sort with those that are devoted to trade and commerce, particularly to navigation. Because less of the latter exists in Germany, than in other regions, we have the more occasion to speak of the other sort. We must know, therefore, that under ordinary circumstances *each region can properly maintain only so many people from its own resources as can get their means of support from its yield.* For example, if we consider a village which has only arable land enough for the cultivation of ten plows, no more than that number of peasants or teamsters can profitably live there, but the others must get their living by artisanship, or get a chance to work outside the boundaries of the locality. If this does not occur, each hinders the others, or there is a scarcity of support. There can also be no more handworkers in the locality than these peasants need, etc. (p. 243).

In this paragraph the author seems to be distinctly on the trail of the law of diminishing returns. He certainly does not squint toward the conception of population which has been attributed to the cameralists of the following century. We shall see that his successors were also much more intelligent on this subject than tradition has testified.

After expanding the propositions quoted, Seckendorff approaches the moral which he wishes to enforce, in this way:

Where the Christian doctrine has been accepted, and ecclesiastics and especially monks have been introduced, from the better cultivated and improved countries, Italy, France, England, etc., also the police, or the more comfortable and at the same time more expensive mode of life, a change has taken place in all localities which could not be properly supervised or controlled, especially because of the many magistracies, but it was allowed in many respects to take its own course. Accordingly no one understands why a given occupation flourishes in a given locality, whether from some particular natural advantage, or from special skill on the part of the inhabitants. The present purpose is to urge that the people chose their course of life almost entirely without reflection, and as a consequence they do not succeed in spite of diligence. . . . . Christianity comes in to improve this state of things, by laying down certain rules about livelihood, and especially about moderation.

The point of interest about this argument, for our purpose, is not the strength or weakness of the reasoning, but the evidence it contains as to the views of the official class at this period about the appropriate aims of government. However practical men or theorists arranged their aims in the relation of means and end, the physical and moral well-being of the population governed was a definite and positive purpose. In the minds of the same men, religion was also both an end and a means with reference to individual as well as governmental welfare. It is not our affair to criticize the crudeness and the confusion in their reasonings about religion, and about its relation to morals and government. The main thing is that they actually recognized desiderata, with some common sanctions of religion, of philosophy, of prudential and political expediency, which positively prescribed moral ideals both for governments and for individuals. These standards of moral value and obligation, which stood for partially developed interests in German populations, were factors, weaker or stronger, in shaping both official and popular programmes throughout the cameralistic period. While other interests were in a sense paramount, these elementary, and in a sense ultimate, human interests were always perceptibly or imperceptibly in the balance along with other considerations of state, and their actual importance, as compared with the interests of rulers as a distinct class, never long at a time ceased to gain an increasing ratio of influence.

It is characteristic of the lack of system in social ideas at Seckendorff's time that from the remarks just quoted he passes immediately to discussion of the sin of tax-dodging, as we now phrase it, and of evading military service in the just wars which Christianity does not disapprove. This leads to discussion of the Christian ethics of conduct in war, and evils both governmental and individual are enumerated and condemned in considerable detail.

In the sixth chapter of this book, the author, with a slight departure from the classification which he made at the outset, enters upon discussion of the ethics of the governing stratum. He at once acknowledges the delicacy of the subject. He says:

> This is a dangerous and difficult matter: partly because inborn human perversity provides that no one hears the truth more impatiently than those who have the power to ignore it, and to insult those who present it; partly because, on the other hand, it is a duty to avoid speaking of the failings of rulers in such a way as to stir up hatred and scorn and even rebellion among citizens toward those rulers who try to act as true Christians (p. 255).

The wise suggestion is made in this connection that preachers would often do better to send to rulers in writing their complaints about bad government, than to utter them in the pulpit, in the presence of those who least need to hear them, and in the absence of those who should be concerned with them most. At the same time Seckendorff betrays very plain symptoms of the prevailing tendency to demand that true Christian subjects shall renounce all claim to a right of bringing direct pressure to bear on rulers if their government is oppressive. The only recourse which his philosophy and theology fully sanction is prayer to God, that He might soften the heart and instruct the mind of the delinquent sovereign. On the other hand, the appeal which Seckendorff makes to rulers to observe the obligations of religion in their conduct of government, puts the final emphasis not on considerations of justice, and the rights of the subject, but on the rulers' hopes of eternal happiness (p. 259).

However we may appraise the force or validity of the sanctions upon which Seckendorff's political ethic relied, he certainly outlined a relatively exacting standard of governmental conduct. It began with the obligation of setting a Christian example to subjects, in personal habits, on the principle of *noblesse oblige*, and covered the whole range of governmental activities. Seckendorff plainly asserts (p. 266) that Christianity puts the origin of ruling authority beyond question. Thus:

The ruling class is ordained of God, although in certain places human means, such as election or investiture, are instrumental in attaining that position, and the specific duties of government are to be learned from the light of reason, and cannot be found in revelation or the Holy Scriptures. When a sovereign therefore according to custom writes "by the grace of God," that is no vain title. It shows rather in part the sovereignty [*Hoheit*], and in part the duty: the sovereignty because of sitting in the place of God, and having to conduct the office according to the divine order. Hence rulers, as such, are accountable first of all to God, and may also hope for his protection. This their sovereignty they may use for the suppression of seditious thoughts of subjects, when the latter presume to override the rulers. The duty may be learned from the consideration that, because they are ordained by the grace of God, rulers are bound to conform to the divine law, and thus to promote the welfare of the people committed to them, and also to observe and fulfill what is promised according to the ancient usage of the land and people. . . . And although in the fewest places external means of compulsion are to be practiced, and thus a ruler, if he disregards his capitulary or his promise, sins before God alone, and is liable to no investigation by his subjects, yet the fear of God will sufficiently, and more than any external compulsion, restrain him, and he will regard those who advise him in a contrary way, and would release him from all laws, as wicked counselors, yes, as tools of the devil. What is true of these high magistrates, who are subordinated to no other human power, is true also in its degree of subordinate rulers, etc.

In the following chapter (vii) the author expands the above theorems about the authority of rulers by going elaborately into the biblical and especially the Pauline doctrine of the relation of rulers to other Christians. In chap. viii, however, he returns to the other side of the case, and argues with equal energy that—

At last rulers attain salvation in one and the same way as other Christians, i. e., by Christian faith, the fruits of which are love and a pious life. There is only one, and that the straight and narrow way, through which is the entrance into life. . . . . Just as the poorest peasant, so also the greatest king, must attain salvation. Everything which people of high degree claim for themselves as emancipation, exemption, and privilege, is sheer deception, and those who help them to these imaginings are their guides and companions toward destruction.

Upon this doctrinal basis, exhibit of specific duties is continued; thus, further duties of setting worthy examples to subjects, for instance, in checking drunkenness and neglect of attendance at divine worship by members of the court; duties of the positive sort, such as promoting the progress of true religion among the subjects; in particular the duty not merely of protecting the institutions of religion but of laying down rules of church government. Christian rulers should reform evils in the church and the clergy.

This duty belongs especially to those Protestant princes who took upon themselves the prerogatives of *Episcopus in externis*, and who administer the other *jura Episcopalia*, which the bishops alone previously administered, either in person or through their *Officiales*, through certain appointed and sworn persons called *Consistoriales* or *Superintendentes* (merely other names for bishops).

On the other hand, it is urged as the duty of rulers to refrain from prescribing articles of faith for their subjects, even when the bishops agree thereto; the duty of abolishing unnecessary display in church worship is expounded; the importance of sound learning and the reading of good books by rulers is emphasized. At the close of the chapter, subjects are exhorted to observe the duties of true Christians in all these matters, even if rulers fail in any of these respects.

Chap. x develops the author's ideas of Christian duty with respect to all sorts of situations before, during, and in consequence of war. It begins with the premise that peace is a good much to be desired, and its preservation is the first work of government. Nevertheless, righteous war being permissible and necessary, it is the duty of governments properly to prepare for it and to carry it on as far as possible in accordance with the behests of religion. The implications of this doctrine are developed with considerable detail. The evils of war are frankly admitted, and remedies pointed out in better observance of Christian precepts. It is urged that "true and right bravery in war must spring from Christian courage, by reason of the assurance of a good conscience, and of a better life after death" (p. 346). Eleven clauses from the imperial articles of war are quoted, to show that Christian principles are recognized as part of the law of the land for soldiers.[1] The chapter contains also an argument for the reinstitution of universal military duty; an essay, in twenty-seven sections, on organization and discipline of a military establishment so created; and concludes that the proposed scheme would lead to successful ending of war with the Turks, and efficient conduct of all necessary minor wars.

Chap. xi applies the test of Christian doctrine to the duties of magistrates in administering justice; chap. xii, to miscellaneous relations of government to subjects, as in excessive taxation, in infringement upon proper liberty, in luxurious living at the expense of subjects, in experimenting with alchemy and other magic arts, in manipulating the coinage, in traffic in public offices, and in establishing monopolies.

The last chapter of this second book returns to one of the initial presumptions of German civic theory, namely, that the government is bound to perform the functions of a presiding genius over the general welfare of subjects. At the same time it reiterates a theorem which in some form and force or other plays its part in all the cameralistic systems. The chapter begins with a brief expression of both these ideas to this effect:

[1] I. e., from "des Heil Römischen Reichs Reuter-Bestallung, *Anno* 1570" (p. 331).

From Christianity, or from Christian love, flows the provision of God-fearing rulers that their subjects shall have all possible encouragement and success in their livelihood and occupations, that their numbers shall increase rather than diminish, because the greatest treasure of the country consists in the number of well-nourished people; and to that end not merely external peace and the moderation of the governing power in collecting taxes, etc., are useful, ... but every other good institution which governments may adopt whereby means of livelihood may be assured to the people, and multiplied in reliable ways, for the more important Christian purpose that they may have something to give to the needy and thus may be and remain able to provide for the support of the community [*Gemeinen Wesens*] and the care of the poor and the needy.

In the spirit of this introduction, the chapter concludes this division of the author's system of ethics with brief reference to the duties of rulers toward vagrants and other forbidden types, such as gypsies, beggars, etc.; toward promotion of profitable occupations through good police organization; toward moderation of duties and imports; toward encouragement of manufactures and commerce; toward selection of competent officials for dealing with these subjects: and two closing sections contain further warnings to subjects about their own delinquencies in commerce and artisanship, with praises of peasants, artisans, and soldiers for their relatively faithful observance of Christian duty, and a final appeal to the self-interest of rulers to guard the welfare of these lower classes.

The third book hews much less closely to the lines of the original plan than the other two. Its title is *On the Spiritual Stratum and Its Reform in Particular*. The author's treatment of the ethics of his two other divisions of activity leads to the expectation that he will follow the same model with reference to the clergy. Instead of this, the book deals with every sort of question which could concern people with ecclesiastical interests at the period of its publication. It has sections which would have to be classed in turn as exegesis, church history, dogmatic theology, homiletics, pastoral duties, clerical ethics, religious pedagogy, the theory of missions, and church polity. It deals briefly with the education of women. In so far as it touches clerical ethics, it is on the same general basis as the earlier books. The most notable fact is the degree to which the relation of the church to the secular government is slurred over. If one knew nothing of Seckendorff's writings beyond this book, the most obvious inference would be that he had in mind an ecclesiastical organization practically identical with that of the Protestant Episcopal church in the United States, and as independent of the civil government. There are passages, e. g., pp. 705 ff., from which one familiar with his previous writings would immediately supply the necessary connections of these details with his whole theory of government. I have found no other passage in the whole succession of cameralistic authors which treats of ecclesiastical questions with so little reference to the relations with the political administration.[1]

A more general comparison than that of one cameralist with another may help to interpret the authors in this group. In one particular not yet referred to Seckendorff was typical of all the cameralists. It may be stated by contrast with Adam Smith. The latter was plainly a philosopher first, and incidentally an economist.[2] The cameralists were first and last theoretical or practical administrators. They betray almost no consciousness that their technique runs back to problems of a fundamental philosophy. The exceptions to this rule are in the form of harkings back to religious premises. According to their ecclesiastical connections, they pay more or less perfunctory tribute to popular Catholic or Protestant religious

[1] Seckendorff's *Vier und vierzig Teutsche Reden*, and *Politische und moralische Discurse über dreyhundert auserlesene lehrreiche Sprüche des Lucani*, I have not been able to obtain.

[2] *Vide* Small, *Adam Smith and Modern Sociology*, pp. 9, 27, 32, 65, *et passim.*

doctrine. The allusions hardly go deeper, however, than to phases of doctrine which might have been derived merely from their pre-confirmation instruction. In short, cameralistics was primarily a system of and for the bureau. It had only indirect and remote affiliations with the academy. We shall find that this fact was a very serious obstacle to the progress of cameralism as a university subject. Dithmar and Stisser will furnish typical evidence.

In this sketch, then, we have presented first of all the conception of a ruler by divine right, and of the government which he should maintain, as it was put into literary form by one of the men best entitled to speak for the system. The sketch is of chief value for this initial element. The secondary features of the régime, although in the germ in Seckendorff's doctrines, will appear in more mature form in the descriptions of later cameralists.

CHAPTER V

THE CAMERALISTICS OF BECHER

The cameralistic series next includes three men, Becher, Hornick, and Schröder, whose chief contribution to the theory was on its mercantilistic side. To the first and third of these men a chapter will be devoted. Since it has proved impossible to make a first-hand study of Hornick, his place in the development of cameralism will be indicated more briefly.

Johann Joachim Becher was born at Speier in 1635. He died in London in 1682. He was the supposed originator of the chemical "phlogiston theory." In the midst of the material and spiritual ruin which followed the Thirty Years' War, struggling against great difficulties, he became a self-taught man of no mean attainments in several directions. He is said to have supported himself, as well as, for a time, his mother and two brothers, by serving as an informer. At the age of nineteen he published a monograph, *De lapide trismegisto;* six years later, a *Metallurgia;* in 1661, a *Universalsprache,* etc. Then he entered into negotiations with the Palatine elector about establishment of various factories in Mannheim; later, with the elector of Bavaria about foundation of a German colony in Guiana, a West Indian colony, etc.; further, about the introduction of a *Commercien collegium*, and other administrative devices. In 1666 he was teacher of medicine and body physician of the elector of Mainz, but in the same year went to Vienna as *Commercienrath*. He was sent to Holland on an imperial errand, and in 1667 wrote in ten days (?) his *Methodus didactica;* and soon afterward, *Regeln der christlichen Bundesgenossenschaft*, his chief cameralistic work, if it may properly be so designated. Meantime he had an appointment as body physician and chemist in electoral Bavaria and here appeared his *Physica Subterranea seu Acta Laboratorii Monacensis.* In the same year he acquired a feudal title for the Count of Hanau to 3,000 square miles of land between the Oronoco and the Amazon, and published a *Gründlicher Bericht* in description of the region. The plan was to form a "High German West Indian Company." Nothing ever came of it. In 1670 Becher was called to Vienna in connection with a silk company and other enterprises. Incidentally, while his personal affairs were developing poorly, he dashed off a programme for setting the world to rights, in the monographs *Psychosophia* and *Einladung zu einer psychologischen Societät.* A location for a demonstrative experiment under the latter head was expected from the bounty of the duke of Güstrow (1674). In 1675 Becher wrote *Theses chemicas veritatem transmutationibus metallorum evincentis*, and experimented in Vienna on extracting gold from the sands of the Danube. His most practical occupation seems to have been at this period as head of a so-called *Manufacturhaus* in Vienna, an institution supported by the government. He fell into disfavor, went to Holland, sold to the city of Harlem a machine for winding silk, and tried to get the Dutch government interested in his attempts to get gold from sand. The enmity of Count Zinzendorf, which had cut short his stay in Vienna, still pursued him, and he went to England in 1680. The imperial ambassador tried to obstruct his plans here, but the body physician Dickinson gave him money, and he went to Scotland to study mines for Prince Ruprecht von der Pfalz. It is said that he wrote his *Närrische Weisheit und weisse Narrheit* in the twenty-eight days (?) while he was on the water making this trip. He returned to London in 1682, and died in October of that year.[1]

While Becher's influence upon cameralism was somewhat indirect, it was actual, and must therefore be duly credited.

[1] *Vide* Oppenheim, in *All. d. Bib., in loc.; vide* Roscher, pp. 270 ff.

He cannot be called in the full sense a cameralist. It is even doubtful if he ever regarded himself in that light at all.[1] This matter of labels, however, is not important. Whatever may have been the differences between Becher and the more typical cameralists, he added something to the content of a theory which at last had a recognized place for his type of interest.

While Becher's title to classification as a cameralist is questionable, his moral rating is still more dubious. Some of his vicissitudes were more his misfortune than his fault, to be sure, as for example when he was ostracized at Würzburg for dissecting the body of a woman who had been executed. He was nowhere in the favor of the clergy. The merchants disliked him for his activities in promoting the theory of the organization of trading companies. He lost his standing in the Palatinate by the failure of a perpetual-motion scheme, and he made himself ridiculous among scholars by a book which promised to teach all *Haushaltungskunst* in twenty-four hours.[2] Taken in connection with odious personal traits, Becher's individual and professional equation has simply the permanent value for our purposes of a factor in establishing a technical tradition.

Becher's most memorable cameralistic work was published in 1668.[3] Its place in the cameralistic series is entirely different from that of Seckendorff. Indeed, as we have seen, it can only by accommodation of terms be said to have had a place in the series. Each petty German state had its little army of func-

[1] *Vide Discurs*, p. 38, ll. 23, 24.

[2] "*Kluger Hausvater, verständige Hausmutter, vollkommener Land-Medicus, wie auch erfahrener Ross- und Vieharzt.*"

[3] D. Johann Joachim Bechers von Speyer, Röm. Käyserl. Majestät Commercien-Raths *Politische Discurs von den eigentlichen Ursachen des Auff- und Abnehmens der Städt Länder und Republicken.* "In specie: Wie ein Land Volckreich und Nahrhafft zu machen, und in eine rechte Societatem civilem zu bringen. Auch wird von dem Bauren- Handwercks- und Kauffmanns-Standt derer Handel und Wandel, *Item*, von dem

tioning cameralists, the hierarchies of the bureaus. Few of them wrote books, but in some particulars such a sorry substitute for a book as this miscellaneous collection of Becher better reflects what they were doing and thinking than the more systematic treatises. Becher's *Discurs* contains no direct internal evidence that the author had ever heard of Seckendorff. It seems to be the record of the impression made upon an unsystematic mind by contact with the workings of bureaucracy in various capitals.[1]

In the dedication to the emperor Leopold, dated September 1, 1672, Becher asserts that his reasons for the dedication were three: first, that the book was largely written while the author was on the imperial civil list, and that the material was largely collected in the course of that service; second, because enemies had scattered the slander that the author was of no visible use in the imperial service, and the book would be an answer to the charge; third, because enemies who were identical with the enemies of the German Roman Empire and of the imperial house had attacked the author for addressing the common German Fatherland in plain vernacular German, instead of academic Latin.

Monopolio, Polypolio und Propolio, von allgemeinen Land-Magazinen, Niederlagen, Kauff-Häusern, Montibus Pietatis, Zucht- und Werck-Häusern, Wechselbäncken und dergleichen ausführlich gehandelt. *Dritte Edition*, mit vier Theilen vermehret, worinnen viel nützliche, wichtige und curiose Sachen begriffen. Franckfurt. . . . . M.DC.LXXVIII." I have used only this third edition. The first is dated 1668.

[1] As a sample of judgments passed upon Becher in less critical scientific periods than ours, we may cite estimates quoted by Roscher from Zincke's *Leipziger Sammlungen* (1758). Becher is spoken of as "the first reformer of German systems of artisanship, manufacture, trade, *Polizei*, and finance." Of the *Discurs*, the same author says: "almost to the present time the only fundamental book which can be used in a certain degree as introduction to *Stadtwirthschaft* and its *Policei* system" (Roscher, p. 435).

Becher adds that he may be reproached for the presumption of dedicating to the emperor a book which contains discussions of commercial affairs, with which nobility has nothing to do. The reply is that his majesty is not expected to concern himself directly with such subjects, but the book is designed to bring more clearly before his eyes the fact that the commercial classes are contributing to the population and wealth of the country, and that ways and means of establishing a populous and self-sustaining community are the most suitable subject-matter of a political policy.

In the Preface to the second edition Becher refers to the contents of the book as *Commercien Materien*. He must be interpreted, therefore, in contrast with Seckendorff, as making the interests of trade his point of departure. While Becher was thus concerned only secondarily with the theory of administrative organization in general, it is no less true of him than of the other cameralists that the test to which he would bring all commercial questions was their relation to the interests of the state as represented by the government.

Becher goes on to say that, although the first edition found many enemies, and was in several places forbidden by the clergy, yet it was soon entirely sold. It appears that the immediate cause of the enmity of the clergy was an innocent quotation upon the title-page from the jurist Calvinus. It was assumed that John Calvin was the author quoted, and that the book must contain Protestant poison!

Perhaps the most significant clause in this preface is that in which the author anticipates charges of partisanship. The implication is that the book contains, perhaps the author would even have said it is, a commercial programme. Such a programme is open to misconstruction or to disapproval from many sides. It will wholly please no party. To the non-Catholics it will seem to be too strongly imperial or Spanish in its leanings; to the Catholics it will appear too favorable to Holland, etc. Becher protests, however, that he has introduced documents into the collection rather as samples of various sorts of instruments, than because he approves the policies in the course of which the documents were executed. He continues: "The sole end of this new edition is on my part to give the reader a formulary of various transactions and political concepts which serve the welfare of the state" (*des gemeinen Wesens*).[1] Further expressions in the Preface emphasize the fact that the book was written in an atmosphere thick with petty political strifes. Prejudice and suspicion would construe it as a party pamphlet, whether it was so intended or not. Under such circumstances, neither the author nor his public could take an objective and critical attitude toward the abstract questions involved. The book attempted to deal with public policy, primarily commercial, as a matter of pure theory. It was in spite of itself to a large degree a discussion of immediate policies. In drawing conclusions about its contents, caution must accordingly always be observed against generalizing specific conclusions into universal doctrines. Becher did not undertake to present a complete social philosophy. His purpose must be gathered from his own professions. "It is enough for me to have done what belongs to an upright German man, namely, conscientiously and faithfully to have served the German Fatherland and its head, the Roman Imperial Majesty."

Becher begins the first section of his introduction with this preamble and definition:

Since I am now to make a beginning of showing wherein the prosperity of a land or of a state consists, I must necessarily at the outset call to mind that man, as the material of the Republic, is an *animal sociabile*, and seeks society, as the sacred text itself says, "It is not good that man should live alone." In order that he may have a society, other and more men are necessary, and that these may be

[1] Reasons for this rendering will be assigned in connection with Justi's employment of the same phrase. *Vide* below, p. 299.

born God has created the female sex and ordained marriage, the end of which is to be fruitful and replenish the earth. I must call to mind further that, next to reason, human society alone distinguishes the life of man from that of the beasts, which society is solely and alone the fundamental cause, beginning, means, and end of all laws and ordinances which men, both pagans and Christians, have made for the preservation of this society. . . . . If then I were rightly to define a state I should call it a *populous, self-supporting community* [*eine volckreiche nahrhafte Gemein*].

The two chief elements in the concept are then expanded in turn, to the effect that, on the one hand, unless a community is populous it cannot defend itself, but must be the prey of every enemy; and on the other hand, that a populous community is impossible unless sufficient means of support are at command. The idea is also emphasized that the people in a community furnish one another mutual support. They live on one another. "When the members of a community arrange their affairs so that the one lives from the other, the one can earn his piece of bread from the other, yes that the one plays his support into the hand of the other, that is the right community."[1] Becher accordingly concludes that the community is the third person of a trinity, people, sustenance, community:

For where the latter exists, there will be no lack of people and sustenance; where this is disturbed [*verstimmt*], however, there will be nothing but hatred, enmity, persecution, oppression of the poor, exaltation of the rich, rebellion, and finally impoverishment and total ruin. Accordingly, just as when one is to play on a violin one must first examine and tune each string, so when its sustenance is to be assured to a community, attention must certainly be paid to every sort of human being that is there, and nothing appears to me more remarkable than that in many places no thought whatever is given to these most difficult points. Each is left to get his living as

[1] It would be unkind to ask Socratic questions of this wisdom. Why not let such simplicity alone and not invent the historical fiction that it is to be understood as political economy!

he may; whether he is ruined and ruins a hundred others with him, or he prospers, with the common gain or loss, prosperity or adversity, no one asks any questions. Because this is the crucial point, however, I will do my best to consider and dissect [*anatomiren*] the members of the community, in respect to the way in which they should work with each other in the matter of support, I will try then to put them together, and to form them into a political skeleton [*sceleton politicum*].

In the second section the analysis continues:

There are necessarily two sorts of people in a community: the first, the majority, the second who are the servants of the former, and here is included the magistracy [*Obrigkeit*], which is a servant of the community, and holds the people in good order and social regulation, so that one may live by the side of another, because the community is not for the sake of the magistracy, but the magistracy for the sake of the community. Also the clergy are the servants of the community in protecting the soul, the learned who protect the mind [*Gemüth*], the physicians, apothecaries, barbers, bathers, who guard the health, the soldiers who guard the body and the whole state and land. All these are servants of the community, and although they help to increase and maintain the *societatem civilem*, they are still not the community itself, but as stated only servants of the same, who must be paid and supported by the community, and hence, in order that they may not become burdensome to the community, they should be made proportional by the community, that they should be neither too many nor too few. For if there are more *Bürgermeister* than citizens in a city, more preachers and confessors than hearers and penitents, more schoolmasters than pupils, more doctors than patients, more soldiers than citizens and peasants, more nobles than subjects, that land is in bad shape. . . . The other sort of people, who essentially constitute the civic society [*societatem civilem essentialiter constituirn*], are those of whom the society most consists, because there are most of them in the society. Such men now, whose servants the former are, may properly be divided into three orders. The first is the largest, namely, the peasant order, the second is the handicraft order, the third is the tradesman's order. The last is the smallest order. . . . . While the peasant order is the most numerous, it is also the most necessary. . . . . In the peasant order there are various classes. . . . . Hence the infallible rule, *Where there is no peasant, the handicraftsman has no material to work over, and where nothing is worked over there the tradesman can have nothing to sell;* moreover, while the peasant cultivates the field, he cannot be at home, and while the handicraftsman works at home, he cannot run about and sell his wares, and while the tradesman does this he cannot be a peasant or a handicraftsman. Hence follows the undoubted conclusion, These three orders should not be mixed together, but it should be possible for them to stand close together and to make a real community; that is, to support each other, for where this occurs, ... the object of a proper *Policey* is attained, i. e., a respectable and necessary human society.

Referring not to the cameralists in general, but to Becher in particular, I cannot refrain from pointing out the resemblance of the first part of this remarkable passage to a pearl in a swine's snout. If we accept the gem as genuine, we must confess that its occurrence at just this point is an unexplained sport of nature. It seems to shed almost pure light of insight into the vicarious character of human society. It is an ungrateful task to inquire in this case if things really are as they seem, but I find myself unable to accept these appearances at full value. The evidence hardly warrants a theory in explanation of ideas which seem to be so at variance with the conceptions of the time. If I were to propose an explanation it would be that this was merely imitation of pulpit conventionalities, and repetition of a stilted form which was not vital with new insight and had not even retained the spirit of the New Testament doctrine of which it was a hollow echo.

I will add but a single query. If Becher actually saw that society is a system of reciprocal services, if he saw that the performance of functions for one another is that which makes desirable citizens, and failure to perform such functions makes the undesirable citizen, if he used the term "servant" as a dignifying epithet for citizens of the former class, by what reasoning or association of ideas did he draw the line between the few whom he classed as servants of society and the many whom he left in the ignominious company of the served? Until we are instructed by what right the tiller of the soil and the artisan and the tradesman are rated as essentially less serviceable to their fellows than those who carry on the relatively non-essential occupations, we must conclude that Becher's apparent penetration must be held under suspicion as tawdry rhetorical embellishment.

We come then to the body of the book, the first part of which treats of "the form of the government, that is, of those who rule and of those who assist them therein." We may repeat that it is not our purpose to investigate the evolution of cameralism. We are not attempting to make out the stages in the elaboration of the system. We are not drawing specific comparisons between the programmes of administration outlined by the successive writers, nor are we trying to appraise the relative merits of their proposals as a governmental technique. We are studying them in turn in order to be justified in presenting what they have in common as a typical attitude toward social problems. We shall present that attitude as it seems to be most characteristically defined in Justi. Our use of the other writers is rather for the purpose of assembling features which belong in a composite picture, than to distinguish degrees of theoretical completeness or variations of technical detail. We refer therefore to his table of contents for more specific indications of Becher's analysis, and we confine our further observations to a few items which may serve as shadings for the picture. For this purpose we find the opening paragraph available, viz.:

As concerns the first point, namely the kinds of civic authorities [*Obrigkeiten*], five sorts are to be distinguished, first spiritual or secular. The proverb runs, "where parsons rule, there is no good in the end." Because their government is not hereditary, their aim is only to enrich their own, *et fit pax in nostris diebus*. If a war comes, they make themselves scarce, after the manner of the hireling in the gospel. A secular lord does not do this, for the sheep belong to him, and since there is a succession, such rulers strive much more for the conservation and the improvement of the land.

Here speaks the partisan, and he reflects one of the sharpest contrasts of his day. The issue was in some respects more acute in Catholic than in Protestant states. In the former, the Reformation had agitated and modified, but had left the social structure externally unchanged. There was accordingly quite as much restiveness under clerical influence, and sometimes even more, than in the Protestant states, where the political power of the clergy was assumed to have been broken. In Catholic and Protestant states alike, the struggle between state and church was not ended, but merely changed in detail. Neither Catholic nor Protestant clergy were by any means cured of their lust for power. Whether openly or covertly there was almost everywhere antagonism between the two types of pretension. In nearly every German state the antithesis between the temporal and the spiritual power was as real if not as evident a political factor as it had been when the immediate form of the issue was Papacy or Anti-Papacy. So long and so far as this conflict was undecided, the cameralism of a given German state was in part one of the military arms of that secularism which was still in battle array against ecclesiasticism.

With entire *sang-froid* as to co-ordination of categories, Becher follows tradition in naming as the other types of government: third, aristocracy, fourth, democracy, fifth, a mixture of these.

The basic theorem of Becher's cameralism is in the proposition:

Monarchical government has the advantage over all the others, and is the most usual. Indeed it is, so to speak, a duplicate of the divine government, established in the Holy Scripture, accepted of all nations, and very profitable for the community (p. 14).

The claim on which Becher chiefly relies to support the theorem is this:

A lord who has a succession is more concerned for his land and people, and makes their interests more his own [*hält bey ihnen stich*] than a government to which the sheep do not belong (*sic*). Consequently a monarchical government is when a ruler has his own land and people, and governs over them according to his own will without interference and limitation [*Einreden und Massgeben*], but has such rule in heredity.[1]

In discussing the merits and demerits of the different types of governments, Becher assembles a list of counts against monarchy and aristocracy which modern democrats have judged to be decisive. A sample of his quality may be cited from the paragraph in which he disposes of democracy:

Namely, where the officials are under obligation to account to the subjects for their government, and the subjects, if they please, are present in council, and contribute their best observations, also see and hear the business that is transacted. But the lacks above found in aristocracies are also found in democracies. In addition to those it must be mentioned specifically that in the democratic government (*sic*) there is no respect for the authorities [*der Obern*], by reason of the multitude there is no secrecy, by reason of the number of voices there is often an unskilful *consultum*, in a word, in this sort of government occur too often factions, seditions and rebellions.

Having considered the pure governmental forms, Becher discusses mixed forms under the two heads *Monarchal* (*sic*)

[1] The parallel should be noted, for further use in other connections, between the argument from succession in the case of monarchy and the similar argument today in the case of property. The first stand taken today against possible modification of our institutions of inheritance is on essentially the same ground as that chosen by the defenders of monarchy of the "benevolent despot" type. Is the ground more tenable in the one case than in the other?

and *Aristocratic* (pp. 16 ff.) and reaches almost the identical judgment in favor of mixed monarchy which he expressed four pages earlier in favor of pure monarchy, viz.:

Among all sorts of governments this mixed form retains the preference, and is most in vogue in Europe. Indeed the Roman Empire itself consists at this moment of such a government. The Roman emperor is the supreme head, and presents a monarch. The eight Electors are the *Seniores Imperii, et Patres conscripti*, the princes, estates, and cities present as it were a democracy. All these three parts secure themselves against one another. Thus the electoral princes require of the emperor the capitulation, while on the other hand they must take the oath of allegiance to him. Princes, estates, and cities of the Empire also co-operate in both ways, and enter into both the above forms of obligation. . . . . This mixed form of government then is the sole *conservation* of the Roman Empire, the guarantee that it will never be an *absolutum purum vel aristocraticum*, or a *Democraticum Imperium*, for if this should happen the remaining freedom would be at an end. . . . . The mixed form is thus the best, but it should be *in superlativo* monarchical, *in comparativo* aristocratic, and *in positivo* democratic. Hence it is evident that the Roman emperor in this mixed government should have the most to say, and that it would not be well if the imperial sovereignty were too strictly held down by capitulations. . . . .

One who had read Seckendorff would instantly decide that in this chapter he was dealing with an inferior order of mind. There is no such discrimination here as that which we found in *Der Fürsten Staat* between the king and the tyrant, although we must confess that the earlier writer was as much in the dark as the later about means of eliminating the one type and securing the other. I cannot believe that responsible statesmen, or even strong thinkers of the academic type, could have regarded this chapter seriously. It bears no marks of derivation from evidence which would have been likely to carry weight with experienced men, even in that less exacting period. It is a jumble of judgments about confused and unauthentic statements of fact. It shows no evidence of insight into the contemporary meaning of the Roman Empire. It speaks of government as though no more personal interests were concerned than those of rulers on the one hand, and princes, estates, and cities on the other. It is in short a schoolboyish essay on a subject of which the elements were not comprehended by the writer. It had approximately the same relation to the more respectable contents of the book which we shall discover below between the historical survey at the beginning of Justi's *Staatswissenschaft* and the portions of which he was competent to speak from pertinent evidence. It was the perfunctory work of a man retained by a type of government which he was bound to support.

The second chapter (pp. 20 ff.) treats of the "qualities and correlations of those who rule and those who serve the ruler." The style suggests the hearsay quality of the so-called "society novel," written by an author whose ideas of society are gained through other novels or the newspapers and observation of supposed representatives of society in public places. One can hardly imagine that the ruling class could have had any use for the book, except to promote its circulation among those in whom rulers and their courtiers would like to inculcate the notion that their superiors consulted such oracles.

For example, the first specification is that a ruler—

> . . . . must before all things consider whether he has come legitimately or illegitimately to his station, for upon this foundation he may infallibly rest all his future weal or woe, and easily guess that he who seizes at government by violence will also usually be expelled by force and he whose cause is just will have God's help, though all the world should be opposed.

A most edifying doctrine, but hardly likely to strike the ruling classes as a novel variation of the stock formulas of the preachers, or to exert great influence against the esoteric practices of their kind. The second specification is a similar platitude, viz.:

The magistracy must preserve order in its affairs, and must observe a strict routine: i. e., not write letters when it is the time to go to church, not hunt when a session of the council should be held, etc., etc.

The third detail is one which a Louis XVI, for instance, found it difficult to arrange, viz.:

A ruler must be sagacious, and himself understand the art of governing, in order that he need not always believe the doctors. There are sometimes rulers who are not sagacious, others are too sagacious. The first do not know how to discriminate between counsels, and must therefore follow all their advisers. The others will never follow advice, and resort to compulsion whenever they are opposed.

It does not seem to have occurred to Becher that, under the régime in which he was employed, it would be just as logical for a writer on farming to specify the sorts of weather to be desired. The specifications would have had as much competence practically in the one case as in the other.

Fourth, some rulers are too diligent, others too indolent. . . . . Fifth, there are rulers who in their action and character are either too deliberate or too hasty. . . . . Sixth, sometimes rulers have too short memories, and sometimes they remember grudges too long. . . . . Seventh, a ruler should be neither too credulous nor too incredulous. . . . . Eighth, in all these things it will be very helpful if a ruler has a care for his authority, does not make himself too common, but is heroic, brave and resolute: but he must not be too distant, arrogant, and proud. . . . . Ninth, a ruler, government, and land should seek the same consideration among neighboring states as at home, but to that end should not be quarrelsome, etc. . . . . Tenth, a ruler must find the mean between prodigality and parsimony. . . . . Eleventh, a ruler should be neither too communicative nor too reserved. . . . . Twelfth, the cardinal virtue of great lords and rulers is, finally, that they should be just and merciful. Too severe is tyranny, too sympathetic is womanish.

There follows, in similar style, a series of ten propositions, which Becher calls "the ten commandments" for the use of rulers in relations with their servants. The illustrations by which the several specifications in the two series are enforced contain rich material for the culture history of the period. They show that the abuses which at length doomed quasi-absolutism were evident enough, even then, to those who cared to observe them. But they show more plainly that they had hardly begun to make for modification of the fundamental political presumptions held by cameralistic theorists. The inference from them is merely, "the wise ruler should do so and so." The fact that the presumptions of quasi-absolutism provide the people with no way of requiring the ruler to observe these precepts had not yet weakened these presumptions in the minds of the cameralists. We shall find that this continues to be the case, with no acknowledged modification, and so far as decisive evidence goes with no great modification even in the private opinion of this type of theorist, until the movement for constitutionalism had won its right to recognition.

On the other hand, the total impression of the collection of commonplaces in the chapter before us is that of a rather strong appeal to the self-interest of princes to observe the rules of prudence and justice in the treatment of their people. There is surprising directness in the hint contained in such words as these:

> A great lord must know that he must deal cautiously with soldiers and learned folk, for sword and quill are two sharp and glorious instruments. The sword has often marred the master whom it had previously served, and the quill can praise and blame, it can write panegyrics and satires, it can also write those things which find their way to the ends of the earth, and no one is exempt from its influence. Hence it is well for great lords to be more careful with their servants and subjects than with their closest kin (p. 27).

The bearing of the material prosperity and moral well-being of the subjects upon the strength of the state and of the prince is repeatedly urged, and indeed is seldom entirely out of sight in the cameralistic arguments. The intimate history of the court of each German principality would have to be investigated in connection with the cameralistic doctrines current from generation to generation in each, if we were to know how actual government and the theories of the cameralists reacted upon each other as alternate cause and effect.

In chap. iii, on "the form and order of a good government," Becher attempts to set forth "the universal political laws by which land and people are conveniently and well governed." He regards it as necessary, however, to begin the chapter with "a short digression, and as a preliminary to show how and whence magistracies and laws are derived, how they must be constituted [*bestellt*] and how far they extend."

The origin of governments is explained upon the traditional dogmatic basis, and there is nothing to indicate that the stilted thought and expression contained anything more than prudent reflection of prevailing orthodoxy. Thus:

Government is said to be the means by which man is enabled to live according to his nature, which is created in the divine image. This nature is made up of five elements [*Stücke*], each corresponding to one of the cardinal elements in the nature of the divine being. These latter are, (1) his existence, (2) his perfection, (3) his omniscience, (4) his omnipotence, (5) his eternity. Accordingly, after "the fall," by which man had lost the ability to realize the divine image in himself, God instituted government, and gave laws to bind men to the laws of nature. Since the laws of nature are of five sorts, so there are now in the world five strata [*Stände*], laws and governments. (1) The spiritual stratum and its laws affect religion. (2) The moral laws affect honor, virtue, good conduct, and the nobility (*sic!*). (3) The doctrinal stratum and its laws affect the learned and sciences. (4) The civil courts pertain to possessions, sustenance, and goods. (5) The criminal court has to do with body and life, under which may be included the maintenance of health, and defense by force and war. The exposition continues:

"Since in these five points all is included which belongs to the maintenance of the human condition, in order to govern these five kinds of laws and their subjects, that is, to hold men in the state of humanity and the natural laws, God has ordained magistracy [*Obrigkeit*] which should be obeyed as God himself. As has been said, it is the office of the rulers by good laws to maintain, protect, govern, and control their subjects in the true religion; love and knowledge of God; in good morals, discipline, honor and integrity; in good and various sciences; with respect to their support and honorable earnings, their health and life, also legitimate increase. In these five points consists the origin of all laws and the foundation of authority and obedience.[1] . . . . Hence arises an important double question, namely, in what form princes, lords and the nobility in their government receive an hereditary succession and complete power over the subjects? Is it that they should make them chattels, and sell them at will to others, incidentally with no respect for the abovementioned welfare of the subjects; i. e., that they should act contrary to all the five points above indicated; and can subjects with good conscience obey rulers of this sort?"

Becher's attempt to answer the latter question throws still stronger light upon the obsession of quasi-absolutism which is the determining factor in the thought of the time. He had no difficulty in entertaining the supposition that a ruler might be oppressive. The possibility does not appear to have shaped itself in his imagination that the oppressed might conceivably govern themselves. When the hypothetical question is put in terms which make obedience to an oppressive ruler intolerable, the only alternative which Becher is able to consider is recourse to another ruler. Thus he says:

Here arises the most difficult question, Who shall pass on the errors of the government? For it is not seemly for the subjects

[1] For further expansion of this theme, Becher refers to his tract, *Bilanx humanae felicitatis et infelicitatis.*

themselves to censor their government. I say therefore they should lay their complaints before their neighbors[1] or other unpartisan judges, and urge their government to answer, and much rather intrust the matter to strangers, than attempt to carry it out themselves (p. 45).

Immediately following this passage, Becher distinguishes between pagan and Christian slavery. He calls the former tyrannical; he pronounces the latter conducive to the good of the subjects. He urges accordingly that peasants have no right to resist their lords, when the latter coerce them for their own (the peasants') good! Thereupon he adds the judgment that rulers will be condemned by the heavenly powers to temporal misfortune and eternal punishment if they are utterly regardless of their subjects' good.

Having thus satisfied his conscience by warning rulers of the supposed consequences of misusing their power, Becher turns to the positive question, By what means are the five departments of government above indicated to be carried on? The reply is that a ruler who purposes to govern with regard to what has been said, should organize five distinct *collegia*, each to have in charge one of the five sorts of laws and administration above scheduled.

The first *collegium* should have charge of the souls of the subjects, their religion, worship, fear of God, etc. The second should care for the moral discipline of the subjects. The third should be charged with the education of youth, promotion of the sciences, etc. The fourth is civil, and attends to ordinary questions touching temporal prosperity of the state, property, outlays, and income. The fifth might be called *collegium vitale*, for its duties are with the health and protection of the subjects, against both secret and public enemies.

The further exposition of the duties of these bureaus consists more of incoherent complaints about evils which need correction in the different groups of activities than of technical

[1] That is, neighboring governments.

details. The inference is that most of this organization, so far as the author was informed, was not yet in existence. Thereupon follows in the fourth chapter a sample scheme of *Policey*. It is a plan approved by the bishop of Mainz for adoption in his episcopal city, but apparently not actually put into execution (p. 60). It is a code of city ordinances, and it is a first-rate source of information about municipal conditions in Mainz at the middle of the seventeenth century.

The speculative and academic character of this first part of the *Discurs* leaves the impression that it was in effect rather hortatory than responsible. The inference which it suggests throughout is that, so far as Becher was acquainted with the facts, provision for all these details of administration was incomplete and inefficient.

Part II proposes an analysis of "the material of the republic, that is, of those who are governed, namely the subjects." In comparison with the first part, this portion of the book seems to reflect less certain conventional forms of thinking, if not of acting, and more of the author's own individuality. Although this second part is amateurish enough, it bears evidence of closer approach to the affairs discussed than is visible in the earlier chapters. The inference that the author was not primarily a cameralist is strengthened. That is, in the course of his occupational mutations he had now become interested in promoting trade. Under the circumstances of the time, the only hope of accomplishing much in this direction was through governmental initiative. Becher accordingly patched his appeal for attention to the promotion of trade into a sort of general cameralistic scheme. It does not appear, however, that the aim to strengthen the government was as distinctly central and paramount in his thinking as in the programmes of the more typical cameralists. Indeed, we may say that, so far as this book is concerned, he was in rather striking contrast with them. His chief purpose could not be called economic in the scientific sense, but it was primarily commercial and secondarily political. If Roscher had not ranked him with the cameralists, the perspective of the literary history of the period would be more accurately indicated by passing him over with a much briefer notice than the undue prominence given to him by Roscher will permit.

This second part of the *Discurs* may be described as an account of the state of trade in Germany. The subject is approached through a characterization of the three strata that make up the bulk of the population—the traders, the artisans, and the peasants. Because this was more nearly fallow ground as a literary theme than the subject of government in the abstract, Becher could appropriate less in the way of current generalization, and the result is a painful exhibition of untrained powers of expression. The style is hopelessly involved. The sentences run distractedly from one predicate into another, and their relation to their subjects is left so largely to the discretion of the reader that the precise affirmation intended by the author is always open to doubt. So far as distinct steps in the argument are discoverable, the following is the main line of thought (pp. 98 ff.):

1. These three strata should be under one administration, not three, else confusion will result.

2. The main end to be aimed at for these strata is increase of their numbers.

3. Consumption is the center and source of the well-being of these strata. The fundamental aim of governmental policy therefore should be to promote consumption. In a word, consumption maintains these three strata. Consumption is their soul. Consumption is the only means of binding these strata together, and it enables them to live upon one another. For promoting consumption, indeed, the trading stratum is necessary in the community in proportion to the size of the peasant stratum. The latter increases the population, but the former nourishes it (*sic*), for as I shall presently show, the sole consumption of these three strata, and thus their

sustenance, depends on the merchant, for the artisan lives on him and the peasant on the artisan. I am best acquainted with such of this stratum as are wholesalers [*Verläger*].[1] . . . . These wholesalers must truly be regarded as the foundation pillars of the community.

4. Trade in foreign goods, when the same could be produced at home, makes for the destruction of the community. Instead of favoring men who enrich themselves by bringing in foreign goods, we ought to deal with them as the meanest criminals (p. 106). On the other hand, those merchants by whom the state gains in money and sustenance are, next to nature, the nursing-mother that makes the desert to bloom.

This theme is elaborated with a zeal that the earlier sections did not betray.

5. These three strata have three dangerous and highly harmful and destructive enemies: the first checks population, viz., *Monopolium;* the second limits means of support, *Polypolium;* the third divides the community, *Propolium.*

In a following section these three abuses are considered in turn; the first being described as "when one member alone in the community has that in the way of support upon which otherwise many others could live." The term *Polypolium* (unrestricted competition for employment) is defined by the statement:

"In order to remedy the evils of monopoly the Dutch have abolished all '*Zünffte*,' and have admitted *Polypolium*, in that everyone is at liberty to earn his living as he may, on which account people flock thither in great numbers and rob one another of work . . . . by which the traders and wholesalers keep the artisans in constant poverty and toil."

Propolium is not directly defined, but Becher evidently uses the word in the sense of the old English terms "forestalling" and "engrossing."

From this general introduction Becher passes to his specific and technical material, the state of trade, and wise methods of

[1] Becher applies the term to the type in the industrial system of the time which combined the processes of the modern manufacturer and jobber. They not only kept large stocks of goods, but they furnished capital to those who produced the goods (p. 103).

promoting it, through a general account of trading companies, as devices by which the evils of monopoly and of *Polypolium* may be avoided. Having specified the general conditions under which he would have the privileges of such companies restricted, Becher divides trade into fourteen types, "to which all others may be reduced." For each of these branches of trade he proposes the organization of a trading company under governmental patronage and control.

This then completes the theoretical part of the book. The remainder is occupied, first, with a survey of the condition of each of these fourteen branches of trade, second, with a miscellaneous collection of documents illustrating commercial and other transactions more or less properly governmental, with which in most instances Becher claims to have had somewhat intimate connection.

We may append all that it is necessary to say about the second of the three men named in the opening paragraph of this chapter.

Philipp Wilhelm von Hornick (sometimes written Hörnigk, Horneck, etc.) was born in 1638. He spent his early years in Vienna, studied law at Ingolstadt, and obtained the Doctor's title there in 1661. He lived a considerable time at Vienna, visited the German courts on a political mission in the company of the Spanish Franciscan and Bishop of Croatia, Christopher Rojas, and about 1690 entered the service of Cardinal Lamberg, Prince Bishop of Passau, as Privy Counselor. He died in 1712. His first political publication was *Hippophili Galeacii de Corneliis Francopolitae wahrer Bericht von dem alten Königreich Australien*, in which he argued for political consolidation of the estates of the German Empire, and support of a common army to resist French attempts at annexation. The book which appears to have made most impression appeared in 1684, with the title, *Oesterreich über alles, Wann es nur will. Das ist: Wohlmeinender Fürschlag, Wie Mittelst einer Wohlbestellten Landes-Oeconomie, Die Kayserl. Erb-Lande in kurtzem über alle andern Staaten von Europa zu erheben, und mehr als einiger derselben, von denen andern independent zu machen.*

From all the allusions to the book which I find in the cameralistic series, as distinguished from later commentators, I discover no reason for crediting the author with firstrate constructive influence upon the theory. Roscher quotes the publisher of the edition of 1784 to the effect that "Austria owes to this book the greater portion of its well-being." If this is not gross exaggeration, it is very strange that the theorists betray so little sense of debt to him. Since I have been unable to examine the book, my opinion is of little value, but all the indications which the succeeding cameralistic books contain lead me to classify Hornick with his brother-in-law Becher by the modern commercial term "promoter." Apparently Hornick made an impressive argument for industrial and commercial development. If he did more than this for cameralistic theory, I have been unable to trace it. (*Vide* Inama, *All. d. Bib.*, *in loc.*, and Roscher, pp. 289 ff.)

The following paragraphs contain the substance of Roscher's account of Hornick's book.[1]

This book was written under immediate influence of impressions made by the frightful experiences of Germany, and especially Austria, in the eastern and western wars between 1680 and 1684. I recall only on the side of Louis XIV "the Chambers of Reunion," 1680, the conquest of Strassburg and Casale, 1681, the French invasion of the Spanish Netherlands, 1683, the seizure of Luxembourg and Trier, 1684: all as humiliating as the contemporary siege of Vienna by the Turks was horrible. "The cunning of the French has brought almost everything into such chaos, that one can reckon one's dates from nothing except God and oneself," says Hornick (chap. ii). But the author hopes for "decisive war with that arrogant nation" which "will find its way into France" (25). The thing to do is to make economic preparations for that alternative, especially as France bases its predominance quite essentially upon economic things. "Would to God we might take the general French programme [*allgemeine Lands-Oeconomie*] in many particulars as a good model (23). No state in Europe can look to its policy, without either in much or in little thereby breaking with hated France" (33). There can be no more dallying in Austria. The might of

[1] *Op. cit.*, p. 290.

a people depends essentially upon the ratio of its means to those of its neighbors. Now Germany, as compared with the mighty advances made by France, England, and Holland in the last hundred and fifty years, has not only stood still (7) but through war, Reformation, loss of population, etc., it has even absolutely declined (17). The greater the necessity of its rise, and especially through the same programme which has made Holland and France so rich, in spite of all the wars, which at this moment is followed by the English against France (24). The state must prevent "loss of our best blood, the very marrow of our strength, our good gold and silver, by the million, by purchase of useless wares from our hereditary enemies."

It cannot be said that Hornick identified possession of money with wealth. On the contrary he made this definition: "The power and excellence of a land is its surplus of gold, silver, and all other things necessary or convenient for its subsistence, and so far as possible derived from its own means, without dependence upon others, and including the appropriate cultivation, use and application of the same" (9). Quite special worth must be attributed to the independence of a land, which to be sure can never be complete, but must always be aimed at as an ideal. Everything pertaining to the thrift of a land falls into two classes: Gold and silver, and indeed copper, "which in their worth and use equal all other things, and on account of their civic use are in a class by themselves;" then the means of food, clothing, shelter, etc. A land that had only gold and silver would be rich, to be sure, but very dependent, since gold and silver can neither feed nor clothe people. A land that has all other things except gold and silver is somewhat more independent, to be sure, but yet not sufficiently so, "because gold and silver are somewhat necessary in the most of human circumstances, while in the rest they are indispensable." A land with neither of the two species of goods in its own resources, like Holland or Genoa, is insecure, even in the most splendid development of its commerce. Most independent is the land which is rich in both classes of goods, for example, China (8). The comparison of gold with the blood leads Hornick to the thought that the princely treasure may play the rôle of the heart (22). Yet he is not consistent. His views on mining and on foreign trade are rather quite mercantilistic. "It were better, no matter how strange it may appear to the ill-informed, to pay two *Thaler* for a ware if they remain in the country, than one if it is to leave the country" (9). It also sounds paradoxical, but it is true, that mining should be continued even when its cost is much in excess of its output. "The outlay remains in the country; what is extracted from the earth remains not less in the country." Accordingly the state is as much richer from the so-called *Freibauzechen* as a merchant who gets 100 per cent. on his capital (31).

Hornick bases these views on the difference between the thrift of individuals and that of countries, or as we would say, between private and public economy: and he even makes the fine observation, somewhat in advance of his time, that the so-called cameral-management (as we say, *Finanzwirthschaft*) is "particular management," thus maintainable only on the basis of the general thrift of the country. This latter is the chief reason why the attention of the state to the general thrift cannot be rated as a mere *parergon* of the treasury (2, 32).[1]

Quite in the spirit of the mercantile system are the "nine chief rules of public economy," which Hornick offers as "a merchant's or cameral alphabet" (9): (1) Precise investigation of a land, also through experiments, and full use of its productive capacity, especially of precious metals; (2) transformation (*Verarbeitung*) in the country itself of all raw materials not fit for use in their natural state; (3) utmost increase and useful employment of population; (4) no export nor useless hoarding of gold and silver; (5) so far as possible, restriction to use of home products; (6) necessary foreign wares should be exchanged at first hand, and not for money, but for home products, and (7) so far as possible (they should be bought [?]) in unmanufactured form; (8) greatest possible export of "superfluous" home products, and preferably for gold and silver; (9) no importation to be permitted, if enough of the same goods, and of tolerable quality, can be furnished at home.[2]

[1] *Vide* the chapter on Schröder, for more explicit development of essentially the same view.

[2] Roscher adds the note: "If we compare these rules with the still very unsystematic mercantilism of a Bornitz, a Besold, and a Klock,

To the author these rules seemed such an obvious version of "eyes open and hands ready to take hold," that he thought "their reasonableness must be evident to everybody. Only a peasant might not be able to understand them" (24). Whoever contradicts them, *sit nobis velut ethnicus et publicanus et patriae hostis* (3).

The bulk of Hornick's book is an attempt to furnish proof that Austria, more than any other European state, possesses the natural endowment for economic independence and wealth. It has at once productive veins of the precious metals (and not so far off as Spain's!) and abundance of the chief necessities of life (10–14). Everything to be sure is still in the highest degree undeveloped. There is no enterprise or venture, the richest natural treasures are allowed to lie unused, raw materials are exported to be brought back at doubled price in manufactured form, the population is sparse, their luxury seeks mostly foreign products, etc. (16–18). Still the inhabitants are by no means lacking in mental equipment for trade and industry (15). It occurs here, as usual, that the raw material countries are poorer than those where manufactures flourish, that the former, if they will, can supply the lack "by proper use of their raw materials," and then can be more secure than the latter (8). Hence there is need in Austria only of earnest grasping of the situation from the highest quarters down, and Hornick urges that this programme should take the form of total prohibition of imports in case of silk, woolen, linen, and French manufactured articles (22). Violations should be punished as treason (23). Then, in his judgment, all the inconveniences of the transition period would be passed in a few years at most. Many foreigners, who have hitherto supplied our market, will settle in the country and continue their industry (21). The necessary amounts of capital will be created of themselves, through discontinuance of the outflow of money. Inordinate rise of prices for domestic goods could be prevented by the government, by establishing scales of prices (24).

Hornick urges further that artists and great *Verleger* should be more honorably treated by the state (28); and he argues that a mari-

who were already acquainted with the great Italian mercantilists Botero and Serra, we get an idea of the meaning of the practical impulse which Colbert also gave to the theory."

time country without naval strength cannot be powerful; while naval power without sea commerce is impossible (30). On the utility of means of exhibiting the resources of the state, on the harm of guild abuses, the classification of traders into the publicly useful and the harmful, he is quite in accord with Becher. *Privilegia privata* are to be regarded with suspicion; their reasonable purpose, namely, control of consumption in the public interest, may be better secured through prohibition of imports, and then free domestic trade (28).

CHAPTER VI

THE CAMERALISTICS OF SCHRÖDER

The third of the group mentioned in the preceding chapter was Wilhelm Freyherr von Schröder.[1]

No writer in the cameralistic series has been portrayed in more conflicting colors. On the one hand, he has been represented as an oracle of cameralistic wisdom, and a model of civic righteousness. On the other hand, so long as his influence was apparent, equally extreme depreciation of his character and doctrines was uttered. This latter estimate is typified by the remarks in a private letter by Seckendorff (quoted by Roscher, p. 294). Speaking of Schröder's book, Seckendorff says: "*stultissimus liber, et pravis repletus opinionibus . . . . a homine perverso; et hos tamen homines fovent principes.*"

In a certain sense this second type of appraisal of Schröder gives him an importance which he would not have obtained if he had always been treated judicially. In spite of his admirers, he occupies on the whole the place of a suspicious character in the literature of the subject. To express it melodramatically, he is the heavy villain, whose shadow ever and anon falls athwart the plot. Even if later writers do not refer to him by name, ideas which were rightly or wrongly attributed to him, and which were not indorsed by cameralists in general, constantly recur. They not only furnish many texts on which the cameralists delivered homilies against tendencies to which they might have given the name *Schröder-*

[1] The title-page of the first edition of Schröder's chief work does not contain the author's name. It reads: *Fürstliche Schatz- und Rent-Cammer, ad Augustissimum & Invictissimum Imperatorem Leopoldum I. Principem Triumphantem. Cum speciali Privilegio Sacr. Caes. Majest.*, ... 1686. Unless otherwise specified, the references are to this edition. I have also used the edition of 1744.

ismus, but perversely enough, these more or less imaginary faults of Schröder have come down to our time as peculiarly characteristic of cameralism. The perversion, the exaggeration, the exception have thus been reported as the rule. In order to reach an objective judgment of cameralism, therefore, it is necessary to form a correct estimate of the man who has been used more than any other to prejudice its reputation. With the help of the article by Marchet, the necessary bibliographical details about Schröder may be summarized.[1]

There has been much inaccuracy in accounts of his life, especially through confusion of his career with that of his father. The latter represented Gotha in the negotiations for peace at Osnabrück in 1643. In 1654 he took a prominent part in the Diet at Augsburg; he became *Kanzler* and *Geheimrath*, and died, 1663. The younger Schröder with whom we are concerned, is known only from the time of his entrance into Austrian service. Possibly as early as 1663, not later than 1673, be became a member of the English "Academy of Sciences," and he maintained rather intimate relations with England throughout his life. One of the faults in his writing was his failure precisely to indicate the English sources which he freely used.

Schröder succeeded Becher as director of the *Manufacturhaus* at Vienna. Becher had lost favor, partly because of his irascible temper and arbitrary manner, partly because he was accused of conducting his office with an eye primarily to his own, rather than the public, interest. Two years before Becher was removed, Schröder was called upon to make a report to the emperor on existing manufacturing conditions in Austria, and he took the opportunity to make propositions about expanding industries and making them profitable for the treasury. Marchet says:

"With Becher and Hornick, Schröder composed the triple constellation which from the seventh to the ninth decades promoted the industrial advance of Germany and especially of Austria. I should arrange the series in the order Hornick, Becher, Schröder. They used approximately the same means, viz., opposition to guild abuses, especially through destruction of the guild monopolies, and

[1] *All. d. Bib., in loc.*

the establishment of a *Manufactur Haus*, high tariff on foreign industrial products, especially French goods, the attainment of a favorable balance of trade, etc. Hornick was most aggressive, and did not stop to think of his own interests; Becher and Schröder acted more cautiously, and with more consideration for their own advantage. The means for attaining these purposes was for all three the absolute prince. Schröder was in the most advanced line in this respect, and swayed between the interest of the prince and that of the people without a fixed point of attachment, although he always affirmed that the prince can be happy and prosperous only when the subjects themselves are well situated. With this conception of the paramount character of the princely power, Schröder takes a rank far behind Seckendorff, and occupies the standpoint of Horn. . . . . In spite of his subservience to princes, Schröder must count as one of those persons who helped to lift Germany from that economic depression and national decline into which the Thirty Years' War and the predominance of the territorial lords had plunged it."

A study of Schröder's writings without previous prejudice leads to conclusions somewhat different from either of those cited. We shall try to present a completely objective judgment.

In the first place, Schröder took the doctrine of divine right, with an extremely absolutistic interpretation of the right, literally, seriously, and as compared with most of his successors, consistently. That is, instead of clinging to the essential doctrine, while glossing it over with all sorts of disguises to conceal its extravagance, Schröder frankly accepted conclusions along with premises. On the whole, we are bound to feel a certain respect for this rugged type of intellectual integrity, in contrast with the perplexed philosophy which insists upon primary theorems but balks at their logical consequences.

It would be difficult to find in the whole literature of "divine right" a more compact and uncompromising profession of the faith than in Schröder's *Disquisitio Politica Vom absoluten Fürstenrecht.*[1] In substance his position is this:

[1] *Vide* pp. 552–69 of 1st ed., *Fürst. Schatz- und Rent-Cammer.*

It is the common madness of scholars to assume that all governments, the monarchical included, are based upon certain compacts between chiefs or rulers, and their subjects. They assume that the rulers are consequently bound to observe these compacts rigidly.

For my part, I fail to see who shall have bound this yoke on the neck of monarchical government, since the same had its beginning not in a compact between the prince and the people, because Saul was made king by the immediate declaration of God, who also caused him to be anointed by his prophets before the people knew the least thing about it. Moreover God had the *jura* and *praerogativ* of this king and his successors put on paper and proclaimed and published by the heralds (I Sam. 8:9). And in order that such *jura* might not in the course of time be obsolete or weakened, the same had to be put aside and guarded in the *archivo* for the Lord (I Sam. 10:25). Moreover the Holy Ghost himself was so careful about this whole matter, that with his own fingers he wrote the whole history and the first origin of the kings, with their rights and prerogatives, in the great book of the unchangeable truth of God, commonly called the Holy Bible, and he saw fit to substantiate the memory of the same to the end of the world. Moreover the people voluntarily abandoned all further pretensions, when God the Lord ordained such *Jura regia*, and thereby made plain that when the king was once chosen, they would no longer be heard (I Sam. 8: 18, 19).

Such princely right now as God dictated to the pen of Samuel may be read in plain and clear words, namely:

Details (Puncta) of the Right of the Prince[1]

"This will be the manner of the king that shall reign over you:

"1. He will take your sons, and appoint them for himself, for his chariots, and to be his horsemen, and some shall run before his chariots, and he will appoint him captains over thousands, and captains over fifties.

[1] Under this sub-title Schröder quotes I Sam. 7:11-19 as a divine code defining princely prerogative in general. The Lutheran rendering is even more drastic than the King James version in the text. For example, we cannot fail to trace an effect of the *Zeitgeist* upon Luther

"2. He will set them to ear his ground, and to reap his harvest, and to make his instruments of war, and instruments of his chariots

"3. And he will take your daughters to be confectionaries, and to be cooks and to be bakers.

"4. And he will take your fields, and your vineyards, and your oliveyards, even the best of them, and give to his officers, and to his servants.

"5. And he will take the tenth of your seed, and of your vineyards, and give to his officers, and to his servants.

"6. And he will take your menservants, and your maidservants, and your goodliest young men, and your asses, and put them to his work.

"7. He will take the tenth of your sheep; and

"8. Ye shall be his servants."

With the puerilities of the exegesis and application we have no concern, beyond recognizing the fact that Schröder simply voiced a certain contemporary orthodoxy, both in the general practice of grotesque construction of biblical material into evidence to support preconceptions, and in the particular doctrine of the divine origin and *quasi*-absoluteness of princely authority. This latter datum itself, however, must be put in its true relations with Schröder's reasoning, and with cameralism as a whole.

Schröder does not mince words in stating his inferences. He declares that, in consequence of Saul's appointment, all Christian princes and potentates derive their position and right to rule immediately from God. Besides that, "most princely governments and monarchies" have in the course of time "conquered and maintained their prerogatives with the sword, and I therefore see no way in which this contradiction

in the gloss which he forces upon the passage, thus turning the episode from its historical meaning, by translating the first sentence: "*Das wird des Königs Recht sein, der über euch herrschen wird.*" In the quotation above, the King James version is adapted to the same liberties which Schröder takes with the Lutheran text.

that rulers are under obligation to some one or other, of which the learned write, can have any basis whatsoever." The author concedes:

There are few monarchs to be sure, who are not involved in a thousand *Capitulationen*, *transactionen*, and *recessen*, but such arrangements cannot be cited as a basis of royal rule. They are rather mere limitations to which rulers were compelled to consent by force of circumstances. They can in no sense be regarded as subtracting from the right which inheres in the royal office, and which is conferred upon the prince by God, not by the people. They cannot prejudice the title "by the grace of God," since, as we have seen, God left the people no freedom by which they were entitled to dispute with kings, or to hamper them with restrictions. Consideration of misuse of royal power is reserved to the divine majesty, and God has already announced the decision that the people's complaint will be rejected, according to the decree published by the prophet Samuel (I Sam. 8:18), "And ye shall cry out in that day because of your king, and the Lord will not hear you in that day."[1] Consequently, although, through many successions, princes and their posterity have consented and sworn to many things, no *jus* has been thereby created, and no prince can be bound thereby, as though he had lost his original divine right. Hence a sovereign prince is authorized, without violation of a good conscience, in re-establishing himself, so soon as he has opportunity, in possession of his princely right, in spite of previous compacts, oaths, prescriptions or whatever the limitations may be called. This does not mean that a prince is released in his conscience from all laws, and that he is not bound as a private person to his private contracts,

[1] It is characteristic of this exegetical method that it had no compunctions about falsifying the very evidence on which it relied. Whatever the bearing of the episode referred to, on its face it lends more countenance to the social compact conception than to Schröder's interpretation. It pictures the people as taking the initiative in demanding a king, and God as reluctantly acquiescing. Schröder not only expurgates this part of the record, in his original statement, but in this clinching passage he omits the clause "which ye shall have chosen you," which would be a sufficient *ad hominem* argument to refute his main contention.

and that he may at will practice all sorts of tyranny without regard to God, and justice and Christian love, for he is a man and has to deal with men, and like his subjects he is a member of the body of Christ. In short, the prince must have respect to the rule (*Eph.* 5:9), "know that your master is in heaven."

The prince must recognize two great obligations as appertaining to his prerogative; first, that he must administer justice among his people: to wit, according to Christian love, and the principles and fundamental doctrines of Christianity; second, that he must be the leader of his people in war, and expose his body and life to defend them against foreign enemies.

The monograph concludes with this summary:

These two obligations of a prince are truly hard matters, since a prince, without violation of his conscience, cannot disregard them. And just as a people, or the subjects, may under no pretext prescribe laws to their prince and king, and as those which are thus *de facto* made have no validity, and do not bind the prince; so on the other hand a prince must so conduct himself in his government that he may be able one day to give account to God alone; as David says, "Against thee, thee only, have I sinned" (Ps. 51:4). And a prince must well reflect with what a rigid law and severe tribunal he must deal, where the judge himself is the accuser, and his own conscience must be the witness against him, where no exception and no excuse can be made, but where no other penalty will be decreed than eternal woe, torture and pain.

In the Preface of the *Schatz- und Rent-Cammer*,[1] the relations of the prince to the state, and thus the landmarks of the theory to be expounded in the book, are still more tersely indicated. Having recapitulated the arguments of the publicists on the question how a prince may best establish his

[1] I refer to the edition of 1744. The *Vorrede* does not appear in the first edition. It purports to have been written by the author of the body of the book, and the fact that it did not appear in the original edition is the only reason I have for suggesting that there is a possible question of authorship. The internal evidence leaves little room for doubt that Schröder was the writer.

power, viz., he must either (*a*) pin his hopes to the powerful class; or, (*b*) he must make friends of the masses; or, (*c*) he should rob and plunder, i. e., he should be a tyrant; the author cancels the last theory from consideration, on the ground that it is essentially un-Christian, and of the remaining two doctrines he says:

Between the two views it is not for me to decide, for each prince will know best where to find support in his own case. For it seems to me that those people are very thoughtless who imagine that a prince can do anything he pleases because he is a prince. Those who talk in this way do not understand the difficulties of government. They judge only from outward appearances. They do not know how many small and large wheels belong in a clock. . . . . To cope with these difficulties of government the statesmen rely upon four means, viz.: (1) *sapientiam summam in constituendo leges;* (2) *summam auctoritatem ut etiam vita religiosa sit;* (3) *vitae diurnitatem;* (4) *bonam fortunam.* If I might take the liberty, however, I would trust myself to hit the mark with two arrows: *first with a standing army, second with plenty of money in the chest.* . . . . The army may be left to others, but I have undertaken to write in this little book of the ways in which a prince may get money. I have taken for granted throughout that the interest of the prince will be joined with the interest of the subjects, and accursed be he who intentionally separates the one from the other, because they cannot prevail unless they are united, and those who rightly examine the chain by which the members of a state are bound together must acknowledge, in accordance with sound reason and experience, *that the prosperity and welfare of the subjects is the foundation upon which all happiness of a prince as ruler of such subjects is based.* . . . The common man is not satisfied with words. He wants good subsistence, cheap times and protection. I have accordingly shown in general all possible means and ways by which a prince may make his subjects or his land rich and prosperous. In order however that a prince, in exacting tribute and in ordering institutions, may make no mistake, I have advised that he make his demands where there is something to take, and where he who must pay can afford it. To that end it is necessary that a prince shall be informed about his land and his subjects, their occupations and their gains. I have accordingly proposed the necessary schedules.

Schröder is half apologetic about his proposals (*Vorrede*, p. 14) and describes his book as a Utopia. Apparently he does not use the word in quite the usual sense. He means by it that while his scheme does not profess to correspond with actual administration in Germany, it is on the other hand not impracticable, and should be set up as an ideal to be attained. He reiterates his general idea in this way:

I think I have shown how the happiness of a prince is conjoined with that of his subjects, and the prince himself may be made rich by ways and means which are opposed neither to God nor to virtue, and that all Machiavellian maxims which are based upon jealousies, mistrust, secret subtle tricks for oppressing the subjects, and other tyrannies, should be avoided in all Christian governments, and in their stead should be introduced, to the advantage of both prince and subjects, mutual confidence and love that would be pleasing to God and would give peace of conscience, and at the last great day of judgment would obtain for prince and subjects the divine blessing.

Those who, after the common fashion, with Adoram who was over the tribute of Rehoboam (I Kings, chap. 12), are accustomed to suck the life blood of the people, may scoff as they will, and may think to gain by it; to me they are like the geographers who measure off the whole world with their circles on paper, without the least concern whether the surface of the earth is made of wood or straw, nor how long it can last, *Latronum, non principum est, omnia auferre.* A robber strips off my shirt. A prince does not even demand my coat.

With this preliminary survey of Schröder's general conception of government, we may attempt to do justice to the main argument of his book. The opening passage was seized upon by later writers as containing a sinister meaning, and the whole book was prejudged accordingly. The paragraph reads:

A prince who has no treasure in the chest, but plans to rely upon the good will of his subjects and lands, is walking on stilts: for the tempers of subjects are lame dogs, with which one can catch no particular hares. Consequently I cannot agree with those publicists who so far neglect care for a full treasury and for accumulating a common fund, that they believe, if a prince only puts himself in the good graces of the subjects by great liberality, or by waiving all gifts, he will always in case of need find abundant treasure among them.

Instead of finding a cause of offense in this passage, the historian who has any sense of social values must give Schröder credit for wise prevision of the necessity of a well-defined fiscal administration. The German states at his time were not yet fully through with the process of evolution from the household to the civic type. The publicists with whom Schröder took issue evidently preferred a régime of hand-to-mouth patriarchalism to an orderly impersonal system of creating governmental revenue. There was no issue between the two types of theorists about the fundamental relations of prince and subjects. The question was simply whether the relation should proceed upon the basis of a sort of happy-go-lucky plantation improvidence, or whether there should be an attempt to anticipate fiscal needs by organizing an adequate system of supplying governmental wants. It would be self-stultifying for anyone in our generation, who believes neither that the social process should have halted with the big-farm type of rural civilization, nor that philosophical anarchism pictures the structure best adapted to secure the utmost development of diversified civilization, to decide against Schröder and in favor of his critics. If he was a king-maker, he was more a Samuel than a Warwick. He cannot be made responsible for the abuses of governmental power by arbitrary rulers. The things which the people of the period most wanted required responsible and capable governments. These governments depended upon relatively fixed sources of income. The creation of such sources of income gave to rulers in turn power to oppress the people. The exercise of this power presented problems with which subsequent stages of civic experience had to deal. Meanwhile it would be hysterical to blame Scrhöder for his meritorious work in planning the sort of civic machinery without which the main purposes of the German peoples of his time could not have been promoted. His critics were of the type who demand the miracle of arriving at ends without use of the necessary means. While we cannot accept as general truth all the reasons which Schröder assigned for his dissent from the policy of relying upon extemporized popular generosity for governmental supplies, we must judge them in connection with the state of opinion to which they were addressed. In other words, the whole issue between him and his critics resolves itself in the retrospect into balancing of *ad hominem* arguments. Briefly, the issue reduces to this: a *quasi*-absolute ruler being by common consent assumed, and *quasi*-absolute rulers being inclined to aggression upon other states than their own, thus constantly jeopardizing the peace and security of all states, and each state assuming that its own ruler is more devoted to its own interests than other rulers are, is it wise or not that the ruler should have control of regular fiscal resources, so that he might act promptly and efficiently for the general weal? In this connection it would be irrelevant to criticize these premises. Whatever their merits or demerits, they were the presuppositions of all theorists who had an appreciable influence upon the passage in political experience which we are considering. None of the subsequent cameralists so much as hinted at a theory of government which essentially modified these assumptions.[1] That being the case, we

[1] I do not mean that no betrayals of views pointing to reconsideration of political philosophy are to be found in the cameralistic books. Instances of contrary impulses, if not insights, may be found between the

are bound to conclude that those cameralists who affected to regard Schröder as a wicked partner impeached either their own mental competence or their sincerity. Whatever room there was for difference of opinion about details, we can have little respect for his contemporaries, or his successors for the next century, who failed to give him credit for foresight and service upon the constructive side of the issue—a fiscal system *vs.* no system.

It has often been repeated to Schröder's discredit, for example, that he made it a part of the right of a prince to prefer his own welfare to that of his subjects, if they came into collision. The fact is, however, that not a single man in the series, from Osse to Sonnenfels, ever stated a fundamental theorem about the rights of rulers of which Schröder's proposition would not be a consistent and necessary corollary. Some of them gave pathetic evidence of an unreconciled conflict between judgment and sympathy, in opinions about specific acts or types of acts. To a modern man some of these opinions would be utterly irreconcilable with an absolutistic theory of government. In this connection the cameralists did not have the courage of their sympathies, however, and they held to their absolutistic theories in general, while incontinently uttering more democratic opinion about particulars. Even the free-thinking Justi never ventured to deny in print the essential theorem which Schröder put in the most uncompromising theological form, viz. (p. 7):

> For that is the right of the prince in the empire of Christ which the prophet David describes, when he says: "He has given thee the heathen for thine inheritance and the uttermost parts of the earth for thy possession,"[1] whence it is seen that the prerogative of kings

lines of almost every one of them. So far as they were willing to state their basic presumptions, however, the cameralists all adhered to substantially the view above indicated.

[1] Again by changing the tense from future to past Schröder alters the text just enough to make it suit his purpose better than the actual language (Ps. 2:8).

is a hereditary right [*jus haereditarium*], that it is a complete and proprietary right [*völlig und eigenthümlich Recht*], and not as it is called by the Cromwellians in England, a royal office [*officium Regium*]. It does not say, "he has given the heathen a king," but "he has given thee the heathen for a possession," whereby the absolute government of princes is evidently established. Accordingly it is impossible that the interest of a prince will not sometimes differ from the interest of the people. . . . . When therefore a prince, in order to conserve his monarchical, not his private interests, must often use means not agreeable to the people, he can in such cases surely look for little help from them, and consequently it is not to be hoped that a prince must rely upon his subjects.[1]

The discussion which follows, of the advantages of absolute over limited monarchy, differs in no essential from the views expressed at length, or implied, by all the later cameralists. It is of course less finished in form than the identical philosophy a hundred years later, and it has less sense of shame to hide under palliating phrase. It is more frank than the same doctrine in later and sophisticated types, but no more justly chargeable with subornation of oppression. The man who believed in the divine origin and absolute right of kingship, and who tried to show what was necessary to sustain such an institution, cuts a much more respectable figure in history than men who still professed allegiance to the premises of the doctrine but hedged on its conclusions. Even a democrat, to whom the dogma of the divine right of kings is a childish superstition, but who prefers logical consistency to mental confusion, must find something to admire in the Bismarckian ring of Schröder's ultimatum (p. 12):

In order now that a prince may be independent of his subjects, and absolute in himself, I regard it as safest and most profitable that

[1] Although this is a literal rendering, the last sentence must be understood as referring to the alternatives presented above, and it means "he cannot rely upon mobilizing the good will of his subjects whenever occasion demands, but must have a regular system of revenue."

he should have the hilt in his hand and money in his chest, whereby he may put his demands into effect, and prostitute neither himself nor his reputation, nor be obliged to put his subjects off with fine words, because he is unable to act from lack of means. As Demosthenes said, "*Opus sunt opes.*" . . . . With gold and silver we can work miracles.

If we fairly consider the civic problems of German states in the second half of the seventeenth century, and if we give Schröder the benefit of his own explanations, we can no more join with those who treat him as the black sheep of the cameralistic flock than we can pass a similar judgment upon Alexander Hamilton for trying to lay a firm foundation for American finance. On the contrary, we must number him among the sane and wise builders upon the structure of German fiscal administration. His second chapter, on the directorate of the income of a reigning prince, begins with a keen analysis of the prevalent unwisdom of European governments in committing both disbursements and the creation of revenues to the *Cammer*. The consequence is, according to Schröder, that when the prince needs money, the tradition-bound *Cammer* knows no other way than to hunt out some new objects on which a tax has not been levied; or to grant some new monopoly; thus causing the subjects to sweat blood because more of their support is taken away; or to exact a new loan; or to demand the ox that has grown fat while working on the lord's estate; or to sell the claim to some future lucrative service for a large sum of money, or some such device. By these means the cameralists have made themselves so hated and suspected in the land that they have frequently been excluded from assemblies of the estates. "Moreover," continues Schröder, "this point, so far as I know, has never been touched. I must therefore dwell upon it, and express my unauthoritative opinion about it." The substance of this expanded opinion is that raising the princely revenues calls for quite other persons and talents from those engaged in the work of disbursement. Schröder accordingly elaborates work for a comprehensive system of *Policey*, although it is not as definitely classified under that title as in most of the other cameralists, and he does not draw sharp distinctions between measures that other writers distribute between "*Handlung*," "*Policey*," and "*Finanz*."[1]

A glance at Schröder's table of contents would disclose that he was interested in a wide range of industrial development, which would make both prince and people richer. He simply concludes (p. 21):

> It consequently seems highly necessary that cameral affairs, at present so called, should be divided into two separate *Collegia*, the one of which, as aforesaid, should have the income and the disbursements, the other should be a *Collegium* which should have nothing else to do but to raise the revenues of the reigning prince.

The remainder of the book is devoted to showing the different kinds of work which such a bureau could do.

As Schröder saw the situation, the treasury officials, from preoccupation, or ignorance, or both, rather than from evil intentions, were effective smotherers of new industrial ventures. An independent organization should therefore be established by the prince, with the special duty of attending to the very enterprises for which the treasury had no competence. Moreover this *Collegium* ought not to be hampered by other bureaus. Hence it is properly to be called "*summum & absolutum Collegium*." The members should have large salaries, in order that they need not be forced by their own pecuniary necessities to prefer their private interests to those of the prince. Moreover a certain fund should be at the disposal of this *Collegium*, so that it might carry out its plans (p. 23). Schröder cites, as an illustration of what he has in mind, the "*Courts of augmentations of the revenues, of the King's crowone*" (27 Hen. VIII). He anticipates opposition to the plan on the part

[1] E. g., Sonnenfels. *Vide* pp. 481 ff. below.

of the existing court functionaries, but he sees promise of accomplishing the establishment of the proposed bureau in the beginnings made "some years ago" by a minister, who is not named, but presumably an Austrian official, whose untimely death postponed the undertaking.

The only plausible hypothesis which remains to account for Schröder's dubious reputation among the cameralists is that the reactionary officials set a fashion of misrepresenting his proposals. A reader of the present day, who should examine his book without knowing the worst that had been said about it, would pronounce the author first and foremost a zealot for establishing a stable fiscal system, but at the same time, and with practically equal earnestness, a champion of popular interests against official greed. The argument is, in the first place, a most judicial analysis of the workings of previous systems of taxation. Schröder admits that the traditional forms of taxation are necessary, and that in extreme cases the rate of the same must be temporarily raised. He declares that they are inadequate for the needs of the state, and that they can never be applied with impartial justice (pp. 29 ff.). The people who rely on them are simply like tenants of the soil, whose only interest is to strip it, regardless of those who must depend on it for their living afterward.

This is well illustrated, in the case of artisans, by the closing paragraph of chap. xcii. The subject under discussion is the reasons for the deplorable depression in German manufactures. The last reason assigned is:

> . . . . the greed of the ruling classes and the consequent bad treatment of laborers and artisans. For no sooner does a foreign or even a native handicraftsman by his science, and art, in the sweat of his brow, earn a better piece of bread than others can ordinarily gain, than the government falls on him like crows on garbage, and tries to take all it can. For it says such a fellow ought not to have more. He should know that he owes his earnings to me as his ruler,

who favors his trade. He should divide with me. Oh! the great foolishness of such magistracies! They have no idea what it means to have prosperous subjects. All that they accomplish is to drive such people out of the country, and at the same time to prevent others from entering.

In the chapter on "*Saving as the Second Customary Device for Enriching the Treasury*," Schröder shows that he had thought much ahead of most of his comtemporaries in tracing out certain economic relations. His exposition of the false economy of hoarding leaves nothing to be said on the essential principle, and his exposure of the penny-wise and the pound-foolish policies of certain penurious types of officials is as merciless as it is just. Incidentally Schröder cites an unnamed "world-renowned publicist" who blames the untimely parsimony of a treasury chief, and adds that he "should distinguish between *Oeconomiam Rusticam & Oeconomiam Politicam*." The latter phrase is notable as apparently anticipating the nineteenth-century conception of economic science. The context shows, however, that the expression must not be taken in its full modern sense. It apparently connoted only an undefined perception that rural management could not be taken in all respects as a model for civic management. This part of the argument concludes with the résumé:

> Although frugality is a great virtue, it should be exercised with a certain discretion, and indeed with a *prudentia politica*. Otherwise it will be called greed or senseless miserliness. If it is greed, it is the root of all evil and misfortune, and is more destructive than all prodigality. If it is unreasoning miserliness, not only the reputation of the prince, but also his interests will be sacrificed, for always to take from the country, and in turn to consume nothing, makes the land waste and barren, the subjects useless, and consequently the prince poor instead of rich (p. 39).

The argument turns at once to an aspect of the situation which has greater interest for its connection with another element in cameralism, viz., the so-called mercantilist theory, of which more must be said later. The author continues:

> Sound judgment shows also that when a prince without great reason takes much money from his subjects, and locks it in his chest, and guards it as a treasure, both prince and land must finally be ruined and impoverished. . . . The result would be that the country would be stripped of money to fill the chest of the prince, and that not a *Groschen* would be left for him to take from the country as revenue. This would be reckoning without the host. Whence it follows that if money, which is the pendulum of the state, which brings all inequality in the life of the state [*Handel und Wandel*] into regular movement, is lost, commerce must collapse, and the people must become poor and needy, and because the means [*Vermögen*] of the country must then grow only from the soil, the fraction of the people, however, who really support themselves from the soil and its produce is always the smallest and poorest portion [*Hauffen*] in a country, the majority of the inhabitants of the country, from lack of support, will depart, and there will remain a barren land and a poor prince; for although the prince has all that money stored in his chest, and alone preserves what was otherwise divided among so many, he still cannot be called a rich prince, although he is called a rich man. . . . For common people are rich in money: a prince, however, is to be regarded as rich only when he has rich subjects (pp. 42 ff.).

This last passage calls for further preliminaries on the subject of mercantilism. In no respect has tradition so grossly failed to understand the cameralists of the books, in distinction from the cameralists of the bureau, as in this connection. The cameralism of the bureau was a policy with reference to the paramount interests of the princely treasury. The cameralism of the books was a theory and a technology of government, with the needs of the treasury taken for granted as the norm of judgment.

It would be useless to question the notorious fact that the policy called mercantilism prevailed in Germany during the cameralistic period. It would be fatuous to question the equally familiar fact that promotion of commerce, with calculation upon a favorable balance of trade, was the most prominent factor in this mercantilist policy. It would be quite futile to question the further fact that the cameralists of the books were virtually unanimous in approving this policy. Our interpretation must take issue with tradition, first, upon the precise meaning of this mercantilist policy, and, second, upon the place which the policy occupied within the whole cameralistic theory of politics.

In the first place, then, mercantilism was a policy, not a philosophy. Speaking for the cameralists of the books only, because this investigation does not go into the evidence about the cameralists of the bureaus, there was a political philosophy after its kind within which the policy had its setting; but the interpretation of mercantilism as a philosophy has the marks of a fixed idea in the modern literature of the subject, and that interpretation is sheer misrepresentation of the cameralistic theorists. The most urgent problem which the cameralists had to solve was that of raising revenues for the prince. In their judgment, the line of least resistance, in cases where it was practicable at all, was through development of commerce. Almost all the literary cameralists, consequently, put more emphasis on the fiscal importance of a favorable trade balance than upon any other single factor in governmental calculation. Incidentally, their arguments treated money in a way which it has proved very easy to distort into a dogma that money is the only wealth. They no more believed, nor intended to assert this, than writers on the financial pages of today's newspapers believe and assert that the bank balances of the money centers are the only wealth of the world. There is rather more *prima-facie* evidence that the congressional and other debaters of the Aldrich-Fowler-Vreeland propositions believed in 1908 that an "emergency currency" is the only wealth, or that the political economists of the United States since the Civil War have believed that a protective tariff is the only means of creating wealth, than there is to warrant the historical fiction that the German mercantilistic theorists held gold and silver to be the only wealth.

In fact, not one of the cameralists generalized the concept "wealth" much more than the ordinary man on the street does today when he uses the phrase "making money." To make the term *Reichthum*, as it was used by the cameralists, equivalent to the term *wealth* in nineteenth-century abstract political economy, is an arrant anachronism. The term was virtually a synonym of the more technical cameralistic phrase, *bereitestes Vermögen*, or "ready means." Instead of giving to gold and silver the final and paramount place which tradition makes the cameralists assign to them, these thinkers were rather remarkably clear in treating them as means to happiness, and under the circumstances the most decisive means, but they did not raise the larger and deeper problem. The whole cameralistic experience was an unconscious preparation for the abstract question, What is wealth? It was a progressively searching analysis of the sources from which the people of a state may procure the means of subsistence, and thus be in a position to turn a part of the output of their gainful occupations into treasure for the support of government. The inquiry was on the whole so concrete in its impulse that there was no apparent tendency to extend abstraction beyond the range of practical transactions. Schröder is nearer than most of the cameralists to the concept "wealth" in Adam Smith's sense, however, when he uses the term *surplus* (*Ueberfluss*). Thus chap. lxviii begins with the paragraph:

Respecting the surplus, whence it is derived, the same consists either *in rebus naturalibus*, or *rebus artificialibus*, that is, first, it comes from the natural fertility of the land; or, second, from the diligence of the men which we make use of in trade when we bring something from one place, and sell it to advantage in another place and thus make trade in all sorts of foreign wares in our country; or third, from the art of men, which is included under the general title *manufactures*, each of which must be treated in particular.

Developing the idea of the former source of "surplus," chap. lxx proceeds in this vein:

Since then so much depends upon the fertility of the land, a prince should pay good heed to the *Curam Rei Rusticae*, in order that the land may be well cultivated, and the inhabitants may not only derive from it their food and drink but also something to sell. . . . . By agriculture (*sic*) is to be understood not merely that which serves for eating and drinking, but also the other things that grow out of the earth and belong to manufactures or to trade.

The proposition is elaborated by citations of the experience of other countries, by specification of particular products, which are profitable articles of cultivation, by reference to the book *Oesterreich über alles*[1] for additional particulars, and by special emphasis upon silk-culture (*Seiden-Oeconomie*) as likely to be as valuable to Germany as it had already begun to be to France. The paramount factor in the calculation, namely, the conversion of resources into ready means, reappears in the summary (§xii):

Here, as in the case of all other surplus which we desire, this principle is to be observed, that the same shall be sought in products which our neighbors need, and which we can best and with greatest gain convert into money. Otherwise the surplus is of no advantage to us, but is often even harmful, since from the same an abuse of the same may arise.[2]

[1] *Vide* p. 129.

[2] The discussion then passes to certain political considerations which should govern the policy of states with respect to promotion of specific kinds of cultivation. The necessary methods of promoting trade, and the value of the same as a source of "surplus" are discussed in chaps. lxxi–lxxix, and the subject of manufactures as means of procuring a "surplus" is treated in chaps. lxxxviii–cv.

Schröder must be given credit for dealing with the relatively concrete problem of putting to most discreet use the opportunities at hand for acquiring ready means. He must not be judged as though he had anticipated a century and had devoted himself to the underlying problem of wealth in general. In the rough, the same proposition applies to all the cameralists included in this study. To confirm this in the case of Schröder, we must notice one of the passages which the traditional interpreters of cameralism always find a conclusive proof-text, viz., chap. xxix. The title reads: "Whence a Prince May Learn Whether His Country Is Gaining or Losing in Riches" (*Reichthum*). Now it would be a waste of time to defend the chapter against the charge of superficiality, if philosophical economists should prefer the charge. The whole aim of the cameralists was on the superficial plane of practical efficiency, not on the deeper level of economic philosophy. Their problem was the development of a programme which would supply the prince with ready means. The general tendency of thought which Schröder represented, and in which presently all the cameralists more or less consciously joined, assumed that ready means for the prince either caused or was caused by ready means for the people. Without analyzing these alternative phases of the idea, we must allow Schröder to speak for his own practical interest, and must not hold him to account for the meaning which his words might have if he were discussing Adam Smith's problem of the sources of wealth in general. When the modern railroad president studies the problem of increasing the net earnings of his road, he may use language which hypercriticism could distort into expressions of belief that freight charges are the ultimate sources of wealth. No one would take seriously an attempt to prove that a railroad president could see no farther, if he should turn from practical business to economic theory. The cameralists were not interested in wealth as a general concept, but they were intensely interested in ready means as an efficient tool for everyday purposes. It goes without saying that their theories would have been much more adequate if they had gone deeper into economic philosophy; but our present purpose is to rescue ourselves from the errors of that tradition which has treated them as though they did pry into that antecedent philosophy and consequently propounded fantastic doctrines. The expressions which have been distorted into the dogma that gold and silver are the only wealth are no more properly liable to that construction than our railroad presidents' judgment that more freight is necessary for more dividends could fairly be construed into the dogma that freight rates are the only source of wealth. Schröder says:

By the different gainful occupations [*Handel und Wandel*] in the country a country supports itself, to be sure, and becomes powerful [*mächtig*], but it does not necessarily thereby increase in riches [*Reichthum;* that is, in the sense of "ready means"]. For such traffic with itself can properly be called only a *commutation*. . . . . Hence the country becomes richer only in the degree in which money and gold are brought into the land either from the earth, or from some other source, and poorer in the degree in which money leaves the country. For since by common consent of nations gold and silver are the universal price of all things, and the value of the same is everywhere in the world reckoned according to the value of gold and silver, for which everything can be bought, we must estimate the riches of a country according to the quantity of the gold and silver in the same. Hence we shall name in order the means by which a land acquires riches, and then those practices through which a land becomes poorer, in order that a prince may promote the former and obstruct the latter (chap. xxix).

The present argument is by no means an attempt to prove that the cameralists had thought out precise economic concepts. They most certainly had not. It is absurd, however, to hold them responsible for use of certain terms in the exact technical sense fixed upon them much later, and thus by forcing an arbitrary interpretation into their concepts to convict them of errors of which they were innocent. It is in principle as unjust to the cameralists to infer from such language as that just quoted that they regarded gold and silver as the only wealth, as it would be to interpret writers in the London *Statist* as believing that the bank balances are the only wealth, while corn and cotton and iron are not wealth. Schröder was talking about the species of wealth which presented the most immediate problems to men who were primarily interested in supplying the treasury. The very fact that he prefaced the passage with the reservation about the occupations by which the country supports itself and makes itself powerful shows that his apparent error about what is wealth and what is not is largely a verbal matter. Not having thought through the concept denoted by the English technical term "wealth," he used a word (*Reichthum*) which we most naturally translate "wealth" for the one species of wealth in which he was peculiarly interested. Thereupon we charge him with identifying his specific concept, most justly represented by the phrase "ready means," with the generic concept "wealth," which he had never found occasion to use at all.

Nor is our argument an attempt to show that Schröder, and the cameralists in general, actually had a perspective of the relation of "ready means" to other wealth, which adequately generalized the facts for all times and places. They certainly had not. The point to be made is that we must abandon the myth that they attempted such generalization. They were not economists in the nineteenth-century sense. They were political theorists dealing incidentally with relatively concrete fragments of economic relations. Those fragments called for generalization later. Meanwhile the cameralists must be interpreted by the conditions of the exact technical task which they proposed, not by the conditions of the subsequent philosophical task which they did not propose.

It is very true also that Schröder did practically nothing to develop the theory of extractive industries. This fact has been cited against him over and over again. It has been interpreted to mean, first, that he did not regard agricultural products as "wealth;" second, that he had no sympathy with the agricultural population, and did not care how miserable its condition might be. However this misrepresentation of Schröder may have come into circulation, a historian who should today assert that his book confirmed this judgment would thereby prove either that he had not read it (e. g., the passages cited above, pp. 152 ff.) or that he was incapable of reading it understandingly.

In the face of his explanation above (p. 142) Schröder might as properly be accused of caring nothing for an army as a governmental recourse. The task which Schröder undertook, in the volume upon which his reputation chiefly rests, was not unlike that which Professors Winthrop M. Daniels and Henry C. Adams had in mind when they wrote their books, *The Elements of Public Finance*, and *The Science of Finance*. Because neither of these modern authors included in his volume on finance a treatise on the improvement of agriculture, it has occurred to no one that they should be accused of omitting agriculture from the sources of wealth, or of heartlessness toward the agricultural population. The charge is equally absurd in the case of Schröder. He evidently knew much less about details of agricultural conditions on the operative side than the majority of the cameralists. So far as he betrays his state of mind on the subject, he seems, it is true, to have had no idea that much could be expected in the way of improving agriculture. Indeed he expressly says as much of manufactures and commerce, and by implication of agriculture, at the close of chap. lxix:

For the fertility of a country brings about cheapness of living, which is the spirit of all trade, and for the reason that cheapness in eating and drinking causes cheap wages for labor, and consequently makes manufactures and wares cheap, so that they can be sold at a lower price than others offer, and hence the market can be held by underbidding others, because everything follows after cheapness. From the examples cited is to be seen what Austria could do, and how rich and powerful it could be if through a good *Policey* it would combine the surplus of nature, with which more than all other lands in the wide world it is endowed, with the diligence of men, and through establishment of splendid manufactures and commerce would apply the bounty of nature to its profit. Details on this subject are to be found in the little book, *Oesterreich über alles wenn es nur will*. I despair of anything adequate in manufactures and commerce in this country however. My reasons I have resolved to set forth in a special tract entitled *Oesterreichs entdeckte Wunden*.

At the beginning of chap. xcii Schröder declares explicitly that Germany has both the materials and the skill to excel England, France, Holland, and Italy in manufactures, if the will were only present. With reference to agriculture as a source of revenue, he was not so wrong as to general theory as he was incredulous about feasibility of improving prevailing conditions. This would in part explain away the traditional inferences from such a passage as the following (chap. lxxxviii):

The third surplus comes from manufactures, and the latter, if conjoined with commerce, must be much preferred to the fertility of the soil, whence we see that unfertile countries where manufactures and commerce flourish are richer than the fertile countries, which have no manufactures. The matter is in itself as clear as the sun. If we appraise a pound of iron in the mine where it originates, it will have very little value. If however a watchmaker or similar skilled laborer takes this pound of iron in his hand and works it according to his art, the pound of iron is worth a hundred times as much as before, etc., etc.

It would be difficult to find in modern political economy a basis for impeachment of the essential conceptions involved in such language. Schröder plainly underestimated the relative importance of the extractive industries; but this was less from misconception of their fundamental nature than from overestimate of the subsequent processes of securing ready means which the endowment of nature made possible, and especially from belief that it would be relatively easier to stimulate necessary use of these latter agencies than to get equivalent results from more intensive cultivation of the soil.

Schröder's position was that it would be unreasonable to expect much more public revenue from the workers on the soil, for they were already as miserable as they could be, without being driven out of the country or out of existence. Without taking up the problem of improving the condition of agricultural populations, which was not his division of labor, he insisted that a wise fiscal policy would drop the idea of further exactions from this overburdened stratum, and would set about developing more fruitful sources of supply.

On the other hand, the very expressions which have been distorted into evidence that Schröder did not regard the soil as a source of wealth, and did not care how much the rural folk were oppressed, are evidently, in the light of the context, first, acknowledgments that agriculture is the first and obvious resource of a people and a state, and second, protests against exhausting this resource.

It should not be necessary for an American democrat to guard himself by repeating that he is not an apologist for the doctrine of divine right. It is no longer necessary nor tolerable, however, for Americans to caricature the doctrine as it was actually held by men in the seventeenth and eighteenth centuries. In order correctly to interpret the cameralism of the books, as a distinct movement in the development of a technology of the state, we must do justice to Schröder, especially against endeavors, prompted by a surviving civic formalism, to discredit his most worthy ideas.

For example, separated from their context, the opening

sentences of chap. vii, "How a Prince May Have as Much Money as He Will," are among the evidences which the opponents of Schröder quoted to prove that he sanctioned unlimited extortion by rulers. He says:

In a well-ordered state, neither metes nor bounds nor times nor seasons prescribe to the prince how much money he shall raise from his country nor how often. For the course of circumstances is uneven, and there is no regularity about the gains of different subjects. . . . . Hence a prince must seek his interest with the parties who are gaining, and are thus in a position to pay, and if a prince always gets a share of the profits of those who gain, he will have a daily source of supply, for someone always gains, and no one can find fault, because only a tithe is sought by the prince of the gains which are made under his protection (pp. 61, 62).

In this passage Schröder simply starts with the common absolutistic premises of all theorists of his time, and as we have said above, his cameralistic critics discredited themselves by attempting to turn against him the very theory which they themselves asserted. More than this, Schröder's use of the absolutistic formula in this connection evidently meant just what an expounder of the idea of eminent domain would mean if he should say today, for the sake of emphasis, "in the last analysis there is no limit to the right of the state to expropriate the private owner of land, with due compensation, if the needs of the state require." The latter expression in the mouth of a modern lawyer would hardly be understood as committing him to a general policy of expropriation. In the same way Schröder first stated in its extremest form a principle to which all civic theorists of his class assented; but this statement was merely to introduce the counterbalancing consideration that *it would be fatal to the prosperity of the state to carry the prerogative to this extreme.* The whole significance of Schröder's book is in its attempt to show how the prince might get revenues more successfully by promoting unexploited sources of supply than by crushing the life out of the primary sources by extorting the last fraction which they could be made to yield.

It would be disingenuous not to quote the most extreme expressions in which Schröder seems to betray a quite different spirit. Perhaps the most difficult case is chap. cviii, which consists of a single paragraph. The title of this chapter reads: "How a Prince May Also Seize and Use the Capital of the Country, and Still Not Ruin the Country Thereby." The following is the entire discussion under that head:

Although I have demonstrated that a prince may hoard in his chest no more wealth than the country has earned [*erworben*], yet I must say something further, namely, how a prince without ruin of the country and of business may also go farther and employ [*angreiffen*] the capital of his land. This takes place if a prince causes the subjects to do business with his own capital. Since now this is one of the secrets of a monarchy, I wonder that princes do not reflect more upon it, because by this means they could gradually obtain an absolute sovereignty, and could make the subjects virtually their body slaves, when the latter in time would see their worldly goods in the hands of the prince.[1]

His language in an earlier passage (p. 66) may be cited as a fairer index of the spirit of Schröder's theory and policy.

And this in my opinion is the inexhaustible treasure of a prince, by means of which he may be a benefactor of the poor, a refuge for the oppressed, a builder of fine cities, and fortifications, founder of

[1] I confess that I am unable to offer a plausible explanation of this passage, beyond the observation that it is too summary and too detached from the rest of the author's argument to reveal his full meaning. On the whole, I classify it as a vagrant conceit which the author did not regard as within the scope of practical politics. From the absolutistic point of view, it was a counsel of perfection; a vision of the absolutistic régime so realized that the prince would be a corporation sole, both politically and industrially, while the subjects would have legal existence merely as his agents. The passage, however, has the effect of a mere fugitive suggestion, without significance enough of any sort to affect our estimate of the author's general purpose.

many churches and schools. This is the treasure with which a prince may equip his capital city with qualified people, and may sustain the magnificence of his court, with all of which the land need not be ruined, as the common man thinks, but it will rather be made prosperous. In all these things a prince has only to see that the money so expended remains in the country. For in this way a prince does only that which is fitting. Since he sees that gains in the country are unevenly divided, he takes from him who seems to have gained from others more than his social position or his merit justifies, and gives it to another. In order, however, that the latter may not enjoy his gains in idleness, he must in return do something which will either contribute to the upbuilding of the land or to the pleasure and magnificence of the prince. Thus I can with complete right call a prince a great national Lord of Exchange, or as Aristotle expresses it, *Custodis et Dispensatoris communium bonorum*. . . . . Accordingly a prince may use the whole capital of the country, and as much more as the whole capital is worth (*sic*), if he only soon consumes it and causes it to course among the people; for a prince is the stomach of the country, the assessments are the foods which it digests. If the foods are not digested in the stomach, and the strength divided among the parts of the body, the members will lose strength and die, but the stomach will die with them.

Since we have said, however, that the prince should take where there is ability to give, and where it can be spared, it follows that a prince must know the means of each person in the country, together with his manner of support and his earnings, in order that he may perceive how the money in the land is divided, and in what direction it tends. This, however, appears to be an impossible affair, and there is no practicable proposition to make it possible.

It is not necessary to notice all the naïve economic conceptions which this language implies. Our attention may be confined to the main line of argument. The strategic point in Schröder's calculation is indicated by the title of chap. viii, "Whether a Prince Can Know How Much Each Citizen Earns or Might Earn, in Order That He May Know How the Money Is Distributed." Schröder does not profess to have discovered a perfect method of answering the question, but he thinks an approach may be made to it that would go far to remove the existing chaos, and increase fairness in demands for payments to the princely treasury. He begins by dividing the population into nine sorts, each to be treated in accordance with their relative abilities: (1) clergy; (2) nobility; (3) peasants; (4) artisans; (5) merchants; (6) court or state functionaries; (7) lenders;[1] (8) usurers;[2] (9) players.[3]

The last section of the chapter presents a puzzle by naming four ways which each of these classes have of gaining money, viz.: (*a*) finding treasure, whether in natural deposits, or hidden or lost goods; (*b*) conversion of the unripe or imperfect metals (*sic*) into good gold or silver; (*c*) inheritance; (*d*) presents. This schedule does not seem to correspond with the subsequent analysis of the gainful occupations of the nine classes. The clue to the discrepancy is, first, that the section is not, as might appear at first reading, a résumé of the ordinary sources from which these classes get their incomes. It is an enumeration of extraordinary sources common to all of them. The precise language is: "All these have still" (e. g., in addition to the resources peculiar to each) "four means of getting money, or of becoming rich, which appertain to one as well as to the others, viz.," etc.

The more one reflects upon the use of language in such passages as this, the more clear it becomes that tradition has forced into it associations which the words did not carry in the minds of the cameralistic authors. As we have said above, it is an unpardonable anachronism to make these authors discourse upon the antecedent problems of wealth in the abstract, when they were discussing merely the most available

[1] I. e., not of money but of other useful articles.

[2] Not necessarily in the invidious sense.

[3] Including not merely gamblers but purveyors of amusement, etc.

method of accumulating ready means for the individual or for the state.

Schröder goes on immediately to cite the schedules in use in the duchy of Gotha, for the twenty years previous to his writing, for classifying the extractive industries within the state, and for purposes of assessment.[1] It is not our affair to pass on the skill or the wisdom displayed in Schröder's attempt to outline a more complete industrial census either for rural or urban taxation. The essential point is that what he did in a relatively crude way became a matter of course with later cameralists; and a large part of their work was devoted either to explanation of the routine methods of assessment upon this basis, or to elaboration of other schemes along lines partly drawn by Schröder. It is impossible to decide from the subsequent literature to what extent use was made in practice of Schröder's calculus of the relative value to the nation of different branches of manufacture (chaps. xv–xviii). At the least, it was a serious attempt to understand a division of industry which was rapidly assuming firstrate importance in the reckoning of all German states.

Schröder's conception of the functions of *Policey* are by means as farsighted as his fiscal perceptions. They do not even seem to be as comprehensive as Osse's. They did not go beyond emphasis of the need of governmental inter-

[1] These schedules are reduced to a conspectus which is numbered as chap. xii, and appears as an insert in the edition of 1744. The insert has been removed from the copy of the original edition which I have used. The table is a complete answer to the irresponsible charge that Schröder ignored the extractive industries as a source of wealth. It should have estopped Seckendorff's denunciation (*vide* above, p. 135). If Seckendorff's master, Ernst the Pious, was not an extortioner and a villain in using this schedule for fiscal purposes, surely Schröder cannot be condemned for making it his point of departure in attempting to outline a more equitable system. Thomasius recorded a fairly judicial estimate of Schröder, in the *Testament*, p. 152, n. 76.

ference to prevent neglect of duties by servants of all classes. The phrase, however, which Schröder applies to *Policey* in chap. xxviii, viz., "*die Grundfeste* upon which all that has previously been said must rest," quite likely furnished the suggestion which gave Justi the title for his most elaborate cameralistic volume, on *Policeywissenschaft.*[1]

If we reach a clear understanding that Schröder, and all the rest of the cameralists, when treating of their central fiscal problem, did not raise the later question of pure economics, but were dealing primarily with problems of immediate application of fiscal means to fiscal ends, and secondarily with problems of adjustment of the people's activities to the need of improved standards of life, whether principally in their own interest or that of the treasury, this perception at once shows that as pure economists or sociologists we have no immediate concern with their conclusions about technological details. Our interest is primarily in the part which they played in developing a general philosophy of society, and the particulars are of value to us only as indexes of their relation to larger conceptions. Enough has been said, therefore, to establish the position of Schröder in the cameralistic series. His main object was to increase the ready means of the prince, while incidentally lightening the burdens of the people. The general scope of his conclusions may be gathered by reference to his table of contents, especially to the titles of chaps. xxx–cv.

Our analysis of Schröder may be completed by a reflection which has also some measure of relevance to all the cameralists. We must distinctly note that the cameralistic estimate of proportions between gold and silver and other goods, which we have discussed, is less a vagary about economic principles than an appraisal of civic values corresponding with contemporary judgments of relative civic needs. If Schröder had been plied with Socratic questions about wealth, in Adam

[1] *Vide* below, p. 452.

Smith's sense, after getting the concept defined, he would have been obliged to retract nothing in principle which he had intended to assert before that more generalized term had been brought to his attention. Maintaining his position, he might have restated his views in this way: "I quite agree that we may give a common name to all the material things which men want to use, and which they may exchange. If we call these wealth, the agricultural products which feed people, the manufactured forms of those products which clothe people, and the other manufactured forms which satisfy people's demands for convenience and comfort, are of course wealth, just as much as the gold and silver which enable the prince to maintain the government, and the people to make their exchanges. My contention is, however, that the need of making the government strong is so pre-eminent that the wealth which satisfies this need is beyond all comparison the most important wealth, and must be provided for whether there is increase of other wealth or not."

Here would be a plain contrast between the cameralistic and the modern scale of social values. It would assign to money a higher ratio of value in the state than it has in modern theory. The reason would be not that cameralism essentially varied from modern theory on the economic principles of wealth, but rather that cameralism varied from modern theory on antecedent political philosophy. It posited an order of precedence between governmental strength and popular prosperity which democratic theory has inverted. That is, the cameralistic theory was that popular prosperity depends on strong government. Modern theory, at least in its democratic forms, holds that strong government depends upon popular prosperity. Thus the cameralistic theory, which systematized mercantilistic practice, did not so much assert fundamentally incorrect economic principles as it transferred emphasis from more to less ultimate principles, for the sake of supposed immediate political expediency. The needed correction of cameralism was less new knowledge of the sources of material goods than new valuations of the scale of ends to which material goods should be applied. Along with the absolutistic major premise, "The fiscal needs of the prince are the paramount needs in the state," went the minor premise, "There is more to be gained for the princely fiscus by exploiting other means of revenue than by depending upon further exploitation of the primary natural resources." This was not a false economic principle, but a specific judgment about the relative availability of an economic principle in a particular situation. The subsequent development of cameralism shows a marked increase of relative emphasis upon the value of the extractive industries. This change does not reflect a revolution in fundamental economic conceptions. It denotes on the one hand increased attention to the technique of agricultural management, with correspondingly enlarged ideas of the maximum resources of nature; and on the other hand, expansion of cameralistic science so that its fiscal division was better balanced by variously classified divisions which brought some of the neglected elements of the civic situation under equally systematic analysis.

Of Schröder as a promoter of the practical economic policy of Austria it does not fall within the scope of this book to speak. Whether his judgment was the wisest under the circumstances, and whether the commercial expedients which he advocated were in the line of general technological prudence, are questions which would be appropriate in a more special study than our programme proposes. The foregoing analysis sufficiently covers the most essential question about him. Objective study permits us to accept the judgment neither of certain interested contemporaries, who would have had Schröder regarded as a prophet of evil, nor of the schematic appraisers of mercantilism in general, who represent all its theorists as teaching grotesque doctrines. These vagaries appear to have been imputed to them first by opponents of the mercantilistic programme, and to have come down to us in place of the authentic opinions of a group of thinkers whose economic conceptions turn out to have been much more valid than their views of political philosophy.

In this connection a few words must be said about four writers who, by general consent of the historians, rank as satellites of the principal group discussed in this and the preceding chapter. We name first the otherwise apparently unknown writer, von Klenck.[1] His book may be called a shorter catechism of mercantilism. It contains 262 pages of large pocket-diary shape. It can be inserted in the vest pocket, and if printed on thin paper, with flexible covers, would be conveniently portable. Roscher says:

A book in many respects enigmatical is the *Fürstliche Machtkunst* . . . . which I have been able to obtain only in the ninth edition, Frankfurth and Leipzig, 1740, under the title: *Tractat von Manufacturen und Commercio*. It is said to have been published in 1702 at Halle or in 1709 at Weissenfels, by the well-known Heinrich Bode, professor of law at Halle. The author, a certain Herr von Klenck, is said to have suppressed it, after it had been severely attacked in 1704, in the monograph, *Das Gold des publiquen credits, welches der vornehme Autor der fürstlichen Machtkunst und unerschöpflichen Goldgruben durch Herrn G. B.'s Gütigkeit und Vermittelung beschauen lassen, auf dem Probierstein der gesunden Vernunft zum Commercio untauglich befunden von einem Lübecker Kaufmann* (p. 303).[2]

[1] *Fürstliche Macht-Kunst, Oder Unerschöpfliche Gold-Grube, Wordurch ein Fürst sich kan mächtig und seine Unterthanen reich machen.* Durch einen in vielen Wissenschafften Erfahrnen Vornehmen Cavallier entworffen, und mit dessen Gutbefinden heraus gegeben Von Heinrich Boden, Königl. Preussis. Rath im Hertzogthum Magdeb. und Prof. Jur. in Halle, Editio III. The editor's preface is dated Halle, July 3, 1702.

[2] The third edition, which I have used, is not dated. It appears to be identical with the original.

Roscher also quotes the statement (p. 303, note), that Klenck's book was republished in 1773 as an appendix to the volume *Klugheit zu leben und zu herrschen.*

Although Roscher finds in Klenck some slight variations from Schröder, and even improvements upon his teachings (pp. 303, 304), they are not important enough to require our attention. In his Preface the author expressly states that he wrote the book in the hope that it would be more successful in attracting the notice of young princes than the more pretentious writings on the subject. He apparently had some particular prince in mind. At the same time he expressly disclaims the purpose of being original, and declares that he has drawn his conclusions from the best authorities. The book emphasizes and popularizes the best in the previous mercantilists. It is especially clear and strong in its assertions that the strength and riches of the prince must be based upon the strength and riches of the people, and that the ancient prejudice against industrial and commercial pursuits as unworthy of the nobility must give place to pride in those occupations.

Whether the author's hope of appealing to young princes was realized does not appear. References to his book by later and influential writers show that he actually did have a share in winning respect for the views which he represented.[1] We need note simply that Klenck leaves no room for doubt that he is a typical cameralist, as described in our general formula.[2] He begins his *Vorrede* with the observation:

All the world knows that in a few centuries France, England, and Holland, not so much through force of arms, as through a special princely art and science, have advanced to such a high power, that the gold and silver streams of the whole world seem to run into them,

[1] For example, *vide* Thomasius on Klenck, *Testament*, pp. 99 ff., n. 41.

[2] *Vide* above, p. 6.

as to an exhaustless sea. To reflect upon such princely power, and with it to serve the Fatherland, is demanded of every true patriot. I accordingly devote this study to the art of princely power, and I feel at liberty to call it a *Studium Magnificum quod Magnos facit*, whereby in our beloved Fatherland hidden springs of gold may be opened. I accordingly call this *Machtkunst* a science highly necessary for princes, of so directing all gainful occupations that, *ex Bono Publico* of the land, the princely treasury may be enriched, and the prince may become powerful. The *finis Primarius* is thus the *Bonum Publicum*, the riches and prosperity of the land, *quo Reipublicae bene fit;* whence flows the *Finis Secundus* or *Secundarius*, the power and great might of the ruling prince, as from the proper source and spring. If the same contains much water, the prince can also have much. Hence the welfare of the prince is so closely bound up with that of his subjects that the one without the other cannot come into being, and still less be permanent.

The second of these lesser writers is Paul Jacob Marperger, 1656–1730. He made an impression by his much writing, but he was the author of nothing of even second-rate importance.[1]

The third in this minor group, "much less known by his contemporaries, but intellectually much the superior of Marperger, was Johann Georg Leib."[2]

While it is not certain that Leib added anything to the theory of his predecessors, writers of his class are important for our purpose. They furnish cumulative evidence of the spirit of the doctrine which they tried to expound. The *Vorrede* to Leib's book begins in this way:

There are many who have such a bad opinion of the *Studium Cameralis* or *Oeconomiae Principis* that they think it impossible to

[1] Roscher seldom packs as much into a few words as in his estimate: "In der Hauptsache ist Marperger als ein Verwässerer des von ihm bewunderten Becher zu charakterisiren. Ein entsetzlicher Vielschreiber, der z. B. in seinem *Ersten Hundert gelehrter Kaufleute* (1717) 35 Bücher aufzählt, die er seit 1698 herausgegeben, und noch 71 andere, zum Druck bereite Schriften." (*Vide* Roscher, p. 301.)

[2] *Von Verbesserung Land und Leuten, und wie ein Regent seine Macht und Ansehen erheben könne* (1708).

raise the revenues of a great lord without adding to the tears and sighs of their subjects. How mistaken this idea is may easily be shown by the fact that the chief and only purpose of this study is to put the whole body of subjects in a permanent condition of well-being, and only from their surplus, and in a just manner, to increase the income of the lord of the land, and to raise his power and repute; . . . . I cannot deny that abuses which have entered into fiscal administration as a common evil have been my sole reason for this writing, out of love for the common good. Accordingly, I have attempted to show how the welfare of the land, or the well-being of the subjects, is inseparably bound up with the interest of the ruler, and this is the true and sole principle of the whole cameralistic study. Moreover, my chief rule for increasing the power of the land is to retain money in the country, and to bring it from other countries. If this rule is observed, it follows without dispute that the welfare of the land will be thereby promoted, and the subjects will be made richer. And if the subjects are made richer, then they can without harm and embarrassment pay to the lord of the land, for the protection which is so profitable, an increased tribute. Then the ampler treasure of the prince must put him in power and repute with other rulers.

The whole book is an amplification of these propositions. Whatever may have been the morale of the typical German government in this period, these theorists represent the standards which the governments were supposed to respect.

Finally, we must select from others who might be named in this connection Theodor Ludwig Lau.[1]

If Lau was not personally a grievous ass, he went far out of his way to misrepresent himself, not only in his dedication, but in his garrulous and "kittenish" *Vorrede*. The one detail

[1] Roscher refers to him (p. 379) as "*Der kurländische Hofrath und Cabinetsdirector.*" His book is entitled *Aufrichtiger Vorschlag: von Glücklicher: vortheilhafftiger: beständiger Einrichtung der Intraden: und Einkünfften; der Souverainen: und ihrer Unterthanen; In welchen: Von Policey- und Cammer-Negocien und Steuer Sachen: gehandelt wird.* Entworffen Von dem Hochfürstlich-Curländischem Hoff-Rath, und Cabinets-Directeur, Theodor Ludwig Lau . . . . 1719.

which is worthy of record about his book is that it made more than any previous text of the classification of cameralistic science into the divisions which were in general accepted to the end of the cameralistic period. That is, the *Aufrichtiger Vorschlag* was divided into four books, treating respectively of (1) *Policey;* (2) finance (*Entwurff einer wohleingerichteten Cammer*); (3) commerce (*Entwurff wohlregulirter Negocien*), in which the first part is entitled "*Von den Manufacturen,*" and the second, "*Von den Commercien;*" (4) taxation (*Entwurff Wohleingerichteter Steuren*). This main part of the volume occupies 324 pages. There follows a monograph of 130 pages treating in detail certain practical phases of the subject of the fourth part of the text. The title-page of this tract is notable for its reiteration of the idea of community of interest between subjects and rulers.[1]

A still more complete account of cameralistic literature at this period would include such writers as Gleichmann,[2] Gundling,[3] and a little later Schreber,[4] and J. A. Hoffmann.[5]

[1] *Practische Vorschläge, Welcher gestalt Steuer und respective Contribution zum Nutzen Eines Landes-Herren, und ohne Nachtheil der Unterthanen einzurichten seye, Damit unter allen steuerbaren und Contribuablen Dingen eine proportionirte Gleichheit, Nach Anleitung der Reichs-Abschiede, gehalten, und kein Unterthan vor dem andern graviret werde, Auch, wie alle Unterschleiffe und viele Kosten vermieden, Und der Steuer- und respective Contributions-Stock in beständiger Richtigkeit erhalten werden kan, Ausführlich projectirt und zum Druck befördert.* Im Jahr 1721.

[2] *Kurtzer Begriff von einer unbeträglichen Fürstlichen Machtkunst* (1711); *vide* Roscher, p. 377.

[3] *Einleitung zur wahren Staatsklugheit* (posth., 1751); *vide* Roscher, *loc. cit.*

[4] "Der Leipziger Professor der Oekonomie, Polizei und Cameralwissenschaft." Hauptwerk: *Abhandlung von Cammergütern und Einkünften, deren Verpachtung und Administration* (1743); *vide* Roscher, *loc. cit.*

[5] *Politische Anmerkungen über die wahre und falsche Staatskunst, worin aus den Geschichten aller Zeit bemerket wird, was einem Lande zuträglich oder schädlich sei* (Latin, 1718; German, 1725); *vide* Roscher, p. 380.

CHAPTER VII

THE CAMERALISTICS OF GERHARD

Gerhard is of value in the first instance as a witness to the influence of Seckendorff. His book is a mere tract of seventy pages.[1] It is notable for mobilizing the term *Staatswissenschaft* as a synonym of the term *Staats-Lehre* used in the title; and this fact evidently corresponds with an enlargement of vision which was widening the outlook of German political theorists, and at the same time giving their views a more coherent content. The author declares that his intention in writing the book is to introduce beginners to the subject, not to address the learned. He also frankly states that he wants the book, and the lectures based on it, to lead up to the study of Seckendorff's *Teutscher Fürsten Staat*. With the book and the lectures on it as a preparation for his course on Seckendorff, he hopes to give his students an adequate idea of "the whole *studium politicum* in general." Gerhard was apparently a member of the law faculty at Jena in 1713, and was among the academic men who were smuggling the beginnings of cameralistics into the universities before special professorships of that subject were founded.

Gerhard's book consists of six chapters, with an appendix on Seckendorff's political writings. If it were to be judged by its size, it would be set down as a negligible factor in the interpretation of cameralism. There is strong internal evidence, however, that the author deserves more attention than he has received. Roscher, for example, devotes to him less than a whole sentence.[2] He was not a mere echo of Seckendorff. In the first place, as a lecturer at Jena, he evidently did more

[1] D. Ephraim Gerhards "*Einleitung zur Staats-Lehre*," *Nebst angehengten Discurs von des Herrn von Seckendorf Politischen Schriften*. . . . 1713.

[2] *Op. cit.*, p. 238.

to prepare the way for admission of civics, as Justi understood that concept, to good standing in the universities than that writer imagined.[1] In the second place, he was a most instructive sign of the times with reference to currents of thought about the whole range of subjects which we now refer to as "the social sciences." His *prolegomena* show that his general conceptions of scientific relationships were far nearer those which we hold today than were those which found expression in some of the more pretentious books. Quite likely this accounts for his inconspicuous place as an author. Apparently he was a man whose insight and outlook surveyed wider reaches of knowledge than he had the constructive power to control. He seems to have had the talents of a scout rather than of a commissary-general. He detected strategic points, but was not qualified to conduct campaigns. Dropping the figure, it seems likely that Gerhard lacked the force or the equipment necessary for writing books which would have accredited his methodological perceptions. It would have required altogether exceptional genius and learning to compose at that time treatises which would have filled out his classification of knowledge. He has consequently left on record merely evidence of a certain precocity which must have affected his students as a liberalizing influence, but he lacked the energy to make much impression upon the slowly developing social ideas of the period.

Not because Gerhard's direct influence can be traced in the later literature of the social sciences, but because he gives expression to ideas which were gathering force among the formative influences of his time, we must give him attention out of proportion to the angle which his book subtends in the literature of cameralism.[1]

[1] *Vide* below, p. 296.

[2] In his preface to Stisser's *Einleitung*, Zincke throws light on Gerhard's influence by the remark that Stisser "sich nebst denen berühmten

The first chapter deals primarily with very elementary matters of terminology. The discussion turns upon the question, What is properly to be understood by the name "Politicus"? The value of the chapter for us is in the light it throws upon the state of mind at that time, both in the general public and among academic people, about subjects which have since developed into the social sciences. The first misunderstanding to which Gerhard addresses himself is that there is nothing in common between scholars and *Politici*, and that there is no room in universities for subjects in which *Politici* would be interested. This error, he declares, is a part of the confusion which has come in with the practice of using the words *Politicus* and *Staatsmann* as synonyms. People at court declare that politics can be understood by courtiers alone; the universities should therefore at most explain languages and the *Institutiones iuris*.

Gerhard's reply is substantially the familiar academic exposition of the utility of general training in theory as a preparation for acquirement of technical knowledge and skill. Attempting to show in particular what sort of knowledge may be acquired in universities as a preparation for practical politics, Gerhard distinguishes first between "the rules of righteousness and love, and the rules of prudence." The latter are usually regarded as the domain of politics, the former, of natural and moral philosophy. Gerhard urges that this division of labor is not wholly wise, because moral philosophy must be the foundation of civic prudence (*Staats-Klugheit*). He says further:

> If I may speak to suit myself, I may be allowed to distinguish between civic science [*Staats-Gelahrtheit*] and civic prudence [*Staats-*

Männern, Herrmanns, Stollens, Dithmars, Struvens, Kressens, Wildvogels und Schröders, sonderlich des Unterrichts-Hausses und Tisches des Herrn D. Gerhards . . . . bediente, unter dessen Vorsiz er auch, 1711, eine Dissert. *de crimine Lenocinii* schrieb und vertheidigte."

Klugheit], while at the same time I want to do justice to each. Civic science is the affair of scholars, and shows the fundamental principles upon which a proper civic prudence rests its observations. Civic prudence, however, consists in skilful application of those rules which are prescribed by civic science. Civic prudence must be learned by grasp of affairs, civic science by appropriate reasoning. The latter is as little the monopoly of the court as the former of the university, although the one is more prominent at courts and the other at universities (p. 9).

Gerhard goes on to say that he is not much concerned about mere matters of words, such as *Staats-Wissenschaft*, *Staats-Klugheit*, *Staats-Kunst*, and *Staats-Lehre*. The main thing for him is "that an upright teacher should not confuse distinct disciplines, and that a right-minded statesman must not despise learning, while he exercises a high degree of prudence in his daily duties."

Advancing in the second chapter to more precise description of civic science, Gerhard proposes at the outset the most compact formula of civic science as he views it, viz.:

"A theory which presents in proper order of dependence the rules of prudence, through which the community [*gemeines Wesen*] is kept in a good state of welfare, and which have as their whole aim the maintenance of the public state." In expanding this definition Gerhard urges that "civic science is thus obviously a constituent part of true science [*Gelahrtheit*] in general, since genuine science is nothing else than a theory through which human thoughts are set toward the attainment and retention of permanent happiness, and moreover it places definitely before the eyes of each this appropriate purpose." The courage of the author's convictions speaks further in the assertion: "I conclude still more that no one has a right to claim the name scholar who has not laid a reasonable basis of scholarship in this very useful division of learning."

In further analysis of science Gerhard proceeds:

The happiness of men is to be sought either in this or in a future life of which God's revelation gives us knowledge, and of which reason itself gives us hope. In a word, it is either temporal or eternal. To the latter we are led by *die hochweise Erkenntniss der Wahrheit zur Gottseligkeit, oder die Lehre der Gottesfurcht*, which therefore is called the science or knowledge of God. Temporal happiness, however, may be sought partly in subjective contentment of mind, partly in external repose and well-being, also health and a competence; hence various treatments of these subjects have become parts of practical learning (p. 15).

Accordingly Gerhard enumerates, with some indication of their respective contents, the theory of virtue, the theory of health, "which cannot be given over entirely to the art of medicine, but is also closely related with the theory of virtue," the theory of justice or natural law, the theory of morals, and the theory of the state, or of prudence.[1] He adds:

> Prudence is accordingly nothing else than a theory which equips man with the rational keys with which he may skilfully and systematically employ the means to his happiness which come in his common life, whereby he may attain the indicated end.

And a little later he further explains:

> Accordingly our civic science is chiefly concerned with finding out good external and voluntary means, through which, without harm or injustice to others, the welfare of the community [*gemeinen Wesens*], that is, the permanence and security of the same, may be properly maintained, promoted, and increased.

On the basis of this explanation the author goes into further details about the various sciences he has named, and especially their dependence upon one another. In this latter respect his views approach much closer to those of methodologists today than his notions of divisions of labor among the sciences. He is especially definite and sagacious in showing (chap. iii) how scholars in each of the faculties in turn, theology, medicine,

[1] This schedule suggests the conceptions which Adam Smith appropriated from the philosophy in which he was trained. *Vide* Dugald Stewart, *Account of the Life and Writings of Adam Smith* (Bohn ed., p. xvii). *Vide* Small, *Adam Smith and Modern Sociology*, p. 32 *et passim.*

philosophy, and law, would profit by the study of social science. It is hardly too much to say that these few pages read almost like a vision of the development of sociological consciousness which has been manifest during the past generation. Upon chap. iv, on "Abuses of Civic Science," a similar judgment may be passed. Although less sophisticated, it is very much in the spirit of Herbert Spencer's essay, *The Sins of Legislators.*

Chap. v, "*On the Purpose, Content, and Sub-Divisions of Civic Science,*" begins with a proposition which in terms is two centuries in advance of the scientific mediocrity of the author's generation. Although we may not read into it all that we should now imply by such language, we must not fail to recognize the notable breadth of view which the most grudging interpretation would have to concede. Gerhard says:

In order to realize the above indicated advantages, and to avoid the contrasted abuses of civic science, it is necessary never to leave the purpose of the same out of sight. The duty of every *Politicus* is contained in the rule: "Whatsoever thou doest, so consider the end and the outcome of thy devising, that thou shalt nevermore do harm" (p. 42).

From the context we can hardly conclude that this precept meant less in principle to its author than was contained in one of Herbert Spencer's wisest sociological aphorisms: "The question of questions for the politician should ever be—'What type of social structure am I tending to produce?' But this is a question he never entertains."[1] Gerhard's next paragraph reads:

As above observed, all the care of civic science should be directed toward the welfare of the state.[2] This consists principally in external peace and satisfaction, so far as these can be maintained by natural

[1] "The Coming Slavery," in Appleton's edition of *Social Statics; The Man versus the State* (1892), p. 312.

[2] "*Wohlseyn des Staates.*" Comments on this and related phrases will be reserved until we reach Justi; *vide* below, pp. 404 ff.

means, without illegal offense to others. It is not to be believed that the first men who subjected themselves to a human scepter surrendered their freedom which belonged to them by nature, without this intention. If now worldly governments are not to be repugnant to the law of nature and the eternal decrees [*Rathschläge*] of Almighty God, their counsels must also seek to maintain this intention. The greatest emperors and princes have most laudably recognized that subjects were not created for their benefit, but they for the subjects. How much more must those who are appointed by them as servants and watchmen of the common well-being [*gemeinen Wohlseyns*] entertain no other thoughts?

In the next paragraph but one the author reduces these generalities to somewhat more specific form in this way:

Everything which preserves, promotes, and makes permanent common repose and peace with pleasing security in the *Republique* in permissible and righteous ways, that must with all care and attention be undertaken and put in execution. It follows, however, that anything which is in any degree capable of hindering common repose and peace must be omitted, prevented, and excluded. Whoever reasonably meditates these two rules, he may arrive in his own head, if he will only at the same time open his eyes and look into the world, at a reflection of all civic science. Indeed, means will often thereby be put in his hand, without his special attention, for putting this science into useful application.

Then follow still more specific reassertions of the ends of civic society as represented by the quasi-absolutistic state, and of the corresponding outlook of civic science as it was coming to be defined in cameralism. Thus:

Since external assaults were probably the chief occasion for the first *raisonablen Republique*, political sagacity must also make this its first care. Hence it has come to pass that the principal attention has been given to the power of a prince. The power however consists in adequate strength to protect the lands which belong to a state against assaults of its neighbors. Since now, in the judgment of all, people and money are necessary for this purpose, it cannot be denied that where these things are in readiness the happiness of a country is thereby quite visibly guaranteed (p. 45).

After referring at some length to the other side of the case, viz., "where there is the greatest power, there it is easiest to do wrong," Gerhard once more formulates the essentials of civic policy as he sees it, in terms of "population, money, and friends."[1]

Returning to the subject of scientific method, Gerhard concludes, quite sanely:

If one is right on these matters, then it will amount to one and the same thing whether one divides civic science into two or two and twenty parts. . . . There is no harm done if, for the sake of grasping the concepts more thoroughly, one subdivides the matter a little. One must however not imagine that the fate of the Holy Roman Empire hangs on such subdivisions; and quarrels about such arbitrary matters are ridiculous. Each is entitled to his own way of dealing with the subject, and although it is well to fall in with the prevailing fashion, yet there is no law to force such conformity upon us; if there were, the fashions could not change so often. In my judgment, there would be no harm in dividing civic science into a general and a special division, for there are rules of prudence which apply to all men alike. Each has on the contrary his own reasons of state, and the special portion of civic science may have as many varieties as there are orders of society in the world. . . .

If God should grant me opportunity and sufficient experience to develop in an orderly written form the thoughts on civic science which I have thus far only communicated orally to my students, I would first set in order the general rules of treatment. I would then discuss the most complete society of the *Republique* in accordance with its purpose, and finally I would point out their duties to the societies that occur in ordinary life, i. e., of married people, of parents and children, of masters and servants, of intermediate rulers and subjects. Especially would I picture to my dearly beloved

[1] Thereupon he quotes with approval "D. Leib, in seinen *vier Proben.*" *Vide* above, p. 172.

students an ideally organized student-state, and I should think that in so doing I was discharging the duty of an upright teacher. . . . . As to the subdivisions of the second (special) part of the science, they would require many sections. It is however not necessary to anticipate them. Whoever understands the science of making the subjects numerous, rich, and moral, in accordance with what has preceded, will easily find out for himself an order for the means thereto necessary. I will at present say only this much: that to this end before all others the didactic method of the incomparable von Seckendorff seems best adapted. In his *Fürstenstaat* he affords so much opportunity for profitable comment that I believe my independent efforts in connection with this science may be long deferred.

Not only in the breadth of comprehension which these observations indicate, but in the detail of seeing a place for a general and a special treatment of the science of the state, Gerhard was well in advance of his time. Justi was most successful among the cameralists in making use of this suggestion. Gerhard deserves credit for perceptions about scientific technique which men of his type did not fully appropriate until a century after he had put them on record. In so far he anticipated the established practice of modern German scholars in all the social sciences.

It is also not too much to say that, in his brief discussion of the subjects which should be studied in connection with civic science (pp. 53 ff.), Gerhard showed breadth of intelligence, if not insight into detail, equal to that afterward exhibited by Justi. Indeed, it is plain that the former had a much broader foundation for his special programme of civic science than the latter. Justi furnishes no clear evidence that his foundations were as strong as those on which Gerhard rests when he says:

Accordingly it is right to say that civic science begins where moral philosophy ends, and it sufficiently appears that the student of politics, before he can become a statesman, must be a student of moral philosophy. Whoever does this with reason and at the right time, while the tree is still capable of being inclined, and thereby is properly molded in justice, good manners, honor, and the fear of God: if he otherwise has good understanding, will not find any portion of civic science difficult. . . . To sum up the whole matter: Whoever will learn civic science to advantage, let him first learn to understand other men, the forces of nature, and the established institutions of the world. Then civic science can teach him besides nothing but the ways in which he may best apply such intelligence (p. 57).

Gerhard may also be observed to advantage as an index of the extent to which there was at his time a recognized cameralistic tradition in academic circles. Those who wish to pursue the subject farther than our present limits permit, should read the Appendix of Gerhard's syllabus. It is a fair index both of the poverty and of the progress of German thought in this subject at the opening of the eighteenth century.

CHAPTER VIII

THE CAMERALISTICS OF ROHR

In a period which discriminated more carefully between dilettanteish and critical writing, the subject of this chapter would hardly have attained prominence among specialists. Because of the attention which was actually paid to him by a considerable number of successors, he cannot be omitted from our account. Intrinsically he does not deserve mention with cameralistic writers of the first rank.

Inama[1] furnishes a biographical sketch to this effect:

Julius Bernhard von Rohr was the son of a country gentleman (*Rittergutsbesitzer*), Julius Albert von Rohr. He was born in 1688 and died in 1742. His education was carefully planned. At the age of seventeen he was sent to the University of Leipzig, where he studied law, mathematics, chemistry, physics, and *Oekonomik*. After ending his studies he went with his father to Hamburg, to get acquainted with the business organization of that city. He became an attaché of the delegation sent to Frankfurt for the imperial election of 1712. The death of his father and the embarrassed condition of the estate presently put him on a very limited income. He went to Halle to study mathematics with Wolf; in 1713 to Holland; in 1714 he received a position as member of the *Stifts- und Erblands-Regierung* at Magdeburg; in 1726 was transferred to a similar position at Niederlausitz; in 1731 became *herzoglicher Landkammerrath;* in 1732 *Domherr zu Merseberg*, but the position seems to have secured his standing rather than to have furnished an occupation. He had been on the waiting-list for this sort of ecclesiastical preferment since he was two years old. He became a member of the *Landkammer* at Merseberg, where he remained till his retirement in 1738.

Rohr somehow managed to retrieve his financial fortunes to such an extent that he accumulated a library for that time rather rich,

[1] In *All. d. Bib., in loc.*

and also in 1720 acquired a landed estate between Dresden and Meissen, where he carried on wine culture, horticulture, and agriculture. He had troubled relations with a mistress, 1724–39. He married another woman in 1739, and wrote his friends an elaborate explanation of his domestic affairs.[1]

Rohr is credited with the authorship of twenty-nine published works, and of nine others left in an unfinished state.[2]

According to Inama, doubtless because of the author's remark on the second page of the *Vorrede* to the *Haushaltungsbibliothek*, Rohr spoke of *Hauswirthschaftskunst*, on the basis of natural science, as the chief task of his life. In his conception of political science he was a devoted admirer of Seckendorff; in his more concrete cameralistics he was equally attached to Schröder. "Under the influence of Wolf's eudaemonism he advanced in many respects beyond either." Under the same influence he escaped some of the poverty of the old *Hausväterlitteratur*, and on the other hand his knowledge of natural science was a factor in promoting the development of cameralism. In particular, he was of service in preparing the way for academic cameralism, which Dithmar and Gasser were permitted to introduce into the Prussian universities.

Roscher (p. 378) speaks of the *Compendieuse Haushaltungsbibliothek* as Rohr's "chief work." If there can be a "chief" among mediocrities, that designation can hardly

[1] In comparison with this account, it is surprising that Roscher did not probe beyond the misleading contents of the note (p. 178): "Er lebte unvermählt, mit viel Büchern, Correspondenz und Reisen, als Domherr zu Merseberg." For our interests, Rohr's life ended before this appointment.

[2] Zedler, *Universallexicon, in loc.* Chief among these were: (1) *Compendieuse Haushaltungsbibliothek* (1716; 2. Ausg., 1726; 3. Ausg., 1755); (2) *Physikalische Bibliothek* (1724; 2. Aufl., 1754); Rohr projected a *Mathematische Bibliothek*, "since these three sciences are united by an inseparable bond;" (3) *Einleitung zur Staatsklugheit* (1718); (4) *Einleitung zur Ceremonial-Wissenschaft der Privatpersonen* (1728); (5) *Einleitung zur Ceremonial-Wissenschaft der grossen Herrn* (1729); (6) *Obersächsisches Hauswirthschaftsbuch* (1722); (7) *Haushaltungsrecht* (1732, 1734; 2 Bände; 2. Aufl., 1738).

remain in this case where Roscher placed it. He does not seem to have been acquainted with Rohr's more pretentious works. The *Haushaltungsbibliothek*,[1] even in the "much enlarged" third edition, is a small handbook of 692 pages. It uses the word *Oeconomie* as synonymous with its general subject-matter. In the dedication to Kreishauptmann Peter Freyherr von Hohenthal, the author says:

While writers on management [*öconomische*] have remained as a rule unread by the learned, because they considered them too low, and by housekeepers, because they found them too high, the useful instruction which you [*Ew. Hochwohlgebornen*] have instituted shows how many objects not only of important but also of ingenious investigation *Oeconomie* contains, and how little one who is uninformed is competent to conduct with success occupations which demand so much knowledge and reflection.[2]

The author's Preface to the second edition, dated August 9, 1726, declares that the first edition had been well received by the public, and that certain scholars in the universities had done it the honor of lecturing upon it. The explanation of the author's intention in citing books which could actually be used in household and agricultural management has an important bearing upon the myth which the critics of mercantilism have propagated, that *there was no attention to agriculture and no thought of it.* At this time there were not only many writings on the subject, but they were not so very difficult to obtain,[3] and Rohr's book refers to the most available of them.

[1] Julius Bernhards von Rohr, Merseb. Domherrn und Land-Cammerraths *Haushaltungs Bibliothek* worinnen die vornehmsten Schriften, die zur Haushaltungskunst gehören, angezeiget werden. Dritte und viel vermehrte Auflage, 1755. I have not seen a copy of the original edition of 1716.

[2] This passage is one of the clearest reflections of the meanings attached at this time to variations of the term *Oeconomie*. It meant plain vulgar thrift, and then the beginnings of systematic thinking about thrift.

[3] We shall return to this point in connection with later writers. *Vide* p. 256 below.

In the *Vorrede* of the third edition, 1755, the editor shows that in his mind the word *Oeconomie* still stands for a very concrete type of technology, not for the sort of generalization which later appropriated the term. He says:

If we think of *Oeconomie*, not as it is practiced by the lowest portion of housekeepers [*Hauswirthe*], but rather as that which it actually is, an art whose prescriptions are based upon knowledge of nature, and which can be properly exercised and extended only by means of this knowledge, then it deserves a respectable place among the learned sciences. It requires also for its completeness the application of various other parts of human knowledge, and the learning of that which predecessors have done; that is, books must be read.

As a cameralistic book, in the proper sense, the *Haushaltungsbibliothek* would not deserve mention. As an index of the relation between the subjects known at the time as *Oeconomie* and *Cameralwissenschaft* in general, it is highly instructive. A glance at the Table of Contents would sufficiently fix this relation. A few sentences from the text may be added without comment. The opening sentence of the first chapter declares:

The art of managing the household [*Haushaltungskunst*] is a practical science (*sic*), which teaches how one in a proper way may acquire money and goods [*Geld und Gut*], may conserve and wisely expend what is acquired, for the promotion or maintenance of one's temporal happiness.

Sec. 2 of the same chapter continues:

The art of managing the household may be divided into the *Oeconomica* of princes and of private persons. In the former case it is called *Cameral-Finanz- und Domainenwissenschaft*. It consists in a prudence not only in administering his own means and revenues and those of his land, and in maintaining the community, but also in adding to the money and goods of the subjects. . . . . The house management of private persons may again be divided into city and country management [*Stadt- und Landwirthschaftskunst*]. Under the former head I reckon knowledge of the coins, of transactions with money, skill in keeping everything in order in the house, and in placing the furniture in the rooms according to symmetry and use, proper supply of the table, temperate use of drinks, wise control of servants, etc. Such things occur also in the country, but because these arrangements can be made without possessing estates [*liegende Güter*], I will not attribute them properly to rural management, which involves immovable landed property. Of this in general the so-called housekeeping books [*Haushaltungsbücher*] treat, and the same consists in knowledge of agriculture, of cattle raising, of fisheries, hunting, forests, gardening, vineyards, etc. This latter is much more comprehensive and difficult than the former, for whoever has the skill to carry on management in the country can quickly learn city management. On the contrary, whoever comes from the city to the country, unless he has particular zeal and guidance, will find it hard to adapt himself to rural management.

Both city and country management embrace three parts, namely skill (1) to acquire money and goods, (2) to retain what is acquired, and (3) wisely to expend it.[1]

As cumulative evidence on the general position of the cameralists, the opening sentence of the second chapter is in order. It is the author's definition of cameral science, viz.:

Cameral science (*Cameralwissenschaft*) teaches princes not only well to conserve and increase their means, but also to promote their subjects' happiness and to order their management (*Oeconomie*).

Then the motive of Schröder's civic philosophy reappears in this form (chap. ii, §4):

The best means of enriching a land is to take care that many people are drawn into the land, and also that all the subjects through diligent labor may have their support and means of gain [*Nahrung und Erwerb*].

These citations show the general character of this book of homely wisdom. After Rohr had written this earlier book, his notions of his vocation seem to have become more ambitious.

[1] This last proposition is notable because, although it seems to be a platitude, it expresses the common-sense which became one of the working premises of nearly all the later cameralists.

He did not confine himself to "management" in the narrower sense of his first programme. We may therefore find an expansion of his ideas in another book. Though it contains nothing original with the author, it won him not a little recognition among later cameralists.[1]

Previous to publication of the books we have named, Rohr had neither academic nor governmental experience to be compared with that of most of the cameralists; and his forms of expression are visibly apologetic toward each of the classes by which he was doubtless rated as an amateur. He writes

[1] Julii Bernhards von Rohr *Einleitung zur Staats-Klugheit, oder: Vorstellung Wie Christliche und weise Regenten zur Beförderung ihrer eigenen und ihres Landes Glückseeligkeit Ihre Unterthanen zu beherrschen pflegen. Mit Königl. Pohln. und Clurfl. Sächss. allergn. Privilegio.* Leipzig, 1718. In his *Vorrede*, Rohr speaks of a previous book, *Einleitung zur Klugheit zu leben, darinnen ich jungen Leuten einige Regeln der Privat-Klugheit beybringen wollen.* The author refers to the present volume as a companion book, designed for the use of beginners in the study of *Staats-Klugheit*. He says that the book is quite different from Seckendorff's *Teutschen Fürsten-Staate*, which had been "up to that time much read by the Germans, and to good advantage." Rohr makes this difference consist first, in describing not only what Christian princes have done in the way of wise and just administration, but also what they might well cease to do; and second, Rohr says that Seckendorff composed his book more as a moral than as a political treatise; that is, he showed what a ruler would do in pursuance of civic law, *if he acted in accordance with his conscience and his duty to God, and his obligations to his country*, but he did not show the means by which the tasks of government are to be carried out in detail. Rohr claims also that his book treats of many subjects which Seckendorff neglected. At the same time he concedes to Seckendorff's works a rank above his own. He explains also that he has had the Evangelical Lutheran states chiefly in mind, because in the Catholic states the doctrines of *Staats-Klugheit* are concerned with somewhat different objects, and rest upon quite different principles. Besides Seckendorff, Rohr says that he has used particularly Schröder, Leib, Marperger, "the learned and eminent authors of the *Unschuldigen Nachrichten*," Herr D. Döhler, Hr. Höm.

rather as an essayist than as a technologist. On the one hand the systematic method of the academic thinker is lacking, and on the other hand the firm touch of the man accustomed to deal directly with affairs. He can be included among the cameralists only as an evidence of the impressions which the cameralism both of the bureaus and of the books had made up to his date upon a university man of a rather refined type. Granting that he helped to gain a hearing for cameralism in the universities, there is no evidence that he exerted a distinct influence upon the development of the theory itself.[1] The *Einleitung*, however, would be an extremely valuable collection of material for the student of the culture history of the period.

The book is a compact volume of 1,474 pages, with a table of contents and index filling thirty more pages. The plate opposite the title-page represents a king upon his throne, at his right female figures symbolizing Religion and Justice, at his left Peace and Prudence, and below the couplet:

> Wenn ein Regente will des Landes Wolfarth bauen,
> Mus er auf Gottesfurcht, Justiz und Klugheit schauen.

The opening paragraph reads:

> Prudence [*Klugheit*] is an adaptability of temper by which actions are directed with reason and foresight toward the promotion of true happiness. It discovers means by which, without prejudice and hindrance to others, one may most conveniently and easily attain and preserve happiness. Because it aims at true happiness, it proposes first eternal and second temporal happiness as its chief and subordinate aim. It is otherwise called *die Politic*, and is either a true or a false prudence.

The looseness of thinking in this paragraph may be taken as

[1] The copy of the *Einleitung* which I have studied was borrowed from the Royal Library at Berlin. While it is much discolored by age, it shows no signs of use. Indeed many of the leaves had evidently never been separated since they left the bindery, and a considerable number, including one containing a part of the Table of Contents, were uncut!

an index of the quality of the book. The ambiguity that is involved in making the same word stand for "adaptability of temper" and "*Politic*" is symptomatic of the style throughout. The author is popular rather than analytic in his treatment. He can be accepted therefore merely as in certain respects a sign of the times, but not as a factor in the development of cameralistic theory or technology. This popular and uncritical quality is even more apparent in the second paragraph, viz.:

The true prudence demands nothing except that to which it may properly lay claim according to divine and natural law; it subordinates the will, as much as possible, when it would go to excess, and for the accomplishment of its purposes it uses permissible means. Its aim is the well-being of itself (*sic*) and of other men (*sic*); yet it recognizes, in case of collision between its own and its neighbor's fortunes, that the preference belongs to itself [!]. It [*Klugheit*] sees from its own experience and that of others that all temporal happiness, however plausible, is associated with much unrest, is fluid and fleeting, and that it quite unconsciously slips out of the hands of its possessors.

Thus while the book contains much that might have been instructive to certain types of mind, in early stages of education, it is not to be taken seriously as a sample of the academic or professional thinking of the author's generation. It belongs in the class once known as "edifying," rather than among technological treatises.

Rohr distinguishes "the prudence of private persons" from "that of the reigning princes" (p. 10). The former was treated in the book named above,[1] the latter is the subject of the present volume. More particularly, the prudence of the reigning prince, or civic prudence [*Staats-Klugheit*] is described as:

the adaptability of the understanding, by means of which rulers are capable of promoting not only their own but all their subjects' true happiness (p. 11).

[1] *Vide* above, p. 190. *Klugheit zu leben.*

The division of civic prudence into general and special, which we find first clearly stated by Gerhard, is adopted by Rohr, but whether or not he was in any way indebted for the idea to the earlier writer does not appear. His distinction, while apparently the same, is really not along the same lines as Gerhard's. Rohr calls application of the rules of general civic prudence to a given state "special civic prudence," instead of grasping the conception of more general and less general principles which may in their way be applicable to all states. Indeed he does not seem to realize that there is a place for general principles, other than religious doctrines or moral truisms, upon which details of civic polity must rest. Instead, he assumes that one may be a specialist in civic science by simply selecting a fraction of it as his task:

Just as it is impossible that a man, however diligent, should cultivate all civic prudence completely: so it is well done if each should pursue those parts for which he has inclination, talent, and opportunity (p. 33).

Rohr bases his essay without hesitation upon the idea of the patriarchal prerogative of the prince:

Just as a ruling prince presents two moral persons, first a private person, who in many acts must conform himself to other private persons, yet also is to be considered as a prince, who has to direct the conduct of his subjects, he must consequently be versed in both private and public prudence (p. 34).

That the book is rather rhetorical than technical is illustrated again in the next paragraph:

The chief task of the prudence of a ruler consists in always seeking to combine his happiness with that of his subjects, and in striving to prevent them from becoming separated. The prosperity of a ruler which is not founded on the weal of his land is of no permanence, as is shown by many ancient and modern histories. He must have the prosperity of his subjects in view in all his actions, and must undertake nothing which is inconsistent with the same.

At the same time, Rohr quite as distinctly affirms the absolutism of rulers. Thus:

In case of a collision between his own interest and the welfare of the subjects, from love for his land, in order to promote the common interest [*gemeinschaftliche Interesse*] he must subordinate his own interest. He thereby not only wins the love of his subjects, but he does that to which he is appointed of God. And while sovereigns are not bound to render account for their actions to anyone in the world, yet they, as well as their subjects, have over them the supreme ruler in heaven, to whom at the great day of judgment they must give answer.

While the author reiterates on the one hand the sonorous principle, "*Salus populi* must be the law of the prince," yet on the other hand he unconsciously betrays the rendering which the spirit of the time tended to give to the principle, when he says:

The art of government is in fact an art above all arts; because it can make kingdoms out of principalities and empires out of kingdoms, can raise a sunken state to its former splendor, and through this rare power of making a prince really great it proves itself the true statecraft.

In the following section (p. 37) Duke Ernst of Gotha, Seckendorff's master, is cited as a type of the Christian prince, and as evidence that piety is necessary for the success of a ruler. No mention is made at this point of Seckendorff, however, from whom it is probable that Rohr derived the substance of his political ideas. For example, the sections in which he describes the duties of a prince in general, especially §§7–19, merely render Seckendorff's views in slightly varied terms, and with trifling additions of detail or illustration. It amounts to no proper acknowledgment to the man who furnished the thoughts when at last, in §18, his name is used in connection with the least important item in the whole programme, viz., the recreations of the prince!

Since Rohr was not a cameralist, but merely a contemporary popularizer of cameralism, we repeat that he is worth our notice merely as secondary evidence bearing upon the impression which technical cameralism had made upon the thinking of men at one remove from the more technical writers.

In a confused paragraph (p. 71) the author raises but does not distinctly answer the question:

In case a reigning prince violates his fundamental pledges to his subjects, have they a right to resist? Rohr first remarks, "It is well known that those who withstand the divinely appointed authorities resist the divine order," and he draws the conclusion that a perfidious prince should be left rather to divine justice than forcibly dealt with by his subjects. Without much assurance that the next recourse is very promising, he points out that the constitution of the Empire calls for judgment by imperial authorities upon a prince who disturbs or threatens the order of the Empire by not keeping faith with his subjects. Pushing the hypothesis to the extreme form, that "the excesses of the prince make the life of a virtuous subject insecure," Rohr ventures the very cautious judgment that in such case one is justified in resisting the prince. He immediately adds: "If the ruler goes only so far, however, as to devise against one and another private person things contrary to God and to natural decency [*Erbarkeit*], such subjects must rather depart from the country, or bear the injustice with patience, than oppose the majesty of their ruling sovereign with violence." The whole discussion of contracts to which a ruler is a party is conducted upon a shifting basis of theological dogma, ethical generality, and amateurish legalism. In modern vernacular, it amounts to a whitewashing report upon the political *status quo*, under the form of an impartial inquiry into alternatives.

The fourth chapter ("*Von dem Oeconomie Wesen*") is worth notice as a further index to the current sense of the term *Oeconomie*. As we try to make evident throughout this analysis, the readiness with which this and similar terms have been translated from German into English words which were equivalent in appearance, but not in sense, has been a serious hindrance to proper insight into the meaning of German sociological evolution. The one point to be emphasized here is that nowhere, in the series of writers interpreted in this study, did any variation of the word *Oeconomie* have the force carried by the English derivative from the same root in the phrase "political economy." In the whole usage of the cameralists *Oeconomie* was primarily thrifty management, as measured by the prevailing standards of household or public prudence. *Oeconomie* was literally housekeeping (*Haushaltung*, *Haushaltungskunst*, etc.), and this conception clung to it, whether the immediate reference was to thrift in the household, on the farm, in artisanship, trade, or government. *Oeconomie* was never, until the period of Smithism, generalized and deepened into consideration of problems underneath rule-of-thumb wisdom. With this in mind, we find in Rohr's approach to the subject of *Oeconomie-Wesen* an instructive guide to the plane of interests which held the attention of men of affairs, both industrial and governmental, before the stage of critical and philosophical interpretation of economics.[1] He opens the chapter in this way:

Just as private persons fill their storerooms by orderly and reasonable management [*Haushalten*], so that they can draw one supply after another; in the same way with ruling princes, if they attend to their *Fürstlichen Oeconomie und Cameral-Wesen* in a proper manner, the happiness not only of their own persons and of their families, but also of their subjects, which must always be connected with their own, will be promoted and secured. In the case of princely persons a double *Oeconomica* must have place, ... first, the *Oeconomica* of private persons. . . . . In this connection they must take care that the sums which they lend [*Capitalien*] are securely invested and kept in good circulation [*rouliren*]. They must administer their domains to good advantage, apportion the outlays reasonably and see that they are balanced by the income, and always take care that a margin remains. That which God has given them they must conserve, in order that it may not be impaired or lost, etc. In all this they must give exact heed to the same rules and cautions which private persons must observe. Beyond this there is, second, the *Fürstliche Oeconomica*, since princes must not only pay attention to increase and preservation of their private incomes, but also to enlargement and preservation of the happiness and goods of their subjects.

Then follows non-technical description of the administrative machinery which the cameralists had begun to analyze more precisely. Rohr explains the *Oeconomie-Wesen* of rulers as an affair of two divisions, *distribuendo et augendo*, on the one hand of applying the revenues, on the other of raising them. He uses the term *Cameralisten* for those officials who have the former division in charge, and explains that a quite different body of persons should be employed in the other division. Thus he thinks (p. 99) that *Cameral-Sachen* should be divided into two distinct *collegia*—the division, by the way, not according precisely with the distribution of functions proposed by the author a few lines before—the one, called the *Cammer* proper, to collect and disburse the reveunes, the other exclusively to deliberate how to increase the revenues. He claims that the usual union of these two *collegia* in a single *Cammer* is harmful and costly.[1] Rohr goes into detail about cameralistic technique as though he were an expert, but our purpose does not require attention to the technological side of cameralism, and if it did we should be concerned not with the expositions of amateurs like Rohr, but with those of men who could speak with authority.

A glance at Rohr's table of contents would show that the personality of the prince, and dynastic policy, are made the center from which the remainder of the book proceeds. While this at once condemns the book, from the standpoint of the

[1] At this point the author appeals to the second chapter of Schröder's *Fürstliche Schatz- und Renth-Cammer*.

modern social theorist, it affords the very evidence which makes the book valuable to the historical interpreter. This paramount value of government, and of the prince as incarnating government, is fundamental in the whole cameralistic régime and theory. It is the pass-key to the whole system. Cameralism as a technique and as a theory was a means developed in the interest of an end visualized first and foremost in the person of the prince, if never absolutely identical with the prince and his interests. In respect to this one factor, the development of German civilization, not to carry the generalization at this point beyond Germany, was a progressive realization of other values in society besides those of rulers and governments, and progressive readjustment of ratios between the several values. All the doctrines and policies of the period which we are considering have to be interpreted in their connection with the ruling presumption of the paramount importance of the prince, who may or may not have been differentiated in thought from the government which he represented. In either case, the ideas of prince and government as values in themselves, not as functionaries and functions to be appraised according to their service for other values, were foremost and decisive throughout this régime. We shall have occasion to ask more than once, as we proceed, To what extent had some suggestion of another scale of values begun to work in the minds of the Germans? It is not a part of the task set for this volume to demonstrate the answer to the question. We shall be obliged, however, to point out frequent incidental symptoms of the workings of more democratic impressions.

Rohr expressly adopts that form of the social contract theory which presupposes nature people contemplating an intolerable social condition, real or impending. To escape or to avert this condition the whole number of individuals make over their wills to one or more rulers. Thereafter the will of the whole community can be expressed only by this single or multiple ruler, and the subject has no rightful alternative but obedience. The ruler summarizes not only the will but the welfare of the state, or of the individuals merged into a unique personality (pp. 248 ff.). By a chain of reasoning which we need not follow, Rohr concludes further (p. 258) that a Christian monarch is bound by divine and human law to take responsibility for both the temporal and the eternal welfare of his subjects. This view of course furnishes the basis for explanation of the ecclesiastical polity of Lutheran states, and the author shows decidedly better acquaintance with church problems, and especially with minutiae of parochial procedure, than with the more strictly cameralistic departments of government. This leaning toward ecclesiasticism is shown in a most painfully smug chapter on the proper course of rulers toward "dreamers, pietists, and new prophets" (pp. 322-65).

It must be admitted, however, that if Rohr's ecclesiastical views belong in a world which Americans cannot understand, his views of the relation of the state to education are at bottom identical with our own. So far as there is a difference in principle it may be traced to his emphasis on the interest of the state in the training of good citizens, while we are inclined to view the matter more from the side of the right of the individual to education. The ecclesiastical factors in education which Rohr had in mind were, both in subject-matter and in machinery, accidental rather than essential variations of educational principles which modern democracies attempt to apply with other details.

In the chapter "*Von Academien*," Rohr partially anticipates Justi in a plea for "*ein Professor Oeconomiae*" at the universities. The chapter is entirely in accord with the other evidence found in the writers of this group to the effect that their references to "*oeconomica*" or any equivalent expression connoted something very different from the implications of the same terms in the nineteenth century, and particularly different from English versions of the terms. In the order in which the items occur in the chapter, we may note, first, that the subjects which Rohr wishes such a professor to teach are at once indicated by the phrase *Stadt- und Landes-Wirthschaft;* second, the principal reason alleged for failure to establish such professorships was difficulty of finding men who had university training who at the same time possessed either knowledge of these subjects or fitness to teach them; third, slightly varying the second point, scholars had seldom given attention to *Oeconomie*, while skilled managers (*Haushaltungs Verständige*) had seldom done much with "*studiis*" in the university sense; third, it ought not to be difficult to find here and there men with experience in administrative offices who understand management (*Wirthschafft*) from the bottom and could teach it passably; fourth, in answer to the claim that *Oeconomica, Politica und morale* ought to be taught by the *Professori moralium*, and that accordingly increase of the number of professorships is unnecessary, Rohr says it is true that diligent *Professori moralium* do not fail to introduce into their political courses all sorts of economic observations, but it is impossible that they could fully explain these three sciences;[1] fifth, quoting Döhler,[2] "In the schools the prejudiced opinion prevails that a student should not concern himself with any sort of *Hauss-Wesen*, that it is even a disgrace for a student to have anything to do with such employments;" sixth, such being the case, it is high time that students in schools and colleges should learn *Oeconomie* from artisans and even from peasants.[3]

[1] At this point appeal is made to Morhoff, "in dem 3. Buche des III. Tomi seines *Polyhistoris;*" and to "der berühmte Professor zu Franckfurt, Johann Christoph Beckmann, in dem §10. des X. Capitels seiner Polit. Parall."

[2] "Herrn Joh. George Döhler in seiner *Untersuchung des heut-zu-Tage überhand nehmenden Geld- und Nahrungs-Mangels.*"

[3] The author refers for further considerations on the subject to the first chapter of his *Haushaltungs-Bibliothek.*

From these citations it is evident that by common understanding among friends and foes of "economic" instruction, the thing intended was technical, not philosophical. It was even more remote from subjects then regarded as within the pale of *Wissenschaft* than manual training is today in the minds of those who are least inclined to welcome it, or its maturer continuations, into our lower and higher schools.

Chap. xvi, "*Von der Gelehrsamkeit*," develops the theorem:

> Since good arts and sciences are fitted in no slight degree to increase and to maintain the happiness of a land and of its ruler, it follows that a ruler who has the weal of his provinces at heart has the best of reasons for desiring that his subjects should be instructed in all sorts of useful disciplines. The more learned and intelligent they are, the more available are they, whether in peace or in war.

The discussion takes a turn which shows the limitations of the time with respect to freedom of thought; that is, it dwells more on what should not be permitted in schools, or allowed to appear in print, than upon promotion of unrestricted investigation; but in one direction it calls for increased liberality. Sec. 12 opens with the remarks:

> In the case of political writings, people are in many places far too scrupulous. State secrets are made out of matters which are quite innocent, and sometimes people fear to make public anything with reference to state affairs, although no good reason for such caution can be found.[1]

Beginning with chap. xvii, "*Von Lastern*," the book invades more and more technical ground, but with the equipment of the essayist rather than of the specialist, and in a style addressed rather to the general reader than to close students. As a mirror of the times, it would be of great value to a culture historian who knew how to use such material. For our purpose it yields nothing which is not to be found in more reliable form elsewhere.

[1] Obrecht has already furnished us a case in point. *Vide* above, p. 43.

Two exceptions to the foregoing must be noted. The first is a negative contribution to our inquiry. In the twenty-first chapter, on the police system of cities, Rohr gives one of the clearest testimonies to be found in the cameralistic or quasi-cameralistic literature, that the police system as outlined later was only in a slight degree in existence at the date of the book. The institution had yet to be developed to meet needs that were felt before the means of satisfying them were created. Rohr quotes "a certain unnamed author, who has described the well-organized state of the hitherto much-sought but never-discovered kingdom of Ophir." He is said to have expressed himself as follows:

Because through observance of good *Policey* the divine blessing and the prosperity of a land are best insured, certain *Policey-Räthe* should be appointed. These should be efficient and learned men in *Moralibus, Politicis und Oeconomicis*, and they should be used for drawing up good police ordinances, and for zealously supervising their execution. Their office demands requirement that agricultural land should everywhere be well cultivated and sowed with the necessary seed, that management [*Wirthschaft*] should be well and thriftily [*häusslich*] conducted; impious, immoral, vicious, dissolute, and infamous persons should nowhere be tolerated; that vagrants and idlers should be made to work, the roads and ways be kept good and secure, the streams be made navigable, cities and villages be provided with good inns, traffic by water and land carried on fairly and diligently, children and servants well trained and provided, the offices properly filled, the unworthy expelled from civic stations, law and justice administered, the wicked punished, the pious rewarded, and the poor relieved. In short, that there should everywhere prevail honorable, Christian and righteous life.

Rohr declares, however, that this ideal must be put in the class of *piorum desideriorum*. He thinks that no more odious programme could be imagined than the prerogatives proposed. His opinion is of no value to us. The important thing is the evidence which the passage furnishes that the *Policey Ordnung* afterward introduced was in a very rudimentary stage when he wrote. His ideas of the standards of conduct which ought to be enforced by government seem to conform in spirit to the standard quoted, and he goes into a mass of details, but the particular machinery recommended by the anonymous author alone meets his disapproval. Rohr apparently felt jealous for the prerogatives of the church in connection with these matters. The progress of events realized more of the system foreshadowed in the quotation than its author appears to have expected. Indeed more than half of Rohr's book is occupied with subjects which Justi afterward systematized under the rubric *Policey*.

The second exception to the general proposition that Rohr affords little light on the cameralistic problem proper is found in chap. xxviii, on "The Riches of the Country." Recalling his earlier assertion that the interests of the prince are bound up with those of his subjects, he premises in particular that the prince has every reason to do his best that the subjects may be rich. Without mincing words, he frankly puts this identity of interest between prince and subjects in the affluence of the latter on the ground that if the subjects have money the sovereign always has means at his command to get it from them. "On the other hand, if the subjects are poor, he can no more get money from them than one can squeeze water out of a dry sponge."[1]

After reciting some of the information which a prince must command, about the wealth and sources of income of his

[1] Rohr cites Schröder, "*Fürstliche Schatz- und Rent-Cammer*, as holding the opposite view, viz., "a prince who has no money in his chest, but relies on the good will of his subjects and territories, is walking on stilts." Our review of Schröder, in which we have quoted the same words (above, p. 144), shows that the contradiction was not so direct as Rohr supposes. He had chiefly in mind one stage in the process, while Schröder put the emphasis at another point, relying however on the same ultimate resource.

subjects, that he may know the location and capacity of the springs which he must tap, Rohr betrays his ideas of wealth itself, and his expressions are rather remarkable. He says:

> A prince must have care that his land may increase in riches. A land becomes richer, in proportion as money and gold (*sic*) are brought into it, either from its own mines or elsewhere, and poorer as money leaves the country. For inasmuch as by general consent of peoples gold and silver are the universal price of all things, and the worth of the same in all places in the world is estimated according to the worth of gold and silver, for which everything can be bought, one must estimate the riches of a land according to the quantity of the gold and silver in the same. Hence a prince must give his thought to means whereby the land may become richer, and he must remove everything through which it becomes poorer (p. 844).[1]

Rohr is not content to let the matter rest with one statement. He repeats it in this form in the next paragraph, almost in the words of Schröder, as indeed the previous quotation was, viz.:

> We find gold and silver in the mines, and this is the most certain increment of the riches of the country, for as much as gold and silver are found, so much has the country increased in riches.

[1] After Schröder's chap. xxx, no equally clear expression of this opinion is to be found in the cameralistic writers previous to Rohr. If the language is carefully considered it will be seen that even this brash assertion of Rohr cannot properly be construed as a generalization of the same logical order as Adam Smith's propositions about wealth. Rohr was evidently not probing beyond immediate practical utility. He was not seeking for a philosophy of wealth, but for a basis of prudence in dealing with the means necessary for practical wisdom. It would be as preposterous to make such a statement, by a writer of Rohr's type, the clue to the economic basis of cameralism, as it would be to take the enthusiastic declaration of some interested politician, in the days of Dingley and McKinley, that a protective tariff is the only way to create wealth, as the measure of the economic insight of Americans in the present generation. As we have seen, Rohr was not an authority upon any technical or philosophical subject. He is not to be taken as representing the cameralists, except in a relatively remote way. Yet it is from such sources that the extreme forms of statement came which were afterward charged, under the label "mercantilism," to the responsible publicists of Germany for most of the rest of the century.

Then follows an uncritical formulation of the theory of the balance of trade. At the same time, without perception of its bearing upon the idea of the exceptional character of gold and silver as riches, the fundamental necessity of making the country as fertile as possible is urged as strenuously as though the author were the extremest physiocrat.

In the chapter on mining (xxxvi), Rohr again falls back upon Schröder.[1] The theorem of the latter is:

> A prince should cause the gold and silver mines to be worked, if they yield anything at all, whether with a loss or a profit, for that matters not to the country, since I have shown [chap. xxx] that this is the most certain approach of a country to riches.[2]

The most direct evidence which we get of Rohr's sources in the next chapter, on forests, is his citation of von Carlowitz' *Sylvicultura Oeconomica*, yet he writes with great confidence, and evidently from a larger range of direct observation than in any other portion of the book, unless it may be the ecclesiastical sections. The essay style and quality prevail in the remainder of the book, and it yields nothing farther that is notable for our purpose.

[1] Particularly on p. 278 of the first edition of *Fürstl. Schatz- und Rent-Cammer*. In the edition of 1744, which I have compared, the passage is on p. 181.

[2] In the same connection Rohr remarks, "Es wäre zu wündschen, dass die Bergwercks-Lehren, die der Herr Abraham von Schönberg in seiner *Berg-information*, Tit. von Berg-Herren, s. 15, vortraget, von allen Potentaten in würckliche Observanz gesetzt würden." Except that Justi does not find occasion to lay stress on the first of Schönberg's six recommendations, viz., gratitude to God, if the country has been blessed with gold and silver deposits, Justi developed his mining policy along the lines of this predecessor. *Vide* below, pp. 358 ff.

CHAPTER IX

THE CAMERALISTICS OF GASSER

We come now to the point at which cameral science was first officially designated as a subject to be taught in universities. Whatever their scientific merits or defects, the men who mark this event in the history of cameralistics are notable.[1]

[1] The most complete survey up to date of the academic phase of cameralism is Stieda, *Die Nationalökonomie als Universitätswissenschaft*, Leipzig, 1906. Within the period covered by the present study, the cameralism even of the book-writers centered in the bureaus rather than in the universities. The reverse became the case in the following period. Stieda (p. 9) credits Thomasius with having been the first to read a course on national economy in a German university. Such judgments do not impress me as at all reliable. In the first place, if we had syllabi of all the courses given at this period, it would be difficult to gain a consensus about the way of drawing the line between those that should be regarded as economic in the general sense of the time, and those that should not. In the second place, judging from Thomasius' notes on Osse (*vide* above, pp. 24 ff.), it seems to me altogether probable that Nicolaus Hieronymus Gundling (*vide* Stintzing *All. d. Bib.*, *in loc.*), although a pupil of Thomasius in *Naturrecht*, may have been earlier and quite as distinguished as he in the economic field. Stieda does not seem to have run down the facts in this instance (*vide* p. 28). Again, it is certain that Gerhard was lecturing at Jena on economics, in the contemporary sense, as early as 1713 (*vide* above, p. 175). Gerhard's name does not appear in Stieda's index. As a sign of the difficulty of obtaining the literature of cameralism, it is worth noting that, in spite of his vantage ground at Leipzig, Stieda says he has been unable to see a copy of Sincerus, *Projekt der Oeconomie in Form einer Wissenschaft nebst einem unmassgeblichen Bedenken, wie diese Wissenschaft, beydes in Theorie und Praxi, mit mehrerm Fleiss und Nutzen getrieben werden könne*, Frankfurt und Leipzig, 1660; he failed also to find a copy of Zincke, *Programm von practischen Collegiis juridico-politico-cameralibus*, 1741–42; he appears to have found in one library only (*Leipziger Stadtbibliothek*) the monograph of Justi (1754), *Auf höchsten Befehl an Sr. Röm. Kaiserl. und zu Ungarn und Böhmen Königl. Majestät erstattetes aller-*

According to Inama,[1] Gasser's father was *Kurfürstlich brandenburgischer Landrentmeister*. The range of ideas within which the paternal duties were discharged must account in part for the interests and limitations of the son. As Inama further says, "he had a clear but extremely jejune intellect, with total absence of higher philosophical, ethical and historical conceptions." Gasser built upon Seckendorff, but was far from appreciating the whole range of the earlier author's wisdom. For our purposes, the fact that Gasser was professor of law, and also a member of the *Schöppenstuhl* at Halle, before he was appointed to the newly created chair of cameralistics, is all that is necessary by way of introduction to his book.

Since Gasser was the first to occupy the economic professorship established at Halle (1727), his book, published two years after beginning the new duties, would deserve attention as a waymark, even if it contained nothing otherwise notable.[2]

untertänigstes Gutachten von dem vernünftigen Zusammenhange und praktischen Vortrage aller Oekonomischen u. Kameralwissenschaften; he found no copy of John Christian Förster, *Einleitung in die Cameral-Policey- und Finanz-Wissenschaft*, 1779 (?); etc. Although I have failed to get access to certain of the cameralistic books, my examination of previous accounts of them leads me to the belief that on the whole they have never been subjected to a more conscientious examination than in this study. At least, I have expressed no judgment as my own upon books which I have not carefully analyzed. There are good reasons for doubting whether even Roscher could have said as much. I venture to hope that this necessarily incomplete survey will provoke German scholars to attempt a completely objective restoration of the cameralistic writers.

[1] *All. d. Bib., in loc.*

[2] Simon Peter Gassers, JCti, *Einleitung zu den Oeconomischen Politischen und Cameral Wissenschaften, Worinnen für dieses mal die Oeconomico-Cameralia Von den Domainen- oder Cammer- auch andern Gütern, deren Administration und Anschlägen, so wol des Ackerbaues als anderer Pertinentien halber, samt den Regalien angezeiget und erläutert werden. Nebst einem Vorbericht Von der Fundation der neuen oeconomischen Profession, und der Allerdurchlauchtigsten Stifters eigentlichen allergnädigsten Absicht*, Halle; In Verlegung des Wäysenhauses, MDCCXXIX (pp. 347 ff.).

The items in the book which mean most for our purpose are contained in the Preface. They may be reduced to a very brief résumé, but the process of extracting this tincture from the fibrous rhetorical pulp which contains it is extremely perplexing.

In the dedication to Friedrich Wilhelm I prominence is given to the statement that the king had both excited the admiration and gratified the wish of many scholars by taking the lead in establishing economic professorships. With respect both to the "admiration" and the "many," Gasser's own account shows that our acceptance of the record must be carefully qualified. All the evidence goes to show that the scholars in Germany who looked with any favor whatever at this period upon the idea of introducing economics into the universities were few and far between. It appears further that some of the credit for the innovation in Prussia is probably due to Thomasius, the editor of Osse's *Testament*, at that time rector of the University of Halle.

In explaining the king's objects in founding the new "economic professorship," Gasser incidentally betrays facts in the situation which are doubtless more apparent to the present reader of his book than they were to his own mind. He states, first, that the king wanted young men to get in the universities some of the elementary knowledge which would make them available as civic employees. With the zeal of a new convert he contrasts this desirable knowledge with the sort of thing which had up to that time been the nearest approach to preparation—"juridical pedantries and lawyers' tricks."[1] He rings many changes on this charge. He thereby shows, first, that the subject which he represented was fighting for its life, and, second, that men of his type had already formulated in their own minds, if they had not widely published, some rather specific counts against the scholastic formalism of the law faculties of the period.

[1] "*Blosse Juristerey oder wol gar Advocaten-Streichen.*"

The next item which we disentangle from the author's labored and involved form of explanation is that he felt himself on the defensive for delaying as long as two years before publishing this book on the subject of his professorship! His explanation is, in brief, that his duties required him to teach "from morning till five or six in the evening,"[1] that his official duties "auf der Kammer und Deputation" consumed his forenoons, that from six o'clock till late at night he had "enough duties connected with the bureau, the faculty and other official labors to occupy two or three men," and that consequently there remained to him for work on economic subjects "only the few morning hours up to eight o'clock!" Furthermore, he contemptuously describes authorship in the legal faculty as a process of picking out passages from ninety-nine volumes and scribbling them into a hundredth. On the contrary, "although a heap of economic rubbish has been brought to light already, there are few if any pioneers in this subject, but everything must be collected with much labor and reflection, also by inquiries and collation."[2] Gasser returns several times to the additional difficulty that "the scholarly and efficient *Hauswirthe* and *Politici* are more at odds with one another than any other scholars can possibly be."[3]

Returning to the reasons why economic professorships had not been established earlier, Gasser quotes Thomasius,[4] first, on the proposition that the jurists had become mere word-

[1] He retained his legal professorship, and his economic teaching occupied only a portion of his time.

[2] Inasmuch as he presently acknowledges Seckendorff as a pioneer to whom he is greatly indebted, it seems necessary to connect this remark particularly with the special sort of material to which Gasser's book is devoted. This conclusion carries with it a judgment as to the sense in which Gasser used all variations of the term *oeconomisch*.

[3] For Justi's comments on the situation at this period, *vide* below, pp. 296 ff.

[4] *Cautele der Rechts-Gelahrtheit*, cap. 17, §1.

splitters and no longer edifying instructors of candidates for civic positions; second, that *Oeconomie* ought to be taught in the universities by professors especially charged with that subject; and third, on the reasons for omission to supply this need. Thomasius covers all the points on which we have already quoted Rohr in this connection,[1] and he adds the following reasons:

First, because Aristotle left us no economic books, and at the founding of the first universities the monks knew nothing but Aristotle; second, the belief has prevailed that the scholar should concern himself with something different from that which the drudge and common man understands; third, it has possibly been partly from fear that the laity would discover the tricks of clerical *Oeconomie;* fourth, scholars of the traditional sorts have little fitness to investigate economic subjects, and so make light of them; fifth, the same, and indeed all scholars, are apt to be poor economists in their own private affairs; sixth, good economy would not tolerate monkish laziness, but is based on the contrary belief that "man is destined for labor, and that he who does not work is not worthy to eat."[2]

[1] *Vide* p. 200 above.

[2] In further explanation of the royal purpose in establishing the professorship at Halle to improve the situation thus indicated, Gasser inserts abstracts from the official correspondence leading to his appointment. The most significant expressions are these: "Es haben Seine Königliche Majest. in Preussen . . . . resolviret auf beyden Universitäten, Halle und Franckfurth, *Professores Oeconomiae* bestellen zu lassen, welche denen *Studiosis* die *principia* der Land-Wirthschaft, wie auch der Policey, ingleichen die Einrichtung der Anschläge von Aemtern und Gütern, nicht weniger guter Verfass- und Regulirung der Städte beybringen sollen." Further, in the final rescript: "Friederich Wilhelm, König, Demnach Wie aus höchst eigener Bewegung allergnädigst resolviret, dass auf der dortigen Universität die *cameralia oeconomica* und Policey-Sachen gleichergestalt, wie die übrige Studia und Wissenschaften, dociret werden sollen, ... damit die studirende Jugend in Zeiten, und ehe sie zu Bedienungen employret werden, einen guten Grund in obgedachten Wissenschaften erlangen mögen, etc., etc. . . . . Berlin den 24. Julii 1727." Gasser also refers to a monograph by the pro-rector of the University of Halle, von Ludewig. *Vide* below, p. 216.

The sense in which the king understood the term *Oeconomie*, and in which Gasser undertook to use it, appears in part, though by no means fully, in the further explanation by the author:

His majesty manifested in the beginning great displeasure at the bad *Oeconomie* which young people were in the habit of practicing in their own affairs, so that when they come back from universities and tours, they are usually already so loaded with debts that they are helpless, and especially those who have landed estates carry on such thriftless management because of aforesaid debts, that they cannot rescue even the most important estates from embarrassment when they at last gradually get some insight into *Oeconomie*, especially because the people who operate and superintend the estates can defraud the uninstructed owners in countless ways.

This being the state of things, continues Gasser, his majesty was zealous to change the proportion of lawyers, who filled the country and sucked it dry. He wanted young men to learn not merely the elements of jurisprudence, but to add the elements of *politica*, *oeconomica* and *cameralia* (p. 8).

Gasser explains that in order to meet this demand, he devotes the first half-year to lectures on Seckendorff's *Fürsten-Staat*. He says that although this *schönes Tractätlein* does not contain much about *Oeconomica* proper, yet it in general corresponds with the royal intention in surveying the whole state, and thus in furnishing a basis for setting the lawyers right. Gasser also mentions Rohr's book as a *compendium oeconomicum*, but he does not agree with the author that it would form a useful basis for university lectures, because it contains too much that is specific and practical in form, but not available until it can be reconsidered and applied after adoption of fundamental rules. "Besides," adds Gasser, "there is nothing in the book in the way of correct formulation of the budgets."

This latter remark is explained by a glance at Gasser's categories of *Anschläge* for all sorts of minor industrial operations. This estimate of the unavailability of Rohr is apparently to be understood primarily by comparison with Seckendorff, because Gasser shows that he is interested in quite as minute details as those presented by Rohr. He finds in Seckendorff, however, the necessary statement of fundamental principles upon which specific rules of management must rest.

After elaborating this claim at some length, Gasser cites "von Schröter,"[1] on the difference between a rich man and a rich prince; to the effect that "much money makes a rich man but not a powerful prince." Gasser interprets Schröder as meaning not that a prince should have no money, but that he should have both money and power. Consequently, Gasser urges that the two supporting pillars of the princely state are "revenues from the country and well-to-do subjects in the country, particularly in the towns." This theorem is the text for a somewhat detailed argument upon the importance of promoting diversified industries.

The author's *Vorbericht* closes with a promise to make his lectures as valuable commentaries as possible, both by explanation and illustration, upon the contents of the book. Although it is aside from our main purpose, we may quote the paragraph in which a pedagogical turn is given to this promise,[2] viz.:

I propose also to set apart a designated hour on Saturdays in which the work of those who commendably choose to attempt practice at once will be examined, their mistakes pointed out and further guidance given. For that purpose I shall assign to some the tasks of drawing up the budgets [*Anschläge*] of estates, and of formulating the special budgets of breweries, mills, brickyards, etc., belonging to estates. Others will be required to draw up the customs schedules, *catastra*, etc., on the lines indicated in the several chapters. When these are read and discussed on Saturdays, other students will be appointed as revisers and examiners, while the lectures will take

[1] *Fürst. Schatz- und Rent-Cammer. Vide* above, p. 152.

[2] *Vide* Justi's related remarks, below, p. 303 ff.

them up further, and they will thus be considered as it were in full session. In a word, each student will be encouraged to do his best in the line in which he shows most inclination, while by listening to the work of all he may gain a general idea of the whole subject.

The body of the book is, in a very narrow sense, technical. As evidence of the progress of administrative technology it would call for careful comparison with previous and following handbooks. For our purpose its chief significance is negative. That is, it shows that the horizon of cameralistic theory, as the author understood it, was bounded by the rules of thrifty management, first of the domains of the prince, and then of the various gainful employments, sometimes viewed as lucrative for the individual citizens, and sometimes as having their chief importance as ultimate revenue creators for the prince.

Even this modicum of meaning is to be found in the book only after patient consideration. The opening chapters, first, on the meaning of domains in general, and especially on the invalid distinction between *Domainen-Güter*, *Taffel-Güter*, and *Cammer-Güter*, and second, on incorporation of new acquisitions into the domains, have only the remotest visible connection with all that follows. They have every appearance of having been revamped from the author's old law lectures, and forced into service in place of a general survey, which he could not extemporize. They are an unkempt rabble of juridical archaeology, homespun philology, current legal usage, and common-sense conclusion. To the modern reader, they are mostly unintelligible. From the references to Seckendorff one derives the impression that, beyond these incongruities, all the definite instruction which the author imparted, after this impotent preamble, was drawn from the *Fürsten-Staat*. One other obvious inference is that the author regarded the word-splitting which he summed up in these two chapters as a bad inheritance from the civilists and the canonists. While he was not sufficiently emancipated from the futile controversy to ignore it, his opinion was as frank in substance as it was Hibernian in form, viz., "If the French writers had not broken the ice of the theorems of the spiritual and secular state, the papal and glossarial yeast would have got the upper hand!" (p. 3).

Without making any visible use of these two chapters on the domains, the author plunges, without a word to account for the abrupt change, into a series of chapters on the most minute details of private thrift.

Chaps. iii–x inclusive begin with analysis of ordinary building processes, and end with details of assessment of tithes and other tributes. Sixty-two pages are assigned to itemized schedules of the cost of different sorts of construction, e. g., a tile roof; a thatch roof; the carpenter's work on a country house; estimate for a pigeon-cote resting on posts; estimate of the cost of mason work; cost of wheelwright's work; cost of pottery, etc., etc. The logic which calls for these exhibits begins with the major premise: "To avoid being cheated, you must know customary prices."

Details of a corresponding order constitute the substance of the chapters just referred to. The aim in the author's mind is made plain again by the opening sentences of chap. iv, "On the budgets of estates in general, and particularly of agricultural lands in three classes, and how such budget is to be constructed, according to the amount of seed furnished or otherwise." Thus:

As Columella observed of his own time, that all sciences, such as military service, scholarship, commerce, building, nautical art, even music, dancing, and such things, have their own guides and teachers, yet agriculture has neither pupils nor teachers. The same holds of our time. It consequently comes about that the minority take occasion to think for themselves, but whoever lives in the country, or has an estate of his own, follows the custom of the majority, and what is still wiser, if a specially good manager is in the locality, the rest observe and try to imitate him.

The passage goes on to say that doing the same thing which the good manager does may not really be doing the same thing; because there is a failure to note the different circumstances of adjacent tracts, and to conform treatment to the varying conditions. Thereupon follows an attempt to analyze classes of soil and to show the processes of culture appropriate to each. The following one hundred and forty pages contain abundant evidence that technical and social administration of rural communities was at this time a highly developed and conventionalized art, but at the same time it was an art consisting of aggregated rule-of-thumb practice. It had no secure basis in fundamental principles.

The chief difference between the first ten and the remaining twelve chapters of the book is not in the method of treatment but rather in the fact that the former deal with technique of more strictly private management, while the latter belong to a larger degree in the realm of public management. In either case the author's effort is to describe actual administrative practice. He has before his mind the private or public functionary, and he tries to schedule the kinds of information which proprietors or managers of farms, or civic functionaries of various grades, from bureau clerks up to the prince, would have occasion to use in their respective positions. All this was *Oeconomie*, as Gasser interpreted the term. It had the same relation to pure economics, as we understand the term today, which instruction in the technique of operating a gas plant or an electric street-railway or a telephone exchange would have to foundations of economic theory.

In order to get at the full significance of the cameralistic foundations at Halle and Franckfurt a. O.[1] the writings of Thomasius would have to be more carefully examined. As our space forbids this, we may merely call attention in passing to another important factor in the movement, Ludewig,

[1] *Vide* below on Dithmar, pp. 222 ff.

professor of law and chancellor of the University of Halle.

On the occasion of the establishment of the new professorship Ludewig wrote a quaint little book of 166 pages, explaining and praising the king's purpose. The tract is a document of firstrate importance as evidence sustaining our main thesis about the center of interest in the whole cameralistic period.[1] Indeed, excess of cynicism could not justly be charged if one should conclude that for reasons of his own the writer had seized the opportunity rather for laudation of the régime of Friedrich Wilhelm I than to promote cameralistic science. At all events, the monograph is vivid confirmation of our diagnosis of cameralism as fiscalism.[2]

The essay seems to ignore the promise of the title-page until forty-five of its fifty-six sections (one hundred and thirty out of one hundred and sixty-six pages) are completed. The argument begins with citation of the alleged dictum of the Persian King Cyrus, "A select army and good management [*Wirthschafft*] of the subjects[3] are the two chief and surest means of making a people rich and a land permanently happy." The authority of Socrates, reinforced by Xenophon, is inserted along with that of Cyrus, "although they were heathen who

[1] *Vide* above, p. 6.

[2] *Die, von Sr. Königlichen Majestät, unserm allergnädigsten Könige, auf Dero Universität Halle, am 14 Juli 1727, Neu angerichtete Profession, in Oeconomie, Policey, und Cammer-Sachen wird, nebst Vorstellung einiger Stücke verbesserter Kön. Preussl. Policey, bekannt gemachet von dem zeitigem Prorectore, Joh. Peter von Ludewig, Ict. Universitäts-Cantzlern. . . . .* 1727.

[3] It is impossible to decide from the context whether Ludewig clearly chose between the subjective and the objective force of his genitive: i. e., whether his thought was "on the part of the subjects" or "over the subjects." From the succeeding discussion it appears that the two aspects of the case were hardly differentiated in his mind, although the emphasis falls heavily on management by the ruler.

must somehow have obtained divine enlightenment," to sustain this argument. Then follows, largely as an interpretation of Columella, a justification of the dictum, chiefly on its economic side, from the experience of the Romans, including the Eastern emperors. As a transition to the immediate application of the theme, Ludewig remarks (§9) that it is very difficult to find in ancient or modern history a ruler who is equally great in war and in promotion of management (*Wirtschaft*). Possibly Henry IV of France is one of the few exceptions. After reciting at some length illustrations of that monarch's wisdom and prudence, Ludewig continues:

> But why should we pause so long upon a foreign and past example? Through a brave and wise king, God has placed this truth before the eyes of our own times and subjects (*sic*). Wherefore we could and should daily admire, honor and thank the perfect [*grundgüten*] God, for such a blessed government of his anointed. So long as the world has stood, as may easily be proved from the authentic history of all realms, no region of the earth has seen an army to be compared with that of Prussia, etc., etc. (§10).

Having continued this eulogy in some detail, Ludewig specifies and partially describes in turn, as items in the excellence of the Prussian system:

the administration of charity (§14); the workhouses and penal institutions (§15); the homes for veterans (§16); medical and sanitary institutions (§17); colonies (§18); the establishment of many industries, and regulation of the same (§§19–24); settlement of boundary disputes (§25); redemption of waste lands (§26); construction of water-ways (§27); development of salt works (§28); profitable farming of certain royal prerogatives (§29); selection of capable young men as subordinates in administrative offices (§30); written ordinances and laws for all functionaries (§31); revision and promulgation of the code of private law (§32); standardizing of weights and measures (§33); transformation of feudal tenures into complete property (§34); introduction of money commutation for cavalry service (§35); removal of capitation, property and other taxes (§36);

reforms of the currency (§37); establishment of the office of comptroller (§38); careful signing of royal decrees (§39); administration of justice and expediting of legal processes (§40); consequent improvement of the royal finances (§41); simplification of ceremonial (§42).

Without notice of transition from eulogy to exhortation, Ludewig ventures to offer three cautious suggestions, viz.:

That it would be well for the government to provide administrative, and especially the *Policey*, bureaus with national and special maps and diagrams visualizing the conditions of the country at large, and, in more detail, of the respective administrative divisions (§43); that certain feudal burdens should be removed (§44); that the military and fiscal administration should in certain features be reorganized (§45).

After this introduction, which occupies more than three times the space reserved for the ostensible purpose of the discourse, Ludewig turns to the supposed theme of the monograph in this way:

But this should be enough about the details of good *Oeconomie* and *Policey*, which by divine grace and blessing are daily before our eyes in these lands. And as we have rendered ourselves liable to all sorts of perverse judgments about this writing, which flowed so easily from our pen and good heart, we will now set forth the motives for the same, instead of offering excuses. For since his royal majesty, our most gracious king and lord, in founding at Halle a new professorship of *Oeconomie, Policey und Cammersachen*, was, so far as I know, the first in the learned world to take such a step; and since he most graciously decreed that the intention and use of the same should be made public; I have believed that neither the new *Oeconomie-Professor* could receive a greater impulse to his labor nor the students and apprentices [*Lehrlinge*] greater zeal for such courses, than if they should turn their thoughts especially in aforesaid *Cameral, Policey und Oeconomie-Lehren*, to the example of the great and wise founder, in his kingdom, provinces, and lands; if they should enlarge upon what I have said, and correct that in which I have been in error, and especially if they should add the larger part which I have been obliged to leave untouched. Besides this, I must call to mind that, along with my administrative duties, the founder of our *Friedrichs-Universität* conferred upon me, along with the professorship of history, the calling of a royal historiographer, in which capacity I felt a strong impulse to use the present occasion for a contribution to *einer Oeconomie- und Policey-Historie*. And as a matter of fact great lords may well be pitied for the money and appointments which they bestow upon *historiographos*. The latter either use their salary for their own enjoyment in learned idleness, or, if they do any work, fall upon obsolete times and forget their founder. . . . . This may be partly, indeed, because the archives are closed to them. . . . . Another extenuating item is that if the historian happens to make a mistake about current affairs, certain people at once seize the opportunity to discredit him at court. Moreover, if anything is written about recent times, it is mostly about wars and rumors of wars, and the great deeds at home [*zu Hauss und im Lande*] are seldom mentioned. Finally, it is urged by the unintelligent that there is no use in writing down what is known to everybody in the land. These do not consider that subsequent times consume and erase the preceding, and that what is now before our eyes and in our hands fifty years hence will have become a secret and forgotten, if not made a part of history. Such being the case, great lords are unfortunate to labor only to be forgotten, and the praiseworthy, wise and tireless princes who have done so much good for their lands and peoples, and have left to good successors so many examples, have no advantages over worthless rulers. . . . . (Sec. 46 elaborates still further the theme, "Make the history of good princes while they are living.")

Sec. 47 goes somewhat more into detail about the developments that led to the new professorship, but in substance it repeats Gasser's account above (p. 208). Sec. 48 discusses the relation of the new professorship to the chairs of "practical philosophy," "ethics," and "politics." Incidentally this section exhibits in the most explicit way the content of the term *Oeconomie*, as officially sanctioned in Prussia in 1727. Expanding the proposition that, while *Oeconomie* at last belongs within the departments named, yet it requires special attention as a subject by itself, Ludewig says:

It is easy to guess the secret why hitherto professors have taught *Oeconomie* who were in doubt whether to look for ears of corn on trees or in the ground. For the sponsor[1] to whom they refer deals in his economic books almost wholly with the morality of father, mother, children, and servants. As to arable land, meadows, streams, forests, gardens, plants; how to treat cattle in the stall; how to increase the supply of manures; how to brew grain and to sell the product; what a manager has to do and what to leave undone every day in the year; what provisions he must keep in store for fire-protection, for food, in storehouse, in kitchen, and in cellar: of all these things Aristotle has not a syllable. Hence his creatures, the *Oeconomie Professores*, up to the present time, have not concerned themselves with these things, but they have considered themselves masters when they could explain the "commandments" which the children recite. This is the reason why among the hundred philosophical books which treat of *Oeconomia* there is not a wholesome and practical line, and thus this name conceals the greatest fraud.

With this indirect definition of the scope of the new professorship we have the substance of the essay, so far as our purpose is concerned. In writers to be noticed presently we shall find intentional or unintentional echoes of these reflections upon belated Aristotelianism. The points to be noted particularly are, first, that the concept carried by variations of the term *Oeconomica* at that time did not by any means make it identical with the scope of contemporary *Cameralwissenschaft;* second, that the term was equally contrasted with the nineteenth-century term economics and its variations; third, that the foundation of the Prussian professorships of *Oeconomica*, etc., was of less immediate significance, either for cameral science in general or for economic science as we now understand the term, than was assumed by the men directly interested, and even by later writers. The horizon of economics in a compre-

[1] Aristotle.

hensive sense dawned on the view of the Germans in a way somewhat parallel with that by which the sociological outlook in our time has widened from attention to certain remedial problems to survey of the entire social process.[1]

[1] In the two following sections (49, 50) Ludewig discusses the need of more exact terms, and especially the possible substitution of the term *Wirthschaft* or *Haushalterschaft* for *Oeconomie.* The remainder of the essay repays careful analysis as an index of the author's knowledge about the bibliography of the subject. He depends chiefly upon Seckendorff and Rohr, both for general conceptions of the sciences with which the new professorship is to deal and for clues to other writers. He is sufficiently explicit that the men who understand *Wirthschaft*, as distinguished from the commentators upon Aristotle, have ignored controversies about mere words and names, and have written some good books about all kinds of practical management.

CHAPTER X

THE CAMERALISTICS OF DITHMAR

Justus Christoph Dithmar was born March 13, 1677, and died on the anniversary of his birth in 1737. We need to know of his personality simply that he was professor of history, then of *Natur- und Völkerrecht*, at Frankfurt a. O., and was designated to the chair at Frankfurt corresponding to that of Gasser, practically at the same time with the appointment of the latter. Both began their new duties October, 1727. Roscher remarks:

While Gasser took his point of departure from jurisprudence, Dithmar passed from history to cameral science. It may be due to this circumstance that he (Dithmar) is as far behind his colleague in practical economic insight as he is superior to him in general culture[1] (p. 431).

The two books which bear their names being taken as the sole basis of comparison, Roscher is justified in his estimate of the relative merits of Gasser and Dithmar. Roscher is clearly in error, however, both when he says that the division into "*Oeconomie, Polizei- und Cameralwissenschaft*" originates with Dithmar, and when he credits him with the distinction between the "*land- und stadtwirthschaftliche Zweige der Volkswirthschaft.*" Both divisions are discoverable in Gasser.[2] The latter is plainly formulated by Rohr.[3] It is true that Dithmar is the first to use these distinctions as titles for subdivision of a cameralistic syllabus.[4] Inama seems to have

[1] This is merely Roscher's surmise. I have ventured (below, p. 229) to locate the differences between them a little farther back.

[2] The former is implied, not quite precisely, in the title-page; the latter is in chap. ii, in the subdivision of rural and town economy in building.

[3] *Vide* above, p. 188.

[4] *All. d. Bib., in loc.*

repeated Roscher on these points, without examining the evidence. Neither seems to have noticed that Stisser confidently attributes to P. Fischer the distinction between *Land* and *Stadt Wirthschaft.*[1]

Although Gasser and Dithmar began the work of their cameralistic professorships simultaneously, the latter does not find it necessary to imitate the former in an apology for delay in publishing on this subject. The book which appeared four years after he assumed his new duties is a mere skeleton of academic lectures.[2] In the Preface he gives virtually the same account of the king's purpose in establishing the professorship which we have already drawn from Gasser and Ludewig with reference to Halle. Dithmar speaks in much more terse and confident terms. He takes it for granted that since "the welfare, power, and repute of a state rest on a well-ordered economic, police, and cameral system," and since people versed in statecraft have long wished that studious

[1] *Einleitung*, 1. Abth., §10. *Vide* below, pp. 238 ff.

[2] *Hn. Just. Christoph Dithmars, des Natur und Völkerrechts, wie auch der Geschichte und öconomischen Wissenschaften vormahligen offentlichen Lehrers und der königl. preussischen Academie der Wissenschaften zu Berlin Mitgleides, Einleitung in die öconomischen, Policey- und cameral-Wissenschaften. Nebst Verzeichniss eines zu solchen Wissenschaften dienlichen Büchervorrathes und ausführlichem Register. Mit neuen Anmerkungen um Gebrauch öconomischer Vorlesungen vermehret und verbessert von D. Daniel Gottfried Schreber.* Fünfte Ausgabe. . . . . 1755. With bibliography and index, pp. 328. According to Inama (*op. cit.*) editions of this book were published in 1731, 1740, 1745, 1748, 1755, and 1768. The author's preface to the first edition was dated "16. Nov. 1731." I have used only this fifth edition, whose preface is dated Halle, September 24, 1755. Of Schreber, the editor, Roscher says: ". . . . the Leipzig Professor of *Oeconomie, Polizei- und Cameralwissenschaft* (1708–77), whose botanical knowledge was valued by Linnaeus, and who showed historical sense in his chief work: *Abhandlung von Cammergütern und Einkünften, deren Verpachtung und Administration* (1743, II. Aufl., 1754)."

youth might be introduced to these subjects before entering the employment of the state, the king's action in providing such instruction settles the matter, so far as the academic rights of the professorship are concerned.

It is more notable that Dithmar says, "since no introduction to such sciences existed." This is a significant reflection upon Gasser, not to mention the earlier writers whom we have noticed. It goes far as a sign that Dithmar perceived the provincialism of previous writers, and had a broader conception than they had shown of the necessary scope of cameralistic theory. He confesses that his Part IV on *Policey-Wissenschaft* takes the police ordinances of Prussia as the material to be explained, with certain notable features of the civil law of other states.

Schreber's Preface to the fifth edition is in some respects more instructive for our purposes than the book itself. The editor says that he has been careful merely to correct the text and to insert such brief notes as would menace neither the size of the book nor the publisher's price. He used Dithmar's book as the basis of his own lectures, probably first at Halle, later at Butzow, then at Leipzig (*vide* Stieda, p. 38). His estimate of the book is expressed in the judgment:

> To the sainted author belongs this honor, viz.: Of the study which he undertook to teach, the mistaken opinion prevailed, that it could not be compressed into certain fundamental theorems, and could not be taught in universities; yet he was a path-breaker in the subject, and he showed, not only that both things were possible, but that they were useful. In spite of its faults, his introduction retains the value of the most convenient reading book on the sciences of which it treats, and is used in various, including Catholic universities.

Schreber continues:

> I do not deny that since the book first saw the light we have had more profound and elaborate introductions to the cameral sciences. . . . . I know the writings of a Gasser, Zschackwitz, Stisser, Hof-

mann,[1] Justi, and others, and I would not detract in the least from the credit due either to them or to the eminent merits of Herrn Hofraths Zink (*sic*), who was the first to go deepest into these sciences, when I nevertheless declare Dithmar's *Einleitung* the most available of all for the purposes of academic lectures.

Schreber states that the day before writing the Preface he had for the third time completed in a half-year the course in which he used Dithmar's *Einleitung* as a syllabus, and he had found no other book with which he could cover the ground in the same time. The technical aims of his instruction appear in his explanation of his pedagogical method. He kept in mind the training of clerks for bureaus.[2] He closes with the advice: "To those who desire detailed instruction in *Kaufmannswissenschaft*, either Lau's *Entwurf wohleingerichteter*

[1] Of G. A. Hoffman, Roscher says (p. 436): "His *Klugheit Haus zu halten oder Prudentia oeconomica vulgaris* (IV, 1730–49) purports to treat systematically all *Wirthschaftslehre*. It pays attention more, however, to the physico-chemical than to the police aspects." I have not seen this work, and it does not seem possible that Schreber could have seen the first edition of Justi's *Staatswirthschaft*, which was published the same year this preface was written. Of Stisser I shall speak below (pp. 238 ff.). I do not think it probable that Schreber referred to Johann Adolph Hoffman, whose book, *Politische Anmerkungen über die wahre und falsche Staatskunst*, was published in Latin in 1718, and a German version by the author in 1725. (*Vide* Roscher, p. 380.)

[2] After explaining that he put before his students all the writers on the subjects in question, he adds: "Sodann lege ich bey denen Theilen wo practische Ausarbeitungen zur Erläuterung nöthig sind, nach vorausgeschickten Grundsätzen, meinen Zuhörern theils selbst entworfene Muster, theils Auszüge aus ergangenen cameral-Acten, Amtsbücher, Manuale und Rechnungen, Anschläge, Steuercatastra, Cammer-Etats, tabellarische Stadt- und Landbeschreibungen, Commercientabellen, Kaufmannsbücher und dergleichen *Schemata* vor die Augen, wobey sie zugleich, wie Tabellen ordentlich zu verfertigen sind, angeführet werden, wovon ich den Nutzen bey meinen ehemaligen Expeditionen einzusehen Gelegenheit genug gehabt, etc."

Negotien, or another system, about to appear in print, is recommended."[1]

Of the syllabus itself little can be said without going into the technical details by means of which comparisons might be possible with those presented by earlier and later writers. Such comparisons are excluded from our plan. In general it may be noted that Dithmar furnishes abundant evidence that analysis of the relations concerned was becoming both more objective and more systematic. The scientific plane which author and editor had reached may be indicated by a few citations.

The first section proposes the following definition:

Economic science (*die Oeconomische Wissenschaft, oder Hausswirthschafts- und Hausshaltungskunst*) teaches how, through proper rural and city occupations, support and riches may be gained for the promotion of temporal happiness.

The editor adds the following leading propositions:

Economic science is not an art.[2]

The purpose of this science does not end with attaining, but extends to preserving and applying, temporal income.

The difference between general and special *Oeconomie* must here be shown.

It should be observed that the definition, and apparently the editor's comments, put the subject of *Oeconomie* quite distinctly on the side of private interests. The public aspects of *Oeconomie* appeared to Dithmar rather under the other two divisions of his subject.

After admitting that opinions differ greatly about *Policeywissenschaft*, Dithmar expresses his own view in this form.

It teaches how the internal and external nature [*Wesen*] of a state is to be maintained, with a view to general happiness [*allge-*

[1] The reference may have been to Darjes, or Justi.

[2] But the suffix *Kunst* was used with great freedom not only by Dithmar in the formula above quoted but by a long line of successors.

meine Glückseligkeit], in good condition and order, and accordingly that the supreme magistracy of the country must have a care that their subjects shall not only be kept in good numbers, God-fearing, Christian, honorable, and healthy life and conduct, and that their support and surplus of temporal goods shall be promoted by flourishing rural and town occupations; but also that a land shall be improved with well-laid-out cities, country districts and towns, and all kept in good condition. Hence *Policeywissenschaft* is a part of *Staatsklugheit*, but it can be taught conveniently with the economic and cameral sciences, on account of its close connections with both (§§viii, ix).

Dithmar's definition of *Cameralwissenschaft* runs:

It teaches how the princely domain and regalian rights [*Regalien*] may be well used, and from them, as well as from the payments [*Prästarionen*] due from subjects, and other public funds, the princely revenues may be raised, improved, and applied for the maintenance of the community [*gemeines Wesen*].

The editor adds:

The difference between *Finanz-* and *Rentwissenschaft* must here be explained (§x).

Dithmar accounts for the neglect of these three important sciences in very nearly the same terms used by Gasser and Rohr,[1] especially in the counts referring to Aristotle and the monks, to the class pride which had relegated knowledge of *Hausshaltungswesen* to the vulgar herd, and he repeats the arguments that all three of these sciences consist of details which must be learned by practice, or by association with experts. Dithmar contends stoutly that the principles of these sciences may be taught to advantage in the universities, while he recommends observation of actual practice in the fields which they severally occupy (§xvi).

Having compressed his main propositions on these general relations into the brief space of twenty-four pages, Dithmar

[1] *Vide* above, pp. 209 ff.

proceeds with the subject of *Landöconomie*. His emphasis is less on the side of manual operation than Gasser's, and more on managerial technique. In his way, he restricts himself as closely to technical details as his predecessor. This remark applies also to Part III, "*Von der Stadtöconomie*." This *Wissenschaft* is said to teach "how, through the occupations of citizens, sustenance and riches may be gained for the happiness of each and of the whole." It would be easy to point out curious combinations between the "science" so marked off and the *Policeywissenschaft* of the same system, but it is enough to remark that these pioneers were not yet much troubled about consistency of classification. They were chiefly concerned with concrete particulars. Dithmar defines cities as "those societies which have *Stadt- und Bürgerrecht*, and are authorized to carry on city occupations [*Stadtgewerbe*] or pursuits that furnish support for citizens" [*bürgerliche Nahrungen*] (§i). The analysis deals consequently with the actual situations only, without attempting anything more fundamental than description of existing urban arrangements.

In the introduction to Part IV, on *Policeywissenschaft*, Dithmar says:

> The *Policey* is grounded in civic society, in consequence of which it is competent for the ruling prince to control the conduct and affairs of his subjects, for the maintenance of the community [*gemeinen Wesens*] (§v).

He continues:

> *Policey* may rightly be called the life and soul of a state, and the importance of *Policeywissenschaft* is therewith evident. The more the grievance that the same has been neglected! In the Middle Ages the Romish clergy were at fault for this. For their purposes good *Policey* was not desirable, and consequently *Policeywissenschaft* was suppressed by them along with other disciplines (§vi). In modern times there is no lack of political books, but little about *Policeywissenschaft* is to be found in them, without doubt because economic

and cameral sciences are lacking, with which *Policeywissenschaft* is closely connected (§vii). Such science is to be gained by knowledge of the police systems of ancient and modern states; by meditation upon what might be good for a state in view of its circumstances; by associating with experts in police affairs; and by personal experience (§§viii, ix).

Instead of attempting to pass upon the value of Dithmar's specific views in this connection, we shall allow Justi to stand for this part of the cameralistic system.[1]

Dithmar again indicates his conception of *Cameralwissenschaft*[2] in the proposition (p. 242):

It teaches how the revenues of the reigning prince may be raised, from time to time augmented, and so applied to maintenance of the community [*gemeinen Wesens*] that a surplus may remain annually.

As a mere outline of the subjects which belong under this head, the syllabus puts its author in wholly respectable comparison with Justi. Of course it is impossible to compare his knowledge of details with that of the later writer.[3]

On the whole Dithmar must be regarded as in certain very important respects more typical than Justi of German cameralistic scholarship at the middle of the eighteenth century. He represents both its weakness and its strength. The stage of evolution through which this division of German social science was passing may be characterized as a struggle for emancipation from a-priori, deductive methodology, into the freedom

[1] *Vide* below, pp. 436 ff.

[2] In a note Dithmar gives the earliest explanation of the origin of the term which I have found in the textbooks, viz., "The science has its names from the word *Camera*, by which, according to the idiom of the Middle Ages, the place was designated in which the revenues of the reigning prince were guarded." He refers to "du Fresne, glos. v. camera." *Vide* Zincke, below, pp. 232 ff.

[3] On the use of Dithmar's book as a text by Ickstatt, at Ingolstadt, 1746, *vide* Stieda, *op. cit.*, p. 241; also by Thom in Giessen, 1757, *ibid.*, p. 153.

of empirical, telic discovery. Dithmar was evidently much more conscientious in every way than Justi. He was extremely respectful toward the past. He was cautious about encouraging innovations. He was the first of the cameralists to present a respectably classified bibliography of the subjects which they treat;[1] and the groups of writers scheduled, ranging from Xenophon, Geoponica, Cato, Varro, Vergil, and a score of other writers on agriculture, to his immediate contemporaries, on subjects which were creating a new literature, vividly reflect the unconscious adjustment that was going forward between authority on the one hand and observation and analysis on the other. Dithmar has fortified the text of his little book with more references to sources than are to be found in all Justi's writings. Still further, there is a perceptible contrast between his mental attitude and that of the legalistic publicists who had no way of determining how to drain a swamp or work a vein of ore, unless a precedent could be found in the law books. On the other hand, Dithmar was no such man of the world as Justi. He could draw upon no such varied experience with affairs. His judgments were those of a scholar rather than of a business man. He was therefore relatively modest and conventional, though evidently intelligent and progressive; while Justi was forceful and self-assertive, partly for the reason that he had a much more restricted historical and literary outlook than Dithmar. The bolder and more aggressive type better visualized the active factors which were expanding administrative theory. The less demonstrative type more fairly represented the form in which the reconstruction was impressing itself upon the universities.[2]

[1] I say this in spite of the fact that there had been many confused lists of books.

[2] A final estimate of Dithmar would have to consider his work as editor and largely as author of the ten numbers of *Oekonomische Fama*, the first German cameralistic journal, 1729. As I have seen none of

these numbers, I must be content to refer to Roscher's account of them (pp. 431, 432). In this connection mention must be made of several men of whose relative merits as cameralistic writers I am not prepared to judge. These are, first, Johann Hermann Fürstenau, 1688–1756, "intrusted with the professorship *Oeconomiae* at the University of Rinteln (*Gründliche Anleitung zu der Haushaltungskunst und denen gehörigen fürnehmsten Schriften, Lemgo*, 1736); second, Andreas Berch, 1711–74, who was not in Germany, to be sure, but was professor of *Oeconomie* at Upsala (an anonymous monograph, 1746, on *Die Art durch die politische Arithmetik die Haushaltung der Länder und Reiche zu erforschen*, and, in 1747, *Einleitung zur allgemeinen Haushaltung, Grundsätze der Policey-Oekonomie- und Kameralwissenschaft*, the latter translated into German, 1763, by the writer about to be named); third, Daniel Gottfried Schreber, 1709–77, "the first to hold a professorship of the economic sciences at Leipzig" (*Abhandlung von Kammergütern und Einkünften, deren Verpachtung und Administration*, 1743, II. Aufl., 1754; *Zwo Schriften von der Geschichte und Nothwendigkeit der Kameralwissenschaften insofern sie als Universitätswissenschaft anzusehen sind: Entwurf von einer zum Nutzen eines Staats zu errichtenden Akademie der ökonomischen Wissenschaften*, 1763). I have been able to see none of the writings of these men. Stieda (*vide* Index) adds important information, particularly about Schreber.

CHAPTER XI

THE CAMERALISTICS OF ZINCKE

No author, in the whole series which this study includes, is more difficult to interpret and appraise than Zincke. The most obvious reasons for this are, first, that he was a somewhat voluminous writer, even if we take into account his cameralistic publications alone. Moreover, his books do much less than is usually the case to throw light upon one another. On the contrary, his variations of terminology and classification from book to book are bewildering. It is hard to decide whether there is consistency and unity in the successive volumes, or whether they are so many distinct trials at a baffling task. In the second place, although Zincke presents his material in highly analyzed form, his style is elusive, and his divisions, subdivisions, and cross-classifications mystify more than they elucidate.

It is also to be said that Roscher has conspicuously failed to place Zincke in his true perspective. While it is necessary to use Roscher in getting back to the facts about the cameralists, he is in this case a stumbling-block as well as a stepping-stone.

From the sketch by Zimmermann,[1] the most salient points in Zincke's checkered career may be summarized as follows:

Georg Heinrich Zincke was born in 1692, and died in 1768. His father was a preacher, and both father and mother seem to have done their best to induce the son to adopt the father's calling. The boy twice interrupted his school career to enter the army. After he had become *Unterofficier* he was captured and taken to France as prisoner of war (1709), but escaped, and went to Jena, ostensibly to study theology, but he gave quite as much attention to the legal sciences. He was made *Master* in 1713, and was allowed to lecture "on German and Latin style, morals and *Gelehrtengeschichte*."

[1] *All. d. Bib., in loc.*

After a short engagement as *Hofmeister* in a family of slight importance, he went to Erfurt, and acquired the right to offer courses and to preach. Presently, "because of love for the law, and a throat trouble," he went to Halle, where he both lectured on his old subjects and attended courses in the legal sciences by Ludewig, Böhmer, Thomasius, etc. In 1720 he received the degree *Dr. juris* at Erfurt. Returning to Halle, he was in turn "*Ordentlicher Advocat; Secretär und Syndicus bei den Coloniegerichten der Pfälzer daselbst, und bei Commissionen in Cammersachen beschäftigt;*" later, "*Fiscal der Kriegs- und Domänenkammer im Saalkreise und im Mansfeldischen, dann wirklicher Commissionsrath und Criminalrath.*" The latter position he retained till 1731, when he was called to Weimar with the rank of *Hofrath*. He gained unusual favor with the *Herzog*, and exerted influence much beyond his proper sphere. Whether this actually injured the *Herzog* and the country, Zimmermann declines to judge. At all events, Zincke made such enemies that a judicial investigation followed, with the result that Zincke was imprisoned for three years.[1] Ill, and weakened by prison life, he was taken up by Herzog Christian in Saalfeld, and after his health was restored he was on his way to take a teacher's position in St. Petersburg when he was persuaded to change his plan and to remain in Leipzig, offering courses in the *Rechts- und Cameralwissenschaften* (1740). Thereupon Zincke developed very influential literary activities. His *Allgemeines ökonomishes Lexicon* (1742) was re-edited in a fifth edition by Volkmann (1780), a sixth by Leich (1800), and Roscher speaks of a seventh in 1820. The scientific reputation which he gained thereby is said by Zimmermann to have been the occasion of his removal to Braunschweig at the end of 1745, to accept an appointment as *Hof- und Kammerrath und ordentlicher Professor der Rechte und Cameralwissenschaften am Collegium Carolinum*, and soon as *Mitcurator* of that institution. In Braunschweig Zincke did not acquire great influence. He was charged with certain functions in the administrative bureaus, and he lectured on *Cameral- und Policeywissenschaft*. The control of the academic administration was entirely in the hands of the "Abt" Jerusalem. Zincke published a criticism of the management in

[1] Roscher has it "nearly six years" (p. 432).

1748, but Jerusalem replied and was sustained by the highest authority. Zincke appears, in consequence of this rebuff, to have abandoned further administrative ambitions. For at least another decade, or till his sixty-seventh year, he continued to be productive as an author.

It is difficult to fix upon an order of treatment which will most clearly represent Zincke's contributions to cameralistic literature. To what has already been said about Roscher's work at this point, we must add that he really dodges the "Zincke problem."[1] He quotes only the earliest and least mature of Zincke's cameralistic books;[2] his reference to the most pretentious of his books is inaccurate, and provokes the suspicion that he knew it only through a catalogue.[3]

We must remark, second, that Roscher's account of Zincke is virtually a description only of the journal which he edited.[4] This emphasis deprives Zincke of his full due. At the same time it calls attention to an important factor in the development of cameralistic theory. Possibly Zincke's influence as editor may have been more effective than the rest of his literary labors. However that may be, his part in the development of cameralistics would be very inadequately represented if we should accept Roscher's showing as sufficient. His account should

[1] Roscher, pp. 432 ff.

[2] *Grundriss einer Einleitung zu der Cameralwissenschaft*, II *Theile*, 1742.

[3] *Anfangsgründe*. *Vide* below, pp. 256 ff. The mere publishers' description, "II, 1755," while technically correct, would hardly have been allowed to stand as a sufficient index of the proportions of the work, if it had been carefully examined. It is nominally in two parts, but each part consists of two considerable volumes. The four volumes contain respectively pp. 806, 1218, 998, and 662+Index 62.

[4] *Leipziger Sammlungen von wirthschaftlichen, Policey- Cammer- und Finanz-Sachen*, of which 184 numbers appeared, 1742–67. As I have seen none of these numbers, I am obliged to depend upon Roscher's testimony with regard to them.

be read by every student of the period.[1] Letting that contribution to the subject count for what it is worth, we must introduce further evidence which at least widens the basis of judgment.

Stieda has presented a much more sympathetic view of Zincke in a compact sketch. A free rendering of the passage will furnish a proper introduction to the later books.[2]

In spite of the fact that he did not reach his aim, for he was never *Professor der Oeconomie*, although he read lectures on this subject at the University of Leipzig from 1740 to 1745, Georg Heinrich Zincke nevetheless belongs in this connection. His views must have had considerable influence upon the further development of the *Wirtschaftswissenschaften* as subject-matter for lectures in universities. In the year 1741 or 1742 he published a *Programm von practischen Collegiis juridico-politico-cameralibus*, the purpose of which was to recommend the lectures which he proposed to give. Since these four sheets met with approval he followed them up, in the year 1742, with a *Grundriss einer Einleitung zu den Cameral-Wissenschaften*. It consisted of two parts. A preliminary discussion dealt with the question how young men should be instructed theoretically in these sciences, and how they might be introduced to the application of them. Zincke had at first the intention of using Dithmar's *Einleitung* as his text, and after the death of the latter negotiations were begun with Zincke, looking to his undertaking, as editor, to bring out a revised edition. For unknown reasons the plan failed. Zincke had come to the conclusion that there were serious gaps in Dithmar's *Einleitung:* e. g., that it omitted too many necessary subjects, that it afforded insufficient explanations to give thorough knowledge, etc. Probably the author himself, if he had lived longer, would have improved the book in these respects. At all events these imperfections made Zincke feel the need of publishing an outline of his own.

[1] *Op. cit.*, pp. 433–41.

[2] Stieda, *op. cit.*, pp. 25 ff. I cite this passage, first, because I have been unable to obtain the two sources to which it refers; and, second, because it coincides with the judgment of Zincke which I had formed from study of his more mature works.

There are but very few, declared Zincke, who at the present time devote themselves with special diligence and with persistent effort to the economic sciences. Most people regard their elementary principles as merely minor considerations. This being the case, there should be a use for the outline. Its aim is the common weal [*das gemeine Beste*], not the advantage of each individual manager. All the doctrines which it presents are connected with the *Policei* or with the public arrangements for support [*Nahrungseinrichtungen*] in a country. In *Kameralwissenschaft* the special relation and purpose of all these doctrines appears in their application to the management [*Wirtschaft*] of the state and of the prince. The total *Polizeiwissenschaft* as a system of management is, however, arranged really with reference to the public and general weal.

It was Zincke's intention to present these sciences in the universities after the following manner. In the first place he would offer every half-year a general fundamental course on the entire science, and second on special portions. Third, he wanted to supply guidance in the application of the science, i. e., a practical course. In the latter it would naturally be impossible to impart to the future official all the technique of economic transactions. Excursions in actual application could be made, however, and the students could be incited to prepare documentary exercises in economic and *Policei* procedure. Zincke had the plan of proposing a subject, of having the same worked up, part by part, through assignments to individuals, and then of having it presented and discussed by the students as a group. In other words, these details show that Zincke was planning essentially the seminar method, and he hoped thereby to make the new subjects particularly attractive. He probably leaned upon Gross, *Entwurf eines mit leichten Kosten zu errichtenden Seminarii oeconomico-politici*.[1]

In the year 1746 Zincke accepted a call as professor and *Kurator* of the newly opened *Kollegium Karolinum* in Braunschweig. With his entrance into the service of Braunschweig-Lüneberg he gave up the realization of the plans contained in the above-mentioned programme. Yet he considered his ideas so important that he hoped they would be generally adopted. Hence in 1746 he returned to them

[1] *Vide* Stieda, *op. cit.*, p. 13.

in the *Leipziger Sammlungen*, which he had begun to publish in 1742. He put them in more general form as *Gedanken und Vorschläge von einem auf Universitäten auf die Cameralwissenschaften einzurichtenden besonderen Collegio Statuum Europae Camerali.*

In this discussion he begins with the explanation of a *Politicus*. He goes back to a concept with which we have become acquainted in connection with Christian Weise.[1] He would not have the word understood to mean a crafty man acting a part to the hurt of his neighbor, but rather a man who possesses the talent, not only in his private station, but also with respect to the common weal, to live justly and wisely. A *Politicus* is thus a statesman. No one can attain this character who is not intelligent about the state and has not carried on political studies. To be sure there are different kinds of knowledge necessary for a chancellor, a civic employee, a minister of war or of finance. All these, however, find something which concerns them in the political sciences. Hence they must in the first place learn the whole in its general principles and rules. Every political function, high or low, has in its affairs a definite relation to the welfare and happiness of the state in general. The state, however, has no other purpose than to improve and perfect all that constitutes the temporal weal of its members. The *Politicus* must learn whatever sciences, talents, and preparation are necessary for the attainment of this purpose.

For this end it is not enough to have the mere knowledge of the laws from the pandects and the theory of civic processes. Rather is it one of the most important and necessary sciences of a *Politicus* to know, in a way that is applicable to practice, how to make a land progressively richer, how to make improvements in the application of the riches to the security and need and convenient life of the members of the state, etc.

The most general theorems and rules of this science are found in the theory of general civic prudence [*allgemeine Staatsklugheit*]. But this great portion of political science needs to be taught much more thoroughly, clearly, and circumstantially than in this general theory. This is done in the *Kameralwissenschaften*, which are composed of *General- und Special-Oekonomie*, of the *Polizeiwissen-*

[1] *Vide* Stieda, pp. 3, 4.

schaft, which is based upon them, and of the science *vom Finanz- und Kammerwesen der Fürsten*.

For further details Zincke refers to his *Grundriss*, in accordance with which he had lectured and intended to continue his lectures. Since however not everybody has the patience in detail, but people rather content themselves with a historical concept and at the same time with other fragments of knowledge in political and civic affairs, that course in general civics is particularly to be desired. He urges, moreover, after he has argued for the study of *Kameralwissenschaft* in general, still another course "*de notitia statuum*," in which, for the sake of general culture, the needs of those shall be supplied who do not purpose to make a career in the departments for which he speaks. He cites Gundling's *Zustand der Europäischen Staaten*, and wishes to add statistics as an enlargement of the study. In this course, which apparently was to have been of a more popular character, the possible and actual condition of a state would be treated, and the relations of the *Policei* and the financial system.

Passing these preliminary and elementary forms of his theory, we must take into account the evidence afforded by Zincke's work upon the second edition of Stisser's *Einleitung*.[1]

Stisser (1689–1739), could be passed over with a few words, if further reference to him were not necessary in order fairly to report Zincke. Stisser was a student of law and philosophy at Jena and Halle and might have gravitated into an academic career if he had not evinced notable administrative talent.

[1] Friedrich Ulrich Stissers, Ehemahligen Fürstl. Braunschweig-Lüneburgl. Amtmanns und nachherigen K. Pr. Krieges- und Domainen-Raths *Einleitung zur Land-Wirthschaft und Policey der Teutschen. Zum Unterricht in Oeconomie- Policey- und Cammer-Wesen eingerichtet. Nunmero aber von neuen übersehen, an vielen Orten verbessert, vermehret und brauchbarer auf Verlangen gemachet, wie auch mit noch mehr Historischen Nachrichten von denen Geschäften und Schriften, auch mit einer neuen Vorrede versehen von D. Georg Heinrich Zincken, Hochfürstl. Braunschweigischen würckl. Hof- und Cammer-Rath, Prof. Juris und Cameralium auf der Universität Helmstädt und des Hochfürstl. Collegii Carolini in Braunschweig Curatore.* . . . . 1746. (First edition, 1735.) Roscher (p. 376) erroneously dates this second edition 1748.

While in practical employment at Jena (1734-35), he was allowed to lecture in the university on the economic sciences, and the *Forst- und Jagd-Wesen der Deutschen.*

Besides the book just mentioned, Stisser published in 1734 *Ein Programma von der Möglichkeit, dass die oekonomischen Wissenschaften in eine Lehrart gebracht werden können, massen ein elendes Vorurteil vormahls auch die grössten Gelehrten von der Unmöglichkeit dieses Vornehmens eingenommen hatte.* In 1737 the work appeared which is rated as the most meritorious of his writings, *Die Forst- und Jagd-Historie der Teutschen.*

It appears from Zincke's testimony that the publication of the two books which marked his professional residence at Jena was the occasion of speedy termination of Stisser's academic career. The book on forestry and hunting was dedicated to the king of Prussia, and that expert in management was so much impressed with the author's knowledge of affairs, as evinced by both this and the *Land-Wirthschaft*, that he called him to Berlin, in order to test his information and judgment orally. As a consequence, Frederich Wilhelm I gave him an appointment at Stettin.[1]

It was Stisser's plan to write a second volume, *Stadt-Wirthschaft*, and a third, *Wirthschaft grosser Herren.* In explaining his relation to Stisser's book, Zincke says (p. 14):

As I began to lecture upon the *Cameral-Wissenschaften* to the students at Leipzig, I looked for a complete hand- and reading-book which would present the subject in brief and systematic form. I found, to be sure, the sainted Herrn Dietmar's *Einleitung*, which surveyed the whole field, but in its special divisions consisted merely of a few scattered observations, with defective fundamental ideas, or none at all, and in many cases employing far too general theorems.

[1] "Krieges- und Domäinen-Rath in der Pommerischen Cammer zu Stettin, mit einem Gehalt von 66 Rthl." Zincke's date for this transfer (1734) is obviously a misprint for 1737. Stisser died two years later, at the age of fifty-one.

The sainted Herrn Stisser's *Einleitung* was in many respects, especially in organization of the material, more according to my taste. It contained more complete conceptions, and united the *Policey-Wesen* with *Oeconomie* in a practical way. At the same time it treated only *Land-Wirthschaft* and *Land-Policey*, and was consequently not complete enough to serve me as an outline of all *Cameral-Wissenschaften*. Beyond that, moreover, I valued highly the practical and still compact arrangement of this little book: yet I was told that it lacked much on the systematic side of pedagogy, that the sainted man was neither a good methodologist nor an adequate philosopher, and that a teacher of these sciences should be both. I was told that certain fundamental ideas might be better defined, and that various of Stisser's particular opinions were not accepted by all specialists in *Wirthschaft* and *Policey*. For these reasons I could not use the book for my purposes. Hence I decided to publish my well-known *Grund-Riss einer Einleitung zu denen Cameral-Wissenschaften*, in two parts, 1742 and 1743. In the first part I presented the general and special principles of the *Land- und Stadt-Wirthschafft* of the Germans, and of *Policey*, with a view to their application by the several *Collegiorum*, and also for pedagogical use. In the second part I presented *die Wirthschafft grosser Herrn oder das Cammer- und Finanz-Wesen*. Yet this was a mere sketch of a much larger work and of a much more complete treatment which would be of no use for beginners. . . . . Before coming to completion of this larger work I fell back upon Stisser's *Einleitung* . . . . which I thought I could make useful for beginners, at least in certain parts of . . . . *Land-Wirthschaft* and *Land-Policey*. . . . .

In his Preface Stisser says that Christianus Thomasius was the first, so far as he knew, to give his hearers a collection of brief propositions, as an accompaniment of his lectures. Then Gentzke, Bierling, Beyer, Gundling, and many others imitated him, including Professor Diethmar at Franckfurt and Herr Hofrat Schmeizel at Halle. Apparently he meant to say that these theorems were in German, for he emphasizes the fact that after some hesitation, he decided to follow the lead of

Thomasius, and present the substance of his teaching "in honest German garb."

After a quaint discussion of the current overvaluation of the advantages to be gained by foreign travel, he urges that Germans may profit most by studying the accumulated practical wisdom of their own country, the ways and means of industrial thrift first of all.

He joins in the discussion of the question why this important subject has had so little attention in the universities, and curiously enough he puts the chief blame on the students. He says they prefer to give their time and money, *Veneri et Baccho*, to learning what would enable them to earn their bread. At all events, they regard it as disgraceful and beneath their dignity to soil themselves with "low-lived economic sciences." Against this prejudice Stisser stoutly maintains:

These sciences are parts of the greatest *Staats-Wissenschaft*, yes the soul in the civic body, and have the special use of showing how a great lord may bring his land and people to prosperity. . . . .

According to Zincke's explanation of his editorial work on Stisser's book, it would be unsafe to pass judgment upon the author, without comparing the original edition. Nothing appears in evidence, however, to show that he was in any way in advance of Gasser in the particular respects with which we are concerned. We may therefore dismiss him from consideration, and turn our attention again directly to Zincke.

The next evidence of Zincke's individual views appears in his modification of the plan of Stisser's book. As he states it in his Preface (pp. 20, 21), this modification consists in presenting "first the *Cammer-Wissenschaften*, then in outlining *Oeconomie* in general, of which the *Land-Wirthschaft und Policey* of the Germans is only a special part." Then Zincke explains that he has assembled "the most general rules of management (*Wirthschafftsregeln*), and has furnished an introduction to the study of *oeconomischen Wissenschafft* itself, in a form which is adequate preparation for these subjects." Certain of the details in the introduction are important way marks for our purpose. Beyond these, the book is devoted entirely to rural management. We should note, however, that Zincke has enriched the book with references to authorities to such an extent that the authors' index fills twenty-four and a half double-column pages. If we had found no evidence of a similar sort in the earlier writers of this group, Zincke's bibliography would alone be enough to demonstrate the absurdity of the tradition which von Mohl repeats in the passage quoted above.[1]

The most significant propositions of the introduction may be epitomized as follows:

The subject of the book is the rural management of the Germans [*Land-Wirthschafft der Teutschen*]. This is a special part of the management [*Wirthschafft*] of this people in general, and this depends to a certain extent upon the whole. It also presupposes various general ideas of *Wirthschafft* and *Hausshaltung* (§1).

The word *Wirthschafft* is sometimes used in a very comprehensive, sometimes in a very restricted, sense. Thus, (*a*) for *Wirthschaffts-Geschäfte* themselves; (*b*) for the ways and means of managing (*Wirthschafften*); (*c*) for a family, considered as managing (*die da wirthschafftet*); (*d*) for *Land-Wirthschafft* in particular; (*e*) for the science and art of understanding one's own or another's management [*Haushaltung*]; (*f*) for the theory and instructions [*Lehre und Anweisung*] which lead to prudent ordering of *Wirthschaffts-Geschäfte*. This last is the meaning which the word has in this book. In the same sense the words *Hauss-Wirthschafft*, *Oeconomie*, and *Hausshaltungskunst* are in common use (§2).

Wirthschaft is thus a practical theory or *Wissenschaft*, in which, according to their wisdom, prudence, and art, almost all learned sciences are applied to proper gainful occupations, to the end that not only necessary and comfortable subsistence, but also a surplus for pleasure or need [*zu Liebes- und Noth-Fällen*], may be gained (§3).

[1] *Vide* pp. 12 ff.

Accordingly *Wirthschafft* in general is a science which teaches prudence in pursuing the callings which provide sustenance and thus justly and prudently not only to gain means of subsistence, but also prudently to hold, expend, and apply the same (§4).

Wirthschafft is variously subdivided: especially into general and special theory; this latter again into *öffentliche Landes-Wirthschafft* and *Privat-Wirthschafft;* or in other words general and special *Policey-Wissenschaft,* which teaches how to order and to promote for their several purposes, through good police laws and institutions, the *Wirthschaffts-Geschäfte* of a country, a city or of an office (§5).

Privat-Wirthschafft teaches how each individual member of civic society may conduct his *Wirthschafft* wisely (§6).

Privat-Wirthschafft is sometimes divided according to the strata and persons that manage (*wirthschafften*), sometimes according to the things which are the objects of management, sometimes according to the basic theorems of the processes concerned, sometimes according to nations (§7).

In the first case we have the *Wirthschafft* (*a*) of princes, rulers, and great lords, with their *Cammer- und Staats-Revenues,* i. e., *die Hof- Staats- und Militair-Wirthschafft;* (*b*) of subjects, since peculiar managerial relations spring from the social stratum and circumstances. These are consequently peculiar rules of *Wirthschafft* for (1) the greater and lesser nobility: (2) soldiers; (3) travelers; (4) citizens of high and low degrees; (5) scholars, at schools, universities, in church, school, and political offices; (6) rural populations of higher and lower degree and peasants; (7) the male sex, e. g., married and single persons, boys, young men, adults, and aged; (8) the female sex, in parallel classes; (9) the poor; (10) the needy; (11) the middle class; (12) the rich; (13) the servant class (§8).

It would be an endless affair to treat of the *Wirthschafft* of each of these strata in detail. Hence, with respect to differences of stratum only the *Haushaltung* und *Wirthschafft* of great lords will be considered. In the theory of *Cammer- Rent- und Finanz-Wesen,* however, their particular maxims will be shown after the basis has been laid in *Oeconomische Policey-Wissenschaft.* And precisely therein consist today the so-called *Cameral-Wissenschafften* in which one learns *Wirthschafft* chiefly with reference to the best common good [*das gemeine Beste*] and for the service of great lords, the *Privat-Wirthschafft* of all others, who live as subjects or as obscure persons, is shown along with the first part of *Oeconomischer Policeywissenschafft* (§9).

Conformably to the objects and transactions of *Wirthschafft*, the same is divided (1) in accordance with the chief branches of business in Europe, into the theory of (*a*) *Land-Wirthschafft*, (*b*) *Stadt-Wirthschafft*, which division was first made by P. Fischer; (2) in respect to the collateral processes (§10).

We may briefly describe *Land-Wirthschafft* as that part of *Wirthschafft* which teaches how one may carry on the cultivation of the earth, both upon and below the surface, especially upon estates and in connection with the appertaining rights, also cattle feeding and particularly cattle raising, so wisely and prudently that one may by appropriate means gain all sorts of profit and advantage, retain the same, and turn it to thrifty application [*hauswirthlich anwenden*] (§13).

Die Wirthschafft consists of various doctrines [*Lehren*]. It contains especially general theoretical and practical theorems, which are final rules. These consist either of fundamental theorems from other sciences, or of fundamental theorems and rules peculiar to *Oeconomia generali*.[1] The former are derived especially from (1) general and special *Rechts-Gelehrsamkeit;* (2) *Natur-Lehre, Chymie, Anatomie*, and *Artzney-Kunst;* (3) *Mathematics*, especially *Rechenkunst, Geometrie, Mechanique*, and *Baukunst;* (4) general *Staats- und Privat-Klugheit* (§14).

Die Wirthschafft consists further (2) of special theorems and rules pertaining to the chief objects and transactions of *Land- und Stadt-Wirthschafft*, to their auxiliary transactions, and to the *Wirthschafft* of this and that sort of persons. Here we present the theorems about the principal and subsidiary phases of *Land-Wirthschafft* and about the persons engaged in the same. This belongs under the head *Specialia* (§15).

[1] Zincke remarks in a note, "These have been presented best by Hr. Lic. Hofmann in his first book, *Klugheit Haus zu halten.*" This is G. A. Hoffmann. The remainder of the title of the book is: *oder prudentia oeconomica vulgaris;* 4 vols., 1730–49. *Vide* Roscher, p. 436.

Finally belong to *Wirthschafft* (3) *Singularia* or the most particular observations and devices. Moreover we must mention (4) the *Wirthschaffts-Termini* or *Kunst-Wörter*, *Redens-Arten*, and explanations of the same[1] (§16).

Die Wirthschafft varies also with respect to nations or peoples, and it is certain that the former [*Wirthschafft*] varies as widely as the latter, their soil and climate. Not to speak of the uncivilized peoples outside of Europe, the *Land- und Stadt-Wirthschafft* of the civilized Europeans, for example of the French, Spanish, Italians, English, Dutch, Poles, Swedes, etc., differs, in respect to very many *Wirthschaffts-Geschäften*, especially in respect to particular arrangements, purposes, and objects, from that of the Germans, and indeed the latter varies not only by contrast between the ancient and the modern, but also by contrasts between the various German peoples and localities at present. Thus there are the differences between the *Ober-Sachsen, der Nieder-Sachsen, der Schwaben, der Schweitzer*, etc. Herr von Rohr accordingly, and not without reason, made a plea for more information and cultivation of *oeconomia harmonica*.[2] Meanwhile it is the duty of Germans to pay special attention to the most common features of the *Wirthschafft* of Germans, and to under-

[1] The bibliography of this part of the subject, as cited by Zincke, is notable: viz., "(1) *Das Cheminizische Oeconomische Lexicon*, new ed., Nürnberg, 1746; (2) Chommel *Diction. Oeconomique;* (3) *Das allgemeine Oeconomische Lexic.*, so vormahls schon bey Gleditschen in Leipzig herausgekommen, *an.* 1744, aber von mir dem jezgen *Editore* dieser *Einleitung*, vermehret und verbessert herausgegeben worden; (4) Savery, *Lexic. de Commerce*, ed. n.; (5) Das bey Heinsio in Leipzig edirte Handels-Lexic. *sub. Tit. Allgemeine Schatz-Cammer der Kaufmannschaff*, in 4 Theilen und einem Supplem., ed. *in fol.*, 1741; (6) Beiers, *Allgemeines Handlungs- Kunst- Berg- und Handwercks-Lexic.*, von D. Struben *ed. in* 4to, *an.* 1722; (7) Das in Berlin von einem Gliede der Societät der Wissenschaften herausgekommene *Real-Lexicon der Wissenschaften;* (8) Das bey Gleditschen herausgekommene *Natur- Berg- Gewerck- und Handlungs-Lex.;* (9) *Minerophili Berg-Wercks-Lexicon;* (10) Mein D. Zinckens *Manufactur- und Handwercks-Lexic.*, so jetzt unter der Presse und von Fuchsen allhier ediret wird."

[2] In his *Hausshaltungs-Bibliothek*, ed. 1726, p. 129. *Vide* also Hrn. von Hohberg, *Adlichen Land-Wirthschafft* (Zincke).

stand it according to the manner, customs, usages, laws, and civic organization of their own country. This book is specially devoted to that purpose (§17).

This passage is at once symptomatic of the whole cameralistic conception of economic problems, and it is a rather exceptionally clear and unequivocal expression of the conception. It is thus one of the crucial exhibits in the body of evidence which sustains one of the principal contentions of our argument: viz., the theories of the cameralists were formulations of different sorts of utility with reference to relatively parochial aims. They were not attempted generalizations of universal economic or civic relations, because universal relations of these orders had not roused their attention or interest in an appreciable degree. They were virtually attempts to answer the question: "Situated as we are, and being what we are, individually and politically, how can we use our opportunities so as most to further our particular purposes?" A stage of experience characterized by this range of generalization must be taken for granted, and accepted just as it was. We turn the reality of experience into myth and fable if we interpret back into such intermediate experience the states of mind which emerged at later stages. In brief, we must interpret the cameralists as they were, not as nineteenth-century economists. We do not satisfy this requirement merely by pointing out that their conclusions differed from those of nineteenth-century economists. That way of stating it covers up and compromises the crucial distinction. In an essential sense, *the cameralists were not concerned about the same problems that engaged the nineteenth-century political economists.* This experience of the cameralists has value for modern men; and historical scholars must find and utilize the value. The experience has been shorn of its value by growth of a tradition which vitiates our interpretation in advance by ignoring the radical contrast between the Smithian and the pre-Smithian attitude of mind toward economic relations. The introduction continues:

Whoever would thoroughly learn *Wirthschafft* in the special department of *Policey- und Cammer-Wesens* must gain the knowledge through instruction and experience. The instruction must consist in part of coherent oral discourse upon *Wirthschafft* as a whole, and afterward upon a portion of the same upon which one proposes to place the chief emphasis; in part through oral instructions incidental to practice itself, and through association with experienced *Hauss-wirthen*, and in part through the reading of good *Wirthschaffts-Bücher* (§18).

Whoever will thus study *Wirthschafft* must have learned previously (1) to write and reckon well; (2) to form a good concept; and the rudiments of (3) *der Moral;* (4) *Natur-Lehre und Historiam naturalem;* (5) *die Chymie;* (6) *die Geometriam, architecturam civilem*, and especially *die Mechanique;* (7) something of *Medicin;* (8) something of the laws. Before all things, however, one must attempt, through the grace of God, to put oneself in the situation in which one can actually exercise the first general *Wirthschaffts-Regel* of the Christians: "Seek ye first the Kingdom of God and his righteousness, and all these things shall be added unto you" (§19).

Beyond this, all depends (1) on very careful consideration and investigation of the *wirthschafftlichen Objecte, Zwecke und besonderer Geschäfte*, and especially upon understanding and choice of the persons concerned: through all this, moreover, upon cautious decisions in *wirthschafftlichen Dingen;* (2) upon a diligent, careful, energetic, and industrious carrying-out of the precepts and applications in general, to the end of gaining good returns from the occupation, of caring well for them through frugality and watchfulness, without greed. Finally, upon applying to those ends all temporal means according to God's law and according to *wirthschafftlichen Klugheit*, and especially upon so ordering outlays that an annual surplus will remain (§20).

We now return to Zincke's own books. Most important for our purpose is, first, the *Cameralisten-Bibliothek*.[1]

[1] D. Georg Heinrich Zinckens, Herzogl. Braunschw. wirckl. Hof- und Cammer-Raths, etc., *Cameralisten Bibliothek, Worinne nebst der*

A general description of these compact little volumes would afford but a vague idea of their contents. It will not be possible to present an adequate outline of Zincke's system, because that would require as much space as can be given to the author who may on the whole most fairly be taken as an epitome of cameralism, viz., Justi. To differentiate Zincke's system from Justi's, it would be necessary to go into comparison of technical details in the two authors; and that would be foreign to our purpose. Without attempting to pass upon the delicate question of the relative merits of the two men, we must confine ourselves here to certain specifications which show that Zincke was among the formative factors in the social science of his period.

Indeed, there are more evident motions in the direction of Smithism, in Zincke's most general methodological observations, than in any other writer in the series. He perceived, in a vague, abortive, fashion to be sure, that the details of cameralistic policy required a center in more fundamental philosophy. His attempts at foundation of such a philosophy are rather pathetic, but on the other hand his contemporaries did not even make the attempt. Whether Zincke actually saw deeper than Gerhard had penetrated cannot be known. At all events he published his ideas much more extensively, and it is plain that his mind was maturing in the direction of such problems

Anleitung die Cameral-Wissenschaft zu lehren und zu lernen, ein vollständiges Verzeichniss der Bücher und Schriften von der Land- und Stadt-Oeconomie, dem Policey- Finanz und Cammer-Wesen zu finden, so theils kurz beurtheilet, theils umständlich vorgestellet worden. Der erste Theil, von der Oeconomie. . . . . 1751 (304 pages); "Zweyter Theil, von der Policey-Wissenschaft, 1751" (270 pages); "Dritter Theil, von der Cammer- und Finanz-Wissenschaft. . . . . 1752" (354 pages); "Vierter und Letzter Theil. Nebst vollständigem gedoppelten Register über alle vier Theile. . . . . 1752" (210 pages). In addition, the authors' index occupies 58 pages, and the subject-index, 36 pages, besides four pages of *errata*.

as Smith afterward proposed. Zincke's place in the cameralistic succession may best be indicated by a few characteristic details.

Zincke was the first German writer, so far as I have been able to discover, to insist strongly upon a sharp distinction between vulgar and learned economic theory. Beginning in the Introduction (pp. 7, 8), and continuing through the classifications in the bibliographies, he tries to show the difference between the folk-lore of familiar occupations, and "learned" theory. His impulse was respectably scientific in its conception. He had not gone very far in his analysis of the kinds of research which would be necessary before "learned" theory could establish a relatively secure base. Zincke maintained valiantly, against the overwhelming academic prejudice of his time, that the subjects properly included within the scope of cameralistics were capable of organization into a group of sciences as methodical and respectable as those which had already won academic recognition.

In supporting this thesis, Zincke argued (pp. 16, 17) that a system of cameralistic science must rest upon applications of doctrines accepted by philosophical, mathematical, legal, and other sciences. "In so far as those theorems are truths established by other sciences, we may take them for granted in cameral science." The list of such truths which he cites as the philosophical antecedents of cameralistic science hardly impresses the modern reader with the solidity of the support, but such as it is we may reduce it to this:

A *means* [*Mittel*] is something in which the sufficient ground is contained through which to reach a given end. We all have a natural longing for welfare. That is an *end* which all men by nature seek. All our lives we strive for this condition, which we call happiness [*Glückseligkeit*]. Progress toward this condition we call temporal happiness, and the things which contribute to it may serve either our bodies or our souls or both. Such things we call our goods. A stock of such temporal goods we call *temporal means* [*Vermögen*].[1] Transactions with these means, or the actual use of the same for the above specified end, we call, in a somewhat narrow sense to be sure, *livelihood* [*Nahrung*].[2]

It need not be argued that the need of using these temporal means for gaining our happiness makes it both the right and the duty both of the individual man and of whole societies, especially of those heads of societies to whom the citizens have intrusted the supreme power over themselves, in order to insure temporal happiness, to apply these means in every proper way to gain the happiness of all. We have then the three most general kinds of transaction in all management [*Wirthschaft*], viz., the gaining, the guarding, and the applying of temporal means. These three kinds of transaction are explained in *General-Oeconomic* (§13).

In the same portion of cameral science this principle will be demonstrated, viz., a prince, as the ruling head of a civic society, whether the same consists of a physical or a moral person, for the maintenance in part of his sovereignty, his house, and his own exalted person, partly the common good [*gemeinen Bestens*] of his state, must strive to gain, keep, and apply a proportional amount of ready means [*bereitestes Vermögen*] (§14).[3]

[1] For reasons already alluded to (*vide* above, p. 76; cf. pp. 367 and 373) and which will appear more fully later, it is necessary to render *Mittel* and *Vermögen* by the same term. We shall have little to do with the former term in the technical sense which Zincke tries to impress upon it, while the latter figures very prominently in the theories that follow. It is necessary to protect it against the unauthorized legal additions forced into it by the rendering "property."

[2] It is impossible to choose a rendering of such terms which can be used consistently even in translating single authors. They vary indefinitely in the usage of the writers in this group (§§10, 11).

[3] One of the incidental questions which this study raises is as to the possible effect of this mere phrase upon the suggestibility of actual rulers during the eighteenth century. The idea of the "readiest" means undoubtedly carried with it the snap judgment of *best* means, and thus one of the impulses was given to exaggeration in practice of the stimulus applied to trade as a producer of national revenue.

The keynote of cameralism is struck by Zincke in the next paragraph:

The more a prince, by observance of this duty, is able to promote his own and his country's welfare and more complete condition (*sic*), the greater will he be. For herein is to be found the true ground of the external greatness of a prince. The greater he becomes, however, the more must he have ready means, and consequently the more must he endeavor to procure, to guard, and to apply the same (§15).

All ready means, and consequently those of a prince, consist of income [*Einkünften*]. Hence there must be *sources* from which it is derived.[1] An irrefutable and indubitable truth is therefore: That a prince is bound [*schuldig und verpflichtet*] to recognize the first general and permanent source of his ready means, and to establish the same upon that source (§16).

Where then is this source to be found? The source of the ready means of the whole human race is well known. Created animate and inanimate nature, especially however the earth with its creatures, its forces, all men themselves, and created things outside of them, are the sources from which they derive everything to be used as means [*Vermögen*].[2] God himself is indeed the first founder of this source, through his wise and beneficent creation, preservation, and care of men. All powers of bodily movement and of the exercise of the soul are to be included in this source. But each individual, and each smaller or larger society, controls only a certain portion of this source of ready means. This control is exercised partly by virtue of the native power of the individual or the society, partly through the two chief natural (*sic*) institutions of the world, namely, property and rulership [*Eigenthum und Herrschaft*]. Accordingly

[1] Zincke uses the French word *fond*, but in apposition with it the German words *Quellen* and *Grund*. The sense is sometimes merely "source" in general; sometimes "fund" in a more special use, and sometimes a close approach to the modern technical concept "capital." Without representing the unstable condition of Zincke's ideas at this point, the term "source" will fairly translate the essential thoughts in this connection.

[2] In this particular passage the author approaches as close as the conceptions of his time would permit to the plain formula, "Nature is the ultimate source of wealth."

no one can bring the whole source under his property or rulership, and it is therefore impossible and consequently foolish to make the attempt (§18).

The portion of the earth controlled by a collection of men must then be the immediate source of their ready means (§19).

Since endeavor after secure and comfortable life has made it necessary for such collections of men to unite their property and powers in the single will of a ruler, and to a certain degree, with respect to these two chief matters, to subject themselves to the same, and thus the concept *state* or *civic society* arises; it follows unquestionably that the immediate source of the ready means of a ruler in general can be no other than his land and people, or so-called *Territorium* (§20).

In order to show the local and temporal shading of this idea in the cameralistic view the next section is translated in full:

I assert with zeal that this is the immediate source of ready means in general. For since lands, and the people in the same, in spite of all this, according to the great law of God respecting the social helpfulness with which human welfare is bound up, are in a certain interdependence, and hence each land and people can and must at the same time make use of the means of another land and people for the welfare of the former, and conversely can and must with its own means and powers help the other land; so one may say that to a certain extent, and in an indirect or distant way, by virtue of this interdependence of lands and peoples, the means and the powers of the same are and must be of assistance as a source of ready means for a ruler over land and people. Moreover one of the most important portions of the cameralistic sciences is that which shows the ways in which other lands may rightly and wisely be made into sources of all sorts of revenues and profits (§21).

Speaking now more precisely, the source of the ready means of a ruler is to be found not merely in land and people, with all their interconnections, but rather in a land and people *placed in a constantly flourishing condition of their means of livelihood.* Hence follows the principle: A prince who would better establish, maintain, and preserve his ready means, must devote all his effort to put his land and people in a constantly more flourishing condition of gaining the means of livelihood, and must thus secure for them increasing prosperity. Accordingly, the more *services*, *things of money value*, *money*, and *credit* increase, the greater and richer is the source and ground of the ready means of a ruler (§23).

Using means of livelihood is called *managing* [*wirthschafften*]. When the produce provides not merely the wants and conveniences of physical life, but also that excess which we call riches, we call it *good management*. If the means of livelihood for a land and people are to be flourishing, good management must prevail among and over them. It follows that the ruler, or those who assist him in these important matters, must have the knowledge necessary to insure good management, and must exert the utmost endeavor to secure the application of this knowledge throughout the land (§23).

This is necessary not only for the sake of promoting good management in the land, and to put the people in the way of ready means, but it is necessary in order to secure the sources of the prince's own ready means (§24).

It follows that a prince needs genuine and skilful cameralists. By this name we mean those who possess fundamental and special knowledge about all or some particular part of those things which are necessary in order that they may assist the prince in maintaining good management in the state (§25).

A land can be put in a flourishing condition of the means of livelihood only through good *Policey-Gesetze und Anstalten*. Whoever would serve the prince well at this point must not only know the existing *Policey-Gesetze*, but he must understand how to invent and introduce such laws and institutions. For this purpose he must also understand the nature and structure of the means of livelihood, or *Wirthschaft*. For the *Policey-Gesetze und Anstalten* have the task of directing and improving the means of livelihood and the management of a people. Hence it follows that the science of making police laws and institutions can neither be learned nor applied without the science and knowledge of management, which is properly called *die Oeconomie* in distinction from *der Oeconomic*, which means the actual application.[1] Whoever, finally, would administer the ready means of rulers, not merely prudently, but in close connection with the constantly improving conditions of livelihood, and with superintendence of the same, which a wise ruler exercises through good police laws and institutions—he must have thorough knowledge of *Oeconomie* and *Policey* (§26).

After rehearsing the argument that all this cannot be left to pure empiricism, but must be reduced to expert knowledge and practice, Zincke compresses his case into this proposition:

Cameral-Wissenschaft is a learned and practical science, first, of inventing, improving, and introducing all sorts of good police laws and institutions drawn from the nature and conditions of the means of livelihood of a land; second, a science partly resting upon *die Oeconomic*, partly upon special rules and maxims which set forth the rights and duties of a ruler, of wisely, prudently, rightly, and skilfully founding, maintaining, increasing, and administering the necessity, comfort, and riches of a land, and at the same time and thereby the ready means needed by the ruler for the good of the state and its ruler (§29).

Zincke explains, half apologetically, that this description, and the book itself, were written not for the learned, but for beginners. He proposes the following as an alternative form:

Cameral-Wissenschaft is a learned and at the same time practical science, having as its object thorough understanding of all means of livelihood and on that ground the introduction of good *Policey*, to the end of rendering useful services to states and rulers in cameral and financial affairs (§30).

Elaborating the idea that *Cameral-Wissenschaft* consists of various *Wissenschaften*, Zincke continues:

[1] But on p. 55 Zincke distinctly defines the word *Oeconomie* as meaning "*die Wirthschaft selbst.*" Again, in the *Anfangsgründe* (I, p. 18), Zincke assigns to the first part of *Cameral-Wissenschaft:* "Die Natur und Beschaffenheit aller Nahrungsgeschäfte insgemein, und besonders deutlich und gründlich zu analysiren und einzusehen. Und diesen Theil nenne ich die *gelehrte Oeconomic.*"

In my *Grundriss* I presented *die Oeconomic* and *Policey-Wissenschaft* in the composite form of *wirthschaftliche Policey-Wissenschaft.* I made *Cameral-Wissenschaft* the first main division, and *Cammer- und Finanzwissenschaft* the second. I have reconsidered, however, and this book will have three main divisions: (1) *Die Oeconomic;* (2) *die Policey-Wissenschaft;* (3) *die Cammer- oder Rent- und Finanz Wissenschaft* (§32).

From the redundant and perplexing variations upon this explanation in the most general part of the work, we abstract only the following items:

Oeconomic attempts to teach the poor how they may advance in means to the middle class, the middle class how they may become rich. *Policey-Wissenschaft* shows not only how to decrease the number of the poor, but also how to promote the interest of all other strata, so that each in its way may enjoy advancing prosperity (p. 60). This does not mean that everybody is to be brought into the middle class, or everybody to be made rich. This is quite as incorrect as the other hateful idea of certain leaches, who teach that all, especially the peasants, should be reduced to the barest necessities of life. It means that all are to be put in the way of gains in prosperity proportioned to the lot of each (pp. 61–63).

The first and most general principle of a good finance system is that the administration shall aim to insure the ready means of the ruler by such arrangements as will at the same time promote the best good of the state. That is, neither (1) the interest of the ruler, nor (2) the interest of the state must be allowed to infringe on the other (pp. 68, 69).

The work as a whole compels the conclusion that Zincke's methodological interests excessively handicapped his cameralistic interests. To use a different figure, his stage machinery is so conspicuous and so intricate that it conceals the play. At the same time it is evident that he was thinking ahead of most of his academic contemporaries. His perceptions were indistinct enough, but his attempt to find a firm basis for cameralistic theory and to organize its parts into a coherent system entitles him to a place with the most intelligent of the series. In one respect he is easily foremost among the cameralists. He published the first bibliography which made a systematic attempt to classify the literature, not merely according to subjects, but according to degrees of scientific merit. He had a code of letters indicating the two main classes of (*a*) "learned," (*b*) "unlearned" books, and in each class the grades, (1) good (2) very good, (3) moderately good, (4) bad, (5) very bad. Besides this gradation, there are numerous quasi-critical and other notes. The bibliography of the first part of *Cameral-Wissenschaft*, or *Oeconomic*, contains 975 titles, of which 295 are on strictly agricultural topics, and 172 more relate to other extractive industries (Part I, pp. 192–304); the second part, "*Policey-Wissenschaft*," contains 502 titles, of which 164 refer to agricultural administration[1] (Part II, pp. 441–565); the third part, "*Cammer- und Finanz-Wissenschaft*," has 570 titles (Part III, pp. 780–916); and in Part IV (pp. 1071–1134). There are 243 bibliographical notes as addenda to specified sections in the body of the work.

At the end of the text (p. 1134), is the devout ascription, which flippant critics might render, to be sure, in a way that would have an appositeness quite undesigned by the author:

"*Gott meinem Schöpfer allein die Ehre.*"

The existence of this bibliographical monument passes into a curious historical problem, when we encounter the contrast presented by the books of Justi and Sonnenfels. We cannot go into the problem here, but must be content with simply calling attention to it.

Passing to Zincke's more elaborate work,[2] we find another

[1] Again attention must be called to the absurdity of the tradition voiced by von Mohl (above, p. 13), in view of this large body of literature on the extractive industries.

[2] D. Georg Heinrich Zinckens *Anfangsgründe der Cameralwissenschaft, worinne dessen Grundriss weiter ausgeführet und verbessert wird. Des Ersten Theils, welcher so wohl die General als Special Land- und*

version of the *Cameral-Wissenschaft*, which however, as the author says (I, p. 7), amounts to the same thing as the formulas quoted above, viz.:

It is a learned and practical science, devoted to thorough understanding of all occupations that procure livelihood, to introducing, in pursuance of this knowledge, good *Policey*, and to making the livelihood of lands increasingly prosperous, to the end however not merely of better establishing, maintaining, and righteously and wisely increasing the ready means of rulers and states, but also, by means of wise income and expenditure, to secure good administration.

The judgment expressed above[1] must explain why it would not be profitable to attempt a digest of this expansion of Zincke's *Grundriss*. The author gives so much space to protestation of what the different branches of cameral science should properly teach, and why, and how, and by what means, and to what ends they should teach it, that it is easy to see how his contemporaries may have lost their patience before they found out whether the science, as he advertised it, actually did any of these things. So far as attention could be held at all at this time by systematized cameralistics, the subject had to be presented with details in the foreground. Very few people cared for the more general methodological settings. Zincke's books give ample evidence of profounder and more comprehensive views of the science than can be credited to Justi. The former, however, was far too cameralistic to win his way very widely with the traditional academicians, while he was much too academic to make a strong impression upon the sort of constituency which was favorable to cameralism. His books cover the whole field of cameralism in a way which

Stadtoconomic (*sic*) *und Policeywissenschaft abhandelt. . . . . Des Zweyten Theils, welche die eigentliche Finanz- und Cammerwissenschaft enthalt*. . . . . Leipzig. . . . . 1755.

[1] *Vide* pp. 252 ff.

was related to the interests of practical cameralists very much as a treatise on the logic of ethics would affect the typical modern legislator. This is not to say that they were on a plane altogether remote from actual application. They contain much, on the contrary, which is at the other extreme of the tediously commonplace; for example, the twenty-three fundamental rules for obtaining "means."[1] As a whole, however, they are emphatically books of and for the study rather than the bureau, and it is not surprising that they failed to make an impression proportioned to their intrinsic worth. As a general proposition, no one engaged directly in any division of the activities which Zincke discusses could fail to be so well informed, or to have such sources of information among his associates in the occupation, that the author's treatment of his interests would seem superfluous. On the other hand, to most of the scholars of the time *Cameral-Wissenschaft* was as much of an impertinence as sociology has seemed to the majority of the same class during the past quarter-century. In the *Vorbericht* to Theil II Zincke seems partly aware of this situation, and to choose his course in spite of it.[2] He declares that he is not writing for the great masters in their subjects, whose pupil he is willing to call himself, nor for those who want a handbook of technical practice, still less for those self-satisfied people who imagine that these subjects are too trivial for their superior minds. He believes that the book will be of use to the students who have listened to his lectures for twenty years, and he also expresses the hope that German rulers, *from whom ministers who disagree with the author do not contrive to keep*

[1] I, pp. 172 ff. *Vide* the nine rules on the relations of occupations to one another (I, 205); the four fundamental rules for *Policey* (I, p. 266); etc. On the other hand, the schedule of 38 "police questions" (I, p. 266) is in spirit and in detail quite typical of the best practical standards of the system.

[2] Especially pp. xiii ff.

the book (*sic!*) will find in it something to approve and apply. Lastly, he speaks as though he had definite expectations that his work would be used as a text by tutors charged with the education of young princes.

To sum up the case for Zincke, one can hardly study the cameralistic sources without astonishment that this writer has been allowed to fall into such an inconspicuous place in the history of German social science. His merit is far above his reputation. His more solid qualities have been obscured by the more brilliant and audacious Justi. There is plenty of internal evidence in the books of the latter that he was both jealous and afraid of Zincke. He might well have been. With all his versatility, his scholarship was not of an order to gain by critical comparison with that of his less showy and apparently less successful contemporary. Stieda has evidently reached a somewhat similar estimate. He is well within bounds when he concludes (p. 31):

Under all the circumstances Zincke seems to have been a very respectable thinker. To be sure he sticks too closely, on the one hand, to details of the particular gainful occupations, and as contrasted with the general principles of national economy he excessively emphasizes *Praxis*. Nevertheless, what he was after was a study of economic relations, and he wanted it to be systematic and thorough. It would surely have been to the advantage of the University of Leipzig, if instead of allowing his migration it had put him in a professorship of the economic sciences, which he would certainly have occupied with all zeal.

In closing his discussion of the economic policy of Frederick the Great, Roscher very aptly remarks:

Whoever would characterize a great general must use, for completing the picture, proportionate details about the qualities of his most important subordinates. Hence something must be said about a group of writers of the second and third rank. . . . .

For the same reason, in order properly to shade our picture

of cameralism in general, we must mention briefly some of the less important writers at the middle of the eighteenth century. First in order, we may name Kottencamp.[1] The most obvious fact about this mere tract of sixty-four pages is that it is a eulogy of Frederick the Great, from the point of view of a military man, to be classed with the similar eulogy of Frederick's father, by Ludewig, speaking as an academician. In the second place, the tract is notable as an apology for the benevolent despot in contrast with the Machiavellian type of prince. Without asking whether Kottencamp understood Machiavelli, we find in him a very graphic sketch of the type of government which cameralistic theory presupposed.[2] If we were confined to this piece of evidence, the picture of the cameralistic régime which could be reconstructed from it would exactly correspond in tone with the account we have thus far given; and there would be more than a suggestion of the main divisions of technical detail which are presented by the text-

[1] *Kurtzer Abriss und wahres Ebenbild eines grossen Fürsten und erhabenen Geistes. Worinnen die allgemeinen Grundlehren der gesunden Staatskunst in natürlicher Ordnung abgehandelt, und mit den neuesten Exempeln der Europäischen Geschichte erläutert seyn. Nebst einigen Anmerkungen über die Lehrsätze Machiavels von der Regierungskunst eines Fürsten, verfasset und entworfen von Christian Friedrich Kottencamp, Auditeur bey dem Königl. Preussis. hochlöbl. Wallravischen Pionnier-Regimente.* . . . 1747.

[2] His subtitles are: "I. Von den verschiedenen Gattungen, und der Gemüths-Art der Fürsten;" "II. Von der verschiedenen Fähigkeit und Arten des Verstandes regierender Fürsten;" "III. Von der Gerechtigkeit, wie, auf welche weise, und wie weit souveraine Fürsten solche gegen ihre Nachbaren und Unterthanen beobachten müssen;" "IV. Wie ein Fürst seinen Staat erhalten und gross werden könne;" "V. Von dem Staatsinteresse, und der Verbindlichkeit der Fürsten in Betracht desselben;" "VI. Von dem Glücke, und dem Einflusse desselben in die Handlungen, und Staatsgeschäfte der Fürsten;" "VII. Ursachen, wodurch die Reiche und Staaten verfallen, und die Fürstenlichen Häuser zu Grunde gehen."

writers with whom we are chiefly concerned. Kottencamp undertakes to show that the principles of true statemanship are equally distant from Machiavellianism on the one hand and from theological ethics on the other. Dismissing at once the assumption that government can be conducted on a prayer-meeting basis, he declares that while "honor, uprightness, and virtue in general must everywhere be bound together with sound politics," yet self-preservation, "which is the natural impulse of all men," is "the plumb-line to which all doctrines of statecraft must conform," and "the actual interests of the state must therefore be placed at the foundation of all civic maxims." "If the precepts of state adopted by cabinets often seem severe, and in outward appearance to insult virtue, they are nevertheless justified by grim necessity in this imperfect human life." It is easy to read between the lines of this essay unrecognized major premises which would in less than a century dictate revolutionary conclusions. In form the monograph rests without question upon the divine-right presupposition. In fact, princes are judged and classified by strictly functional standards.[1] We shall find cumulative evidence of this conflict between old and new standards of value in Justi and Sonnenfels. Men at this time still expressed their belief in princes in terms of divine right. They were already unconsciously learning to form their working estimates of princes by the criterion of their benefit or injury to their states. Kottencamp formulates the first great commandment of statecraft in the precept: "Seek to maintain thyself and thy state, and to promote the best good of thy state."[2] While the first clause was still paramount both in political policy and in political

[1] E. g., p. 19. Still more distinctly, p. 44, "Das wahre Staatsinteresse besteht in den Nutzen, ... aber . . . . dieser Nutze . . . . könne von der Gerechtigkeit auf keine Weise getrennt werden."

[2] "Suche dich und deinen Staat zu erhalten, und deines Staats Beste zu beförden" (p. 19).

philosophy, the great dynamic fact in this period was the gathering force of the second clause. Rulers and their advisers regarded it as the formula of a gratifying incident of absolutism. In the retrospect we can see that it was a revolutionary principle, destined to supplant absolutism.

The prevailing assumption of the universal enmity of states is presented in the essay as a matter of course. "To tell the truth, it is with peoples and states as with the animal kingdom. The stronger overcome the weak, and grow still stronger by devouring them" (p. 20). Therefore, "a prince never transgresses justice if he only restrains his desire to oppress others and to appropriate their powers; and on the other hand has only the purpose of his own preservation in all undertakings against his neighbors" (p. 30).

Turning to principles of government Kottencamp bases political wisdom on three "maxims":

A prince must rule his realm according to its own genius and the disposition [*Gemüthsart*] of the people, and must understand how to stop the sources of all internal unrest and disturbance (p. 33).

Then internal concord provided for the prince has the comparatively easy task of dealing with foreigners. Therefore, second:

A prince must always put himself in such a condition as compared with his neighbor that he is at least his equal in resources and power, or, if this is impossible, that the inequality may be offset by alliances and other arrangements, so that he need not fear destruction or subjugation by his neighbor (p. 34).

In the third place, a prince who would provide against his own fall and the destruction of his realm, must in his prosperity moderate his desires and not covet more than he would be able in a natural manner to protect and permanently retain (p. 37).

The thesis of the second part of the same chapter (iv), on the question, How may a prince become great? is:

The true greatness of princes is inseparable from the prosperity and growth of the fortune and welfare of their lands (p. 39).

To modern republicans such propositions are platitudes. Their historical importance consists in their demonstration that the times were generating essentially republican energies while the absolutistic régime was superficially unquestioned.

Again, Kottencamp voices a deeper political philosophy, rather than the creed of a governing class, when he defines the interest of the state:

The interest of the state . . . . is whatever belongs to the growth, prosperity, and welfare of a state (p. 43).

To be sure, the Germans had not yet fairly entered upon that stage of their political education in which a thoroughly rational content was to be given to the concepts "growth," "prosperity," "welfare," and the like. The meaning of these forms of expression may easily be exaggerated. They may not be taken to mean all that they would suggest to modern men. We argue from them here no more than that men were well on their way toward abandoning the will of the prince as the last norm of political desirability. They were learning to set up more essential popular values as the valid ends of civic action.

A second minor writer of this period is von Loen.[1] Roscher says:

The extent to which at this period (1747) popular feeling had adjusted itself to police guardianship may be seen from M. v. Loen's *Entwurf einer Staatskunst, worin die natürlichsten Mittel entdeckt werden, ein Land mächtig, reich und glücklich zu machen* (1747, III. *Aufl.*, 1751). The author recommends *freedom* as the first means of promoting population, "this essential ground of all the power of the prince and happiness of the state." Freedom is "the true happiness of a state, the most precious possession of man, a part of his life. He cannot be robbed of it without violation of justice and violence to nature" (pp. 3 ff.). Yet according to von Loen

[1] As I have been unable to secure copies of his books, this reference is wholly a quotation from Roscher (p. 441).

much constraint is consistent with this freedom. Tradespeople, for example, "should not be allowed to bring any foreign wares into the country which are unnecessary and useless, and on the other hand drive money out of the country." The manufacture of too much gold and silver and of too much liquor should be forbidden; likewise the founding of too many printing establishments, because "most books are good for nothing, but merely make the common people discontented, turbulent, and confused" (pp. 6 ff.). A marriage bureau should forbid marriages "whenever the parties are not suited to each other" (p. 23). There should be sumptuary laws regulating the costumes of the various social strata (p. 154).

Von Loen died in 1776. His best-known book is the novel, *Graf Rivera, oder der ehrliche Mann am Hofe*. Its motive was the improvement of life at courts.

The third writer to be recalled in this connection is Philippi.[1] This exponent of Prussian civic ideas is of the same general class and type with Kottencamp. He adds nothing to the theory of cameralism, but he is good evidence of the kind of commonplaces which had become orthodox tradition in the quasi-absolutistic states of which cameralism was the theory. Philippi's books contain not a little material which goes much farther than he imagined in throwing light upon details of political opinion as held in Germany at this time. Our limits permit only a few indications of points in his argument. The fundamental proposition is:

Everyone is bound to take care for the improvement of his temporal circumstances and princes especially for the righteous aggrandizement of their states.[2]

The essay calmly takes for granted that the temporal happi-

[1] *Die wahren Mittel zur Vergrösserung eines Staats*, 1753. (166 pp.) This essay is dedicated to Frederick II of Prussia. *Der vergrösserte Staat*, von Johann Albrecht Philippi, Königl. Preussischen Auditeur Finckischen Regiments. . . . . 1759. (372 pp.) Dedicated to the Prince of Prussia.

[2] *Die wahren Mittel*, chap. i.

ness of subjects depends more upon providential care by the prince than upon any other human means, and it is therefore primarily a discussion of this cardinal factor. "The first means of blessing and aggrandizing a state is a good prince." It is also presupposed that there is divine guarantee of good princes in hereditary succession, while there is no such guarantee in an elective monarchy. Next to a good prince, *true and wise counselors and administrators* promote the aggrandizement of a state (chap. ii). Chap. iii begins with a typical formula of the factor of population, viz.:

The great author of the *anti-Machiavelli* says with the greatest justice: "He is not the greatest and most eminent who possesses the most land. If he were, many an owner of agricultural land would outrank a counselor of state, but on the contrary, we may say with certainty that he is the richest prince who has unlimited sovereignty over the most subjects." Accordingly, for the aggrandizement of a state, all legitimate means must be used to maintain a constant increase of the popualtion.[1]

Next in importance for upbuilding a state is the maintenance of armies (chap. iv); after these essentials, important means are freedom of conscience (chap. v), freedom in gainful occupations (*Handel und Wandel*), except possibly to the Jews (chap. vi), promotion of commerce through promotion of agriculture (chap. vii).[2] The remaining chapters on taxation (chap. viii), the judiciary (chap. ix), the treasury (chap. x), the improvement of higher and lower schools (chap. xi), and *Policey* (chap. xii) contain nothing which calls for comment.

The second of the essays mentioned is merely a variation

[1] Here and elsewhere Philippi cites von Loen as conclusive authority.

[2] This part of the argument corroborates our generalization that the traditional accounts of this mercantilist theory are largely fabulous. *Vide* p. 14. Philippi quotes with approval a remark attributed to Pliny: "The more diversified crops a land has, the greater its happiness and wealth."

of the first.[1] The date of the Preface is May 21, 1759. Although, as it proved, the third Silesian war was to drag along nearly four years more, this Prussian militarist wrote in an exultant tone. The second essay may be called an I-told-you-so version of the first. The chapters are the same in number as in the earlier essay with the exception of an added thirteenth in the later, "*Gedanken über die Kameral- und Finanz-Wissenschaft;*" they treat of the same topics; but now the point of view is no longer prospective, it is retrospective. The recommended means for aggrandizing a state had been used a half-dozen years longer by the great Frederick, and Prussia was now the already aggrandized state. This view of the situation furnishes the occasion for elaboration of the eulogy upon Frederick's régime, which had been more moderate in the earlier essay. At the same time, there is reason for the suspicion that this confident tone was merely a rhetorical device. The author wanted to do his part toward keeping up the courage and stimulating the ardor of his fellow-Prussians. Whether the essay was merely a specimen of the "point-with-pride" type of campaign literature, in which the pride is often in inverse ratio with its real occasion, or a genuine expression of belief about the assured results of Frederick's rule, it has the same value for our purposes. It is the *credo* of a mediocre man, in which we find such a man's reflection of the doctrines taught by more eminent authorities.

[1] I have used both a separately bound copy of the first, and a copy in the same covers with the second. It should be added, however, that the binding, though not very recent, is apparently of a much later date than the publication.

CHAPTER XII
THE CAMERALISTICS OF DARJES

Roscher speaks of Darjes as "undoubtedly the most important of the cameralistic professors patronized by Frederick the Great" (p. 419).

Like many Germans at this period who afterward gained eminence in other spheres, Joachim Georg Darjes (1714–91) devoted a considerable portion of his attention as a university student to theology. He even preached a short time after gaining his Master's degree. Turning, however, to jurisprudence he received the degree of *Dr. der Rechte* (1739), offered courses on the Institutes and Pandects, and in 1744 was made *ordentlicher Professor der Moral und Politik*, with the title *Hofrath*. According to Richter (*All. d. Bib.*, *in loc.*) Darjes' academic success was so great that in his twenty-seven years at Jena, he had more than ten thousand hearers. On the invitation of Frederick the Great, he migrated (1763) to Frankfurt a. O. as *Königl. preuss. Geheimrath und ordentlicher Professor der Rechte*. Here he founded the *Königliche Gelehrte Gesellschaft*. He did not, however, acquire the same influence as a university lecturer which he had enjoyed at Jena. He became (1772) *Direktor* of the university, *Ordinarius* of the law faculty, and the ranking professor of law.[1] Richter says: "Darjes was of great service to the cameral sciences by introducing them into university instruction." (Richter

[1] Of his numerous writings (scheduled in Meusel's *Lexicon*), we may name, in addition to the book to be discussed below: *Elementa metaphysica*, 1743; *Institutiones jurisprudentiae universalis*, 1745; *Philosophische Nebenstunden*, 1749–52; *Erste Gründe der philosophischen Sittenlehre*, 1750; *Via ad Veritatem*, 1758; *Discurs über Natur- und Völkerrecht*, 1762; *Einleitung in des Freyherrn von Bielefeld Lehrbegriff der Staatsklugheit*, 1764 (on J. F. von Bielfeld [sic] *vide* Roscher, pp. 426 ff.).

doubtless meant at *Jena.*) "As an author Darjes does not stand particularly high. He lacked thoroughness, precision, and talent for clear presentation."[1]

This estimate by Richter is by no means to be accepted as final. Indeed, if we recall Zincke for the sake of comparison, we experience a deep sense of relief in passing from his much less perspicuous, if more profound and comprehensive books, to Darjes' clear and intelligent outline of cameralistics.[2] Roscher further says (p. 419):

> Darjes was an eminent pupil of Wolff, who wanted jurisprudence, medicine, *Wirthschaftslehre*, etc., to prevail only as applied philosophy, but on account of his severely demonstrative method of exposition J. J. Moser contemptuously labeled him "*Modephilosoph.*" With respect to the fundamental concepts of national economics Darjes had learned much more from Hume than the majority of his contemporaries in Germany.

Roscher cites only the second edition of the *Erste Gründe*, published after the author had moved from Jena to Frankfurt.[3] In his estimate of Darjes' rank Roscher evidently did not include Justi in the group of "Frederick's professors of cameralistics." He doubtless classed Justi as an administrator or author, rather than as a professor.

[1] *Vide* Stieda, pp. 52 and 78.

[2] *Erste Gründe der Cameral-Wissenschaften, darinnen die Haupt-Theile so wohl der Oeconomie als auch der Pòlicey und besondern Cameral-Wissenschaft in ihrer natürlichen Verknüpfung, zum Gebrauch seiner academischen Fürlesung entworfen von Joachim Georg Darjes, Hoch-fürstl. Sachsen- Weimar- und Eisenachischen Hof-Rathe, der Philosophie und beyder Rechten Doctor, wie auch der Sitten-Lehre und Staats-Klugheit ordentlichen Professor zu Jena, des Senats der Churfürstl. Maynz. Akademie nützlicher Wissenschaften ordentlichem Beysitzer, der Jenaischen Akademie z. d. Z. Pro-Rector und der Philosophischen Facultät Decano.* . . . . 1756. (Pp. 664, exclusive of the Index, which fills 54 pages.)

[3] All references in this chapter are to the first edition. I have not seen the second.

Darjes' own account of the origin of his book, as contained in the *Vorrede*, is substantially this: He says that from boyhood he had been eager to search into the secrets of nature, to find out how natural forces work, and thus to learn what must be done when the attempt is made to imitate nature by art. Following this impulse, he found frequent occasions, in the course of lectures on other subjects, especially morals and politics, to introduce practical reflections upon rural and urban management. His hearers recognized the importance of such considerations, and at length a petition came from them for a separate course on the subject.

In adopting the suggestion, Darjes selected as his guide, first, Dithmar's *Einleitung*. He pronounces the book admirable [*schön*], but finds it somewhat too "remote" from the aspects of the subjects which he wants to treat. That is, he regards it as not sufficiently concrete. "It describes things which occur in all departments of these activities [i. e., *Wirthschaft*, *Policey*, *Cammer*], but he does not explain how they are to be carried out and improved." Then followed "the excellent work which bears the title, *Klugheit zu leben und zu herrschen*."[1] He says:

I have more than once lectured with profit upon this work, and I doubt if anyone can read it attentively without becoming more useful. It lacks nothing except more specific explanation of the grounds on which the activities of rural and civic management must be judged.

Darjes says that he had also several times used Schröder's *Fürstliche Schatz- und Rent-Cammer*,[2] and Seckendorff's *Fürsten-Staat*,[3] as the basis of his lectures, but at length he was prevailed upon by his students and the publishers to print his own ideas in systematic form.

[1] Rohr's digest seems to have had an influence out of proportion to its author's merit. *Vide* above, p. 190.

[2] *Vide* above, pp. 135 ff. [3] *Vide* above, pp. 61 ff.

The author's views of the instruction in cameralistic subjects most appropriate to universities, and consequently to be introduced by such a book, call for treatment midway between abstract methodology on the one hand and details of administrative routine on the other. He points out very clearly that it would be an endless task to describe in detail each of the separate processes that occur in the different divisions of management. He is equally clear in his judgment that such detailed description would be undesirable if possible. He declares that many managerial processes must be comprehended under a common idea; that the important thing is to understand this fundamental idea, in a single typical case, and then anyone capable of independent thinking can find for himself the relation of other cases to the same idea. He also draws a very definite distinction between the science of management and actual management itself, and he adds:

> Those who carry out operations are often incapable of comprehending the science fundamental to the operations. They simply do what they are told, and their reasons for doing it do not extend beyond the fact that they are told. Those who have charge of operations, however, must necessarily understand the science of the same.

Accordingly, Darjes calls his book "philosophical introduction to *Wirthschaft*" and he explains that his purpose is:

> to dwell on the connection of truths which will make us capable of judging all questions that would arise in practice, on their real grounds, and to form clear and intelligible ideas of everything which occurs in *Wirthschaft*. . . . . The science of *Wirthschaft* should make us capable of making an orderly *Wirthschaft* possible where it has hitherto been impossible, and of guiding the same to the advantage of human society. If we add that wisdom has its purpose in promotion of the welfare of men, and second, that a great part of the welfare of the state is founded in an orderly *Wirthschaft*, we have the motives for applying the science of *Wirthschaft* to the state; viz., first, to derive from the constitution of the state those means

by which the establishment of an orderly *Wirthschaft* in it is possible; second, to describe those means through which an orderly *Wirthschaft* will be capable of promoting the prosperity of the state. The first of these purposes is treated in the first and second parts of this book, the second in the third part, the third in the fourth part.

Darjes concludes with the specification:

The source from which I have drawn the special ideas is experience. Hence I may rightfully demand that the ideas be judged not in accordance with the conceptions which others have constructed, but in accordance with experience. That which experience teaches us I have combined with general truths, partly in order to establish a correlation, partly to confirm rules, the observance of which will conduct us securely toward attainment of the end which we have proposed.

As we have intimated before,[1] this appeal to experience, particularly in the sense of personal observation, may be taken as one of the authentic finding marks of the cameralists. Beginning with Osse, we find increasingly evident tendencies to break away from mere repetition of tradition and precedent, and to consider state policy as means to certain rather clearly defined ends not contained in conventional definitions. With exceptions, and with varying degrees of emphasis on this phase of their reasoning, the men whom we recognize as cameralists have exhibited this trait. They were not equally aware of the importance which they actually assigned to the empirical element in their systems. Darjes is notable, however, as one of the most outspoken in this respect.

But we must judge Darjes still more specifically. The succession of cameralists furnishes several marked cases to point the moral that reputation is not always in accordance with an objective measure of merit. If we were to make out from the type of evidence now under review the most exact

[1] *Vide* p. 4 *et passim.*

estimate possible of the growth of scientific consciousness among the cameralists, the most significant signs would by no means always be found in those writers to whom tradition, as we have it, has awarded the most conspicuous place. Darjes is one of the most notable cases in point. In spite of the phrase quoted above,[1] readers of Roscher who do not compare the authors discussed will hardly gain the impression that Darjes marks a distinct stadium in the development of German economic insight. My own judgment is that the *Erste Gründe* contains the most striking evidence to be found in the cameralists thus far reviewed, that attention was turning toward economic relations conceived approximately as in Adam Smith's formulation of economic problems. A casual reading of Darjes' book would detect in it merely insignificant variations in form and content from the analysis and treatment of previous cameralists. More careful scrutiny discovers such differences of precision and clearness in the perception of relations, that one feels bound to credit Darjes with having advanced a long distance toward the standpoint of positive science. Not only is his style more direct and business-like than that of most of his class, but clear and objective thinking furnishes a substantial content for his language. Nor is progressiveness the only trait for which Darjes is notable. His epitome of the aims and outlook of cameralism is remarkably concise and comprehensive. No single writer in the cameralistic succession gives a brief account of the scope and purpose of their discipline which better reflects the genius of the whole movement.

Although it may not be immediately apparent that it is more than mere repetition of ideas which had become stock properties among the cameralists, we should leave a serious gap in our outline of the development of the subject, if we failed to present, in a faithful rendering of his own words,

[1] *Vide* p. 267.

a digest of Darjes' introduction. He first pays his respects to three objections, already familiar to us, urged by his contemporaries against *Cameralwissenschaft* or *Haushaltungskunst*, viz.: first, it is useless to try to make a science out of these subjects—they must be learned by experience; second, whether worth while or not, a science of these subjects is impossible, because so many contingencies are concerned, which cannot be foreseen, and cannot be brought under general conceptions; third, it is beneath the dignity of scholars to concern themselves with subjects which are matters for peasants and plain citizens.

In answer to the first objection Darjes forcibly maintains the proposition (§2): "All works which men carry on for the advantage of human society become at once, if not perfect, at least less imperfect, if they are ordered and controlled by those who have a science and a philosophical understanding of these works." In support of the proposition he urges, in a spirit much more of the future than of the past: "It is not difficult to prove this theorem, both from reason and from experience. Reason draws this conclusion: a thing is perfect when it is arranged according to its nature and its idea. If then we are not to expect that a work shall be perfected by blind chance, its completion must be governed by those who are skilled enough to investigate the nature and idea of this work, and from this understanding distinctly to conclude what determines the perfection and imperfection of the work. This is the idea of a science and of a philosophical understanding. Is not this enough to furnish conclusive support for the thesis: A science and philosophical understanding of *Cameralwissenschaft*, or of *Haushaltungskunst*, in the general acceptance of that word, is not only necessary, but also profitable?"[1]

To the second objection Darjes replies (§4): "People who say that *Cameralwissenschaft* is impossible fall back on a prejudice created by those who have proposed untenable conclusions in the name of such

[1] In expanding the argument, Darjes cites, "for the benefit of those who allow themselves to be influenced more by celebrated men than by reasons, ... *die vortrefliche Streitschrift* . . . . *de excolendo studio oeconomico*." (By Rohr. *Vide* Roscher, p. 378.)

science. The answer must be given: We must distinguish the grounds from inferences drawn from them. The alleged grounds are not to be repudiated completely. In the first place it is true, and I can prove it from my own experience, that in the application of economic science [*öconomischen Wissenschaft*] many circumstances emerge which we could not have foreseen and which demand that we must, if not completely abandon, at least in certain particulars modify our plan. Among such circumstances I count the various states of mind and capacities of men, by means of which our project must be carried out; the various sorts of soil, determined partly by their inner constitution, partly by their location; the various accidents due to weather conditions, etc. In the second place, it is true that in various writings which purport to treat *Haushaltungskunst*[1] scientifically, matters are included which partly contradict experience, and which partly, although they may be possible, are impracticable. . . . . This does not prove that a scientific treatment of *Haushaltungskunst* and the cameral sciences is impossible. On the contrary, the following causes compel rejection of such a conclusion: first, no one who acts intelligently rests his judgement of a thing upon the mistakes of those who represent it. Second, mistakes made by the intelligent deserve special attention. They may show how to discover what has been concealed, and how to make that which was well known more useful and applicable. Who can make use of such mistakes, however, but he who already has a science of such things? Such mistakes then are no proof of the impossibility of the science now in question. They may rather extend and complete the science. Third, he who possesses no science in the art of management (*sic*)[2] must conform to old tradition, and it will be hard for him to adapt himself to unexpected and altered circumstances. If things go well in such a crisis, it is his good luck; if

[1] The substitution within a few lines of the term, "*Haushaltungskunst*" for "*öconomische Wissenschaft*" is strictly typical. The clearest thinkers in the group did not get their objects of attention so definitely related that such terms as these received a precise and invariable content.

[2] "*Wer in der Haushaltungskunst keine Wissenschaft besitzet.*" However sane the fundamental thinking of men who expressed themselves in such fashion, they were outside the threshold of scientific

they go ill, it is his misfortune, and the essence of it is his own stupidity. Whoever on the other hand has a philosophical understanding knows how these unexpected circumstances are to be considered, how one may compare them with the nature of the matter, and thus determine the general theory more exactly, and thereby make it more useful. What then is proved by this addition of special circumstances? That a philosophical science of *Haushaltungskunst* is impossible? It rather confirms the contrary, and the necessity of such a science. This may then be concluded that without experience a philosophical science of management [*eine philosophische Wissenschaft der Haushaltungskunst*] cannot be made sufficiently definite and applicable." Darjes assents to this conclusion, and declares that his book will be composed accordingly.

To the third objection the answer is substantially this: The people who regard attention to *Haushaltungskunst* as beneath the dignity of the learned, appear to have a very great soul but a very petty mind. They call themselves learned, but do not know what learning [*Gelehrsamkeit*] is. They have perhaps forgotten that the true learning is that which proves itself profitable among men and in human society, and that the eminence of this learning depends upon the quantity of this advantage.[1] To put it briefly, a philosopher constructs general concepts, he infers from these the qualities of things, and he consequently builds up a correlation of truths which represents the essentials of all particulars which are to be treated in this special division of learning. A philosopher will then become practical if he determines his general understanding more accurately through history and experience, and this is the natural way of building the special sciences.

Thus one determines one's ideas of what is right and wrong through the customs of peoples and through the decisions of rulers,

precision, and without special evidence for each particular case, none of their propositions are to be interpreted as carrying the same content which their terms would connote in later, more critical, stages of social theory. If Richter (*vide* above, p. 267) meant to accuse Darjes of lack of precision in this sense, there is surely no reason for treating him as exceptional. It was the fashion of the time.

[1] Is "pragmatism" then a recent discovery!

and one becomes a *jurist.* The philosopher determines his understanding of the forces of things through learning how the human body is put together, and through that which he is taught by experience in this connection, and he becomes a *physician.* Another philosopher determines his understanding of the nature and workings of things through that which experience in affairs ["*Beschäftigungen*"] teaches him, and he becomes a *manager.*[1] Why now is the dignity of the scholar more in question in the last case than in the others? Is he who constructs a science of preserving and extending the riches of the state and of its inhabitants less useful to the state than he who makes himself skilled in preserving the health of people, or he who learns how to decide what is right and wrong in the quarrels between people? The external welfare of men is related to three factors, to riches, to the enjoyment of rights, and to health. Each who is zealous so to determine his philosophy that it may be useful in promoting any of these purposes (*sic*) is thereby zealous in promoting the welfare of human society. Is it not a clear proof of confusion and prejudice if one looks upon one of these factors as opposed to the dignity of a scholar? That which is really beneath the dignity of a scholar is to deal in confused ideas, and to draw conclusions from prejudice.

But, continues Darjes, I may have misunderstood these men. Perhaps they merely mean that plowing, manuring, brewing, baking, etc., are not proper occupations for scholars. If that is their meaning, I have misinterpreted them, but it is their fault. Of course we do not have these practical manipulations [*wirthschaftliche Handthierungen*] in mind when we speak of a philosophical science.

[1] The word is *Wirth.* Shall we translate it "economist"? If we do, we introduce an ambiguous middle term which falsifies our whole subsequent interpretation of evolution in German theory. One of the constant motives of this book is to set forth enough selections from the mass of evidence to show that English assumptions about the history of German thought have almost completely failed to take account of the actual process. In fact, the conception of the *manager of economic relations* was much later than this, and with great difficulty differentiated from the conception of the *generalizer of economic operations.* Consequently the arts of economic management, and the science of economic

We turn then from these objections to a positive description of cameral science (§9). In the first place we must define certain uses of terms. The chief theorem is this: *Whoever wishes to count upon a certain annual income, must look out for the source from which the income may flow.* The theorem is supported as follows: Our yearly incomes flow either from an established source, or they depend upon chance, and are thus beyond our control. Since it is self-evident that in the latter case we can make no certain calculation upon the yearly revenues, wisdom demands that we look out for a source that is capable of producing our revenues. In a note Darjes explains that he uses variations of the word "certain" or "assured" in this connection in the general sense in which such terms are employed in the theory of morals and prudence; that is, not complete certainty, but a high degree of probability is the meaning.

There are two possible sources of annual income (§10): (*a*) skill in the application of our powers, or (*b*) an already secured "good" which is capable of producing a yearly profit. This latter is called in a special sense the source of annual revenues, the fund [*Fond*], the capital.

"I am uncertain," says Darjes, "whether to give precedence to the former or to the latter of these sources, or whether they are equivalent in respect to yearly income (§11). Thus A has a capital of 10,000 *Thaler* and this yields a yearly profit of 500 *Thaler*. B can earn with his skill 500 *Thaler*. Accordingly the one has as great an income as the other. For many reasons it might be inferred that in respect to yearly income the two sources are indifferent.

relations were (also much later than this, and never with quite the same abstractness in Germany as in England) set distinctly over against each other. Between the cameralistic period and the economic period in the nineteenth-century sense, an evolutionary process intervened in which the center of attention was shifted a long distance away from particular operations and details of results toward correspondences of many operations, and formulas of relations between operations and results. German experience before this process was matured has a value of its own, but we have misconceived most of the value, because we have assumed it without proper reckoning with this evolution of purpose by which it must be interpreted.

On the other hand it is urged that a capital is exposed to various vicissitudes. We may lose it by fraud, fire, flood, and other accidents. Our skill on the contrary is secure against these attacks. Persons of the opposite view reply: 'We can earn nothing with our skill if we are sick; moreover it depends in many ways upon the opinions of other men whether we shall be able to apply our skill. It is not always within our power to rouse the necessary opinions. A capital, however, may show itself effective whether we are sick or well, and whether men are of one opinion or the other.' "

Most people would conclude that capital and skill should be combined (§12). Darjes expresses his own judgment, however, that between capital and skill the former is the more secure source of revenue, and for these reasons: The greater the number of accidents which may interfere with the sources of our annual revenues, the more easily these accidents may operate, and the more independent they are of our control, the less securely can we reckon upon our yearly income. This uncertainty is greater in the case of skill than of capital. Hence we can more securely count upon a yearly income from capital than from skill.

In a note (§13) the author specifies that he uses the word "capital" not in the narrower sense in which it is applied to a sum of money which we borrow for the sake of making a profit, but in the general sense, of those acquired means which we assume to be permanent, so that they may annually be efficient for our advantage. This use of the word, he says, is usual in all writers on *Haushaltungskunst* whom he has read. "If there is no objection to the term, I prefer to use the word *Fond*. I have no objection to any freedom which others desire in this respect."[1]

The foregoing must be applied to the revenues of a prince (§14). It is known from the law of nature that the prince, as a member of civic society, must be distinguished from a prince as such.[2] In the latter character the prince must be considered in his

[1] Darjes gives no hint of the writers whom he had in mind in this connection. The probability is that they were French, for I have found in the earlier cameralists no direct attempt to define the use of the term.

[2] This distinction seems to have been assumed by all the cameralists more or less consciously. The most definite previous formulation of it is in chap. vi; *vide* pp. 143 ff. above.

relation to the state and the subjects. This gives us a ground for dividing the yearly revenues of the prince into the personal and the princely income.

The capital or the "Fond" of the princely revenues is the riches of the state and of the subjects (§15).

Whoever attempts to increase his yearly revenues either draws upon his capital, or he seeks to increase his capital and make it more fruitful (§16). The former means is unreasonable, because it either defeats the purpose or makes permanent attainment of the purpose impossible. Hence the theorem: *The increase of yearly income is unreasonable when it is brought to pass by impairing the capital.*[1]

In order that our attempts to increase our revenues may be reasonable they must aim either to increase the accumulated capital or to make it more fruitful (§17).

To appraise the riches of the subjects, we must determine either the sum of their already accumulated capital, or the amount of their yearly revenues. If, accordingly, we understand that the capital of the princely revenues is the riches of the subjects, these revenues are taken either from the capital, which the subjects have already acquired, or from the yearly revenues of the subjects. If the former method be chosen, the income of the prince each time impairs the capital of the subjects. This is unreasonable. If one will accordingly follow reason, one must assume in this case that the capital or the *Fond* of the princely revenues is the yearly income of the subjects. Hence the general rule (§19): *The first care of him whose task it is to raise the princely revenues, must be to discover how the yearly income of the subjects may be increased. Accordingly a prince is a rich prince when he has rich and skilful subjects.*

In the Middle Ages the word *Camera* designated the place where the princely revenues were kept (§21). Hence it occurred that men

[1] The importance of this argument can hardly be estimated unless it is connected with chap. cviii, in Schröder's *Schatz- und Rent-Cammer*. We must allow for the persistence in practice, to a certain extent confusing theory, of the less mature idea of which Schröder was the spokesman. *Vide* above, pp. 135 ff.

understood by *Cameralwesen* those ordinances which defined the *Wirthschaft* of a prince. An orderly *Wirthschaft* consists of three chief points (*sic*) viz.: the maintenance, the raising, and the administration of the yearly revenues. This is enough to show why we understand by *Cameralwissenschaft* that science which shows us the reasonable way of preserving, raising, and applying the annual revenues of a prince. There may be some who disapprove the separation of these purposes, instead of combining them in one expression. To satisfy them we may define *Cameralwissenschaft as a science of the reasonable Wirthschaft of a prince.*

A cameralist is one who understands *Cameralwissenschaft* (§22); more particularly, he must be able to solve the following problems: (1) How may an established source of the yearly revenues of a prince be preserved? (2) How may the yearly income of a prince be reasonably raised? (3) How is a reasonable application of the yearly revenues of a prince possible?

Cameralistic technique consists then, first: (*a*) in finding means capable of realizing the riches of the state and of the subjects; (*b*) in bringing the yearly incomes of the subjects into certain classes, and in determining their amount as accurately as possible (§23); second, in finding reasonable ways of raising the annual revenues of the prince, and consequently (*sic*) of making the subjects richer and more skilful (§24).

Our yearly revenues are either direct workings of nature or the output of the latter is based upon our occupations, which in turn presuppose a certain skill which we have acquired by our efforts (§25). These occupations either put nature in a condition to accomplish that which is possible for her, or out of natural products they produce other things which are useful for the human race. This taken for granted, it is clear that in respect to the second point, a true cameralist must understand: (*a*) the true qualities of natural objects, and what can be brought to pass by means of them; (*b*) how nature can be made more skilful in bringing forth what is possible for her; (*c*) how other things for the use of men may be produced from the yield of nature. And the author adds in a note: "We speak of 'the use of men' not in a moral, but in a political sense, according to which everything is useful for the human race which may bring about its preservation, happiness, and the improvement of welfare. The science with which we are now concerned demands that we should attach such a meaning to the word."

It is hardly necessary to point out that we have here a seed of the sort of thinking which developed later into pure economics of the nineteenth-century type. The argument continues:

By these signs we may distinguish between a true cameralist and a despoiler of the country [*Landverderber*] (§26). There are people devoted to raising the revenues of a prince, who either through wantonness or stupidity are restrained from taking the way which wisdom prescribes, i. e., *the way of increasing the yearly revenues of the subjects*. They think they have fully discharged the duties of their office if they find schedules which would increase the annual payments of the subjects. These people increase the annual revenues of the prince by weakening the capital. This increase is of no duration. The subjects and the state must eventually grow poorer. This is enough to show that such people do not deserve the name cameralist. They are the plague in the state, and for this reason are called despoilers of the country.

On the contrary (§28), the true cameralist proposes to increase the yearly incomes of the subjects. The subjects must accordingly not only be put in a situation in which it is possible for them to increase their incomes, but their will must lead them to the necessary occupation. This latter demands an awakening of their zeal for labor. The former demands, first, an understanding of the possible increase of revenues; second, possession of those means through which the understanding may be skilfully applied; third, removal of all those circumstances which might obstruct the execution of this purpose. Accordingly, in respect to the second main task, a cameralist must further understand how the *state is to be arranged* (*sic*) in order (*a*) to rouse in the subjects a zeal for labor; (*b*) to enable the subjects to gain adequate understanding of the possible increase of incomes; (*c*) to insure to the subjects adequate provision of means and opportunity skilfully to apply the acquired understanding; (*d*) to guard the subjects against hindrances to convenient disposal of the things which they have produced.

The reason why a cameralist concerns himself with these points is to raise the annual revenues of a prince (§29). This is the principal occupation through which he is distinguished from another scientific manager [*Wirth*]. But this peculiar occupation demands that he shall observe more than one rule. It follows immediately that he must understand (*a*) how a prince may raise his yearly revenues from the yearly incomes of the subjects, without weakening the source of the same; (*b*) how, through the reasonable use of the yearly revenues of a prince, the yearly incomes of the subjects may be preserved and increased.[1]

We come then to the third main task, viz., the reasonable use of the annual revenues of a prince (§30). Whoever manages wisely brings his revenues and his outlays into certain classes. He distinguishes the necessary outlays from those that are less necessary. He compares the outlay with the income, and designates for each class of outlays a particular class of revenues. Hence, in respect to this third task, a cameralist must understand (*a*) how to bring the revenues of a prince into certain classes; (*b*) how to determine the yearly outlays of a prince, and how these are to be divided in certain orders; (*c*) how to compare the annual outlays of a prince with his annual revenues, and how a special class of the revenues may be assigned to each sort of outlay.

It follows that an introduction to *Cameralwissenschaft* must first outline the operations of nature. Accordingly we have as the first part of the science, *Landwirthschaft* [*Oeconomia rustica*] (§31).

A note upon this section offords another instructive sign of the progress of analysis in this field. Darjes says:

Many who treat of *Oeconomie* interpret it in a moral sense, since they regard us as in an interdependence of those rules in accordance with which a reasonable *Wirthschaft* must be arranged, and we have made a brief sketch of these in the philosophical theory of morals.

[1] Throughout this discussion, and in the same connection in other cameralists, there is ambiguity in the words which I have translated "raise the revenue," etc. The meaning is sometimes "increase the revenue," but it is not always clear to the writers themselves which they mean.

The cameralist presupposes this treatment, and he goes farther. He investigates how these general rules can be applied to the works of nature. For this reason he busies himself with *Oeconomie* in the physical sense, yet not as a peasant, but as a philosopher. He works out a conception of the workings of nature, of the natural causes of these workings; of completeness in the workings of nature, and of the means of making these causes capable of rendering the workings complete. From these conceptions he deduces general theorems which serve him as rules in a specific case, and hereby he becomes a philosophical *Land-Wirth*, who is able to regulate the *Landwirthschaft* in a country, and to make it more complete for the profit of the state.

The passage calls for the observation that the development of thought in Germany at this time, upon subjects afterward differently allotted among nineteenth-century social sciences, was by no means confined to the cameralists. We must remember, while analyzing cameralistic thinking, that this was merely one of the factors in the whole thought-movement of the time, within the range which we may call in general sociological.

Darjes accordingly classifies the first part of *Landwirthschaft* in three divisions, dealing respectively with (*a*) the workings of nature and the means of making them more complete; (*b*) agriculture; (*c*) cattle raising (§32). He calls the second part of *Cameralwissenschaft*, dealing with those things which may be produced by artificial control of the workings of nature, *Stadtwirthschaft* or *Oeconomia urbana* (§33), and its subdivisions deal with (*a*) *Gewerken* in which the forces of nature are employed in producing certain goods, such as beer, alcohol, and starch; (*b*) *Manufacturen und Fabriquen*, which produce things which nature by herself could not produce (§34).

Darjes makes *Policeiwissenschaft* the third part of *Cameralwissenschaft*, and he explains:

The Greeks understand by the word πολιτεία those laws of a

state upon which its beauty and well-being rest.[1] The state is accordingly beautiful, and its well-being is assured, if its subjects have flourishing means of subsistence. This is sufficient to show why the name has been given to this third part of *Cameralwissenschaft.* This part of the science is concerned with: (*a*) the population of the state; (*b*) establishment of schools and universities; (*c*) political establishment of the *ecclesiastical* system: (*d*) incitement of subjects to labor; (*e*) arrangements of the state preserving the health of subjects; (*f*) beauty of the country; (*g*) promotion of security; (*h*) care of the poor, etc. (§36).

The cameralist must finally apply the sciences thus described to the *Wirthschaft* of a prince, as prince (§37). This application makes the fourth part of *Cameralwissenschaft* which has appropriated the name *Cameralwissenschaft* in a peculiar sense. Its subdivisions are: (*a*) determination of the various sources of the princely revenues; (*b*) devising of ways and means to draw from these sources; (*c*) description of the regular application of the annual revenues of a prince.[2]

We are not concerned with comparative techique in any part of the cameral sciences, and we may allow this general description to represent Darjes' professional equation in the cameralistic group.[3]

[1] Substantially the same explanation is given more at length, with quotation from Xenophon's *Athenian Republic,* in Justi's *Grundfeste,* I, 5.

[2] The author promises to name, as occasion requires, books on the various subjects; but he refers in general to Rohr's *Haushaltungs-Bibliothek* and "Zink," *Cameral-Bibliothek.*

[3] If the sources had been accessible, I should have added an estimate of Johann Jacob Moser as an index of the spirit of cameralism. I have as yet no means of testing the reliability of Roscher's account (pp. 441 ff.).

CHAPTER XIII

THE CAMERALISTICS OF JUSTI

Since we have referred to Seckendorff as the Adam Smith of cameralism, we may carry out the conceit by calling Justi the John Stuart Mill of the movement. In each case, however, the analogy rests upon points of resemblance which would be rated as trivial after critical investigation. It is true, nevertheless, that, as a pioneer in reducing an administrative programme to literary expression, Seckendorff occupies very much the same relative position in the development of cameralistic theory which Smith occupied later in the evolution of an abstract theory of wealth. It is also true that Justi organized the cameralistic technology which had been developed up to his time into a system of theory which correlated the different phases of cameralism, very much as Mill gave to the doctrines of classical economics their most impressive rendering. It would hardly be profitable to pursue farther the quest of likeness or unlikeness in either case.

The original plan of this book proposed to present Justi alone as the type of cameralism in general. Further reflection led to change of the plan to the programme here followed. The principal reason was that, if the first intention had been carried out, it could not have forestalled the criticism: "One case cannot justify a generalization. Nothing appears in evidence to prove that Justi was not an exception rather than a type." Since the literature by which this objection is removed is so inaccessible to Americans, mere assertion that it exists, or even copious references to particular passages, would fail adequately to present the cameralists to English readers. The alternative chosen was an attempt to survey the whole cameralistic period and to divide attention in proportion to the relative importance of the principal writers.

The most convincing biographical study of Justi has been made by Frensdorff. We follow his conclusions in reducing to the lowest terms such details as are necessary for our purpose.[1]

Johann Heinrich Gottlob von Justi, son of the *Gerichthalter* Georg Heinrich Justi, was baptized December 28, 1717, in the *evangelisch-lutherische Kirche* at *Brücken an der Helme* (*Regierungsbezirk Merseburg, Kreis Sangerhausen*). The story that he was born on Christmas eve of that year is thus not improbable. Of his earlier years little is known. The traces of his university career are rather dubious. The most reliable of them are at Wittenberg. Partly within his student period he had some army experience. "Although Justi's military period was no longer than his academic career, it left traces which may be observed for a long time in his writings. He often made use of observations collected (1741-42) during the war of the Austrian succession" (Frensdorff, p. 363). Justi credited the lieutenant-colonel of the regiment to which

[1] F. Frensdorff, "Ueber das Leben und die Schriften des Nationalökonomen J. H. G. von Justi," *Nachrichten von der Königl. Gesellschaft der Wissenschaft zu Göttingen.* Philologisch-historische Klasse, aus dem Jahre 1903. Göttingen, 1904. (Pp. 354-503.) It would be an unfortunate misdirection of energy to enter upon examination of Justi's career under the guidance of the previous accounts of his life: e. g., the article in *All. d. Bib.;* Roscher's essay, in *Archiv für die Sächsische Geschichte*, 6ter Bd., pp. 77 ff.; the digest of that essay, *Gesch.*, pp. 444 ff., etc. My first loss of confidence in the reliability of Roscher in matters of detail came from discovery of numerous inaccuracies in his biography of Justi. These related to items on which the text of the author's works is final. Frensdorff has used sources of other kinds, not accessible in this country. He has not only discovered Roscher's mistakes in cases of the type just referred to, but he has proved that previous biographical sketches of Justi were largely fabulous. An earlier monograph by the same author should be consulted: *Festschrift zur Feier des hundertfünfzigjährigen Bestehens der Königl. Gesellschaft der Wissenschaften zu Göttingen.* "Beiträge zur Gelehrtengeschichte Göttingens" (Berlin 1901), pp. 495 ff.

he belonged with turning the course of his life to legal and scientific pursuits.

Justi's first publication was *Die Dichterinsel* (1745), a combination of Utopia and satire feebly resembling Swift's *Gulliver*. At about the same time, Justi began to publish in Dresden a monthly magazine, under the title *Ergetzungen der vernünftigen Seele aus der Sittenlehre und der Gelehrsamkeit überhaupt*. During the remainder of his life Justi seemed never content unless he was addressing the public through one or more journals of various types.

In the course of the year 1747, Justi removed to Sangerhausen, where his name is known first as *Advocat*, then as *Rath der verwittweten Herzogin von Sachsen-Eisenach*. Although the term *Witthumsrath*, used in flippant allusion to this incident, seems to indicate that the sonorous title was not everywhere taken seriously, on the other hand, perhaps without exceeding the privileges which at the time went with any title whatsoever, Justi evidently regarded the designation obtained from the *Herzogin* as an available asset, and he made good use of it as a help to something better.

Justi's next step toward distinction was the composition of a monograph on a subject calling for review of Leibnitz' theory of monads. The subject was proposed for a prize contest by the *Berliner Akademie der Wissenschaften*, and the prize was awarded to Justi in 1747 (Frensdorff, p. 371).

Presently Justi changed his residence to Vienna. Of this episode Frensdorff says (p. 375):

The period of his stay here is the most important of his life. From this point dates the turning of his mind to the science which was to give him his place in history. Up to this time he had traversed many fields with his facile journalistic pen—polite literature, philosophy, history, jurisprudence, etc. He now began to cultivate the economic sciences. His removal to Vienna had much to do with this transition.

Justi arrived in Austria at precisely the time when Maria Theresia had put her improving hand upon all departments of the inner life of the state. The system of taxation and the organization of civic functionaries were reconstructed, so that the government was independent of the estates, and a central control of internal affairs was possible. These reforms reached their most definite expressions through Haugwitz, head of the political and cameral administration. . . . . The reforms which he introduced in general administration were also beneficial to the educational institutions founded at the same period. Both the *Theresianum*, founded in 1746, and the *Savoysche Ritterakademie* proposed to furnish a training for aristocratic youths which would provide the state with more competent servants both civil and military.

No sufficient explanation of Justi's initial success at Vienna has been found. At all events, he was appointed, August 31, 1750, to the "*Professura eloquentiae germanicae*" in the *Collegium Theresianum*. In connection with this professorship, Justi was instructed to offer lectures entitled "*collegium oeconomico-provinciale*," which included "*Finanzen, Handel, Contributionale (Steuerwesen) und Manufacturwesen*." The immediate occasion for this course, which was incidental to a larger educational porgramme, was similar to that which had led the king of Prussia, a quarter-century earlier, to establish the cameralistic chairs at Halle and Frankfurt a. O., viz., the desire to supplement the traditional courses at the university by instruction which would be direct preparation for official service.

The document which marks Justi's entrance into the cameralistic series was in the nature of a report to the empress (1752), containing a prospectus of cameralistic study.[1]

At particular command of the empress, Justi was commissioned to deal specifically with the subject of mining.

[1] *Auf höchsten Befehl an Sr. Röm. Kaiserl. und zu Ungarn und Bohmen Königl. Majestät erstattetes allerunterthänigstes Gutachten von dem vernünftigen Zusammenhange und praktischen Vortrage aller Oeko-*

Thereupon he gave his attention not merely to the theory, but to the actual development of the mineral resources of Austria. This particular element in his activities may have had much or little to do with the brevity of his stay in Vienna. At all events his connection with mining administration proved to be his final undoing. For reasons which are as confused as the explanations of his coming to Austria, among them friction with the ecclesiastical authorities, Justi returned to North Germany in 1753. Stieda thinks (p. 33) that he did not even begin his lectures on cameralistics in Vienna. Frensdorff, on the contrary, is quite sure he was the first teacher of the economic sciences in Austria (p. 389). Unless we presume that Justi had forgotten the facts in less than eight years, or that he deliberately lied, his own assertion, which Stieda seems to have overlooked, is decisive.[1]

Light is thrown on Justi's reasons for leaving Vienna by his hints that the Jesuits were hostile to him, and had spies at the doors and windows of his lecture-room.[2] He also says that the rector told him flatly, "There is no need of *Cameralwissenschaft und Policei;* Austria has been prosperous a long time without anything of that sort. If people are only pious and say their prayers, God will bless the country without such stuff."[3]

Reviewing the Austrian passage in Justi's career, Frensdorff says (p. 389):

nomischen und Kameralwissenschaften . . . . von Herrn Hofrat u. Professor J. H. G. edlen Herrn v. Justi. Herausgegeben von Dr. E. W., Leipzig, 1754. According to Stieda's description (p. 32) this document contains virtually the same programme afterward proposed in the Preface of *Staatswirthschaft*. In the latter form it will be discussed below.

[1] It is quoted below; *vide* p. 336, note.

[2] *Staatswirthschaft*, I, 119. It does not seem to me that Frensdorff has given due weight to this evidence.

[3] *Grundriss einer guten Regierung*, p. 324.

Brief as was his stay in Austria, the time was not lost for Austria nor for himself. As one line leads back from him to the most eminent representatives of *Volkswirthschaft* under Kaiser Leopold I, so another connects him with those who followed. Justi continued the work of Becher, Schröder, and Hornick. . . . . Each had at heart the question how Austria might be made more prosperous by means of *Landesoekonomie* or *Volkswirthschaft*. They solve the question according to the principles of the mercantilists; and the difference between them and Justi is his more abstract procedure. He is not concerned in the first instance with a particular country. He tries to lay down principles of universal validity, and while they handle their material in a popular way, Justi puts his in the form of a dogmatic and schematically complete exposition.[1]

Justi left Austria during the year 1753. On New Year, 1754 at Mansfeld, he signed the prospectus of a new monthly journal;[2] he appears to have been for a short time in Leipzig, but in 1755 he appears in Göttingen. The reasons which account for these movements remain unexplained. In Göttingen Justi combined the activities of *Polizeidirector* with the academic function of lecturer on cameralistic subjects.[3] In June, 1757, however, Justi left Göttingen. Again the reasons are largely matters of conjecture. The action for divorce brought by his wife doubtless had something to do with the brevity of his stay. He next appears (1757) as *Bergrath* in the service of the king of Denmark. This Danish episode lasted less than a year. He moved to Altona, then to Hamburg, where he made the acquaintance of the Prussian resident von Hecht. From this time to the end of the Seven Years' War, Justi did a great deal of political writing. He affected a

[1] This estimate must be considerably qualified, especially as to the contrast of purpose between Justi and his predecessors. I note my partial dissent, however, without further comment.

[2] *Neue Wahrheiten zum Vortheil der Naturkunde und des gesellschaftlichen Lebens der Menschen. Vide* Frensdorff, p. 391.

[3] Frensdorff, p. 393.

manner which purported to set the issues of the day in the light of a comprehensive political philosophy.

Justi appears to have remained in Hamburg until some time between 1758 and 1760. From the spring of the latter year[1] his books are dated at Berlin, and the title, "*Kgl. Grossbritannischer Bergrath*," disappears.

Justi's occupations and status in Berlin are extremely uncertain up to 1765, when he was appointed *Berghauptmann*. From this vantage ground he secured the notice and favor of the king, who indorsed rather extensive plans for the development of mines. On the other hand Justi seems almost immediately to have made enemies. These were partly personal creditors, partly bidders for the opportunities which his office controlled or influenced. Presently more serious trouble came. Questions were raised about Justi's financial administration. The outcome was judicial investigation which resulted in his arrest and confinement at Küstrin (February 9, 1768).[2] At the time of his death, probably from apoplexy, he was carrying on the legal fight for release. He maintained that the whole case was trumped up by enemies, and according to his daughter's statement, he expressed his confidence, the evening before his death, that the process would result in his favor. Although it is possible, and even probable, that in the whole matter Justi was "more sinned against than sinning," we must admit that the incident at best deepens the impression left by the most favorable version of his earlier life. With all his intellectual versatility, Justi never shows a sign of moral strength.

Returning to our main interest, viz., the cameralists as authors, not as individuals, we are obliged to disentangle

[1] Roscher says "from 1762" (p. 444); but the *Vorrede* of Vol. I of the *Grundfeste* is dated "*Berlin den 25. April 1760;*" of Vol. II, "*Berlin, den 6. April 1761;*" while the *Vorrede* of *Natur und Wesen der Staaten* is subscribed, "*Geschrieben zur Leipziger Michaelis-Messe 1759.*"

[2] *Vide* Frensdorff, pp. 449 ff.

Justi's cameralistic works from a mass of miscellaneous writings. Meusel's *Lexikon* schedules forty-eight works which he published between 1741 and 1771, many of them in several volumes. They fall into six groups: (1) aesthetics and *belles lettres;* (2) philosophy; (3) natural science; (4) history; (5) law and statesmanship; (6) cameralistics in the wide sense.

Most of his books were dashed off with genial carelessness, and with notorious disregard of the literature of the subjects treated. He despised all science which could not be turned to tangible uses, philology, mathematics, astronomy; in the latter case showing his ignorance by sneering at the inaccuracy of astronomical opinions.[1] Such reaction against earlier one-sidedness probably had a certain value. At the same time it became itself very plain one-sidedness when, for example, Justi admitted the right to kill in self-defense, but merely to preserve one's own life, not however "to preserve those chimeras and absurd treasures which we have constructed out of honor, and property, which is probably not in accordance with the will of God, or out of female virtue, and perhaps even of virginity"[2] (Roscher in *Archiv für Sächs. Geschichte*, Bd. 6, pp. 77 ff.).

One might read Justi's cameralistic books a long time without happening upon express recognition that anything worth notice had previously been written on the subjects treated. Tardy and grudging references to other authors occur, but they do not by any means give due credit for Justi's drafts upon his predecessors. He succeeded in eclipsing them partly because he had rather unusually acute political instincts. Besides this, he was a skilled organizer of literary material. If he was not a plagiarist in the strict sense, he was a persistent absorber and purveyor of other people's ideas as his own. While this fact foredooms certain tendencies to idealize Justi as an originator in the social sciences, it indicates his value as a summarizer of previous social science. Justi

[1] *Staatswirthschaft*, I, xxiv.

[2] *Natur und Wesen der Staaten*, pp. 176 ff.

repeatedly excuses his omission to cite other writers, on the ground that such references merely serve to parade an author's learning.[1] He has a euphemistic substitute for frank confession in the following passage:[2]

> I have never owned a book which I have not read entirely through, and my memory was so strong that in case of all notable passages I not only knew the volume in which they were to be found, but also the chapter and usually the page. Indeed, I have often introduced into my writings from memory passages many lines long without again referring to the book. This extraordinary memory has been growing weaker for several years, and I am learning the value of good tables of contents.

Our plan requires a review of the most important of Justi's cameralistic books, as nearly as possible in their chronological order. We shall find at least the elements of all his subsequent books in the *Staatswirthschaft*.[3]

We must give more than passing notice to the strategic force of the expression on the title-page, "which are requisite for the government of a country." The phrase at once puts to the front the purpose and viewpoint of cameralism, viz.:

[1] E. g., in the last paragraph of the *Vorrede* of the first edition of *Grundsätze der Policeywissenschaft*.

[2] *Vorrede* to the "*zwoten Ausgabe*" of the book just cited, 1759.

[3] *Johann Heinrich Gottlobs von Justi Staatswirthschaft, oder systematische Abhandlung aller Oekonomischen und Cameral-Wissenschaften, die zur Regierung eines Landes erfodert werden. In zweien Theilen ausgefertigt. Erster Theil, Welcher die Lehre von Erhaltung und Vermehrung des Vermögens des Staats, und mithin die Staatskunst, die Policey- und Commercien-Wissenschaft nebst der Haushaltungskunst in sich begreifft.* Zweyte stark vermehrte Auflage. . . . . 1758.

The title-page of the second part of the book, bound in the same volume, is varied as follows: *Zweyter Theil, Welcher die Lehre von dem vernünftigen Gebrauche des Vermögens des Staates, und mithin die eigentliche Cameral- oder Finanz-Wissenschaft in sich begreifft. Nebst einem vollständigen Register über beyde Theile.*

I have seen Professor E. R. A. Seligman's copy of the same edition. It is bound in two volumes, but the binding is evidently much later than that of the copy which I chiefly used.

first, the paramount state—whether the princelingdom of Reuss or the kingdom of Prussia, is immaterial—a dominant conception of what belongs to thrifty state-housekeeping, and *Staatswirthschaft* as the tradition of the technique which accomplishes that species of thrift.

We must set it down as a fixed fact that this is an element in the historical development of German social science, and of German government, which accounts for certain of the typical contrasts with English theoretical and practical tradition.

In order to obtain a general conception of the range of *Staatswirthschaft* as Justi and others taught it, and as most of the higher civic officials in Germany learned it, till a more modern organization of science was brought into vogue by Rau (*Lehrbuch der politischen Oekonomie*, 1826, etc.), the Table of Contents should be examined.

The first impression which the book would make upon any fairly intelligent person, who happened upon it with no previous hints about its contents, would be that it was intended as a digest of knowledge useful for civic functionaries. The primary thesis which the book and all the other writings of Justi on related subjects justify is that social problems presented themselves to the author principally as problems of civic administration. That is, the autonomous, patriarchal petty state was the ever-present working assumption. Justi is thus strictly in line with cameralistic tradition as we have made it out from the beginning.

Since Justi's work is in effect a recapitulation of cameralism, we are justified in reproducing rather fully his own review of the state of cameralistic knowledge at the time of writing. The Preface to the first edition of *Staatswirthschaft* clears the ground in this way:

The economic and cameral sciences are very old in the world. The application of them occurred indeed the moment property was introduced among men, and republics came into existence.

This delightfully unconstrained style of historical free-lancing at once illustrates Justi's irresponsibility to authorities. Yet it would be unfair to treat him as exceptional in making hearsay a sufficient basis for historical generalization. Europe was still in its age of fable. It was half a century after the writing of this preface when Niebuhr's first volume on the history of Rome marked the dawn of the era of historical criticism. If Justi felt at liberty to spin historical formulas out of his imagination, he was exercising a liberty which was at his time under no serious ban of disrepute.

It is important to notice that the word "republic" in Justi's vocabulary is not an anachronism. It is merely the unprecise term in frequent use at the time to denote any civic society.[1] Justi goes on to say that:

People have always been obliged to observe appropriate rules in exploiting their estates, and rulers of republics have found themselves constrained to adopt expedient measures both for organizing the state and for thrift and order in the same. This is the essential in the economic and cameral sciences.

Then Justi cites Aristotle as evidence that theoretical treatment of these subjects was very ancient, and we need not challenge this phase of his retrospect. He proceeds to bemoan the neglect of this branch of science:

All other sciences have workers in superabundance. To these alone have they given little thought, and if we had not been able to collect certain practical observations from people active in these pursuits, but little devoted to learning, these sciences would be everywhere barren and empty. There has been scarcely a thought of teaching these sciences in the universities, and, although teachers

[1] *Vide* Index, title "Republic." Justi applies the designation to the beginnings of civic society, apparently making the origins of the institution of property and of "republics" simultaneous, if not identical. With Justi, as with his predecessors, the word "republic" was a purely generic term of the most general application to all sorts of civic societies in which the relations of ***meum*** and ***tuum*** had begun to receive social sanction.

in excess have been provided for all other branches of knowledge, centuries elapsed after the founding of these institutions before it was found necessary to devote a single chair to these sciences.

From the following passage it is probable that Justi used the same sources which we have quoted above (viz., the books of Gasser and Dithmar, and possibly the tract of Ludewig); but his readers would find no hint of these means of verifying his statements. For the contents of the passage in addition to the data given above, Justi offers no evidence beyond his own assertion. He says (Preface, p. xii):

It was thirty years ago when the former king of Prussia, who was himself a really great manager [*Wirth*], who appraised learning wholly according to its use to the state, and consequently had no very high ideas of the scholars of his time, set the example of establishing in his universities chairs devoted to the economic sciences. This occurred in fact in Frankfurt a. O. and in Halle. That at Halle remains; and in this case the king was so fortunate in his first appointment as to find as an incumbent Privy Counselor Gasser, who really had much talent for these sciences, although he did not think with enough order and system to develop them thoroughly. The king thought so much of his teaching that a Prussian subject stood little chance of promotion if he could not show a certificate from Gasser that he had regularly attended the latter's lectures. This example of the Prussian king at last drew the attention of other states to the advantage of economic professorships. Similar chairs were accordingly founded in Upsala, in Göttingen, and some other German universities, as well as in some academies, as in Vienna and Braunschweig.[1]

Justi expresses himself as highly dissatisfied with the results of this movement. In the first place, cameralistic chairs were still too rare. In the second place, when they exist they treat

[1] While Justi is literally correct about the foundation of cameralistic professorships, he overstates the neglect of these subjects. They were treated more or less formally, oftener, however, on some other than the cameralistic basis, by many men in Germany: e. g., Gerhard, as early as 1713 at Jena. For further details *vide* Stieda (*vide* p. 206 above).

"only *Haushaltungskunst und Landwirthschaft* with less incidentally about *Policey*, and the *Regalien*." That is, to express the idea in today's idiom, Justi regretted that the emphasis had been placed on the operative rather than on the managerial side of gainful occupations. He supported this judgment by referring to the textbooks which Gasser and Dithmar had published in connection with their lectures.[1] These are the only text-writers whom Justi mentions here by name, although the vague reference to "others" shows that he knew more than he cared to tell or was willing to make exact, about path-breakers in the subject. Enlarging upon the criticism just quoted, Justi declares (p. xiii) that it is mere patchwork to deal with these fractions of *Cameralwissenschaft* and to neglect the rest.

> Indeed [he exclaims], thanks to such samples, the statesmen and practical cameralists have the idea that in these sciences no orderly system of theory is possible, and this opinion has been uttered to my face. On the other hand, the students find little that is important in such books, but discover that they have to do mostly with rural economy, which they expect to learn by experience, if they have occasion for it. They therefore look upon these sciences very coldly, and conclude that they can get along without learning them.

Justi adds that another obstacle in the way of these sciences is found in the teachers themselves. They are apt to be people not trained for university careers, and taken from the administrative service. They accordingly are seldom good instruct-

[1] *Vide* above, pp. 207 and 223. He mentions Gasser and Dithmar again (Preface, p. xliii), where he also refers to "a new cameralist" (*vide* p. 309 below). On p. viii of the Preface to the second edition it appears that some reviewers had compared the first edition unfavorably with Zincke's *Grundriss*. Unless the latter writer was the "new cameralist" referred to (and such a phrase would have been both inaccurate and insolent), I have no surmise about the man intended. Justi takes up the matter again in the Preface of the second edition of *Grundsätze der Policeywissenschaft* (*vide* below, pp. 437, 438).

ors (p. xiv). On the other hand, the trained scholars of the academic type who are charged with teaching these subjects do not know enough about them in detail to make their instruction valuable.

At the same time Justi finds a brighter tint for the picture. He thinks there is no doubt of the superiority of the Prussian bureaus to those of other states, and some of this excellence is due to the teachings of Gasser and his colleagues. The establishment of cameralistic chairs had also been accompanied by more publication on the subject, and in most parts of Germany there had been an evident increase of interest in cameralistic science. The same appeared to be true elsewhere, notably in Sweden, and Justi credits Sweden with more progress than Germany in this field. He draws the inference that progress in these respects would everywhere have been still more creditable if instruction in the universities had been more adequate, and the remainder of the Preface is devoted to expansion of this proposition.

Justi goes about his task of establishing the claims of cameralistic science in a way that is quite in accord with the methodology of the time. At first glance it seems not unlike the general argument of Adam Smith. It is impossible, however, not to infer that the preliminary moral part of the argument sits more lightly upon Justi than upon Smith. In the case of the former, it has rather the effect of an *argumentum ad hominem* addressed to people whose conventional views were inhospitable toward his subject. It attempts to show on their own grounds that cameralism has valid claims. He begins with the proposition that there are different kinds of knowledge appropriate to the different uses of life (p. xvi). If we refuse to cultivate the kinds of knowledge necessary for the fulfilment of our diverse duties, it is just as though we had deliberately declined to perform the duties themselves (p. xvii). Included in this necessary knowledge are "natural and revealed religion, morals, or the theory of virtue, and the science of civic law, which shows us our duties in our various stations."

Dividing knowledge into the "necessary," the "useful," and the "attractive," Justi urges that the "economic and cameral sciences" should be recognized as belonging in the first class. "They give us precisely that insight which we most need for the purposes of civic and social life (p. xix). The government of republics cannot endure without them, and there is no social institution or class or mode of life which could do without them entirely."

Advancing to another premise of his argument, Justi predicates of the universities as follows:

> It will be enough if we attend to their ultimate purpose. This, in so far as they are public foundations of the state, can be no other than that of affording to youth properly prepared in the lower schools adequate instruction in all intelligence and science which will be needful for them, in order that they may some time, as servants of the state and upright citizens, render useful services to the commonwealth,[1] and be in a position fully to discharge their duties (p. xx). It follows from the foregoing reference to the ultimate purpose of the universities that it should be one of their principal efforts to teach the economic and cameral sciences (p. xxi).

The argument is then developed by going into detail in expanding the proposition:

> There are very few positions of responsibility in the state in which expertness in the economic and the cameral sciences would not be the chief matter, if the duties of the position were fulfilled and good service to the state performed (p. xxii).

We get something like a direct view into the state of thought at the time by finding that it was necessary for Justi to argue

[1] I give under protest this rendering to the phrase, "***dem gemeinen Wesen.***" It has no exact equivalent in our idiom, and must certainly not be understood to carry the associations which we attach to the expression that must serve us as translation.

against the idea that, while instruction was necessary in law and medicine, civil servants could pick up casually all that they needed to know about economics and cameralistics. While we have a precise parallel with this situation in many universities today in the case of sociology, the academic conditions against which Justi argued have been transferred, in England and America more than in Germany, to business and government. That is, the universities are now eager to teach these subjects, but the practical men are skeptical whether the universities can teach anything about them which cannot be learned better in practical life.[1]

Justi's estimate of the part played by knowledge of the Roman law in German civilization, and as substitute for more specific cameralistics, is also instructive. He says (p. xxv):

The recovery of the Roman law, and provision for teaching it, was the first step which Providence allowed us to take, in leading us out of the thick fog of ignorance which everywhere surrounded us. We therefore owe deep gratitude to Roman legal learning, and it is remarkable that for several centuries it was believed that all human wisdom was to be found in the body of Roman laws. To knowledge of these laws it was chiefly due that we became intelligent enough to begin the extermination of barbarism. Today's fortunate organization of states according to the fundamental principles of economic and cameral science is by no means old. Less than two hundred years ago there was no knowledge of a cameral system in Germany, and at that time men could scarcely have believed that the prosperity [*Aufnahme*[2]] of the trading classes, the encouragement of the classes producing raw material, and the administration of the revenues of the sovereign could occur in accordance with permanent principles and methods. Consequently nothing was known of cameralists. The most eminent magistrates [*Justizbedienten*] of the prince at the same time managed his revenues; or the matter was

[1] *Vide* Spencer's argument in *The Study of Sociology.*

[2] This is one of the ambiguous terms which a literal translation would not fairly render.

held to be of such slight account that the consort of the prince took charge of it, just as today the spouse of a well-to-do private person manages his household. The good arrangements in the police and other bureaus, which we now find in most states, came only gradually into being, perhaps more through accidental suggestions than in pursuance of coherent principles of the governmental sciences. The organization of states is itself perhaps not yet brought to perfection, and perhaps it is only a beneficent fruit of our enlightened century that we at last perceive that the great housekeeping [*Wirthschaft*] of the state, in all its economic, police, and cameral institutions, rests upon coherent principles, which are derived from the nature of republics, and incidentally are veritable sciences.

Justi at once reiterates the moral that these sciences are now worked out in somewhat complete shape, and consequently it would be a dereliction in high places if there should be further delay in making them the subject-matter of university instruction (p. xxvii).

One of the passages in the Preface indicates that Justi's idea of cameral science pictured it as a social polytechnic, and the cameralist as an all-around expert in this complex science of government. Thus he says (p. xxxi):

We may admit, to be sure, that a merely practical cameralist, if he has good natural intelligence, and industriously makes himself acquainted with the institutions of other lands, may become a good particular cameralist (*sic*) in this or that branch of civic administration, but he can never become a good universal cameralist (*sic*). From lack of coherent basic principles he will never walk with secure steps. At every unusual occurrence he will waver and seize upon questionable decisions. If he thinks he has introduced important improvements in this part of the administrative organization, he will at last come to the perception that he has thereby caused disproportionate injury in another part of the great housekeeping of the state, because he did not sufficiently understand the correlation of this great system and the influence which all circumstances of the entire system have upon one another. What can however be more indispensable to a state than perfect universal cameralists? The welfare of the state rests heavily upon them. Most lands appear in this respect to be seriously lacking.[1]

Justi frankly puts the sciences of civic administration, as professed technologies, in direct antithesis with "the other sciences which merely serve to enlarge the human understanding" (p. xxxiii). He urges, however, against the contrary opinion of some scholars, that the former would not interfere with the latter, but on the contrary, "the more we discharge and respect our duties to the state, the more shall we be inclined to improve our understanding."

But Justi is not content with arguing that the universities should undertake instruction in cameralistics. His argument is so cogent in his own mind that it carries him much beyond his premises. Apparently inflamed by a zeal that is kindled in the course of his discussion, he demands still wider scope for his science. He concludes the first branch of his arugment as follows (p. xxxiv):

In my opinion I have sufficiently shown that it is necessary to teach the economic and cameralistic sciences in the universities. This theorem has the corollary that we must prepare youth for such instruction in the lower schools, and there can be no doubt that every new academic citizen[2] should bring with him at least the general theories of *Haushaltungskunst*[3] as the basis for all the sciences which are necessary for promoting the great housekeeping of the state. Indeed, in the very meanest schools, in which the children of the lowest rabble are instructed, at least the most comprehensible precepts should be taught, and the duties which they at some time, as citizens and inhabitants of the state, and as fathers of families, will have to observe. In the case of institutions of this class, we seem never to have thought that it is not less needful to educate good and useful citizens than good Christians.

[1] The rest of the paragraph (p. xxxii) reads like a memorandum for Spencer's *The Sins of Legislators*.

[2] I. e., every matriculant at the university.

[3] Without trying to make too much of it, we may notice that he uses the *art* rather than the *science* concept.

Justi then passes to a second consideration, viz., the proper organization of cameralistic instruction. His proposal is worth quoting at length (pp. xxxv ff.):

It will hardly be supposed that I should regard a single man as sufficient to teach the economic and cameralistic sciences in universities. At least two teachers should be appointed, of whom the one should deal chiefly with police and commercial science, the other with economics and finance. For if these sciences are to be taught completely, fundamentally and to real purpose, each of these professors must have time to treat of this or that portion of his sciences in detail in separate courses of lectures, in order that each may have opportunity to make himself proficient in that branch to which he proposes to devote himself. Some will want to make a career in the manufacturing system, some in the bureaus of taxation and revenue, some in forestry, or the forestry bureau, and all must have opportunity to get detailed instruction in the selected specialty.

The traditional professorship of politics in the universities should be so filled that future ambassadors and ministers could profitably hear the occupant discuss statesmanship, and so that the doctrines taught would not seem ridiculous to actual ministers and statesmen. The professor of chemistry should be of such a character that he would be prepared to teach ***Probier- und Schmelzkunst***, and should not give his time merely to the theory of compounding medicines, which any apothecary's boy can learn without trouble. Likewise, the teacher of mechanics should be prepared to explain the machinery of mining operation and construction, and the professor of natural science [*Naturkunde*] should be able to impart adequate knowledge of ores and of fossils in general. These six professors, to whom we might add the professor of civil and military engineering [***bürgerlichen und Kriegsbaukunst***], if talented, experienced, and expert men were chosen, would compose a faculty that would be uncommonly salutary for civic life. It would amount to an oracle which could with great advantage be called upon in many affairs of state for which it is now often necessary, at great cost, to procure advisers from foreign countries.

In respect to instruction in the economic and cameral sciences, there is first of all needed a *Collegium Fundamentale*, in which all these sciences are presented in a single coherent theory. This is necessary in order that young students may get an insight into the whole, that they may gain a coherent idea of all contrivances in the great housekeeping of the state, and may be filled with correct principles derived from the nature of republics. When they have laid such a ground they will never be entire strangers in any part of the housekeeping of the state, although it may be their intention to emphasize some particular part of civic administration. This will under all circumstances accrue to their advantage, because all affairs of state have an inseparable influence upon one another and an interconnection with one another. This course should properly be heard by every student, unless he is determined not to become a member of the civic organization. Should we not get acquainted with the structure and nature of the civic body in which we live? Should we not make ourselves acquainted with our obligations toward the republic, and is there a scholar to be found who does not need at least the rules of ***Haushaltungskunst?***

The many-colored naïveté of this passage gives it a high value. The cross-lights upon the state of knowledge in general, though not directly in the line of our inquiry, are altogether worthy of attention. The observation most immediately pertinent is that, although Justi's range of effective vision covered only the operations of a system of bureaus developed in the service of an obstinately statical type of state, yet the soul of truth in his contention has gone marching on. We now see that adequate social science presupposes analysis of all the processes within which government is a mediate process, until we have a survey of the whole cosmos of human purposes in the whole complexity of their activities. In other words, we have here an outcropping of the social logic which had never been generalized in its present form until the last half-century. The perception that we need to understand the social activities of which we are factors permits no stopping-place until we have compassed the whole range of activities within which there are traceable connections of cause and effect in human lives.

Our primary interest with the cameralists, however, is in tracing the progress from their preoccupation with a mere administrative technology to an economic theory which would have the same relation to such technology that the science of physics has to civil engineering.

Justi goes on to say (p. xxxvii) that the first part of his *Staatswirthschaft* is for use as a textbook in such a *Collegium Fundamentale*.

It contains in a coherent system the chief principles of all economic sciences. First of all the chief theorems of statecraft [*Staatskunst*[1]] are presented. Then the police administration is explained, which in a broad sense includes the science of commerce. These two sciences occupy the first book. The second book teaches principally the immediate duties of subjects, in which duties are involved the grounds of financial science, and then follow the general rules of management, with the chief theorems of agricultural science.

Justi thinks that this part of the book can be covered in the university in a semester (p. xxxviii).

This fundamental course taken for granted as an introduction, Justi would proceed to develop the involved particular sciences. First of these he says is "*Oekonomie*," and the term is thus put in the place of a specific designation under the generic terms "*Staatskunst*," "*Staatswirthschaft*," "*Haushaltungskunst*," etc. Justi at once explains his use of the title "*Oekonomie*":

It includes not only the general rules of management [*Haushaltung*], but also the theory of municipal management, and especially

[1] The undifferentiated conception of which the word was a symbol at that time cannot be indicated by any English word now in use. The rendering "statecraft" does not quite correspond with Justi's idea, yet it would be more unfair to use the modern term "political science." In the rough, *Staatskunst* as Justi knew it, was the methods of keeping the civic machinery running and of assuring the ways and means on which the machinery depended; including, however, much more management of private affairs than Americans or Englishmen would admit into political science.

of agricultural management. It is necessary to begin the special sciences with these two, because they in turn are fundamental in this field (p. xxxviii).

Again we must make the comment that the apparent validity of this position is shaken by the fact that the "*Oekonomie*," as Justi knew it, was systematized rule-of-thumb. It was the procedure which had become the routine of the traditional bureaucratic state. Its foundation was the sand of assumption that this state was the universal state. "*Oekonomie*" was thus essentially stereotyped usage, while "political economy" as proposed by Adam Smith was essentially an inquiry into principles of economic relationship antecedent to usage, and destined to control usage. We must admit that usage on a different plane set bounds to Smith's objective analysis,[1] yet the contrast between the two systems was at bottom this: Justi was formulating usage, Smith was referring usage to underlying principles. Each procedure had justification after its kind. Neither procedure has yet come to its full fruition. On each side criticism has both brought out incompleteness and found approach to correlation with the opposite procedure.[2]

Of this first fundamental science of the second order, "*Oekonomie*," Justi adds (p. xxxviii):

It not only affords adequate ideas of the subject-matter concerned in all these specific sciences, but its theorems are at the same time an epitome of all the measures which are necessary in the great management of the state. The great management of the state rests virtually upon the same rules which other management must observe.[3]

[1] *Vide* Small, *Adam Smith and Modern Sociology*, pp. 56, 107, 125, 148, 160, etc.

[2] This passage contains a part of the reply which I would make to Frensdorff's generalization. *Vide* above, p. 290.

[3] While this proposition suggests the remark which Herbert Spencer somewhere makes, to the effect that "the problems of the state are merely the problems of the household enlarged and extended," the inferences drawn by the two men from the same generalization were quite contradictory.

In both establishments the ultimate purposes are to acquire "means" [*Vermögen*], to assure what has been acquired, and to use reasonably the goods possessed. The housekeeping of the state is merely of incomparably greater extent than that of a private person. A student who wants to learn the economic and cameral sciences thoroughly, and at the same time wishes to end his studies early, might therefore hear the *Oekonomie* while also hearing the *Collegium Fundamentale*, yet it would always be better if he would begin the more special courses after completing the more general. The course on *Oekonomie* may also easily be completed in a semester.

Next to the economic lectures [continues Justi] should follow in order the course on police science. This is also the first part of the great *Oekonomie* (*sic*) of the state, since it includes the chief measures intended to preserve and increase the general means of the republic. All the methods whereby the riches of the state may be increased, in so far as the authority of the government is concerned, belong consequently (*sic*) under the charge of the police.[1] The science of police is consequently the more immediate basis for the cameral and finance sciences proper, and the expert in police science must sow, as it were, in order that the cameralist in turn may reap. Since this science is very comprehensive, the lectures on it will demand a whole year, if one treats the subjects involved with the proper thoroughness and completeness.

Then cameral and financial science proper completes the series. This is, as it were, the second main division of the great *Oekonomie* of a republic, since it deals with the reasonable use of the means of the state, and the entire internal housekeeping. . . . . This science also is so inclusive that it can hardly be covered properly in less than a whole year.

All these sciences are demanded if one is to attain thorough knowledge of them, and to become a universal cameralist. But if one is destined to become only a particular cameralist, one or the other of these sciences may, if necessary, be dispensed with. For instance, one who purposes to give his attention chiefly to the com-

[1] The "consequently" is obviously a term of reasoning in a circle. But why call attention to a spot on the outside of this cup and platter, while the whole contents were a *ragout* of begged questions?

mercial system may omit the *Oekonomie* and *Cameralwissenschaft*, and after the *Collegium Fundamentale* may turn immediately to police science, etc. (p. xl).

Another specification shows that Justi's perceptions were in more than one direction prophetic. He adds (p. xl):

It is not to be denied that it would be of great advantage if one would begin this study with a course on the history of the police, commercial, economic, cameralistic systems. This sort of history, however, is not yet at all worked out, with the exception of a slight beginning at Berlin, and there is a special lack of a suitable text-book for this purpose. Meanwhile, each of the above-scheduled courses should begin with a brief history of the subject. Thus in the lectures on police one may introduce a discourse on the police arrangements of ancient times, and of the rise and fall of countries and cities; in commercial science one may rehearse the history of shipping and trade, and similarly in the case of the other sciences.

The technological and vocational trend of Justi's ideas is more evident than before in the paragraph in which he begins to discuss the limitations under which instruction in these sciences must proceed. His first proposition may be rendered in modern academic jargon, "It is of course impossible to conduct these courses by the laboratory method" (p. xli). And he continues:

For in these sciences practice would not amount to much if it consisted in preparing cameral documents or acting as a commission in cameral affairs. That is perhaps not the hundredth part of the practical labors in these sciences. In the case of each main division there are numerous side applications. If one were to give specially practical lectures, one would be drawn into repetition of exposition and explanation which would amount to a review of the whole body of science, and a series of years would not suffice for such a course. Consequently every course on a special economic science must be planned in a practical way, especially the courses on police, commerce, and finance, and so soon as the instruction has reached the end of a main division the instructor must exhibit pieces of work of the sort that apply what has been explained. He must require the students to imitate these samples, and he must pass judgment on them publicly. This should be the practice at least with the more diligent students, who have an interest in getting thorough mastery of the subject. It would be impossible to treat in this way all the exercises that might be submitted.[1]

At the close of the Preface (p. xliii) Justi again refers to Gasser and Dithmar, and expresses the hope that his work will be found superior to theirs. He thinks these latter are too defective to be used with advantage. Then occurs the phrase, "a new cameralist," already noted. Justi says that so far as extent of material is concerned this writer is measurably complete. "But it would not be in accordance with the truth if one should attribute to his work an organization firmly based upon the essence of the subject."

In the Preface to the second edition, less than three years later than the first, Justi says that the first edition was exhausted a year and a half before the time of writing.

He betrays a rather innocent idea of the growth of science, when, in apology for enlarging Part I, he says that an author ought not to publish a book until he has reached his limit of ability to treat the subject, so that changes will not be necessary in later editions. He ought at most to publish additions as appendices, but in separate sheets, so that the owner of the first edition could use them with it. He conformed to this requirement in part by making the changes chiefly in the notes (p. iv).[2]

Before entering upon an analysis of the text of *Staatswirthschaft*, mention must be made of the syllabus which

[1] As an item of evidence bearing on the growth of the seminar method in German universities, sec. xlii is worth consulting.

[2] Secs. vi–ix of this preface contain curious circumstantial evidence about the author's attitude toward other writers, and about the sort of liberty which a commentator on political subjects might at that time assume.

preceded it. The main outline is identical with that of *Staatswirthschaft*, and the latter evidently incorporated the substance of the lectures given on the basis of the former. The most notable feature of this outline is the prompt and definite statement of its fundamental thesis: viz., after declaring (§2) that the ultimate purpose [*Endzweck*] of the economic and cameral sciences is the common happiness [*gemeinschaftliche Glückseligkeit*], Justi declares (§3):

Hence follows the first and universal principle, namely: all the governmental activities of a state must be so ordered that by means of them the happiness of the state may be promoted.

Our interpretation of this principle must be deferred.[1]

In accordance with his theory, Justi begins *Staatswirthschaft* with a "short history" of the financial systems and commerce of all peoples. It occupies twenty-six pages. The status of its historicity may be inferred from a note on the second page, in which Whiston's estimate of the population of the antediluvian world is cited as proof that navigation must have been practiced during that epoch, because without it a population twenty times as numerous as that of the modern world could not have been supported!

[1] *Vide* p. 319. The syllabus is entitled: *Kurzer systematischer Grundriss aller Oeconomischen und Cameralwissenschaften*. It is reprinted in Justi's *Gesam. Pol. u. Finanzschriften*, Vol. I, Abth. 2, pp. 504–73; and in Vol. II, Abth. 2, pp. 303–77. A note to §2 says: "I used this outline as the basis of my lectures at Vienna, and it had to be submitted to the previous censorship of the ministry. Graf von Haugwitz was so much pleased with it that he caused it to be circulated among all the members of the *General-directorii*." This seems to settle the case with Roscher as to Justi's academic activities at Vienna. *Vide* above, p. 289.

Both in the essay referred to above (p. 286) and in the *Geschichte* (p. 444) Roscher says that *Staatswirthschaft* was dedicated to Maria Theresia. Frensdorff (p. 385) assumes that such was the fact. I have been unable to find a copy of the first edition, but have used the second (1758). My copy seems to be in the original binding, but it contains no

The character of the historical propositions is seen in the following samples:

The Phoenicians carried on extensive trade both on land and sea; . . . . because her finances were not well administered, this powerful republic in consequence, and also because of party spirit, at last suffered total destruction; . . . there were at the time [of the first Ptolemies] in Egypt 33,339 flourishing cities (p. 7); . . . the Romans, as the rest of their constitution was wise and excellent, had also a well-ordered constitution of the financial system (p. 7), etc.

Justi mentions Livy, Josephus, Suetonius, the Capitularics, etc., but not in a way which shows whether he had first-hand acquaintance with them. The notes do not furnish evidence of the authorities behind the statements in the text, but add illustrative or cumulative material backed by nothing but the author's assertion.

In the sixth section (p. 10) Justi declares:

The Roman commerce declined, just as this realm tended toward its fall, on account of the bad administration of the emperor; and although the Roman Empire in the Orient, especially in Constantinople, in the beginning had a considerable trade, yet this declined in proportion as the realm was weakened by the Arabians or Sara-

dedication whatever. The same is true of other copies of the same edition on which I have obtained reports from libraries in this country. As the Preface to the first edition was dated "Leipzig 11 April, 1755," i. e., in the second year after Justi left Vienna, it does not accord with the circumstances of his departure, so far as theyare understood, to suppose that he would have been in a state of mind to waste any veneration on the empress. Roscher seems to have been in error about the dedication. It is possible that the original of the *Grundriss* may have been dedicated to Maria Theresia, and that Roscher confused the syllabus with the expanded work.

After the foregoing was written I received the following from the library of the British Museum: "The first ed. of Justi's *Staatswirthschaft* (1755) is in B. M. *and is dedicated to Maria Teresia.* His *Kurzer systematischer Grundriss* (1752 ?) is not in B. M." This puts Roscher right; but it also shows that he missed the significance of the omission in the second edition.

cens. On the other hand all commerce passed over to these peoples, especially after they had conquered Egypt.

Then in a note upon this paragraph Justi continues:

Not the division of the Empire, as many writers on history believe, caused the fall of Rome, for both empires remained after the division stronger than the most powerful realms. We must seek the true cause of the fall of both empires in the insecure occupancy of the throne and in the irregular succession, etc.

These platitudes and generalities are below the standards of a modern "finishing school." They are mere space-fillers in a book ostensibly introducing young men to practical governmental careers. It is hard to believe that they could have been regarded by their author as more than rhetorical flourishes.

Coming to the period of discovery and colonization, the information vouchsafed contains this item concerning the English possessions in America:

They possessed there Virginia, Carolina, New England, Scotland (*sic*) besides several other lands and islands (p. 17).

The more serious and practical purpose of the book might be inferred, perhaps, from the points to which Justi calls attention in the case of Germany. He says (p. 24):

In respect to the finances, Germany has been very careless for several hundred years. Only at the end of the last century were manufactures to some extent re-established through the Protestant French refugees, and the former king of Prussia, who was himself a very great administrator [*Haushalter*], by good management, increased his revenues by one-half, and he gave equal attention to manufactures. The present great and wise Prussian monarch has not only retained the former management, but by forming great maritime trading societies he has laid the foundations for sea commerce, etc.

A note to this paragraph declares:

In the Middle Ages, when almost all the revenues of the German princes were derived from the crown estates, which produced little enough, as a rule the consort of the prince, or the prince himself, took charge both of the income and of the expenditure, without the help of bureau employees. In modern times, and even within 200 years, questions of justice and finance, neither of which bulked very large, were dealt with by one and the same body of officials. Landgrave Philipp of Hesse, as appears from his will, had for all his administration two dignified officials, each of whom received fifty florins salary. Elector August of Saxony (1526–86) is, so far as I know, the first of the German princes to have organized an orderly cameral system.

So far as a serious scientific or practical purpose may be supposed to have stimulated this "historical" survey, so far as it is to be regarded as something more than a mere rhetorical embellishment, there appears to be but one object which it can have served. It advertised the importance of administrative thrift. It did this not by analysis of cause and effect which was above the grade of puerility, but merely by calling attention to the matter-of-fact elements of ways and means which romantic or speculative or heedless tradition had formed the habit of neglecting. Perhaps the present state of mind in the United States on the subject of forestry may be cited as the most instructive parallel. Until very recently it was almost impossible to make anyone of the academic or of the political type take the slightest interest in the subject of forest preservation. It was regarded as a matter that would take care of itself, or if not, it was no concern of people whose chief interest was in taking care of themselves. Justi's public was in a somewhat similar state of mind about national revenues. Evidently there was a reason for this in the fact that public revenues were not in the same sense "public" that they are today. They were the revenues of the prince and of his government. While there had been great changes in the technique of administration, and while the problems of productiveness of different sources of revenue had been systematically calculated by the governmental bureaus, it was about as hard, apparently, to create non-official interest in these subjects, as with us at present in the subject of forestry. People then said, "It is the prince's affair; let him look out for it;" just as we now say, "What has posterity done for us? Let future generations look out for themselves." Accordingly, this historical retrospect, utterly without value as a contribution to knowledge, for it was merely a recital of scrappy hearsay, was a bit of homiletical practice. It was an appeal to the suggestibility of hearers, and an attempt to put them into a receptive attitude toward the technological considerations which were to follow.

CHAPTER XIV

ARGUMENT OF JUSTI'S "STAATSWIRTHSCHAFT"

It is now in order to summarize Justi's epitome of cameral science, not with reference to its technological details, but especially with a view to the larger scheme of purposes which these details, and cameralism as a whole, presupposed. In this résumé much reappears that has been said or implied either by Justi or his predecessors.

The argument begins with assertion of the necessity of starting the teaching of any science by laying down fundamental principles (p. 29), as distinguished from the programmes of teaching merely through examples, or practice, or memory.

The importance of basing a system of teaching on principles is peculiarly evident in cameralistics (p. 30). The forethought of a wise government must extend to a thousand sorts of matters which are most intimately connected with one another. If then one lacks a general and connected idea of these governmental affairs, one will in many ways cause injury to the body politic [*gemeines Wesen*], when one attempts to be of use.

Again Justi implies, without dogmatically asserting it, that these affairs of state have never yet been treated in a single book as details growing out of fundamental principles. His note on this proposition still more clearly reflects the situation as he saw it. He says (p. 31):

We cannot assert, to be sure, that there has been a lack of books along these lines. If we consider both home and foreign countries, we may collect quite a library. Yet we cannot find a book among them all which attempts to teach one or more of these sciences on the basis of their correlations with the whole subject. Even the *Compendia* are not exceptions. Usually they treat somewhat of economy and of the royal revenues. If they are very ample, there will be a few sections about the police, but in the fragmentary fashion and disorderly arrangement in which they accidentally occurred to the author. I am by no means inclined to blame others, and I therefore refrain from mentioning names. The facts however are open to the eyes of everyone. Without doubt the reason of it is that, through some ordering of destiny which I do not understand, philosophical minds have paid no attention to these sciences which so intimately concern the welfare of social life.[1]

We call the sciences dedicated to the government of a state the economic as well as the cameralistic sciences, or the economic and cameralistic sciences.[2] Economics or *Haushaltungskunst* has for its aim to teach how the means of private persons (*sic*) are to be preserved, increased, and reasonably applied. What economics attempts to do in connection with the goods of private persons, the governmental sciences aim to do in the case of the total means of the state. Hence they properly bear the name, the economic sciences.[3] We give them the name cameralistic sciences, however, because the high *collegia* which the sovereigns have established, to manage the preservation, expansion, and use of the means of the republic, are usually called *Cammern* or *Cammercollegia* (p. 32).

Our times are so fortunate that almost all rulers are eager to secure for their states a flourishing trade, and for their subjects all kinds of subsistence and temporal welfare. I do not venture to say that this providence always springs from genuine sources, that is, from love for the subjects and from paternal impulse to make them happy. Self-love is here and there the chief motive. Yet there is rather satisfactory consciousness on the part of princes in general that they cannot be great and powerful if they have a land that is poor and resourceless. All courts accordingly use language consistent with the genuine sources of motive for political action. It is

[1] Zincke's *Cameralwissenschaft* appeared the same year with Justi's first edition. I fear he was a cad to publish such a reflection three years later.

[2] In *Adam Smith and Modern Sociology*, pp. 189 and 210, I have called attention to the strange turn of affairs which led von Mohl to declare that political science had nothing to do with political economy. This antithesis must be looked into later.

[3] The unsteadiness of the conception in Justi's mind is evident.

our business to set in order the principles of these governmental sciences, which the nature of things, truth, and sound reason demand. These principles must be derived from the ultimate purpose of the state. What then is a state, and in what does its ultimate purpose consist? (p. 33).

It is evident that Justi is to a certain extent aware that he is proposing ideal principles rather than those which are actually accepted by the ruling classes. It is not so plain that he saw the inherent antagonism between contemporary political policies and abstract principles. He was apparently concerned with generalizations primarily as a rational basis for existing practice, and only secondarily, if at all, as a leverage for change of practice. Yet the moment one begins to formulate human society, in general, or a state, in particular, in accordance with rational categories of whatever sort, one inevitably initiates a reconstructive impulse. The problems are thereby presented: Why does not the actuality conform to the theory? and, What is to be done, either to the actuality or to the theory, in view of the discrepancy?

Justi answers his own question in this way (p. 33):

It is usually asserted that republics have been derived from fear of incursions. It is more probable that they grew out of the governing skill of families; that is, the patriarch must necessarily have had a certain prestige and power over his children and servants, which descended at his death to his eldest son, until in the course of time it amounted to a real rulership. We have many evidences that this was the fact, but of course they do not account for great empires, which have always been formed by force of arms.

With no further fact or theory or criticism as a basis, Justi proceeds to the following definition (p. 34):

A republic or state is a unification of a multitude of people under a supreme power, for the ultimate purpose of their happiness; or we may say, a republic consists of a multitude of people who are combined with each other by means of a general interdependence and certain fixed institutions, in order, with their united energies, and under a superimposed supreme power, to promote their common happiness. Republics are accordingly distinguished from *Gesellschaften* or *Societäten*, which, to be sure, have a certain best, and sometimes happiness in general, as their aim, but have never subordinated themselves to a supreme power. The supreme power in the state accordingly originates without doubt from the people; a principle which today is as universally recognized as true as it was formerly regarded as dangerous by little minds.

Hamlet's reflection, "What a piece of work is man!" might be parodied from the opposite point of view, with such generalizations as the foregoing as the point of departure, With what Pickwickian states of mind do men fool themselves! In a political society in which government was primarily of, for, and by the sovereign, a theorist could still suppose he was dealing with realities in basing a technological system on the presumption that the power of the sovereign is derived from the people. Perhaps the anomaly is most striking when inverted. Sovereigns could persist in acting as though they had absolute rights as sovereigns, for generations after men of thought had discovered that the powers of sovereigns come from the people. The wonder is not so great as it seems, because the anomaly does not by any means last so long after the discovery as appearances seem to indicate. It is altogether improbable, for instance, that to Justi the formula, "The power of sovereigns is derived from the people," meant what it means to us. Nor did it have precisely the psychological sense in which it is a truism. It had rather a vague, dreamy, mixed sense, made up in part of purely idealized notions of the relation, partly of the historical hypothesis above expressed. The thought-medium in which this idea was carried, however, was a strong tincture of superstition about some sort of foreordained fitness of certain hereditary lines to be the repositories of these powers over their fellow-men; and accordingly it carried an energetic presumption that the well-being of these multitudes was to be thought of in terms of the pleasure of the sovereign, rather than of the wants of the subjects.

Yet Justi seems to be very much in advance of his time when he continues (p. 35):

> The ultimate aim of each and every republic is therefore unquestionably the common happiness. . . . . It is unnecessary to enlarge upon the proposition, therefore, that the subjects do not exist for the sake of the ruler.

But it was precisely this principle which was to be the bone of contention between sovereigns and subjects for the next hundred years. The system which Justi was trying to interpret, and for which he wanted to train recruits, was historically an assertion of the contrary principle.

As previously in the *Grundriss*,[1] Justi formulates as "the first and universal principle of all economic and cameralistic sciences" the following proposition (p. 35):

> All the administrative transactions of a state must be so ordered that by means of them the happiness of the same (i. e., of the state) shall be promoted.[2]

To what extent we have here a clue to the conflict of ideas in Justi's mind, and in the civilization of the time, it would be unsafe to infer with much positiveness. The confusion is notorious, both in abstract thinking and in the current social practice. Neither the psychology nor the logic nor the sociology of it is our immediate concern, beyond mere observation of the fact. We are at present interested in tracing the development of scientific consciousness out of this situation. Merely as a symptom of the situation, as a sign of the lack of precision and consistency of view, we may note that in the previous paragraph Justi had been talking about the well-being of subjects, as the end for rulers to subserve, or "the common

[1] Above, p. 310. [2] *Vide* below, p. 327.

happiness." In the formula which he now constructs to embody that idea, the center of attention is the happiness of the state. No long argument is necessary to show that there was room for endless incongruity and inconsistency in theory and practice so long as such variable common denominators were used as "subjects," "the common happiness," and "the happiness of the state."

In other words, there was not yet a precise and consistent analysis of civic relations. Conceptions of civic relations were fluid and shifting. As Hegel might have put it: Experience was only partially self-conscious. Theory was accordingly in many ways in contradiction with itself and with practice. Both theory and practice were unsystematically feeling their way toward precision and consistency. Justi bravely declares that the sequel will prove the theorem just quoted to have the character of a universal principle, and to be the source from which all doctrines of the state and of government may be coherently derived (p. 36).

Then Justi classifies all "republics or forms of government" (*sic*) into the three types:

(1) The monarchy or autocracy, in which the power resides in one alone; (2) the aristocracy, or the government of the better class [*Vornehm*]; (3) the democracy, or the rule of the common people. Then there are mixed forms.

This whole type of analysis, not yet by any means outgrown, makes form of political structure the decisive matter, and does not press back to the psychological or even the sociological meaning of the form. Commenting on the analysis, Justi adds:

It is easy to prove that the monarchical form of government is far preferable to all others, in consideration of the rapidity with which it can grasp the means of happiness of a state, and because many domestic disturbances and discords are thus prevented. It is also certain that a single good monarch can do more good than free republics could bring to pass in centuries (p. 38).[1]

Since the monarchical form of government is taken for granted in this book, it is necessary to consider the various constructions of the monarchical form: viz., (1) with reference to succession of rulers; (2) with reference to unlimited or limited power; (3) with reference to the connection of realms and territories which belong to a monarchy (pp. 39–43).

The analysis under these heads is of the most elementary and obvious sort, and dynastic convenience is throughout the principal test of value. Thus Justi says that there are ample grounds for the conclusion that women are not fit to govern a state; yet he adds that the same reasons would exclude an incompetent or ignorant man from the succession. Without saying it directly, he implies that the fixed succession in the male line is notwithstanding a lesser evil than uncertainty about the succession. In a note he makes a remark which throws light on the preconceptions which lead to this judgment:

A realm is in its essence nothing but an estate [*Landgut*], which might fall into the hands of an alien heir (p. 39).

The discussion is so general in its character that it is a famous object-lesson in the futility of deciding upon social arrangements by means of academic generalizations. Whether a monarchy, limited or unlimited, an aristocracy, or a democracy is the best government, proves to be a question quite co-ordinate with the problem whether a saw or a hat or a loaf of bread is the best piece of property. There is no universal "best" in either case. The historical judgment in both cases, that is, the actual working judgment, the judgment that holds, is the judgment not of types but of workings. The academic method thus illustrated by Justi must always sooner or later

[1] As we have pointed out before, this is today one of the most confident presumptions of *industrial* monarchy.

give way to the pragmatic method best illustrated on a large scale by British history.

At the same time it must be admitted that there was much more pragmatism in fact than in form in Justi's theories; and this is almost universally the case with social philosophers. That is, he dealt with universal propositions, but they were universals of which particular cases were given in the current problems of German states, and more than he was aware he was really asking: "Which of the possible alternatives will work best in this situation?" Questions of checks upon the ruler, of succession to the throne, of relations between territories politically connected only through a common ruler, were everyday affairs. The judgments passed upon them, both by practical and theoretical reasoners, were in this form: So and so works best with us just now: *ergo*, so and so is a universal principle. This type of fallacy is long-lived. In slightly less naïve shape it underlies the Smithian political economy. Adam Smith knew, yet he did not know, that the capitalistic order of society in which he lived was merely a stage in historical evolution in the same series with community ownership, and with feudalism. He believed, however, that the social division, landlord, capitalist, and proletarian, worked well. Hence he canceled the historical factor and concluded that the stratification, landlord, capitalist, and proletarian, is eternal; and he proceeded to draw all further conclusions with this premise reckoned as a finality. The judgments which Justi expresses are defective in a much more elementary way, because they are based on a presupposition of a much more precarious type. The corollaries which he immediately draws are as follows:

(1) The fixed form of succession is necessary to the happiness of a state, because otherwise the state can expect nothing but unrest, wars, and disruption; (2) the territorial possessions, and the freedom of those classes that are not harmful to the welfare of the state must

be preserved; (3) no new liberties and privileges must be conceded which interfere with facile control of the means of happiness of a state (pp. 43, 44); (4) various realms and lands belonging to a monarch must be combined in a union and a general organization, because separation hinders the use of the full powers of the state, prevents complete employment of means of revenue, especially in commerce, and leads to antipathy and jealousy between the different territories.

In qualifying this conclusion Justi betrays the opportunism that is really decisive in all his judgments (p. 46).

Further light falls on the standpoint of the whole system in the elaboration of these clauses. Thus Justi observes that some states seem to assume as a principle the opposite of (2), i. e., liberties are suppressed as much as possible. Thereupon he remarks that "there are weighty considerations making for the conclusion that a monarch does no wrong in adopting this policy: for usually such liberties are no good to the state, but are merely for the benefit of individuals." The two terms, "state" and "individual," here brought into comparison, were relatively unanalyzed concepts; and judgments between them were necessarily rough. The leaning in favor of the state as contrasted with private persons is, however, plain and characteristic. When Justi puts into German the familiar Roman epigram in the form: "The happiness of the state is its highest law," we must understand him to mean not what a Roman tribune would mean, nor what an American democrat would mean. He meant: "The successful carrying-out of the policy which the ruling power in the typical German state sets up as its aim is the paramount consideration." It is impossible to determine precisely how much his frequent partial formulations of more popular standards should modify this proposition.[1]

The nature of the presuppositions on which Justi's system

[1] *Vide* below, p. 327.

rests appears further in his analysis of the monarchical factor in the state. Thus he begins with the definition (p. 47):

A monarch or ruler [*Regent*] is the supreme head of the state, or of the republic, who possesses the highest power in order that by means of it he may take care of all the affairs of the community and may apply efficient means for promoting the common happiness.

These words could of course be fitted out with an utterly democratic meaning. Their connotations at the time were at best patriarchal, and as a rule the patriarchalism was of a sort which inverted the personal relations actually concerned. That is, state policy was incarnated in the ruler, whose success was identified with "the happiness of the state;" while the individuals subject to the ruler were in the last analysis not regarded as having any well-being which deserved to weigh against "the happiness of the state" so conceived. This appears always only in part, in formulas of the royal character or powers. These theorems are never perfectly clear either way. They contain elements of contradictory views. They can be interpreted correctly, therefore, not by mere linguistic rules, but by the light of the conduct in which they were applied. Such partially ambiguous propositions follow, e. g.:

The chief duty of the monarch consists therefore in guardianship of the happiness of the subjects.

But in the next sentence the other conception reappears, viz.:

We should form a very erroneous idea of the monarch if we thought of him as an administrator or superintendent of the supreme power and of the affairs of the community. In this way we should make of the monarch merely the servant of the state, and place the republic over him, so that he could not be distinguished from a *Staathalter*. This is the false notion held by the *Monarchomachi*, from which so many harmful and dangerous conclusions follow.

In the note to this paragraph, the idea is made still plainer, viz.:

> The enemies of the supreme power, and especially of absolutism, whom we are accustomed to call the *Monarchomachi*, adopt as their chief principle the theorem that the whole people is above the ruler, and hence may either call him to account for acts prejudicial to the welfare of the community, or may resist him. From such damnable principles came the unhappy tragedy of the unfortunate Charles I of England, and from the same cause Henry III came to his death in France. Nothing is more detestable than these ideas which are evidently contrary to the nature of a republic and open the doors to all sorts of uproar and disorder (p. 47).

Here then we are dealing with the familiar fallacy of passing judgments first on fragments of situations, and then promoting those judgments to the rank of principles with universal validity. With such beginnings, modern social science is still not too far along in the juvenile grades of its education.

The supreme power [*die höchste Gewalt*] is next defined as consisting "in the use of the total means and powers of the state in order thereby to attain the ultimate end of the same, viz., its common happiness" (p. 48).[1]

Again we must not take these eighteenth-century words as indicating twentieth-century ideas. Every shade of meaning has to be challenged, to be sure that the real thought is detected. The clue to the difference between the earlier and the later conceptions is in the antithesis between the conception of the monarch and the state, as incarnations of the community in a sense which left the people in a status of tributary externality, and on the other hand, the conception of ruler or chief magistrate as merely the representative and the agent of the state, which is simply a name for the people in their political relations. If this latter idea were forced into Justi's further explanations, they would in a general way command present

[1] *Vide* pp. 327, and 372, 373.

assent. But the other idea has to be understood in connection with the words, and they then describe what actually was in German states at the time, but has to a considerable extent been revolutionized out of them meanwhile. Thus Justi says (p. 48):

We should limit the supreme power much too narrowly if we should make it consist merely in laws, ordinances, penalties, etc. To the means and powers of the state belong not only all sorts of goods, both fixed and movable, within the boundaries of the country, but also all the talents and abilities of the persons who reside in the country. The reasonable use of all these things, then, and the prerogative of such use, is therefore the supreme power.

The judgment passed above on Justi's generalization of particular utilities into universal principles, in the case of the monarch, would have to be paralleled if we went into particulars about his opinion of the relations between the lawgiving, the judicial, and the executive departments of government (pp. 49-51).

Following these most general observations about the organization of states, Justi returns to the fundamental proposition which dictates the divisions of his book, viz.:

The business of a ruler falls into two great divisions, to wit: (1) the preservation and expansion of the means of the state; (2) the wise application of these means, both in use and in thrift.[1] Hence all the sciences concerned with the government of a state fall into a twofold division. The first contains statecraft, *Policey*, and commercial science, along with economy (*Oeconomie*), all of which aim either to preserve or to increase the means of the state. The second comprises the cameral sciences proper, which teach how to use these means wisely and in promotion of the happiness of the state.

Since the paramount aim of the state is to preserve and extend

[1] I translate the phrase "*gebrauchet und damit gewirthschaftet*" in this clumsy way, to avoid premature use of the technical concepts "consumption" and "production."

its means [*Vermögen*], this purpose must be regarded as the chief responsibility of rulers, and Justi accordingly deduces the following theorems (p. 53):

1. The monarch must make use of means and measures through which the resources of the state may be preserved and expanded, and his subjects may be made happy.

2. The subjects must facilitate these measures by their obedience and diligence [*Fleiss*].

From these principles another follows, viz.:

3. The welfare of the ruler and the happiness of the subjects can never be separated, and the one without the other can never permanently exist.

There is more pathos and naïvité than conscious hypocrisy in this third proposition. It is true in the same sense in which the familiar classical economic dogma about the unity of interest between employer and employee is true; and it is false in the same way that this economic dogma was false. If there were some infallible arbiter of the interests concerned in either case, the formula might be so construed as to express the truth. The well-being of subjects is by no means necessarily harmonious with the well-being of rulers, when the rulers have power to determine both; any more than the interests of employers and of employees are necessarily one, when the employers have the power to pronounce upon both.

Justi's note on Machiavelli at this point is instructive (p. 54). He cannot understand how his Italian predecessor can possibly have meant some of his doctrines seriously; and therefore adopts the theory that *The Prince* was a heavily veiled satire. The more probable alternative from our present point of view is explanation of Machiavelli and Justi on precisely the same grounds. Each was a product of his environment, with a sufficient force of variation to betray innovating impulses that looked toward a modified environment. Contradiction and inconsistency were in both cases an inevitable part of the situation.

That Justi mixed much sentiment and idealism with his programme of objective analysis, may be illustrated by citation of the next paragraph (p. 55) viz.:

From the combined welfare of the ruler and the subjects alone springs the real strength of a state. This strength consists principally of the reciprocal trust and love which the wise ruler and the fortunate subjects of a considerable state have for each other, while they endeavor with united energies to preserve and extend the resources of the state. For neither the well-filled treasury and the formidable army of the ruler, nor a land living in riches and abundance makes this strength. Such a condition, however happy it appears to be, is by no means sufficient against all accidents. History is not empty of examples of the most powerful and flourishing realms which unexpectedly came to destruction. A monarch has accordingly met with a great loss if he no longer enjoys the love and confidence of his subjects.

It is impracticable to give an adequate account of Justi's work without succumbing to his own tediously repetitious style of exposition. We have already had occasion to notice two or three variations of his general scheme. We come now to still another explanation which we may reproduce in brief. Of the sciences to be treated in the first part of the *Staatswirthschaft*, Justi says (pp. 60–62):

The chief purpose of *Staatskunst* is to assure complete security for the community, both against external and internal dangers. The immediate reason for this purpose is that these dangers threaten the common welfare, and weaken the resources and powers of the state. Statecraft thus obviously seems to preserve the resources of the state.

Policeywissenschaft is concerned chiefly with the conduct [*Lebenswandel*] and sustenance [*Nahrung*] of the subjects, and its great purpose is to put both in such equilibrium and correlation that the subjects of the republic will be useful, and in a position easily to support themselves.

The name "commercial science" is applied to two distinct

sciences. The one teaches the ways and means of conducting commerce, and the composition of goods with which commerce is carried on. The other treats of the measures by means of which commercial enterprises may be established and made to flourish, so that as a result the sustenance of subjects may be more ample and the resources of the country may be increased. The latter presupposes knowledge of the former, so that it is not dependent merely on the reports of traders themselves, and it (the latter) is peculiarly appropriate for those persons who are charged with the government of the state. Accordingly it may be called, in distinction from the first, civic-commercial-science [*Staatscommercienwissenschaft*]. Fundamentally it is a subordinate science of *Policey*, and it is a subject which we shall presently discuss. It is evident that this science, too, ends with extending the resources of the state.

Management [*Haushaltungskunst*] is particularly devoted to showing how the resources of private persons may be preserved, increased, and well used: and since rural thrift is of great importance to the state, this branch of science, after referring to all classes and vocations, gives special attention to the ways and means of cultivation. The more thrifty the private persons, the greater and securer the resources of the state. Again there can be no doubt that the science of management is tributary to the preservation and extension of the resources of the state.

Since the co-operation of ruler and subjects is necessary for these ends, the subject-matter of these sciences involves two chief considerations, viz.:

1. What means and measures has the ruler to adopt, in order to preserve and increase the resources of the state, and thus to promote the happiness of his subjects?

2. What duties have the subjects in order to lighten the responsibilities of the ruler?

The treatment is divided into two books in accordance with this latter subdivision.

As a special introduction to the former of these subjects, civics, or statecraft, on the side of the ruler, Justi attempts to define the concept "happiness" [*Glückseligkeit*], which is the goal of statecraft (pp. 65 ff.). He distinguishes it in the first place from the philosophical concept, "happiness," which he describes as "perfection of our moral condition, and the consequent felicity of the soul." On the other hand, the happiness here in question is either the perfection of our external condition, or some specially advantageous occurrence which could not properly have been expected from our situation. More definitely expressed, Justi means by the happiness of subjects in the present connection:

such good arrangement and structure of a state that everyone may enjoy a reasonable freedom, and by his diligence may be able to attain those moral and temporal goods which the demands of his social station make necessary for satisfactory living.

In spite of himself Justi includes much more than material goods in this concept, yet the moral elements which he inserts in the specifications have to be scrutinized with great care to distinguish them from the concepts which the same terms now suggest to us. For instance, he explains that "the *freedom* of the subjects is indispensably necessary to their happiness," yet the whole treatise is in principle and in detail a definition of relations between ruler and subject to which our generation would deny the predicate "freedom." We must emphasize our previous observation that the essence of the situation of which Justi was a symptom must be formulated as an effort to express, in theory and in practice, the purposes involved in the situation in terms of the paramount governing factor of the situation. This is a social solecism. Social logic is a progressive demonstration of the fallacy. The interaction of the interests represented by these two terms, ruler and subject, or more generally, social control and individual initiative, is the process actually going on, so far as these two terms at any moment are active factors of the process. Justi accordingly had in mind a relatively local, temporary, provisional phase of the social process, and he virtually attempted to generalize this transient situation as a universal condition, and to lay down the laws of its equilibrium as laws of universal equilibrium. When we have pointed this out, we have really closed the rational verdict upon the system, and upon all others of which it is a type. But we are at work upon something more than the mere appraisal of a piece of archaic philosophy and technology. Our main interest in it is as it functions as a term in the evolution of social science in general. With this purpose in view, we must continue the analysis. We must try to discover how the fallacies of attributing a static character to the evolving, and a universal validity to the particular, progressively discredited partial science and forced more valid representation of reality.

Justi specifies "freedom, assured property, and flourishing industry," as the three chief factors on which the happiness of the state and of the subjects depends.[1] These specifications completely omit the factor which modern democracies have placed at the head of the list, viz., government of, for, and by the people. The cameralistic conception of the state was that of a population free to conduct their private affairs for themselves, but not presuming to have thoughts or actions about public affairs except as they were dictated by the ruler. This arbitrary distinction between private and public interests could not withstand the wear and tear of the social process; but before the artificiality of the distinction was discovered civic life had to struggle on a long time under the embarrass ment of the provisional absolutistic theory and practice.

Entering upon discussion of the security of the state, Justi urges (p. 70) that:

more must be understood under this head than the condition of the subjects in which, freed from all violencc and fear, they may peace-

[1] In *Grundriss einer guten Regierung*, p. 65, Justi makes the constituents of happiness, "freedom, internal strength, and security."

fully enjoy their goods and pursue their vocations. The state itself must be in such a condition that, without fear of a stronger power, it may make use of all means and measures which it finds necessary for its prosperity and for the happiness of the subjects. The fact that such danger to the state itself may come from either external or internal assault, makes it necessary to develop the theory of state action with reference to each type of contingency. This gives the classification of the material of this division into two sections.

We come then to the specific teachings of the book. Since Justi is much more significant as an epitomizer of the whole cameralistic movement than as an original contributor to the theory, it is necessary for our purpose to present the most complete survey possible of his principal doctrines. We have therefore compressed the most important sections in the volume into a series of brief propositions, viz.:

1. A republic enjoys external security when it is fortified against conquest and even against the excessive power of a neighboring state (p. 72).

2. Interest is the moving spring of all actions of states, and when two peoples insist on their irreconcilable interests war is the consequence (p. 72).

3. Hence two things are necessary: first, discreet conduct toward other free powers; and, second, a sufficient army (p. 73).

4. Discreet conduct toward other states involves: first, knowledge of all other European states; second, adequate knowledge of the home state, its physical and personal make-up (p. 74).

5. A state must perfectly understand the nature of its relations to other states, the previous history of those relations, etc. (p. 76).

6. The so-called "balance of power" in Europe is an academic invention. If there were such a system no one would have less cause to conform to it than the house of Austria (p. 77).

7. A state must observe natural law, the law of nations, and the social duties toward other states (p. 78).[1]

[1] A note qualifies the proposition by asserting that this must never go so far as the making of apologies by one state to another.

8. A state must seek to discover the movements and intentions of other states (p. 79).

9. For the foregoing purpose the most able and discreet men must be selected as ambassadors (p. 80).

10. But no pains must be spared to get the necessary imformation by secret means (p. 81).

11. No state should invent schemes for the disadvantage of others which would be disgraceful if discovered (p. 81).

12. When a state discovers such secret machinations, it often performs a good service by informing the court of the country in whose interest the plans are made, that the plot is known. This usually leads to abandonment of the scheme (p. 82).

13. When the plan is abhorrent to natural and international law, or to fidelity and faith, it may be made known at other courts (p. 82).

14. Discretion demands that the blame be put on the ministers, not on the sovereign (p. 82).

15. A state must be particularly on its guard against another state in which such a plot has been discovered, even though it was dropped. The same animus is likely to hatch another (p. 82).

16. Measures for the foregoing purpose consist usually in advantageous alliances, which are of two sorts, offensive and defensive, each of which requires its own sort of consideration (p. 83).[1]

17. Allies against a hostile power must be sought among those whose interests and policies are identical with ours (p. 86).

18. Guarantees, and other treaties, by which free powers promise aid in stipulated cases, are also means of security for a state (p. 89).

19. Another protection against outbreak or extension of war, is the treaty guaranteeing the neutrality of a given territory (p. 87).

20. Frequently some European power, under a particularly energetic prince, threatens to subordinate the rest of Europe. Then a wise monarch is both privileged and bound to adopt means to keep such a prince within proper limits (p. 88).

[1] Justi has a long note on this subject in which he takes decidedly advanced ground against war except for the most important reasons. *Vide* §56, p. 88, last sentence.

21. Such measures vary according to circumstances, but they must not include treachery (pp. 88–90).

22. Discreet conduct toward the other free powers is not a guarantee of external security, but other means of defense will be required (p. 92).

23. The chief of these is an adequate army (p. 92).

24. Recruits from the inhabitants of the state are preferable to foreign mercenaries (p. 93).

25. The army must be in constant readiness for war (p. 95).

26. There are three ways to make an army brave and invincible: (1) By honors and rewards, together with appeals to love of country, after the example of the Romans; (2) by granting license to plunder and ravish, as in the case of Tamerlain, Attila, etc.; (3) by maintaining discipline through fear of punishment. The third only is to be recommended (p. 97).

27. In a well-ordered state the military budget must take precedence of everything else (p. 98).

28. The monarch should be commander-in-chief of the army (p. 99).

29. Fortifications are another means of security (p. 100).

30. Maritime nations also require a fleet (p. 101).

31. Incidental to these latter, various munitions of war must be collected (p. 102).

32. Resort must be had in extremes to troops furnished by allies, and to mercenaries (p. 103).

33. It is most advantageous when the allies make separate invasions of the enemy's territory (p. 104).

34. It is a question whether subsidizing revolt in an enemy's territory is a permissible means of security (p. 105).

35. It is permissible to destroy an enemy's trade and commerce (p. 106).

36. Non-permissible means of defense are: assassination of the hostile monarch or his ministers; bribed incendiarism, murder, or similar treacherous violence; poisoned weapons; violation of truce.

ON THE DOMESTIC SECURITY OF A STATE

37. The domestic security of a state consists in such a well-ordered constitution of the same that all parts of the civic body are

held in their appropriate correlation, and in the consequent repose, while the persons and property of individuals are protected against all injustice and violence (p. 108).

38. For the above purpose each class in the state must be required to keep its appropriate place (p. 108).

39. The relation which subjects must observe toward the state, as well as toward each other, is based on a moral foundation. A wise government therefore will have a care for the religious faith which the people profess (p. 109).

40. The state must care for the administration of justice (p. 110).

41. The state must protect the subjects against frauds and violence (p. 111).

ON THE ATTENTION OF THE RULER TO THE EXTERNAL CONDITION OF CLASSES AND THEIR RELATION TO THE STATE AND TO ONE ANOTHER

42. No one should be permitted to gain so much power and wealth that he might be dangerous to the state or to his fellow-citizens (p. 112).

43. The ruler has nothing to fear from the wealth of his subjects if it is not too unequally distributed (p. 113).

44. The ruler must first of all give his attention to securing the best talent for the high offices of state and of the army (p. 114).

45. No officer should be allowed to gain enough power to be dangerous to the state (p. 114).

46. Hence no officer should be intrusted with *lettres de cachet* (p. 114).

47. Offices should not be hereditary (p. 114).

48. Neither at court nor in the state should there be different parties (p. 115).

49. No special class, family, or single person should be allowed to gain so much power that disobedience to the supreme power would be safe (p. 116).

50. No one should be permitted to possess fortifications or maintain an armed force (p. 116).

51. Subjects should not be allowed to attach themselves to foreign powers (p. 116).[1]

[1] A note applies this proposition particularly to the Jesuits.

52. No privileges should be permitted to subjects which are harmful either to the state or to other subjects (p. 117).

53. No class should be permitted to monopolize the riches of the country (p. 119).[1]

54. The ruler must not disregard the feelings of the subjects toward himself or his ministers (p. 120).

55. The ruler must use all the wisdom possible in governing his conduct in case disorders arise (p. 121).

ON THE ATTENTION OF THE RULER TO THE MORAL CONDITION OF SUBJECTS, PARTICULARLY THEIR RELIGION AND CONDUCT

56. The moral condition of the subjects must be such as will accord with the welfare of the state (*Wohlfahrt des Staats*), and promote internal security (p. 122).

57. The ruler must not allow his own religious opinions to be the sole criterion of the goodness or badness of the religion of his subjects; but he must always treat that religion as true which has been introduced by the fundamental principles and constitutions of the state or by the treaties of his predecessors (p. 123).

58. The regent must nevertheless attempt to establish unity of faith among his subjects (p. 124).

59. On the other hand the welfare of the state must be preferred to unity of faith (p. 124).

60. The ruler must prevent the introduction of opinions about religion which are blasphemous and disgraceful, and which tend to demoralize the character of the subjects (p. 125).

61. For the forgoing reason, a censorship of books must be established (p. 126).[2]

62. The ruler must try to stimulate the intelligence of his subjects (p. 128).

63. The ruler should use the thousand means which are at his disposal to put premiums on personal virtues of all kinds (p. 128).

[1] Again a note states that this has special reference to the Jesuits, and intimates that the author's teaching in this spirit in Vienna was one of the causes of his becoming *persona non grata*.

[2] The qualifications which Justi adds would seem to the modern mind sufficient to nullify the proposition itself.

64. Yet the ruler must not go so far as to pry into the family life of unsuspected persons (p. 130).

65. The ruler must not deny the subjects innocent pleasures (p. 131).

ON THE ADMINISTRATION OF JUSTICE

66. The supreme power must adjust strife between subjects over property, pursuits, and transactions, and the decision must rest on the constitution of the republic and on the principles of morals (p. 132).

67. The administration of justice is to be distinguished from the science of law. It belongs partly to statecraft, partly to *Policey* (p. 132).

68. The laws must correspond with the condition of the community, with the character of the various groupings of the subjects, and with the particular purposes which a wise government proposes (p. 133).

69. The laws must be plain and intelligible (p. 134).

70. The laws must be brief and simple (p. 135).

71. Good laws will be in vain unless the government selects men of high character for judges (p. 137).[1]

72. Even then the judges cannot be trusted without careful supervision (p. 138).

73. Before all things the administration of justice must be non-partisan (p. 139).

74. The judicial procedure must be prompt and brief (p. 139).

75. It would promote justice if the costs of court procedure should be defrayed by the state and not by the litigants (p. 140).[2]

ON THE MEASURES OF THE RULER FOR SECURING THE PERSONS AND GOODS OF SUBJECTS

76. Domestic security demands that the persons and goods of subjects shall be safe (p. 141).

[1] Justi cites the French Parliament as an example of a wise arrangement of influence upon the ruler in an unlimited monarchy, from the judicial department. He apparently had no suspicion of the verdict which the Revolution was about to pass upon that same Parliament.

[2] Justi speaks on this point as though he considered his opinion utterly impractical.

77. This safety must be assured both against domestic and foreign violence or fraud (p. 142).

78. Nations frequently regard the traders of another nation as legitimate booty (p. 142).

79. Nations sometimes kidnap the subjects of other nations for soldiers (p. 143).

80. Nations sometimes encourage special sorts of lotteries, or other fraudulent schemes for obtaining the property of the subjects of other nations (p. 144).

81. The worst sort of domestic violence is nocturnal robbery and murder, whether on country roads, the streets of cities, or in private houses (p. 145).

82. If we seek the sources of these evils, they are to be found chiefly in the defective education of youth, and in the consequent excesses of adults, the scarcity of food in the country, or the defective impulse to perform remunerative work, the oppression of the land under heavy taxation and other wrongs of government (p. 145).

83. A wise ruler would not have much difficulty in adopting measures which would remove these conditions (p. 146).

84. Meanwhile the minor civic officials must be required to keep sharp watch of criminals (p. 146).[1]

85. Frequent visitations of roads, forests, and suspicious houses, and the use of the militia on country roads and at night in the streets of towns, are advisable. Also the closing of public houses at an appointed time, and sharp watch of them after that hour, while the watchmen themselves must be subject to the severest punishments, if they take bribes to allow criminals to escape (p. 147).

86. Thieves are on the whole more dangerous to security than robbers and murderers, and must consequently be zealously traced and punished (p. 147).

87. Vagabonds of all sorts must be driven from the country (p. 148).

88. Watch must be kept at the boundaries against such classes,

[1] Again Justi, whether facetiously or as a mere excursus in academic utopianism it is impossible to decide, suggests that it would be well to imitate the Chinese custom of docking the pay of officials if they failed to apprehend robbers or murderers within six months of the crime.

and householders must be required to report the names and circumstances of the people who lodge with them (p. 149).

89. It is a question whether a wise government should tolerate Jews. They surely cause much harm by their usury and sharp practices. Yet it is also a question whether they have not been forced to these and even criminal practices by the policies of governments toward them. Probably if they were admitted to all means of gaining a livelihood they would be as useful to a land as other subjects (p. 150).

90. A wise government must finally punish with severity all other kinds of violence, such as duelling, outbreaks of apprentices, and all ways of taking private steps to supplant the law in meting out justice (p. 151).

91. To prevent these evils, the law itself must efficiently treat the conditions which they are intended to correct (p. 151).

ON THE RICHES OF THE STATE

92. Besides security, sufficient wealth is necessary to the happiness of a state (p. 152).

93. By the wealth of a country we understand a sufficient supply of goods to satisfy the needs and conveniences of life, and by means of which the subjects by diligence and labor may find adequate sustenance (p. 152).[1]

94. Such being the nature of wealth, if a land yielded an abundance of such useful things, and had no trade relations with other lands, we might call it rich, even though it contained no trace of gold and silver (p. 152).

95. Because of international transactions we need a ware [*Waare*] which is rare, to which all peoples assign equal value, which is durable and easily carried, to be used as a universal means of payment (p. 153).

96. Gold and silver possess these qualifications. Consequently a land cannot be regarded as rich today unless it possesses a sufficient supply (*genugsame Menge*) of these metals (p. 153).

[1] It is obvious at a glance that this description is an unanalyzed compound which presently had to be decomposed into the concepts, "wealth" and "capital."

97. Token currency is in no proper sense an addition to national wealth, although it may be a means of increasing wealth (p. 154).

98. If a ruler could circulate token currency at will, he could gradually absorb the whole national wealth (p. 155).

99. Such currency ought not to be used unless a definite term is fixed for its redemption (p. 155).

100. We must distinguish (*a*) the wealth of the ruler; (*b*) the wealth of private persons; (*c*) the wealth of the land (p. 155).

101. Gold, silver, and costly ornaments stored in the treasure-chests of the monarch are of no use to the country and would not alone tend to remove the land from poverty (p. 155).

102. The same is the case if there are many rich persons in a country who either hoard their wealth, or keep it in foreign banks (p. 155).

103. The true conception of national wealth then is that it consists of an adequate supply of money, distributed among the subjects, employed in gainful pursuits, and constantly passing from one hand to another (p. 156).

104. In order that the people may be able by labor and diligence not only to support themselves but to supply the needs of the state, the ruler must see (*a*) that all measures are taken which secure the necessary means of increasing wealth; (*b*) that all necessary means are used to insure the constant employment of this wealth in gainful ways, and the circulation of it from hand to hand (p. 156).

ON INCREASE OF THE WEALTH OF THE STATE

105. A state cannot increase its wealth without guarding what it already possesses. The first rule of a wise government therefore should be to prevent by all possible means the unnecessary removal of money from the country (p. 157).

106. This involves stopping, by the court, of purchases of foreign goods and discouragement of customs which tend to take the money of private persons out of the country (p. 157).[1]

[1] The item chiefly in Justi's thought at this point is the custom of deposit in foreign banks, and the antidote which he proposes is such a firmly established domestic bank system that a premium will be put on keeping the funds at home.

107. The second fundamental rule of a wise government must be that there should be constant effort to increase the wealth of the state, for a land cannot be too rich (p. 158).

108. On the other hand riches must not be increased at the cost of oppressing other peoples, for such means of obtaining wealth demoralize those who so obtain it. The chief cause of the fall of the Persian and Roman monarchies is to be found in their disregard of this principle (p. 158).

109. There are three chief ways of increasing the wealth of a land: (1) the increase of population; (2) foreign commerce; (3) mining.

ON INCREASE OF THE POPULATION OF A COUNTRY

110. Increase of the population increases the means of a country both because the newcomers bring goods into the country, and because they stimulate circulation of money (p. 160).

111. It is thus certain that large population makes a state prosperous provided its constitution is beneficent.[1] The talents of the persons in the republic, indeed the persons themselves, are among the resources of the state. The larger the number of people living in the country therefore, the greater will be the means and power of the republic. Hence the duty of the ruler to promote increase of population (p. 160).

112. It is often asked whether a population cannot become too great, so that some will obstruct the happiness of the rest. Nothing is so unfounded as this objection. Given flourishing commerce, manufactures, and trades, with well-administered police and government in general, and there is no good reason why the population should stop at any particular point. Holland and China are evidence to this effect (p. 161).

113. There is no reason to fear that population could overtax the food supply. Europe could feed six times its present population (p. 162).

[1] The expression is "*seine Beschaffenheit und Regierungsverfassung.*" This seems to be one of the rare cases in the cameralistic books of use of the term *Verfassung* very nearly in the modern sense. *Vide* above, pp. 34, 70.

114. If we had wise police and economic administration, there would be no need of allowing emigration to America (p. 163).[1]

115. To encourage increase of population the government in the first place must be beneficent and mild (p. 164).

116. As a particular under this generalization, reasonable freedom must be permitted to the subjects (p. 165).

117. The growth of population is scarcely possible unless the ruler permits complete freedom of conscience (p. 165).

118. Freedom of conscience must be distinguished from complete freedom of religious liberty. The latter is to be granted only under approved conditions. The former, consisting of rights of belief and household worship, should be allowed in so far as it is not harmful to the state (p. 165).

119. A wise ruler will not leave the food supply and employment of subjects to take care of themselves, but will see that they are systematically made abundant (p. 167).

120. Still further, the government must encourage the immigration of rich and talented people of all kinds, and may resort to titles, honors, positions, and privileges as premiums to them (p. 168).

121. So far as possible, the government should relieve newcomers who wish to build, of the taxes, building-permit fees, etc. (p. 168).

122. Special encouragement must be given to skilled foreigners who wish to introduce into the country desirable industries (p. 169).

123. The ruler should see that the laws are favorable to the marriage relation (p. 170).[2]

124. A wise Catholic ruler will try to limit the growth of the clerical orders, for they are largely responsible for the unfavorable contrast in population between Catholic and Protestant countries (p. 173).

[1] The pious reflection is subjoined: "Nevertheless we must bow to the wise providence of God, which perhaps in this way will make the most remote regions of the earth moral, reasonable, and enlightened in religion."

[2] Certain fines and penalties for celibate men are suggested, and it is further hinted that instead of requiring a payment to the government for permission to marry, a reward should be given for marrying.

125. A wise ruler will consider seriously the point of view of population, before entering into war. He will especially encourage all means of diminishing sickness and of preventing plague (p. 173).

126. A wise government will check drunkenness and other demoralizing vices (p. 173).

127. The art of medicine must be brought to the highest efficiency (p. 174).

128. Surgery, midwifery, and pharmacy must for the same reason be encouraged and regulated by the government (p. 175).

129. Provision must be made for assuring purity of foods (p. 175).

130. The cleanliness of cities must be assured, and this requires attention to the building regulations (p. 176).

ON COMMERCE WITH FOREIGN PEOPLES

131. Commerce is transactions in means of sustenance in which the goods and wares are exchanged with advantage either against gold and silver, or against other wares, and by this process the needs and conveniences of human life are satisfied. This explanation includes everything which belongs to the nature of commerce and to comprehension of it (p. 177).

132. Only foreign commerce can increase the wealth of a land (p. 178).

133. The first principle of commerce must be that more gold and silver shall be brought in than carried out by it (p. 178).

OF KNOWLEDGE OF THE NATURE OF COMMERCE

134. The first distinction to be made is between goods produced at home and those obtained from abroad (p. 179).

135. When commerce is carried on with domestic wares, the wealth of the land always gains something by it, but this kind of commerce may nevertheless be very disadvantageous to the state; for if the wares are carried from the country in the raw and untransformed condition, or are drawn from foreign nations, the land loses considerably from the earnings and support of subjects which might have been enjoyed from the same (p. 180).[1]

[1] This paragraph is translated as literally as possible; the obscurity is in the original.

136. When commerce is conducted with foreign wares alone, this is either because these wares are to be consumed at home, or because they are to be traded, with profit, to other nations. The first sort of commerce is wholly harmful to a country; for although the special traders, certain commercial cities, and the tariff and excise accounts of the ruler may temporarily profit, the land as a whole cannot gain anything by such trade. On the contrary, if it has no other sources of wealth, it must gradually lose all its gold and silver, and this harmful trade must at last stop from lack of means of payment (p. 180).

137. The second sort of foreign trade is incomparably more profitable for the state (p. 181).

138. There is a great difference in goods with respect to the source, or the lands from which they are derived. The trader must know all about the differences, and he must know whether he receives them from the first, second, or third hand, and where they can with profit be sold. The cameralist, however, must know them so far that he can judge what sorts are most advantageous for the entire system of commerce, and for domestic manufacture, or with which kinds the land may most easily carry on profitable trade (p. 182).

139. Another difference in wares springs from their essential nature and composition. That is, they may be rough or fine, useful or useless, superfluous or necessary, genuine or spurious, fresh or spoiled, etc. Of all these differences, a trader must be fully informed. A civic official in the commercial department must also be somewhat intelligent about these things, in order to promote the transportation of the wares, and properly to assess the duties and excises (p. 182).

140. There are also differences with respect to their external and accidental condition; i. e., packed or unpacked: to be counted, weighed, or measured; salable or unsalable and contraband—the latter only temporarily and in time of war forbidden. Both merchants and cameralists need to be informed about these details (p. 183).

141. These various sorts of goods occasion many sorts of trade; e. g., the customary classification is: (1) Cloth; (2) Silk; (3) Spices; (4) Groceries [*Materialien*]; (5) Hides and furs [*Rauch- und Pelzhandel*]; (6) Gold, silver, or jewels; (7) Books. This however is

merely an approximate classification, for there may be as many sorts of trade as there are separate sorts of wares. Indeed it is advisable for a trader not to deal in too many wares. If he dares to confine himself to a single one he can more effectively master the conditions of that trade. Small traders who have to look out merely for cost and sale may carry a miscellaneous stock (p. 183).

142. Trade comprises two chief types of transactions: (*a*) obtaining the wares; (*b*) marketing them (p. 184).

143. All domestic goods come either from cultivating the earth, or from stock-breeding, or from industries [*Gewerben*]. As to agriculture, a wise merchant will either himself engage in it, or by advancing loans, storage, and favorable contracts will seek to get the wares at a good price. As to products of stock-raising, he may, by cash payments, by courteous conduct and minor attentions [*eine kleine Ergötzlichkeit*], get the good-will of the shepherds and other country folk who have such things for sale. The wares, however, which come from the trades, are procured best through the establishment of manufactures and factories. Sometimes advances to the manufacturers and hand-workers will secure the goods. A wise government, on the other hand, will always see to it that all these domestic wares are supplied at the required quality and price, in order that the favorable balance in other countries may be retained (p. 184).

144. As to obtaining foreign wares, they come either by wagon or by boat from neighboring lands, and in such cases the factors involved are essentially those just named; or they are brought from long distances across seas. For that purpose the merchant must either have ships of his own, if commerce is free to all, or he must buy shares in trading associations, or in the great auctions he must provide himself with the needed wares (p. 185).

145. By "shares" [*Actien*] we understand those participating parts which a great privileged trading society at its organization sells at a fixed price, in order thereby to bring in the sums which must be used in the trade of the society. These shares, which thereafter may be resold, rise or fall in price, according to the success of the society (p. 185).

146. Since seafaring is beset with many dangers, a wise mer-

chant will never risk his whole resources, or a large portion of them, at one time upon the waves. Consequently it is not only customary for many merchants to join in fitting out ships, but many forms of contract have been invented, such as shares in ships, insurance, etc. The most important of these is insurance; that is, another party undertakes to assure the cargo of a ship for a payment of 3, 5, 10, 20, 30, or more per hundred, according to the degree of danger to be feared, and in case of loss to make it good (p. 186).

147. The second chief type of transaction, sale, depends principally upon good correspondents, who protect the merchant by giving him timely notice of rise and fall of prices and other circumstances which affect his trade. A good merchant must be able to distinguish between a correspondent who can be relied upon to serve his employer's interests and one who is seeking chiefly his own advantages. The bourse, a house where in great trading centers the merchants daily meet to transact business, is very prolific of such reports, but they cannot be regarded with much confidence (p. 187).

148. Actual sale is of various kinds: e. g., for cash payment, on credit, on instalments, on exchange, on venture, or on speculation [*a l'aventure ou en l'air*], or by means of commission merchants, factors, fairs [*Messen*] or similar devices. A merchant must be well instructed about these different sorts of trade, together with the cost of transportation, tariffs, probable dangers, and the prices to be expected, in order that by weighing these items over against one another he may be reasonably assured of profits. He must also assure himself about the reliability of the persons intrusted with the transportation, also concerning the warehouses and other circumstances of the towns and roads through which the goods must pass (p. 186).[1]

149. To keep all these things straight, bookkeeping is necessary. It is customary to use the following books: The inventory book; the manual, or memorial, or chief book; the journal; the debt book; the credit book; the treasury book; the secret book; the stock book; the expense book. All of these must be kept in the greatest

[1] To those who imagine that commercial dishonesty is of recent growth, Justi's note on types of rascality which have to be counted on would furnish valuable information.

order, and they must exactly correspond with one another. For this reason, in large concerns a special bookkeeper is appointed (!) (p. 188).

150. The ultimate purpose of all these transactions is, on the side of the republic, to export goods produced in the country, and not needed, and therefrom to gain increase of wealth, as well as to provide the land with all those goods which are required for the needs and convenience of human life. On the side of the merchant, however, gain is the single purpose of all his endeavor. In view of the service which he renders to the state, of the danger which he incurs, and of the labors which he undertakes, we should not begrudge his gains. They consist in the increase of his goods and of his means. The amount of his goods depends entirely on the value which they have in terms of gold and silver. Consequently the single aim of the merchant is to increase his resources in gold and silver, or in goods which in comparison with these metals have a great value (p. 188).[1]

151. Gold and silver is also in fact the ground (*sic*) of all commerce[2] carried on in the world or at least among civilized or somewhat intelligent peoples (p. 189).

152. Because merchants have constant occasion to transfer gold and silver to one another, a large number of devices have been invented to serve their purposes. Thus the important exchanges, and the system of bank credits, whereby gold and silver are transferred only in imagination, yet with the same advantage to the merchant as though the metals were actually delivered. The essence of the matter is that one gives to a third party notice that the sum due can be drawn at a certain place. This simple and natural way of payment is then by the laws, by the different moneys, and other circumstances, surrounded with a multitude of formalities and special details, which today compose a considerable part of the

[1] In such propositions as this, mercantilism seems to be less false than crude and unanalyzed.

[2] Transliteration of the vague term *Grund* is probably the best way of indicating the altogether immature character of the thought in this connection.

science of commerce, not only for the merchant, but also for the cameralist (p. 189).

153. A bank is a public institution of the state in which merchants and other private persons may at will securely deposit sums of money, in such a way that they may withdraw the same any hour, or may use their deposits for payment to other persons by means of the bank-credit system. Banks of this sort are called deposit [*Giro*] or exchange banks, in distinction from loan banks (p. 190).

153A. It must be repeated that not money, but gold and silver, is the chief price and the universal means of payment for all goods. Money, so far as foreigners are concerned with it, is in fact itself nothing but a ware worth just what the gold and silver in it will bring (p. 191).[1]

154. Those rulers who coin depreciated money miss their calculation in expecting to gain by it. Foreigners will take it only at its true value, and even something less. The bad money therefore returns to the land that coins it. It is paid back by the subjects into the treasury of the ruler, and he deceives himself if he supposes he has in the treasury more than the actual gold and silver. This flattering idea disappears as soon as the attempt is made to purchase abroad. Meanwhile the subjects who have received the money from the ruler at the imaginary value, and who must make foreign purchases, suffer (p. 191).

155. The persons engaged in trade are either principals, subordinates, or auxiliaries. The duties of each of these classes must be treated in the special textbook on commercial science (p. 192).

156. The fundamental principles of merchants must be distinguished from the measures and purposes of the government. While the merchant aims only at gain, and is not always concerned whether his gain corresponds with the advantage of the state, a wise government, on the contrary, must give the chief attention to this latter consideration. Hence the merchants may be much dissatisfied with the regulations of trade. Domestic manufacture and trade are far less inviting to them on this account than the welfare of the

[1] It is rather remarkable that Justi does not state in the same connection that gold and silver are themselves essentially "wares" like any other.

state demands. It is not to be assumed, however, that the advantage of the whole state is incompatible with the prosperity of the merchants. The former may, however, require that the advantages enjoyed by the latter shall be less than at some other periods. Even in this case the merchants may offset the restrictions by interesting themselves in promoting mining, manufactures, etc. (p. 194).

ON THE FOUNDING AND THE PROSPEROUS CONDITION OF COMMERCE

157. No European country is entirely without foreign commerce, but some of it is very harmful, and cannot continue without adequate increase of wealth from other sources (p. 195).[1]

158. The establishment of commerce presupposes that it will obtain a condition which promises permanence with advantage to the state (p. 195).

159. The founding of commerce is not a mere matter of appointing and encouraging fairs and markets (p. 195).

160. If at these markets more foreign than domestic goods are sold, then they are only a great vortex from which more gold flows out than comes in, and the town where the fair is held is the only gainer, and it consequently holds on to its advantage as long as possible, in spite of the general poverty of the country (p. 196).

161. Prohibition of the exportation of money does not secure profitable commerce. In the first place it cannot be effective, in the second place it would deprive the subjects of many things which their present standard of life requires, and in the third place it could accomplish nothing of itself in the direction of establishing commerce (p. 196).

162. The first principle of advantageous commerce with foreign nations is, that more gold and silver shall come into the country as a result than goes out, and on this principle must all measures for establishing useful commerce be founded (p. 198).

163. Since commerce must be carried on either with domestic or foreign goods, and since the mere importation of foreign goods cannot possibly constitute an advantageous trade, there follows naturally another principle, viz.: The value of the domestic products

[1] *Vide* Proposition 135, above.

exported must exceed the value of foreign wares imported. The inferences from these two principles will give us all the measures necessary for the establishment of commerce (p. 198).

164. The excess value of exports over imports can be secured in only two ways: first, the quantity of imported foreign wares must be diminished; or, second, the gaining and exportation of domestic products must be increased (p. 198).

165. In fact these two methods must be combined in order to assure the result (p. 199).

166. For this purpose a wise ruler must inform himself precisely about the exported and imported wares and their aggregate values. These facts must be exhibited in tables drawn from the tariff and excise registers, so that they can be reviewed at a glance. For greater exactness the contents of the tariff and excise registers may be tabulated separately and compared with each other. To be still more certain, all merchants, artists, manufacturers, and artisans may be required to report what kinds of wares they imported during the previous year, and what domestic products they sent abroad. By these three processes together the facts may be somewhat exactly ascertained (p. 199).

167. We call this casting the general trade balance. The special trade balance is a similar showing of the imports and exports between the home and a specified foreign country. A wise government will every year keep both accounts (p. 200).

168. A wise ruler or his ministers will study these tables to discover whether among the imports there are any which could be produced at home, and thereupon it must be made a fixed rule that nothing which can be produced at home shall be imported. The necessary measures must then be adopted to promote production of those wares (p. 200).

169. In this connection all kinds of textiles call for attention, since they are for clothing and are accordingly necessaries of life. Every land either has materials for these, or can easily get them. Silk-weaving is also possible in northern countries. Wool may be grown everywhere, and the fine wool to be mixed with it may be had through trade, as the English importation of Spanish wool. Hence such manufacture ought not to be omitted (p. 201).

170. Yet foreign trade in such fabrics is not to be expected. Our neighbors, England, Holland, France, and Wales, have already too long start of us. But it will be advantage enough if we check the import of foreign textiles (p. 201).[1]

171. The only variation from the last conclusion is in case we can invent such improvement in the fabrics, that we can make foreigners our debtors (p. 202).[2]

172. The same principle holds in the case of every sort of ware which might be produced at home. As everything cannot be done at once, beginnings should be made in the case of those wares which are most used at home, and for which the largest sums are now sent abroad (p. 203).

173. A second rule must be kept in mind along with the first, viz., preference should be given to those industries which would employ and support the most men (p. 203).

174. A third rule should also be followed, viz., to prefer those industries for which the raw materials are produced at home (p. 204).

175. On the other hand, those industries must be stimulated which will produce goods that foreign nations need (p. 204).[3]

176. In order to exploit these resources it is necessary for the government to rouse a commercial spirit among the subjects.[4]

177. No monopolies in such domestic products, and no similar privileges should be granted (p. 209).[5]

[1] In such propositions it appears that Justi's generalization was even narrower than its usual form would indicate. The problem was not even that of the type of state then regarded as permanent, but of the author's particular state.

[2] Justi's note on this section is a plea for governmental encouragement of inventors.

[3] A considerable list follows of German resources for such supply.

[4] The picture of unthrift and indifference which follows is an important piece of culture-historical evidence. There is also a plea for industrial education which has a truly modern ring, and also suggestions about stimuli to individual effort.

[5] The reasons assigned for this rule make against protective tariffs, and all the consequences which Justi suggests have been illustrated on an enormous scale in recent years. Justi adds that this last principle

178. Assuming such measures for promoting domestic production, a wise government must give its attention to measures for inducing foreigners to take the wares. Two factors must be assured: (1) The wares must have the desired quality; (2) the price must be satisfactory. It may be added that the beauty of the wares is also a factor (p. 211).

179. In order to insure the quality of wares, the government must not merely promulgate certain ordinances and rules, but it must also appoint certain inspectors who will examine the completed wares, and will mark with a distinguishing sign those which conform to the standards and those which do not. In case, as is certainly advisable, complete freedom from tax shall be permitted to exports, this immunity should extend to those wares only which satisfy this test (p. 212).

180. It is also often necessary to stimulate production by certain prizes and rewards, and when the court learns that science or skill is lacking for the production of certain wares, every effort must be made to attract people with the necessary qualifications, or by the necessary money payment to get the lacking information from a foreign artist, since everything may be had for money (p. 212).[1]

181. If the wares are to be supplied at a favorable price, not only must the articles requisite for supplying the necessities of life be purchasable at moderate prices, for on this depends the amount of the wages of the laborers, but the raw material of the wares must also not be dear. The ruler must accordingly take all possible care that not only agriculture but all the industries that supply the neccessities of life shall be in good order, so that no scarcity shall occur, as one industry always sustains another. Before all things, however, those crafts which deal with the necessities of life must

had come to be recognized in practice at his time. He also remarks that "such privileges can have no validity in themselves," for it is presumed that they are to be allowed only in so far as they make for the welfare of the state, and the successor to the throne can in no way be bound to continue them. He recommends the formation of a special company for exploiting the mineral resources of the country (p. 210).

[1] In a note Justi goes into considerable detail about the sort of specifications that should be prescribed.

be held under strict supervision, in order that they may not raise prices by charging excessive profits, or by buying up the supply, and other underhanded means (p. 214).[1]

182. When so much has been done for stimulation of domestic production, it is time to establish fairs and great markets (p. 214).

183. But flourishing commerce must be described as something more than enough to sustain fairs and markets established under the foregoing conditions. The expression is properly used only when flourishing trade in all sort of wares is carried on with all parts of the world. This is hardly to be thought of unless it is in connection with extensive merchant marine and foreign trade (p. 215).

184. Assuming that the land borders on the sea and has good harbors, or at least the possibility of making them, or is crossed by a navigable river which is at the command of the country to its mouth, the beginnings of sea-trade may be made by the formation of a great trading society, which can collect the guarantee or the capital for its transactions by the sale of a certain number of shares (p. 216).

185. In order to induce both natives and foreigners to take shares, either very great privileges must be granted to the society, or the bad condition and management of foreign companies must furnish the necessary stimulus, or the court must offer the company material support.

186. The success of such a company depends principally upon good management of its affairs. The court must consequently do its best to insure the election of directors whose insight, talent, diligence, and integrity are grounds for confidence; and the minister of commerce and marine, who should possess all these qualities in the highest degree, must know how to lead these directors in accordance with his purposes (p. 217).

187. Such a company must be guarded against dangerous enterprises and needless outlay. A few unfortunate investments will not only ruin the company, but it will be much harder for the state afterward to bring about the formation of a new company (p. 217).

188. The power and prestige of the monarch go far toward the

[1] This paragraph gives more evidence of economic insight than any that have preceded.

success of such a company. Other nations that carry on foreign trade look with jealous eyes on such a company, and try in every way to put obstacles before it. The power of the monarch, however, restrains them within such limits, that they cannot openly antagonize it (p. 217).

189. It is proper that possession of a certain number of shares should be a condition of sitting and voting in the meetings of such a company. It is not so certain that a similar condition should hedge election of directors, because it is not at all certain that wealth enough to own shares is combined with the necessary qualifications for such an office (p. 218).

190. It is a prime condition of success that such companies start with sufficient capital for large operations (p. 218).

191. It must be insisted that the predominant effort of such companies should be to sell domestic goods in foreign lands. If they only bring in goods directly from foreign lands which have previously been bought from middle-men, a saving of middle-men's profits and of transportation charges of foreign ships is made, to be sure; but nevertheless the money to defray the first cost of the goods goes out of the country (p. 219).

192. Such a trading society must not count on founding establishments in distant lands at once, but must plan to gain them gradually; i. e., not until they can pay good dividends to the shareholders, and until there is a comfortable capital in reserve, so that the cost of foreign establishments may be covered out of the reserve without diminishing the dividends (p. 221). Such gains take large fractions of the capital; societies formed by other countries, and already operating there, conduct minor warfare with competitors, and the monarchs cannot regard their quarrels as sufficient grounds for actual war. If one such society is ruined under these conditions, it is all the harder for subsequent ones to succeed (p. 219).[1]

193. When the trade of such a commercial company becomes flourishing it is possible to organize other companies to operate in the same territory in particular lines of goods. It is preferable,

[1] Justi testifies to scruples, which must have passed as altogether utopian, about the grounds in justice for exploiting the territories of weaker people.

however, to sell more shares and expand the operations of a single company. This prevents harmful jealousies, cross-purposes, and manifold loss of advantage by the home company (p. 223).

194. After all, such companies are not absolutely essential to the promotion of foreign commerce. Even if they have been used to establish trade, the time may come when expansion of trade will be best assured by opening it freely to all mariners and merchants (p. 223).[1]

ON THE AUXILIARIES [*Hülfsmittel*] TO COMMERCE

195. First of all we must name among the conditions of promoting commerce, a mild government, and reasonable freedom of conscience and action, as in the case of domestic prosperity.[2] People engaged in foreign trade must for special reasons enjoy these immunities, because they have special facilities for withdrawing their wealth from the country (p. 225).

196. Second, a wise ordering of the tariff and excise system is the principal means by which a wise government can guide foreign commerce according to its purposes. Instead of being detrimental to trade, since traders always have their own interest in view more than that of the state, and it would be ruinous to leave the ways and means of commerce to their enterprise, no trade can be carried on in a way that is advantageous to the state which is not in this way guided, controlled, and to a certain extent promoted (p. 226).

197. For purposes of tariff and excise, wares are of three classes: (1) for export; (2) for import; (3) for transport. Wares of the first class are either fully manufactured, or in raw or partially manufactured condition; those of the second class are either indispensable or dispensable. Accordingly the tariff and excise laws must take account of five classes of wares, and this makes five primary rules necessary (p. 227).

198. RULE I.—*All exports of manufactured goods must be*

[1] Justi fortifies this opinion by citing the opposition in England to the great trading companies, and he expresses the judgment that they had become more harmful than useful to the British Empire. On the other hand he thinks it is not time for Holland to abolish the Dutch East India Company (p. 225).

[2] *Vide* above, Propositions 115–18.

burdened with light imposts. The one profitable kind of trade consists in commerce of this class, and a wise ruler must not merely take care that the goods themselves are of high quality, but he must see that foreigners are stimulated to take them. It is poor encouragement to foreign buyers to lay a tax on such goods. The exportation is of itself such an advantage to the state, that it is unnecessary to burden it with imposts which make against the ultimate use of exportation (p. 227).[1]

199. The only exception to this rule is in case the home products are so cheap, or transportation is so cheap and easy, that the exports can undersell competing products of foreign countries. Even in this case, export taxes should not be imposed on articles the home production of which is capable of indefinite expansion. It is better to give the home merchants the opportunity to make the profit, so that they will be stimulated to increase the volume of trade to the utmost (p. 228).

200. Another corollary from this rule is that very low imposts should be placed on raw materials when they are moved from one part of the country to another for the purpose of being manufactured (p. 229).[2]

201. RULE 2.—*Export of raw material which is a home product must either be heavily taxed or entirely prohibited* (230).

202. RULE 3.—*All imports of dispensable wares must carry heavy imposts; for if they are really dispensable the importation brings the country great harm by useless foreign expenditure of money* (p. 231).[3]

203. RULE 4.—*Imports of indispensable wares should bear only light imposts.* Tariff and imposts should not be the ordinary way of collecting tribute from the subjects. They are justified as a source of revenue only by some subsidiary purpose. *Their main purpose should be to direct the course of commerce* (p. 231).

[1] Justi cites the wisdom of countries which put premiums on exportation.

[2] Justi's illustration of harm to the book trade through taxation of paper might be quoted as prophetic.

[3] The author's discriminations between degrees and types of dispensability are sociologically interesting.

204. It follows that foreign raw material needed for chief or subordinate purposes in home manufacture should be free of import duties (p. 232).

205. RULE 5.—*Goods in transport should be free of imposts, with the exception of trifling tolls* (p. 232).

206. The only exception to this rule is when the carriage of an article through the country takes a market away from a home product, in which case we must be sure that imposition of high taxes would not lead to reprisals (p. 232).

207. All the servants of the taxing system must be held under strict discipline, both against peculation, and against needless vexation of travelers (p. 233).

208. Commercial treaties with foreign countries are the next most important means of promoting commerce (p. 235).

209. Next in order are good harbors and roads, and passable rivers and canals (p. 236).

210. A well-organized system of posts, boats, and land carriers is a further desideratum (p. 237).

211. The coinage is an essential factor of flourishing trade (p. 238).[1]

212. Unpartisan and prompt rendering of justice in all trade litigation greatly promotes business (p. 240).

213. To this end special commercial courts, both original and

[1] For its bearing on the content of Justi's mercantilism, the note at this point is worth translating in full, viz.: "There can be no doubt that a low rate of exchange is very harmful for a country, and there are two chief circumstances which put the exchange of a country on a bad footing: (1) when it must annually pay a large sum to other nations to settle the trade balance; (2) when its coinage is depreciated. A land which finds itself in these bad conditions is in a sorry plight. Bad will go toward worse through the workings of exchange. All in all the coinage today is in an unspeakably bad condition. Under it twenty million people suffer extreme disadvantage, and only in the neighborhood of fifty dealers in coin [*Münzlieferanten*] and fifty money-changers enrich themselves as leeches by sucking the blood of their neighbors. In such a situation it would be a thousand times better that we had no coinage at all, but simply settled our balances in gold and silver by weight" (p. 239).

appellate, should be organized. They should be composed in part of legal experts, in part of merchants, capable of bringing the most exact technical knowledge to interpretation of the laws (p. 240).

214. The most flourishing commerce is hardly possible unless the ruler organizes a special bureau of commerce. This must be composed of members who, along with proved integrity, fidelity, and wisdom, possess complete knowledge of trade, and especially of civic-commercial science; and it is particularly advisable that no merchants should be members of the bureau, because their purposes are often different from those of the state.[1] In the largest countries a special subordinate bureau may be organized for manufactures. In this bureau former merchants and mining experts may be useful. In both bureaus individuals must be placed in charge of divisions of operations with which they are particularly acquainted, and consequently only the most important and general matters should be handled by the whole body. In every important seaport or commercial center there should be at least one commercial councilor, to supervise commercial and manufacturing relations at that point under the provisions of the two bodies (p. 240).

215. Finally, a wise government must take care to remove all obstacles which may embarrass commerce. These may come either from foreign or domestic causes. Thus, under the former head, war between other powers, with incidental hindrances to our commerce; secret machinations of other powers against our foreign traders, etc.[2] Among domestic hindrances may be named: Scarcity of materials for shipbuilding and other production; lack of capital in the country; existing privileges of certain lands and towns in the matter of imports and exports of staples; the envy and jealousy of certain lands and towns toward one another, etc. (p. 241).

ON MINES AS A MEANS OF INCREASING THE WEALTH OF A COUNTRY

The plan of this study excludes, as far as practicable, consideration of opinions about merely technical, adminis-

[1] *Vide* Prop. 156.

[2] A naïve discussion follows in a note, as to whether the spirit of the Christian religion permits a state to buy immunity from piracy of non-Christian powers; and the comforting conclusion is reached that the Christian religion surely cannot oppose any arrangements which make for the real welfare of the state (p. 243).

trative, or operative details. We are concerned with the main problems which cameralism proposed, and the relation of the formulas and solutions which cameralism offered to the development of social science in general. In order to fix with certainty the meaning of the essential theories, we must admit much evidence that is contained in subordinate details. The importance of these minor applications in the routine rules of the cameralists diminishes from this point, as we have already epitomized the cardinal doctrines which reflected the peculiar circumstances of the period, and which were modified after the circumstances changed. At the same time, we have seen in these characteristic theories some of the presumptions, both theoretical and practical, which have retained, and in some ways have gathered force in later German thinking. These views have encouraged tendencies in German policy which, for better or for worse, have produced evident contrasts between the civic and economic systems of Germany on the one hand and of England and America on the other. It will not be necessary to reproduce the remainder of Justi's system as fully as the sections have been represented thus far. It is in point however to translate in full the opening paragraphs of the portion devoted to mining. The redundancy of statement is a fair index of Justi's usual style. He says (pp. 243 ff.):

We come now to the third chief means by which the riches of a country may be increased, viz., mining, whenever the natural resources of the country include mineral deposits. In Germany these resources are by no means rare. Few states of any size in our Fatherland are without them. Yet the population of most parts of the country lacks inclination to develop the mines, and the governments have not taken adequate interest in this source of riches. Nevertheless this is almost the sole way in which well-founded hopes may be cherished of increasing the riches of the country. Germany has at only a few points facilities for navigation. In this respect, as well as in manufactures, our neighbors have such a long start of us, that we should be very foolish if we reckoned on more through these means than merely retaining our money at home. Since, moreover, the neighboring countries are giving more and more attention to keeping their rich inhabitants at home, our mining operations are in fact the only probable means by which riches in the various states of Germany may be increased.

Since in our enlightened times the intelligence requisite for the government of states has greatly increased, almost all European states are exceptionally alert to prevent the outflow of money from the country. In France, England, and Holland, careful reckoning is kept of the wares annually sold to foreign nations, and of the wares bought from the same nations. If attention to these subjects continues, in fifty years it may easily occur that commercial treaties will set limits to the amount of goods that a nation may annually take from another. The same foresight will be used with reference to the other ways by which money is drawn from the country. Thereupon the mines will be the only means of increasing the wealth of the country. This resource alone is completely in our power, and no counter-enterprises of foreign peoples can restrict us in exploiting the same, or can make it valueless.

The mines not only increase the treasure of the country with respect to the amount of gold and silver which they extract from the earth, but they also furnish us the principal wares with which we may expect to establish advantageous foreign commerce. In addition to this the mines will support a multitude of people, and this will have further an important influence upon the plane of living in the whole population. Especially will the mountainous regions be populated and exploited to the benefit of the revenues of their districts and of the whole state, while the same districts, without mines, would usually have a barren and empty appearance. All this, it seems to me, furnishes more than superfluous proof of the great utility of the mines.

Who then can doubt that the mines deserve the special attention of a wise government? So soon, therefore, as minerals are found in a country, or as good evidences of them appear, or when information is at hand that in earlier times mines had been operated there, a ruler who is really concerned for the best good of his state will make it a principal rule to establish mining and to develop it to the utmost. To that end he must seize upon all useful and efficient measures. I shall now do my best to show what such measures must be.

Propositions more summary in form than those in the series up to this point will sufficiently indicate the scope of the discussion, viz.:

216. Precious metals should be mined with the aid of governments even at a loss (p. 246).[1]

217. This is not a loss for the state as a whole. The sums expended remain in the country and support many people. The country as a whole will be richer by the amount of gold and silver that is taken from the earth (p. 246).

218. In case of the other metals, even a small profit should justify mining. By furnishing material to be sold abroad they add to the nation's wealth as truly as the mining of gold and silver.

219. The measures to be adopted by rulers for promoting mining fall into three groups: (1) for stimulating the population to engage in mining; (2) for standardizing the operation of mines; (3) for promoting mining science (p. 247).

220. Although all mining rights belong to the ruler, yet he cannot work them, because that would too greatly enlarge his budget, and make his income uncertain. The first requisite, then, is proclamation of free mining rights, subject to the laws of the land, at least to citizens, with reserve of the rightful royalties to the government (p. 247).

221. The ruler should give assurance that he will not himself, or through his ministers, engage in mining (p. 248).

222. The ruler must take care in many ways that those who operate mines shall be free to carry on their enterprise under the most favorable conditions (p. 249).

223. The government must assist unprofitable mines, by remitting dues, etc. (p. 250).[2]

[1] This doctrine goes back to Schröder, *loc. cit.*, chap. lxv.

[2] The idea here proves to be, not that mines should be operated if the net outcome is to be a loss, but that mines *at first* unprofitable should be assisted until they can be made to pay.

224. Many changes in the mining laws are necessary, especially because the introduction of machines, etc., has changed conditions (p. 251).

225. An area of "at least two miles" should be assured for the operations of a new mine (p. 252).[1]

226. This plan is recommended only for the precious and base metals (p. 253).

227. For salts, coloring matter, and clays, commercial societies are preferable (p. 254).

228. Schools of mines should be founded to train future managers of mines (p. 256).

229. It will be useless to count on mines as a permanent source of wealth unless provision is made for keeping up the supply of wood.

ON THE CIRCULATION OF GOLD IN THE TRADES

230. It is not enough that there should be wealth in the country, but the ruler must take care that this wealth is constantly active in the trades, and that it passes from hand to hand, for the true wealth of the country depends wholly upon this. In this way the subjects are put in a position not merely by diligence and labor to provide for their need and comfort, but also bear their share toward supplying the needs of the state. In fact it is quite natural to represent a republic under the figure of a human body. Wealth is the blood, the trades are the arteries, and the government is the heart, into which from time to time the wealth circulating in the arteries flows, and thence again pours into all parts of the civic body through the outlays of the state. We have now to treat of the means by which this circulation is promoted (p. 259).[2]

231. The chief means of promoting circulation of money in the trades are four, viz.: (1) that the sources of subsistence shall be kept in good correlation; (2) that the land shall keep its credit high;

[1] This apparently means two German miles square, and Justi recommends that such a reservation should be divided into four or five hundred parts, whether for separate operation or merely in dividing the proceeds is not clear.

[2] This paragraph is translated in full because it is a characteristic expression of mercantilism, and contains its own evidence that the theory was not so definite as tradition has made it.

(3) that manufacture and artisanship shall be kept prosperous; (4) that idleness and beggary shall be abated (pp. 259–330).[1]

One or two incidental symptoms occur among the technological rules, in these sections. For example, while reiterating the precept against allowing money to flow out of the country, Justi adds: "A flourishing condition of the occupations by which the necessities of life are gained is, however, the real strength and health of the state." This perception again challenges the current reputation of mercantilism.

Justi denounces abstract science, and demands that the learned class shall abandon profitless refinements and devote itself to the useful arts. He would also have the government weed out the student ranks by examinations difficult enough to reduce the numbers of would-be scholars (p. 274).

After discussing at length the desirability and means of preventing idleness and luxury, he adds a qualification which is symptomatic of mercantilism in particular and of the prevailing economic naïveté in general. He says (p. 328):

I will go further, and assert that the government has no need of prohibiting extravagance and luxury. According to all rational principles it is entirely a matter of indifference to the state in whose hands the wealth of the country rests, if it is only in the country and is distributed in proper proportions among the different classes and orders of the subjects. Moreover, if the things with which extravagance is practiced are not imported from foreign countries, it is a blunder to suppose that extravagance is harmful to the state. On the contrary the circulation of money and the support of the citizens are promoted by it. Everything therefore which the government needs to care for, is that those wares and things which are used in

[1] These sections are almost exclusively composed of rule-of-thumb conclusions about practical details. They presuppose the essentially patriarchal conception of the state which we have called the major premise of cameralism. The state being the housewifely patron saint of the people, specifications of the supervision to be exerted depend on their efficiency in promoting the chief end of such a state.

extravagance shall be produced at home, not imported from abroad. A state composed wholly of misers, or frugal people, and in which no luxury existed, would necessarily be the poorest, weakest, and most miserable state under the sun. It would not be able to employ and support a fourth part of the population of present states. How many occupations would remain if we should restrict ourselves strictly to necessities? Luxury in the use of domestic products, if it is conjoined with industry, is the natural heat and fire in the civic body, which gives it activity and vitality. Very few cases will be found in which repression of luxury is required in the interest of the welfare of the state. I have treated these cases in the *Grundsätzen der Policey.*

OF THE DUTIES OF SUBJECTS IN ORDER TO ASSIST THE RULER IN PRESERVING AND INCREASING THE RICHES OF THE STATE

232. The nature of a republic necessarily involves common and harmonious obligations, for *when the subjects have placed over themselves a supreme power* (*sic*),[1] from which they demand that it shall promote their happiness, they are naturally bound to conform to those arrangements which that supreme power adopts for their happiness, and to promote them in every way, otherwise they would obstruct their own ultimate purposes (p. 333).

233. By subjects we understand all those who enjoy the protection of the state. This brief proposition gives us the clearest idea of the essential characteristics of a subject, and in fact no more essential finding mark can be determined than the enjoyment of protection (p. 334).

234. The right cannot be denied to a ruler to demand that all those who possess estates in his land shall either be permanently domiciled upon them, or shall sell the estates to some person agreeable to him (p. 340).

235. Subjects owe their duties to an unlimited monarch only when he does not act as an enemy of the people. This situation may never have occurred, because even the greatest tyrants had apparent excuses, and it is consequently never quite clear that an autocrat is acting as the enemy of his people (p. 345).

[1] The Italics are mine, and the proposition is quoted for its bearing upon our interpretation of Justi's fundamental political conceptions.

236. Under mixed forms of government the subjects owe duties not to the monarch alone, but also to the whole state, and to the fundamental laws of the same. Consequently duty to the monarch is not a valid plea in extenuation of action harmful to the estates (p. 347).

237. Duties of subjects are accordingly of two classes: (*a*) *immediate* duties to ruler or state, springing from the essential nature of the relation of subjects; (*b*) *mediate* duties toward ruler and state, i. e., such as subjects owe primarily to themselves, and thus secondarily to ruler and state.

OF THE IMMEDIATE DUTIES OF SUBJECTS TOWARD RULER AND STATE

238. The immediate duties of subjects toward ruler and state are those which are necessarily connected with the ultimate purposes of the republic and with the relation of subjects, and which subjects owe to the supreme power in the state alone (p. 349).

239. These immediate duties fall into three chief classes: (*a*) exact obedience to the laws, commands, and ordinances of the supreme power; (*b*) unimpeachable loyalty to the same; (*c*) contribution according to ability to the support and best welfare of the state (p. 349).[1]

240. Loyalty [*Treue*] consists of complete devotion, attachment, and reverence toward the supreme power, with careful endeavor to avoid, and so far as possible to assist in preventing everything which might be harmful to the external and internal security of the state and of the person of the ruler (p. 376).[2]

241. Subjects are released from loyalty to a ruler (1) through absorption by conquest or otherwise into another country (p. 393); (2) when the ruler abdicates (p. 397).[3]

[1] The immediately following sections are a diversified homily on the fundamental virtue of obedience, with extreme claims for the arbitrary rights of rulers (pp. 351–73).

[2] Again the treatment is rather hortatory than scientific.

[3] The third type of duty (*vide* Prop. 239*c*) is discussed in variations of commonplaces adapted to the particular conception of the state on which cameralism was based (pp. 402–28). The following division, "On the Indirect Duties of the Subject," exploits the homely virtues of the thrifty type (pp. 429–35).

242. In order to treat at length of the mediate duties of subjects, we must elaborate the whole housekeeping art [*Haushaltungskunst*] since the obligation to operate well with our resources can be fulfilled in no other way than through the rules which this *Haushaltungskunst* teaches. But *Oekonomie*[1] belongs in the system of the sciences which we have undertaken to expound, because through the exercise of the same the resources of the state are maintained and increased. On that account it is the more evident that all the sciences pertaining to government and to the large management [*Wirthschaft*] of the state hang together most exactly in a single system. Attempting therefore to treat of *Haushaltungskunst* completely and thoroughly, so far as the limits of the present work permit, we shall in the first place present the general doctrines of the same, then we shall treat particularly the two chief topics of *Oekonomie*, viz., *urban economy* and *rural economy*, and shall apply to them the general rules (p. 435).[2]

243. The name *Haushaltungskunst* or *Oekonomie* may really be applied to two distinct sciences. When we speak of the *Oekonomie* of the country, or of the great management [*Wirthschaft*] of the state, all the sciences are involved which we treat in this book. When we talk of *Oekonomie* or *Haushaltungskunst* simply, we mean that science which we are now about to explain, and which is concerned with the goods and with the gainful occupations of private persons. *Haushaltungskunst* is, however, a science of so ordering the gainful occupations and the thrift in town and country that means [*Vermögen*] will thereby be preserved, increased, and reasonably used, and the

[1] Apparently used in this paragraph as a synonym for the former term. In the following paragraph this is certainly the case, i. e., Prop. 243.

[2] Of the whole following division, which has certain necessary resemblances to political economy as Adam Smith used the term, yet differs from it as kitchen work from chemistry, we may say that it contains nothing beyond commonplace material which genius and humor like Benjamin Franklin's might have coined into pithy Poor Richard's proverbs. Sufficient samples are given to show the quality. It should be observed that the presence of this department in *Staatswirthschaft* again demonstrates the absurdity of the traditional accounts of mercantilism as a theory.

temporal happiness of private persons will be promoted; or more briefly expressed, it is the science of applying our "means" to the promotion of our temporal happiness (p. 437).

244. One sense of "means" [*Vermögen*] signifies everything that is within our power, or that which we are able to bring to pass. In ordinary thinking "means" signifies all goods and aptitudes which we possess and which we may employ in order to provide for ourselves the necessities and conveniences of this life. In the narrower sense we understand by "means" the possession of a sufficiency of movable or immovable goods, which put in our hands, according to our social position and make-up [*Beschaffenheit*], all the conveniences and advantages of life. When we here use the term "means," it is in the two last senses, principally in the third (p. 438).[1]

245. Except through accident, no obtaining of "means" is possible unless our aptitudes and already-possessed goods are the beginning and ground of the acquisition (p. 439).

246. By "goods" we understand in *Haushaltungskunst* only those things which have a certain value and use for the need and convenience of human life, and which at a certain value or price can be transferred to others; i. e., things that have a money value (p. 440).

247. Credit is to a certain extent to be reckoned among goods, for it can be used as the ground and beginning of "means" (p. 440).

248. By "aptitudes" we understand those acquired capabilities and skills by which we may be useful to others and to ourselves in business and trades, or in social life in general (p. 441).

249. All "means" must be gained either by services [*Dienste*], or by trades [*Gewerbe*]. The former require only "aptitudes;" the latter require "aptitudes" and goods together (p. 441)

250. Services are a certain compact between the principal and the servant, by which the latter, in return for a certain salary or compensation, promises to apply his "aptitudes," in certain assigned

[1] This paragraph sufficiently accounts for choice of the vague term "means" instead of a more technical term as a rendering for *Vermögen*. We should misinterpret egregiously if we smuggled a later precise and constant concept into the word. *Vide* pp. 76 and 250.

occupations, for the benefit of the principal. These services are either honorable or menial; they are also morally legitimate or illegitimate (p. 442).

251. The two great classes of gainful occupations are (1) those that procure livelihood in the town; (2) those that procure livelihood in the country (p. 443).

252. From services or trades come "earnings" [*Gewinnst*]. This is the advantage which accrues to us from a thing after deduction of our applied outlay and effort. The justification of earnings must have at its basis the revenue which the other can, and probably will derive from the thing, for we are surely entitled to demand that the other shall allow a just portion of the return to accrue to us which he would not have acquired without our co-operation (p. 444).

253. In order to gain "means," one must first of all make a plan of his mode of life, and of the ways by which he is to acquire earnings. In this plan account must be taken of his aptitudes and goods. Most men make the mistake of making no plan, and of seeking their fortune in a merely haphazard way. Still others fail because they draw back in fear from every obstacle (p. 453).

253A. Before all things we must so apply our "aptitudes" and our goods that they will actually promote our purposes (p. 455).

254. Further it is necessary to know all the details involved in the success of our plan (p. 457).

255. This knowledge will enable us to choose the necessary means for carrying out our plan (p. 457).

256. It is further necessary to combine these means in a skilful way (p. 458).

257. By this skilful combination of "means" it is often possible that one may at the same time accomplish several sorts of purpose, and earn in several ways (p. 458).

258. But one will not acquire "means," either by service or trade, if one has not learned to save (p. 460).

259. In order to exercise this great art of saving, the first thing in every establishment must be a budget or correct estimate of income and outlay (p. 461).

260. The savings must then be used further to increase "means" (p. 464).

261. After all, the increase of "means" will be a tedious process unless one takes some reasonable chances, and occasionally exposes a part of his "means" to the hazards of fortune (p. 465).

262. Those who make such ventures should first possess considerable "means," so that they could lose what they risk without being reduced to want (p. 466).

263. Then the anticipated gain should be in proportion to the danger to which one is exposed (p. 467).

264. The reasonable use of "means" is the chief purpose of acquisition and of *Haushaltungskunst*.

265. "Means" contribute not a little to the end of a social happy, and virtuous life. One is thereby much more qualified for service to the community, and one can fulfil the duties of social life in a much higher degree than those who have no means (p. 471).

266. The reasonable use of means depends upon three chief rules: (1) The "means" must be so used that the substance (*sic*) of the same will not be impaired (p. 471); (2) one must apply one's "means" to the support of one's life and to the promotion of one's temporal happiness, according as the social position and constitution of each demand, and as the condition of one's "means" permits (p. 481); (3) besides using our "means" for our own needs and the convenience of our life, we must devote them also to the use of our needy neighbor, and to the advantage of the republic (p. 485).

ON MANAGEMENT IN TOWNS

267. The life of towns has the most intimate connection with human society and with the constitution of the republic. The towns both form the bond of connection between the rural sustaining system and the whole sustaining system of the country, and in them quite unique occupations are pursued, which have immediate influence on the weal of the state. The fundamental rules of management can be applied here therefore only in a general way, because otherwise it would be necessary to discuss each particular occupation. In the case of rural management, on the contrary, there must be specific application of the general rules (p. 490).

268. A town is a combination of societies, families, and single persons, who live in a guarded [*verwahrten*] locality, under the over-

sight and direction of a police bureau, or other persons charged with administration of the police system, in order with better success to maintain the operation and co-operation of those gainful pursuits which are immediately demanded both for the needs and conveniences of the country and for the unification of the whole sustaining system. The protection [*Verwahrung*] is the essential finding mark of the town, without which no locality can be called a town, however large and well built it may be (p. 490).[1]

269. The essential difference between towns depends therefore on the fact that one kind must be guarded by art, that is, by walls and ditches, another kind by nature, that is, by oceans, seas, rivers, and inaccessible mountains, so that entrance may be had only at certain places called gates or portals expressly designated for that purpose. Otherwise the requisite police arrangements for the chief purpose of the town are not available (p. 493).

270. Towns must accordingly be classified in various ways: (1) Into (*a*) commercial towns; (*b*) manufacturing towns; (*c*) mining and salt towns; (*d*) brewery and distillery towns; (*e*) market towns; or (2) into (*a*) residence towns (i. e., of the court); (*b*) university towns; (*c*) fortified towns; (*d*) border towns, etc.; or (3) into (*a*) large; (*b*) medium; (*c*) small; or (4) into (*a*) capitals; (*b*) provincial towns (p. 496).

271. At bottom there are two principal types of occupation for towns; first, the assembling of persons capable of carrying on the various pursuits; second, the accumulation of all sorts of wares and goods, and to this end all their establishments, measures, and endeavors must be directed (p. 497).

272. Since we are here exclusively concerned with the economy of private persons in towns, we have to do principally with two subjects, viz.: (1) What the general rules of management have to say about management and organization of the sustaining occupations; (2) how management itself, without reference to occupations in the town, may best be conducted (p. 497).[2]

[1] It is needless to comment on this typically cameralistic inversion of essence and accident.

[2] This programme results only in slight variations upon the generalities indicated by Props. 253–64. Passing to treatment of occupations

273. Rural management is a complex of sustaining occupations' to the end that through agriculture and stock-raising the resources of the soil may be best used, and that all sorts of raw wares and materials may be extracted from the same for human need and convenience. The rural sustaining occupations consequently differ from those of towns principally in this: in the former the effort is to produce raw wares and goods, in the latter men are chiefly engaged in transforming the raw wares and materials. While this latter purpose requires unified societies and efforts, with police supervision, the former can be carried on by separate families either scattered at considerable intervals, or living in village groups"[1] (p. 523).

THE THEORY OF THE REASONABLE USE OF THE "MEANS" [*Vermögen*] OF THE STATE, INCLUDING CAMERAL OR FINANCIAL SCIENCE PROPER

On the Reasonable Use of State Revenues in General

On the second title-page of the second part, or volume, the clause is inserted, "in which cameral science proper is treated." It is not our present affair to debate with Justi the insufficiency of his economic foundation, nor to go into details about the overlapping and confusion of economic, cameralistic, and police problems as they appear in his system.[2] We are attempting to present this typical cameralist just as he was, and to show how cameralism as a so-called science reflected the immaturities and prejudices of the type of state in which it was developed. We come now to a portion of the system in which actual administration had worked out a technique that was relatively precise. In so far as such a

which are not necessarily peculiar to towns, Justi lapses into extended pseudo-technical discussion of brewing, distilling, vinting, truck-gardening, and milling (pp. 505–17).

[1] Then follows an academic version of the wisdom that every farmer's boy is supposed to acquire (pp. 526–606). This then is as deep as Justi goes into the theory of economics on the side of production proper.

[2] *Vide* II, 63, and Prop. 219.

technique, not guaranteed by a conclusive economics, can have a value for science, it is the most important part of Justi's system. We must repeat, however, that the problem of cameralism was not yet consciously the problem of modern economics, and still less the problem of modern sociology, viz.: What is the value of all mediate processes for the trunk-line process of promoting the evolution of persons? The problem of cameralism was merely the ways and means problem of the quasi-absolutistic governments of that period, viz.: the quasi-absolutistic type of state being given, in which, in effect, the state is the government, and the government is the prince, how may the resources of that type of state be so managed that its perpetual motion will be assured?

We shall show this in further detail by continuing the series of propositions condensing Justi's argument.

274. To recapitulate: The common happiness, the ultimate purpose of all republics, for attaining and realizing which the supreme power exists in states, demands that the care and endeavor of this sovereign power shall be directed chiefly toward two great activities, viz.: first, securing and increasing the "means" of the state; second, the reasonable and wise use of the "means." The great management of the state consists then of these two chief employments. Part I having been devoted to the former of these, Part II will deal with the latter (II, 3).

275. The "means" of the state consist not merely in all sorts of movable and immovable goods, possessed primarily either by the subjects or by the state itself; but rather in all talents and skill of the persons who belong to the republic. Even the persons themselves must in a certain sense be included, and the general use of these means of the state constitute the supreme power.[1] All ordinances of the supreme power have for their object therefore the wise use of the means and forces of the state for the realization of the common happiness (II, 5).[2]

[1] *Vide* I, 19, and this book, pp. 76, 250, 367.

[2] This proposition is typical of the vagueness of undifferentiated cameralistic ideas. The original reads: "*Alle Anordnungen der ober-*

276. In the widest sense, the reasonable use of the "means" of the state includes all the rules laid down in Part I. In the special sense we understand by the reasonable use of the "means" of the state the wise measures of the ruler, to the end that the general "means" of the state may be made to yield certain revenues, and constantly available resources, without impairing the "means," and in accordance with the demands which from time to time the essential needs of the state may enforce (II, 6).[1]

sten Gewalt kommen also darauf an, dass sie von dem Vermögen und den Kräften des Staates zu der Bewirkung der gemeinschaftlichen Glückseligkeit einen weisen Gebrauch machet." I attribute the thoroughly noncommittal force in this connection of the phrase "*kommen darauf an,*" to an unreconciled antithesis of ideas. As it stands, the proposition distinctly means neither, "The objective goodness or badness of the acts of a government is to be decided by its use, etc.," nor, "The *intention* of the government is to use, etc." The former meaning would lead to a corollary which is abhorrent to Justi (*vide* I, 47, above, pp. 325 ff.). The latter meaning is always the reserve presumption on which to rest the claim of the government to unquestioning submission. Yet, so long as the latter claim maintained its orthodoxy, it was by smuggling into its assets some of the credit which the former proposition would establish, while that proposition was not admitted at full force. In other words, the stage of thinking represented by Justi was a dodging between affirmative and negative answers to the question, Are governments absolute, and so unimpeachable, or are they fallible, and consequently to stand or fall on the merits of their acts as determined by some objective standard? The quasi-absolutism which Justi represented resorted, when hard pushed, to the affirmative. Cromwellism and the French Revolution, and the American Declaration of Independence vindicated the negative. We shall miss the full meaning of this treatise and of cameralism in general, if we fail to keep in mind that they were straddles on this fundamental problem, with the working balance toward the arbitrary side (p. 513.)

1 It should be remembered, that this discussion is in terms of *Vermögen,* not of *Reichthum.* One of the most subtle questions in future historical criticism of the literature of economics will to a large extent turn upon the fallacy of interchanging the two concepts. When Adam Smith founded systematic study of problems of *wealth,* he carefully delimited the concept. The subsequent confusions in English thinking

297. The first condition of reasonable use of the "means" of the state is adequate knowledge of them (II, 6).[1]

298. The wise ruler has a conception of a true happiness of the subjects and of the state constantly before his eyes, and he has a

were not quite indentical with those in German theory, and one of the reasons for the differences was strictly verbal. I am not prepared to express a judgment about the relative importance of this factor. I have not collected sufficient evidence to prove that much of the confusion in English economic theories came from taking over arguments expressed in unwarranted translations of German terms. I am convinced, however, that this is the case. It is enough at present to point out that it would shunt us on to a side track if we should render Justi's word *Vermögen* by the primarily legal term "property;" still more if we should use the more restricted economic term "wealth." The work of reducing this and similar ambiguous terms to constant values has been a considerable part of the difficulty of promoting the various social technologies assembled as "cameralism" to relative distinctness and precision.

The idea of the divine foreordination of hereditary sovereignty reappears as the constant *motif* in the cameralistic doctrines. We illustrated this in its most dogmatic form in the case of Schröder (above, pp. 137 ff.). Thus Justi says: "The Eternal Being whose Providence has appointed him to the government of the people put under him as subjects will hold a ruler to strict accounting, etc." This was not merely a pious phrasing of social order. It was literal interpretation, and it carried the corollary that the Almighty alone, not the people of a state, had the right to call the ruler to account. Justi employs formulas of the ruler's responsibility which would mean to a twentieth-century man almost all that we should assert about the responsibility of chief magistrates (e. g., II, 10); but we must always construe these propositions in the light of the reserve clauses in the author's mind. These latter virtually nullify those phases of democracy in the formulas which a twentieth-century man would regard as crucial.

[1] Much of the development of the proposition in subsequent sections has already appeared in substance in our citations from Justi's Preface and Introduction, and need not be repeated. For instance, a section (II, 13–15) is devoted to the proposition that a ruler ought not to use the "means" of the state without having a correct estimate of them. It amounts only to a more pedantic way of reading the New Testament moral: "*What king going to make war against another king, sitteth not down first and consulteth whether he be able, etc.*"

correct judgment of the relative proportions of the different needs (II, 15; *vide* I, 66–69).[1]

299. The wise ruler must take no steps for the welfare of the state without taking care that "means" enough are devoted to the purpose to insure its success (II, 17).

300. For the purposes of the state, great sums must be expended. These "means" are mostly in the hands of private persons. The portions necessary for the purposes of the state must be obtained from the individuals in ways which will not impair the substance of their "means," i. e., they must be taken from earnings [*Gewinnste*]. Enough, however, must be left so that the subjects can live from their earnings (II, 8).

301. The "means" so obtained must be at all times available in the form of money, and we call it then "the readiest means" of the state (II, 20).[2]

302. This "readiest means" of the state is the great subject-matter of cameral or finance science proper, in so far as the same is regarded as a subordinate science under all the economic and cameral sciences required for the government of a state. All measures and transactions of cameral science have to do merely with this "readiest means," and have for their aim either the systematic raising of the same or wise application or administration. Otherwise expressed, *Cameral or finance science is an adequate knowledge and facility* [*Erkenntniss und Geschicklichkeit*] *in those transactions whereby*

[1] Although the proposition is supported only by the most commonplace generalities, it indicates, along with stalwart faith (for publication) in the virtues of paternalism, a rather comprehensive view of the sorts of interests which the benevolent despot should try to harmonize. Incidentally, Justi again has his fling at the relative unimportance of the learned class.

[2] Justi has evidently used the term "means" now in a special sense, i. e., the reserve plus the current revenues of the state. Whether this idea is more cause or effect of the general mercantilist position it would be fruitless to inquire. It is a typical case of fallacious transition from a concept defined to include both goods and persons, to a concept symbolized by the same term, *Vermögen*, but defined to mean gold and silver coin.

"the readiest means" of the state, for promotion of the common happiness of the same, are well and economically managed (II, 21).

303. We easily see that cameral science is closely connected with all other economic sciences which are treated in this book. It teaches not merely how to use wisely and for the good of the state those "means" of the republic which are founded, preserved, and increased by *Staatskunst, Policey, die Commercienwissenschaft und Oekonomie,*[1] but in the great management of the state it conducts, so to speak, the internal management, to the effect that without its co-working no governmental business of any kind can be undertaken; because for all such undertakings "readiest means" are necessary. In short, cameral science is absolutely indispensable to the happiness of the state, because the greatest "means" of the state would yield nothing, without skilful administration. Hence it has its ground in the common fundamental principle of all the sciences which pertain to the government and general management of the state.[2] It is particularly based however on *die Staatskunst und Policeywissenschaft,* since it must derive its chief working principles from them. Moreover it must make use of *Haushaltungskunst* and jurisprudence as principal auxiliaries. The former will furnish the elementary rules of managing "means," the latter will guard against unjust procedure (II, 23).

304. The fundamental principle of cameral science is this: *"In all transactions with the 'readiest means' of the state, the aim must be to seek the common happiness of the ruler and the subjects"* (II, 24).[3]

305. The rules of raising the revenues without harm to the

[1] As we have seen, these are categories which do not correspond with recognized classifications in current social science. The essential reason is that they were impossible as scientific categories. At a venture we may offer as equivalents the terms, civic policy, police and commercial science, and economy.

[2] *Vide* above, pp. 298 ff.

[3] In spite of the arbitrary conception of the state in terms of which this formula must be interpreted, it contains much saving grace of correct moral valuation, while the context shows that the principle was not always evident in actual cameralistic practices.

subjects, and from current earnings, must also be applied to provinces, so that the chief division of the state will not be favored at the expense of minor divisions (II, 30).[1]

306. The theory of cameral science may be divided into three chief parts. We accordingly divide this second part of the *Staatswirthschaft* into three books: (1) On the raising of revenues; (2) on the disbursements of the state; (3) on the organization and administration of cameral business. This classification leaves nothing lacking which is necessary for a beginner in cameral or finance science, and in general about the reasonable use of the "means" of the state (II, 39).

ON COVERING THE COSTS OF THE GREAT OUTLAYS OF THE STATE

307. A state often finds itself in need of resources which are not supplied by the rules already given for raising the "readiest means." This book is devoted then to the problems which those extraordinary requirements involve (II, 40).

308. The problems of cameralism accordingly fall into three chief divisions: (1) The establishment of the "readiest means"—which calls for the greatest skill and strength of the cameralist; (2) the raising of the regular income of the state from the sources that are common to almost all states; (3) the raising of emergency funds (II, 42).[2]

309. Establishing the "readiest means" of the state depends

[1] In this connection (II, 33) Justi admits that he is repeating rules that have already been laid down, but he solemnly adds, "But in those passages we were not yet treating cameral science proper. Since it is now necessary particularly to define the fundamental principles of this science, we must not be content with mere citation of the fundamental principles reviewed above. Indeed these are not the same, since in the former case we were talking of the use of the general "means" of the state, while now we are speaking of the administration of the revenues of the state. Nevertheless, everything that could be called a "principle" is the same, even in Justi's version, and he was close to the perception that cameralistics was not a science at all, but merely a technology without a peculiar scientific content.

[2] From this point the treatment becomes more narrowly technical. To what extent it was practical rather than academic, according to

first upon developing a populous land, with the maximum amount of wealth circulating in the gainful occupations (II, 44).

310. A second and more immediate foundation is necessary, viz., either certain estates the proprietorship of which belongs immediately to the state and to the ruler, and the whole revenue of which accrues to the "readiest means," or certain rights reserved to the supreme power. The proper name of these rights is the regalia (II, 45).

311. The foundation of the revenues of the state is laid then, first, in good management of the estates immediately appertaining to the state or to the ruler (II, 45).

312. In the case of the *regalia*, the desideratum is a reasonable use of the rights, in consideration of the common "means" of the state, and of the common welfare of the ruler and of the subjects (II, 46).[1]

313. The best standard of taxation is the persons of the subjects in general, according to a just proportion of their immovable "means" and industry, and especially the laborers and assistants employed in such gainful occupations. In such case the commerce, the industry, and the freedom of the subjects would not suffer the slightest hindrance, as the number of the persons employed could not possibly be concealed (II, 52).

314. It is possible for the state to raise so little revenue by taxation that the total "means" of the state will fall far below the normal level, and the welfare of the subjects will be harmfully restricted (II, 53).

contemporary standards, it does not fall within my province to decide. The technical programme proposed has diminishing pertinence to the purposes of this book. I shall accordingly ignore the larger part of its contents, and, as in the account of Adam Smith's purely economic chapters (*vide* Small, *Adam Smith and Modern Sociology*), merely call attention to incidental symptoms.

[1] While our aim does not permit attention to details of fiscal technology, it should be noted that for investigators of the subject of taxation, the rule-of-thumb conclusions scheduled by Justi are by no means unworthy of consideration. For example, Justi's rules are quite close approaches to the doctrines of free trade afterward promulgated by Adam Smith (e. g., II, 48, 49).

315. The *Regalia* should be so administered that the welfare of the state and the convenience of the subjects would remain the first consideration, and the revenues the second (II, 54).

316. A reasonable cameralist will accordingly follow two rules: (1) Direct management by the administration of complicated economic processes must be avoided by arranging with competent *Entrepreneurs* (*sic*) to carry on the enterprises at their own risk, at a certain rate of dividend on the proceeds; (2) all needless extra expense, such as unnecessary employees, must be avoided (II, 56).[1]

317. Subsidies from foreign rulers are not to be rejected, especially if they do not entail more costs than they amount to (II, 61–63).

318. The best and surest increase of the revenues of the state comes from encouraging the laboring class [*Nahrungsstand*] (II, 63).

319. A cameralist should at the same time be a police expert and an economist (II, 63).

320. The first care of the cameralist must be for the development and cultivation of unimproved and thinly populated sections (II, 64).

321. A considerable budget must therefore be annually at the disposal of the bureaus (II, 66).

322. Even without such capital the domains may by good management be made to yield large revenues (II, 69–74).

323. Returning to the *Regalia*—the most harmless increase of revenues through extended use of the *Regalia* occurs (1) when they are used in places where they had previously not been enforced. Hence the intelligent cameralist must be on the watch for such undeveloped sources of revenue (II, 75); (2) through improvements of public works affected by the *Regalia* (II, 76); (3) through increase of the rate of impost and of prices of products covered by the *Regalia* (II, 77).

324. The problem of increasing the revenues of the state in the form of contributions, taxes, and other payments by the subject can be solved only by improving the condition of the laboring class, and

[1] A highly idealistic excursus follows on the possibility of painless taxation. Justi declares that democracies might easily realize such an ideal (II, 57).

by increasing the population (II, 81), but this just portion of revenue should be collected only when the needs of the state call for it.

325. The only exception is when a new impost may restrain or cure a police evil, or may evidently benefit and enlarge the laboring class.[1]

326. The second chief responsibility of the cameralist is the raising of the ordinary revenues of the state.[2] By the ordinary revenues we understand the established arrangements for covering the ordinary needs of the state by levies upon designated objects (II, 88).

327. Following the Roman law, it has been customary in Germany to distinguish between *Fiscum* and *Aerarium*. Under the former are classed the revenues of the cameral estates and of the *Regalia*. These are supposed to be for the support of the person of the ruler and of his family, court, and servants, with all other expenses necessary to maintain the princely dignity. It is the traditional idea that the cameralists were to deal especially with these revenues, and they are accordingly known as cameral revenues. The revenues of the *Aerarium* are supposed to be especially for the protection and security of the country, and for promoting the general welfare of the state (II, 89).

328. This distinction is groundless (II, 90).

329. Knowledge of the distinction is necessary, however, in order to understand certain existing survivals and consequences of the distinction in the present cameral organization (II, 92).

330. It is best to divide the revenues of the state according to their four chief sources, viz.: (1) Those from the crown estates, the cameral estates, or the domains (as they are variously named); (2) those from the *Regalia;* (3) those from payments by the subjects, in general taxation; (4) those which indirectly accrue in the course of attaining other chief purposes (II, 95).[3]

[1] Justi's examples would fall in the class of sumptuary laws.

[2] *Vide* Prop. 208.

[3] The sections devoted in turn to these subjects contain almost nothing pertinent to our purpose. They are strictly technological (II, 97–305).

OF CONTRIBUTIONS, TAXES, AND IMPOSTS

This portion of the *Staatswirthschaft* is also chiefly technological, and thus not primarily germane to our purpose. Since policies of taxation have their roots, however, so deep in social philosophy, and since the theories of taxation occupy so prominent places in the social sciences, we present a digest of Justi's more general opinions.

331. The three chief sources of the necessary income of the state are: (1) the contributions; (2) the taxes; (3) the excises paid by the subjects. The domains and the *Regalia* are not sufficient to cover the expenses necessary for the welfare of the state, especially in the present armed condition of Europe. The magnificence of courts has also greatly increased. To cover these costs the subjects must contribute from their private means (II, 306).

332. There can be no doubt that the subjects owe this contribution to the great expenses of the state. In so far as all subjects, in respect to their common welfare, are in close unity with one another, and represent a single body, or moral person, their private means are at the same time the general, although mediate "means" of the state (II, 307; *vide* I, 415, Prop. 239).

333. It is a fundamental rule to seek such ways and means of levying the taxes now in mind, that the subjects will pay them with willing and happy hearts, and at their own initiative. This is possible even in monarchies, if wise use is made of the passions of the subjects; e. g., if the people, with the exception of nobility and scholars, are divided into classes, according to the amount of tax which they pay; or, if certain lucrative occupations are permitted only to persons who pay a certain minimum tax, as is stipulated for example in the case of brewers in Frankenhausen, Schwarzburg, etc. (II, 309).

334. A second fundamental rule is that the taxes must not interfere with the reasonable freedom of human conduct, with the credit of merchants, with the trades, and shall in general not be oppressive to the industrial system or to commerce (II, 311).

335. A third rule is that the taxes must be levied upon all subjects with righteous equality, since all are equally under obliga-

tion in this connection, and all share in the protection and other benefits of the state. Yet the application of this rule must have due respect to the second, for, although all subjects should pay taxes in just proportion to their means, yet the nature and purpose of the different species of goods does not permit that all objects can bear equal rates of taxation (II, 312).

336. A fourth rule is, that the contributions and excises shall have a sure, fixed, and unfalsified ground, and consequently should be levied upon objects not only upon which they may be promptly and certainly collected, but in connection with which fraud and concealment is not easy for the subjects, nor peculation for the officials (II, 313).

337. A fifth rule is, that the taxes shall be based on such objects as will permit limitation of the number of collectors' offices, and therewith of officials (II, 314).

338. The sixth and last fundamental rule is that payments must be made as easy as possible for the subjects, and hence must be divided into convenient parts, and made payable at appropriate times (II, 315).[1]

339. It is not easy to hit upon an impost which satisfies all these requirements. Vauban, Schröder, and others have proposed a royal or general tithe, which should combine all desirable qualities. Tested by above rules, however, the plan will be found wanting. Others have proposed a combined poll and income tax, etc. (II, 316).

340. The nearest approach to application of the rules will be through selecting three classes of objects for taxation, viz.: first, immovable goods; second, the persons of the subjects; third, the gainful occupations (II, 318).

[1] *Vide* Adam Smith's "four maxims," *Wealth of Nations*, Book V, cap. ii, part ii, Bax ed., p. 351. *Vide* Small, *Adam Smith and Modern Sociology*, pp. 229 ff. Smith's first maxim is approximately Justi's third rule; the second maxim is nearly Justi's fourth rule; the third maxim is almost identical with Justi's sixth rule; the fourth maxim may be compared with Justi's second rule, but is much more fundamental and precise. Justi's Rule 1 is nebulous; Rule 5 refers to one class of consideration only which, with many others, enforces the much wider generalization of Smith's Maxim 4.

OF CONTRIBUTIONS AND TAXES ON IMMOVABLE GOODS

341. The propriety of taxing land rests on two facts: first, it is mediately a part of the general property of the state; second, the revenues from it are least concealable. Nor is there any hardship in liability of the land for a portion of the expenses of the state (II, 320).[1]

342. Lands of the different kinds, e. g., meadows, vineyards, forests, etc., must be divided into three classes, good, medium, and bad; and houses must also be classified as large, medium, and small. Again, the regions in which the lands lie must also be classified, and in like manner the towns which contain the houses. A calculus of these different factors will give the rate of taxation (II, 324).

343. The productiveness of the land must be precisely reckoned, and the tax must be levied accordingly (II, 324).[2]

344. The revenues of the houses should also determine the amount of levy upon them; and it should correspond with the just rate upon the interest which would be derived from the selling value of the same (II, 325).

345. An important duty of the bureaus relates to remission of the taxes in case of providential losses by fire, flood, storm, drought, etc. (II, 333).

346. It is a mistake for the ruler to reward services by grants of freedom from taxation (II, 335).

OF PERSONAL TAXATION

347. The second chief taxable object is the person of the subjects themselves. Not all subjects possess immovable goods. All are however members of the community, and enjoy its benefits; all consequently owe something in return. Personal payments to the state even by those who also pay land taxes are therefore proper, if they are rightly graded (II, 340).

348. The personal tax may be the chief tax of a country, virtually

[1] The details which follow deal with the technique of assessing and collecting land taxes.

[2] It is not clear whether Justi regards this precept as a further elaboration of 342, or as something distinct. There is no meaning in the classification proposed in 342, unless it is a part of the process intended by 343.

summing up all the forms of income tax, or it may be an accessory of the principal forms of taxation (II, 341).

349. There is no adequate standard of personal taxation (II, 343).

350. Personal taxes may be regarded as a means of collecting a portion of their dues to the state from subjects who otherwise would be wholly or partially exempt from taxation (II, 344).

351. Poll taxes on Jews are to be specified as one of the forms of personal tax. They are levied at the same rate upon rich and poor alike, and they are left to equalize the matter among themselves. Usually the whole Jewish community is held responsible for payment of an aggregate sum reckoned in proportion to the numbers. Since it is the choice of this unfortunate race to remain aliens among us, we need not bother ourselves about strict propriety and exact justice (II, 346).

352. In some countries protection-money [*Schutzgeld*] is paid by those subjects, or aliens, who possess no immovable goods. It is sometimes reckoned by families, sometimes by polls. In either case it is to be reckoned as a personal tax. This is an undesirable levy in addition to a poll tax (II, 347).[1]

353. Various other taxes have been levied as personal, which are really occupation taxes or excise (II, 348).

354. In the same way, salt and tobacco taxes have been levied as personal taxes (II, 348).

355. The chief duties of the cameralists in connection with these personal taxes consist in so administering the same that the system will be reasonable, conducive to the welfare both of the subjects and of the state, and duly respective of the equality of the subjects. In this respect a cameralist has an opportunity to show great skill and wisdom. Decisions must be rendered as to cases in which personal taxes should be remitted. The ground for this concession should be services.[2] Particularly must the cameralists take care that personal

[1] Justi makes the *Schutzgeld* appear as a species of the genus now known as "police graft."

[2] Justi broadly hints that "the benefit of clergy" had German forms which amounted to serious abuses, e. g., in freeing from personal taxation as "*Gelehrte*," men who had made no good use of their time in the university.

and other taxes are collected by the same officials, so that the expense of separate employees shall be saved (II, 351).

OF TAXES ON OCCUPATIONS, OR SO-CALLED EXCISE AND IMPOSTS

356. Since immovable goods can be burdened with taxes to the extent of only one-fourth or one-third of their earnings, and since no very considerable sum can be raised from personal taxation, the gainful occupations must be the next source of revenue (II, 352).

357. Occupations may be taxed (*a*) on the materials which they use, and on their output (excise); or (*b*) directly, according to the extent of their operations (II, 353).

358. The former method is almost universal in Europe (II, 353).

359. The latter has a minor place (II, 353).

360. Various causes contribute to the vogue of excises in Germany: thus (*a*) the limitation of tariffs by the laws of the Empire gave occasion for excises as the most convenient and productive substitute. Again (*b*) it was observed that large industries were growing up in the towns without paying much into the national treasury; (*c*) they are means of getting revenue from individuals who have no immovable goods (II, 355).

361. It is not true that the owners of real estate can make the taxes which they pay fall upon other subjects, because customary price defeats this shifting of the incidence of the tax (II, 355).

362. A further reason for the use of excise is that it gives the ruler a much freer hand than in levying land taxes (II, 356).

363. Excise is either universal—falling upon all articles without exception which are used for the support of life or come into the channels of trade; or particular—falling upon selected articles of consumption or wares (II, 356).

364. Excise does not conform to the rules above given for taxation; for (1) it limits the reasonable freedom of human action (II, 358); (2) it is detrimental to crafts and commerce (II, 359); (3) it does not spread the burden of taxation equally (II, 361); (4) it has no secure basis, since fraud and peculation are afforded large scope (II, 362); (5) its collection requires many officials and large expense (II, 364).

365. The claims for excise are insufficient; viz.: (1) It puts a

share of the common burdens upon all; (2) by limiting his expenditures each may ease the burden at will; (3) it calls for only a fraction of earnings a little at a time; (4) but almost without the knowledge of the subjects it increases the "readiest means" of the state; (5) no sheriffs' process (*execution*) is required to enforce it; (6) aliens must bear their share; (7) it is a means of controlling the commerce of the country, and of promoting manufactures (II, 365).

366. Since immediate abolition of excise is hopeless, the rules for its employment must be stated, viz.: (1) All the rules previously laid down in the case of tariffs, etc. (II, 288–300); (2) excise rates must respect the rate of earnings of the different occupations, and must call for only a small fraction of the earnings of those that deal in the necessities of life (II, 368); (3) in order that moderation of excise be not misused for unwarranted increase of profits, the police must interfere and fix the price of necessities (II, 369); (4) larger demands may be made upon luxuries (II, 369); (5) but the three grades of luxury must be respected (II, 369; *vide* I, 231); (6) excise is surely excessive when it amounts to more than the remaining earnings of the craft, or when it amounts to a half or two-thirds of an article on sale (II, 369); (7) excise must vary according as the transactions are first, second, or third hand, and whether a craft contributes or not to the completion or improvement of a thing (II, 370).

367. Occupation-taxes [*Gewerbe-Steuer*] might be introduced, in harmony with the fundamental rules of taxation, and to the advantage both of ruler and subject (II, 373).

368. The essential principle of this type of tax is adjustment to the scale of income of the occupation (II, 374–92).[1]

OF THE RIGHT OF THE SOVEREIGN TO IMPOSE SPECIAL TAXES

369. These revenues may be called accidental in a double sense: First the sovereign power finds occasion to raise certain revenues without making the revenues themselves the ultimate purpose, and at the same time without prejudice to the actual ultimate purpose of the state; second, these revenues may be called accidental because

[1] Justi elaborates a scheme of occupation taxes in considerable detail, and seems to regard it as wholly practicable and wise.

they are based merely on accidental arrangements and certain incidents, either of the whole republic or of the supreme power; or of those subjects who contribute to these revenues. Such occasional circumstances are so various that some of them are likely to be present always, and their revenues consequently aggregate an appreciable sum (II, 400).

370. These accidents may be grouped in five classes, and we may arrange them in the order of their probable value in yielding revenue, viz.: (1) Revenues from overlordship of the state over certain properties, to be distinguished from the *Regalia* (II, 401–11); (2) rights of revenue that are incidents of the administration of justice (II, 412–16); (3) the revenues accruing through administration of the police system (II, 417–21); (4) revenues incidental to the war-making power, including subsidies (II, 422–25); (5) revenues from sovereignty over the ecclesiastical system (II, 426–29).[1]

ON THE COLLECTING OF EXTRAORDINARY SUMS FOR THE USE OF THE STATE

371. In case of war, or other crises, exceptional demands for money arise. It is not for the cameralist to decide whether the occasion actually demands the exceptional sums, but if the ruler has so decided it is the task of the cameralist to find the ways and means. These are chiefly two: (1) Extraordinary contributions of the subjects; (2) the credit of the ruler and of the country (II, 430–33).

372. There are two ways of levying extraordinary contributions, viz.: (1) By increasing the rates of ordinary contributions and taxes; (2) by levying a new sort of contribution. The preference is to be determined by the circumstances of the state. If the sums to be raised are not too great, if there is no need of instant payment, and if the ruler can assure the subjects that the increase will be only temporary, the former method is preferable, because the technique for raising such contributions is already in operation. The existing taxes must, however, be at such rates that they do not absorb one-third of earnings, or the other form must be adopted (II, 435).

[1] These items as treated by Justi are so largely reflections of temporary conditions, that the details yield nothing for our purpose that has not appeared elsewhere.

373. The best form of extraordinary levy is a tax on social position [*Würdensteuer*], that is, all subjects, lay and clerical, are to be arranged in classes and subdivisions, and the higher the social rank and dignity the higher must be the rate of this tax. Thus the levy falls to a considerable extent upon persons who were not burdened before, and who have the ready means of payment (II, 443).[1]

374. One of the first rules of a wise government must be to preserve its credit, and this depends, first, on integrity in its transactions; second, on prompt payment of interest (II, 452).

375. The establishment of a bank is also a useful means of obtaining control of extraordinary sums (II, 455).

376. Another means is the provision of annuities, the capital of which falls to the state on the death of the annuitants (II, 455).

377. So-called "*Tontines*," invented in France, and named after their originator, Tonti, are also to be considered (II, 456)

378. Lotteries may also be used when exceptional sums are needed (II, 458).

379. Scruples about the fundamental morality of annuities, tontines, and lotteries are not sufficiently valid to estop the state from using them (II, 459).

380. Although it is impossible to exclude aliens from investment in annuities, tontines, and other forms of state debts, yet so far as possible subjects should be preferred as investors, so that the interest will not go out of the country. Whether money should be borrowed abroad for the sake of winning other nations to our interest is another question which belongs to *Staatskunst* (II, 461).

381. When the credit of the country makes borrowing difficult, then one of the more common devices is to farm out certain fixed revenues, and to obtain advances from the parties to whom they are farmed (II, 461).

382. A similar device is to make over certain domains or other revenues of the state to a lender (II, 462).

383. A still more desperate device is the pawning of domains or even provinces (II, 463).

384. A cameralist will today scarcely recommend the absolute alienation of territories and people for the sake of money (II, 465).

[1] Additional minor taxes are discussed (II, 445-49).

OF THE EXPENSES OF THE STATE

385. The second chief responsibility of the cameralist is with the disbursements of the state, and this is quite as important as responsibility for the revenues (II, 469).[1]

386. Instead of being expended for the common happiness, the means of the state are (1) often wasted; (2) used with shortsighted niggardliness; (3) applied at the wrong point for the best results; (4) unsystematically administered (II, 471).

387. In order to avoid these errors, the rules laid down in the introduction must be applied, viz.: (1) Outlays must be in accordance with the circumstances and revenues of the state; (2) the "readiest means" of the state must be used for no other purpose than the best good of ruler and subjects (II, 473).

388. From the previous fundamental principles we derive *the first rule* of wise expenditure, viz., No outlay must be undertaken without the most thorough previous consideration, and estimate of the involved cost, and of the income likely to accrue from the same to the state (II, 476).

389. *The second rule* is, that the outlay should never exceed the income (II, 478).

390. *Rule three.*—For all outlays the "readiest means" must be already in hand, and in no case should a start be made with a debt (II, 479).

391. *Rule four.*—All expenditures of the state must be made certain (II, 480).

392. *Rule five.*—No outlay should be made which tends permanently to diminish either the available or the total "means" of the state (II, 481).

393. *Rule six.*—So far as possible, outlays should be so ordered that the money will be expended within the state, and will get into circulation in the sustaining system of the country (II, 482).

[1] Justi accuses the cameralistic writers of having failed to give this subject proportional attention, and assigns as one of the reasons that they have had little faith that rulers would pay attention to cameralistic precepts on the subject. Justi disclaims the purpose of instructing courts as to their duties, but thinks it the duty of cameralists to systematize wise rules of administration, whether rulers adopt them or not.

394. *Rule seven.*—The importance of every proposed outlay must be measured by the amount of income that it is likely to return for the welfare of the state (II, 484).

395. *Rule eight.*—Outlays must be arranged in the order of their usefulness for the common good of ruler and subjects (II, 486).

396. The great management of the state bears much similarity to the housekeeping of private persons; hence the rules that are valid in private housekeeping apply, with changed details, to the use of the "means" of the state (II, 487).

396A. *Rule nine.*—The necessities of the state must take precedence of all other demands, and necessities must be reckoned in the following grades, viz.: (1) Those on which the stability of the republic depends; (2) those which are of qualified necessity, i. e., from omission of which the community would suffer great harm, such as loss of industries through failure of proper promotion; (3) those which might be omitted without positive injury, but without which the maximum happiness of the state cannot be reached (II, 488).

397. Even expenses of the first grade should not be covered so extravagantly that outlays of the other grades would be impossible (II, 489).

398. *Rule ten.*—Only when all the necessary expenses are provided for can the means of the state be appropriated to conveniencies (II, 490).

399. *Rule eleven.*—After all outlay is provided for which is required for the needs and conveniencies of the state, attention may be given to comfort, dignity, display, and ornamentation (II, 491).[1]

400. *Rule twelve.*—The aim should be to put the finances of the country in such condition that not merely the necessities and con-

[1] Justi adds: "I have no hesitation in giving the preference to outlays for the display of the court: for since the chief purpose of these outlays is to impress foreign nations with the prosperity and power of the state, no better place of using the money can be found than at the court of the monarch, where it most directly appeals to the eye of foreigners. Still, that which is appropriate for the comfort and elegance of the country in other places must not be forgotten. It is not consistent if the residence charms the eye of foreigners, while the rest of the country has a poverty-stricken appearance.

veniencies, but also the comforts and elegancies may be secured (II, 492).

401. *Rule thirteen.*—If the government is to be in a situation to make fair appropriations of all kinds, it must in all its outlays observe reasonable economy (II, 493).

402. *Rule fourteen.*—Care must be taken that economy be not turned into greed, especially through contempt of the ruler for certain needs of his subjects, while his passions lead him to favor other outlays (II, 495).

403. *Rule fifteen.*—The finance bureau must constantly have the most exact information about the condition of all the funds (II, 499).

404. *Rule sixteen.*—No disbursements should be made except upon strict account (II, 500).

405. *Rule seventeen.—Entrepreneurs* should be used in all cases which involve employment of a large number, and many minor outlays (II, 501).

406. *Rule eighteen.*—Nothing which can be obtained with a lump sum should be subject to several charges (II, 305).

407. *Rule nineteen.*—The persons expending the money of the state should not themselves make additional costs necessary (II, 504).

408. *Rule twenty.*—Everything must be supplied at the proper time, with foresight and advantage, and by cash payments; and when it is profitable stocks of goods needed by the state should be kept.

409. *Rule twenty-one.*—Strict accounts, in perfect order, must be kept of the outlays of the state (II, 507).[1]

410. After provision for the military budget (II, 527–57), and for the court budget (II, 560–86), the cameralistic expenses proper may be divided into eight groups: (1) Moneys for the civil-list and dowries (II, 588); (2) appropriations for the various admin-

[1] The following section, viz., Division Two, "Of the Proper Ordering of Expenditure, or the General Budget," contains simply considerations still more strictly technical and does not call for analysis. We may note one important precept, viz., *If a European state wants to have influence, it must devote at least two-thirds of its revenues to the military budget* (II, 523).

istrative expenses (II, 589); (3) the expenses of levying and collecting the revenues, and of maintaining the sources from which they are derived (II, 592); (4) the salaries and pensions of all civil servants in the state, finance, police, and justice bureaus (II, 597); (5) the expenses of bringing land under cultivation (II, 602); (6) the expenses of buildings for the use of the state (II, 607); (7) the support of the ecclesiastical and school systems (II, 609); (8) expenses for the comfort and adornment of the country (II, 613).[1]

411. The organization and the correlation of the cameralistic system, and of the bureaus belonging to it, is one of the most important elements in the government of a state. The whole management of a community rests upon it, and to a certain extent its whole internal constitution rests upon it. The administrative police institutions of the state are a part of the cameral system. At all events the two are inseparable, because the former constitute the ground of the "readiest means" of the state and must in turn be supported by the same. In this most general signification of the cameral system, it comprehends not merely all police institutions and measures, and consequently the commercial and agricultural administration, but also the administration of justice, at least so far as concerns the technique of the same, and the nature [*Beschaffenheit*] of the laws, as well as the management of the military system. There remain therefore only foreign affairs, which may be contrasted with cameral business, and which constitute the second essential element in the government of the state. Important as the constitution of the cameral system is then in itself, it is especially so on account of the peculiar traits of our times. Since the European powers have placed themselves on a constant war footing, since they have made it a part

[1] The remainder of this subdivision (II, 614–60) is entirely devoted to the routine of cameralistic functions. Justi makes the topic of correlating the different kinds of cameral administration co-ordinate with (*a*) the raising of funds; (*b*) the reasonable use of the "means" of the state. The technique of this organization as outlined in the remainder of the *Staatswirthschaft* contains nothing directly material to our purpose. Nevertheless, as a bit of shading for the picture of the state which we have already found in the book, an abstract from Justi's introduction to the section, is added.

of their programme to encourage commerce and manufactures and the sustaining class, as well as the general culture of their countries, the cameral system has taken on a quite other form. Those states in which the rulers two or three hundred years ago either left the finances to their consorts, or intrusted them as a minor duty to a privy council or court, now have various great and important bureaus for the administration of the same, and meanwhile the revenues have increased five, six, and ten times (II, 664).[1]

[1] The remainder of the book contains (1) a general sketch of the administrative organization of the chief European states (II, 666–84); (2) a brief discussion of propositions looking to improvement of the cameral organization (II, 684–88); (3) Justi's own programme of reorganization (II, 688–702); (4) the fundamental ordinances and technical processes of cameral administration (II, 702–44). In this portion of the book a conspicuous trait of Justi's method is particularly prominent, viz., an appearance of studied effort to avoid giving credit to previous writers. This peculiarity cannot be overlooked as a symptom of the literary practice of his time, as the usage of previous cameralists sufficiently shows. Justi was exceptionally unwilling to give other writers their due unless they were safely dead. Montesquieu is the only author whom he frequently mentions by name. Only three or four others are mentioned at all in this volume, and never with precise reference to passages by which the correctness of the judgment passed upon them might be decided. When Justi refers to "other cameralists" who have proposed modifications of the system, he gives no clue to their identity, so that their own grounds for their propositions might be examined. In this respect his methods are as crude as his manners.

I regret that I have been unable to secure a copy of the work in which Justi expanded his views of fiscal science; viz., *Das System des Finanzwesens*, 1766.

CHAPTER XV

JUSTI'S POLITICAL PHILOSOPHY

As we have seen from various points of approach, cameralism was not primarily a philosophy, nor was it an economic theory in the modern sense. It was a technique and a technology. In so far as it rested on a basis of principles, they were primarily political rather than economic generalizations. That is, political purposes were chiefly in view, and economic means were enlisted in the cameralistic technique to promote those purposes.

If would be easy to cull out of Justi's books sentences from which we might infer that he was, in the last analysis, a full-fledged democrat. Such an inference, however, would be as unwarranted as the contrary conclusion that he manifested no democratic opinions or sympathies. The plain fact is that his thinking had, so to speak, special apartments for as many different orders of opinions, which would have treated one another roughly if they had met face to face. Occupying separate quarters they could ignore actual incompatibilities.

In his apartments devoted to the most general aspects of life, the conspicuous motto on the wall was: "The Happiness of Ruler and Subjects."

In the apartments assigned to the primary necessities of life, the fireside talk was a ringing of changes upon "Earn and Save!"

In the apartments reserved for plans and programmes of political life was an undertone, always audible, droning variations of the constant theme: "The clue to life is a good king, with well-trained civil servants and docile subjects."

Now, it would be folly to class a house as "disorderly" simply because its tenants were of such diverse types, but the moment it becomes necessary for the lodgers to decide upon a common standard the problem of harmonizing these conceptions is imminent. It by no means follows that their different outlooks upon life are essentially incompatible. In composing them, however, it is inevitable that different forms and contents and implications of each will from time to time control, and that one of the main conceptions will dominate the others. Men will ask one another, What is happiness? How is it composed? What does it involve? Is it one and the same thing for everybody, or does it vary from man to man, from time to time, from place to place? To what extent is it simply our own affair, and to what extent does it depend on other people? Again, they will ask, How many ways are there to earn and save? What do these ways have to do with one another? How do they depend on one another? What advantages has one over another? How far may the arts of earning and saving be developed beyond present methods? To what extent may we discover more fundamental and inclusive principles of earning and saving and of guaranteeing to each all that he earns and saves? Still further, men will ask, What proof have we that kings are essentials to life, any more than stone hatchets, or bone fish-hooks? Why may not kings and paternalism be outgrown, just like wooden plows, and bows and arrows, and flint and steel? When are kings and kingcraft good and when are they bad? What recourse have men when kings and kingcraft fail?

Men need not have asked all these questions by any means, nor others equally obvious, before they would be capable of seeing that Justi's system, however useful for its purpose, was very far from a conclusive science of the things with which it was concerned. It contained rudimentary moral and economic and political philosophies but neither of these philosophies had been thought through, and the relations between them had been subjected to no critical analysis whatsoever. In effect it was plans and specifications of the best paternalistic government that could be devised, with the reservation that no questions were to be asked about the finality of that paternalistic government as an irreducible minimum. It was accordingly a system of operating the paternalistic type of state, first and foremost, so that it could maintain itself in the rivalries of similar neighboring states, through systematic superintendence and stimulation of approved thrift, without prying behind the precepts of commonplace prudence, and with such resulting happiness to the people as was to be gained in the course of making the permanence and power of the paternalistic state the supreme end. In other words, so far as Justi's type of cameralism held the center of attention, it postponed all larger questions of social science, and substituted for them a catechism of the routine to be observed in governmental bureaus, of the attitude which the ruler would maintain toward government and subjects if his views agreed with Justi's, and of the attitude which the subject should maintain in any event toward ruler and administration. Otherwise expressed, all the social science there was within the sphere of cameralism was first, as we shall see presently, a more or less explicit political philosophy, then a managerial ritual, with no positive provision either for revising the ritual itself or for reappraising the purposes which the ritual was supposed to serve. It had the same relation to the problems of society in general that a book on tactics would have to statesmanship.[1]

In applying the term "ritual" to Justi's cameralism, I do not mean to assert that it was necessarily arbitrary in detail. On the contrary, the larger number of its precepts were emi-

[1] Parts of the contents of Justi's books might be cited as proof that the comparison is an exaggeration, especially the volume, *Natur und Wesen der Staaten*. If substance, not form, is decisive, the parallel is exact.

nently reasonable. The ritualism came from its relation to the major premise, viz., the finality of the paternalistic state. As items in the operation of such a moral economy as present analysis discovers in human experience, these same precepts might be no more ritualistic than valid rules of hygiene.

This appraisal of Justi's system may be varied as follows: It was an undigested mixture of judgments about means and ends. It did not consciously encounter the previous question, viz., How shall we know when such means as the type of state, and ruler, and bureaucracy which we now take for granted, and which are at present assumed to be indispensable for the types of ends which we also take for granted, lose their value as means, to such an extent that we can no longer take them for granted as approximate ends? The parallel question would also have challenged the authority of Justi's system, but it had not appeared above his horizon; viz., How may we know when the types of ends which we take for granted cease to satisfy the conditions of life, and consequently impeach the means on which we have relied for the conduct of life? That is, the autocratic state and ruler and bureaucracy had so imposed themselves on the thoughts and feelings of the time that they were virtually valued as both means and end of human purposes, and criticism of them to discover how far they were merely provisional means to mediate ends was marking time in the cameralistic technology. Meanwhile, such larger social philosophy as ventured to show signs of life within or around this technology was in its primary characteristics more prominently political than economic. We shall attempt to justify this judgment by an examination, first, of the *Natur und Wesen der Staaten*, and second, of the *Grundriss einer Guten Regierung*.

Of these two books, which we shall notice not in their chronological but in their logical order, we may first observe in general, that they merely elaborate themes which were contained in *Staatswirthschaft*. Indeed that volume in principle exhausts Justi's cameralism. The later volumes contain nothing except illustrative material which was implied, if not expressed, in the earlier synoptic book. We shall therefore be able to do justice to these volumes, as expansions of Justi's system, without the detailed analysis which was necessary in presenting his general survey.

We turn to the more fundamental of these special treatises.[1] If this book had been written for the purpose of supporting our main thesis about cameralism as essentially a political rather than an economic theory, it could hardly have been more unequivocal.[2] For our purposes the Preface is most important, because the body of the book merely enlarged upon principles which are sufficiently prominent in our account of *Staatswirthschaft*.

The contents of the Preface may be summarized in this way:

Montesquieu's *Esprit des Lois* is in many respects an exemplary book, but it contains certain errors which should be corrected.

This book may be regarded as an alternative treatise on the spirit of the laws [*Geist der Gesetze*]. "After I have discussed the essence and nature of states, and have pointed out the errors of Montesquieu in this connection, I come to the essence [*Wesen*] of the laws, which are the means through which states must attain their essential purpose, namely, the common happiness [*gemeinschaftliche Glückseligkeit*], which means can be derived nowhere else than from the essence and nature of states as their chief source."

[1] *Die Natur und das Wesen der Staaten, als die Grundwissenschaft der Staatskunst, der Policey, und aller Regierungswissenschaften, desgleichen als die Quelle aller Gesetze*, abgehandelt von Johann Heinrich Gottlob von Justi, Berlin, Stettin und Leipzig. . . . . 1760 (488 pages + index of 32 pages).

[2] It was not from this book, however, that I arrived at my interpretation. Long before I discovered it, I had reached my conclusion from equally decisive but less obvious evidence.

"It will easily be seen that this book contains the fundamental science of all the economic and cameral sciences, and that it constitutes, so to speak, a sort of political metaphysic for all the governmental sciences. For there can be no doubt that all these sciences must be based upon the essence and nature of a (*sic*) state, and therefrom alone, as from their fountain-head [*Hauptquelle*], must be derived."

We have inverted the order of Justi's paragraphs, so as to place his more general propositions first, without affecting his thought. The more specific reason which he assigns for writing the book is in the earlier paragraphs of the Preface, viz.:

I made the plan of this work five years ago.[1] Meanwhile it has reshaped itself in my mind, in accordance, as I think, with a better general idea which I have meanwhile formed. The necessity of such a work was evident to me from the time that I began to write upon the economic and cameral sciences.

All these sciences, and all those which are required for the government of a state, must in a word be derived from the general nature and essence of states, and nothing can be securely established in them if one does not constantly look back to the nature of civic institutions [*bürgerlichen Verfassungen*]. If accordingly I would justify this or that principle or rule in *Staatskunst*, in *Policey*, in *Finanz-Wissenschaft*, and the other economic sciences, I had to trace the grounds of the same very remotely [*weitläuftig*] from the essence and the nature of states; and when this principle or rule emerged in another portion of these sciences, it was necessary to repeat the most important grounds, in order to show the harmony of the same with the essence of civic institutions. I judged accordingly that a special treatise on the essence and the nature of states would serve my own as well as my readers' convenience, since I would not then be under the necessity, in all my subsequent works,

[1] If we take the statement literally, it would locate this passage in Justi's thinking during the interval between his departure from Vienna and his arrival in Göttingen, i. e., about a year before publication of *Staatswirthschaft*. It is not unlikely that revision of his notes for that volume clarified his ideas in the direction of the book before us.

repeatedly to show the correspondence of my fundamental propositions with the nature of a state.

Thus we have Justi's own direct testimony that all the sciences embraced in the general sense of the term cameralism were, in his view, deductions from a fundamental political philosophy. Moreover, all activities in civic society were to find their *rationale* in this a priori, viz., the presupposed "essence and nature of states." This concept served in Justi's thinking as the finality back of which analysis could not penetrate. A large part of the difference between this type of thinking and modern sociological inquiry is a consequence of penetration by the latter into the social processes antecedent in time to the existence of states, or more general in content than civic activities. The resultant perception that states are but one of the many variations of means by which men seek to accomplish their purposes displaces the concept "essence and nature of states" as the ultimate term in explanation of civic activities, and substitutes the essence and nature of associating persons, whose purposes give the sliding scale of values to all their machineries.

The argument of *Natur und Wesen* may be compressed into the following résumé:

First, the assumption of an original condition of "natural freedom" (chap. vii). Justi's particular version of "natural freedom" need not be analyzed in detail. While he does not arrive at a plausible hypothesis of reconciliation between the notion of the freedom of individuals and freedom of groups. within which there was no freedom, he satisfies himself that there is enough in the idea for a major premise, and he proceeds to build upon it.

Second, the derivation of social life from an inborn "social impulse" is denied (§5). On the contrary, perception of advantage from social reciprocity, i. e., in the last resort, reason [*Vernunft*], is the cause of social life (§6). With the development of circumstances, and corresponding development of wants, the utility of extending social combinations appealed to developing reason. Fear was one of the tributary motives. Some more intelligent men began to see the advantage of using compulsion upon weaker men, subjecting them to their laws, and making them serve their own advantage and conscience. Thus the condition of compelling or being compelled, the condition of war, took its origin. Hence come consolidation of related societies into larger societies, in order to offer more resistance to less closely related societies (§7).[1]

Third, these aggregations of people in societies do not yet constitute republics. Mutual aid [*Beystand*] is the purpose of societies, but republics have an incomparably greater purpose. In these societies all men lived still in the state of natural freedom. Each was subject to his own will and laws in so far as he was not constrained by others. Since they had not yet merged their will, the will of each was entirely free. It was within the free choice of each to make use of the advantage of reciprocal support, or to forego the same and to live each for himself. This freedom to step out of society at will is common to all societies which have no overlord, or which do not live under the laws of a republic. Particularly, however, the difference between societies and republics consists in the latter having a supreme power set over them, while the former have not. When therefore the societies compel one of their members to conform to their purposes and to the social compacts, this occurs according to the laws and the condition of war, not however according to the nature of a supreme power (§9).

It may be asked whether it were not possible that men could have lived in the condition of natural freedom in such societies, without creating republics. In my opinion that is precisely the question which is put in theology when is is asked whether it were not possible that men might have continued in the state of innocence, ... (§10).

Rather is it probable that increasing vice and license, which disturbed the internal peace of these societies, was the immediate cause of adopting civic laws and institutions. When such disorders occurred the most reputable and reasonable must naturally have set themselves up as arbiters, in order to abate the evils and to restore peace.

[1] Justi rejects Hobbes's theory of the inborn propensity to domineer.

. . . . This was a way to laws, or a beginning of them. The approach to civic institutions became closer and closer, while people were probably not conscious of it. . . . (§11).

The actual institution of republics was probably not after one fashion, but (1) through the growth of patriarchal power into actual overlordship (§12); (2) through the respect and eminence which certain men gained in their societies (§13); (3) through instruction of the people by skilled and experienced men, in the ways of attaining the comforts of human life (§14); (4) the leaders of new colonies have thereby at the same time founded states (§15). . . . . The earliest states were small monarchies, these being the most natural transition from freedom to civic institutions (§16). All these little monarchies were very mild and differed very little from the condition of natural freedom. . . . The people in their assemblies always retained the law-giving power in their hands. . . . . The kings and princes had only the right to propose and to convince by argument (*vide* Tacitus, *Germania*, chap. xi). Only in time of war had the magistrates, according to the testimony of Julius Caesar (*de bello Gal.*, lib. vi), right over life and death. This however was demanded by the nature of the case, if a commander were to accomplish anything (§17). From this slight removal of the first states from the condition of natural freedom, as well as from the unobserved growth of the civic organization, it follows in my opinion indubitably that men never chose to subject themselves to a severe form of government. This intention of the peoples is also founded in the nature of the case. Men would have been the most insane fools if they had been willing deliberately to exchange their most precious possession, freedom, for a government under which they would be slaves. The will of the peoples, upon entrance into republics, was thus doubtless this: that they would surrender their natural freedom and subject themselves to the government and laws of another only in so far as necessary for the ultimate purpose of the republics. Who however would deny that this will of the peoples must not be regarded in each and every government?[1] Besides this, the impulse

[1] Justi's frequent use of the double negative without the affirmative force makes a puzzle of such a sentence as this, in which the meaning cannot be positively fixed by the context. I think the above rendering

to dominate over others is not grounded in human nature. It is merely a consequence of a mediocre understanding. Men undoubtedly presuppose that they wish to be ruled by a perfect understanding. This advantage, this quality, can alone move them to intrust to another the government over themselves. Indeed, since finally God has put us in the world with equal freedom, dignity, and rights, I derive from all this the conclusion that it is the duty and obligation of every government to limit the natural freedom of its subjects, only in so far as the ultimate purpose of republics requires, and that always the best government is the one which without interference with the ultimate purpose of republics most nearly approaches natural freedom. This conclusion, which follows from the origin of republics, I regard as a fundamental principle, which I shall often use in treating the sciences of government (§18).

Justi appears to have entertained no doubt of the cogency and conclusiveness of this patchwork of guesses and irrelevancies and *non-sequiturs*. In contrast with Schröder, Justi had exchanged the theological for a pseudo-rationalistic major premise. There is no change in the finality, for practical purposes, of the pseudo-absolutism which the premise supports. The twentieth-century mind finds extreme difficulty in believing that an adult accustomed to reflection could ever have rested content with the puerilities of either argument. We flatter ourselves, however, by underestimating the capacity even of the sophisticated mind for self-deception. The psychological situation, in the case both of Schröder and of Justi, was first the unquestioned concrete datum, the existing absolutistic state; and second, the problem, to find a thread of association which would act as binding-twine and hold together with this datum the remaining assortment of ideas in the

faithfully reflects the ambiguity. The original reads: "Wer wollte aber wohl läugnen, dass dieser Wille der Völker bey allen und jeden Regierungen nicht in Betracht gezogen werden müsste?" I understand Justi to urge the antecedent probability that every government would regard the will of the subjects.

minds of the authors themselves and of their contemporaries. The effectiveness of the notions which proved to serve this purpose was evidently derived, not from logic but from suggestion. The datum "absolutistic state" was no more deduced from Schröder's or Justi's premises than the earth was deduced from Atlas. A plausible justification for the cameralistic state was set up, not so much in the uncritical explanation of its origin, as in the presumption that it was supernaturally devoted and adapted to its purpose of serving the general interest.

Throughout Justi's writings the idea of the common good, as the ultimate end of the state, repeatedly recurs. The implications of the idea are indefinite, but it unquestionably contains elements which went into the structure of later democratic conceptions.[1] A suspensive veto, so to speak, was held over these democratic elements by the inveterate assumption that the government was actually conforming to its destiny of preternatural wisdom and righteousness in the interest of all concerned, whatever might be the immediate appearances to the contrary. Thus the actual order of thought in Justi's political philosophy was, first, the state as it is must be accepted as the ultimate human recourse for promotion of temporal happiness; second, the details involved in the conception "temporal happiness" must be learned by experience; third, rulers must be relied upon to show the wisdom and righteousness requisite for setting in operation, in due time, the measures which will secure their subjects temporal happiness.

In a later paragraph (§23) Justi emphasizes the crucial conception in this philosophy, viz., the merging of the wills

[1] This may be inferred from the very significant fact that Justi sometimes uses the still more democratic phrase, *Glückseligkeit der Unterthanen*, as designation of the ultimate purpose of the state (e. g., §36). The whole conception was as yet, however, a matter of rhetoric rather than a decisive factor in statecraft.

of many free individuals into a single will. This conceit was not the democratic idea of a constantly re-established consensus between the members of the state. It was a notion of transference of the individual wills to the ruler, and their fusion in him into a transcendent will. This occurred once for all. Subsequent generations had nothing to do but accept the arrangement. The use to which this conception is put is indicated in general in the opening paragraph of the third chapter, as follows:

> The merging of many wills into a single will is the first moral ground of republics, and that which chiefly constitutes the civic condition. If many wills are to be consolidated in a single will, they must all have one and the same paramount purpose, and this chief purpose of each must include all their special and incidental purposes. In short, those who merge their wills must all have a common paramount purpose which leads all their transactions. The question then is, Wherein does this paramount purpose consist which produces the merging of the wills in the founding and building of republics? This ultimate purpose can be no other than the universal best [*das allgemeine Beste*], the welfare of each and every one of the families which as aforesaid merged with one another, in a word the common happiness [*gemeinschaftliche Glückseligkeit*] of the whole state.

At this point a single comment will be sufficient. If Justi's conception of the general welfare had actually been the prime consideration in his reasoning, he would have been forced to make it the major premise of an objective critique of the competence of absolutism to attain the involved results. This plane of reasoning was beyond Justi. It turns out that, in effect, the perpetuation of the absolutistic state is the ultimatum in his system, and that the general good comes to its own only as a secondary consideration, in so far as it can subordinate itself to the actually paramount interests of the quasi-absolutistic governments which posed as embodiments of the welfare of their peoples. The striking peculiarity of the transitional type of thinking which Justi represents was not its insistence upon the welfare of the people as the ultimate aim. It was rather its constant resort to the assumption that actual governments were more inerrant in their pursuit of this end than any other available civic system could possibly be. Herewith we have in principle the whole of Justi's political philosophy. His elaboration of it, on the institutional side, in the remainder of this volume is merely an expansion of the corresponding sections in *Staatswirthschaft*. We shall find more explicit description of civic well-being itself, as Justi conceived it, in the second of his volumes on political philosophy.[1]

A general estimate of another factor in Justi's thinking is pertinent at this point; viz., the evident line of cleavage between the technological and the idealistic elements in his books. Justi was apparently only half-conscious, if even so much, of the mixture of elements. On the one hand he was systematizing the actual technique of governmental administration. On the other hand he was describing the spirit and details of governments as they should be. If one were to read him without this distinction in mind one might reach utterly unwarranted conclusions about the modernness of his philosophy. The reservation must always be remembered that his theory had no place for an ultimate appeal beyond the authority of the constituted government, as the last resort of peoples. The government was the final moral arbiter, against whose decrees the citizens had no recourse. This was not merely the working condition, but the philosophical theory supported the conditions. At the same time, parallel with this theory and practice, a body of ethical judgments was taking shape which constituted a standard of political attainment destined pres-

[1] *Der Grundriss einer Guten Regierung*. In Fünf Büchern verfasset, von Johann Heinrich Gottlob von Justi, Königlichem Grossbritannischen Bergrath. Frankfurth und Leipzig, 1759.

ently to hail existing rulers before the bar of a more highly evolved justice. This more far-seeing justice shows itself in Justi's accounts of the purposes and technique of administration. The dilemma presented by these two elements had not yet been frankly admitted. The French Revolution first brought it into distinct view. In a word it was this: The proper moral standards of governments are such and such; the actual moral standards of governments are much inferior; there is no recognized means of compelling governments to adopt the higher standards; does the logic of the civic relation then require men to leave moral standards at the mercy of governments, or have men a deeper right to enforce subordination of governments to the higher sovereignty of morals?

In the philosophy which Justi represents this inevitable conjunction of ideas had not been reached. The two antithetical, yet necessarily related conceptions and their corollaries were in existence side by side, but they had not been reconciled, and the need of a reconciliation was not yet distinctly formulated.

The book just mentioned begins with a version of the same argument which was presented in *Natur und Wesen.* Avoiding repetition as much as possible, we may draw from the present volume certain details in completion of the account of Justi's system.

Without the proviso just urged, we should be inclined to believe we had stumbled upon a prophet of modern democracy when we read (§1):

The nature, essence, and ultimate purpose [*Endzweck*] of states are the only criteria by which to decide what is a good government.

Passing propositions which have already been quoted in other connections, we read (§4):

Every human being has an energy [*Kraft*] of his own. If many human beings combine in a society, there results a composite energy, which is in proportion to the number of persons. Every person in society has a share in this composite great energy. He is thus much stronger than the isolated man. Participation in the great energy of society is thus the ultimate purpose of societies.[1]

The will of each human being is to promote his own happiness. When therefore many human beings combine their wills, and resign to this combined will the use of their energy, i. e., when they set over themselves a supreme power, and subordinate their particular will to it, there can be no other intent than that each identifies his own happiness with the happiness of the whole society. The common happiness is accordingly the ultimate purpose of civic structures (§5; *vide* pp. 51 ff.).[2]

[1] Justi's form of expression seems to imply in the first place that the "great energy" of societies is merely the arithmetical sum of the energies of the individuals. This being the case, one wonders just how he pictured the process of getting out of that total more than was put in. He evidently assumed that something more than a mere addition took place in society, but his account of the situation leaves the essentials to be desired. The chief crudeness in this section of Justi's philosophy is not in the description of the central fact of a state, but in the absence of analysis of the sources of the "general will" or "supreme power." The *non sequitur* is at once in operation that a certain representative or repository of this "general will," say the monarch of a European state, being given, the concurrence of social forces by which that monarch came into existence has served its day and generation, and has gone out of business, leaving the monarch virtually absolute. I find no direct evidence that Justi consciously borrowed anything from Hobbes, but the assumptions of the former are quite in accord with the philosophy of the latter. Justi feels at liberty to tell when rulers ought to be ashamed of themselves, but he has no recourse short of judgments of God if they do not mend their ways (*vide Grundriss*, pp. 77 ff.).

[2] From this point the fallacy of confounding means and ends is constantly on duty. The *particular mode* of uniting the associated wills is assumed to be identical with, if not paramount to, the concept "common happiness." Consequently this *particular mode* of controlling association, the absolute state, is substituted as paramount purpose, for a developing idea of "common happiness" which would hold any *means* of its own realization, e. g., any form of civic constitution, as constantly liable to answer for its results, and to modification as the actual paramount purpose from time to time seemed to demand.

Hence arises a state, a republic, a "common being" [*gemeines Wesen*].[1] These three concepts are identical, if one takes the word republic in the most general sense, as its chief significance demands. A state or republic, however, is a society of human beings who have combined with one another in order to promote their common happiness under a sovereign power; or, in other words, a state consists of many families, that have united their energies and their will with one another in order to combine the happiness of each particular family with the common good (§6).

Such a society of human beings is called a people [*Volk*], and it is a ground of the state without which a state cannot be thought, that such a people occupies a certain portion of the earth's surface, which is their peculiar possession, and which we call the country or land [*Land*] (§8).

When a people thus unites its energy and its will, and intrusts the use of the combined energy to the master-will; that is, when it establishes a supreme power, this power rests in the beginning unquestionably with the people, since it originates through the unification of their energies and wills. The people can accordingly either exercise this power themselves and make ordinances about that exercise, or it can transfer such exercise to others. All power in the state springs therefore from the people [*Volk*] which is always the source of the same. The power therefore, by virtue of which the people makes ordinances about the exercise of the supreme power, or transfers such responsibility to others, is called the fundamental power [*Grundgewalt*] of the people, and is distinguished from the active supreme power, which originates only through the ordination of the former. This fundamental power of the people is a part of the essence of the state, and is always present, even with the most unlimited supreme power. It can be overthrown only by destruction of the state, either through total subjugation by an alien enemy, or through internal tyranny (§9).[2]

[1] No precise English equivalent for the content which Justi put into this phrase can be found.

[2] This is perhaps the most distinct formulation of fundamental democracy to be found in Justi's books. It would be misrepresentation if I should try to explain it away. It is simply a partially assimilated

When a people, by virtue of its fundamental power, determines how the active supreme power shall be exercised, it ordains fundamental laws. These institutions for the exercise of the supreme power are called the government, and the external ways and means in which the supreme power is exercised are called the form of government.[1] The form of government of a state can therefore be established only through the fundamental laws (§10).

In the establishment of the fundamental laws and of the form of government, the fundamental power of the people acts as law-giver. But when this fundamental power, according to the standards of the established fundamental laws and form of government, makes over the supreme power to others, it acts not as law-giver, but as party to a contract, i. e., it makes a contract [*Vertrag*] with the assumers of the supreme power, to the effect that they will take upon themselves and exercise the supreme power according to the standards of the fundamental law. The fundamental power of the people can thus not be a judge over the active supreme power, but all affairs and controversies between them must be adjudicated according to the nature of the contract (§11).[2]

The supreme power of the state consists in the use of the united energy by a united will (§5). The supreme power then amounts

element of his system. It reflects a phase of reality which has always haunted men's thinking, and which may be counted on to reopen every supposed closed system of social philosophy so long as there remains anything to adjust between the individual and the social factors in the human process. What happened, however, in Justi's system, was that working necessity so completely outweighed in his judgment the claims of popular sovereignty in any applicable sense that political absolutism was the unimpeached result.

[1] Thus Justi identifies fundamental laws (*Grundgesetze*) and government (*Regierung*).

[2] Here Hobbesism comes into the open in contrast with the democracy of §9. How and by whom adjudicated, if not by the fundamental power? Justi avoids that question here, but he has given his practical answer in the passage already noted in the *Staatswirthschaft*, viz., "The king can do no wrong," which any other power in the state has a right to resist. The unconscious humor of the reasoning is appealing when

to the performance of two great activities, viz., law-giving and the execution of law. Hence the supreme power may be divided into two branches, each of which may be subdivided (§13). The various combinations of these subdivisions give the mixed forms of government (§14).

The body thus formed has at most only the means [*Vermögen*] of activity. To be really active, it must have a peculiar ground of movement or activity. This can be none other than love of the fatherland or of the form of government. The ground of all moral actions of men is self-love, and the state, as a moral body, can have no other ground of activity than love for itself, or for its essence and form. This love, which is so natural in itself, must fill rulers and ruled, and thereby all parts of the civic body will be vitalized (§15).[1]

Although self-love is the ground of all moral action of human beings, yet this self-love requires very judicious guidance if human beings are really to attain happiness. Man must be virtuous, and live according to the natural laws if he wishes to be happy. Just so the civic body would fail to attain its happiness if love for the Fatherland were not judiciously guided toward this end. The mov-

we reflect that the "contract" alleged is purely unilateral. In exchange for total transfer of the citizens' freedom to the newly constituted supreme power, no *quid pro quo* is provided for in the nature of an enforcible obligation on the side of this new trustee to discharge the trust according to the intention of the alleged grantors.

[1] In pointing out the defects of Justi's reasoning I am of course not blaming him for being merely a reflection of his time. Blame and praise are not in question. The point is to detect precisely the strength and the weakness of the methods of thinking of which Justi was an exponent. The object is always to make use of these discoveries in criticism of current methods of thinking. We must observe, then, in connection with this paragraph, that it is a long leap to a conclusion which is not contained in the previously adduced premises. Between self-love and the love of the state the minor premise is implied, as already indicated (§9, note), that the *only* means by which self-love can attain its ends is through the state as traditionally constituted. Logically the reasoning is the vicious circle. Psychologically, the relation between self-love and love of the state is unanalyzed. This latter is no wonder, as the analysis is still incomplete.

ing spring of virtue is necessary, and this virtue consists in fulfilment of duties toward the state and fellow-citizens (§16).

The form of government is the special nature of each civic body. Each body can move only in accordance with its special nature. Each form of government requires its special spring of action, e. g., monarchy, honor; aristocracy, moderation; democracy, love for equality (*vide Staatswirthschaft*, above, p. 320) (§17).

All forms of government are equally good, so long as they preserve their ground of activity and their springs of action in full strength (§18).

If the springs of action are corrupted, well-organized mixed forms of government are preferable (§19).

Good organization of the mixed governmental forms depends on a just balance between the different branches of the sovereign power (§20).

Despotism is not a special form of government, but merely an abuse (§21).

Every state consists of rulers and ruled. This division alone is essential, and is peculiar to all states. All other divisions are merely accidental. In monarchical states these two classes are ruler and subjects. In republics all are subjects of the supreme power, but not of the persons at the head of the government (§23).[1]

The people, which in the democracy is everything, shrinks in importance in the mixed forms of government, until in the aristoc-

[1] Justi thus implies plainly enough the personal rulership of monarchs. In effect there was nothing in his political philosophy which differed from the *Stuart* view of divine right. Such passages as p. 159, in which legislation by a representative body is treated as best, do not nullify this proposition. Weighed against the whole tenor of his system, these flashes of modernness must be regarded as a sort of mirage, which played about the edges of his theory but were not actually assimilated with it. Justi's views of a representative legislature seem, moreover, to have been not unlike those of the present Czar. In 1907 the latter allowed the third *Douma* to be called, but he refused to acquiesce in its declaration that he was no longer an autocrat. The boundaries which Justi draws between the executive and the legislative powers leave the former still in possession of a different type of sovereignty from that which today goes with genuine representative government (*vide op. cit.*, p. 163).

racy and the monarchy it is only a very trifling something. Finally, through abuse of monarchy in tyranny the people and its fundamental powers are reduced to nothing. The people consists of thinking beings. A thinking being, however, can never wholly and blindly give over the care for its happiness to another. The people therefore should in all states be something (§27).[1]

The sovereign power and the people are parts of a whole because the one necessarily demands the presence of the other, and because neither can exist without the other. So soon therefore as the one part undertakes anything which is harmful to the other it harms itself (§29).[2]

The substance of all duties of the ruler is accordingly to make his people happy, or to unite the happiness of each several citizen with the general good. All duties of people and subjects may be reduced to the formula, *to promote all the ways and means adopted by the ruler for their happiness by their obedience, fidelity, and diligence* (§30).

The happiness of individuals and of the state consists of freedom, internal strength, good conditions, and security (§31).

Freedom may be separated into two concepts, political and civic; or the freedom of the state and the freedom of the citizen. The state is free when it is independent, i. e., when it is neither wholly nor partially subject to another state. The citizen is free when he can without hindrance realize his will. But the citizen has merged his will into another, and this combined will can express itself only through the laws. Consequently the citizen is free when he suffers no other limitation of his will than through the laws. The citizen is therefore really free because he is restrained by nothing except rules for his happiness, rules to which every free and thoughtful being must subject himself (§32).[3]

[1] Was Sieyès' famous *mot* after all a plagiarism?

[2] Substitute for "sovereign power" and "people," "employer" and "employee," and we have the familiar dictum of the classical economics on the absurdity of supposed conflict of interests between wage payer and wage taker.

[3] Justi omits his apologies to the spider and the fly. The other elements of happiness are described in terms that have already been specified. *Vide* above, pp. 330, 331.

A ruler must not impair the reasonable freedom of his subjects, nor allow it to be impaired by his favorites and servants. No one in his whole state must be directly or indirectly compelled to do or to forbear from doing anything which the laws, made for the welfare of the state, do not prescribe (§39).

The property of the subjects must be the most sacred and inviolable object in the eyes of the ruler and his servants. Hence the ruler may regard it as his greatest glory if in his private transactions the subjects refuse to make over their property to him. That is always the most royal mark of the goodness of a government (§40).[1]

The ruler and his ministers should neither directly nor indirectly interfere with the due process of law (§41).

Never, except in the most extraordinary need, should the contributions of the subjects be increased (§42).

No war should be fought unless the preservation of the state makes it unavoidable (§43).

The text is then divided into five books, viz.:

I. On the ultimate purpose of a good government, and consequently the general idea of a good government.

II. On the fundamental arrangements by means of which governments are made good by nature.

III. On the goodness of the government which springs from its own moderation.

IV. On the wisdom of a good government.

V. The errors and faults of bad governments.

It is unnecessary to go into further details of the argument. From these generalizations it would be easy to anticipate the substance of the elaboration of each topic. The state which Justi outlines is an organization of people whose conceded legal and moral rights do not include a voice in making the laws which they must obey, and they do not include legal or moral right to call ruler or ministers to account if the laws which they decree are unjust, or if their administration of them is oppressive. The few further passages to be cited will

[1] E. g., the story of Frederick the Great and the miller at Potsdam.

serve chiefly to illustrate this proposition. In general the fact is that Justi's ideal of the achievements of a good state was in the main intelligent, if no account is made of the stultification involved in this conception of the means by which the ideal was to be attained. But in such a case we cannot separate the end thus abruptly from the means. Freedom to do our own experimenting with freedom is one of the proximate ends which thinking beings propose to themselves if their thinking is not suppressed; and this freedom to find our own way to something that may be thought of as an ultimate freedom is a more importunate aim than the conceivable ultimate freedom, if it could be conferred by a superior power.

Justi lays down the major premise: "No one can rule over reasonable and free beings except with the intention of promoting their welfare and making them happy" (p. 33).

Of the possible meanings of this sententious proposition, the substance of Justi's system forces us to select this version, viz., It is impossible to suppose that a ruler would desire anything but the best good of his subjects. That is, it was a purely *ad captandum* appeal for acquiescence in the prevailing type of absolutism. With so much granted, all the rest of the reasoning is unanswerable.[1] Once given an absolute ruler with his existence justified, and no logic can depose him. The only refutation possible is through destruction of the major premise; and of course this was the actual first step

[1] I find no evidence that there was intentional or conscious sophistry in Justi's argument. He was apparently a convinced advocate, at least to the extent that he had not clearly thought out a feasible alternative; and he was not aware of weakness in his method of proof (*vide op. cit.*, p. 35). Whether his occasional praise of the English system impeaches his sincerity as an absolutist, or merely punctuates the incoherence of his political philosophy, is, to be sure, an open question, but on the whole, I incline to the view that these irreconcilable elements in his thinking show that he had not faced the necessity of adjusting the incompatible doctrines.

in abolishing absolutism everywhere. Rulers being human are both intellectually so narrow and morally so fallible that they are incapable in the long run of performing the function which absolutism assumes. Then another functionary and another technique and another philosophy must be substituted.

Justi begins his detailed discussion with a proposition which reflects the fundamental political conception of which cameralism was an incident; viz., "To govern is to guide the actions of other people in accordance with certain purposes."[1] The affair in which Justi was engaged, both as advocate and as bureau official, was the operation of a legislative and executive organization conceived as something over and above and superior to the people, although perforce in certain relations of and for the people. So far as the relation had been thought out and realized, it was not by the people, and it was for them only so far as the persons who wielded the power of the organization were sufficient centers of light and leading to use it for the real benefit of the nation in a democratic sense. The first and typical idea and aim was to magnify the governing power itself, and the rest of the nation was accordingly rated as tributary to that paramount purpose. Justi proceeds to build on his foundations of political philosophy after this fashion:

Those who govern other men in the unobserved way, if they are rightly constituted and honorable, will always have as their object the best good of those whom they rule. . . . . If the ruled discover that they are controlled in another spirit, no matter how simple they are, they will sooner or later break the fetters. Invisible or unconscious government must consequently have the best good of the people at heart; or, what amounts to the same thing, it must succeed in keeping the people under the spell of assumption that its best good is the foremost purpose. We have then to inquire what

[1] "Regieren heisst die Handlungen anderer Menschen nach gewissen Absichten lenken" (p. 34).

must be the ultimate aims of those who openly govern other men (pp. 35, 36).

Thereupon Justi constructs an argument along these speculative lines; not an induction of the actual character of states as they are, not a frank idealization of kinds of government as he thought they ought to be, not even a modest inference as to the requirements to which governments must eventually conform. Instead of either of these, he actually expatiates upon considerations partly of the second, partly of the third, types, and then, as though such considerations were pertinent evidence, he derives the basic inference that governments *as they are* conform to those specifications of morals and long-term expediency, which entitle them to the implicit acquiescence of subjects. In short, his major premise is that actual governments are essentially what they would be if the men in power were divinely good and wise.[1]

Justi constantly appealed to religious sanctions for beliefs and actions. No evidence appears that this was a phenomenon

[1] Three distinct questions emerge here: *first*, Whether the policy which this doctrine prescribed was the one best adapted to the stage of evolution then in progress; *second*, Whether the philosophy expressed by the doctrine was a valid generalization; *third*, What were the actual effects of the doctrine upon the theories and practices of the period? We might answer the first of these questions in the affirmative, as indeed I am inclined to do, yet we might most confidently answer the second question in the negative, and we might find that there were most unfortunate and confusing results to be scheduled in answer to the third question. Our present study has no further reference to the first of these questions. We are dealing with the second, principally, and with the theoretical, more than the applied, aspects of the third. That is, we are attempting to get first a clear view of Justi's political philosophy, because it was the setting in which his cameralism has to be interpreted; and we are to use this analysis of the principal and subordinate factors of his system as a guide to the effects that the system, and others of which it was a type, had upon the course of development in the social sciences at large.

with deeper roots than mere acceptance of the conventionalities of his surroundings, and instinctive perception that this was the type of *argumentum ad hominem* which would meet with least express opposition. It is accordingly a matter of course that he relies upon the claim that goodness will in the long run be successful, and badness unsuccessful. Upon this ground he urges that no ruler would be so unwise as to rule simply in his own selfish interest. Even Machiavelli, he thinks, did not teach that (p. 36 *et passim*)[1] and the worst tyrants were probably not primarily enemies of their people, but they found that without intending to rouse their hostility they had done so, and thereafter supposed themselves to be unsafe unless they ruled with a high hand. This is all a-priori reasoning, monarchy being taken for granted, and the attempt being made to show that the aim of monarchy must be the common good. There is no trace, even in the last book of the volume, which at hasty glance might seem to furnish the exception, of a genuine attempt to measure the strength of this probability by induction. In a word, as Justi expresses it, the outcome of this a-priori reasoning is, that because it is stupid and wrong for a ruler to govern with selfish aims, *therefore*, "His final purpose can be no other than to guide the ruled to their best good, to promote their welfare by wise measures—in a word, to make them happy."

The chapter ends with a homiletical exhortation apparently intended both as a play upon the suggestibility of the people on the one hand, and as the most direct appeal permitted by good form to the better impulses of princes:

When a ruler in this manner makes his subjects and at the same time himself happy, something grand is before him in their eyes. That is the honor, which accompanies all his ways and the glory which attends the footsteps of all his actions. How beautiful, how lordly, how glorious, how commendable is it to govern men, when

[1] Justi thinks *The Prince* was a deeply veiled satire. *Vide* p. 327.

one makes them happy! That is the greatest, the most exalted of all human activities, to which a reasoning being can attain, and other kinds of human honor and glory are not to be compared with it (p. 50).

The method of proving that men united in societies for the sake of promoting their happiness is equally speculative, but the more pertinent fact is that the conclusion did not go so far as to justify the continuance of an effectively teleological attitude of subjects toward their governments after they were once formed. For practical purposes Justi's philosophy meant that the people must depend on the government to promote their happiness, but more than that, they must in the last resort trust the good intentions of the government even when it is not apparently working in their interest. That is, Justi posited absolutism mitigated by laws which the government itself had made, by considerations of prudence, of religion, of benevolence, of reputation, each and all to be valued in case of collision, not by the people, but by the ruler.

This is the typical confusion of ideas in the philosophy of absolutism, and especially in the conflict in Justi's mind between tradition and a valid estimate of social values. His judgment of political ends reads almost like fundamental democracy. The limitation of his reasoning is found in his inability to accept the conclusion of social logic that the historically developed means of attaining human ends must, in the long run, command the approval of the groups in which they function, or be repudiated. He could not advance beyond the dogma that the government, as constituted, must be accepted by the people as an automatically self-correcting agency, not to be interfered with by the subjects. That is, in creating it men acted as practical utilitarians. In their attitude toward it since it has been created, they must be essentially acquiescent. Throughout Justi's writings standards of governmental action are expressed which are prophetic of inevitable change of attitude toward governments. The crucial matter for his views as a political philosophy, however, is that these ideals are scheduled merely as standards which it is proper for the people to desire, and right and wise for rulers to adopt, but not as rights which citizens are free to enforce.[1]

Then Justi reiterates his generality that the common happiness of the state depends on "the three ideas, freedom, inner strength, and security." Then these ideas are expanded in a way which makes them quite compatible with the virtual absolutism previously assumed (pp. 65 ff.).

The discussion which follows (pp. 67–109) of the means of securing these three elements of happiness, is in substance nearly identical with the treatment of the same subject in *Staatswirthschaft* and we pass over all but a few incidental variations.

For example, the "law of parsimony," of which so much has been made in later economic theory, is recognized in the fundamental theorems about political means, viz., first, the means must correspond with the nature of the thing to be attained; second, of the possible means they must be the best; third, they must be the easiest, "for it is a law of nature and reason that we do not accomplish a thing by means of a greater force, which might be adequately brought about by a lesser" (p. 67); fourth, they must also be just, "for reason, justice, and virtue command us not to apply bad means for good ends." "These are to be regarded as so many fundamental principles of a good government, by disregard of which one will always fall into notable errors" (p. 68). Justi nowhere contemplates

[1] He says, to be sure (p. 64), "Whatever is plainly opposed to the ultimate end and nature of a society can without doubt not be binding upon the society." In the immediate context, however, he appears to imply that this cannot be thought of anything that occurs under the regular forms of law. He has elsewhere expressly denied that sovereignty can at last be in the people as opposed to the government (*vide* p. 325).

any more effective sanctions of these virtuous generalizations than the conscience of the monarch. If he is not so minded, there is no appeal except to the inscrutable workings of divine Providence.

Another betrayal of the abortiveness of the conception of freedom posited in Justi's philosophy occurs in his elaboration of the concept in §85. He says: "Freedom consists in the unhindered exercise of his (the citizen's) will. But the citizens who constitute a state have merged their separate wills in a single will. This single will can show itself in no other manner than through the laws." Thus freedom is defined only in the same breath to be denied. In the state which Justi contemplated, freedom had only an imaginary existence. It was a fiction of the philosophy of consolation applied as a balm to the feelings of subjects whenever they were wounded. The reality which occupied the place of freedom was just as much tether for the individual will as the will of the monarch, expressed through laws which he made, saw fit to allow.

The light in which the factor of population was contemplated in Justi's philosophy appears in the same context. It was primarily a military consideration, and only secondarily industrial. That is, in facing the prime problem of the strength and security of the state against foreign aggression, the necessary factors are found to be, first, well situated and fortified territory, and enough of it; second, a sufficient population living in such close community that they can act effectively together. For, says Justi (84):

Few people, scattered over a wide territory, cannot repulse enemies invading from all directions. Thus they have much less activity than the same number of people who live closer together in a smaller country. It is easy to show mathematically how much weaker a million people are who live scattered over a thousand square miles than another million occupying two hundred and fifty square miles, other circumstances being equal. It is consequently essential to the strength of the state that its territory must be peopled according to the measure of its greatness. Accordingly, the internal strength of a state depends upon the situation of its territory, upon the number of its inhabitants, upon the goods at its disposal, and upon the talents and moral qualities of the people.

Enlarging, two pages later (p. 86), upon the second of these conditions, Justi adds:

> Two million people have of course more aggregate energy and strength than one million, other things being equal.

The doctrine of population, taken in this obvious relation, would seem to have had much less of the character of a distinctive dogma than the commentators upon the history of economic theory have represented.

The same may be said of the factor of wealth in this philosophy of the state. It was less a dictum asserting some occult potency of wealth than a matter-of-course reckoning upon the obvious. Thus Justi says (p. 87):

> The internal strength of the state depends further upon riches of all sorts which are required for the needs and conveniences of human life. . . . . Just as it is beyond doubt that those states have a much more permanent ground for their welfare whose soil is by nature adapted to the production of the necessities of life, so may we also assert that, other things being equal, that state is always the strongest and happiest which has to satisfy the fewest needs from other states. Such a state is in no way dependent upon other peoples, and it will have within itself all the means which are demanded for strength. A good government must therefore give its weightiest attention to the production of such riches and abundance of goods within the country.

Justi continues (p. 88):

> I have here with great deliberation based the internal strength of the state not upon riches in gold and silver, and upon the ways that lead to such wealth, namely, commerce, mining, etc., but entirely upon wealth in goods. This wealth in goods is also alone the true wealth of the state which is requisite for internal strength. The

Spaniards, who imagined that they would be the lords of the whole world, if they had all the treasures of America in their possession, and for that reason entirely neglected wealth in goods, were in gross error. With all their treasures they have since been the poorest nation in Europe, and they could not be anything else, since they lacked the real wealth of peoples. . . . . If, however, a state possesses the real wealth in goods, and is sufficiently populous, it can have all the internal strength of which it is capable, with neither gold nor silver nor commerce nor other intercourse with foreign nations, in so far as this isolation is compatible with its natural situation, its circumstances, and its form of government. . . . . Riches in gold and silver is only a relative wealth of the state, which relates entirely to commerce and the interconnection with other peoples, and is necessary merely on that account. It belongs to the external strength of the state, and to aggressive power [*Angriff*], but not to internal strength and defensive power, to which alone I now refer, because aggression is not to be included in the happiness of a state. If a state finds it in accordance with its circumstances and happiness to have such connections and intercourse with other nations, then its internal strength will require that it shall seek to export as much as possible of its surplus in order to increase its relative riches in gold and silver. Under these circumstances that is the strongest state which has to look to other states for the fewest satisfactions of its wants, and which exports the most of its surplus.[1]

In confirmation of the general thesis as to the qualified absolutism which was the ultimate term of Justi's political philosophy, we may quote from a following section. Having elaborated the proposition that the internal strength of a state depends, first, on the fundamental virtue of obedience in the subjects, Justi continues (p. 93):

The moral quality of rulers, which is demanded for the internal strength of the state, may be expressed in one word. It is wisdom.

[1] The relation between cameralism and mercantilism is reviewed in the closing chapter (pp. 586 ff.). It is enough to say here that intimate acquaintance with the cameralists punctures the myth that their conceptions of wealth were utterly bizarre.

But this concept contains very much. If rulers are wise, they are everything necessary to make their state strong and their people happy. This quality, moreover, is so essential to the strength of the state that all previous means to internal strength in the largest measure lose their force, so soon as wisdom is lacking in rulers. . . . . The perfection and wisdom of the government is accordingly the chief means and the foremost quality whereupon the true power and internal strength of the state rest. It is the soul of all previously mentioned means, and it gives to them their full effect. . . . . The wisdom and perfection of a government, however, consists in the positing of a wisely chosen plan and programme of government, and the genuine fundamental rules: in government by the monarch himself, through his own insight, not merely through his ministers, and the concentration of all affairs in his strong hand; in his wise choice of ministers and servants, and assignment of each to a post of duty in accordance with his qualities and capabilities; in holding all business and affairs in the most precise order and coherence and the fighting forces in like order and discipline; and finally in putting the state in the utmost possible condition of preparation against all the misfortunes and accidents which must be anticipated. If a state is governed in this way, and if it possesses at the same time the before-mentioned means and qualities for internal strength, it is certainly the most perfect machine for exerting an unspeakable energy. . . . . Meanwhile, although a perfectly wise and complete government will never exist in the world, it is always an indubitable truth that, of two states which are otherwise completely equal, that one will always overcome the other, the government of which is most wisely and perfectly conducted.[1]

[1] The bathos of this conclusion is characteristic of the whole conception of which the paragraph is an epitome. It involves the two factors pointed out above: first, absolutistic government as the final term in civic relations; second, homiletical moralizing upon the character that rulers would have if they knew their best interests, with the implication that actual rulers are enough like this ideal to make obedience to them the ultimate duty and recourse of citizens. This remark applies also to the chapter (pp. 109–28) on "General Idea of a Good Government."

In the introduction to the second book, on "The Fundamental Constitution of States, by Means of Which Governments Are by Nature Good," Justi promises to sketch "a sort of Platonic republic, which to be sure never will be realized. Meanwhile it is never useless to know how far human provision can go in a probable way in the direction of the goodness and excellence of the government" (p. 132). Before fulfilling the promise Justi estimates in some detail the merits and defects of different types of government (pp. 132–82). If this passage were read without checking it up by the rest of his political philosophy, the conclusion would be necessary that he was in favor of a form of government more like that of England in the Victorian period than that of the Stuarts (p. 175). It would falsify the record to explain away the implications of this chapter. They are plainly and rather unreservedly democratic in the modern sense with the monarchical element retained as an offset to democratic faults and inefficiencies. If the whole system were contained in a compendium a thousand years old, the higher critics might without remorse assign this chapter to some interpolator of strange doctrines. The actual explanation is in harmony with traits which are quite evident in Justi here and there, particularly in the *Staatswirthschaft*. He allowed himself short flights of fancy which he did not take much care to guard from confusion with his working technology. Inasmuch as he opened the discussion with the notification that he would end it with a castle in the air, it is easy to infer that his feet left the ground much earlier than he proposed. He simply permitted himself to rhapsodize. The chapter is half-conscious *Wahrheit und Dichtung* throughout. It is of a piece with the ideal ethics which the author had previously held up to rulers as a righteous standard, with no thought of winning for it available political sanctions. He meant it, in the unofficial, irresponsible compartments of his mind which were open to the play of imagination. He was sincere about these unassimilated conceits, with a sort of other-worldly longing that took refuge in them from literal affairs; but as he gave partial notification in the confession above quoted, he did not expect to be held accountable for supposing that such visions could ever be actualized. Even in the course of this excursus, when he is speaking of the checks which must be put upon the different branches of government, he touches his familiar earth with the reservation—

The executive power, however, or the king, must, to be sure, always be so sacred and so inviolate that he himself can never be required to render such an account of his acts (p. 167).

In his summary Justi says:

If the legislative, executive, and judicial powers in the fundamental constitution of a mixed governmental form are so ordered, as above pictured, we may declare that the government is good in its nature. The king has all power which is requisite for execution, and on reasonable grounds he can demand no more. In all external affairs of state he has completely free hands, and nothing hinders him from taking the resolves and measures which he regards as necessary for the true welfare of his state. Since in matters of execution he is not bound to obtain the consent of anyone, he can give to all his undertakings the utmost swiftness, vigor, and efficiency, and it is his own affair if his intentions and measures do not remain secret. In short he has all power to do good, but no power at all to do evil (p. 173).

Coming to the avowedly utopian part of his discussion, he begins as follows (p. 183):

Is then a governmental form possible, in which no errors and imperfections would inhere, but which by virtue of the excellence of its fundamental constitution would represent a type of government which by its very nature would be always and completely good? If the question were to be taken in all its severity we should be obliged to answer without reserve in the negative. People themselves are subject to a thousand limitations and weaknesses. All their actions are led by their passions, and all too often do these passions raise a storm which drives the wisest and best men hither and thither like so much chaff. How is it to be expected, then, that people can erect a mode of government which in the strict sense would be completely perfect? It is people who erect governments, and who are governed. They are the stuff for the whole work. How can a highly perfect work be composed of such meager and feeble material? If, however, we understand by the question, whether a form of government is possible which is freed from all the major mistakes and failures which we so often find in civic institutions, a form which can assure to citizens all the security, freedom, and happiness to which by means of their weak nature they can ever attain, and which at the same time possesses all the strength and permanence against contingencies within and without of which a state is capable, then we must answer, Yes. We said above that we would construct a sort of Platonic republic, which it would be ridiculous to expect to realize in the present condition of realms and states. Nevertheless, we hope to give our proposal such a form that fewer faults can be found with it than with such idealistic structures in the past.

Reducing Justi's fantasy to the lowest terms, it is as follows (pp. 184–207):

1. We must take men as they are, with all their desires and passions. Accordingly, when a reasonable and moral people, living by the side of similar peoples, wishes to choose a constitution, it must base its plan on the existence of these desires and passions. They must be reckoned upon in the plan as the means of making the structure of the state strong and durable. If we except love, which is rather a natural impulse than a passion, the strongest among all human passions is the desire for prestige [*Vorzug*], or the passion for honor and glory.[1] Nothing is so natural to man as this passion. The impulse which the wise Originator of nature implanted in every man, to hold his own being most precious, in order that he might

[1] This passage then is of more than curious significance merely as presenting a Utopia. It is a first-rate piece of evidence on our fundamental theorem that Justi had not focalized the economic interest proper. He had not heard of "the economic man." His fundamental assumption was the personally ambitious man.

take pleasure in maintaining himself and in fulfilling the designs of the Creator, is that which brings forth the longing for prestige. Consequently this is the passion of which chief use will be made in a wise design for a civic constitution (p. 184).

2. Yet we must seek to establish and maintain virtue. All passions may be evil as well as good, in the degree in which they are guided and governed; and when they are left to themselves they always tend rather to bad than to good. The desire for prestige needs therefore another moving spring, whereby it is guided and, as it were, geared, in order that it may be held back from excesses. This second moving spring is virtue (p. 185).

3. A mixed form of govenment, composed partly of aristocracy and partly of democracy, would serve best in employing these two motive springs in all their strength. I see no probability that virtue would be preserved in a form composed of king and democracy. I would therefore forego the efficiency of a monarchy for the virtue of a republic. To be sure, Sparta had kings, and virtue was perfectly maintained there. But our times are so different from those of the Spartan republic, that we could not think of such a thing as subjecting the king to the judicial judgment of the people, and his morals and management to the guardians of the state. Our times are so accustomed to combining with the royal dignity great outward splendor and display, that a king without this frivolous, to be sure, yet, on account of prejudice, necessary glitter, would be the laughing-stock of all his neighbors. It will, however, never be possible to banish vice from a state if it contains that degree of luxury which so closely borders on vice, if the king and his court are not subject to the institutions of the state for the maintenance of virtue (p. 187).[1]

4. It is non-essential what marks of distinction a government adopts to stimulate the desire for prestige, so long as sufficient skill is used to create a prejudice in their favor. To this end three means

[1] What business Justi has to embarrass a Utopia by consideration either of Spartan times or of "our times," it would be cruel to ask. He was evidently not aware that he was trying to stand with one foot in the clouds and one on the earth. This attempt at a free flight of fancy only brings out more clearly his conviction that for mundane purposes the quasi-absolute kings of his experience were necessary.

must be adopted: (1) the symbols of honor must be publicly bestowed; (2) they must be given for actual merit only; (3) they must not be made too common. Under these conditions a laurel wreath is as effective as a golden crown bestudded with gems. The reason why our times show so few heroic deeds is that our marks of distinction are not bestowed according to these specifications (p. 188).[1]

5. Nobility should not be hereditary, and being obtained for life only it will be a powerful spur to virtue (p. 190).

6. Virtue must be maintained by laws and morals which are identical, and there must be a moral censorship [*Sittenrichter*]. This college must consist of the most eminent, virtuous, and honorable men in the state, and the members must have a right of veto upon an election by the people to a vacancy in the college in case they know anything to the discredit of the person proposed. These censors must not have the slightest connection with the government. They must be the protectors of the fundamental constitution of the state, the defenders of the laws, the maintainers of virtue and good morals, the promoters of skill, of the arts, and of science. In all these particulars they must have a quite unlimited power subject to the fundamental laws, a power which should extend indeed over all the administrative colleges of the state, and even over the representative of the people. They must have power to suspend or depose and imprison any member of the government who is guilty of treasonable or corrupting practices. There must be in front of the place of assemblage of this college a receptacle in which citizens could deposit testimony about anything of which the censors should be informed (p. 191).

7. In the form of government which I here propose no one has a peculiar interest in the welfare of the whole people. It is therefore not necessary that the people should possess law-giving power. The power of the people is never free from deficiencies and faults. The people [*Volk*], however, which has (*sic*) little capacity for governing, is excellently endowed for selecting those who may be charged with governing. I consequently propose that the whole work of

[1] As our plan is to exhibit Justi's system objectively, as an attempt at social science, rather than to examine its psychological presuppositions, it is needless to comment on this naïve mental philosophy.

government, both law-giving and execution, should be reserved for the personal nobility, and that the people should have no part in governing beyond election of the officials (p. 194).

8. The common rabble should not be allowed to take part in elections. Electoral right should be based upon the rates paid to the public treasury. The man who pays 20 *Thaler* yearly should have one vote; he who pays 100 *Thaler* yearly should have two votes, and for each additional 100 *Thaler* there should be one vote. This would not only be just in itself, but it would bring about a more willing payment of the rates. The personal nobility, as the only class eligible for election, would not be permitted to vote, because of their self-interest. In large states a representative system of election must be adopted (p. 196).

9. The number of the nobility should be one hundred and fifty in small states, three hundred in medium states, and six hundred in large states. Each of these should receive from the state an annual allowance of three hundred to six hundred *Reichsthaler* (p. 200).

10. The officials should be divided in the first place into three chief colleges: (*a*) for law-giving, (*b*) for execution, (*c*) for judicial functions. Members should be divided into three classes, one class retiring from office each year (p. 200).

11. There should be in addition as many other colleges as are at present customary in European states, but they should be subordinate to the three principal colleges (p. 201).

12. In case of disagreement between the three chief colleges, which cannot be arranged by conferences within thirty days, it shall be the duty of the chairman of the colleges, on pain of banishment, to lay the matter before the college of censors. The latter must then summon the whole body of the nobility to investigate the difficulty and to decide it by majority vote. The contending colleges must adopt the decision at once, for the total nobility is the body in which the unlimited power should reside, although it does not exercise it except in an extremity. Even then it must sometimes proceed by choosing from its own number a dictator, who for a short period should unite in his own person all might and power, in order to save the republic from threatened destruction (p. 202).

13. Universal liability to military service for a term of six years would be necessary (p. 204).

It is not worth while to analyze the implications of this conceit, as Justi himself a third time (p. 206) reminds his readers that it is aside from the serious purpose of his book. Even the specifications of this Utopia, however, serve to emphasize the literal preconceptions of Justi's working philosophy. It was in the first place a presumption of static order in the state; second, a reliance upon some institutional absolute; third, an overestimate of the relative importance of civic structure in the whole economy of life.

Passing to Book III, "On the Goodness of the Government Due to Its Own Moderation," Justi begins with the proposition that if we cannot have such "governments good by nature," the only hope of good government is in the self-enforced moderation of such governments as actually exist, "for every unlimited and great power is by its very nature terrible, and it has harmful effects on the subjects (p. 211).

In dealing with a body of thought which from our modern point of view is so crowded with half-developed and arbitrarily correlated ideas, there is always danger of making the anomalies more extreme than they were. No other interpretation can be put on this section, however, than the following: first, we must in practice take for granted the absolutism of government; second, "a government which has unlimited power in its hands, and can use that power as it pleases, can never be good unless it moderates this power by its own initiative" (p. 211). In other words, this is the literal formulation of the fundamental political conception which is known by the proverbial phrase "benevolent despotism." This formula expresses the cameralistic conception, as the legend, *l'état c'est moi*, symbolizes the *ancien régime* in France. Justi assumes that the world being what it is, an absolutism embodied in a king is a necessity. Yet many things go to make up that other conception, "happiness," which royal absolutism might easily frustrate. This philosophy does not thereupon reconsider its conclusion that political absolutism is necessary. It leaves "happiness" at the mercy of absolutism, with the hope that the absolute monarch actually will be merciful. The present section then is virtually a series of memoranda from the side of "happiness," calling the attention of absolute monarchs to points which they will observe if they want their rule to result in the largest output of advantage for the state, in distinction from their own absolutism.

In other words, this political philosophy started with the lame and impotent assumption that it is desirable for absolutism to be good, rather than the assumption that absolutism is not a good. Then it proceeded along the cautious path of specifying how an absolutism would conduct itself if it were good. If we were immediately engaged in tracing the course of political evolution, we should have here an important clue to the process. Even these dutiful reminders had a cumulative force. Specifications of happiness presently came to have another logical value. The inference drawn was no longer that it is desirable for the absolute government to promote these things, but that an absolute government is intolerable because it can jeopardize these things. This is the gist of the whole matter involved in this part of Justi's argument, and we shall notice only one or two details.

The first chapter of Book III is dedicated to proof of the proposition that "unlimited and great power is in its nature terrible and dangerous." It takes as its point of departure the theorem: "Every man is inclined to misuse his power" (p. 212). The moralizings and mental philosophizings which form the medium of the discussion need not be called to account. For our purposes it is enough to set down the specifications of danger which Justi discovered. In the first place, he concluded that even virtuous men who are able to extend their power fall into the way of thinking that such extension of power is good in itself, regardless of consequences to others. As Montesquieu says, "Even virtue needs limitations" (p. 213). Great power tends to become arbitrary power (p. 214). Hence such power is always to be feared (p. 215). The outcome of arbitrary exercise of power is despotism in which the mere will of the ruler is the highest law (p. 215). The whole power of the state in the hands of one person is in itself to be feared, apart from its resting upon the will of the ruler alone (p. 216). Platitudes are Justi's specialty, but he seldom puts it on exhibit more plainly than at this point.

The same level of bathos is maintained in the following chapter "On the Moderation and Fixing of the Will Whereby an Unlimited Government Becomes Good." It consists of such "copy-book commonplaces" as these:

The misuse of unlimited power which is so harmful to the state consists in the exercise of the will of the ruler according to his pleasure and caprice (p. 222); hence a good unlimited government must have two chief qualities: (*a*) its will must be moderated, (*b*) its will must be constant (p. 223); the proper moderation of the will of an unlimited government is through the guidance of reason, which has no other aim than the best good of the state (p 223); a good ruler must clearly distinguish his personal will from his will as a ruler (p. 224); even if convinced that his personal will is a good will, a wise ruler will not try to make it his governmental will; e. g., he will not try to impose his religion upon his subjects (p. 226); constancy of will in the government is necessary to prevent uncertainty among the governed (pp. 227–32).

In the same general tone Justi proceeds, in chap. iii, to schedule "the fundamental principles and rules of a good government." These turn out to be:

The first and chief principle of a good government is unquestionably that of benevolence and moderation [*Gelindigkeit*] (p. 233); (2) Since it is the aim and duty of a good government to make the people happy, one of its chief principles must be to make the people rich (p. 237);[1] (3) General diffusion of wealth, rather than its concentration in a few hands, is to be promoted (p. 239); (4) Fraud and treachery as devices of statecraft are to be rejected on grounds both of morals and of utility (p. 241);[2] (5) Cunning not involving treachery may be used (p. 242); (6) "A good government will observe five fundamental rules: (*a*) To assure the subjects a reasonable freedom, (*b*) To regard their property as inviolable, (*c*) To withhold its hands from interference with justice, (*d*) Not to increase the imposts, (*e*) Except in actual necessity not to declare war (p. 243).

[1] For its value as evidence in another connection the context is worth translating, viz., "We understand here riches in all sorts of goods which are based chiefly on a flourishing sustaining system [*Nahrungsstand*], and without the same no people can properly be thought of as happy. . . . . Today there is no doubt about this principle. If a corrupted statecraft once believed that the wealth of the subjects must be hindered in order not to feed the spirit of uproar, or at least of opposition to the supreme power, we have today gone beyond that petty principle. We have found that an impoverished people, which has nothing to lose, is much more inclined to disorder than well-to-do citizens, and the credit [*Ansehen*] of the supreme power is today so well established by reasonable rules of government, and by standing armies, that there is little to fear from subjects in this respect. . . . . There can be no doubt that the riches and welfare of the subjects should be the main purpose, and the consequent power and strength of princes the subsidiary purpose, and not the reverse." (This last proposition is a plain negation of my fundamental theorem about cameralism. My justification throughout is appeal to the whole system against its parts. I repeat that we must not force upon inconsistent elements a coherent unity which did not exist. Judged by the rest of the system as contained in Justi's books and in the workings of the type of government which they formulated, the proposition quoted must be taken, along with the other idealistic elements, as a symptom of partially assimilated insight, which would presently give both to social science and to governmental policy a changed perspective.)

[2] Justi compares his own with earlier times in this respect in terms which, taken literally, claimed that this theorem was the contemporary working rule. Here again was an uncritical mixture of relative truth and of sheer assertion of ideal value. The latter is demonstrated by the admission which Justi makes at the close of the paragraph (p. 242).

The fourth chapter of the book, on the restraint which a good government should exercise in the matter of expense, is merely a variation of commonplaces which governments of the type that he had in mind observed or not, according to the temper of their rulers.

Book IV, "On the Wisdom of a Good Government," is a very slight variation upon corresponding passages in *Staatswirthschaft.* It contains nothing which in principle modifies our previously expressed estimate of Justi's political philosophy. As we intimated above,[1] Justi's confessed knowledge of abuses in actual operation did not lead him to the conclusion which has since become self-evident, viz., that the quasi-absolutism of the eighteenth century was an intolerable anachronism, In the last book, Justi catalogues enough faults of that type of government to condemn it without remorse, but his expressed inferences amount only to the impotent reflection that rulers who permit such abuses ought to be ashamed of themselves, and God probably has in reserve for them such averted glances as are thinkable in the case of his anointed. It would be profitless to rehearse specifications of delinquencies which had no further meaning for human programmes.

[1] E. g., pp. 406 ff. *et passim.*

CHAPTER XVI

JUSTI'S "POLICEYWISSENSCHAFT"

We now come to the most peculiar division of cameralistic theory, the portion which, next to the fundamental absolutistic political philosophy, contains most that is antithetic with English and American theory and practice. In order to represent it most vividly we shall digest Justi's treatment, translating as nearly as possible his own words. This will involve not a little repetition. We cannot fairly represent Justi, however, without reporting some of his self-iteration. We deal first with *Grundsätze der Policeywissenschaft.*[1]

The Preface to the first edition of this book is dated, Göttingen, May 11, 1756. A second edition appeared in 1759. Beckmann says the book had been used by various eminent teachers as the basis of their lectures on the subject. Meanwhile, several such introductions had appeared. The editor refers to Justi's disregard of other writers,[2] and promises to do his best in the notes to supply the gaps. In his own Preface to the first edition (reprinted in the third) Justi discusses the literature of the subject, and in order to show the state of his information and opinions about other theorists his remarks must be cited. In substance he says:

[1] *Johann Heinrich Gottlobs von Justi, ehemaligen Königl. Grossbritannischen und Braunschweig-Lünebergischen Churfürstl. Berg-Raths, und Ober-Policey-Commissarii, wie auch Mitgliedes der Königl. Societät der Wissenschaften in Göttingen, Grundsätze der Policeywissenschaft, in einen vernünftigen, auf den Endzweck der Policey gegründeten, Zusammenhange, und zum Gebrauche academischer Vorlesungen abgefasset. Dritte Ausgabe, mit Verbesserungen und Anmerkungen von Johann Beckmann, ordentlichem Professor der Oekonomie in Göttingen . . . .* 1782. All references are to this third edition.

[2] *Vide* above, p. 292 *et passim.*

This book is the first instalment of the promise to write textbooks on each of the cameralistic sciences. It is the outline of a course to occupy one semester. It is the first complete treatment of *Policeywissenschaft*. The common error has been to boil this subject in one broth with *Staatskunst*. We have a countless number [*eine unbeschreibliche Menge*] of books which contain the elements of *Staatskunst*, but they do not assort their material. *Staatskunst* has nothing for its purpose but the internal and external security of the state, and its chief attention must be given to the conduct of states toward each other, to increase of the power of the state in relation to other states, and especially to wise conduct toward other states. In like manner *Staatskunst* is concerned, on the other hand, with adjusting the conduct of subjects toward one another and toward other states.

Policeywissenschaft, on the contrary, is concerned with nothing but the preservation and increase of the total "means" [*Vermögen*] of the state through good internal institutions [*Verfassungen*] and with creating all sorts of internal power and strength for the republic: e. g., through (1) cultivating the land; (2) improving the laboring class; (3) maintaining good discipline and order in the community. In the last task it is the tool of *Staatskunst* in maintaining inner security.

Other books have treated *Policey* in connection with principles of *Cameral- oder Finanz-Wissenschaft*, to the disadvantage of each science, though they are nearly related. *Policey* is the ground (*sic*) of genuine cameral science, and the police expert must sow if the cameralist is to reap; yet each science has its fixed and indisputable boundaries. The one seeks to increase the total "means." The other seeks to get from this the "readiest means," without harm to the former.

In other books, *Policey* is treated along with *Oekonomie;* e. g., Zink,[1] both in his *Grundriss* and in his *Anfangs-Gründe*, starts with certain general principles of *Oeconomic*, and then of *Policey*, and then treats of more special economic questions first from the economic, second from the police standpoint. This leads to constant

[1] I have not observed an instance in which Justi follows his contemporary's spelling of the name.

repetitions. Moreover, *Policey* cannot be completely treated in this way, because it has a much wider scope than economic subjects. In his *Anfangs-Gründe*, which is very diffuse,[1] Zink either wholly forgets many important police subjects, or gives them only a few lines.

The late *Herr Canzler von Wolff* wrote a large number of books,[2] and as, according to his profession, he wanted to be a system-writer of *all* sciences, it was to be expected that he would write a *Policey*. But the *social life of human beings* was the mistaken chief subject of his work, which did not fit into the proper boundaries of the sciences. His book therefore contains many valuable teachings about *Policey*, but consistently with his ultimate purpose he mixed them with so many principles of moral philosophy [*Sittenlehre*], of the law of nature, and of prudence [*Lebensweisheit*], in general, that the work is of no use as a system of *Policey*. Sciences must be separated from each other to be complete, because many useful doctrines will be overlooked if they are treated together.

Of the few books that remain on *Policey* proper, we name none until the present (eighteenth) century. There has been, until late years, no adequate idea of *Policey*, as is proved by such examples as Boter, *Gründlicher Bericht von Anordnung guter Policey*, Strassburg, 1696; Schrammer, *Politia historica*, Leipzig, 1605; Reinking, *Bibliche Policey;* etc.

Others in this century have a correct idea of *Policeywissenschaft* but are not at all complete: e. g., Law, *Entwurf einer wohleingerichteten Policey*. The author was not equal to his undertaking. With the exception of certain observations about the *Policey* of various states, the book contains little that can be used. Again a pseudonymous "C. B. von L." published (1739) *Ohnverfängliche Vorschläge zu Einrichtung guter Policey*. It is not a system, and contains much that is chimerical and not pertinent to the science. Lucas Friedrich Langemack published *Abbildung einer vollkommenen Policey*, Berlin, 1747. In this brief work the fundamental principles are very well and philosophically presented, but on the whole it is not specific

[1] The pot is scandalized at the color of the kettle.

[2] Again "*eine unbeschreibliche Menge*," which is a trifle strong for a critical treatise.

enough for a system. The Mecklenburg *Hofrath* Velter published several monographs on Policey: e. g., *Unvorgreiflichen Gedanken von Einrichtung und Verbesserung der Policey*, 1736; more important was *Unterricht von der zur Staats und Regierungswissenschaft gehörenden Policey*, 1753. The author flatters himself, in the prospectus of the latter book, that he is the first to treat this science systematically, but no one with an orderly mind will admit this. The book is not only confused, but leaves out much that should be included, and has much affectation of wisdom from the ancients, while betraying defective judgment.

The English and French have produced nothing better. De la Marc's *Traité de Police* contains certain excellent and useful things, but has no well-grounded and connected system.

It has been said that Zink's book is more available as a text, because it describes the police systems of other lands, and applies the general principles of *Policey* to this or that particular state. On the contrary, this ought not to be expected of such a textbook. We should rather require of a textbook on the *öconomischen Wissenschaften* only the general principles, without this or that concrete application.

"In this book I have followed my usual rule of not citing other authors. A dogmatic writer[1] must present the subject conclusively, and if he does this he does not need the authority of earlier writers. Such citations smack of pedantry, unless they contain historical facts, or unless some special circumstances call for them."[2]

Passing to the body of the book, our task is to abstract the more general conceptions, within which the technology had its setting, from the applications, which of course make up the bulk of the contents. The material so abstracted is cumulative evidence for our interpretation of cameralism. Reducing Justi's propositions to the most compact form, we have the following general outline:

[1] Probably "didactic" would be nearer to Justi's thought than the word thus literally rendered.

[2] These observations by Justi tell their own story about the state of the social sciences at his time, and comment would be superfluous.

§1. The name *Policey* comes from the Greek word πόλις, a city, and should mean the good ordering of cities and of their civic institutions.

§§2, 3. Two uses of the term *Policey* are common today: first, and most generally, "All measures in the internal affairs of the country through which the general means [*Vermögen*] of the state may be more permanently founded and increased, the energies [*Kräfte*] of the state better used, and in general the happiness of the community [*gemeines Wesen*] promoted. In this sense we must include in *Policey die Commercienwissenschaften, die Stadt- und Landöconomie, das Forstwesen*, and similar subjects, in so far as the government extends its care over them for the purpose of securing general correlation of the welfare of the state. Some are accustomed to call this *die wirthschaftliche Policey-Wissenschaft*. This name is a matter of indifference so long as it is not supposed to designate a particular science.

§3. In the narrower sense we understand by *Policey* everything which is requisite for the good ordering of civic life, and especially the maintenance of good discipline and order [*Zucht und Ordnung*] among the subjects, and promotion of all measures for the comfort of life and the growth of the sustaining system [*Nahrungsstand*]. We shall treat here the general principles and rules of *Policey* according to the comprehensive idea. In the special elaboration we shall not stop to consider those things which are the subject-matter of other economic sciences, and meanwhile we shall discuss chiefly the objects of *Policey* in the narrower sense.[1]

[1] The difficulty which we find in getting a distinct conception of Justi's meaning is due to the fact that his own ideas were not clear. His classifications have largely been abandoned, even by bureaucratic theorists. The change begins to be visible with Rau, *Lehrbuch der politischen Oekonomie*, 1826, etc. In England and America the distribution of activities, and consequently the theory of them, left no place for *Policey* in Justi's sense.

The editor of the third edition adds as his own definition of "*Policey*," the following (p. 26): "The science of governing the various occupations [*Gewerbe*] according to the purpose of the state." Of course "Smithism" was fundamentally a protest against the thing itself, but the thing itself was the very genius of the cameralistic state. There consequently had

§4. The purpose and consequently the essence of all republics rests upon promotion of the common happiness. The general "means" of each republic is the resource which it must use for promoting its happiness. Hence the general "means" must be assured, increased, and reasonably used, i. e., applied for the promotion of the common happiness. This is the content [*Inbegriff*] of all the economic and cameral sciences. The maintenance and increase of the general "means" in relations with other free states is the affair of *Staatskunst*. *Policeywissenschaft*, on the other hand, has for its object the maintenance and increase of the same general "means" of the state in connection with its inner institutions, while cameral and finance science has for its task to raise from the general "means" of the state, by a reasonable use of the same, the special, or "readiest means," and to put into the hands of *Staatskunst* and *Policey* the means of accomplishing their purposes.

§5. The purpose of *Policey* is therefore to preserve and increase the general "means" of the state; and since these "means" include not merely the goods, but also the talents and skill of all persons belonging to the republic, the *Policey* must have constant care to have in mind the general interdependence of all these different sorts of goods, and to make each of them contribute to the common happiness.

§7. *Policeywissenschaft* consists accordingly in understanding how, under existing circumstances of the community, wise measures may be taken to maintain and increase the general "means" of the state in its internal relations [*Verfassung*], and to make the same,

to be a technology of it. The editor continues: "The occupations are agricultural pursuits, artisanship, trade, and personal services. The first part of *Policey* accordingly treats of the responsibilities of the ruler with respect to rural employments. . . . . The second part of *Policey* is urban, i. e., the *Policey* of the handicrafts and trade, as the two occupations peculiar to towns. . . . . In the third part I reckon, for example, medical practice, the ecclesiastical and educational system, etc. The fourth part, or at all events the appendix, should treat of those abandoned or unfortunate persons who will not pursue any of the occupations mentioned, and hence will or must live upon the diligence of other people; i. e., beggars, almshouses, houses of correction, and workhouses.

both in its correlation and in its parts, more efficient and useful for promotion of the common happiness [*gemeinschaftliche Glückseligkeit*]. More briefly, *Poeiceywissenschaft* consists in the theorems for preserving and increasing the general "means" of the state, and for so using them that they will better promote the common happiness.

§8. The general principle of *Policeywissenschaft* is accordingly: *The internal institutions of the community must be so arranged that thereby the general "means" of the state will be preserved and increased and the common happiness constantly promoted.*[1]

§§9–16. Hence follow three fundamental rules, viz.:

1. *Before all things the lands of the republic must be cultivated and improved.*[2]

The development of the territories may take place in two ways: (*a*) through external cultivation; (*b*) through increase of the population, which may be called the internal culture of the lands. The second sort of culture must be of three chief kinds: (1) Through attraction of foreigners as settlers; (2) through means which promote increase of the native inhabitants; (3) through prevention of sickness and premature death.

2. *Increase of the products of the country and the prosperity of the sustaining system* [*Nahrungsstand*] *must be promoted in every possible way.*

3. *Care must be given to securing among the subjects such capacities and qualities, and such discipline and order, as are demanded by the ultimate purpose, viz., the common happiness.*

Book I is devoted to the subject of "the external cultivation of the land," i. e., to all measures conducive to (1) removal of impediments to occupation of the soil; (2) utilization of the material advantages of the land in all its parts; (3) providing the citizens with means of obtaining shelter and support. Chap. i treats of the improvement of the soil for the abode and

[1] *Vide* below, p. 450 *et passim*.

[2] *Vide Grundfeste*, I, 21. I cannot decide what difference in meaning, if any, Justi associated with the two words *Cultur* and *Anbau* which he sometimes seems to use merely as synonyms in *oratio variata* and sometimes as cumulative expressions.

support of the inhabitants. Under these heads, means discussed are, in general: clearing superfluous forests, draining ponds and swamps, protecting against flooding from seas or rivers, bringing barren land under cultivation, construction of harbors, making streams navigable and digging canals, exploiting mineral and rock deposits, utilization of land formed by recent action of the sea, or of islands, distribution of land, provision for both large and small estates, establishment of villages and attached arable areas [*Fluhre*], etc.

Chap. ii deals with the improvement [*Anbau*] and growth of cities, and does not vary in substance from the corresponding passage in *Staatswirthschaft*. The purpose of cities is said to be to work up raw material and to carry on foreign commerce. All other institutions of cities must end in these two purposes. Sites should be chosen which are favorable, the general plans should conform to the needs, the dwellings should not be left entirely to the caprice of the citizens, protection in the shape of walls, gates, harbors, canals, water supply, and drainage must be furnished, decisions must be reached about extensions of the city, those who furnish material and labor must be looked after, means must be taken to secure circulation of sufficient money, wealthy and talented foreigners and artisans must be attracted, the immediately neighboring land must be made productive, diligence must be stimulated, means of stimulating foreign trade must be devised, laws and statutes must be passed, in accordance with the primary and secondary purposes of the towns, and with the other characteristics of the locality, city councils must be so organized that proper correlation of all police activities will be promoted, there must be special courts for manufactures and for trade, *Zünfte* and *Innungen* must be discouraged in new factories so far as possible, and in old hand-trades kept in close bounds.

Chap. iii deals with the convenience and ornamentation of country and city, and discusses such subjects as roads, streets, postal systems, bridges, fountains, reservoirs, water-mains, paving and cleaning and lighting of streets and alleys, marking of time by bells, and by night watchmen, inns and other places of refreshment, market-places, public conveyances, aesthetic regulations, parks and pleasure gardens, amusements, etc.

Chap. iv begins the subject of "inner cultivation of the land, or the increase of population." At the beginning of this chapter another of the passages occurs to which von Mohl referred.[1] It is as follows:

All external improvement of a land would be of little avail, if the same were not satisfactorily settled and populated. This populating is the internal cultivation which must give to external cultivation its soul and life. Hence increase of population is the second main aim in the cultivation of countries, and just as the sustaining system will always be more flourishing, the more people there are in the country, so we must regard it as a fundamental theorem in this division of the subject that *a land can never have too many inhabitants*. It is easy to protect this theorem against all objections.

However we may disagree with Justi's presuppositions and with subsequent conclusions, we do not do him justice if we charge him, as von Mohl and many others have done, with teaching the opposite of Malthusian conclusions. The fact is that he never considered the Malthusian problem at all. He confronted a condition of under-population. The states for which he spoke needed more population for their purposes, and it was those purposes for which Justi was the spokesman. He would have put the case precisely as he meant it if he had said:

For the purposes of a practical cameralist today, the probability of over-population may be canceled from the reckoning.

Although it had never occurred to him to pry far into the relations that determined the limits of population, there is

[1] *Vide* below, p. 477.

nothing in his books to show that he supposed population could be increased indefinitely.

§§86–96 develop devices for attracting immigrants.[1] §§97–108 develop a programme, first, for increasing population, second, for checking emigration.[2] §§109–21 are on public hygiene.

Chap. vii, *Von der Landwirthschaft*, approaches the subject rather from the approximate standpoint of the agronomist, than of the economist. It begins (p. 109):

The promotion of the sustaining system in the country demands in the first place that a sufficient number of rural products shall be gained. To that end the rural *Policey* must constantly pay great attention to those sources through which rural products are derived. Here then the rural *Oeconomica* come first to attention, as the chief means through which the raw materials for the products of the country are brought into existence. These[3] are: agriculture, the exploiting of natural and cultivated forests, the mines, and the thereto appertaining smelting and refining works. In this subdivision we deal first with agriculture.

Perhaps no part of Justi's cameralism exhibits better than this division the contrast between the régime which he represented and the other extreme illustrated by American policy. We must again call attention to the main question, viz., *What should government do about these matters?* The American answer from the beginning has been, "Nothing! Every man knows best what he wants, and government has no right to interfere, so long as each lets his neighbors alone." We have therefore taken absolute individualism as our presupposition, and have tried in every way to cover with soothing phrases and fictions each departure from actual individualism which changing conditions have required. The most important factor in bringing about in reality, through our voluntaristic system,

[1] *Vide* corresponding passages in *Staatswirthschaft*.

[2] Also parallel with same topics in *Staatswirthschaft*.

[3] The reference goes back to *Oeconomica*.

some approach to scientific use of our agricultural resources, has been our legislation establishing agricultural experiment stations, and systematic instruction in rural economy. The thing that we have thus tardily and cautiously attempted on the ostensible theory that it is primarily the affair of the individual, has from time immemorial been frankly regarded in the German lands as primarily the affair of government. It is no part of the present study to inquire about the relative efficiency of the two policies. Two general remarks only are in point: first, Englishmen and Americans would have treated German social science in the nineteenth century more intelligently and would have gained more from it, if they had been more willing to judge it on its own grounds, and had been less prone to damn "paternalism" and all its works; second, whether on a paternalistic or an individualistic theory, much that cameralistic administration worked out, especially in its latest forms in modern Germany, is evidently enlightened wisdom for a commonwealth. Bureaucracy, or no bureaucracy, the things themselves need to be done, or at least a constructive and coherent policy with reference to them needs to be adopted. Study of the bureaucratic way of doing them may tend to confirm most Americans in dislike of that way, but it ought at least to make them more able to perceive that in point of results we are at a disadvantage, and that our system is not vindicated until its technical results compare more favorably with those of the more paternalistic German system.

We have then in cameralism a body of officials presiding over agricultural programmes just as a general staff conducts the administration of a modern army. The *Landes-Policey* deals with such subjects as the organization of larger and smaller rural estates (§124), the regulation of acreage devoted to different crops on these estates (§125), the adjustment of taxation so as best to stimulate agriculture (§126), the protection of cultivators against the interests of hunting or forestry

(§127), regulation of other occupations which might draw the peasants from cultivation of the soil (§128), stimulation of agricultural talent in the peasants (§129), inducing production of raw materials which would not be raised without special stimulus (§130), improvement of the quality of products (§131), employment of "economic inspectors" to supervise all these things (§132), adoption of uniform systems of measuring land (§133), adoption of rules of rotation of crops and other regulations, like the wages of laborers, etc. (§134), adoption of special standards for particular products, kinds of seed to be used, etc. (§135), enactment of ordinances to protect growing crops from thieves, etc. (§136), particular attention to cattle-raising (137), also to vineyards (§138), and to horticulture (§139).

In chap. viii cameralistic duties regarding forestry, mining, and minor industries are analyzed (§§140–49). "Manufacturing and factories" are treated in the same relation in chap. ix (§§150–80), and on these two presumptions (§152):

A wise government must consequently have two theorems constantly before its eyes, viz.: (1) *Everything required by the need and comfort of the inhabitants of the country is to be produced as far as possible within the country itself; (2) the government shall see that, in the interest of the sustaining system, and of foreign commerce, everything that the land produces shall, so far as possible, be worked over to its complete form, and shall not be allowed to leave the country in a raw and unfinished state.* To this end the government must have precise extracts from the tariff, excise, and license sheets, on such points as (*a*) all imported goods, in order to judge which of them might be produced within the country; (*b*) all exported goods, in order to discover whether domestic products in the form of raw materials, or partially manufactured, are exported.

Thereupon the technique of keeping check upon raw material produced or producible in the country, of materials which must be supplied by other countries, and of tools, etc., needed for working up the materials is discussed (§§153–

55), and then the programme for developing manufactures (§§156–80). The whole is merely a somewhat expanded reproduction of the corresponding part of *Staatswirthschaft*.

Chap. x treats very briefly the hand industries (§§181–90), and chap. xi claims to offer only fundamental principles of commercial administration, with the intention of devoting a separate volume to the subject. Justi divides commerce [*Commercien*] into domestic and foreign, applying to the former the name trades [*Gewerben*], and repeating that a land might conceivably be happy if the trades flourished, even if there were no commerce. Then the fundamental condition of a favorable balance is mobilized as the basic principle of commercial administration. The details are not greatly in excess of those indicated in *Staatswirthschaft*.

Chap. xii, on the circulation of money, contains little, for our purposes, which does not occur elsewhere in Justi's books. The fundamentally correct conception of gold and silver money as a "ware," the weight and fineness of which are accurately given, is repeated (§221–23). The last of these paragraphs is worth quoting as cumulative evidence:

> If money and goods are to retain a constant ratio to each other, no change should occur in either; and if such change could be totally avoided, it would be a matter of entire indifference whether there were much or little money in a country. A state which had no relations whatever with other peoples, and whose inhabitants consumed all that they produced, would have a constantly unbroken circulation of money. It would have all the power and strength of which it was capable, and it would be as fortunate as another state of like population with ten times as much gold and silver. But since no state in our part of the world is in such circumstances, changes in the value of money and of goods with respect to each other often occur. We must explain the effect of these changes upon circulation.

In general Justi continues (§§224 ff.):

> If the amount of money in circulation diminishes, the price of wares will increase, beginning with the most needless, the influence

extending gradually to all. If the quantity of money in circulation increases, the most necessary wares will grow dearer. This stimulates the activity of laborers and has its influence upon all wares. Money becomes less desirable, interest falls, more wares are produced. Gradually wares will again become cheaper, and thereby exportation is promoted, whereby the quantity of money in circulation is more and more increased and the diligence of laborers more stimulated. Accordingly it must be a first care of the government to prevent diminution of the amount of money in circulation (§226). Lack of confidence and external dangers are prime causes of diminished circulation (§228). Unfavorable trade balance is the most effective cause (§230).

Chap. xiii, on credit, is interesting for the historian of economics proper, but is not immediately significant for our purpose. The same is true of chaps. xiv and xv on means of encouraging the laboring classes.

Book III, on the moral condition of the subjects, and maintenance of good discipline and order, has value for our present inquiry simply as cumulative evidence that the problem which Justi formulated was essentially patriarchal. The point of attachment between this division of labor and the whole purpose of the cameralistic state, appears at the outset, as follows (§270):

If the means of the state in its internal constitution are to be used for the promotion of the common happiness, the subjects, apart from the cultivation of the land and the promotion of the sustaining system, must also themselves possess such qualities, capacities, and talents that they can contribute their part to the realization of the common welfare. In this view religion deserves first to be considered. The members of a community are made by religion incomparably more capable of fulfilling their duties as citizens; and a state can hardly attain all the happiness of which it is capable if public institutions of religion [*äusserlicher Gottesdienst*] are not introduced. The more this cultus harmonizes with the nature and essence of men, and with the paramount purpose of republics, the more excellent will it be, and the more capable will it make the citizens of the state to work for the common welfare.

The same point of view is adopted in considering the morals of the people (§§285 ff.), and also in treating science and education (§§295 ff.).

Whether religion, morals, and education are to be regarded as primarily affairs of the individual, and thus not to be interfered with by government, is a question to which Germany has always assumed one answer, while the United States has tried to apply the opposite answer. Our business in the present connection is not to open the question of principle, but merely to show the attitude of cameralism toward the question. The state and its power to maintain itself against all assault from within or without being the central aim, of course it was a strictly logical inference that everything which could have an effect on the strength of the state was properly within the sphere of state supervision.

It is beginning to be possible for a few people to discern that the old dilemma between the individual and the state was purely fictitious in the abstract, and that neither horn of the dilemma could be taken as the symbol of a concrete programme without surprising results. Religion, morals, science, and education have both individual and social relations, if we choose to retain that distinction. We are at once in the region of absurdity if we attempt to run a legal boundary line between their individual and their social phases. The real question for governmental theory is not whether they are the one or the other, but to what extent and in what ways either phase must be taken account of by the law. The arbitrary character of the traditional criterion might be inferred from the historical contrasts between theory and practice. The German presumption at once runs counter to individual aspects of each, which dictate a thus-far-and-no-farther to government, while the American presumption not only gives itself curious things to account for in our actual practice toward religious institutions, moral conditions, and scientific needs, but it almost wholly disappears in our systems of state education.

The chapters on administration of justice (§§339–59), and preserving the peace and checking the lesser nuisances and crimes (§§360–80), are notable only as indexes of the place which cameralism assigned to these subjects in the civic structure.

The last book is a brief discussion of the technique to be operated by the branches of government concerned with applying the foregoing principles of police science. Justi says that in a certain sense the subject-matter of this book forms the practical part of police science (p. 327). The following paragraph confirms our account of the cameralistic state (§382):

> The law-giving power in police affairs, since the internal arrangement of the state chiefly rests upon it, can unquestionably be exercised by no one but the sovereign power, the destiny of which is to administer the affairs of the state for promotion of the common happiness. In whosesoever hands the sovereign power is lodged, he has also to enact the police laws which are to bind the state as a whole. If now the sovereign power rests not alone in the hands of the ruler, but at the same time also with the estates of the realm, or with representatives of the people, obligatory police laws must be agreed upon and promulgated by these conjointly. On the same principle, the police laws which should affect the whole German Empire should be enacted by the Kaiser and the estates assembed in the *Reichstag*.

Again, §384:

> Since the territorial sovereignty which the estates of the German Empire possess is nothing else than the sovereign power in each particular state, which finds its limitations merely in the proviso that its exercise shall not extend so far as to prejudice the general coherence and common welfare of the Empire; the estates of the German Empire accordingly possess the law-giving power in *Policey* affairs; and the above limitation does not prevent them from adopt-

ing such *Policey* institutions and ordinances as will serve the advantage and prosperity of their respective lands; even if this advantage and prosperity might not harmonize with the interest of other German states. Thus they could ordain that no wares should be imported from neighboring German states for consumption within their own territories. On the other hand, they could not forbid the mere transportation of the wares of their neighbors; because thereby the total coherence of the German states united in a common civic body would be utterly destroyed.

The following sections (§§385 ff.) explain how this power is actually exercised in the name of the sovereign.

To complete our account of Justi's *Policeywissenschaft* we turn to the work in which the author has expanded the outline just reviewed. With the possible exception of the *Finanzwissenschaft*, the *Grundfeste*[1] is the most elaborately wrought-out of Justi's works. We must nevertheless allow our résumé of the *Grundsätze* to stand as the best index which our space permits of the general contents of the more complete treatise. The system of control outlined in the *Grundfeste* reflects a régime which the people of the United States have thus far, by almost unanimous consent, refused to reflect upon judicially. They have dismissed it without a hearing, as "unamerican." Nevertheless, it is safe to predict that the time will come when thoughtful Americans will be able to deliberate about the system exhibited in an immature form in these books, to weigh the purposes which the system was designed to serve, and to conclude that although the methods of control which the purposes presuppose are impossible in America, yet the purposes themselves must in principle be organized somehow into the most highly civilized life.

This conclusion must be allowed to rest on the exhibit thus

[1] It is a fair surmise that Justi got this title from the heading of chap. xxxiii, in Schröder's *Fürst. Schatz- und Rent-Cammer*; *vide* above, p. 167.

far made of the different police systems. We may add merely a few notes from the *Grundfeste*.

In the Preface to the first volume Justi says:

> I have often noticed that there are very few people who have a correct idea of *Policey*. That which in the narrowest sense is called *Policey*, namely the *Policey* in the cities, is regarded by the majority as the whole scope of this science. If this very limited signification were the whole, I should have insufficient ground for calling the *Policey* the main defense of states. Both the *Grundsätze* and the present work should make it plain that the scope of the science is much wider.

Justi complains that most writers on *Policey* have not sharply separated the subject from *Staatskunst*.[1]

> It will be found [he says] that as a rule those who have treated *Staatskunst* have at the same time discussed *Policey* with *Commercien- und Finanz-Wissenschaft*. This is the case, for example, with the latest writer on *Staatskunst*.[2] If our conception of *Staatskunst* or *Politik* made it include not only all knowledge necessary for the government of a state, but also all the details of institutions necessary in civic society, those would be right who include in one system of *Politik*, *Policey*, the *Finanz-Wissenschaften*, and all the other

[1] *Vide* above, p. 328.

[2] "Baron von Bielfeld, born 1716, Hamburg, of an aristocratic merchant family, died 1770. He was a friend of Frederick the Great when the latter was crown prince. Was for a while guest of the latter in Rheinsberg, and immediately upon his accession entered his diplomatic service. After 1741 he was *Legationsrath* in the foreign department, later second *Hofmeister* of a Prussian prince; after 1747 *Oberaufseher* of the Prussian universities, but without the least loss of the king's favor retired presently to his estates. His writings, the most important of which, the *Institutions Politiques*, appeared in 1760, suggest not merely by their French dress, but also by their genial cosmopolitan tone, Frederick the Great, much more than contemporary academic specialists. Schlözer credits him with the immortal honor of having first introduced learned politics at courts!" (Roscher, p. 426.)

economic sciences.[1] But, in that case *Staatskunst* would be no special science at all. It would be nothing but a general name for almost all other sciences. *Die Rechtsgelehrsamkeit, die Bergwerks-Wissenschaften, die Mathematik, die Mechanik*, and almost all other sciences would belong to *Staatskunst*. For all these furnish knowledge which is applicable in the government of a state, and necessary for the institutions and practices of civic society. In a word, they all contain knowledge of means whereby the state may be made powerful, and the citizens happy. That is the explanation which Baron von Bielfeld gives of *Politik*.

Justi declines to accept this description of *Staatskunst*. He contends that it has been at all times not a general name for many and almost all sciences, but a special and self-sufficient science, sharply distinguished from *Policey, Finanz- und Commercien-Wissenschaft*. Then he restates his definition of *Policey* thus:

"*It is that science which has for its object permanently to maintain the welfare of the separate families in an accurate correspondence and proportion with the best common good.*" This definition is supported by the comment: "The best common good [*das gemeinschaftliche Beste*] is the ultimate aim of all civic institutions. But, we can imagine no best common good without the welfare of the separate families. To make these correspond with each other is accordingly in fact the main defense of the state, out of which its power and happiness must chiefly arise."[2]

Justi elaborates in this connection his theory of the division of labor between *Staatskunst* and the other "sciences." We have already quoted from the *Staatswirthschaft* his principal propositions on this classification.[3]

[1] In this case it is clear that the phrase "*die öconomischen Wissenschaften*," which I have rendered "economic sciences," had a meaning for Justi which would be more exactly represented to our minds by the phrase "social technologies."

[2] This definition is amplified on p. 4, also pp. 6–9.

[3] *Vide* above, p. 328 *et passim*.

A curious measure of Justi's sense of proportion may be found in the fact that he occupies five out of the fourteen pages of his Preface with a discussion of the relative merits of different printing establishments. His laudation of the publisher chosen for this work, after relation of sad experiences with others, one of them named, rouses the suspicion that a motive less disinterested than zeal for improvement of the art of printing was beneath this discourse. Incidentally he betrays a characteristic trait of the whole *Policey* régime, as well as of his personal theory, in this suggestion:

Perhaps we find here a lack in our *Policey*. It is without doubt the duty of the *Policey* to look out for the quality of wares and work, and to set the standard below which work shall be regarded as entirely unfit, and to be made good to the person who suffers injury from it. I doubt, however, if there is a country in which a standard of passable quality in printing is enforced. The more our publishing system becomes a staple ware (*sic*) the more will such laws be necessary.[1]

Having discussed the evils of putting the emphasis in the state either on the interests of the government, or on those of the separate families, to the prejudice of the other, Justi offers the following "general fundamental principle" of *Policeywissenschaft*, viz.:

In all the affairs of the country, the attempt must be made to put the welfare of the separate families in the most accurate combination and interdependence with the best common good, or the happiness of the whole state.[2]

[1] Justi's most explicit attempt to explain the etymology of the term *Policey* occurs on p. 5, Part I. He quotes from Xenophon's *Athenian Republic* to show that the word Πολιτεία meant "not only the internal institutions of a state, but the whole governmental system of a community: and even what we now express by the word republic."

[2] The author calls attention to the divergence of this proposition in form from that in *Grundsätzen der Policeywissenschaft Einleitung*, §8, p. 7. He explains that the two formulas do not essentially differ. (*Vide* above, pp. 442.)

In the most emphatic terms he declares that this is the single great object of police institutions, and that all the major and minor rules of *Policey* must be derived from this central purpose.

Less fundamental, but more significant for the matter upon which tradition has most stupidly misrepresented the cameralists in general, is the main theorem which the first part of the work supports, viz.: "*The strength and the permanent happiness of a state rest principally upon the goodness of the climate and soil of the country.*" Justi is not among the writers whose attention is given chiefly to agricultural technique. He evidently knew comparatively little about agriculture proper. Of the extractive industries, mining was the only pursuit about which he professed to write as an expert. Yet the place which he assigned to agriculture in his theory leaves no valid excuse for applying to him the label "mercantilist," if it carries the traditional meaning "believer in trade as the sole source of wealth." Instead of accepting this doctrine, Justi urges (§27) that "economic trade," as the phrase went, that is, the trade of a nation of middlemen, like Holland in the seventeenth and eighteenth centuries, is a precarious source of national prosperity and wealth. He says:

> Economic trade is always based on the stupidity and laziness of other peoples. So soon as a people perceives that it does better when it gets its wares from the first hand, it is all over with this economic trade. Upon quite as uncertain ground rest the manufactures of such a country. A wise and industrious people will always seek to manufacture its own raw materials. Hence this source of riches rests on the stupidity and laziness of other peoples, and so soon as these peoples get their eyes open, they will no longer furnish to the trading nation a source of riches. . . . . A nation which, by virtue of its good and well-cultivated soil, exports a great quantity of domestic products is also in a situation, according to the nature and course of commerce, to draw to itself much easier and to retain even the economic trade, than another nation which has few domestic products.

From all this it is clear in my judgment, that the success and permanent happiness of a people rest in a very important degree upon the good character of its soil and climate, and that a people which itself produces all its needs (*sic*) and many domestic goods is incomparably more powerful and happy than a nation which must obtain its necessities and wares for consumption from other peoples, and thus is in a certain sense dependent upon them.

These considerations lead us to two theorems which will be of great importance in the whole treatment of *Policey:* First, *a prudent nation must always take care to put itself in such condition that it is not under the necessity of obtaining its most important wants* [*Bedürfnisse*] *and materials from other peoples;* second, *a nation must seek in every possible way to cultivate the area which it occupies and to improve its climate.*

This proposition is not only repeated in slightly varied form in the following paragraph, but the body of the book expands it, and Justi's whole philosophy presupposes it.

Along with this fundamental principle, Justi next reiterates his second main theorem (§30), viz.:

Since there can never be complete cultivation of the soil without dense population, our second working theorem is, that *a state must in every way promote population.*

These theorems are insufficient without a third, viz.: *If a state has only inhabitants devoted to cultivation of the surface of the earth, its population can never be dense. . . . Consequently we have the third fundamental principle: that government must constantly pay the strictest attention to the building and growth of cities and villages* (§31).

A fourth theorem must be added, viz.: *The Policey must devote itself to works and institutions for the comfort of the inhabitants and the ornamentation of the land* (§32).

Each of the four books of the first part of the *Grundfeste* develops one of these four theorems.

In the Preface of the second volume Justi professes an entire reversal of literary policy. He says: "The attentive reader will be able to judge how great pains I have taken to seek out the most excellent thoughts of the greatest minds, in order thereby to strengthen my discussion." The fact is that Justi was from the start the most expert recoiner of other people's thoughts that German political literature up to his time had developed. He had not before approached so near to a confession that he was more a codifier than a first-hand investigator. The Preface is chiefly devoted to a defense against the criticism of Baron von Bielfeld that Justi had included altogether too much in *Policeywissenschaft.* The passage is so characteristic of the time and of the author that no independent student of the subject should neglect to read it.

Probably there is no more accurate and detailed contemporary picture of the policy behind Frederick the Great's type of benevolent despotism, at least no picture of the policy as it was idealized in the minds of theorists, than the views presented in these two volumes of the *Grundfeste*, together with the later work, *System des Staatswesens* (1766). As the evidence already presented is more than sufficient to support our main contention, we must pass these volumes with the remark that their contents are cumulative proof of the correctness of the view we have taken of cameralism in general.

CHAPTER XVII

JUSTI'S CAMERALISTIC MISCELLANIES

To complete the exhibit which the compass of this book permits us to make of Justi's views, we must draw from his collected miscellanies. Without attempting to organize these extracts into systematic form, we shall present them in the accidental order in which they occur in the three volumes.[1] This chapter is therefore in effect an appendix, consisting principally of notes which serve to emphasize certain features already referred to in the author's theory.

The Preface to Vol. I of this collection is dated Berlin, Sept. 3, 1760. It refers to "the present war" (i. e., the Seven Years' War, 1756–63) as hindering the correspondence with Austrian publishers, who wanted to get out a new edition of some of these papers previously published in *Teutschen Memoires*.

The Preface to Vol. I repeats the theme of cameralism in this form:

Money is today so largely the ground (*sic*) of all the activity of the state, that the greatest courage and the greatest bravery of a people in our time can have little success if it is not provided with sufficient money, that great motive spring and nervous fluid of all undertakings which are to attain fortunate results. We must go farther; we must indeed affirm that the most wholesome and excellent arrangements and institutions of a state will have little success along with a bad condition of the financial system of the state.

Again, in the same preface (the pages are not numbered):

I believe that we still lack a species of history which would be peculiarly useful. The historical books of all peoples are concerned

[1] Johann Heinrich Gottlobs von Justi, *Gesammelte Politische und Finanzschriften über wichtige Gegenstände der Staatskunst, der Kriegswissenschaften und des Cameral- und Finanzwesens. . . .* 1761.

almost entirely with extraordinary and unfortunate occurrences with wars and slaughters which peoples have waged against one another, with narration of extraordinary rascalities and villanies, and the succession of rulers. In my opinion this is of least value and least instructive in history. We should have a history from the earliest times in which the chief attention would be given to the origin of realms and states, to the efforts to found them and to bring them into a flourishing condition, to the principles of government in political, financial, and police affairs, to the attempts to cultivate and people the lands, to the causes of the growth and decay of realms and states, and especially to the governmental mistakes which rulers and ministers have committed. On the other hand, the wars and other matters which heretofore have filled the histories should be mentioned only in passing, in so far as they have had a greater or less influence upon the welfare or decline of civic societies. If a history were so constructed, we could say that history is a mirror of human transactions. As histories are now written I believe they have very little claim to such a title. I have made up my mind to write such a history. I will give it the title: *The History of Mankind as Citizens* [*Die Geschichte des Menschen, als Bürger*].[1] In my opinion such a history, if it satisfied its purpose, would go far toward extending a knowledge of true governmental and financial principles upon which the happiness of peoples largely rests, and such a book could incidentally not fail to be useful to civic society.

Again, in the same preface the author says:

If my efforts in the economic and cameralistic sciences have thus far received the indulgent favor of the world, I do not credit this to my own skill. I believe I owe it entirely to my efforts to establish all the theorems and rules upon the essential purpose of all states, namely the happiness of the peoples. These are also the principles on which I base the financial treatises in this collection. In fact, one can never have other principles in finance. A cameralist who bases his measures upon other principles cheats his master, the state, and himself.

Examining these papers in turn, and selecting items which

[1] The book never appeared.

are most significant for our purpose, we have the following details of varying importance:

A usage that was common in this period, not in Germany alone but throughout Europe, is illustrated in I, 1, in the employment of the word "philosophy" as equivalent to "science."

The main point of I, 2, is in the paragraph on p. 17:

That which is the decisive factor in human affairs is "the allwise Providence of the Highest which always has a hand in human activities and which orders the outcome of all things according to its great wisdom."

A side-light on the application of Justi's theories to actual conditions is in I, 6:

Should sumptuary laws be enacted in the interest of the happiness of the state, especially when it is desirable to encourage commerce and trade? Of course superfluous display and waste or luxury [*Ueppigkeit*] are contrary to the principles of sound morals. What degree of outlay should be regarded as extravagant is a question. It is not at all certain that the outlays which would harm a single family are for that reason harmful to the whole state. For strength against possible enemies the state needs available means. If money were hoarded by the subject, to that extent the sources of available means would dry up. The good of the state demands that money should circulate. If the outlays for display and luxury do not leave the country, they are not harmful to the state (p. 80). Neither the power of the sovereign nor the total means of the state lose anything by it. Hence such outlays should not be forbidden. In the case of luxurious consumption of foreign goods, the best regulation is by prohibiting import of the same (p. 89). Yet certain luxuries should perhaps be forbidden: e. g., those that consume gold and silver in perishable ornaments, or in gilding wood or the baser metals. Probably, however, even the trades that furnish these should be allowed freedom, as the amount of gold and silver permanently lost to the state is trifling compared with the amounts which craftsmen are able to earn in these trades.

The silver plate owned by the upper classes is so much dead treasure. It is certain that this is not contributing to the welfare of the community [*gemeines Wesen*], and it is to be wished that this sort of display could be restricted (p. 91). Yet I cannot conclude that possession of such things should be prohibited. A special tax on luxuries would be a wiser means of restraining extravagance.

I, 8, compares the government of a state to a machine, and makes the analogy a text for an argument for strict ordering of the civil service. I, 11, enters the field of social psychology in this vein:

Peoples are governed by the help of prejudices [*Vorurtheile*]. The passions are the first sources and motive springs of all human actions. If we were controlled by reason only, we should need neither republics nor forms of government. The strength and weakness of a state depends accordingly upon the character of the prejudices with which its citizens are filled, and the wisdom of the government consists chiefly in producing prejudices by means of which the state may attain to all the possible power of which it is capable.

If ever there was a people that needed to change its prejudices, we poor Germans are the ones. Since the Saxon emperors (919–1024), our strength has been steadily on the wane, and for two hundred years we appear to have been the prey of all neighbboring peoples. Our prejudices cannot be of the sort that put us in possession of our full strength. It is not the least of our lacks that we are wanting in the impulse and genius that are necessary for commerce. We must change our prejudices so that commerce and manufacture will rank higher, and will not be beneath the dignity of the nobility. Is a nobility in general consistent with the nature of republics (p. 151)? A hereditary nobility stops up a source which could furnish a great number of rewards for services.

Justi seems to discuss the question seriously (I, 170, *et passim*) whether it were not better to give up the idea of developing commerce and to resume the idea on which the old German nobility was based—power and happiness by conquest. The chief idea would then be—not to have a sufficient army to repel attacks, but an aggressive policy of conquest. This would be to turn the nation into a robber among nations. After referring to somewhat more admissible causes of war, Justi continues (p. 175):

Moreover, in our day war is extremely costly. It is more a sacrifice of unmeasured sums of money than of blood. If therefore a poor nation should today determine to make conquests its chief purpose, it would come to a very ridiculous resolve. A people that today wants to be militant must accordingly also seek to be rich.

There is no other way whereby a people can become rich than through commerce. If a people had in its power the richest gold mines, without carrying on flourishing commerce, it would not thereby be rich. Those foreign peoples who get control of its commerce will also indirectly have its gold mines in their power. Spain furnishes a very conclusive example.

Accordingly no people can today reasonably make conquests its chief purpose without proposing commerce as an equally important affair. . . . But let us suppose that a militant folk has brought all Europe under its yoke. Would it therefore be happy? By no means. It would without doubt acquire vast plunder, but these very riches, instead of promoting its happiness, would cause its ruin.

All riches which do not come into the state by way of commerce, which do not make the industry of the citizens active in their vocations, and which do not incidentally pour themselves into all parts of the civic body, are the source of all disorders, which will presently draw after them the corruption and total destruction of the state. Not the German peoples were the real destroyers of Rome, but the treasures of Attalus (*sic*) and other riches which came to Rome through the plundering of so many peoples. . . . This destruction would have been even more rapid if the Romans, after their conquests, had not become merchants. But even this medicine could not restore the humors once totally corrupted. They were only a strengthening by which the wholly emasculated body was able to endure for a period. . . . .

All this amply proves, it seems to me, that a people can never make conquest its chief aim, and thereby promote its happiness. It proves that no people can be powerful without wealth, and consequently not without commerce, that a people without sufficient power would be very foolish if it dreamed of conquests, that the other European powers would soon enough make it repent of its silly idea; yet, it proves that if a poor people, contrary to all probability, gained the conquests it had desired, still without commerce it would neither be happy, nor would it be able to retain the advantages it had gained.

If, accordingly, all this is established, it naturally follows that the militant origin of the nobility cannot be sufficient ground for its devoting itself exclusively to the purpose out of which it originated.[1]

In I, 13 (p. 198), Justi again explains his doctrine of the importance of the factor of density of population as a component of the strength of a nation. In brief his assertion is that, other things being equal, a country with a million inhabitants scattered over a thousand square miles of territory is much weaker than a country of two hundred and fifty square miles, with the same population. He continues (p. 199):

The more populous a state, the more prosperous will be its food industries and trades, and the more active will be the circulation of money, because all men have need of reciprocal aid and of a thousand kinds of necessities from each other. If a state has foreign commerce, it will constantly acquire more riches, with the greater number of hands that labor on the domestic products and wares. This increased

[1] The whole foregoing passage (I, 175–79), it must be remembered, is incidental to discussion of the question, What is the relation of the nobility to the state and commerce? The main point in Justi's mind was to establish the position that on the principle, *noblesse oblige*, a nobility should justify itself by the sort of service which the state most needed. His argument was that war was not the most radical employment of the state, that commerce went much nearer to the roots of happiness, and that, when promotion of commerce was needed, the nobility ought to serve the state by assuming commercial responsibilities. The context does not warrant any confident inferences from the passage in its bearings upon mercantilism. There are traces in it, in the reference to stimulation of domestic industry, of the actual association of ideas with the more fundamental processes of production. We find the same cropping out elsewhere in qualification of the supposed extreme mercantilist theory.

wealth will always set the industrious hands of the population into more active motion, and the wealth of the state will the more increase. This wealth will at the same time attract much folk from the neighboring states, that barely support life: and thus this wealth will increase the power of the state. The superiority of a people depends today as much and more upon its wealth than upon its numbers. A land which is wisely ruled, and has a flourishing sustaining system, can accordingly never have too many inhabitants.

A moral state must look to wedlock for the increase of its population. How important to the state therefore are its marriage laws (p. 200).

The monograph I, 19, is almost the modern "pace-making" generalization which Professor W. I. Thomas has done so much to develop. The paper glorifies the type that we now call "promoters," while it denounces the merely adventurous varieties of the type. I, 24, expands previous suggestions about getting the most out of people by a system of honors.

Of the papers in the second division of Vol. I on financial questions, we need note merely that (1) expands the view previously expressed, that it is better to farm the *Landesherrlichen Cammergüter und Aemter* than to administer them directly; (4) adds details on wise forms of taxation; (5) discusses excise, and a proposed substitute in the form of an occupation tax; (6) gives further details of the duties of a cameralist in connection with forests and forestry; (7) elaborates a detail under the same head; (8) expands the discussion of the proposition that subjects are not necessarily happy by reason of low taxes; (9) enlarges on "*Mauthen und Zölle*," as means of promoting commerce; (12) treats of taxation as a means of developing and managing the sustaining system.

Passing to Vol. II, the first paper deals with division and balance of power between the main branches of the government in the fundamental constitution of the state. Justi makes two primary divisions: first, the law-giving, second, the executive power. The former has for its object both the main purpose of the complete happiness of the state, and also the subsidiary purposes. Justi slides over, however, into the conventional legislative, executive, judicial classification, and a main proposition is that neither all nor two of these branches of power should be in the same hands. The most tolerable combination is that of legislative and executive powers (p. 10).

If the executive power is entirely independent of the legislative power, if the former has at its disposal all necessary resources, the executive power will certainly attain such preponderance that the legislative will presently be suppressed (p. 12). Either it will not be convened at all, or it will be permitted to concern itself merely with the most insignificant matters. "In all German nations legislation rested at first mostly with the *Volk*."[1]

The paragraph continues:

But, because they[2] put permanently in the hands of the executive power, or of their kings and princes, the means of execution, namely the revenues of the state, in such a way that the executive power had no more need of their co-operation, the result was that in Spain and France nothing remains of the legislative power of the *Volk*, and in most of the German states only a bare shadow. If on the other hand the legislative power is entirely unlimited, and not at all dependent upon the executive power, the former will presently abuse its strength to suppress the executive.

[1] I imagine that such a proposition, even with the explanations immediately to follow, was possible only because of the ambiguity of the term *Volk*. Some of the political philosophers of the time could interpret the personal acts of their own ruling princes as constructively the action of the *Volk*. That is, the latter term carried a content of metaphysical theory. It did not necessarily mean the "people" in an unequivocal democratic sense.

[2] The implied antecedent of the pronoun is the plural "nations" in the preceding sentence, not the collective and metaphysically construed noun *Volk*. The whole explanation would go to pieces under analysis.

The indubitable conclusion is it seems to me that a well-ordered fundamental constitution of the state will be so arranged that the two highest powers will always be in a certain sort of interdependence or equilibrium. This equilibrium depends entirely on their having the right to hinder each other when the one or the other goes too far and loses sight of the welfare of the state, or tends to repudiate the fundamental constitution.[1]

The true freedom of the citizen in monarchies would be represented principally by two circumstances, viz., first, if the laws were so clear and distinct that the decisions would be rather the decisions of the laws than of the judge; second, if the accused, especially in penal cases, were allowed to choose his own judges, or at least to reject so many of them that the remainder would seem to be of his own choosing.[2]

Another passage occurs (Vol. II, p. 26) in which a leaning toward the English form of constitution is expressed. More important than symptoms of this kind is the touch of color which we find in II, I, 9, Justi's inaugural address at the begin-

[1] As in other passages, Justi goes on to speak of details which would enable the ruler to commit the nation to policies that would constrain the legislative power to acquiesce—in the last instance on the principle "my country right or wrong." It is not to be denied, however, that Justi's theory in this passage really in a large measure anticipates the demands of the constitutionalists of the following century (*vide op. cit.*, pp. 21, 22). Yet his illustrations of acts which would make an absolute sovereign into a despot are far from indicating limitations that would remove the conditions which to the modern mind amount to practical absolutism. For instance, when Louis XIV declared his natural sons eligible to the throne, and when Peter I of Russia claimed for the crown the prerogative of designating the successor, each was an attempt to alter the constitution, and beyond the proper rights of the unlimited monarch. That is, Justi argued in most cases for limitation of the monarch *by the constitution*, not otherwise, and the constitution which he had in mind must not be thought of as going into any such details as the written or unwritten constitutions of modern states.

[2] I. e., Justi had his eye so closely trained on personal freedom that he did not properly estimate the degree of its dependence upon political freedom.

ning of his professorial work at Vienna. It contains among other things, an anticipation of the idea of division of labor, and the dependence of each upon the labors of all, so much more minutely worked out by Adam Smith.

The address further glorifies "republics," as against the fantasy of "the state of nature," and is in effect a plea for acquiescence in the type of rule which the House of Habsburg represented.

In the course of the address, after an outline of the tasks that a state must perform in order to insure its happiness, a passage occurs which is so full of the time-temperament that we are unwilling to weaken it by translation. It reads (p. 135):

Ohne Zweifel, *hochgebiethende geheimde Conferenzminister, und wirkliche geheimde Räthe, gnädige Herren, wie auch höchst und hochgeehrteste Anwesende!* hat Ihnen allen dieser geringe Abriss nur Gelegenheit gegeben, sich unterdessen an der geheiligten Person unserer allerdurchlauchtesten Monarchin, eine weit würdigere und erhabene Vorstellung von der Sache zu machen. Ich bin versichert, dass sie unterdessen in ihren Gedanken diejenigen weisen und unermüdeten Bemühungen welche diese wahrhaftig grosse Regentin vor die Wohlfahrt ihrer anvertrauten Völker anwendet, an die Stelle meiner unzulänglichen Beschreibung gesetzt haben: und was vor eine weit lebhaftigere und vollkommenere Abschilderung ist ihnen nicht dadurch gerathen? Die österreichischen Staaten haben zwar allemal das Glück genossen, das ihre Monarchen den anvertrauten Zepter mit weiser Vorsicht, mit unermüdeter Sorgfalt, mit einer Gütigkeit ohne Beyspiele, und mit der zärtlichsten Liebe gegen ihre Unterthanen geführet haben. Allein die Hand des unendlichen Weltbeherrschers, wenn er es seiner allgemeinen Haushaltung gemäss befindet, dass die Gestalt der Zeiten verändert, der Wuth der Verwüster des Erdbodens, die sich die Schwäche ihrer Nachbarn zu Nutze machen, Einhalt gethan, und die Ruhe des menschlichen Geschlechts dargestellet werden soll, bildet manchmal in dem Schoosse seiner Vorsehung ausserordentlich grosse Seelen, welche geschickt sind, ein Reich auf einen viel höhern Grad der Macht und der Glückseligkeit zu setzen. Wenn also die glücklichen österreichischen Länder ihren Zepter jemals in weisen Händen gesehen haben; wenn jemals die besten und wirksamsten Mittel ihre Glückseligkeit zu befördern, angewendet worden sind; wenn sie sich jemals dem wahren Punkte ihrer Grösse, Macht und Glückseligkeit genähert haben: so ist es itzo, und die gegenwärtigen Zeiten werden das Glück geniessen, dass unsere späten Enkel den Zeitlauf von Oesterreichs vergrössertem Zustande bey ihnen anfangen werden.

Of course this impossible fulsomeness was largely a matter of prescribed and perfunctory form. It would be absurd to draw the conclusions from it which literal interpretation of the language would suggest to modern democrats. At the same time the fact remains that Justi was a pliant servant of a régime which called for that sort of conventionality. Discount whatever is necessary for the demands of ceremony; discount too the reservations in Justi's mind, and betrayed frequently in his books; he remains the spokesman of the type of state of which Maria Theresia is a symbol. In the remainder of the address from which the passage is taken he employs rhetoric of almost equal extravagance to express his pride in the vocation of preparing youth for service in the administration of the Habsburg state (p. 137). When a little later he found himself no longer *persona grata* in Vienna, he went from state to state of the same essential type, and left behind no credible evidence of ever in his responsible moments having entertained the thought that in Germany an essentially different type of state was feasible. The relation of Justi to the modern type of political theory may be indicated in a perfectly fair illustration. Suppose that in a hundred years Great Britain shall have moved as far from her present type in the direction of socialism as continental states, in becoming constitutional, have moved from the absolutistic type in the direction of democracy. Suppose that a historian at that date should take John Stuart Mill's record in connection with the *Land Tenure Reform Association* as proof that he was not a nineteenth-century conservative, but a twenty-first century radical. The guess would be no wider of the mark than an interpretation of Justi as other than a technologist of the Maria Theresia type of governmental theory.

In this same address (p. 142), in speaking of the conditions which enable a state to accomplish its purposes for its citizens, Justi puts "adequate riches" first, and "complete security" second, and he continues:

We must not, however, form the same notion of the riches of a state which we have of the riches of a private person. Not all riches which a land may contain can be regarded as wealth [*ein Reichthum*] of the land. Not chests filled with money in the treasury of the monarch, not the heaped-up piles of gold in the houses of private persons, accumulated by greed and oppression, constitute the riches of the state. Gold and silver, these lustrous metals, which seem so beautiful to the eager eyes of men, lose all price and all worth previously credited to them, and they turn again to trifling parts of the globe, if they lose their ultimate purpose: namely, to be a universal means of determining the worth of all other sorts of goods, and to serve for the establishment and promotion of the business of men. Only that wealth is therefore the real wealth of the state which is grasped by the busy hands of the inhabitants, and is daily moved from one employment into another.

Apparently Justi had to defend his claims for the cameral sciences against suspicion of being on a level with alchemy, fortune-telling, etc. With changes of detail, his lot was not unlike the situation in which even now sociology finds itself when it presents its case to representatives of the older social sciences. Apparently in part to outflank this phase of opposition to his subject Justi explained (*op. cit.*, pp. 155–60) the three methods of obtaining national wealth which he assumed to be worth considering, viz., (1) mining; (2) commerce; (3) inducing rich foreigners to become citizens.

The essay, "Proof that a Universal Monarchy Would Make for the Welfare of Europe and the Human Race" (II, I, 17), was first published anonymously in 1748. Justi acknowledges that it is punctured by the consideration that there would be no assurance of a succession of fit monarchs. It amounts then merely to a fancy picture. He meant it, however, as a means of expressing indirectly certain opinions which could not be published unveiled. In general, he wanted to ring changes on the idea that princes had no right to govern arbitrarily, but that right reason must control them. He took the round-about way of arguing that it was not necessarily a misfortune to subjects to have their prince subordinate to an overlord, because he might enforce the reasonable principles which might not otherwise prevail.

Justi argues that the present *status quo* of some hundred and twenty ruling princes was regarded by the princes themselves as synonymous with the happiness of Europe; but he argued that the personal preferences of these one hundred and twenty are of relatively little moment (II, 246).

This essay tends to raise the suspicion that Justi was much more of a skeptic in his early manhood about the prevailing type of government than he found it expedient to remain. He very explicitly declares that the curse of Germany is its multitude of independent princes (II, 257).

The last 167 pages of Vol. II (i. e., 406–572) are devoted to a technically very important monograph on causes of the debasement of the currency, and means of removing the evil. The view of gold and silver money which Justi expresses (II, 427 ff.) is essentially sound. The heading of §16 is: "The supreme power cannot arbitrarily fix the price of gold and silver." Again (§22), he says: "The conditions of European states make gold and silver necessary as the material of money." There were, just before Justi's time, "silver campaigns" in Germany. It was claimed that the currency evils were due to the fact of the unfair ratio of gold to silver, while the ratio established by other nations did not correspond. An act of the Empire in 1737 fixed the ratio at $15\frac{1}{10}$ to 1. The ratio in England and most other countries at the same time was $14\frac{1}{2}$ to 1 (II, 468; *vide* II, 544 ff.).

Justi makes the coinage right a consequence of sovereignty over mines (II, 472–86). From Vol. III we gather the following: First, a passage in the second paper (p. 23):

To be rich is to possess in abundance all that is demanded for the needs and comforts of human life, just as he who can procure for hmself in sufficiency the comforts of life is a well-to-do man. [*Wohlhabender*]. According to the foregoing concept, a rich state is the one which has within itself superabundant provision for all the needs and comforts of life for a dense population. A well-to-do or opulent state is one which produces an adequate quantity of the goods which a dense population requires for its needs and comforts (III, 26).

In the following pages Justi explains at length that money is not merely the symbol of goods, but that it is itself a "ware." "Gold and silver are in a certain sense necessary as money only in trade with foreign peoples" (III, 31).

If a land possesses only one sort of wares, viz., gold and silver, in superabundance, the surplus must be enormous if all the needs and comforts are to be supplied by exchange for it to such an extent that the gold and silver country will be properly called rich. Of course in such case the price of gold and silver in the country would be very low. . . . . The foreign nations which supplied other goods in exchange for these metals would make large profits, the metals would go into the foreign lands, while no surplus of goods would remain in their place to make the land rich. This is the case with Spanish America (III, 34).

Another consequence of the supposed conditions is that such a land is very thinly populated (III, 35).

All this sufficiently proves, in my opinion, that a state which produces a surplus of only gold and silver, but not of other goods demanded for the needs and comforts of life, can never be called rich. On the other hand a state is always to be regarded as rich which itself produces these goods in abundance. It possesses the true riches of nature, which are much superior to those fanciful riches which arise from the silent conventions of men. It possesses the essential and the thing itself, and needs not to trouble itself about the symbols of the same. It is quite independent of other nations, and need fear no unfortunate consequences if its commerce with them is cut off. Indeed, if it pleases such a state, it can terminate all trade with other peoples, and enjoy by itself all happiness which a wise government can procure.

We may even assert that such a state would be truly rich, if not a pound of gold and silver were to be found in it; and such a state would be able to continue all its connection and trade with neighboring nations. This appears to be a paradox, because gold and silver are necessary, particularly on account of foreign trade, and the relative wealth as compared with other states has always been regarded of great importance. Yet, since I have considered the matter more carefully, I find that what I here affirm is strictly correct.

If it is presupposed that such a state produces in superabundance all the goods pertaining to the needs and comforts of life, there will certainly be many in the number which the neighboring nations do not have in such abundance, which they must constantly seek in the state in question. It is natural that such a state, which itself satisfies all the needs and comforts of its people, requires few wares from other peoples, and hence must have the balance of trade in its favor, so that it has to pay little to other nations. Now let us assume that such a state has no money in circulation, but only paper. Sure enough! This paper, as the sole representative symbol for which the wares of this state can be exchanged, will be eagerly sought by the neighboring nations. It is so untrue that this paper will pass at a lower value than real money, that in proportion to profit anticipated a premium will be paid for the paper above the value of the gold that it represents. This is a natural and familiar experience with all paper money and bills of exchange of a land to which neighboring nations must pay more than they collect. Both the government and the merchants and subjects of this state will accordingly do the same and more with their paper than if they used gold and silver coins in their transactions with other nations (III, 36 ff.).

The third paper in Vol. III contains a translation of the letter alleged to have been written by Colbert to Louis XIV in 1672, and first published in the *Guardian*. It has a scheme of reasons why the French monarch could not subdue the Netherlands. On the general question of the true power of states, the essay premises: The state is not powerful because of extensive *territories* (pp. 57 ff.); nor because of *population* alone (pp. 60 ff.); nor because of territories, plus population, plus riches (pp. 62 ff.); nor even because of invincible armies (pp. 65 ff.), with frequent and strong fortifications (pp. 73 ff.).

Then the positive doctrine follows:

The true strength and power of a state rests entirely upon the wisdom and completeness [*Vollkommenheit*] of the government (p. 74). This theorem involves very much. It means not only that the whole correlation and fundamental constitution of the state is good; but the wisdom of the government must display itself in all parts of the civic body; and it must neglect no kind of affairs. . . . . A state will always be powerful in the degree in which its government is completely organized [*eingerichtet*] and wisely exercised; and of two states, equal to each other in population and riches, that one will always overcome the other the government of which is the wiser and more complete (p. 74).

The development or justification of the theorem, which Justi says will be new to many, is virtually a glorification of cameralism as the technique of a wise and complete government; although Justi admits that all lands are not to be governed in the same way.

In the sixth essay of the same volume, Justi schedules the services of religion to the state. In brief these are: (1) It may stimulate the citizens to cultivate the soil, and to increase the population. In this respect Catholicism is pronounced least efficient (p. 147); (2) it may promote diligence and skill (p. 151); (3) it may promote civic virtues and stimulate people to practice them (161).

Justi proceeds to consider the relation of Christianity in particular to these services (pp. 169 ff.), and he does not think that this religion is well fitted to be the dominant force in the state because:

It is entirely heavenly, entirely spiritual, entirely devoted to God, entirely withdrawn from this temporal life, and dedicated alone to the future life. It is all too passive, patient, humble, with respect to the earthly life, and so strongly and openly despises everything which constitutes the welfare of citizens, that a civic constitution could not be maintained among other powers by true Christians only (p. 170).

The first paper in the second division of the volume, a prospectus of the economic courses to be offered at Göttingen, is dated June 20, 1755. It has the following variation of scientific classification:

The sciences either contribute something directly to the discharge of our duties and the improvement of our external condition or they serve those purposes indirectly, and put us in a condition better to fulfil our duties; or they are merely capable of amusing our immortal soul (p. 222).

The economic and cameralistic sciences are those which teach management on a large scale with the means of the state, or which put us in possession of the measures by which the general means of the republic may be preserved, increased, and reasonably applied to its ultimate purpose of happiness (p. 223).

One of the impressions which the paper makes, from our point of view, is that Justi was beginning to increase his attention to the economic emphasis, and second, that the presumption of the prime and necessary first claim of *the state* was still decisive.

Justi urges that the cameralistic sciences belong in the first of the three groups just distinguished. He calls attention to the lively movement at the time in favor of getting these subjects taught in the universities (p. 226); and he repeats his frequent reflection that, until recently, the learned were simply engaged in exchanging esoteric views with one another, chiefly in a language not understood by the people, instead of doing something that would be of service to the general good.[1]

In the sixth paper of the second division there is discussion of problems of state revenues with respect to different circumstances of states and forms of government. In the seventh paper an open secret of the cameralistic régime is confessed in this wise:

The distribution and direction of the means of private persons belong, to be sure, among the subjects which demand the special care of the government. If the government could bring it about that no citizen or resident should become entirely inpoverished, it would thereby perform a service of the highest importance to the welfare of the state. Ancient governments looked out for this. Modern governments have neglected it almost completely. It has been taken for granted that it was entirely a matter of indifference for the state whose hands held the means and the wealth, if they were only present and remained in the country. The contrary is true wisdom.

Special and peculiar measures are demanded of the government in the case of movable and immovable wealth respectively. Movable goods are fruits of diligence and skill (p. 343). It is wisdom for the state to add its encouragement in every way to stimulate diligence and skill. Immovable goods, on the other hand, belong to the total means of the state, and the means of a state is the chief ground of its energies, its strength, and its power [*Kräfte, Stärke und Macht*].

[1] An explanation which occurs on p. 243 confirms and partially explains a detail of our knowledge of Justi's personal history, viz.: "Sr. Königliche Majestät von Grossbritannien und Churfürstl. Durchl. zu Braunschweig-Lüneburg haben allergnädigst geruhet mich in diesem berühmten Musensitze als Dero Oberpoliceycommisarium zu bestellen, etc., ... zugleich . . . . Erlaubniss ertheilet in den Oeconomischen und Cameral Wissenschaften . . . . Vorlesungen zu halten."

It cannot thus be a matter of indifference to the state whether this portion of its total means, which is in the hands of private persons, is in good or bad condition, or whether it is well or ill employed. . . . . The use and the good condition of private estates, however, rests to a great extent upon the direction of a wise government over the same, and upon the proper proportion and distribution of private estates in the country. . . . . If the movable goods belong, so to speak, to the whole world, and circulate from one country into another, the immovable goods are the real fixed and assured property [*Eigenthum*] of the state. They are the *terra firma* [*Grund und Boden*] of the *Volk*, because they belong to the country which peculiarly pertains to the total *Volk* (p. 358).[1]

As a primary principle, government must see that lands shall be in the possession of those who will live on them and cultivate them (p. 359). It is also desirable that the peasants shall have a proprietary tenure (p. 362). This will tend to increase the rural population (p. 366).

In the eighth paper in the second division Justi tries to make his views about population as emphatic as possible. He says (p. 379):

If one should ask me whether the chief consideration of a genuine and wise cameralist—to which, according to the general principle of the happiness of the state, his chief care must be directed, and back to which he must refer in all his measures and operations—could be expressed with a single word and concept, I would without a moment's hesitation cry out the word POPULATION. Yes! Truly! POPULATION must be the apple of his eye, as compared with all other measures.[2]

[1] The form of expression in the last sentence has a bearing on the sense in which Justi thought of *Volk*, i. e., not in the ordinary modern distributive sense, but as a more artificial collective concept.

[2] *Vide Grundriss der Policey-Wissenschaft*, p. 77 (*vide* above, p. 444), and von Mohl, *Gesch. u. Lit. d. Staatswis.*, III, 471. Von Mohl quotes the second edition. I have referred to the corresponding passage in the third. It is very evident that von Mohl had practically no knowledge of the setting of the doctrine of population in Justi's system. In fact,

Many cameralists who glance at this monograph will certainly not have expected this word. If they had been asked for such a leading concept, they would certainly have called out in the loudest voice: MONEY! REVENUES! "PLUS!" or something of that sort. Most of them are so entirely convinced that the whole reason for their existence is to bring together MONEY, or revenues, that all the philosophers in the world could not convince them otherwise. I am not now writing for these people. I will at this point attempt to convince only those cameralists who, along with a good head, have also a good heart, that money and revenues should at least be only their second great aim, if they are not to fail of both population and revenues (p. 379).

Someone will perhaps reply that my theorem might lead too far. It might be possible for a land to be very well populated, and to have a surplus of all goods required for the need and comfort of human life, while still lacking money; or gold and silver, and consequently to be poor in comparison with other states, as a result of which it would be exposed to various harmful consequences. We must therefore conclude that riches in gold and silver, if not more necessary than population, are still equally necessary, and thus deserve equal attention.

I reply: If a country possesses a surplus of all sorts of goods, and therewith the true riches, there is scarcely a possibility that it can suffer a lack of the representative signs of goods, namely gold and silver. The signs automatically follow the thing which they represent. The surplus of goods in this country will stimulate other nations to exchange the same among us for the representative signs, because the goods will be cheap among us, and the quantity of gold in the country will presently be in proportion to the quantity of money.[1]

he qualified it sufficiently to make von Mohl's criticism gratuitous. He no more believed that population could be fed in unlimited numbers than Malthus did. For the practical purposes of the states in whose interest he was elaborating a technique, population was the first consideration, until, as he indicated in *Staatswirthschaft*, population should reach three, four, or six times the number at his time. He never formulated the more general Malthusian problem of population.

[1] The last word is apparently a misprint for *goods*.

We have no instance of a country with a great surplus of goods, which was still poor in money, *provided* that such a country carried on commerce with other peoples. On the other hand, we have examples of countries which possessed the richest silver and gold deposits, and still were very poor in the goods of life, and thus in the true riches. The representative signs at once followed the thing, they entered the country which had the surplus of the goods of life, and such a (gold-producing) country remained poor in spite of its gold mines.

Justi's opponents in the above argument are men of straw so far as evidence appears in the cameralistic books. He must have had in mind cameralists of the bureau, men of affairs rather than of theory, who wanted policies to be shaped according to the contrary hypothesis. In the next paragraph (p. 385) Justi continues:

But suppose that a well-populated land, supplied with a surplus of goods, has not an adequate proportion of the "representative signs" in gold and silver. This would be a very slight disadvantage. In the country itself it would have not the slightest harmful effect. In respect to domestic circulation [*Umlauf*] the proportion of money in the country is wholly indifferent. If the land is only well populated and has a surplus of goods, exchange will be as lively with little money as with much. Indeed, it may be dispensed with entirely. Such a country could, without money, have all the happiness and strength of which it is capable.[1]

Then Justi goes on to say (p. 386) that of course the quantity of money becomes important so soon as we consider relations with other states. That is, it is important chiefly when a state is in an aggressive attitude toward others, and its policy is to harm them.

[1] This passage is notable as proof that Justi was not the sort of mercantilist described as the traditional type. The naïveté of his ideas about the relative importance of a circulating medium is to be noted, but it does not immediately concern our purpose, except that it was a very natural incident of his predominantly administrative conception of the state.

The true relative defensive strength of a country depends always upon the larger population, other things being equal; although the relative aggressive power depends more upon wealth in gold and silver; or at least the relative wealth has in this connection the most effect.

In the following pages (pp. 387 ff.) Justi resumes his main line of argument on population, and elaborates rules for encouraging a high birth rate. These are: (1) Means of earning a living must be made abundant; (2) the government must not be oppressive; (3) the laws must encourage marriage; (4) the chief means of promotion is that the rights of the *pater familias* and of the husband, namely the lordship over his house and his wife, which so undoubtedly belongs to him according to the law of nature and of civic society, should be restored (p. 393; *vide Natur und Wesen der Staaten*, 8. *Hauptstück*, §§240, 241);[1] (5) the state must exercise great care over the education of poor children, and the training of children in general (p. 395).

The remaining papers in the collection are so strictly technical that they add nothing to our knowledge of Justi's more fundamental reasoning.

[1] It is more than possible that the first Frau Justi may have had a mind of her own at this point, and that the domestic troubles of the house of Justi may have turned on this issue.

CHAPTER XVIII

THE CAMERALISTICS OF SONNENFELS

("INTRODUCTION")

The reasons for treating Sonnenfels as the last in the cameralistic series must be reserved for a later volume. More conventional usage extends the present group to the time of Rau.[1] This summary measure of convenience is possible only by ignoring the essential distinctions of purpose which distinguish theorists of successive periods.

Roscher divides the history of German economic theory into three great periods: First, the *theologico-humanistic*, from the early humanists to the end of the Thirty Years' War; second, the "*polizeilich-cameralistische*" to which no date of expiration is assigned; third, the *scientific*, for which no distinct birthday is designated, but the implication is that it begins with the favorable reception of physiocratic doctrines in Germany, that is, during the last quarter of the eighteenth century. As divisions of this sort are mere uncritical superficialities at best, we need waste no time upon them, after pointing out that they are worthless for purposes of precision. They magnify accidentals, instead of penetrating first to the purposes which are the ultimate marks of distinction between theorists, and second, to the methodologies which are the variants of their procedure.

If we compare Roscher's main analysis with the titles of his subdivisions, we find that he falls back upon a collection of uncorrelated characterizations after all. For example, he treats Dithmar, Gasser, Zincke, and Justi, with others of lesser note or of equal importance if studied primarily in relation to their proper groups, under the subtitle, "*the older eclectics of the*

[1] *Lehrbuch der politischen Oeconomie*, 1826, etc.

eighteenth century."[1] He makes a subdivision under the "scientific period," for Sonnenfels, with two or three others of trifling consequence thrown in to keep up appearances, with the label, "the later absolutistic eclectics."[2] This all amounts to the veriest parody of analysis. Roscher gravely declares that in the period from the predominance of Wolff to the influence of Kant all German philosophy was eclecticism, and at the same time national economy, from the end of the Seven Years' War to the outbreak of the French Revolution, was predominantly eclectic. We should say rather that "national economy" was still what it had been for two hundred years, an increasingly circumstantial and subdivided technology of management of the state, considered as the patriarchate of the prince, and that it was no more eclectic in principle than it had been from the beginning. It is always uncertain whether Roscher's term "*Nationalökonomik*" amounts to anything more than a synonym for Justi's "*Staatswirthschaft.*" If Roscher meant to imply that there was in Germany, at the period designated, an economic science of any sort differentiated from the general system of civic management, in which the power of the government was the decisive aim, no evidence appears that the wish was not father to the thought. In this period, and notably in Sonnenfels, a new spirit is evident. The more obvious and extreme corollaries of quasi-absolutism are challenged, indirectly at any rate, by sentimental rather than formulated variants consisting of higher valuations of the claims of citizens as such, in contrast with the older presumption that whatever the supposed good of the government demanded must as a matter of course prescribe the terms of individuals' rights.

Yet Roscher is correct in a way when he continues:

In such a time criticism is far from serious examination of fundamental ideas. It is rather busy rubbing down the sharp points,

[1] Roscher, *op. cit.*, pp. 430 ff. [2] *Op. cit.*, pp. 533 ff.

reconciling petty contradictions; that is, it is essentially eclectic. Before the discussion of the Smithian system, all the German teachers of public management [*Volkswirthschaft*], the apostles of physiocracy and the historical-conservative opponents of the new spirit excepted, may be classed in two groups—absolutistic and liberal eclectics, the former attached to the two major German powers, especially Austria, the latter to the medium and petty states of North Germany, particularly the Hanse cities.

For more than two generations Austrian national economy was dominated by Joseph von Sonnenfels (1733–1817). He undertook his professorship of *Finanz- und Policeiwissenschaft* at Vienna in 1763. His significant literary influence began still earlier, and a little later his political importance. The latter constantly grew under Joseph II. In the troubled times of the French Revolution it encountered opposition, but on the whole it maintained itself so long that until the publication of his own handbook in 1845 Kudler followed the tradition of making Sonnenfels' works the basis of his lectures. This, to be sure, does not speak well for the intellectual productivity of Austria, and the fact is that the country had to rely largely on thinkers from the other German states.

Sonnenfels was the grandson of a Berlin rabbi. His father moved to Austria, submitted to baptism, and assumed the name Sonnenfels. He was a pioneer of German culture in Austria, and some of his experiences remind one of the reception which Adam Smith found in Scotland for the Oxford English which he had acquired during his university residence.[1]

Of Sonnenfels the younger, Roscher further says:

His general political view is a theoretical and insecurely founded absolutism, mitigated by the sort of philanthropic ideas which were prevalent in the second half of the eighteenth century. In a monograph dedicated to Maria Theresia (1771) and entitled "On Love of the Fatherland," he has much to say about monarchy, aristocracy, and democracy, but with express adherence to the words of Pope,

> For forms of government let fools contest,
> The best administered is the best.

[1] *Op. cit.*, p. 534, n.

He explains the origin of the state in the sense of Rousseau, and the mottoes of all three volumes of his chief work were taken from Rousseau.[1] At the same time he declares that the natural condition of men is the social condition, and following Rousseau's own words, to be sure, he compared the state with the organism of the human body. Meanwhile, because "irresistibility is the most essential trait of the sovereign power, the governments nominated by the aggregate will are as unlimited as the will was whose place they have taken." Religion itself is by no means a positive limitation of the will of the ruler. It is conceived rather quite in the sense of Joseph II, as a guiding thread in the hand of the ruler, which the latter should never neglect, and which was especially necessary in dealing with ordinary people. Freethinking is also politically a crime, and there is no ground for the fear that attachment to the laws of society could ever harm religion and morality. Sonnenfels calls the censorship of books one of the most necessary police regulations. He urges the shortening of processes before the courts, and the payment of advocates by the state: thus impressing the most natural and expert organ of the opposition into the service of the government. A favorite idea of Sonnenfels was that in criminal cases the penalty of ascertained guilt should be determined by the vote of the majority of the judges; the question of guilt or innocence however, as well as of the mitigating or aggravating circumstances, should be settled only by a unanimous vote. In practice this proposition would in most cases simply lead to the release of the accused.

On the other hand, Sonnenfels gained a reputation in Austria for his efforts to abolish torture.[2] This reform was decided in 1775 by the publication of a tract which was at the same time in defiance of a decree of 1769 against "all too great freedom in writing," the

[1] This is only partially true of the fifth edition, which I have used. Roscher cites the third. The motto of the fifth edition of Vol. I is from Cicero, *De divin.* i–iii, and on the page opposite the beginning of the General Introduction, is a paragraph from Richard Hey, *Observations on the Nature of Civil Liberty.* The motto of the third volume is from Horace; while only the second takes its motto from Rousseau.

[2] Among the more creditable facts about Becher is his adhesion to the same view. (*Vide* Roscher, *loc. cit.*, p. 284, n. 2.)

same being occasioned by his publications on the death penalty and torture. Sonnenfels also opposed treatment of the pensions of civic servants as charity. Again his curt demand that every obsolete law should be repealed, ran counter to a well-known maximum of despotism according to which the ruler is never to admit that he has erred, and reserves the choice between various fundamental principles in dealing with a specific case. That in the case of every law the purposes of the law-giver should be discussed so as to protect right principles, is much more emphatically urged by Sonnenfels than by Justi.

At the same time, it is characteristic of Sonnenfels' absolutism to be more liberal at the expense of private rights than at the expense of governmental power. Thus in the case of the obligations attached to peasant holdings of the soil, he speaks, for example, of the ancient imprescriptible human rights, in contrast with the traditional rights of possession.[1]

The foregoing passage from Roscher has been cited not for its value as an interpretation of Sonnenfels, but as a commentary on Roscher's use of the term eclectic. The details recited furnish a content for the word as he employed it. This usage is to be distinguished from another which to some minds at least is more appropriate. That is, we understand by eclecticism an attempt to construct a system of thought by combination of two or more systems which are held by their extreme adherents to be mutually exclusive, as for instance the Kantian psychology and the Benthamite ethics.[2] According to Roscher's specifications, he meant by eclecticism a certain degree of independence in deciding whether traditional conclusions about details necessarily follow from principles still regarded as fundamental. It is in the latter sense alone that Sonnenfels can be called an eclectic. It is not true that he was a mediator between the traditional philosophy of quasi-absolutism and a rival political philosophy. It is true that his attempts to mitigate the

[1] *Vide Handlung*, 5te *Aufl.*, p. 53; *vide* below, p. 549.

[2] *Vide Century Dictionary*, title "Eclectic," II.

consequences of quasi-absolutism must be read at this distance as clear signs that a new thought-era was in the making. The times were ripening for a system of political philosophy which would openly challenge tradition. Specific valuations were forming in men's minds which would presently amount to repudiation of the old general theory. The reconstruction, however, in the case of men like Sonnenfels, had gone only so far as to produe a half-conscious conflict between the cognitive and the emotional sides of political judgments. To put it in paradox, Sonnenfels thought as an absolutist, but he felt as a democrat. Like every other paradox, this is a very loose statement. It more correctly characterizes the breaking-up process of which Sonnenfels was an index than any label which purports to assign him a precise position in a schematic classification of theorists. The justice of this dissent from Roscher will appear as we deal directly with Sonnenfels.

The work which is most important for our purpose, as reflecting, so to speak, a *fin de siècle* phase of cameralism, is in three volumes, entitled, *Grundsätze der Policey, Handlung und Finanz.*[1] The volumes are closely related, but each is a distinct unit, devoted respectively Vol. I to *Policey*, Vol. II to *Handlung*, Vol. III to *Finanz*. According to the author's explanation in the Preface to Vol. I, the books were what we should now call syllabi of the courses which he gave in the unisity at Vienna on the corresponding subjects. This description must be commented upon further in connection with the several volumes.

A single observation should precede analysis of these books, viz.: One feels in passing from Justi to Sonnenfels that a watershed has been crossed, and that one is within the borders

[1] The title-page has the further legend, "*Zu dem Leitfaden des politischen Studiums.*" The center of the page is occupied by a vignette of Montesquieu, in itself a critical index of first-rate importance. The first edition was published in 1765. I have used only the fifth edition, 1787.

of another territory. Speaking literally, the mere fact that Sonnenfels makes the conscious attempt at modernism involved in adopting a corrected orthography makes the reader aware of a transition. Typographically these volumes are not an improvement upon the mechanical style of Justi's publications. In their contents one detects a somewhat freer spirit. Judging wholly from the internal evidence, one would by no means rank Sonnenfels as Justi's equal in intellectual strength. The later writer appears to have been of a more receptive than creative type, but although they were in part contemporaries the impressions which molded him contained elements which were less active in Justi's world. If one were called upon to defend this estimate, it might be said that while Justi seems to have been intellectually more virile, he seems also to have been less open to persuasion by the comparison of moral values. Justi's personality betrays some of the signs of quasi-absolutism at its worst. Sonnenfels shows affinities for something superior to quasi-absolutism at its best. In spite of this contrast, we should go astray if we followed the example of Roscher in affixing a distinctive label to Sonnenfels. We cannot make such men fit into any schematic classification. They show that a new type was in the process of evolution. They do not quite correspond with any general description or definition. They are not entirely consistent with themselves. They are partly of one tendency and partly of another. They show survivals of traits which are logically incompatible with the presence of other traits, yet the incongruities exist. Historical veracity consists in reporting them just as they were, without attempting to conventionalize them in the image of any conceptual type whatsoever.

Turning to Vol. I, *Policey*, we find at once in the Preface literary symptoms rather favorably contrasted with those observed in Justi. Sonnenfels begins by explaining why he finds himself obliged to add a textbook to those already in existence. Some of them he thinks are too comprehensive, others too narrow in their scope. At the same time he names none of these works at this point, and we are obliged to search the body of the book for desirable information about his connection with other writers.

The Preface to the fifth edition discusses the criticism of a reviewer that the importance of rewards as means of securing good civil service had been overlooked in the earlier editions. Sonnenfels replies that he did not forget the subject, but that he intentionally omitted rewards from his schedule of means of obtaining good government. He urges, however, that the best way to stimulate a high quality of service is to make distinction the prize of excellence. Rewards of any other sort are really premiums to the unworthy who do not become worthy in return for such payments. He contends that civil servants should be punished for neglect of duty, but should not receive premiums as means of making them perform the duties that belong to their positions, and he supports his view by citing Hume without locating the quotation.

This first volume contains 552 pages, of about 125 words each, and is divided into 432 sections. As a rule, one of these sections is a succinct statement of the substance of the author's view upon the matter to which it refers, and elaboration rather than addition was attempted in the lectures. The point of view is partially indicated in the opening sections of the "general introduction,"[1] viz.:

> The isolated human being is not the human being in the state of nature; his condition would be a condition of constant helplessness. But he feels his lack. He feels that he is capable of remedying the

[1] This "general introduction" occupies forty-nine pages. It includes the chapter on computing the population. It was evidently intended to introduce the three volumes as a whole. It is followed (p. 50) by an introduction which relates specifically to *Policey*, the subject-matter of the first volume.

lack, of improving his condition. Reason, which distinguishes him from the beasts, enables him to perceive the means by which he may reach an improved condition. This means is socialization with his kind [*Vergesellschaftung mit seines Gleichen*]. The natural condition of man is thus the condition of society: the domestic, the conjugal, the paternal society, are so many steps whereby he comes nearer to the great society, which includes all others, and which, since the minor groupings direct their gaze toward the weal of the separate members, has adopted as its aim the best good of all societies.[1]

[1] In a note Sonnenfels comments: "The notion of the isolated human being is perhaps merely a literary abstraction. Man is always in society, and as Ferguson, in his *Essays on the History of Civil Society*, acutely observes, 'a savage caught somewhere in a forest, no more proves that man by nature lives alone, than a sheep straying in a forest would prove that sheep do not flock together.'"

In the Preface to the third volume (5th ed.) the author says: "I have cited only those books that I have read, and of which I can give assurance that it will pay to consult or read them." The books which he explicitly mentions will be carefully noted. He seldom locates the passages to which he refers, and I am unable to decide whether the remark quoted applies to all three volumes, or whether he intended it to include authors cited in this casual way. He later refers to Smith's *Wealth of Nations*. Although a German translation of the *Wealth of Nations* bears the date 1776, the same year in which the original was published, I am not sure that the version appeared as early as the date would seem to indicate; and I have no conclusive reason for believing that at the time of making his first printed allusion to Smith's work Sonnenfels knew it except by title. If he had actually read Smith and Ferguson in 1787, the leaven was working in Germany rather earlier than is usually supposed. Even Ricardo did not discover the *Wealth of Nations* till long after that date.

The phrase "so many steps, etc.," might be turned into evidence that Sonennfels repudiated the "social contract" idea, and held the evolutionary view of the origin of human society. A monograph recently conceived in Berlin and published in Leipzig employs exegesis of this sort to read into Adam Smith and Adam Ferguson a considerable catalogue of sociological concepts which their philosophy had never dreamed of, viz.: Hermann Huth, *Sociale und individualistische Auffassung im 18. Jahrhundert, vornehmlich bei Adam Smith und Adam Ferguson. Ein Beitrag zur Geschichte der Sociologie.* If Sonnenfels had consistently

Sec. 2 continues:

The great society is the state. The transition into the same has given the members a new name, has put them into new relationships. The human beings have become citizens, beings who, through the nature of their self-chosen (*sic!*) status, have now, as parts, their relationship to a whole, are united as members in a moral body. The effect of this unification is *unity of ultimate purpose*, *unity of will*, *unity of force*.

The three following sections expand the three principal concepts in the last sentence. Thus (§3):

Unity of ultimate purpose, or of welfare, of the best, which now is called the best good of the community *das gemeinschaftliche Beste*] whereby the best of the single member, that is, private advantage, remains constantly subordinated to the former, and cannot be otherwise brought into the account than in so far as it constitutes a part of the common best of the whole body. In case their private advantage could not be reconciled with "the common best," the former must necessarily be subordinated to the latter. Fortunately, however, in the precise sense, there can be no thought of a contradiction between the true permanent private welfare and the general welfare. For upon closer examination it will always appear, either that what is regarded as private advantage ceases to be such so soon as it works in opposition to the general advantage; or frequently that a supposed limitation of the common weal is not actually such. . . . The welfare of the parts is based upon the welfare of the whole; but at the same time the welfare of the whole springs only from the welfare of the parts.[1]

applied *our* logic, some of his phrases would have carried him nearer to Darwin than to Rousseau. But—!!

The next section contains typical evidence that interpretation of an author by phrases isolated from the general tenor of his thought is impossible.

[1] Again, if we might credit the eighteenth century with the associations of the twentieth, we should say that here was a profession of the most modern democratic political philosophy. What we actually find here is evidence that valuations were coming into vogue which were logically incompatible with the prevailing quasi-absolutistic political

Sonnenfels continues (§4):

Unity of the will, which, in case something is involved whose effects extend to community interests, suspends all contradiction, upon the principle that no one can at the same time will and not will, and makes the separate will of the individual subordinate to the community decision.[1]

In §5 the explanation continues:

Unity of force. In so far as the individual energies are necessary for the attainment of the ultimate end of the community, they should be exerted in no way except that toward which the community energy is devoted. Whoever withdraws his share of this energy, in case the common ends require a given quantity of force, leaves the

philosophy, and that they were accelerating the motion of the social process toward retirement of the more arbitrary philosophy.

The perception had not yet been reached that this interdependence of private and public good demanded a different means of adjusting in practice the claims of the co-operating factors. That is, the rulers still decided for the people what was for the people's good. This technique presupposed that the rulers were not only superior in wisdom, but that they were disinterested judges. Whether the former assumption was valid or not, the latter was directly contrary to fact. The rulers were to a considerable extent competitors with the citizens for things desired by both. That the former should be perpetual arbiters about relations in which they were perpetually interested parties, was the essential fallacy of the old régime. I discover no evidence whatever that Sonnenfels was aware of this weakness in quasi-absolutism. Until theorists arrived at this perception, they were intellectually with the old régime, however symptomatic their emotions may have been of a changing order.

[1] Again the approximateness of Sonnenfels' philosophy must be pointed out. The alleged principle was thoroughly modern in its abstract statement. It proves to be still archaic when interpreted by the implications which clung to it. The crucial matter was to get a technique which could properly ascertain the social will in contrast with the individual will. The old régime simply seized the power to make the will of certain individuals subvert the will of the overwhelmingly larger number of individuals and count as the will of the society. The essence of quasi-absolutism remained in force in political theories until the full significance of this dilemma was admitted.

general activity too weak; but if he turns his energy against the general purpose the disadvantage is doubled, because the energy of another person is thereby nullified.

In the sixth section Sonnenfels distinctly asserts the right of each member of society to take part in deciding what measures should be taken to attain the common ends, and the consent of all the members is necessary if this decision is to appear in a law.

In the seventh section, however, doubt is cast upon the connotations which the generalization had for the author's mind. It seems to be more a historical hypothesis in the sense of Hobbes, Locke, and Rousseau, than a moral principle by which to test the technique of existing societies. By means of this generalization Sonnenfels accounts for the transition "from the multitude to society, from anarchy to the simplest democracy." He goes on to say, however, that confusion must soon have appeared in council, universal agreement must have been impossible. Decisions of some sort were necessary. Out of this practical necessity grew the different forms of government. Then follows (§8) enumeration of democracy, aristocracy, and monarchy, with the comment (§9) that:

in these three forms of government nothing essential to society is modified, but merely the form in which the common will expresses itself, i. e., either through the majority or through the élite, or through the autocrat. . . . . Thus, just as the decisions of all were binding upon each individual, the same must be the case with the decisions of those who take the place of all. This obligation on the one side implies on the other side the right of compulsion, and irresistibility, and thus the relations between rulers and ruled, between subjects and the supreme power, were more specifically determined. Originally (§10) the use of the combined forces was determined by the will of all the citizens. Since now the supreme power combines in itself the community will, its prerogative is likewise to determine how the community energies shall best be used for the common welfare.

Gratitude is due to Sonnenfels for reducing this reasoning to such a bare skeleton that its most serious dislocation is evident. We can see at a glance, and it is hard to understand why thinkers of Sonnenfels' ability did not perceive, that this was merely an illusive collocation of a generalization about political rights, a hypothesis about historical sequence, and an utterly arbitrary begging of the essential question of fact about the institution of monarchy. This special pleading was a perfunctory excuse for taking quasi-absolutism for granted, and proceeding to inquire how to make the best of it. If each member of society has a right to his share in making up the will of the society, nothing but sheer assertion appears in Sonnenfels' reasoning to justify the conclusion that the monarch must be accepted as vicariously exercising that right for all the citizens, and must be obeyed because his will is virtually the will of all. Thus, in spite of sentiments which make for reconstruction of ideas, Sonnenfels' major premise was the same old impotent makeshift of absolutism, the presumption that royal power summarizes all the fundamental rights of citizens, and that it is a political datum back of which our theories of social technique must not pry.

In §11 Sonnenfels further elaborates his concept "welfare," and it is in this direction that we find evidences of a force that was generating as a variant both of the theory and the practice of quasi-absolutism. While criticism of the social logic summed up in benevolent despotism was not admitted into this type of social science, the concept "welfare" was becoming more intensive and was thus looming up as a factor in the modification of theory and indirectly of action. The syllabus continues:

The ultimate purpose for the sake of which men enter society is that best which they possess neither enough moral nor physical power to attain alone; which in itself considered is, to be sure, the separate best of each member. Since, however, this separate best is sought by each at the same time, and each by promoting the best of the other thereby also confirms his own, it is called the community best. The ultimate purpose of men entering into combination might be expressed therefore as the *individual best;* the ultimate purpose of combined men as the *general best.* In civic societies this best, this ultimate purpose, has been security and convenience of life, which combined constitute the *public welfare.*

Security is defined (§12) as:

a condition in which we have nothing to fear. The condition in which the state has nothing to fear is called public security, that in which no citizen has anything to fear is called private security. When the state is safe against attacks from without, the condition is called public external security, and if no danger threatens from its own citizens, there exists public internal security. If neither the state, from within nor without, nor the citizens have anything to fear, this fortunate condition is called the general security.

The convenience of life [continues the author in §13] is the facility of providing one's support by diligence. Diligence will find its support the easier the more diversified the gainful occupations. The general convenience of life depends therefore upon diversification of the gainful occupations.

The general welfare [as explained in §14] cannot be maintained without cost. . . . . The ruler must be provided with revenues, which must be in proportion to his dignity. This outlay is made for the best good of all the citizens. It is therefore proper that the expense should be borne by all the citizens, but that it should be drawn from them in a way that will promote the ultimate purpose.

Thereupon follows the definition (§15):

From manifold observations and experiences it is possible to refer the various rules through which the general welfare may be maintained, to reliable fundamental principles, and to give them the form of a science, which is *Staatswissenschaft* in the most comprehensive sense; that is, the science of maintaining the welfare of a state, the science of governing. . . . We are convinced that the problematical and the variable does not reside in the principles of the science, but in the circumstances and occurrences to which the principles are to be applied. The mere empiricist in politics is therefore as little to be regarded as a statesman as the empiricist in the healing art is to be regarded as a physician.

When Sonnenfels takes care to warn against confounding the practical administrator with the empiricist (§16), and when he describes the former as the man who is trained and experienced in applying the rules of *Staatswissenschaft* to actual conditions, he completes his demonstration that he is dealing with a technology pure and simple. Sonnenfels took for granted a certain general standard of life. He did not go to the trouble of justifying the standard, but he counted on it as a conceded major premise. Then his problem was to set forth the governmental processes by which that standard might be reached. Just as there was no question about the authority of the standard, so there was no inquiry into the assumption that responsibility for maintaining it belonged to the government. In principle, therefore, as we have said above, Sonnenfels was simply one of the series of spokesmen for the dominant régime of quasi-absolutism. His humanitarian sympathies called for qualification of the system in detail, but they did not produce the slightest variation in essentials from the typical position of the earlier cameralists.

Sonnenfels replies (§17) to the possible objection that politics is too inclusive to be the subject-matter of a science:

> The ultimate purpose of states may be divided into four cardinal subdivisions, which are connected with one another, to be sure, and must join hands with one another, each of which stops, however, with a subordinate end. *Staatswissenschaft* has accordingly been divided into four sciences, viz.: *external security; internal security; diversification of gainful occupations;* and *raising the revenues* necessary for the expenses of the state.

The first of these sciences he calls (§18) *Staatswissenschaft* in the special sense; otherwise known as *Staatsklugheit* or *Politik*. The second is his *Polizeywissenschaft* (§19). The third he calls *Handlungswissenschaft* (§20). The fourth is *Finanzwissenschaft* (§21). The extent to which this classification varies from Justi's may be seen by comparison with pp. 303 ff. above.[1]

There is a surprisingly modern appearance on the surface of §22, the last of the Introduction. It reads:

Natural science [*Naturlehre*] in all its parts, the mathematical sciences, physical geography [*Erdbeschreibung*], the history, laws, languages, are to be regarded partly as an indispensable preparation, partly as reinforcing auxiliaries of the theory of *Polizey*, *Handlung*, and *Finanz*. But the man of affairs, in actual administration, must know the customs, habits, and statutes of peoples, the reciprocal advantages and disadvantages of lands, the political conditions of states, and if he is to participate with advantage in law-giving, he must know men.

We should compare this dictum, however, with Justi's prospectus of a school for cameralists, and we should not jump to the conclusion that Sonnenfels had really advanced beyond him in discovery of the proportions and relations of governmental technology.

[1] The note to §17 is an important literary landmark, viz.: "It may be for this reason that numerous as are the writers upon special parts of *Staatswissenschaft*, the catalogue of those who have undertaken to cover the whole is extremely small, even if we add to Justi's *Staatswirthschaft*, and Bielefeld's *Institutions politiques*, St. Real's *Staatskunst* and Stewart's *Staatswirthschaft*, together with certain so-called outlines and elements of the *Polizey- und Cameralwissenschaften*, and if we honor the Aristotelian and also the Hanoverian edition of the Wolffian political books by allowing them to count as principles of *Staatswissenschaft*."

The "Stewart" mentioned in the note was evidently Sir James Steuart, and there is more than merely verbal significance in the use of the term *Staatswirthschaft* as translation of his title, *Inquiry into the Principles of Political Economy*. Probably no German was fully aware at this time that the term "Political Economy" stood for a sort of analysis which had not yet been proposed in Germany, and that its lines of demarkation ran in quite distinct directions from those of *Staatswirthschaft*.

The second chapter of Vol. I, *Polizey*, is entitled, *Fundamental Principle of Civic Science, and its Branches.*[1] The chapter begins with a brief homily quite in the spirit of its time, upon the importance of a principle to serve as an *a priori*, and the qualifications which such a fundamental principle must possess. In §24 Sonnenfels adds: "The only one who has referred *Staatswissenschaft* with all its branches to a universal principle is, so far as I know, Justi." If Roscher discovered the bearings of this remark and of the context, he certainly failed to make them plain to his readers.[2] The passage is really one of the most compact illustrations to be found, in any literature, of the crossings of judgments in a period of scientific reconstruction. If the passage had been made to order it could hardly have reflected more typically the confusion introduced into theory by attention to new valuations.

On the one hand, Sonnenfels truly interprets Justi as building his whole theory upon the principle of "general happiness" [*allgemeine Glückseligkeit*].[3] On the other hand, the point of the paragraph is its attempt to show that it is a fallacy on Justi's part to depend on such a principle. In spite of more evident sympathetic leanings than previous cameralists had shown in the direction toward which Justi's principle points, Sonnenfels rejects it as a major premise for civic science.

As we have seen, of the two men, Sonnenfels was far and away more inclined than Justi to decide, in the concrete, in favor of the alternative which promised most in the way of general happiness in the modern or democratic, as distinguished from the absolutistic, sense. Yet in this connection, instead

[1] *Hauptgrundsatz der Staatswissenschaft und ihrer Zweige.*

[2] *Op. cit.*, p. 444. Roscher leaves the impression that Sonnenfels commended Justi in this passage. The precise contrary was the fact.

[3] The sense in which Justi interpreted the concept has been discussed above, p. 323 *et passim*. Cf. Index, "Welfare."

of praising Justi, Sonnenfels really blames him. His contention is that "general happiness" cannot be made a test of civic measures, but that a more ultimate test must be found. Thus Sonnenfels deliberately commits himself to a form of reasoning which subordinates in theory the element which in the historical perspective makes him most conspicuous: and he reproves Justi for an element in his formal reasoning which had much less effect on his concrete technology than it had on that of Sonnenfels himself. As a literary landmark the passage must be cited in full. We must remember that it occurs as a part of the argument on the necessity of an adequate *logical* principle as the basis of a science. It reads:

The only one who has referred *Staatswissenschaft* with all its branches to a universal principle is, so far as I know, Justi. He assumed as such a principle the promotion of general happiness. That is a true, but not a conclusive principle. The promotion of general happiness is the object of all states, to be sure, in the period of their origin, and it is their perpetual aim; for that very reason, however, it cannot be taken as a principle of verification, or as the general fundamental, *because by means of this fundamental the goodness of the measures, which consists in their harmony with the ultimate purpose, must be tested.*

To bring out Sonnenfels' thought as distinctly as possible, we must translate the note to this section, viz.:

In his [Justi's] *Staatswirthschaft* when a law is to be given, or any other device is to be decided on, about which it is doubtful whether it would be advantageous for the state, the question is, "does the proposed law promote the general happiness?" Hereupon it must be tested by that principle, as the moral touchstone, and when the judgment of benefit or injury is reached, the ground for the judgment is given through that principle (i. e., "general happiness"). In case, therefore, the promotion of general happiness is assumed as the chief fundamental principle, the decision will amount to this: "It promotes the general happiness because it promotes the general happiness."

This passage, by the way, may serve also as a sample of the evidences which might be cited in support of the estimate above expressed of the relative intellectual strength of Justi and Sonnenfels. The former had few qualms about adopting a frankly opportunistic principle and getting the benefit of all the conclusions it would yield. The latter tried to be more profound, but succeeded only in being confused. We shall see in a moment that Justi's *a priori* was no more and no less reducible to an identical proposition than Sonnenfels' substitute. The chief meaning of the section then is its profession of faith in a deductive *a priori* rather than a functional test of social values. The next section shows how far Sonnenfels was capable of going toward a test which was absolute in form without being functional in essence. Sec. 25 is as follows:

Observation of how civic societies have arisen, and through what means they have reached their end, will more surely guide to the real fundamental principle. The isolated man was at the mercy of every attack by a superior power. His security was not greater than the forces with which he could defend himself against the attack. Two men whose physical strength exceeded his own were already dangerous to his security. He therefore sought to increase his strength by combination with others. The isolated man felt wants for the support of his life, sufficiency to satisfy which was within the compass neither of his strength of body nor of soul nor yet of his time. He sought to satisfy these wants by putting his diligence at the service of the wants of other men, from whom he received as compensation the supply of necessaries which he lacked. The isolated man was deprived of a thousand comforts, the lack of which he felt, the possession of which would make his external condition more complete. He sought the comforts through socialization [*Vergesellschaftung*] with others. The larger the society into which he was merged, the greater was the quantity of the resistance which he could exert in every case, and thereby assure his security. The more numerous the society, the more frequent its wants, the easier he found ways, by supplying what was lacking to somebody, to get trom the same person what he wanted. The more numerous the society, the more various were its products, and the easier was it for him to supply each of his wants and comforts. Through the enlarging of the society therefore, and according to its bulk, was the aim of civic societies reached, viz., *the security and comfort of life*. In later times this aim remains ever the same. The same means will also remain effective.

Continuing the argument in §26, Sonnenfels adds:

The enlargement of the society thus contains in itself all subordinate special means which in the aggregate promote the general welfare. So soon then as it is proved of an institution [*Anstalt*], or of a law that it makes for the enlargement of the society, or at least does not hinder the same; this proof at the same time carries the higher conclusion, viz., that the measure promotes, or at least does not hinder, the general welfare either on the side of security or of comfort.[1] I take, therefore, *the enlargement of civic society, through promotion of the increase of population*, as the common fundamental principle of *Staatswissenschaft*, with its included parts: and the validating principle [*Prüfsatz*] of every measure which is adopted for promotion of the general happiness is this: *Does it tend to increase or diminish population?*[2]

Further comment upon this explicit statement is unnecessary. It confirms our proposition about the uncertain character of Sonnenfels' underlying philosophy. It is not our affair to probe the logical fatuities of the cameralists beyond discovery of their actual ways of thinking. It is not even necessary to note that by turning Sonnenfels' method against himself his

[1] I will not enlarge on this unconscious confession that the author at last, in spite of himself, relied upon "general happiness," to give value to "enlargement of society," rather than the reverse. I simply let him speak for himself. (*Vide* pp. 493 and 531.)

[2] "Of that school of populationists which, after the middle of the eighteenth century, may count as a revised edition of the mercantile system, Sonnenfels is unquestionably the most important exponent in Germany."—Roscher, *op. cit.*, p. 536.

supposed ultimatum is at once reduced to the identical proposition "Promoting population is the main principle because it promotes population." We go far enough for our purpose when we find that Sonnenfels was content with the generalization that increase of population promotes the general happiness, and thereupon he persuaded himself that increase of population is the *ultima ratio* of civic science. His system turns out to be a technology in the interest now of "the general happiness," now of "the promotion of population;" with more inclination in practice than previous cameralists had shown to treat the ill-defined concept "general happiness" as the ultimate end, with corresponding tendency, inadvertent but real, to revise valuations of all means whatsoever by judgment of their adaptation to that end.

In the same connection, however, we find a methodological indication of a more gratifying kind. It adds to the evidence scheduled above to the effect that, so far as the cameralists are concerned, it is very easy to overestimate the distance between previous theories of population and that of Malthus. Thus, in §27, Sonnenfels speaks as follows:

I must seek to avoid indefiniteness. The population contains all the means which the common welfare [*gemeinschaftliche Wohlfahrt*] demands. All institutions of the ruler should accordingly be directed toward maintaining and increasing the numbers of the population. This number, nevertheless, has its limits, or a so-called maximum: and these limits are drawn by the nature of states, by the political and physical situation, and by the circumstances. Genoa will never reach the populousness of France. The bare rocks of Malta will never maintain as many inhabitants as fertile Sicily, the sandy Mark Brandenburg never so many as Bohemia. This, however, should not, on the other hand, prevent the Senate of Genoa, the Order of St. John, the king of Prussia, from using all means to assure for their territories the largest population which they are capable of supporting. If man with all his efforts can never be quite perfect, yet it always remains nevertheless a principle of morals that man must strive for the highest perfection! In politics, as in morals, if small states, less favored than others by nature, never can become as populous as those which combine larger area with rich soil, this does not invalidate the principle, *the government should always concern itself with promoting population to its highest level:* that is, the highest level which the means at its disposal make possible. This explanation will remove most of the objections which can be made against the fundamental principle of population. I come then to the application of this principle to the separate branches of *Staatswissenschaft.*

Thereupon Sonnenfels indicates, in a merely formal way, the application of this fundamental principle of population in the different divisions of the science. Thus (§§28–31):

"The greater the number of the people, the greater is the quantity of the resistance upon which the external security rests." A note adds: "The smaller states are consequently of their own strength capable of no high degree of external security. They combine with others, so that with the same, in respect to the ultimate purpose of defense, they may constitute a numerous society. Even the promptness of diplomatic action is affected by the amount of power at the command of the conferring parties." Then follow the conclusions:

(1) "Hence the fundamental principle of *Politik.*"

(2) "The greater the number of the people, upon whose ready assistance one may count, the less has one to fear from within—hence the fundamental principle of *Polizey.*"

(3) "The greater the number of people, the more the needs, hence the more various the gainful occupations within the society. The more hands, the more abundant the products of agriculture and industry, the stuff for external exchange. Hence the fundamental principle of *Handlungswissenschaft.*"

(4) "The greater the number of citizens, the more are there to help bear the public expenses. The smaller therefore is the share of each taxpayer, without decreasing the total amount of the public revenues. Consequently the fundamental principle of *Finanzwissenschaft.*"

"The knowledge of population is therefore, in all parts of public administration, indispensable. The means of surveying it, as a whole and in its parts, belong therefore to no branch of *Staatswissenschaft* exclusively. They belong as introductory knowledge to all."

If we were relying on the proof-text method of supporting a foregone conclusion, it would be somewhat difficult to explain away the formal principle either of Justi or of Sonnenfels, so as to justify their inclusion in the cameralistic series, as above defined (p. 6 *et passim*). We have not in any case relied on detached propositions, but we have attempted to interpret each writer's single propositions by the whole content of his writings. We have made his promises and his performance confront each other, and have tried to find the resultant. In fact both these writers were centered about the fiscal needs of governments, and their principles of "welfare" and "population" respectively were in effect rather less distinctive of a particular type of cameralism than regimental colors are of distinctive military tactics.

Chap. iii bears the title "*Means of Computing the Population.*" It does not profess to contain a contribution by the author to the statistical method, and is significant merely an as index of the extent to which statistical theory had impressed men of Sonnenfels' type. Beginning with the observation that, from the earliest times, whether the doctrine of population was taken as fundamental principle or not, states have been interested for practical purposes in ascertaining the size of the population, the author distinguishes two methods of computation, viz., "political calculation," and "actual enumeration." Under the former head he briefly discusses the uses and uncertainties of estimates based on (*a*) the number of deaths, (*b*) the number of births, (*c*) the consumption of grain. We need notice merely that the authors to whom Sonnenfels refers as the sources of his information about statistics are the following: Bielefeld (*sic*), *Institutions Politiques*, 1760;[1] Zanoni, "VI. Band seiner *Briefe dell' agricoltura dell' arte e del comercio, etc.;*"[2] Süssmilch,[3] Kerseboom,[4] and Melon.[5]

[1] *Vide* Roscher, p. 426, "Jacob Friedrich von *Bielfeld.*"

[2] These two writers are referred to as having furnished a brief history of political computation, tracing it back to the middle of the seventeenth century.

[3] *Göttliche Ordnung in den Veränderungen des menschlichen Geschlechts aus dem Geburt, dem Tode und Fortpflanzung derselben erwiesen.* 1st ed., 1742, 2d ed., 1761; *vide* Roscher, *op. cit.*, p. 421.

[4] *Abhandlung zu einem Versuche der wahrscheinlichen Menge des Volkes von Holland und Westfriesland*, etc.; *vide* Roscher, *op. cit.*, p. 421, "Kersseboom."

[5] *Essai politique sur le commerce*, 1734; German, 1756.

CHAPTER XIX

THE CAMERALISTICS OF SONNENFELS ("POLIZEY")

The special introduction to the first volume bears the title: "The Simplest Concepts of Polizey and Consequently an Outline in Accordance with Which They Will Be Treated."

Assuming that political institutions were, to a much greater degree than appears probable today, premeditated anticipations of evils, Sonnenfels makes this formula:

When these measures and devices are assembled, and referred to certain principles derived from the nature of the social purpose, there results the science of founding and maintaining the internal security of the state; that is, die Polizeywissenschaft.[1]

The author's own comment will best indicate the relation of this formula to previous conceptions of classification within the boundaries of *Staatswissenschaft*. He says:

"By this formula I take issue with all authors who have previously treated the subject. To a certain extent I give *Polizey* an entirely different meaning. Perhaps I should say, my reason is because the formulas hitherto offered seem to me too vague, too ill-defined, some of them too limited, not including all which belongs within the scope of *Polizey:* others too general, embracing much which does not belong in *Polizey*. My intention is not, however, to repudiate other formulas, but by means of my own to draw the proper boundaries of *Polizey* according to my own views, and to exhaust the concept. I think I have a right to demand that after the work itself has been read the judgment should be passed whether I have acted in accordance with my intention." In a note the author adds: "This intention is to treat the internal constitution of a state in its interdependence, and in all parts of the public administration, and at the same time to investigate the sources of law-giving. Consequently I shall frequently use the words *Polizey* and *Gesetzgebung* as synonymous."

[1] He refers to Montesquieu, *Esprit des loix*, Vol. I, chap. xxiv, p. 26.

Sonnenfels' further analysis of his method of treatment will afford the most direct means of comparing his outlook with that of Justi.

The author proceeds to indicate his line of approach by pointing out, first (§44):[1]

that in a certain sense *Polizey* is principally defense against either intentional or fortuitous occurrences of a harmful nature; second, every occurrence which hinders the accomplishment of the ultimate purpose of society must be regarded as harmful; third, from this point of view *Polizey* regards every transaction which does not *promote* this ultimate purpose as harmful.

In order to perform a harmful act, the will and the ability must coincide. The law-abiding man has constant opportunities to perform harmful acts, but he does not want to. The imprisoned criminal has the will to perform harmful acts, but he is deprived of ability. Hence *Polizey* falls into two parts, first, directive, the intention of which is that no one shall wish to perform harmful acts; second, preventive, which seeks to make it impossible for anyone to commit harmful acts even if he has the desire.

The will of the actor is determined by impulses [*Beweggründe*], and the more certainly and effectively the oftener the impulses toward or against an action occur, or the greater the weight of the single impulse which operates upon the actor. This is the invariable principle of will, in which alone the great secret of law-giving resides. If the law-giver only knows how to offer his people preponderating impulses toward the good, he may be assured that he may lead them as he will.[2]

The impulses to action are of two sorts—first, *attractive* [*einladend*]; second, *preventive*. Again, the nature of the advantages or disadvantages to be anticipated from actions divides impulses into *general* and *special*. The general impulses include all actors and actions. For that reason they deserve the first rank in law-giving. There is another reason, viz., there are actions in connection with which it is difficult or impossible to discover a special attractive

[1] The author's own forms of statement are now epitomized.

[2] Speaking of identical propositions!

or preventive impulse. In such a case there remains for the law-giver only the motive power of the general impulses, which may be grouped in two classes: *morals*, and *the high idea of the excellence of the laws*.

Morals, in the relation in which they are regarded by the law-giving authorities, are devotion to the general order. As Toussaint well says, "they very well supply the place of laws, but nothing is capable of supplying the place of morals." Devotion to the general order is the effect of combined institutions, which enlighten the understanding of the citizen to the end that he may pass correct judgments upon everything which affects the general order, which guides the inclinations, which controls the passions and directs them to worthy actions. The whole system of devices to this end I refer to under the phrase *attention to the moral condition*.

Next in importance is effort to propagate *a high idea of the excellence of the laws;* that is, to raise it, among all the citizens, to the rank of an accepted, incontestable principle, that whatever the laws command is good; that is, with respect to the whole, necessary; and with respect to each individual, profitable. Whenever the supreme power succeeds in establishing this presupposition, it is the most reliable guarantee for the observance of the laws, through the violation of which each will then believe that he will harm himself.

But given the willingness to obey the laws, insight into the special actions that would conform to the laws is not thereby assured. The ruler must consequently supply this lack by laws which specify what is to be done and left undone. This is what Hume had in mind when he said that the laws are to be regarded as reinforcement of the insight of the individual. The subject-matter of these laws is internal *public* and internal *private* security.

As previously defined, internal public security is a condition in which the state, that is, the public administration (*sic!*), whatever the governmental form, has nothing to fear from the citizens. Voluntary obedience to the law, and thus public security, is brought about through the devotion above discussed. Compulsory obedience springs from the consciousness of weakness against the superior powers of the sovereign, or from impossibility of resistance. What Montesquieu in another connection makes the fundamental principle of a civic structure [*Staatsverfassung*] may be applied here with great accuracy, viz., "it is essential," he says, "that through the order of nature one force holds another in check;"[1] that is, the quantity of possible powers of resistance on the side of the citizens must always be smaller than the quantity of the powers of coercion on the side of the state. Hence the chief attention of the *Polizey* and law-givers is demanded to prevent any stratum or single citizen from attaining to such power that the public authorities may be successfully opposed.

In §52 Sonnenfels repeats the definition given above of internal private security, and he proceeds:

All good, which can accrue to the citizen, all bad, whereby his happiness may be endangered, may be traced back to his business, his person, his honor, and his goods.[2]

It is difficult to understand why the elementary observations which followed upon the workings of legal mandates and sanctions were necessary or even tolerable in a university lecture-room. As we have said above in the case of Justi, the most plausible explanation is that they were of a piece with the homiletical style of the period, the method of magnifying the obvious.

The foregoing discussion furnishes the reasons for the sub-

[1] *Esprit des loix*, Vol. I, Part II, chap. iv.

[2] "*Auf seine Handlungen, Personen, auf seine Ehre, und seine Güter*." The ambiguity of the term *Handlungen* might be used as one of the *stigmata* of the untenable analysis in which it figures. The same is true of the plural *Personen*, of *Ehre* as having a possible content not gathered from the other three categories, and of *Güter*, in distinction primarily from *Handlungen*, and secondarily from the other two concepts. The classification serves as basis of the technology which follows, but the confusion which corresponds with the superficial analysis does not much affect the larger relations which we are emphasizing, and we may pass it with this notice. Sonnenfels adds the note (p. 63): "The English writers compress all into the words *Liberty* and *Property* [*Freyheit und Eigenthum*]. *Freyheit* has special connection with *Handlungen*, *Personen*, and *Ehre; Eigenthum* with *Güter*."

divisions of the book. Except in details of classification and of judgment about minor means, the remainder of the volume affords little material for our purpose. Roscher has digested the technical contents of the three volumes in which Sonnenfels varies somewhat from the other cameralists.[1] The most noticeable contrast with Justi, in respect to technique, is the creation of the division *Handlung* co-ordinate with *Polizey*, instead of treating subjects falling under the former as subdivisions of the latter. In respect to the spirit of the treatment I am able to adopt Roscher's judgments with but slight modification.[2]

"For the development of German national economy, Sonnenfels may be characterized most accurately in this way: his standpoint reminds us essentially of Justi's ideas," but he gave to the ideas an apparently firmer setting in the sort of reasoning which was conventional in his day; and he was rather more systematic in developing the consequences of the ideas. "At the same time the demands of the ought-to-be play with him a much more significant rôle than explanation of the existing. Suggestion of practical propositions is in bulk, as well as in the interest of the author, much more notable than the scientific analysis of the subjects in question."

Although we shall be led into somewhat extended discussion of numerous details, we have thus covered in principle all that our main purpose calls for in the case of Sonnenfels, and what follows amounts merely to illustrative specifications under previous propositions.

The first section in the chapter on "Attention to the Moral Condition" is worth quoting as a summary of Sonnenfels' ethical preconceptions. He says (§61):

Morals are a common subject-matter of religion, of ethics, and of law-giving; but each treats them in the light of its own purpose;

[1] *Op. cit.*, pp. 536 ff.

[2] The original should be compared, *op. cit.*, p. 536.

the first two as an end, the last only as a means, satisfied if correspondence of conduct with the laws can be procured not by the most lofty motives, but also merely by hope of an advantage or by fear of punishment. Hence arises the idea of *political virtue*, which differs from the concept of virtue demanded by *ethics* and *religion*. *Political or social virtue is the facility of ordering one's conduct in correspondence with the laws of the society.* The motor machinery, whereby this correspondence is procured, does not fall within the scope of the present explanation, since virtue of a higher order is not to be dispensed with. Meanwhile there is no ground for the anxiety that *political virtue* may be dangerous for religion and ethics [*Sittenlehre*]; that would be the case if political virtue and religious virtue were in antithesis with each other: but this is by no means the case. For the purpose of the law-giver, to be sure, the first is enough; yet the second is not thereby excluded; but to a certain extent it is presupposed by the first. A wise law-giver will always seek to base social virtue [*Gesellschaftungstugend*] upon moral virtue, yet from inadequacy of the means at his command he cannot always discover whether each member of society in practice bases his social virtue upon moral virtue. He must therefore be content to take knowledge simply of the body of the transactions, and he leaves it to the spiritual teacher to introduce the vitalizing spirit of religion.

Of course Sonnenfels is at this point merely a symptom of the ethical and theological dichotomy which still succeeds in keeping most of the population of the world under the impression that virtue is an affair of separate circuits, which may be operated independently or be brought into communication with one another. It was no peculiar demerit of his that he could treat social virtue as different in kind from ethical or religious virtue. It would simply plunge us into conflict with speculative moral philosophy in general if we should enter upon discussion of this part of the analysis. We may simply allow him to show further, in his own idiom, what working relation he presupposed between social virtue on the one hand and religious virtue on the other. In §63 he says:

The chief and most effective means for the building-up of morals are *religion*, *education*, and the *sciences*. Among these religion deserves the first place. Religion is the gentlest bond of society. Religion instructs through her venerable teachings in goodness. Religion stimulates to the application of the same through promises. Religion deters from evil actions by threats. Religion brings about thorough repentance, which she produces in the sinner, and forgiveness, which she offers to the penitent, the improvement of the vicious. Religion increases therefore the determining as well as the deterring motives. Law-giving would in countless cases find itself inadequate, if religion did not beneficently come to its aid. Whenever the eye of the law-giver, and consequently also the penalty of the judge, fails to accomplish the end, the exalted principle of the omnipresent God, as witness and judge of all, even the most secret evildoers, is the sole means of arresting evil undertakings. The whole world is consequently in agreement with Warburton, that *the doctrine of a future life of rewards and punishments is utterly indispensable for every civic society*. The ruler may not disregard this leash [*Leitriemen*] given into his hand, and he must take care that every citizen in the state has religion. From this point of view (§64) freethinking appears as a political crime, because to a certain extent it robs the state of the means of guiding its citizens most completely. The chancellor Bacon, and President Montesquieu have never been under suspicion as persecutors, yet the former writes: "No one denies God, except those who have an interest in there being no God;"[1] the latter: "From the opinion that there is no God comes our independence or our revolt."[2] Accordingly to them the atheist becomes either a criminal or a disorderly citizen. Consequently the concord and happiness of the state depend on intolerance of the declared *freethinkers;* and circumstances might often make it necessary for the public authorities to demand of everyone a visible sign of the religion "to which he adheres."[3]

[1] Sonnenfels simply refers to "*sermones fideles, etc.*"

[2] *Esprit des loix*, Vol. XXXIV, chap. ii.

[3] A note to this section reads: "During the reign of Queen Elizabeth, a penalty of twenty pounds was imposed upon anyone who absented

The argument continues (§65):

From the necessity of religion, even for the temporal happiness of the citizens, and the common security, are derived the right and the obligation of the *Polizey* to extend its attention to the education of the people in religious duties, to prevent abuses, and to watch over the external order of religious functions and worship. The instruction in the duties of religion, in the rural regions particularly, is worthy of so much attention, because with the rural population religion must largely take the place of education, and at the same time it is the only means of making an impression upon their ways of thinking. The first object to which the care of the *Polizey* should be given in this respect should be sufficient and skilful curates.[1]

On the ground of necessity for public morals, education is then discussed as a section of the duties of *Polizey*. The author says (§70):

After religion, education has the greatest influence upon morals. It is, to be sure, a peculiar duty of parents; but not only a son, a citizen is also to be educated. Education can therefore, on account of its connection with the common welfare, not be a matter of indifference to the law-giver, and cannot be left by the state to private whim. Parents must be compelled to give their children the necessary education (§71). In order that dependent children may be educated, academies, foundling and orphan asylums are necessary (§72). It is desirable that public schools should be attended by children of the upper as well as of the lower classes, for the sake of making these classes acquainted with each other (§73). Secs. 74–79 go into some detail about alternatives in the administration of foundling and orphan asylums, with respect to influence upon public

himself for a month from public worship." The authority for the statement is given as, "Hume, *Hist. de la maison de Tudor*, *Tome* V." Evidence of this and like kinds, in spite of occasional appearances to the contrary, makes it probable that, whenever English sources were cited, they were usually known to Sonnenfels by name only, or through translations, usually French.

[1] The four following sections elaborate the last proposition, and specify problems and duties for *Religionspolizey*.

morals, and §§80–82 attempt to answer the question whether it is worth while to enlighten the people through "the sciences." Sonnenfels urges instruction in the lower schools about ordinary civic duties, and he argues for favors, like separate jurisdiction, for the higher schools, in order that their prestige may be increased. Then follow hints, rather than programmes, about the availability of various minor means for promoting good morals (§§83–98); distinctions for exemplary citizens, the stage, with necessity of censorship, and as another negative means, the censorship of books. In connection with this last subject Hume is quoted,[1] to the effect that the freedom of the press is absolutely assential to England's form of government, in order that mind and talent may without any hindrance act in defense of liberty. "But," answers Sonnenfels, "this author himself admits that this same means allows the spirit of resistance, of revolt, and other harmful influences to be spread abroad. He consequently holds the censorship as necessary for other forms of government, especially for the ecclesiastical state. Perhaps we are justified in replying to the Englishman, that the goodness of a constitution which is capable of preservation only by such dangerous means, must be very equivocal."

But Sonnenfels presently reaches conclusions which have a firmer psychological basis, whatever be the estimate of them in current economic or political theory. In §100 he begins with the premise that law-giving wisdom must provide the general and special means of preventing vagrancy and idleness in general. The previous §99 lays down, as a major premise for this dictum, the proposition that idleness produces immorality. Whether we should agree or not with the inference that the government must prevent idleness, there is little doubt among social theorists today that an occcupation is one of the primary conditions conducive to morality in Sonnenfels' sense of the term. The special arrangements which he recommends for repressing idleness fall under the heads: prevention of begging; careful inspection to see that everyone in the state

[1] *Political Essays*, Vol. II, Part I, "Essay on the Liberty of the Press."

is earning a living; checking of all useless occupations akin to vagrancy; diminution of the number of students (because in Austria they were said to be in excess of the positions requiring highly educated men); good discipline of the servant class (§§107–14), and as a means of making all these efforts efficient well-ordered workhouses and penal institutions (§§119–21). Everything of the nature of free soup, and indiscriminate alms-giving, including gifts to begging students, is protested against almost in the spirit of modern scientific charity (§§101–6). The degree to which Sonnenfels relies on constraint, as compared with his belief in attractive measures, is noticeable at every step. The second phase of laws relating to the servant class, viz., their protection against unjust employers, is treated in §§115, 116; and the third phase, provision for reducing the number of the unemployed servant class, in §§117, 118. While he emphasizes the danger to good morals from all tolerance of pandering to sexual vice, Sonnenfels has only the following as a programme (§122):

All that can be demanded of a reasonable *Polizey* is, not that its attention shall be carried to the extreme of increasing its numbers for the purpose of spying and house-visitation, nor that by excessive severity toward weaknesses it shall give occasion for greater and more dangerous crimes, but that the *Polizey* shall restrict itself to preventing public indecency, and outbreaking offenses, and that it shall co-operate with parents, relatives, married people, who make complaints about seduction of their relatives, or disturbance of domestic order. Beyond that, religion, education, and reduction of the number of the unmarried must do the most toward the restriction of an evil which it will be possible for no foresight entirely to uproot.

Finally the chapter concludes with this omnibus paragraph (§123):

The *Polizey* must, however, exert itself to remove all occasions through which, directly or indirectly, moral disorders of another sort may be increased. Here belong, for lessening drunkenness, and the evils that flow from it, the restriction of the number of dram shops; the ordinance that after a certain hour (at night) nothing more shall be sold in such shops, and at no time to intoxicated persons; exemplary punishments for confirmed drunkards; prohibition of lodging strangers except in recognized inns; and further, measures approved by monarchs of insight, and readily granted by a head of the church worthy of immortality, viz., for decrease of the number of feast days. For it is certain that all time devoted to labor will be rescued from vice and excess.

The spirit of chap. ii, "On the Means of Awakening a High Idea of the Laws," may be indicated very briefly. The fundamental proposition is that:

"on the average in a nation high respect for the law will be less a result of persuasion than of antecedently formed opinion, that is, of a favorable prejudice" (§124). This prejudice must be aroused and strengthened. It may be weakened or destroyed. The means in either case are in the hands of those who give the laws. In republics, where laws are examined by representations of the people before they are enacted, the presumption of the goodness of the laws springs from the *nature of the constitution*. That is, it is supposed that the law would have been rejected if its advantages had not been beyond all doubt. In monarchies, that which occurs in republics before the acceptance of a law should occur at the promulgation of the same. This may take place in two ways—first, by giving assurance that consultation with estates, parliaments, councilors, etc., preceded the decree; second, that every law should have a preamble, setting forth the reasons why it was necessary for the public weal and beneficial for the individual. "A government which imposes upon itself the rule of accompanying its laws, so far as possible, with reasons, shows confidence in its measures, honors the intelligence and integrity of the citizens, appears less to command than to persuade. The people itself imagines that it obeys less the law than its own insight." Again (§128) it is added: "Even if the law bears only some such legend as 'moved by the public good,' the people will be inclined to believe it." Furthermore, the conviction which assumes that the laws are good is produced by laws of great age, and the *invariability* of laws is the condition of their attaining great age (§129). Conflicting interpretations of the law by experts weaken the presumption in its favor (§131). Nothing weakens the prestige of the laws more than a distinction between obligation before the judge, and absence of obligation in conscience (§132).

Chap. iii, "On Provision for Holding Private Powers in a Subordinate Equilibrium with the Powers of the State," may also be epitomized very briefly. The main proposition is that:

the powers of resistance on the side of the citizens must always be kept inferior to the powers of compulsion on the side of the state (*sic*) (§136). This persistent antithesis between the citizens and the state is one of the most essential traits of the pre-democratic political philosophy. "The forces or means, which might hinder the state in the exercise of its powers, consist of ***wealth***, of the ***strength of a stratum of society***, and of ***privileges***." "While security of property is one of the principal advantages to be gained by civic society, wisdom seeks to prevent the accumulation of excessive private wealth" (§138).[1] It is not wise to prescribe the limits of wealth which individuals or families may possess (§139); but the state may set precise bounds to the wealth of deathless societies. "This necessity has been recognized in all states,[2] especially since Edward I set the example with his 'amortization laws' " (§140). "In case the laws have neglected to provide against too great accumulation of wealth in families, indirect measures may be adopted with advantage to correct the evil; as when Henry VII of England *allowed* the division of the estates of the nobility among several sons. If he had ordered the division, it would have been resisted. The permission was regarded as beneficent. Similar indirect measures may be taken to limit the growth of deathless societies (§141); and parallel action is wise in the case of societies, parties, and organizations of many sorts which tend to acquire excessive power (§142 ff.). Secs. 149 ff. deal with cases in which sedition of more or less violent sort breaks

[1] Hume is again cited rather vaguely, p. 181.

[2] Illustration cited from Hume, "*Leben Edwards I*," *Geschichte von England*, *T*. 2.

out, from actual violation of laws against accumulation of riches or power, to reflections on the government by public speakers, preachers, teachers, actors, writers, etc.; and different kinds and degrees of censorship by the police are rather vaguely recommended. The duties of the police in case of disorderly assemblies are rather hinted at than specified (§§155 ff.).

Chap. iv, "On Security of Action," is notable, first, because it gives evidence that some of the concepts of an innovating popular philosophy were beginning to call for attention in one of the more conservative universities of the German countries. Sonnenfels begins by saying that "security of action" and "freedom of action" are identical ideas. "They refer to the condition in which we have nothing to fear with respect to our actions." Thereupon he undertakes an analysis of the distinctions to be made between "freedom," "licentiousness" [*Zügellosigkeit*], and "independence" [*Unabhängigkeit*]. The presuppositions of his argument are, first, "the laws of nature;" second, "the social compact." These make "freedom" a limited, not an absolute condition, and *per contra* they estop licentiousness and independence. Regardless of the method of the argument, the author urges the sane view, which he phrases after Pope, that "he who obeys reason is free." He finds that reasonable freedom or security of action may be endangered, first, by the ruler, considered as law-giver and judge; e. g., when he transgresses the limits of the law-giving power, or when he falsely accuses, or unfairly conducts a process in court; second, by fellow-citizens in various relations. The succeeding discussion of the limits of the law-giving and judicial power is literary rather than technical, but it marks a rising tide of demand for laws and administration of them, in conformity with needs which citizens feel to be reasonable. In this connection (§§165–69), Sonnenfels presents his famous objections to torture as a judicial measure. The infringements upon security of action by fellow-citizens are scheduled under the heads, "servitude," "chattel slavery," "constraint by parents, guardians, etc." (§§171-75).

Chap. v, "On the Security of the Person" (§§176-293), covers a wider range of detail with a greater number of specific topics, than any other main division of the book. Although in many cases it indicates rather definite policies about particular problems, yet on the whole it has rather the force of a catalogue of subjects than of a codification of rules. Its importance is technological, and a proper estimate of its value could be made only by technologists in the different subjects of which it treats. It does not furnish material which falls directly within the scope of our inquiry. It should be said, however, that it is another remarkable reflection of the degree of attention which German administrative theory had already given to details affecting public welfare. It discusses a surprising number of relations by which physical well-being is affected. These range from crimes of violence, to methods of relieving poverty, caring for the sick, promoting public hygiene, and securing pure food or pure air. It should be noticed too that the chapter includes a strong and explicit argument against toleration of duelling, and also against all methods of procuring abortions. In the latter connection Sonnenfels shows farsighted views about the policy which the government should pursue toward mothers of illegitimate children.

Chap. vi, "Security of Honor" (§§294-304), proposes to treat of honor "considered as respect for the integrity [*Rechtschaffenheit*] of a citizen." The viewpoint is indicated by the propositions: "Whatever deprives the citizen of honor, therefore, robs him of actual advantages, harms him seriously: and the legal authority is bound to defend every citizen against such injuries." The chapter accordingly specifies the following subjects which should be taken into account in applying the principle: supposed hereditary dishonor (§§295-97); supposed dishonor on account of certain occupations, court servants, spies, executioners, etc. (§298); loss of honor through insult and slander (§§300–303); loss of honor through seduction (§304). It should be observed that, whatever be the value of the means recommended in these connections, the content of private and public welfare in particulars of which this chapter contains samples was much more justly estimated in the German civic theories of the cameralistic period than in the practice of modern democracies. We have by no means improved in all particulars upon the civic theories of the eighteenth century.

Chap. vii, "On Security of Goods" (§§305–51), contains nothing that calls for special remark, except that it groups with the crimes against property as ordinarily understood, various injuries to possessions through oversight [*Versehen*] (§§337 ff.). Under the latter head, Sonnenfels discusses protection against damage by fire, including building-ordinances, fire-departments, fire-insurance, protection against lightning, use of firearms and fireworks, ordinances against vagrants, and various minor devices.

Chap. viii, "On Penalties" (§§352–88), although not strictly pertinent to our purpose, deserves brief notice because it contains symptoms of the independence of thought about details which led Roscher to apply the term "eclectic."[1]

Sonnenfels begins by questioning the sufficiency of Grotius' explanation of legal penalties, viz.: "Punishment is an evil of sensation because of malice of action." The author comments:

> This aphorism, handed down from writer to writer, has given a one-sided direction to reflection upon the subject. The viewpoint from which the judge who enforces the penalty regards it, and that of the law-giver who ordains it are quite different. The first punishes because the law was disobeyed. The second threatens a penalty in order that the law may not be disobeyed. With the former the

[1] *Vide* pp. 481 ff. above.

penalty is a consequence of the conduct. With the latter the conduct is a consequence of the penalty. With the first the affixing of penalty is inculpation, with the second it is stimulus. Penalty therefore, considered as an auxiliary, to protect the law, namely, by exerting an influence upon the resolutions of actors, and by supplying the place of other determining motives, is *an evil which is attached to the law as a means of influencing against infraction of the same.* In determining penalties, attention is to be paid, first, to the quantity; second, to the kind of the same.

The attempt to find a principle on which to decide the former question proceeds by considering four possible criteria, viz., the conduct itself, its relation to the state, its consequences, or its motives; and it reaches the conclusion (§357): "The general means of measuring punishment is, therefore, to be sought only in the motives of the crime." The following specifications are deduced:

"(1) The penalty must be as great as necessary to procure the lawful action or restraint; (2) The penalty must not be greater than necessary to procure the lawful action; (3) The strongest deterring motive, that is, the most effective penalty, will always be that which threátens an evil in direct antithesis with the motive which solicits to the crime." In explaining the application to be made of these principles, Sonnenfels recurs to his classification of evils to be avoided, or of "securities" to be gained. As the evils have reference in turn to civic freedom, honor, goods, and corporal integrity, the penalties should correspond. Thus, they should be variations of—"loss of all civic rights; loss of social standing [*Standesrechte*]; loss of rights of the family; loss of legal rights; or, in special cases, banishment from the country; expulsion from the locality; infamy; degradation [*Standesentsetzung*]; confiscation of goods; fines; corporal punishment, from minor inflictions to the death-penalty."

Respecting the extreme penalty, Sonnenfels energetically opposes the prevailing opinions and practices. He repeats the theorem which he had published in 1764:

Death penalties are contrary to the purpose of penalties. Hard, incessant public labor promises much more for that purpose, and at the same time makes the punishment of the criminal profitable for the state.[1]

One paragraph in particular, in discussion of this question, is notable more for its wider implications than for its immediate bearings. Whether its author was aware or not that he was betraying tendencies which were ominous for the old régime, it is evident enough from our present viewpoint that we have here one of the signs that absolutistic preconceptions were losing some of their hold. On justification of the right of capital punishment the author says (§377):

The first question which must be investigated is without doubt in respect to the *right*. Has the law a *right* to punish with death? If questions have been raised over this point, it was because writers have fawned upon princes, and have sought the source of this right in no one knows what form of a majesty derived immediately from heaven, and assigned to them an unlimited right over life and death. The source of this awful right is to be sought nowhere except in the individual man, whose combination constitutes the state. Man, thought of in the natural condition, has the right to protect his security in every way, and if the violence of attack cannot otherwise be warded off, it is his right to carry his defense even to the death of the assailant. In civil society each separate member has made over this right of defense to the whole, that is, to the sovereign power that represents the whole; that is, not a right over his own life, which no one possesses, but the right of each over the life of every other who might become an assailant. In that way the sovereign power acquired the right over all.

Our concern is not with the validity of this reasoning, but with the fact that Sonnenfels exhibited a tendency to think

[1] Reference is made to "*die vortreffliche Abhandlung des Marchese Beccari: Von Verbrechen und Strafen,*" which appeared almost simultaneously with the publication of Sonnenfel's first edition, and supported his position on this subject.

for himself about certain parts of the traditional philosophy of the state.

The purpose of chap. ix, "On Institutions for Maintaining Internal Security," is particularized in the opening paragraph (§389), viz.:

Under the name institutions we include all persons and devices which aim at prevention and discovery of every action harmful to civic security, including the higher as well as the lower stations and functionaries that have to do in any way with guarding the peace, with detecting seditious intentions, or dangerous persons, and finally everything which has to do with punishment of the same.

As a survey of the civic structure which all the cameralists have contemplated with variations of detail, the following paragraph (§390) is useful, viz.:

As the prerogatives of *Polizey* have been treated in this work, the law-giving as well as the executive power lies within the scope of its functions. The supreme administration of the same can consequently be accredited only to the highest station in the state, whatever be the name under which it exists. This is the directing guidance of the state, where the principal laws and ordinances are enacted. Execution, however, is, according to the variety of the objects, committed to subordinate divisions. Moreover, the public administration usually subdivides affairs, and retains for itself law-giving, at least in general affairs of the country, or respecting other more important matters; it turns over the civil and criminal judiciary functions to special bodies, or so-called *Stellen*, and restricts the operations of *Polizey* in the narrower sense to maintenance of the public peace, good order, and discipline, to superintendence over measures, weights, markets, cleanliness of cities, institutions necessitated by the various dangers and accidents, and especially over everything which demands emergency action. Since mention has already been made of the different judicial offices, it remains for this chapter to treat only of this last significance of *Polizey*.

The chief difference between Justi and Sonnenfels in this division of the subject is not that they disagree in principle, but that Sonnenfels has scheduled a larger number of concrete details to which the principles apply, and that these specifications have the effect of considerably extending the apparent consequences of the principles. A striking instance of this is the argument for abolition of places of refuge (§§410–15).

Chap. x, "Use of the Institutions in Case of Great Accidents" furnishes a sort of title for activities which in the nature of the case cannot be thoroughly analyzed nor formulated, and no very explicit prescriptions about them are possible. The reference is to occurrences which may be anticipated in kind, but cannot be foreseen in time and place, and cannot be averted by human power. The sort of foresight to be exercised is suggested by the questions, What sort of accidents are probable in a given locality? How does the situation affect the probability of such accidents? What variations of the probability are there at different times? Among such accidents, which permit of provisional prevention? Then action with reference to such accidents may be in part thought out in advance by dividing the calamity into stages, and by determining the sort of conduct appropriate in each, viz., (1) before the actual case; (2) during the same; (3) after the same. As an illustration, Sonnenfels takes the case of a freshet in the Danube at Vienna, and specifies a programme for minimizing the calamity, before, during, and after. It is evident that this sketch is not a mere academic exercise, but it has the same importance for civic conditions which the plans of a commissary department have for an army.

With reference to the volume as a whole the curious fact is to be noted that no one who had not been advised of the author's alleged fundamental principle would discover a sign of it in any paragraph of the book after the passage in which it is discussed in the abstract.[1] From that point it disappears, and no use is made of it whatsoever. A student of Justi who

[1] *Vide* above, p. 500.

omitted the first forty-two sections of the present volume, and carefully studied the remaining three hundred and ninety, would probably find no occasion for doubting that Sonnenfels was completely in accord with his predecessor in making "the general happiness" the criterion of civic procedure. The argument does not close here, to be sure, and the author will find a use for his alleged criterion later. We shall return to the subject, and shall find it instructive about the unsettled condition of the philosophy of which it was a symptom.

CHAPTER XX

THE CAMERALISM OF SONNENFELS ("HANDLUNG")

The title-page of Sonnenfel's second volume, *Handlung*, is identical with that of Vol. I, *Polizey*, except that the vignette represents "Fortbonnais."[1] If Sonnenfels did not translate Forbonnais' term *commerce* by the word *Handlung*, the scope of his book would call for the version "industry," in the more general sense connoted by ordinary American usage, not in the more technical sense of the German "*Industrie*." Although the activities discussed include gainful occupations in general, Sonnenfels prefers to consider them as "commerce," and that term will be used as a translation of his word *Handlung*. If all the passages in which it occurs were collated, they would show a curious lack of precision in his analysis. To what extent this classification of economic activities of different kinds under a name proper to some of them and not to others is cause or effect of important economic misconceptions is a query which we merely register, without attempting to offer an answer.

This second part is very largely a discussion of technical phases of different kinds of business, more than investigation of economic principles at the basis of all business. The introductory portions of the book, however, show traits that are highly useful in marking theoretical tendencies.

The Preface declares that this "outline of political commercial science[2] was not written for men in business, whose

[1] On p. 4 of the Preface the edition of Forbonnais' book which Sonnenfels used is referred to as "*Elémens du Commerce, zweyte Leydner Auflage.*"

[2] *Umriss der politischen Handlungswissenschaft.* I have not found this expression in the earlier cameralists. It seems to me to be in itself a sign that there was increasing instability in the notions of classification

theories have been established by long experience, and have become complete. If I wish to leave the book in their hands, it is only in order that I may be corrected by them if any errors have escaped my knowledge."

The Preface continues:

> My ambition limits itself to the young friends to whom my calling commissions me as a guide. If I have in some measure smoothed their way to their duty, if I have made their preparation for their calling easier, I have accomplished my purpose.

As an index of the intellectual conditions within which Sonnenfels wrote, the next paragraph is instructive, viz.:

> There is no lack, to be sure, of thorough writings on the subject of commerce. The English and the French have always recognized the importance of a subject which may be regarded as the foundation of public welfare[1] [*der öffentlichen Wohlfahrt*], since through multiplication of means of subsistence it is the basis of population. The greatest men in all sciences, publicists [*Staatskündige*], historians, philosophers, have made contributions to the explanation of commerce. Mathematicians have believed that they were no less useful to the world and to their fatherland when they spoke of the advantages of a cloth factory than when they analyzed the profound theory of the infinite. Their writings meanwhile are rather for the already educated readers than for beginners. It appears that men of such ability have been unable to put themselves on the level of the untrained. Hence the obscurity of their writings. They presuppose knowledge of which the uninitiated have no comprehension. The latter cannot grasp conclusions from principles which they do not understand.

and methodology. Although Sonnenfels is far from generalizing economic problems in the spirit of an abstract science, the prominence and relative independence of business questions, as distinguished from fiscal problems, is a still more meaning sign that general economic problems were approaching the threshold of consciousness.

[1] Perhaps it is mere fancy, but in Sonnenfels' usage this expression seems to me to connote a less governmental and more popular center of gravity for the concept "welfare" than was indicated by the corresponding terms of the earlier cameralists.

The profound author of the *Elements of Commerce* declares at the outset that he did not write for those who read only to save themselves the trouble of thinking. If Forbonnais would admit only thinking readers, did he reflect that his excellent book would remain almost unread? I take the liberty of confessing that my intention is precisely the opposite of his. I write for those who are not yet capable of thinking for themselves on this subject. This book is to introduce them to it. My purpose is to prepare readers for Forbonnais.

Sonnenfels presently schedules the Austrian literature of the subject as follows:

The catalogue of writings to which we can make claim as a national possession may be read at a glance. It comprises in all *Oesterreich über alles*—mostly credited to Horneck, but partly to Becher;[1] Schrötters *Fürstliche Schatz- und Rentkammer;*[2] Meixner's *Anmerkungen über die Beschaffenheit der k. k. Erblande:*[3] a book which only arouses the wish that such a work might be undertaken by a more competent and better informed man; and an anomymous book entitled, *Wahre und vortrefliche Mittel, wodurch die k. k. Erbkönigreiche und Länder in einen glücklicheren und florissanteren Zustand gesetzt werden könnten*, under which much-promising inscription everyone would be likely to expect more than five pieces[4] which are shoved together without connection as without choice, and of which, for the author's sake, I will attribute the much-professing title to one of the usual publishers' tricks to make eight paltry sheets salable.

[1] *Vide* pp. 129 ff. above. [2] *Vide* pp. 135 ff. above.

[3] Not mentioned by Roscher.

[4] Sonnenfels' note: "I. *Beweis, dass es den österreischen Fabriken eben so leicht seyn werde, ein Konsumme in Pohlen zu finden, als der Churbrandenburg.* II. *Gründliche Anleitung zu regelmässiger Sprengung fester Steinfelsen u.s.w.* III. *K. K. Verordnung Kirchengelder und Kirchenrechnungen.* IV. *Ganser's Abhandlung von Torferde.* V. *Vorschlag zur Beleuchtung der Städte.*" The author adds: "This Preface was written in 1769. Since that time several works have been written which have relations to the Austrian states."

Four books, or eight, if we reckon Becher's *Bedenken von Manufacturen in Deutschland*,[1] von Vogemont's (or Bogemont's) *Deutschlands vermehrten Wohlstand*, Boden's *Fürstliche Machtkunst*,[2] and Jörger's *Vota Cameralia*, from all of which no one would be able to gather particularly important information. These are all of this species, however, which Austria up to this time has to show. The rest of Germany is not rich in writings of distinction, while other nations are taught about all parts of commerce and finance by the most excellent works.[3]

Not less instructive is Sonnenfels' hypothesis in explanation of Austria's backwardness in this respect (Preface, p. 8):

This lack may have its cause chiefly in the difficulty of access to those sources which occasion the speculations of writers, which guide them, which must necessarily be made fundamental by them, in so far as their works are not to remain merely indecisive and mostly inapplicable thoughts. The strength and population, the condition of commerce, of manufactures, the various changes, the occasions of the same, the hindrances, the encouragements, the increase of diligence, the condition of the public revenues, of the national credit, all this is in other states known in detail, either from public registers and tables, or it is readily made known to those who desire to inform themselves about these matters. Competent men then look upon it as their duty not to withhold from the state their observations about the same, and their advice. In this way, as it were, a whole nation unifies its insight. The number of its councilors is in certain respects not smaller than the number of its thinking patriots.

With us such facts are still regarded as state secrets. There

[1] I am unable to explain this title except on the assumption that Sonnenfels quoted from memory and meant the *Diskurs*. *Vide* above, pp. 109 ff.

[2] *Vide* above, pp. 170 ff.

[3] It is to be noticed that Sonnenfels does not claim Justi's *Staatswirthschaft* for Austria, although it was a product of the author's work in that country. It was not devoted particularly to *Handlung*, to be sure, but covered the subject to such an extent that the omission is surprising.

may be many important grounds for this reticence, which are unknown to me. Meanwhile I can cite this secrecy in general as the cause of that dearth of political writings, the number of which I wish to increase by publishing these elements. My merit may perhaps be very slight, if a one-sided estimate is put upon the worth of my labor. If, however, judgment is so generous as to consider the intention, the endeavor, to be useful at my post, I have thereby earned at least a certain measure of thanks.

In the evolution of the methodology of the social sciences in Germany, no writer seems to me more symptomatic than Sonnenfels of the tendency toward transition from a technology of civic management, with the interests of quasi-absolutistic governments as the determining aim and norm, to a technology in which a co-ordinate position among the aims and norms would be assigned to the interests of economic production, and of popular welfare in a more modern sense than that which was the content of the concept "welfare" in the philosophy of the quasi-absolutists. For this reason, the entire introduction to this volume—*Handlung*—must be adopted into this survey. The alternative title given to the volume at this point is: *Elements of the Science of Commerce*, and the particular subject of the introduction is "The Simplest Concepts of Commerce, and its Branches."[1]

From one point of view, the work in a pure science upon which all the subsequent details and applications are based, is discovery of the categories in which the facts of the science have to be thought. The methodology of a positive science is a rhythmic reaction between observation of isolated facts and generalization of those facts into categories. From any stage of discovery the way to an advanced stage is through processes of further analysis of facts and assembling new facts, to learn whether the relationships in which the facts occur are

[1] *Grundsätze der Handlungswissenschaft, Einleitung. Die einfachsten Begriffe des Handels und seine Zweige.*

generalized in a valid manner in the categories in use. A history of economic science might with advantage be written as an expansion of this proposition. Logically antecedent to all quantitative formulation of economic laws must be static formulation of the structural phases of economic processes. Whatever other merits or demerits may be attributed to the Smithian type of economic theory, it was the most potent factor in nineteenth-century thinking in stimulating analysis of the elementary economic relationships, and of bringing into use relatively precise terms as symbols of those relationships.

In other words, a first step in passing from every less critical to a more critical stage of a positive science consists in displacing less adequately analyzed categories for more adequately analyzed categories, as the qualitative conceptions of the science. From our present point of view, the value of Sonnenfels' introduction to this second volume consists in its exhibit of such economic categories in a relatively early stage of their evolution. Their crudity is cumulative evidence in support of our theorem that the cameralists are radically misunderstood if we interpret them as economists in the classical sense of the term. They were political scientists in whose minds distinct economic categories were not differentiated until the Smithian influence became a variant of German thinking. Sonnenfels' own language is the most effective commentary on this thesis which could be cited. We translate his introduction in full:

The beneficent influence of commerce upon general happiness [*allgemeine Glückseligkeit*] was long overlooked by political philosophy [*Staatsklugheit*]. No attention, no care, no promotion was supposed to be due to this subject. Not as though Alexander, even in the irresistible course of his victories, had not cast a glance upon commerce, and after the destruction of Tyre had not built Alexandria as the emporium of eastern and northern wares: but ministers and monarchs recognized in the son of Philip only the conqueror, and only in that character did he seem worthy of imitation. Charles V, Sully, Elizabeth, Colbert first enlightened cabinets about the true advantages of commerce. World-wisdom lent statecraft its insight. Men who had received from Providence the calling of being teachers of the nations instructed the world on this subject in deathless writings. Finally, as the principle gained prevalence—*the happiness of the state consists in the number of its citizens*[1]—people began to recognize the worth of a business [*Geschäft*] which, through multiplication of the means of support, contributes such a large portion to this happiness. Thereupon commerce became an affair of the cabinets. Attention was given to the principles *by whose application the largest number of people may be supplied with occupation.* The collection of these principles constitutes the *political science of commerce.*[2] Mercantile [*die kaufmännische*] science is distinguished from this subject, because the private merchant has for his purpose the increase of his own private means, without thought whether thereby anything accrues to the general advantage of the state, or whether the general advantage is endangered. Yet the *political* commerce by no means works against private advantage. The former seeks to use the latter as a tool to subordinate it as a means to the general end: that is, to combine the advantage of the state with that of the individual citizen.[3]

[1] *Vide* above, pp. 500 and 523. This is the first recurrence of the proposition.

[2] *Die politische Handlungswissenschaft.* The phrase is a snapshot at the struggle for survival among concepts. The predominant problem still was, What shall the government do about commerce? There was not yet independent analysis of commerce itself, apart from state policy.

[3] Sonnenfels' note to this paragraph is not a model of lucidity, but it must be quoted to complete the evidence which we must consider in deciding about the precise stage in the process of critical analysis which the author represents. The note is on the phrase, *politische Handlungswissenschaft*, and it reads as follows: "The multiplication of means of support, through advantageous exchange of that which nature [*das Erdreich*] and diligence produce, is taught by *Handlungswissenschaft*," (the adjective "political" does not appear at this point). With reference

The occupation [*Beschäftigung*] of human beings has for its purpose the placing in their hands the means whereby they may provide their support. They derive this support through receiving something as compensation for that which they produce by their occupation.[1] Thus *barter* comes into existence, and this is the business of commerce in the most proper sense (§2).

What one should accept as a compensation for that which one has given must be of such character that one *wants it.* Want [*Bedürfen*] is here not to be understood in the restricted sense which misanthropic worldly-wise have given to the word. Desire [*Verlangen*] for greater comfort, the means to gratify this desire, the ability to find pleasure in possession and enjoyment of the same, are not without a purpose in the plan of nature. They are, to the same extent, not without a purpose in the plan of *Staatsklugheit* (*vide* §10 below). Want [*Bedürfniss*] means accordingly everything the use of which can give us advantage of any sort whatever, the possession of which is meanwhile desired; and these wants, whether they are real wants, without which human beings could not exist, or imaginary wants, which the customary mode of life, the standard of comfort or enjoyment, the pride of men, have made

to this definition, and to the paragraph just quoted, the work proceeds (Vol. II, p. 3): "This explanation appears to vary from the ordinary one; i. e., the most advantageous exchange of products. In fact, however, it leads to the same. For precisely this more advantageous exchange occurs in order to keep a great number of people employed. Moreover, exchange itself is the business of commerce, and in this fact is to be found the explanation of the science which guides this business. Commerce will also be regarded as the means of increasing the resources [*Vermögen*] of the state. The increased wealth of the state is a constant consequence of commerce, but not the ultimate purpose in the estimate of the state to which riches without citizens would be useless."

[1] Even the word "produce" is likely to have the effect of an anachronism when used as a translation of terms employed at this period. The word in this case is "*hervorbringen.*" "*Erzeugen,*" "*erzielen*" (*vide* below, pp. 534, 551, and 558), "*verdienen,*" "*gewinnen,*" and similar synonyms, with their derivatives, occur without the precise technical force of the English "produce," "production," etc.

desirable, are equally an object of exchange through which wants are traded for wants (§3).[1]

If that which one can give for that which is offered were of such a sort that it were everywhere found in abundance, it would have no compensating worth, and by means of it, therefore, no exchange could occur. The object offered in exchange must accordingly be something which he, with whom the exchange is to occur, wants and does not possess, or at any rate does not possess *in the quantity* which he desires. That is, it must be relatively rare. Commerce is thus a business which owes its origin to a reciprocal want. What one may offer to another for the satisfaction of a want, is called a ware [*Waare*] (§4).

In the exchange of wares many sorts of hindrances presently appear. It is possible that he who desires to acquire a ware cannot offer for it precisely the ware which the other party wants at the moment, or in the quantity in which it is offered, and the offered ware is either entirely incapable of division, or the division diminishes its worth. In such a case one must seek to secure what one wants through a series of exchanges. Then again, that which one possesses may be of such a nature that it cannot, without difficulty or deterioration, be transferred from one place to another; the want may be so imperative that one cannot wait for the circuit of exchanges. These difficulties presently led men to look around for a means by which the difficulties might be avoided, and exchange be made easy. Something was sought which might, as it were, take the place of all wares, and be regarded as a universal equivalent [*Entgelt*] for the same. Not any stuff whatever could be adopted arbitrarily as such equivalent. Each of the qualities which was sought in the same should be a recourse against one of the indicated difficulties of exchange, and these difficulties pointed to that stuff in which the qualities were found united (§5).

In order to relieve wants in as small portions as was necessary

[1] In a context of this sort *Bedürfnisse* might more properly be rendered "necessities," but in other cases the translation "want" is nearer to the sense. I use it, therefore, as the most available equivalent, although the subjective and objective phases of the words cannot always be fitted in the translation to the original.

according to circumstances, that which was adopted as the general equivalent must necessarily be capable of very great divisibility without loss of worth. Since, especially after the extension of commerce, the objects of exchange often had to be carried long distances, durability and imperishability were demanded, both in order that in the exchange itself, or in going from hand to hand, it might not be used up, and also in order that, without danger of deterioration, it might be saved up. In order that the carriage should not be difficult it must be rare. In this way a small piece became an equivalent for a considerable bulk of wares. At the same time a great sum could be sent in a small space. But it is probable that only after many unsuccessful attempts would the peoples discover the combination of these qualities in the precious metals, which had elsewhere been sought in vain. And therein lies the cause of the almost universal agreement of the nations about gold and silver, which now are regarded as the representatives of wares, and are called money (§6).

After the introduction of money, to be sure, the turn-over [*Umsatz*] was no longer called barter,[1] but purchase. But this change in the words (*sic!*) did not essentially change the "commerce." The money did not thereby come otherwise into consideration than in so far as it represented those wants, or wares, which at another time could be procured for it. The thing accomplished by the "commerce" is still always the exchange of one ware for another, or for the representative of a ware (§7).

Wares with which exchange is effected are either immediately usable in their original form, or they must be transformed for use by artificial labor. The occupation which devotes itself to obtaining [*Erzielung*] the former is rural management [*Landwirthschaft*]. It embraces the natural produce of the earth, of grazing, and of the waters. The occupation which makes the natural products usable through imparting an artificial form, or which multiplies their use, is called *Manufaktur*.[2] The manu-

[1] In the previous sections Sonnenfels had several times used the same word—*Tausch*—in the more general sense of "exchange." This is the first time in which the restricted meaning is strictly correct.

[2] In a note the author adds: "Purists" (I do not know whether his use of the term "Puritaner" in this sense was an intentional or an uncon-

factures are dependent upon land management. The first attention of the state must therefore be given to this latter. What land management furnishes to the manufactures is called raw materials or stuffs (§8).

The original commerce consists therefore in the produce of the earth and of artificial labor,[1] so far, that is, as both come to the assistance of wants; and in those who devote themselves with their produce, who furnish the means, of providing in turn their own wants. This enables us to determine the extent of general commerce. It is equal to the sum of the wants of all consumers [*Verzehrenden*].[2] In order to extend commerce, either the wants or the consumers must be increased (§9).

The wants of human beings, as already observed, are very limited, if we attach to the word the strictest concept of *real* wants. But in that case the occupations of the citizens will be kept within the same narrow bounds. The multiplication of wants occurs through introduction of comforts and of superfluity, both of which make luxury. All declamations against luxury, therefore, are either not well considered, or the objections which are urged against it are not really directed so much against luxury, as against the one-sided wastefulness on the part of a few, while the other portion of the nation ekes out a miserable existence. Luxury, in so far, on the one hand,

scious solecism) "in the vocabulary of commerce speak of *Manufaktur* when hammer and fire are not used, as *Tuchmanufaktur, Cottonmanufaktur*. On the other hand, where these two are necessary, that is called *Fabriken, Stahlfabriken, Messingfabriken*. Usage has almost abolished this distinction. The word *Fabrik* is more general. We hear daily *Tuchfabrik, Cottonfabrik*."

[1] An explanatory note adds: "The word *Kunstarbeit* will constantly be contrasted with *Landwirthschaft* in order to indicate the class of *Manufacturanten*." We may translate this obviously inappropriate term, "suppliers," as a mean between "manufacturers" which offends modern usage if it includes farmers; and "producers" which would attribute to Sonnenfels a generalization that he had not made. "The word diligence [*Aemsigkeit*] will also be used."

[2] The author's note reads: "The total of commerce is thus the sum of two magnitudes, the wants and the number of consumers."

as it increases the wants of citizens, and thereby perhaps makes it harder for some to support themselves, increases on the other hand the occupations; thus it incidentally makes gainful occupations easier and more numerous; that is, the superfluity of one satisfies the wants of others. And if here and there a citizen does not know how to limit his outlays by the rules of private prudence, and ruins himself, his wasted resources are, in the first place, no loss for the state, because they merely pass out of one hand into the other, or are transferred to many persons; second, the ruin of the one may perhaps have provided the support of ten families of the laboring class of the nation. With this explanation all, even the most plausible, objections to luxury may be answered (§10).

At the same time, however, the boundaries between useful and harmful luxury may be determined. For without doubt there is a sort of luxury which is harmful. All luxury, for example, is harmful, which contradicts the purpose for the sake of which the state should encourage it, which does not increase the sum of national occupations, but diminishes it. This occurs in the case of unnecessary foreign articles of luxury and also in the case of those which are not made in the country itself, because these foreign wares always take the place of a national ware, and crowd the latter out of the sum of national occupations. One case only deserves to be regarded as an exception, viz., when the foreign article of luxury has come in, not by purchase but in exchange for a ware produced at home. In this instance justice is done in advance both to national consumption and to all demands of the foreigners who wanted to acquire it by purchase or in exchange for wants. In this case, however, it is only the extension of a branch of the occupation. The foreign article of luxury takes the place of the national product (§11).

The outlay that is restricted to domestic products cannot be increased without end. The resources of those who use these products, and their number, constitute their necessary limits. Commerce would thus not be greater than the possible national consumption. There remains, however, the extension of the same on another side, through increase of consumption. Takers of the wares will be sought outside the country. The effort is made to supply other nations with what they need, and through their consumption to increase the sum of national occupation. Commerce thus divides itself into domestic and foreign. Domestic commerce is that which is carried on between the members of a state (§12).

Foreign commerce is carried on with foreigners. It must necessarily be based on domestic commerce, and it must give up something to foreigners only when it has first satisfied the national wants. Thus foreign commerce is carried on only with the surplus; that is, with that which the national consumption can spare. On the other hand a nation will take either only such wares as it really needs, or those to the taking of which it is drawn by powerful stimuli. These two grounds determine takers in general, but a state will be moved to take from precisely *this* nation, inasmuch as the same wares may actually be had from several sides, only through the most advantageous, or the least disadvantageous conditions under which a ware is offered. These conditions affect the price of wares, or their qualities (§13).

Scarcely any state or nation, at least under present circumstances, and with the once introduced mode of life, will be sufficient unto itself. What it does not possess, it must try to get from abroad under the least oppressive conditions. To this end external commerce furnishes its aid, and in accordance with the division of its occupation it is divided into two branches, viz., export and import. It carries out, from the surplus; it brings in for a double purpose, either to use the imported articles itself, or to export them again, with advantage, to other nations (§14).

This last makes a third branch of commerce, re-export [*Wiederausfuhr*], called economic commerce [*ökonomische Handlung*]. If its advantage consisted only in the occupation of persons engaged in trade, and in the increase of navigation or of wainage, re-export would even then be highly important for a state. It would be giving occupation to a part of the citizens at the cost of other nations. But this is not the whole of the advantage, and the re-exporting state increases thereby the national stock [*Nationalhauptstamm*] to the extent of the excess of the selling price over the price of purchase, which is always a nation's gain if it may not always be the gain of the merchant (§15).[1]

[1] A note explains the last clause as follows: "A merchant buys cloth for 10 in England; the national capital is diminished by 10. The

The less a nation has to receive from others for its own wants, and the more sales it can make to other nations, the more advantageous is its commerce. But the situation in different regions does not always afford to countries either the requisite quantity or the variety of wares necessary for their own consumption and for export. The commercial states, particularly the maritime provinces, turned their gaze in consequence toward the islands, sought to subjugate the same, and to secure possession through settlers transplanted thither, whence they have the name colonies, or settlements [*Pflanzörter*]. Thence they may now draw a part of their wants, independent of other states and under self-imposed conditions, and they may increase without limit the stuff to be exported thither (§16).

The wants which are obtained from other states, and that which is sent abroad, must be transported to the place of sale. This transportation, which is denoted by the word "carriage" [*Fracht*], may occur in various ways. The nation receives its own wants through foreign carriage; and foreigners bring that which they are to receive by their own carriage; or the nation brings in by its own carriage what it receives from others, and returns by its own carriage what other nations buy. In the former case the nation loses the whole advantage of the occupation, which reciprocal carriage was capable of creating; and its commerce is thus in a certain sense passive. In the second case the nation appropriates this advantage and its commerce becomes more active. Every nation must therefore seek to receive its wants through its own carriage and to deliver exports to other nations with its own carriage (§17).

Carriage is by land or by water. Land carriage depends on good commercial roads and a well-conducted carrying system (§18).

Water carriage is on rivers or on the sea. River navigation is promoted by making and keeping rivers navigable, and by uniting rivers by means of canals and locks. These arrangements cannot be extended beyond the boundaries of a state. Sea carriage, on the

merchant pays for freight 1, for storage, handling, etc., 3, so that the cloth stands the merchant at 14; but because the ship was a national ship, and the other outlays were within the country, or paid to citizens, the national capital has not lost these 4. The merchant sells the cloth for 18. The nation gains 8, the merchant, however, only 4."

contrary, is of incomparably greater extent. It depends upon a well-organized and supported merchant-marine (§19).

The danger of carrying, especially at sea, would of itself frighten from undertakings, because only few have enough courage to risk their whole resources, or a considerable portion of them, for a gain which is in no proportion to the possible and often very probable loss.[1] The costs of carriage would also mount very high on account of this consideration, because the carrier would take into account the risk which he undertook. The danger of carriage may be approximately estimated, and according to this estimate the goods and ships may be made secure for a proportional compensation. From this making secure the business has the name insurance or assurance, whereby the courage for commercial undertakings is produced and increased (§20).

In the most favorable situation of a state, it is not possible greatly to extend commerce, or to maintain already extensive commerce, without a corresponding sum of money. The presence of money is necessary from two points of view: the state must in general not lack money as a promoter of national exertion; in particular commerce must not lack an adequate fund for its undertakings (§21).

The physical presence of money in a state does not give to enterprise the energy which comports with the purpose of commerce. It is necessary that the money shall do its work, and shall circulate among the members of society. It is therefore a special duty of the state to promote the circulation, and to remove all hindrances which might obstruct the same (§22).

In case, however, for whatever cause, the circulating sum of money is either insufficient, or diminished, means must be sought to replace the deficiency. The work [*Verrichtung*] of money is as follows: *to be to its possessors the reliable representation of a certain quantity of wares, to the effect that whenever it pleases them they may exchange the representation for that which is represented.* If it is possible for a state to succeed in procuring, for verbal consent, or for certain other signs, the same confidence, that, as money represented the wares, these signs represent the money, these arbitrary signs will then accom-

[1] This is almost an exact repetition of Justi, but the proposition was probably a commonplace at the time.

plish the work of money, and will temporarily make up completely for its absence. No care will therefore be too great which the ruler may devote to the maintenance of public confidence (§23).

If commercial enterprises are to be carried on energetically, they will require great sums. Only a few individual citizens in a state have the means or the credit, and those who have both have not always resolution enough to risk so much in undertakings from which to be sure great gain may be expected, which however are always exposed to an uncertain outcome. Where the means of individuals are not sufficient, an association is formed, each member of which risks only a small sum the more resolutely because in any event the loss would not impair his fortune; and yet the total of these separate contributions procures for commerce the adequate fund. The commercial associations accordingly contribute a large portion to the extension of commerce (§24).

Through export to foreigners and import from foreigners the commercial nations become reciprocal debtors. The discharge of these debts with ready money would be expensive, through the carriage of the money to the place of payment, and also dangerous; the money in carriage would be a considerable time unused, and the business of commerce would be plunged into tedious straggling [*Weitläufigkeit*]. It is possible to avoid these difficulties in whole or in part, if a state exchanges its claims with another, whereby it discharges its debts in so far as the condition of their commerce with each other permits. This exchange of reciprocal claims gave rise to the business of dealing in exchange, which to be sure is only a private affair, but it is always worthy of public attention, because it either facilitates or retards general commerce, and in addition furnishes useful information for the guidance of the same (§25).

In the present situation of science and knowledge, all cabinets are in such wise enlightened about the great influence of commerce that each nation must expect to be crossed [*durchkreuzt*] in all undertakings by the states with which commerce is carried on, or through whose territory the commerce will take its course, whenever it runs counter to their purposes. It is necessary to anticipate these hindrances, and at favorable opportunities, by means of negotiation, to assure advantageous conditions both for oneself and against other rivals. Commercial treaties consequently constitute an important part of *Handlungspolitik* (§16).

In order to know the status of commerce in itself and relatively and therefrom to conclude whether the course of affairs conduces to the utmost expansion of population, states compare the amount which they have supplied to others with that which they have received. This comparison of import and export is called the *balance:* the plumb line in the hands of the state to show where and in what parts commerce requires special aid (§27).

From the foregoing merely general concepts we see how numerous and far reaching are the knowledge, purposes, combinations, and plans which must be made the basis of advantageous commerce; and the necessity of controlling this important business through the combined insight of capable men, and incidentally of establishing for the conduct of commerce a special *Kollegium*, or a special *Stelle*, is thus very obvious. The name in itself is a matter of indifference, but this *Kollegium* must embrace in the circuit of its activity everything which can promote the advantage of commerce (§28).

The most important features of the main argument in this volume are discussed in the next chapter.

CHAPTER XXI

THE CAMERALISTICS OF SONNENFELS ("HANDLUNG UND FINANZ")

In two or three particulars more direct light is focused on factors of firstrate importance for our argument by chaps. i and ii of Sonnenfels' second volume, than by an equal portion of any of the works thus far reviewed.

In the first place a relatively minor matter of methodology deserves passing remark. Chap. i, on rural management, occupies 116 pages, and chap. ii, on manufactures, 157 pages: a total of 273 out of the 564 pages in the body of the book. Attention is called to this division as a commentary on the lack of precision in the title *Handlung* which for reasons stated above we are obliged to render "commerce."[1] It must be said, on the other hand, that a considerable portion of chap. ii is concerned with relations of manufacture to trade, primarily domestic, so that commerce in the strict sense creeps into the discussion earlier than the titles of chapters would indicate. Nor is the mere proportion of pages given to various topics a safe guide to the logical value assigned to different portions of subject-matter. It remains true, however, that Sonnenfels' classification of material under the term *Handlung* was extremely uncritical.

In the second place, it must be admitted that we are not entitled to infer from a book of this type anything very specific about the actual administrations for which the book offers a technology. To what extent the government of the German states as a whole, or of any of them, approached the ideal set forth in Sonnenfels' theory must be determined by other sorts of evidence. Neither the original sources nor even the second-

[1] *Vide* above, p. 525.

ary authorities on this line of evidence can be brought within the compass of our present argument; the former, because they are inaccessible to investigators on this side the ocean, the latter, because a digest of the material would require a separate volume. We must repeat then that we have to do merely with the theory of cameral administration as it appeared in the literary versions.

With these qualifications, we may state positively, third, that one must be disqualified by invincible prejudice if candid study of this book did not arouse a certain degree of admiration for the comprehensiveness, and prudent attention to details, involved in the ideals of cameralism. By comparison with administrations which attempted anything approaching the systematic and thorough management here outlined, democracy as practiced in America has been slovenly, improvident, and reckless.

In the fourth place, this second volume reflects at its best the fundamental cameralistic conception of the state. Without referring to the more abstract legal theories of the relation of the concepts "state," "government," "people," etc., the working resultant of all these was an assumption of a community pictured as a great landed estate, which was such a unity that every part and member had to be considered as having an importance for the whole, and the task of the administration of the whole was to see that nothing was neglected which might serve to insure that efficiency of every resource within the whole which might contribute to the well-being of the aggregate. Whatever our philosophical preconceptions, they are tending toward a common expression in terms of values ascertained and agreed upon in the course of experience. Certain things are found to be worth while. If other things interfere with those which we judge to be worth while, they must drop out of competition and give place to the more highly valued things. Suppose a modern democrat has no tolerance whatsoever for the basic political philosophy of cameralism. He could hardly be intolerant enough to deny that in this book Sonnenfels has done something worthy of praise. He has drawn a wonderfully farsighted and inclusive sketch of things that people must learn to provide for, in some way or other, before they can make the most of life. It is difficult to show this without reproducing his discussion in detail, but the following pages contain an attempt to digest the argument in a way that will confirm this estimate.

At the same time our purpose calls for attention to the embryonic state of the concepts employed in the argument. We must keep in mind that Sonnenfels' problems were not our problems. His social science did not correspond precisely with any division or definition of social science today, much more than the "rhetoric" of the schoolmen tallied with any field of knowledge recognized in modern classifications. Especially must we discriminate between the administrative problems which he proposed and problems of pure economics. The latter are implicit in the former, but as we have repeatedly pointed out, we misinterpret and misvalue the theories of this period if we construe them as theorems applied by their authors to the more general problems of the abstract economists.

The last proposition is in order at once, when we begin to examine the concept *Landwirthschaft* (chap. i). Neither in England nor in America does anything exist today which quite corresponds with the activities which Sonnenfels included under the term. Let us render it as we have in previous cases, "rural management." The term applies, however, to a conception of the situation which it is difficult for Americans to keep in mind. The whole national territory is presumed to be virtually a farm, to be operated for the advantage of the state; and it is the right and duty of the government to see that every foot of the farm is thriftily cultivated. The occupants of the soil are regarded as indentured to the state, and it is the right and duty of the government to dispose of their labor-ability so as to make the land most fruitful, just as it is the business of the managers of a modern factory to organize the help so that their combined labor will be most profitable for the company. That is, "rural management" connoted to the cameralist, and to the governments of the quasi-absolutistic states, a plane of administrative function which correlated individual extractive occupations in a way virtually unknown in America. Our Department of Agriculture, our Geological Survey, our irrigation and forestry enterprises, our agricultural colleges and experiment stations are recent and partial approximations to certain features involved in the German system; but they rest upon a quite different theory of the relation of the state to individuals, and for that reason are essentially unlike much that cameralistic "rural management" included. On the other hand, this phrase did not include the special technique of extractive industries. Both sides of this formal description of the concept will be illustrated by details in the following résumé.

Sec. 30 begins with betrayal of the complexity of the classification which the author adopted. He says:

> Rural management is regarded in *Polizey* as the occupation which provides means of life; in its *commercial* functions [*Handlungsleistung*] as also providing the material [*Stoff*].

It is added at once that the phrase is used to include the procuring of raw material from all three realms of nature, "the vegetable kingdom, the animal kingdom, and the mineral kingdom." Sonnenfels proposes, however, to deal principally with agricultural management, including stock-raising, in so far as the latter is combined with the former; and "only in the political aspect, not in practical technique, which it is the business of the so-called *Oekonomie* to treat." The standpoint from which the discussion starts is further indicated (§31) by the specifications:

"Considered from the side of the state, the perfection of rural management consists in the best possible utilization of the earth[1] in accordance with the demands of subsistence [*Unterhalts*] and of commerce." A note adds: "From the side of the proprietor, it is the best combination of the largest yield with the least expenditure" [*Vorauslage*].

This result will have to be sought:

I, by utilizing all the earth; II, by utilizing it in the best way as respects systems of cultivation; and III, by utilizing it as required by relations to the other connected or dependent occupations. The use of *all the earth*, and the *best* use of the same, coincide in many ways in obstacles and in furtherance.

Sec. 32 seems to start upon the trail of a cardinal sociological distinction, but it is immediately dropped, and nothing is done to follow out the fundamental implications of the distinction. The first sentence reads:

The earth is either private property, or the means of the state.[2]

The dictum follows that:

In order to make full use of private property, the proprietor must have first the necessary power, and second the necessary motives.

[1] The word is *Erdreich*. We might of course render it "land," but this would immediately force upon it an interpretation as equivalent to that term in its later technical sense. Our version is chosen to avoid that anachronism and to preserve the archaic connotations of the term.

[2] "Das Erdreich ist entweder Privateigenthum oder Vermögen des Staates." This juxtaposition of *Eigenthum* and *Vermögen* brings out the fact previously noted, that the two terms are sometimes used interchangeably, and sometimes with an approach to respect for their etymological distinctions. The result is uncritical and fallacious German usage. Translation into English usually makes the matter worse. It is a correct general proposition that at this period the class of writers we are dealing with were unconcerned about precise discrimination between the ethical, the legal, and the merely objective material connotations of the two words.

Lack of means for rural management may be regarded from two sides (§33); namely, the poverty of the rural folk as a class, or of the particular cultivator. The former condition comes from such unavoidable circumstances as first, wars, loss of cattle, failure of crops, the poverty of the present possessor, or only from his temporary embarrassment.

Each of these types of misfortune is treated as deserving of public attention. Means of extinguishing fires are to be provided by the local administration; the dwellings are to be in village groups, not scattered over the land, and the garden plots are to be located between the houses instead of behind them, the barns to be separated from the houses, etc., in order that there may be the minimum danger from fire with the maximum facility of controlling it. Districts should also maintain systems of mutual fire insurance; proprietors should be made to see that their interests demand such precautions. In case such protection is lacking, the cultivator who is embarrassed must be assisted either by the proprietor or by the state. Mere negative help, which is customary, i. e., remission of the dues, does not meet the case. Active help must be given, e. g., lumber, building materials, farming implements; seed must be furnished gratuitously, or at least on the easiest terms. If the individual proprietors are not in a position to do this, it must be done by the state. The alternative is sterilization of the soil, declining value of the revenues of the state, and diminishing population. To remedy these conditions is more expensive than to prevent them. The direct and indirect consequences of cattle diseases are among the important objects of public attention. To prevent them veterinary schools should be introduced (§36), and the causes of the diseases should be investigated.[1] The price of salt, and provision that farmers shall have easy access to it are important in this connection, and should be carefully looked to by the state. In case of failure of crops, as in case of fire or war, the cultivator must be helped either by the proprietor or the state to raise his crops the following year. The state must take measures to prevent exorbitant or oppressive terms in case of loans by individ-

[1] A note states that the so-called *Ecole vêtérinaire* was opened in Vienna in 1766. At first only treatment of horses was attempted, but attention was later extended to all species of farm animals.

uals (§37). In case an individual proprietor is too poor properly to cultivate his tract, the state is in danger of suffering loss of a portion of its dues. There is therefore no reason why the state should not have the right to require that the proprietor should permit others to cultivate the land on shares, or to purchase it. The very circumstances which have caused the embarrassment of the proprietor may make such purchaser or farmer hard to find. The flocking of persons of means to the cities leaves the cultivation of the soil to an inferior class of people. In case forced sale is necessary, the state should provisionally take over the property at a fair price, in order that the possessor may not be compelled to make too great sacrifice (§38). Land is often uncultivated, not by reason of the permanent but the temporary poverty of the possessor (§39). It is an unpardonable mistake of the law-making power to aggravate this helplessness by exaction of the usual dues. The proprietor who has allowed the tenant to fall into arrears should be declared to have forfeited the amount.

Laws should seek to prevent excessive debt by setting a limit to the amount which may be borrowed (§40). An exception should be made in case the loan is necessary for actual cultivation of the land, and the conditions of loans for that purpose should be made especially favorable, and should be under the oversight of the proper officials.

Unthrift on the part of proprietors will be checked by the introduction of supervisors of rural management [*Landwirthschaftsaufsicht*] (§41), consisting of the officials of the circuit [*Kreis*] to whom a subordinate might be added, and the private managers subordinated to these.[1]

A second means of preventing neglect of proper cultivation is afforded by the dues to the state (§42). That is, every piece of arable land should be taxed on a moderate estimate of what it would yield if properly cultivated. Thus the occupant will be compelled to cultivate the land or to pay dues for land which yields him no crop, while the industrious cultivator receives as it

[1] The word *Oekonomieaufseher* is used later in the section apparently as a designation for the officials constituted supervisors of agricultural management.

were a reward for his industry, in being assessed only on a medium rate of yield.

If these means are not sufficient to secure good cultivation, a third remains. It seems severe, but it is not if the others have failed (§43), viz.: In case a piece of land has remained uncultivated two or three years, unless the proprietor can offer to the supervisors an adequate excuse, it shall be declared forfeited, and transferred to someone who will cultivate it. Such a provision is based on the claim which the state has upon the private property of the citizens, for proportional contribution for maintenance of the whole. The forfeiture here proposed can no more be regarded as an invasion of property rights than the law of limitations. The security of property is only conditionally assured by the state, viz., in case the private proprietor does not impair the property of the state.

The lack of courage on the part of the cultivator has its ground in the opinion that his labor is lost, and that he will not reap its fruits (§44). The insecurity of property, the rate of taxation, and the excessively favored love of hunting, on the part both of the sovereign prince and of the private owners, may be regarded as the chief causes of this lack of courage, and the multitude of idle days may be added.

In case the insecurity of property has its origin in the defective fundamental order [*Grundverfassung*] of a country, it will always be difficult for the laws to limit the evil (§45).[1] If the private possessors considered, however, that such fundamental order made against their own advantage, they would not oppose abrogation of the same. The right which is based on ancient possession is made very questionable through the older and imprescriptible rights of mankind.[2] Where the tenants in a certain sense are regarded only as farmers

[1] The term *Grundverfassung*, in the idiom of this period, had the effect of a pun. It seems to have carried partially a literal and partially a derived meaning. That is, the concept in the author's mind seems to have been a blur of the two notions, *land tenure* and *constitution* in something approaching the modern sense.

[2] This is the passage cited by Roscher in support of the proposition: "It is characteristic of Sonnenfels' absolutism to be more liberal at the expense of private rights than at the expense of governmental power." *Vide* above, p. 485. Roscher's point appears to be well taken.

[*Pachtinhaber*] the lords of the soil think they do wisely when they transfer a thrifty farmer to the holdings of a negligent one. Instead of increasing the industry of each, they ruin both. The negligent one shirks work because he is negligent, because this negligence is rewarded, and he keeps hoping for the same reason to be transferred to a better cultivated location. The thrifty one is discouraged and refuses to make improvements which would give occasion for another transfer. Since this right has such great influence upon the condition of rural management in general, we cannot but approve a system which would assure to the peasants a tenure for life at least, and the abolition of this freedom of transfer.[1]

The evictions [*Abstiftungen*] which the officials are sometimes empowered to make must also be reckoned as unfavorable to the security of property (§§45, 46). They must consequently never be a one-sided procedure. Even the economic supervisors must have their hands bound in this respect; how much more the private owners.

The tiller of the soil will work only hard enough to maintain life, if all the rest of his produce is taken from him by landlord and government (§47). Experience proves how little statesmanship there is in the proposition, "The peasant is most industrious when he is miserable."

Secs. 48 and 49 recite some of the hardships which hunting rights inflict on cultivators of the soil, and point out the depressing effect of these hardships upon cultivation in general. The author observes that the restrictions which the laws ostensibly put on these rights are always ineffective in practice. The indemnities allowed to the farmers are awarded by the parties who inflict the losses, and consequently do not compensate the loser, while it is impossible to repair

[1] A note (p. 55) speaks of "*Die ökon. Gesellschaft zu Petersburg.*" The note continues: "The organization in 1765 offered a prize on this subject: 'Is it to the advantage of the state that the peasants should possess property? Does this question do credit to a government? to our century? to mankind?' The better solutions are the monograph which received the prize, under the title, *La Félicité publique* and another by Bearde de l'Abbaye. Meritorious also were those of Woelnor, Mark, Oeder, and Merkel."

the damage done to the national productiveness in general. The time and loss of rest expended on protecting crops against game are a great drain on the resources of the country. An ordinance of Joseph II, dated January, 1786, is called a long-overdue attempt to protect the general welfare of many against a very equivocal pleasure of the few.

The depressing influence of fast days and other holidays upon agriculture is referred to again in §49, and complaint is made that "the obstinacy or the caprice of the pastor" determines whether the peasants shall be permitted to take advantage of good weather on such a day, after protracted rain, to make sure of the crop for which they have toiled earlier in the season. While Sonnenfels here betrays independence of ecclesiastical tradition, yet one detects in his tone no such bitterness toward the clergy as is frequently exhibited by Justi.

In §50 the author verges upon economic generalization in the Smithian sense. Thus he says: "The more incentives to labor are presented to the farmer, the greater will be his diligence. The first motive for him is the support of self and family; the second, the tribute [*Entrichtung*] to which he is bound; the third, the desire to lay by something in case of need, for the improvement of his condition, or for his family. The products of the soil must not fall below a value which affords the hope that all three motives may be satisfied. In determining this price the interests of agriculture seem to be to a certain extent opposed to those of other kinds of business [*Handlungsgeschäfte*]. If the price of agricultural products is high, the price of every manufactured product must rise, whereby one of the principal qualities of a ware, cheapness, is lost. If the price of agricultural products is low, it is not sufficiently encouraging for the farmer, and he finds it to his advantage to produce[1] less, because from half the crop he can then receive a like sum, and save himself trouble, time, seed, etc. Only the medium price remains therefore where the interests of both branches can be combined. This medium price may be considered in its essence or merely numerically."

The subject is continued in §51: "In its essence the medium price is always and everywhere the same: the price, namely, which

[1] *Erzielen; vide* above, pp. 532 and 534.

stands in such relation to the condition of commerce in general[1] that thereby land management may get its proportional share of the gain which comes from commerce. This sharing in the general advantage is not only just, it is also necessary. The state is under obligations to observe and maintain equality between the members of society according to the degree of their reciprocal contribution to the general welfare. Where this equality is not observed the neglected part lacks those encouragements which must be the spur to and the real soul of diligence. It is also unavoidably demanded in order that the worth of the agricultural products may procure for the seller adequate means of satisfying his other wants, that—in the degree in which the wants either rise in price, or otherwise, as through the prosperity of commerce, the prosperity of the working class, and with the same the number of their wants increases—the farmer shall find enough in the price of his products to procure either the higher-priced or the more numerous wants. If his way to this result is closed by an arbitrary fixing of the price, it would follow in the one case that his wants would not be satisfied, whereby he would be forced to interrupt his labor; or, in the other case, his condition would be at least relatively more unfortunate than that of the other working classes. The peasant class would consequently be abandoned, because it would be eager to improve its lot by going over to the other classes. Those that would remain in the class would be without means, or would avenge themselves by indolence for the unrighteousness of society."

The conclusion is drawn in §52: "It is consequently necessary from so many grounds to assure to land management through the medium price its share of the gains of commerce. But the regulation of the medium price cannot occur through the taxes, but through the reciprocal agreements of purchasers and sellers in the market place, if no hindrances are otherwise placed in the way of the freedom of these compacts.[2] If the varying market price of several ordinary years is compared, and the average reckoned, this will be

[1] The word is *Handlung*, and with the variation noted in §50 it illustrates the lack of uniformity in usage throughout the book.

[2] A note cites as such hindrance the ancient right of the lord to an option on the produce before it is taken to market.

taken as the numerical mean, which is variable according to circumstances."

Still further, in §53, Sonnenfels has an elementary statement of the demand side of price, with the corollary that "the state must see that the number of sellers is not too great, and also that a proportional number of customers for agricultural products may be assured." In §54 natural variations of demand and supply are further discussed in contrast with forced variations, e. g., through constraint upon the peasants to pay their taxes at a certain time. The closer this date is to the harvest the greater the disadvantage to the farmer. The cheapness of farm products at such a time is one of the principal causes of the ruin of agriculture. "The state has therefore not merely to moderate the fiscal burdens upon agriculture, but to prevent cheapening of the produce by spreading the payment over various periods."[1]

The sections just epitomized (§§50–54) are notable for several reasons. In the first place, they present the familiar conception of the state as a something which is set over against the component elements of the nation. In the second place, they consistently presume that the state can and must regulate prices. In the third place, they show that some of the elementary facts of market valuation, which eventually show the impotence of statute law against economic law, were beginning to make an impression. Sonnenfels does not go very far toward drawing the involved conclusions, but the difference between him and Justi in this connection is not so much in variations of view about particulars, as in the extent to which Sonnenfels betrays a sort of premonition that something deeper than laws of the state is the key to the situation.

Sec. 55 analyzes demand into that of national and that of foreign consumers. As to the former, it is not enough that there should be a favorable proportion between agricultural products and consumers, i. e., a large population; it is at the same time necessary that

[1] A note names Michaelmas (September 29) as the time shown by experience to be fairest for the payment of agricultural taxes.

this population shall be distributed so that local demand and supply shall be balanced. Otherwise the purchasers will control prices at one point, and sellers at another. The former situation tends to ruin agriculture. Hence disproportionate flocking of people to chief cities is the main cause of the decline of agriculture (§56). Those states therefore are most prosperous in this respect which have numerous provincial cities in which the landed gentry reside. Here manufactures will also spring up, and become middle points of consumption, through which money will circulate uniformly in all localities. If these intermediate cities did not exist, this division of consumers might be otherwise secured, e. g., by forbidding the nobility not in the service of the government permanently to leave their estates, and by distributing over the country those consumers that are not necessarily located in the capital, e. g., factories, almshouses, universities, a great number of cloisters, etc. From the same point of view §57 discusses the operation of intermediate tariffs between provinces of the same state; the inference is that both agriculture and the state suffer if artificial barriers limit the extent of the market.

But the demand of national consumers cannot, at the present rate of population, assure to agriculture the price necessary for its encouragement (§58).[1] Hope of foreign markets alone can stimulate the farmer to cultivate all his land, and give him courage for better cultivation. This hope will be animated by freedom of export.

"Opinions about the advantage of free trade in grain, and about the limits of the freedom, have varied among times, states, and writers (§59). Early times did not consider agriculture in connection with commerce, and fear of scarcity long restricted export of grain. On the contrary, writers of eminence have urged unlimited freedom in this respect at all times and places. The purpose and the effect of free export of grain must be to assure a sufficiently remunerative price for agricultural products without embarrassing national consumption. This combination is secured in a freedom of export which is not directly limited in quantity but by rise of price above

[1] The number that the land could support per square mile (German) is estimated by Sonnenfels as 1,500; this after comparison with Süssmilch's estimate of 2,750, and Vauban's of 2,361.

an accepted mean. In application this principle will have the expression: *Everyone has freedom to export grain so long as the price at such and such markets does not exceed such and such figures.*"[1]

"If administrative policy adopts this view, it rests on the principle that the mean price is a sign of adequate supply [*Feilschaft*] (§60). If this is not the case the state is infallibly and immediately informed of it by the advancing price. At the same time the counter-influence begins to work. Export ceases, and the national market contains what had been exported. Thereupon the price falls. The mean price and therewith freedom of export are restored.

"England began in 1689 to furnish the other nations an illustration that freedom of foreign trade in grain not only supports the cultivator in this industry, but is also capable of bringing agriculture to perfection (§61). Since that time other nations have tried still harder to promote agriculture, and through this effort foreign trade in grain has been greatly hindered. All the more must the law-giver remove the internal hindrances and must assist the merchants by external means, e. g., premiums on export, etc., so that they can compete with the merchants of other nations."

These sections have been reviewed at such length because they contain a neglected link in the chain of evidence which accounts for the tendencies in political theory, both abstract and technological, for the following half-century. The remainder of the chapter is of minor importance for our chief purpose. If affords cumulative evidence, however, of the minuteness with which cameralism analyzed elements of national prudence.

The immediately following sections (§§62, 63) refer to the problems of utilizing lands that for various reasons are wholly or partially uncultivated. Secs. 64–79 develop the same problem in connection with such details as means of assuring a proper proportion between cultivators of the soil and other classes; discouragement of luxury; restriction of the numbers of the servant class; the loss of labor

[1] A note begins with the words: "Die Oekonomisten, ein Zweig der Encyklopedisten, fodern eine unter allen Umständen freye Ausfuhr." The same use of the term *Oekenomisten* occurs in a note to §61.

through military service; colonization of laborers; means of making new settlements prosperous; reclamation of waste lands through clearing of forests, the draining of swamps, the construction of dykes and protection of the same. Secs. 80–107 elaborate the following proposition: "In order that the earth may be used to the best purpose in respect to cultivation, it is necessary: *I, that the rural folk shall possess the necessary knowledge of cultivation and of agricultural improvements; II, that no hindrances shall stand in the way of applying their knowledge; III, land which is devoted to other purposes than cultivation must be managed with skill.*"[1]

The center of attention under the first clause is the introduction and development of various sorts of agricultural schools, and means of scattering the information gathered by such schools among the peasantry.[2]

The second clause deals chiefly with hardships that come from the methods of concentrating or dividing the land, from the taxing system, or from survivals of feudal liabilities. On the first subject it is asserted that "the French economists are in general in favor of cultivation on a large scale, and assume

[1] In this part of the book the following are referred to: "Wiegand, der Verfasser des *vernünftigen Landwirths;*" no further clue is given; "Young, *Politische Arithmetik;*" Ingram, in *Enc. Brit.*, title "Arthur Young," says: ". . . . in 1774 his *Political Arithmetic*, ... was soon translated into several foreign languages." Other references are: Nickols, *Avant et Defavant, de la France*, etc., édit nouvelle d'Amst.; *Principes de la législation universelle*, author not named, but cited as representing "die französischen Oekonomisten;" Arbuthnot, *Sur l'utilité des grandes Fermes et des riches Fermiers*, traduit par Freville; *Traité politique et œconomique sur les communes, ou observation sur l'agriculture, sur l'origine, la destination et l'état actuel des biens et communes*, etc.; Götting, Preisschrift in dem *hanoverischen Magazin*, p. 764; Peningthon, *Réflexions sur les avantages qui résultent du partage des communes pour être défraichis et mis en clos;* Schlettwein in dem *hanov. Magazin*, 704.

[2] For instance, "An ordinance of the Austrian states, to the effect that the calendars for the common people should not be printed, without previous approval of the *öconomischen Gesellschaften*. These societies are considered among the most important of these educational agencies.

as certain that it is not possible to cultivate small holdings profitably" (p. 128). In the same connection Arbuthnot is cited as representing English opinion to the same effect. The third clause is devoted to three classes of uses of the land by which agriculture is the loser: meadows, common pastures, and tracts reserved for beauty.

Chap. ii, on manufactures, begins with the definition: "Manufactures, in the most extended and literal sense, are all occupations which give a new form to any stuff whatsoever." Millers, bakers, and all similar workers are expressly included in the class of manufaturers. More specifically, manufacturers are those species of artisans who make a stock, or so-called merchants' goods.[1] In the more proper sense,

Manufacture is the correlation of all the kinds of labor which are demanded in order to make a ware complete, that is, to make it marketable. The manufacturer is accordingly the citizen who guides this correlation.

The purpose of manufactures, from the standpoint of the individual manufacturer, is to provide support and gain; from the standpoint of the whole state, to increase the occupations; in other words, through manufactures to give work and employment to a part of the people which land management does not employ.

The paragraph continues:

From this point of view, from which manufactures must be contemplated by the public administration, the designation by which the economists[2] mean to depreciate the value of artisanship and of the whole class of manufacturers, is a senseless play on words. The amount advanced to manufactures is called by them "an unproduc-

[1] *Welche Verlag oder sogenanntes Kaufmannsgut machen.*

[2] The context brings out most clearly the shade of meaning which Sonnenfels associated with this particular use of the term *Oekonomisten;* that is, it was pretty nearly coextensive with the class *Physiocrat* and it did not mean, as it did later, "one who is studying problems relating to wealth." It meant "one who adheres to the peculiar theory about sources of wealth advocated by the physiocrats."

tive outlay" [*unfruchtbare Auslage*]; the class of manufacturers, "the unproductive class," because, in the physical sense of the word, they do not create [*hervorbringen*] anything. The essential thing is, however, not whether manufactures create, but, whether they enlarge occupation, that is, whether they increase the means of support for the people, and herewith the population, the welfare of the state from within, the security and prestige of the same from without. This is the effect of manufactures. They themselves really originate [*erzielen*] nothing; they are however the immediate occasion for the origination of the stuff, which without the transformation of artisanship would have no worth and consequently would not be originated.

A note illustrates the author's meaning by the specification:

"Without the prospect of linen, flax would have little or no use. Worked into Brabantian lace the price rises to such an extent that the worth of the stuff entirely disappears." The text continues: Manufacturers "are the immediate occasion for the enlargement of agriculture, for they increase the consumption of the necessities of life, which would otherwise be reduced to the demands of the cultivating families, and consequently would be without value. They even occasion a real growth of national wealth. For, although, according to the calculation of the physiocrats, in the case of an artificial product all parts of the investment [*Vorauslage*] can be resolved into products of the soil [*Erdreich*], yet in the case of wares disposed of abroad the gain of the merchant cannot be classified under that head, but is a real addition either in equivalents of wealth [*Numerarien*] or in wares taken in exchange.[1] More than that, when the Genevan clock-maker constructs of brass and steel worth perhaps two gulden a clock which he sells abroad for thirty gulden, and then in exchange for the thirty gulden imports fifteen measures of grain, is not his skilled labor quite as fruit-bringing for Geneva as that of a farmer who has got fifteen measures from his field? On the other hand, when a state raises a surplus of agricultural products, but is

[1] A note adds the illustration: "A bale of cloth stands the merchant in the marketplace of *Sinigaglia* 1,500. He sells it for 2,000. The gain of 500 is increase of the mass."

surrounded by states that are devoted to agriculture, its surplus will find no sale, and because there is no prospect of disposing of it no surplus will be raised. But a silk factory is established. The laborers engaged in it consume the produce of the field. The silks are exported. The state receives in exchange their worth. Is it not indifferent to the state whether it exports grain in its original form, or grain transformed into silk? Only, that the skilled labor obtained a sale which agriculture could not have obtained; only, that the skilled labor furnishes a growth in occupation and so a growth in population."

Sec. 110 draws the conclusion, which serves as the presumption of the rest of the book:

Manufactures are thus, in the economy of the state, not unfruitful, but a useful and an indispensable enlargement of occupation. In the arranging [*Anordnung*] of manufactures the grades of promotion are to be measured according to their contribution to the purpose of the state, that is, according as the general mass of occupation is enlarged and made more permanent. The general mass of occupation, however, gains only when artisan labor is a means of multiplying the products of agriculture.[1] Those manufactures accordingly deserve the first attention for which national stuff is either actually in hand, or might be had with little trouble. Without observing this consideration, agriculture not only loses a possible sale, and consequently a portion of the occupation which it could appropriate; but the manufacturing labor will be dependent upon those nations which furnish the raw stuff. Therefore the occupation of the people, from this side also, will exist only by favor [*bittweise*], that is, only so long

[1] A note expands the argument in this way: "The harm which may come to a nation in the various branches of its welfare is affirmative or negative. The affirmative is diminution of the greatness which it possesses: if, for example, one thousand of the citizens emigrate, or a half-million capital flows out without compensation. The negative is failure to realize the growth which is within the power of the nation: if, for example, the foreign trade is conducted with foreign carriage, whereby the nation loses the cost of carriage in the selling price. In the calculation of political commerce, gains not made are entered on the debit side. That is, what might have been gained and was not is reckoned as a loss."

as the nation from which the raw stuff is received either does not work it up itself, or it is not taken under more favorable conditions by another nation, or for some reason or other the supplying nation makes the export of the stuff more difficult, or finally for political reasons the supplying nation stops production of this stuff altogether.

Continuing the argument, §111 proceeds:

It is worth while to draw out the consequences of such a situation still farther, in order to reach conviction of another truth, viz.: that it is less harmful never to have extended occupations above a medium number, than ultimately to lose something from a greater number. In the former case, to be sure, the state will enjoy only a moderate degree of prosperity, but it will maintain itself on that level. In the other case the reversal of its prosperity will be almost without limits. In such circumstances many people lose their occupation. That is, they no longer receive the sum of money which they previously used for their support. Since it is not easy at once to absorb an unemployed number into the ranks of the general gainful agencies, the laborers who have lost their employment will be reduced to the most miserable circumstances, and perhaps find themselves compelled to emigrate in order to find ways of earning a living. I will not follow out the consequences of diminution of the number of marriages and other harmful accompanying effects, but restrict myself to the most immediate.

The section closes with a brief but clear indication of the different effects of a contraction of the market through withdrawal of the purchasing power of the unemployed.

It would be difficult to epitomize the remainder of the chapter, and a very general description must suffice. It must be said with emphasis that this chapter would repay study today. The men who are engaged in callings which apply this sort of knowledge usually prefer to get their information by doing the thing itself, rather than by consulting books. The men who are responsible for the parliamentary process of enacting public demands into law do not as a rule in this country attain eminence as students of comparative legislation. The programmes of more than a century ago do not appear to impress them as likely to throw light on the problems of modern life. The fact is that democracy has yet to learn how to co-operate as effectively on the basis of its fundamental conceptions, as quasi-absolutism did on the basis which democrats repudiate. The German benevolent despotisms of the eighteenth century took a more comprehensive survey of the different factors which must lay the foundation of general prosperity than American democracy has learned to take. These benevolent despotisms accordingly planned more intelligent co-operation of their interests and agencies than Americans have yet devised. The German system wasted at the governmental end, on the expenditures of the court, and on the military system, much that this prudent thrift at the popular end enabled states to save. On the other hand, we lose in actual convenience, comfort, and security of life much that the German paternalistic system secured. Without surrendering any principle of democratic political philosophy whatsoever, Americans may well study the details of German quasi-absolutistic administration, in order to learn from it elements of public and private prudence which our pride of individualism has caused us to neglect, and greatly to our own hurt.

The remainder of the chapter elaborates an analysis along these lines:

A manufacture occupies more people in proportion to the amount of preparation necessary before the stuff which it handles becomes complete wares, and in proportion to the generality of its use (§112). The more common use of a ware depends upon its sale to the greater part of the people; that is, it must be of a quality and price which the small means of the great numbers can purchase (§113). It would be at bottom to the advantage of manufacturers to give to their wares the four features: cheap price, good quality, external beauty, and variety. Shortsighted manufacturers should be compelled to recognize this principle, so that they would not in the end make foreign purchases more desirable, and thus diminish the amount of home occupation (§114). In order to be able to sell wares of a poor quality at a high price, the manufacturer must be in a position to control the supply, and it must be something that the public needs. If competitors enter into rivalry, the conditions are reversed. The conjunction of the above conditions alone can insure to manufactured articles those qualities which will multiply their sale (§115). So soon as an occupation yields profits, it is attractive enough for itself; hence, to promote the active combination of factors above named, not only affirmative means are necessary, but also negative, i. e., removal of all hindrances to industry and zeal, e. g., monopolies, exclusive societies, special privileges, manufactures supported by the prince, exclusive guilds, and disproportionate levies upon a manufacture. Examination of these hindrances in order will call attention to principles which may never be neglected in conducting manufactures (§§116–32).[1]

Throughout this discussion the word *Zusammenfluss* defies translation. Collating all the passages in which it occurs one would decide that the concept which the author generally associated with it was "concurrence of all the conditions necessary to insure the four qualities of manufactured goods enumerated above." In certain cases it is plainly used in the sense of "concourse," either of buyers, or sellers, or laborers, or capitalists, as the case may be. In other passages it means "agreement between competitors;" in others it apparently puts the emphasis on the competition itself; while again the

[1] While containing no distinctly new view, these sections show decided advance in maturity over Becher's treatment of *Monopolium* and *Propolium*. *Vide* above, pp. 128 ff. Sonnenfels' major premise throughout the discussion is that the maximum powers of the state are not developed unless the conditions are maintained in which goods are manufactured within the nation in conformity with the four specifications. A very fair anticipation of the modern argument against governmental conduct of industry appears in §§126 ff. In §130 the reference occurs: "Sur les compagnies et les maitrises traduit de l'Anglois. Chinki histoire Chochin chinoise, p. Coyer."

chief reference seems to be to the idea of a confluence of manufacturing enterprise into channels that would provide a sufficient supply of goods. Sonnenfels apparently regards the word as a sort of technical term, but it is not confined to a precise idea.

Passing to another phase of the subject the analysis continues:

If the hindrances mentioned are out of the way, the zeal of industry will be unrestrained, and its fortunate consequence will be the perfection of manufactures. Each of the qualities which we have specified as necessary to this perfection springs from a multitude of separate parts, knowledge of which is necessary, and it will not be practicable in considering them not to cast side glances at foreign commerce (§133).

Thereupon still more intensive analysis is undertaken of the qualities of wares posited as essential, and of the conditions requisite to insure them. Secs. 134–68 might be set apart under the title, "The Elements Which Enter into the Price of Manufactured Goods." Secs. 169–82 might be entitled, "The Elements Which Enter into the Quality of Manufactured Goods." Under the corresponding title, "The Elements Which Enter into the Beauty of Manufactured Goods," we should mark off a briefer passage, §§183, 184. In a general way an appropriate designation for the remainder of the chapter (§§185–202) would be, "Factors Involved in Assuring Variety of Goods." The details are largely technical primarily on the side of manufacture, or trade, or administrative policy, as the case may be; and so do not fall immediately within the scope of our inquiry; but the underlying criterion gives the discussion its principal significance. The persistent question is always by implication ultimate: "What line of conduct will conduce to the largest consuming ability of the largest number of people, and so to the strength of the state?"

The passage cannot be dismissed without certain minor

observations. Thus, the discussion of the terms "cheap" [*wohlfeil*], "price," and "value" reflects a critical spirit quite in accord with that of Adam Smith.[1]

The proposition with which Sonnenfels covers the whole subject of the price of manufactured goods is:

> The price at which the manufacturer can part with his wares comprises the sum of all the separate outlays which were made up to the time of sale, with addition of the profit (§136).

This decidedly empirical formula is then translated into detail. The elements of price upon what the author puts emphasis are:

> buildings, lumber, and all other common necessities, purchase of material, wages, carriages, insurance premiums, import and export duties, interest on the capital, exchange, in case of wares requiring foreign purchases, and profit.

The discussion does not deal with abstractions, but generalizes business prudence. The spirit of the whole may be illustrated by such a passage as the following:

> Not even for the advantage of a manufacture established in the province is it advisable to put restrictions on removal of raw material to another province. For this outgo will not occur so long as buyers are to be found in the locality of its origin who offer acceptable terms of purchase. If it were desired however to give the manufacturer a one-sided advantage, this would amount to promotion of industry [*Aemsigkeit*] at the cost of land management. Then only can the state hope for permanent advantage when it supports both at the

[1] As evidence we may quote the note to §135, viz.: "Die Oekonomisten erklären den Werth: Das Maass des Bodens welches in der Erzielung enthalten ist. Dieser Begriff, ist eben so undeutlich, als unrichtig. Das nämliche Maass Erdreichs von besserer oder schlechterer physischen Beschaffenheit mit besserer oder schlechterer Bestellung trägt mehr: also würde die nämliche Sache von verschiedenem Werthe seyn. Der Verfasser des Werts (Werks?) *Essai sur le commerce en général*, Part I, chap. i, setzt dem Maasse des Erdreichs noch die Arbeit bei, welches den Werth zwar näher bestimmt, aber immer zu metaphysisch ausdrückt."

same time . . . . ; so long as the producer can get a proper price for raw material, constraint is unnecessary; so soon however as the manufacturers take advantage of the constraint of export duties and try to oppress the producer, the latter abandons the unremunerative production, and the manufacturer suffers from lack of material (§141).

The effect upon cost of raw material of duties on imports and exports is discussed at considerable length. Again, the effect of numerous holidays upon the price of manufactured goods is analyzed, and on the ground of the advantage of the state, the term in this case meaning the necessary material prosperity of all classes, the advisability of reducing the number is urged, in spite of the church.[1] Further (§153), different situations in which scarcity of laborers is the decisive factor are intelligently treated. A paragraph follows (§154) on the advantages of the division of labor. It refers to the classical passage in Adam Smith's *Wealth of Nations*,[2] and it borrows from that passage the illustration of pin manufacture. Smith is referred to merely as "one of the more recent English writers," and no indication appears that Sonnenfels had discovered in him any radical importance. The inventiveness of manufacturers, turned to construction of machinery which saves labor and diminishes that item of cost, is next in order (§155). In this connection a qualification is entered which plainly illustrates the difference between the purpose which Sonnenfels had in mind and the sheer capitalistic standard:

> For the state, cheapness of manufactured goods is merely a secondary purpose, which must not be opposed to the paramount purpose, viz., the multiplication of occupations. Everywhere, therefore, where the ways to occupation are in such precise equilibrium with

[1] In this connection we read (§152): "Man liest bei Goldasten in den Reichshandlungen;" and a little later, "Fortbonnais in *Disc. praelim. zum Négotiant anglois*."

[2] Book I, chap. i.

the population that the portion of people whose place would be taken by machines could not be utilized for other labor, the introduction of machines would be harmful. This would be approximately the situation of a state which had no foreign commerce of any consequence. The same consideration is to be kept in view in the case of agriculture. The introduction of agricultural machinery would diminish the class of rural folk, and for the state nothing is so desirable as to see this class as numerous as possible.

In connection with the subject of export and import duties, as a factor of the price of manufactured goods, another indication to the same effect appears (§157). Referring to "the almost universal assumption that customs dues are to be regarded as a profitable branch of the public revenues," Sonnenfels says:

Since increase of price in the first instance contradicts the paramount purpose of commerce it is necessary to criticize this theorem. As certain as it is that the revenues of the state must cover the expenditures, so certain is it also that inappropriate means may be selected for raising these revenues. Those objects then will be inappropriate in which the first purpose of the state, viz., to have a large population, is hindered, because the impost has an influence on occupation; in which case what may be gained on the one side may be more than lost on the other, and in which by virtue of their very nature, no fixed basis of assessment can be assumed; in which, finally, the collection of the money revenues is not in accord with the main purpose, for the reason that although large sums are collected the main purpose is not promoted; or if this purpose is reached, the revenues would have to be raised to an impossible amount. All of this may be proved in the case of customs [*Mäuthe*].[1]

The argument is continued in §§158–65. The claim is urged that import duties are taxes on consumption and tend to diminish the output of wealth. They are only admissible, under ordinary circumstances, when they do not have this

[1] The author refers to his *Abhandlung vom Mauthwesen* in the tenth volume of his collected works.

effect. An export tax discourages foreign use of the ware, and so limits domestic occupation.

Consequently the finances purchase their momentary advantage at a much too high price, through the loss of land management whose stuff is in less demand, and through the harm to industry whose earnings are in the same degree lessened.

On the distinction between two kinds of commerce noted above, a passage (p. 242) is a commentary. Speaking of the part played by general frugality if it does not descend to a stinginess which limits the national output more than foreign trade extends it, Sonnenfels says:

A state which in the last analysis possesses only an economic trade, cannot carry exclusiveness [*Häuslichkeit*] in its mode of life too far without provoking other states, whose trade is based upon their own products, to imitate this policy with equal vigor.

A sample of a different sort will show how minutely Sonnenfels' technology calculated cause and effect from the standpoint of the state. It occurs in the sections on the relations of the qualities of goods to price. The custom of requiring of young artisans a certain number of *Wanderjahre* before they were allowed to work at their trade in their own locality had been referred to as on the whole tending to vagrancy. The author, however, adds (§174):

Considered from one point of view, however, these migrations should not be abolished, but better regulated. Only the most talented should be sent abroad, and that with the previous knowledge of the state, and with certain assistance. According to their branch of trade the places to which they should go should be designated, and they should be recommended to the embassies at those places. In this way the emigrations would be profitable in gaining for domestic wares the envied perfection of foreign goods.[1]

[1] In continuing the subject of the effect of the *quality* of products on price, Sonnenfels cites (note to §176) Savary, *Dictionaire du Commerce*, T. IV, art. "Règlement," and Justi, *Abhandlung von Manufacturen, Fabriken Reglements.*

A little later (§179) Sonnenfels epitomizes the objections to *Meisterrecht*, and particularly to *Manufacturreglement, die Inspektionen und Beschauanstalten*, in a volume translated from the English, with the title rendered from a French version, *Versuch über die Meisterschaften*. The author's name is not given. The book urges the abolition of the institutions named. The reasons are evidently those of very narrow selfishness. Sonnenfels takes the position that every one of them may be answered in favor of continuing existing or similar regulations and supervision, by consideration of the general welfare. A little later, speaking of the policy of encouraging settlement of skilled laborers from abroad, Hume, *Geschichte des Hauses Tudor*, T. III, is cited as authority for the statement that Henry VII, instigated by an outcry of women, drove 15,000 artisans, mostly French, from London. Sonnenfels charges England with still maintaining essentially the same attitude.[1]

[1] Further references in the chapter are as follows: "In den Briefen des La Porte," cited from memory, p. 273; in a note on p. 279 the author remarks: "Die Errichtung der Manufacturhäuser ist vor Justi schon von Boden in seiner *fürstlichen Machtkunst*, von Schrödern in seiner *fürstlichen Schatz- und Rentkammer*, u. a. m., als ein nützliches Mittel angepriesen worden;" then follows reference to Justi's monograph, *Von Manufacturen und Fabriken*. Justi is blamed for giving Schröder an empty compliment for proposing that manufactures should be assisted by a scheme of *landesfürstlichen Wechsel*, an impracticable notion, in Sonnenfels' opinion. Fortbonais, *Elém. du Com.*, chap. iii, reappears, p. 283, and, in the same note, Hume, *Polit. Essays of the Balance of Trade (sic); alle Physiokraten* are referred to at the same point, the implication being that they universally support a prohibitive policy with respect to imports; Reimarus, *Handlungsgrundsätze*, is named without indicating the reason; a second note on the same page (p. 283) contains a rather pointed criticism, viz., "England, France, even Holland, has prohibitions of imports, and what amounts to the same thing, high entrance rights. When therefore many a writer confidently asserts that commerce flourishes most in states where universal freedom of trade rules, we are justified in demanding that these states shall be specified;" and finally (p. 299), Nickols; *vide* above, p. 556.

We pass to chap. iii, "On Foreign Commerce." In the previous chapter Sonnenfels had shown a decidedly opportunistic attitude toward regulation of foreign trade. On the whole, he is inclined to assume that artificial restrictions of the spontaneous course of trade are likely to work more harm than good. At the same time he holds firmly that it is entirely within the competence of the state to enforce all sorts of restrictions, provided they actually tend to promote the main end, viz., the multiplication of "occupations," and thus the increase of population. Besides details under this principal proposition, and technical specifications with which we are not concerned, the chapter contains little that is germane to our purpose. A leading theorem is that, "The ground of speculation is knowledge of foreign countries" (p. 205). The author's expansion of the idea shows sagacity of a high order, and again it must be said that Sonnenfels might be read at this point with profit by everyone who is directly or indirectly connected with foreign trade or the diplomatic intercourse which is based upon commercial interests. The rudiments of the duties of diplomatic and consular representatives, as so long and well understood in Germany, and so tardily practiced in America, are distinctly set forth. Sonnenfels writes rather as a learner from other nations on this subject than as a eulogist of German policy. For example, he remarks (§207):

England especially has selected as ambassadors men of fundamental insight into the commercial system; such were "*die Keene, Castres, Fallquener, Porter, Walpole*," in Spain, Portugal, Turkey, and France.[1]

[1] A bibliographical item is to be noted. Sec. 221 expands the conclusion: "Summing up both sides, we may say with Raynal: 'Fairs and markets in themselves are a mischievous recourse, but occasionally they are serviceable.'" A note adds: "*Histoire polit. et phil. des établissemens de deux Indes*, T. IV. Der Verfasser führt die Erfindung der Messen zu dem 7ten Jahrhundert zurück: als durch die Einfälle der

The drift of the chapter may be gathered from a part of the closing section (§223). The opening sentences read:

In order therefore not to diminish the useful class of merchants, the state should make common cause with them. Instead of granting letters of nobility to rich merchants upon retirement from business it should rather ennoble the merchant only upon condition that he shall continue to carry on commerce, and shall bring up his children to the same occupation. The state should offer nobility to him who, with certain resources, passes from another stratum into the ranks of the merchants. On occasions where distinctions are to be drawn between classes of the people, for instance, at court festivities, the state should include the merchant class among the distinguished. The protection of the state must be extended to the large, as well as to the small trades, etc.[1]

The standpoint of chap. iv, "On Colonies" may be indicated in brief in accordance with the analysis in §224, viz.:

Colonies have the significance and the purpose, first, of promoting *external security;* second, of promoting *commerce;* third, of promoting *navigation*.

A fundamental presumption is frankly expressed in §225, viz.:

The mother state will have the preference over every other country in drawing from the colonies those wants which it will either use itself or again export. And in general, whenever a decision must

Franken und Barbaren in Gallien die Handlung durch ungeheure, und unzählige Gebühren gehemmet ward. Die erste Messe war zu St. Denys gestiftet worden. S. den Art. *Foire* in der Encyclopedie, welche Turgot zum Verfasser hat." The following section (§222) has a reference to "Coyer, *La noblesse commerçant.*"

[1] This note follows: "Die Selige Kaiserin liess einst dem ganzen Handelsstand die Adelung anbieten. Viele aus demselben machten von diesem Anerbieten Gebrauch, und führen dann auch geadelt den Handel immer fort. Die Erhebung in den Freyherren, und nachher in den Grafenstand, und die Stelle eines K. K. Hofraths hielt H. Fries nicht ab, seine Geschäfte mit eben demselben Eifer fortzusetzen, als er vorher gethan hat."

be made between foreigners and the colonists, the state will seek to secure the advantage for the latter. Whenever, on the other hand, a question arises between the state and the colonies, the state appropriates the advantage to itself, and deals with the colonies in complete accordance with the principles of foreign commerce. That is, everything which the colonies supply will be accepted only in the simplest form. On the contrary, whatever is supplied to the colonies they must consent to take in the most complete form. Thence the mother state derives the increased advantage: it gets its wants in the easiest and supplies the wants of the colonies in the most profitable way, since it increases occupation at home through the consumption of the colonists. These advantages are all the greater since the home government prescribes laws for the colonies, and can exclude all rivals from trade with them. Consequently the merchants of the mother state are to be regarded as to a certain extent monopolists as respects the colonies.

After a few more specifications to the same effect, Sonnenfels shows that he is by no means in sympathy with the policy which he faithfully analyzes. He says (§228):

Such are the chief principles in accordance with which mother states treat their colonies: principles of armed power, against defenseless weakness, to the injustice of which the lust of expansion and the mercantile spirit blind all nations. . . . . When the English, who regard private property in their own island as so inviolable, but treat with contempt the property of inoffensive peoples in other parts of the world, when they, even yet in our century, take possession of every island on which they land, in the name of his British Majesty, are they nevertheless in the eyes of mankind the honorable [*achtungswürdig*] nation in which the concepts of freedom and right seem almost exclusively to have been preserved? . . . . But however many the advantages which are drawn from the colonies, their possession will continue only so long as the colonists are kept in the ignorance, out of which time, the efforts of rival nations, and the confluence of favoring conditions, will sooner or later, but certainly, some time remove them, and will put an end to their dependence.

A note comments:

This was written in the year 1763; the outcome of the war with America converts it into a prophecy.

Chap. v, on "Land Carriage," calls for two observations only. In the first place, we may note its bibliographical citations.[1]

In the second place, we must recognize the continued attentive elaboration of administrative detail. The chapter contains hardly more than titles of subjects which have to be dealt with in securing all possible advantage to the state from means of internal communication by land, but merely as a programme or as a catalogue of items to be kept in view by the state, it is a notable reflection of the cameralistic spirit. The details to be dealt with by government under this head are all considered as "means of increasing the national occupation." They vary from construction and repair of roads, the encouragement and control of carriers, the provision and regulation of inns, stables, and storehouses for the men, animals, and goods engaged in transportation, to maintenance of the various trades, wheelrights, saddlers, smiths, etc., necessary for conducting the repairs incidental to land traffic.

Substantially the same is all that need be said of each remaining chapter in the book. In the first place, the printed

[1] Viz.: first, referring to Cromwell's "Navigation Act" of 1651, a note remarks (p. 351): "Ich kenne nur den Verfasser der *Handlungsgrundsätze zur wahren Aufnahme der Länder*, etc., §13, welcher gegen wahren Vortheil dieser Akte einen Zweifel zu erheben scheint." On p. 356 the following occurs: "Das Werk von Bergier, *Histoire des grands chemins d'Empire*, ist allen unentbehrlich, die diesen Theil der Verwaltung zu besorgen haben. Gautier, *Von Anlage und Baue der Wege und Stadtstrassen* aus dem Franz., ist eine kleine Schrift von vieler Brauchbarkeit." Again, p. 358: "*Sur les Corvées* ist bereits in der Sammlung von Mirabeau aus Schriften unter dem Namen: *Ami des hommes*, eine schöne Abhandlung eingeschaltet." On p. 363 the vagrant observation appears: "Eines ungenannten *Anmerkung über den Gebrauch und Nutzen des Intelligenswesens*."

sources to which the author acknowledged himself indebted must be noted.[1]

[1] In general it may be observed that dependence upon Forbonnais becomes more evident from this point. On p. 367 is this note: "Es kann meine Absicht nicht seyn, von der Marine anders zu handeln, als nach der allgemeinen Verbindung derselben mit der politischen Handlung. Um wenigstens sich nur einen Begriff derselben zu machen, wird *La Science de la Marine* par Villeneuve, und das *Dictionaire de la Marine* zureichen."

On admiralty law, the author remarks (p. 375): "Die Quellen dieser Seerechte sind des Harmenopolus *Sammlung der legum Rhodiarum;* die Spanische Sammlung von 1057, welche unter dem Namen *consolato del Mare* bekannt, das wisbysche Wasser- und Seerechtsbuch, die oleronischen und hanseatischen Seerechte, die lübekischen Seerechte, von denen Stein eine Abhandlung entworfen hat; die englische Akte; die ordonnance de la marine von Ludwig dem XIV. Hierzu sind die Verträge, und das Seeherkommen zu rechnen: von welchen in dem für die innerösterreichische Schiffahrt entworfenem Editto Marino einige Anwendung gemacht ist." A sentence or two before this passage, Sonnenfels refers to Curland, *Grundsätze des europäischen Seerechts*, and this work was apparently his leading authority.

Referring to the history of men's efforts to improve inland water communication, a note (p. 382) says: "Diese Geschichte hat H. Oberlin in 3 lateinischen Werken gesammelt und bis auf unsere Zeiten fortgesetzt. I, *Prisca;* II, *media aevi;* III, *jungendorum marium fluminumque omnis aevi molimina.* Die österreich. Staaten sind von vielen Flüssen durchströmt, deren Vereinigung möglich ist, und worüber viele Entwürfe gemacht worden. Besonders müssen irgend in den Archiven, oder Registraturen die Entwürfe vom Philibert Luchese, über einige Flüsse der Monarchie aufbehalten seyn. Vielleicht sind die Entwürfe, welche H. Maire über die Vereinigung der Flüsse, in den sämmtlichen Staaten des Hauses Oesterreich heraus gegeben, und in einem sogenannten *Mémoire raisonné sur la circulation intérieure du commerce*, etc., erklärt hat, nicht durchaus ausführbar; aber dass es ein grosser Theil derselben ist, kann nicht gezweifelt werden und die Entwürfe zeigen: wie vortheilhaft die Handlung aller erbländischen Provinzen unter sich verbunden werden könnte."

In chap. vii, on "Insurance"—chiefly marine insurance—the only writer directly referred to is Forbonnais (p. 394, *et passim*).

In chap. viii (ix), on "Money," Justi is apparently the guide whom

In the second place, these chapters are cumulative evidence that the center of gravity in Sonnenfels' system was shifting its position. It does not appear that he was conscious of it. He does not directly substitute another aim for the strengthening of the state which had been ultimate with the other cameralists. He returns frequently to some variation of the constant theme that the state must look out that the proper thing is done in all these relations, but the reader cannot fail to detect an infusion of more of the spirit of gain for the sake of gain, which distinguishes the specifically commercial from the typi-

Sonnenfels mainly trusts. On p. 423 he mentions him, and in a note (p. 426) he says, of the particular monograph referred to (*Ursachen des verderbten Münzwesens in Deutschland, und Mittel dagegen*): "Dieser Vorschlag ist eigentlich nur eine Zurückführung der Münzenbenennungen zu ihrem Ursprunge." In a previous note (p. 525) he says: "Die Schriftsteller welche von den Grundsätzen der Münzprägung handeln, haben über diesen Gegenstand so viele Dunkelheit verbreitet, dass sie Anfänger ganz kleinmüthig machen. Diese Dunkelheit rührt daher, weil sie den Grundsätzen eine Menge angewendeter Rechnungsbeispiele mit untermengen, die nicht zu den Grundsätzen, sondern Zum praktischen Theile des Münzwesens gehören."

Sec. 291 cites Melon, *Essai politique sur le commerce*, 2te. Aufl.; also, Dutot, *Réflexions politiques sur les finances et le commerce*, and Fortbonnais, *Anfangsgründe*, II. Tom., chap. ix, "De la circulation."

In chap. ix, on "The Circulation of Money," there is a reference to "Montesq., *Esprit des loix*, Liv. 22, "Principes sur le commerce;" to Hume, *Essay of the Balance of Trade;*" to "folgende Stelle Ustaritzes," viz., *Theorie & pratique du commerce*, Cap. III am Ende; Vol. III, p. 150, has the reference: "Ustaritz, *Consider. sur les financ* (*sic*) *d'Espagne;*" to "Plinius, *paneg. Traj.*," to "X. Band meiner gesammelten Schriften: *Abhandlung von der Ursache der Theurung in grossen Städten und dem Mittel, ihr abzuhelfen;*" on p. 494 Hume is quoted again as authority for the statement that although during the minority of Edward (VI ?) interest was prohibited in England, the rate was 14 per cent. (Incidentally we may note that Sonnenfels uses "*die Interessen*" interchangeably with "*die Zinsen.*") Raynal is cited (p. 496) as authority for tracing disbelief in the justice of interest to the Middle Ages. The Justinian Code is cited (p. 499): "4. Buch, 31. Tit., 26. Gesetze," and five pages

cally political standpoint, and which was, consciously or unconsciously, the animus of the Smithian political economy. Although Sonnenfels had only in the faintest degree begun to generalize economic problems in the Smithian manner, his dealing with the technique of the subjects treated in the last half of this volume was distinctly an approximation to the Smithian method.

For various reasons, Vol. III, *Finanzwissenschaft*, must be much more summarily treated than the other two. A few of its general characteristics, however, should be pointed out, and this may be done in the form of disconnected notes.

later "der Verfasser des Werks, *Des corps politiques*." On p. 508, referring to the advantages of a low rate of interest, a note begins: "Dieser Gegenstand ist vorzüglich in englischen Schriftstellern behandelt worden." Child and Culpeper are named. Then follows the remark: "In der Sammlung von politischen Abhandlungen, die in V Bänden 1750 zu Amsterdam bei Schenchzern erschien, sind die verschiedenen für und wider die Interessecherabsitzung in dem Parlemente gehaltenen Reden, aufbehalten, am ausführlichsten sind Lockes Briefe, welche unter dem Titel: *Betrachtung über die Münze, Geldzinse, Finanz und Handlung* gesammelt sind. Auch die Vorrede, welche Fortbonais der Uebersetzung des *British Merchant* vorausgesendet hat, ist eine eigene und mit vieler Gründlichkeit geschriebene *Abhandlung über die gesetzmässige Zinsherabsetzung*." On p. 519, "Dio Kassius" is drawn upon for an illustration of the effect of a sudden increase of money in circulation in raising prices, and at the same time lowering the rate of interest, and Hume's "Essay of the Balance of Trade" is again referred to (p. 520). In chap. xi, on "Trading Companies," Raynal, "*Hist. polit. et Philos.*, etc.," is again used as a source; in chap. xii, on "Exchange," Fortbonais, chap. viii, again appears to be the author's point of departure, and Dutot (*op. cit.*) is once more named. Siegel, *Einleitung zum Wechselrechte*, and the same author's "*Corpus juris cambialis*, welches Herr Usal fortgesetzet hat," are listed at the end of the chapter. Chap. xiii, on "Commercial Treaties," mentions "die kleine Schrift *Les avantages que le Portugal pourroit tirer de son malheur*." Chap. xix, on "The Balance of Trade," quotes Hume "in dem *Versuch über die Handlungsbilanz*." At the same time it is asserted that "die Physiokraten halten die Berechnung der Bilanz für überflüssig." The volume closes with the note: "S. X. Band meiner gesammelten Schriften Abhand. von der Mauth."

The title-page is a duplicate of that of the first two volumes with the exception that the vignette represents Maximilien de Berthume, duc de Sully.

In the Preface of the first edition the author indicates his purpose to occupy an intermediate position between two classes among the numerous writers on the subject, viz., first, those who have exaggerated their systems into Utopias; second, those who have tried to reduce policies of oppressive exploitation to an art. These latter talk only of enriching the treasury. They ask how much may be taken from the citizen without bringing him to the threshold of extreme poverty.

These contemptible hirelings of tyranny resemble the hunting-dog that scares up the game for the hunter in order to feed on its entrails.

A third type which, to be sure, is very small, aims at a quite different purpose, viz., the honor of standing for the interest of the people [*des Volkes*]. These have to reckon with the ruler, and to challenge every expenditure which exceeds reasonable needs.

In this passage Sonnenfels applies the word *Kammeralschriftsteller* to a class of writers on finance who correspond to the term *Oekonomieaufseher*, as used above.[1] That is, he asserts that they knew nothing of the broad principles of finance but fill their books with the most minute details of private thrift. These petty people should have confined their pride entirely to writing for zealous administrative employees, who might have read their books with advantage. According to this passage, then, Sonnenfels repudiated the name "cameralist;" but that was a matter of words, and it does not separate him in fact from the series of writers whom we are considering.

As between the types thus characterized Sonnenfels hints, rather than directly says, that he intends to write with a view to the general prosperity, rather than chiefly in the interest of the national treasury. He declares that he proposes to

[1] *Vide* p. 548.

write principles of finance, not a finance encyclopaedia; and he advertises the freedom and independence with which he intends to treat the problems. In this last respect he gives the impression of protesting too much. His language serves chiefly to remind the reader of the difficulty of making any presumption except the governmental one tolerable to rulers. Although Sonnenfels praises the magnanimity of the empress, which had protected his freedom of teaching, we read between the lines that he was consciously approaching delicate subjects, and he wanted to conciliate the civic powers as much as possible.

The Preface to the present edition contains a paragraph which expresses the author's attitude toward bibliography, viz.:

> In respect to the books to which I have referred in this as well as in the first and second parts, I have this to say: that my intention in such references was not to furnish a literary encyclopaedia. The reader or student does not want a mere list of writings, brought together from catalogues and unreliable journals, without selection and very often without knowledge. He wishes to get acquainted with good writings, from which he may extend the principles which he has gained, and in which he may find further information about this or that subject. With this purpose alone in view I have listed books, and none others than those which I have myself read and of which I can give assurance that they will repay the trouble of consulting or reading them.

It is perhaps a virtue rather than a fault of the first two volumes, that they appear to have been drawn more from observation than from previous writers. Whether it is a virtue or not, the internal evidence does not strongly sustain a literal version of the above claim to personal acquaintance with all the books cited in the parts already discussed. In this third part the citations are more frequent, but this fact merely reflects the state of the available literature.

It should be noticed too that the volume now before us is

full of vivid side-lights upon the issues which were then seething in all the political pots of Europe. Nowhere did the fundamental issue, government for the sake of the citizen or the citizen for the sake of government, come to more distinct definition than in policies of taxation. The day after the Preface to this fifth edition of the third volume was written, the Assembly of Notables at Versailles was dissolved. Reduced to the concrete, the Revolution was an assertion that taxes should thereafter leave Frenchmen a living. The Revolution told the rest of Europe that the battle could be won. In this academic book one feels the tug of the vested interests upon the earnings of the masses, but what is better, one feels the force of a moral judgment that the masses must not be sacrificed to institutions. There is no assertion of a new social principle here. There is, however, assertion that old social principles must be applied with changed emphasis. So understood the book is a vivid document of political reconstruction.

On p. 2 Sonnenfels gives his definition of the science of finance, viz.:

> The more necessary is it, therefore, for those interested in this important part of administration to be guided by well-considered *principles according to which the revenues of the state may be most advantageously raised.* These collected principles are the science of finance [*Finanzwissenschaft*].

The author's formulation of the standpoint from which these principles are to be considered may be summarized as follows: In the first place, we may reduce the general process of financial administration, according to his analysis, to four stages, viz.: first, estimate of the needs of the state, and drawing up a corresponding budget [*Staatsaufwandsüberschlag*]; second, determination of the resources of the state; third, by comparing the former with the latter, discovery of the proportion of the resources which it will be necessary to use in order to cover the needs; fourth, the technique of assessing and collecting the revenues. Without attempting to reproduce the author's doctrines of the limits within which the idea of the ordinary and extraordinary needs of the state must be defined, we note, first, that the sources of revenue are divided into two classes, viz.: the mediate and the immediate contributions of the citizens (§15). The former class includes revenues from all those sources which are the common property of the citizens: crown estates, regalian rights, etc. The second class includes all revenues which are derived from payments by individuals. As an ideal principle, the former class should cover the ordinary expenses of the state, while the latter should be the means of discharging the extraordinary expenses (§§18, 19).

Then follows a most characteristic and illuminating proposition, viz.:

The contribution to the extraordinary expenses must be arranged according to the multitudinous circumstances in which the state finds itself, always however without allowing attention to wander from the *well-being of the citizens*, which remains under all circumstances the ultimate purpose of every expenditure (§20).

More than a mere verbal variation is involved in this dictum. Instead of the conventional *Wohl des Staates*, or the noncommittal phrase which occurs in the Preface of the first edition, "*die Sache des Volkes*," we now have "*das Wohl der Bürger*." Of course it would be absurd to rest an important conclusion upon a single phrase. It is hardly probable that Sonnenfels was distinctly aware of meaning anything different by this phrase from the ideas conventionally associated with the terms in more frequent use. A difference between two stages of civilization might be expressed in the contrasts between the conventional concepts connoted by the technical phrases *der Staat*, or *das Volk*, and the democratic phrase, *die Bürger*. The two former presuppose an entity in antithesis with the individual citizens, or a mystic collectivity in which the rôle of the individual citizen is an after consideration. The latter phrase connotes a conception that there is no whole except that composed of the individuals whose co-operation gives reality to the state. Even conceding that Sonnenfels consciously meant less by substitution of the new phrase than it means to us, the fact that he made the substitution may legitimately be taken as a straw showing the direction of his own thought and of current opinion. A change of emphasis was taking place. The state as a self-existent entity was becoming less real. The individual was becoming relatively both more real and more important.

As a means of locating Sonnenfels with reference to another important principle, the opening of §32 is significant, viz.:

> The sources of national income are agriculture and industry [*Aemsigkeit*], under which latter everything is included which increases the so-called numerical riches [*numerären Reichthum*] of a state.

Sonnenfels has been called the "systematizer of mercantilism." Such a phrase would have to be defined very precisely, and so as to remove most of its proper meaning, before it could be accepted as covering the facts.

There is no more vigorous nor progressive passage in the three volumes than the discussion (§§85 ff.) of exemptions from taxation. Sonnenfels tersely disposes of the claims to freedom from taxation on the part of nobility, clergy, and scholars respectively. In a word, his argument is: first, these classes either are citizens or they are not; second, if they are, this general designation, and the consequent advantages from the protection of the community, carry with them the general obligation of sharing in the costs of government; if they are not citizens, then it would be well for them to consider whether they would gain by release of the state from the obligation of protection which it owes to all citizens. As to the claim that these classes perform a special service to the state, which entitles them to exemption, Sonnenfels declares with rather unusual warmth:

I at least lay my hand on my conscience, in order to concede that the community could do without my writings better than it could dispense with the labor of the rustic who produces our bread by the sweat of his brow. But I am treating the matter more seriously than it deserves. Every social stratum contributes after a certain proportion its share to the common well-being. These contributions therefore cancel one another, and the duty to contribute remains the completely equal responsibility of all.[1]

In the course of the discussion of clerical claims to exemption from taxation the author incidentally utters another opinion, which may not properly be construed as intentionally asserting all that would now be found in it. As a symptom, however, of the fluid condition into which political philosophy was lapsing it is decidedly instructive. Sonnenfels had shown his reasons for concluding that no claim to exemption could be maintained by the clergy on the ground of special divine right or through the claims of an external power, such as the Roman court, and he continues:

The concessions of princes are the only remaining ground for the claim. Now, in so far as this exemption is a concession of the ruler, it carries with it, like every concession of this sort, the tacit qualification, ***provided the public welfare is not too nearly affected thereby;*** in which case it is not alone revocable, but it ***must*** be revoked, because no power extends so far as to [be free to] harm the community for the sake of an individual or a class (§91).

Quite as democratic in form, but perhaps even more vague

[1] A note refers to "Justi, *Staatswirth.*—§407," with the comment: "He is the only writer in whom I remember to have read a claim for this exception in the case of scholars. He demands it also for the clergy, but for both only in the case of their personal dues; and he later finds himself obliged, for the same reasons, to call for the same exceptions in the case of all in the military and civic service of the state."

in application, were Sonnenfels' principles for distributing the burdens of taxation. Thus he says:

The payments of the individual citizen must be reckoned according to a double relation: to his own means, and to the means of the other tax-payers. . . . . With reference to the former, this principle must govern: the dues must not be so great as to impair the earning-power of the citizen, or to affect his courage to continue earning. That is, whatever is necessary to the continuance of his earning must be free from tax; e. g., first, the necessary support; second, the advance [*Vorschuss*] or the necessary and useful outlays without which the income cannot be gained at all, or at least in full; third, a portion of income large enough to stimulate the citizen to continued labor.

In pursuing the argument, the author adds:

Men whose hearts are of steel and whose temper is hostile to the citizens have tried to make it a principle that *a people will be the more industrious, the more it is loaded with taxes*. . . . . The difference between stimulating and discouraging taxes consists in this: the former increase the motives for industry, ... the latter diminish the motives to labor. . . . . Even if the state had a right, therefore, to extend the taxes to the limit of support and advance, the self-interest of the state would forbid use of this right. The greater sum of one year would be purchased too dear at cost of the deficit of the following years through loss of energy and decrease of national zeal for labor [*Arbeitsamkeit*] (§99).

In the same connection Sonnenfels betrays uncertainty bout the precision of the two tests of taxation which he has proposed. Thus he says:

Certain writers have ventured to define numerically the fraction of income which may be taken for taxes. Men of insight cannot fail to have seen the impossibility of finding such a general numerical ratio. . . . .

In the following section another angle of the subject is encountered:

In order to determine the ratio of the payments for taxes to the means of other tax-payers, this seems to be taken for granted as an infallible principle, viz., The portions to be paid should be to each other as the incomes of those who are liable to taxation (§100).

That is, as the context explains, if one citizen has an income of 100, and another of 1, the tax of the former should be 100 times that of the latter. But Sonnenfels at once points out that this principle cannot be accepted without modification, for, "suppose we consider not the sum which this principle would take from the two citizens respectively, but the sum which would be left to each after the payment." The one might still be left in affluence after the payment, the other might be crowded below the means of subsistence, and the exact principle is still left in question by the conclusion:

One sees that no point can be assigned for even an approximate comparison of the abundance of the one with the misery of the other.

In the next paragraph the attempt is made to help out this vagueness by another specification, viz.:

Nevertheless one must be fair enough to admit that this striking inequality is not the consequence of the disproportion in the tax, but of the incomparability [*Unebenmasses*] of means, i. e., of the difference in the strata of civic society, and that the demand to reduce to equality, by means of a finance system, this difference which, at least in larger states, is not accidental, would be senseless. The thing to be considered, in the case of definition of the reciprocal relation between citizens, is that this inequality shall not be increased by a disproportionate burden of taxation. This end will be approached as near as possible by applying the following principle: "The sums to be paid shall be to each other as the *net* incomes of the taxable citizens; that is, as the sums which remain to each after subtraction of support and advance."

In the closing section of the chapter (§104) the general marks of a good financial system are summarized as follows:

The same will have to raise the sum reckoned with reference

to the general national income and adequate for the needs of the state, in so far as the domains [*Regalien*] and accidental revenues do not yield the same according to a provincial apportionment corresponding to the balance of money, from the citizens assessed ***without exception, in proportion to their net incomes***, covering short specified periods, at the time which is least inconvenient, through its own system of collection, which must be as simple as possible.

Sonnenfels regards the *Regalien* as either essentially taxes, and to be treated as such, or as auxiliaries of *Polizey* and *Handlung*. He declines to elaborate the subject therefore on the ground that Justi was strongest at this point, and may be regarded as the best authority.[1]

This epitome of Sonnenfels' views about finance in general contains all that is necessary for our purpose about his ideas of taxation. He enters at some length into argument with the physiocrats, but his position may be inferred from what has preceded. We may note his use of the phrase, "*die einzige Abgabe*," for the physiocratic *l'impôt unique* which has passed into the modern "single tax." We may also note that while the critique by which Sonnenfels defended his position was quite different from the major premises of the modern single-tax argument, his discussion contains the rudiments of all that has been said for and against the "single tax" as an expedient.

On the whole, Sonnenfels regards the consumption tax [*Verzehrungssteuer*] as the least oppressive to the tax-payer, and for these reasons:

First, because it is in proportion to earnings; second, because it is collected at the time when the citizen has the means of payment; third, because it is collected in rates which the payer feels less than any other form of tax (§180).

[1] Reference is made to "*Staatswirthschaft, System des Finanzwesens* und seine 2 Quartbände über die Polizey, unter dem Titel: ***Die Grundfeste zur Glückseligkeit der Staaten.***"

A single quotation from chap. x, on "Financial Schemes," may complete our study of Sonnenfels. He says:

Financial schemes are in great part the offspring of the spirit of selfishness, which clothes itself, however, in the garb of zeal for the public good. This must arouse the distrust of the financial administration, and as the anonymous author of the *Versuchs über die Staatseinkünfte* says, always rouse the more suspicion against them the more they promise. Every proposition looking to the improvement of the income of the state is a financial scheme. However they may be dressed up, these schemes fall into three classes: I, those which propose to facilitate collection, and incidentally to diminish cost of collection; II, those that propose to increase the amounts raised on actually assessed objects; III, those that propose to assess new objects. Before dealing with these in detail, the following two observations may be advanced: I. *Every proposition which promises no other advantage than increase of public revenues in general*, or as the hirelings are accustomed to express themselves, *den Nutzen des allerhöchsten Aerariums, deserves no attention.* For the incorrectness of the principle, *the public revenues must constantly be raised*, has been exposed. A proposition which aims at the one-sided advantage of the treasury is a scheme for exaction. II, Every proposition which promises larger sums for the state treasury, in spite of the fact that the payers are to pay less, unless it discovers fraud or incompetence in the collection, is at first glance to be rejected. It promises a numerical increase by means of a subtraction. That is, it promises a monstrosity.

CHAPTER XXII

SUMMARY

1. It would be superfluous to argue with students of the social sciences that German experience is instructive. Whatever our opinion of the purposes which German polity has proposed, or of the methods by which the purposes have been pursued, the efficiency of the German civic system is beyond dispute. As an adaptation of means to ends, it operates with a remarkably low rate of waste.

2. In order to give this factor of efficiency its full valuation, we must look back of German polity to German political philosophy. Here too, for purposes of interpretation, we are under no necessity of approving or disapproving the German conception of the state. We are merely bound to understand it. Americans cannot interpret German polity correctly so long as we assume that its basic thoughts are identical with our thoughts. Whether they ought to be or not is beside the mark. The Germans have done what they have done while aiming at a somewhat different goal from ours, while assuming a somewhat different social reality from that which we presuppose, and while consequently applying a somewhat different scale of values to details of available ways and means.

3. In spite of the necessary inaccuracy of a brief theorem, especially when it is antithetic in form, the contrast between German and American conceptions of civic experience may be stated approximately as follows: *From the beginning the Germans have regarded the state as primarily a unit, and only secondarily an aggregate. From the beginning Americans have regarded the state as primarily an aggregate, and only secondarily a unit.* This contrast is the necessary starting-point for American interpretation of German polity. The theorem

is commonplace enough to American students of comparative politics. It is indeed merely a variation of the familiar proposition that German political theory is primarily collectivistic, while American political theory is primarily individualistic. Americans have not given all the attention that would be profitable to the bearings of this fact upon valuation of German political experience.

If rigid and consistent logic ruled human conduct, the foregoing formulas would not be as true as they are, nor on the other hand would the degree of truth in them have permitted the degree of similarity which actually exists between individualistic and collectivistic states. In all social affairs we are dealing with relativities, not with absolutes. We have to do with proportions, and emphases, and emotional attitudes, not with fixed quantities. We find accordingly that there are certain collectivistic types of civic conduct, but they are by no means confined to states properly classed as primarily collectivistic. In certain types of situations the most individualistic states, as though with one accord, have recourse to the most extreme types of collectivistic conduct. In like manner, the most collectivistic states tend, in certain situations, toward individualistic types of conduct. No state, therefore, can be truly described as a product of either collectivism or individualism. Each state is a resultant of individualistic and collectivistic factors in the mental operations of its citizens and of other peoples. To use a different figure, we may say that in Germany collectivism has been the constant predicate, while individualism has furnished the varying modifiers. In America individualism has been the predicate, while collectivism supplied the modifiers.

4. Nor must we allow ourselves to be distracted by the fact that the German conception of the unity of the state has often lent itself to perversions which no theory could excuse. The state has not only been regarded as exterior to the citizens,

as above and beyond them, as identical with the government, but the government has sometimes been regarded as merely an emanation from the prince, and the prince has been accepted as a ruler by divine right, even when he respected no law that might have restrained his arbitrary will.[1]

We must remember, on the other hand, that individualism as we know it in America has, in its turn, too often degenerated into license of some to invade the rights of others. The argument from perversion cuts about as deep on the one side as on the other. This argument is insufficient either to cast down collectivism or to set up individualism. The legitimate conclusion from the facts is that neither policy is a self-sufficient principle for control of civic action. Neither policy has been finally correlated, in theory or in practice, with its necessary correctives. The purpose of this book has not been to argue for the one policy nor for the other, but simply to summarize the evidence contained in the cameralistic books as to the way in which the collectivistic idea was interpreted by the Germans during the cameralistic period. This retrospect is a necessary preliminary to intelligent interpretation of subsequent developments in German civic theory and practice down to the present.

5. According to the cameralistic conception then, the state was a magnified family with a big farm as its property.[2] The unity of this family with its estate was symbolized by the prince. Its interests were represented by the prince in such a way that no one could very clearly discriminate between the personality of the prince and the interests of the state. The unity of this farm-patriarchate-principality was so impressive that at first very little occasion seems to have been found for distinguishing between the concepts "welfare of the prince," "wel-

[1] *Vide* Index, titles "State, Theory of," "Quasi-absolutism."

[2] *Vide* Index, titles "Cameralism as Political Theory and Practice," "Cameralism, Meaning of," "Cameralists," etc.

fare of the state," "welfare of the people" (considered collectively), and "welfare of the people" (considered individually). It is approximately true that the cameralists did not distinctly entertain the last of these conceptions. They implied it from the beginning. They insisted upon valuations which became motives of the German democratic movement after the Napoleonic period.[1] They furnished schedules which might be adopted as the programme of a rather thorough individualism; yet on the whole their theory, as far as it was published, treated all civic problems as questions of situations within a literal or mystical unity of prince and people. In the last analysis, the knowing and feeling and willing for this unity was to be done by the prince. On the other hand, the good citizen lived and moved and had his being as a sort of organ of a body whose center of consciousness was the prince.[2]

Of course the relationship did not present itself in precisely this form to the cameralists. We are expressing it in our terms, not in theirs; yet it is not sure that a single one among them would have rejected our form of statement.[3]

In general it may be said that political evolution in Germany, as everywhere else, has been a variation of adjustments between the extreme conceptions, on the one hand that the citizens may, can, and should exist only as functions of the state, and on the other hand that the state may, can, and should exist only as functions of the citizens. The latter conception was latent rather than patent among the cameralists. It is not within the scope of this book to inquire whether there is a possible synthesis of the foregoing thesis and antithesis. We are dealing with men who would have said, and after a fashion did say, that the two views are mutually exclusive.

1 *Vide* Index, title "Democracy, Symptoms of."

2 *Vide* Index, title "Welfare and Kindred Terms."

3 *Vide* Index, title "Biological Analogy." Similar references might have been multiplied.

6. Considering the state then as an organism of which the prince was the head and (again in modern idiom) of which territory and population composed the tissues, the cameralists easily reduced the questions of civic polity to this double problem: *How may it be well with this state-organism in its internal operations and in its external relations?*[1]

By a process which does not fully appear in its elements in the cameralistic books, the cameralists arrived at the major premise that all the problems of "internal and external security" resolved themselves into the question of the princely revenues. We must remember that the social preconceptions of the cameralistic period were thoroughly static. Publicists were apparently no more certain than every other social class that the human lot was a permanent arrangement of social strata. It was assumed that a certain standard of life was appropriate to each stratum, and that, maintenance of this standard of life being assured, it would be impertinent and presumptuous for members of any stratum to long for satisfactions in excess of the norm for their social level. If then the conduct of the different strata of society could be so ordered by the state that the total activities of the people could be made to result in an increasing margin of material return, above the aggregate demands of the different class standards, *the state might appropriate that surplus without injustice or hardship to the individual.*[2] This, in a word, was the programme which the cameralists undertook to formulate. It might be expressed in this way: *Given the resources of a territory, the labor capacity of the population, and the customary wants of the different strata, how may the state so exploit territory and people that the customary wants may be supplied, with an increasing surplus which may be claimed as public revenue?*

7. Cameralism was accordingly in no sense an abstract

[1] *Vide* Index, title "Security."

[2] *Vide* Index, title "Taxes, Burdensome vs. Non-burdensome."

philosophy, except as every human action connotes to the philosophical onlooker some implied preconceptions. Cameralism was an administrative technology.[1] It was not an inquiry into the abstract principles of wealth, in the Smithian sense.[2] It was much more closely analogous with grub-staking a prospector or financing a street railroad. It was a theory of managing natural resources and human capacities so that they would be most lucrative for the prince in whose interest the management was conducted. To be sure, just as any other human activity tends to suggest generalizations, this cameralistic technology visibly expanded its conceptions from rule-of-thumb thrift to somewhat comprehensive industrial, commercial, and political principles. It even cast its conclusions occasionally at last in forms which seemed almost to anticipate abstractions of the classical economists. On the whole, however, cameralism remained a technology, not a philosophy. It was analogous with the rules of banking which one might learn in the course of practical business. It was not like the philosophic reasoning in the economic treatises. Not until the Smithian influence began to be felt in Germany did questions of material ways and means cease to be treated on the one hand merely as matters of domestic thrift, on the other hand, merely as matters of political expediency.[3] It is accordingly a fundamental error to treat the cameralistic technology as a system of economic generalizations in the nineteenth-century sense. The theoretical setting of the economic ideas was the paramount political opportunism of the period. The provincialisms of the cameralists were more essentially political than economic.

8. In expansion of the last proposition we may specify that tradition has very seriously misconstrued cameralism, in

[1] *Vide* Index, title "Cameralism as Political Theory and Practice."

[2] No one in the cameralistic series came as near to the Smithian type of generalization as several British predecessors of the author of *The Wealth of Nations*.

[3] *Vide* Index, title "Economy and Related Terms."

consequence of treating it as a system of doctrines about nineteenth-century economic problems. The truth is that the cameralists had not come within sight of those problems. They were trying to answer the questions of expediency proposed to them by the political opportunism which animated the statecraft of their period. The controlling principle of that type of politics was, *let each state look out for its own interests*. This meant a policy of readiness for aggression or for resistance to aggression. The foremost consideration was ways and means to protect the state in the constant struggle with other states. In this situation there was no more use for doctrines of abstract economics than there was in the latest special session of Congress, when the main concern was not scientific tariff legislation but the most skilful trading of votes in the interest of particular constituencies. The wonder is not that the cameralists held narrow economic views, but that their ideas of economic relations contained such a small proportion of error.

The supposed economic fallacies of the cameralists might be expressed as details of the policy known as *mercantilism*. It would be irrelevant to open the question of the merits or defects of the mercantilist policy in its historical time and place. It would be futile to deny that the cameralists were mercantilists. The significant fact, however, for the development of the social sciences, is that mercantilism was not an economic generalization at all, as we now understand that phrase. It was a fiscal expedient. It is as fallacious to infer fundamental economic doctrines from the mercantilistic programmes as it would be to impute strange notions of essentials of economics to the American legislators who prefer a tariff to an income tax.[1] There is not a line in the cameralistic books which forbids the conclusion that their authors under-

[1] *Vide* Index, titles "Mercantilism" and "Mercantilism, Its Relations to Cameralism."

stood as clearly as the physiocrats, or as modern economists, that the extractive industries are the ultimate sources of wealth. The mercantilists did not differ from the physiocrats about the ultimate sources of wealth, but if they had expressed themselves in the modern way they would have said that was "a purely academic question." The real difference between mercantilists and physiocrats was on fiscal policy. The former held that it was wiser fiscal policy for governments to put their strength into promotion of commerce than into encouragement of the extractive industries. The latter insisted on inverting the proposition. This disagreement about practical policy no more proved a difference of opinion about basic economic relations, than opposite views about the expediency of a corporation tax in America today would prove that the opponents believed in antagonistic systems of abstract economics.

In particular, it has been supposed that the mercantilists, and especially the cameralists, held fantastic views of the nature of wealth. This tradition is not supported by the cameralistic books. Their essentially sane assumption about wealth does not appear more clearly anywhere than in Justi's propositions.[1] If a reader had heard none of the misrepresentations of mercantilism, however, study of the cameralistic books would impress him from the start with the authors' sense of the urgency of fiscal needs; but he would find nothing which could legitimately be interpreted as an essentially different view of what constitutes wealth from that which the most enlightened modern economist would exhibit if he owned an elevator full of corn, but needed to raise ready money.[2]

Less prominent in the list of alleged errors of the mercantilists, and particularly of the cameralists, is their supposed misconceptions on the subject of *population*. It is frequently implied, rather than positively stated, in allusions to these

[1] *Vide* above, p. 339.

[2] *Vide* Index, titles "Gold and Silver," "Money," and "Wealth."

writers, that they supposed increase of population might go on without limit. In fact, so far as they are to be judged by their books, they knew as well as Malthus did that population must always be in proportion to the food supply.[1] They believed that the German lands were undercultivated and therefore underpopulated. They believed that there was no immediate prospect of exhausting the resources of German soil, and therefore it was good govermental policy to promote increase of population by every possible means. They were no more guilty of economic misconception because of this judgment than Kansas farmers are when they advertise for laborers from outside the state to help harvest their crops.

But the gravest of all the errors of cameralism is supposed to be its connivance with *paternalism*. On this count we may as well confess judgment at once, but our plea is that the facts do not constitute a fault in the historic sense. The Germans three or four hundred years ago confronted a task which was hardly less appalling than that which Russia is facing at present. The statesmen of the time saw certain elements of the problem much more clearly than we can see them today. In a word, the great masses of the Germans were infants—infants in knowledge, infants in experience, infants in feeling, infants in judgment about the conduct of life. They lived in straightened circumstances. No affluence of natural resources stimulated their ambition and allured them to effort. They loved the pitiful measure of comfort which they could command, and they were timid, even if they were wistful, about enterprises that might improve their condition. How might the dormant powers of these unaroused folk be awakened and enlisted in the task of making the most of themselves and of their material conditions?

The method by which the German leaders undertook this task was something like the method by which a levy of raw

[1] *Vide* Index, title "Population."

recruits is made over into a regiment of disciplined soldiers. The Germans were divided up into some hundreds of squads, each controlled by a territorial prince who was within limits absolute in his own land. This was of course not a scheme invented out of hand. It was a stage in the historical evolutionary process. The arrangement corresponded to the conditions and fitted the conditions. Populations largely of peasants, and the remainder mostly artisans who had been incubated in the quasi-communistic guild organizations, and had never learned to walk alone, populations politically and economically in their swaddling clothes, and needing, first, nursery care, then tutors and governors to bring them to maturity—this was the situation in which that paternalism culminated which Americans have been taught to despise. The régime would have been impossible in America, because of the difference in conditions. It has been more than justified by its results in Germany.

9. As was intimated in the Preface,[1] the chief motive for this study was a desire to find out whether history had treated the cameralists fairly, and if not to learn the lesson of this unfairness for methodology in the social sciences. So far as the facts are concerned, it is unnecessary to enlarge upon the statements in the Preface. The cameralists have been misunderstood and misrepresented simply because their own center of attention was ignored, and they were judged as though they were trying to deal with the problems which interested their critics. The consequence has been that a series of writers, unsurpassed by authors of any other period as exhibitors of the social forces which were conducting the evolution of their time, have either been neglected altogether, or they have been represented as freaks, with unimportant relations to the social process in which they occurred.

The cameralists not only gave voice to the constructive

[1] Pp. xxi, xxii.

civic ideas of an era, but the system which they formulated contains all the essentials of German polity today. From the close of the cameralistic period, and the turning of German political thinking from its natural course by the Revolution on the one hand and Smithism on the other, down to the formation of the *Verein für Socialpolitik* in 1871, so many factors enter into the reorganization of German social science that it is easy to overlook the permanent cameralistic elements. To understand modern Germany which is directly and indirectly exerting such manifold influence upon the whole world, it is necessary to take account not only of present activities in Germany, but of those formative purposes and tentative institutions which the cameralists represent.

The wider methodological generalization is that every process of thought has its telic coefficient, which must be accurately computed if the thought is to be objectively estimated. In other words, we must know what the thinker is consciously or unconsciously trying to do with his thought, in order to value it correctly in the scheme of intelligence.

If the cameralists had been trying to determine the laws of wealth, or value, or distribution, their thinking would have had one force. Since they were attempting no such thing, but were trying to work out a civic technology which would incidentally provide for the necessities of citizens, and thereby furnish the prince with money enough to pay his bills, their thinking has a quite different force. *Historical interpretation of the cameralists not only turns the strongest light upon the later evolution of civic theory and practice in Germany, but it furnishes a typical case for illustration of the theorem that every system of thought must be interpreted in connection with its peculiar purposes.*

INDEX

INDEX